Movements, Currents, Trends

494-500
+ Intro on 489

Sources in Modern History Series

BARTLETT *The Civilization of the Italian Renaissance*

LEVY *Antisemitism in the Modern World*

LUNENFELD *1492: Discovery, Invasion, Encounter*

SAX AND KUNTZ *Inside Hitler's Germany*

WEBER *Movements, Currents, Trends*

Other titles forthcoming

Movements, Currents, Trends

Aspects of

European Thought

in the Nineteenth

and Twentieth

Centuries

·

Eugen Weber

University of California, Los Angeles

D. C. Heath and Company

Lexington, Massachusetts / Toronto

Address editorial correspondence to:

D. C. Heath
125 Spring Street
Lexington, MA   02173

Designer: David Ford

Published simultaneously in Canada.

Printed in the United States of America.

International Standard Book Number: 0–669–27881–5

Library of Congress Catalog Number: 91–71288

10 9 8 7 6 5 4 3 2 1

For Jacqueline
again, as ever.

A Few Words to the Reader

Thirty years and a lifetime ago I published the first version of this book under the title *Paths to the Present*. The present, at that time, ended with Existentialism. A great deal of ink has flowed under the bridges since 1960, and *Movements, Currents, Trends* reflects changes and novelties. Old chapters have been revised and trimmed; new chapters have been added.

I hope that those who liked *Paths to the Present* will enjoy *Movements, Currents, Trends,* and that those unfamiliar with *Paths to the Present* will appreciate this fresh attempt to collect and discuss the more striking expressions of European art and literature since the days of Romanticism.

E.W.

Contents

Introduction   1

I. Romanticism   13

William Wordsworth: Preface to the Second Edition of the *Lyrical Ballads*   18
William Hazlitt: *Wordsworth and the Lake Poets*   29
René de Chateaubriand: The *Génie du Christianisme*   31
Victor Hugo: Preface to *Cromwell*   39
Victor Hugo: Preface to *Hernani*   63
Charles Baudelaire: *The Salon of 1846: To the Bourgeois*   65
A Romantic Painter   68
Charles Baudelaire: *The Life and Work of Eugène Delacroix*   69
Théophile Gautier: Preface to *Mademoiselle de Maupin*   76
Alfred de Musset: *Reflections*   103
Henri Murger: Preface to *The Latin Quarter*   114
P.S.: Germany   124
Bettina Brentano: *Letter to Goethe*   126
Ludwig van Beethoven: *Letter to Bettina Brentano*   131

II. The Positivistic Reaction   135

Realism and Naturalism   135
Charles Sainte-Beuve: *Hopes and Desires of the Literary and Poetic Movement after the Revolution of 1830*   141

Champfleury: *Letter to Madame Sand, concerning M. Courbet*   147

Gustave Courbet: *Realism*   155

Edmond and Jules de Goncourt: Preface to *Germinie Lacerteux*   156

Hippolyte Taine: *The Principles of Historical Analysis*   158

Emile Zola: *The Experimental Novel*   179

Impressionism   194

Emile Zola: *The Realists of the Salon of 1866*   196

Emile Blémont: *The Impressionists*   198

Emile Zola: *Naturalism in the Salon*   199

Oscar Wilde: *The Influence of Impressionism upon the Climate*   200

III. Consciousness and Confusion   203

Eclecticism and Aestheticism   208

Walter Pater: *Coleridge*   208

Walter Pater: *Art for Art's Sake—The Aesthetic Approach*   214

Oscar Wilde: Preface to *The Picture of Dorian Gray*   217

Symbolism   218

Charles Baudelaire: *Correspondances*   220

Jean Moréas: *A Literary Manifesto*   222

Expressionism   227

Wassily Kandinsky: *Concerning the Spiritual in Art*   229

Hermann Bahr: *Expressionism*   243

Hermann Hesse: *The Brothers Karamazoff,* or *The Downfall of Europe*   248

Cubism   254

Guillaume Apollinaire: *On Painting*   255

Futurism   264

Filippo Marinetti: *The Foundation of Futurism*   265

Dada   270

Tristan Tzara: *Dada Manifesto*   271

Surrealism   278

André Breton: *What Is Surrealism?*   279

The Freudian Revolution   307

Jacques Rivière: *Notes on a Possible Generalisation of the Theories of Freud*   308

IV. Social Awareness: The Reintegration of Art   321

John Ruskin: *The Nature of Gothic*   326

William Morris: *The Aims of Art*   341

Bauhaus   353
Walter Gropius: *The New Architecture and the Bauhaus*   353
Michael Roberts: Preface to *New Country*   363
Cecil Day Lewis: *The Conflict*   372
Cecil Day Lewis: *On the Twentieth Anniversary of Soviet Power*   374
Arthur Koestler: *An Intellectual's Conversion*   376
Ignazio Silone: *Bread and Wine*   382

V. A Literature of Disillusion: Anti-Utopia   397

Paul Valéry: *The Intellectual Crisis*   403
Aldous Huxley: Preface to the 1946 Edition of *Brave New World*   408
George Orwell: *Nineteen Eighty-Four*   415
Andrey Sinyavsky: *Socialist Realism*   423

VI. A New Individualism   443

Friedrich Nietzsche: *Loneliness and Its Possibilities*   447
André Gide: *Advice to Nathaniel*   456
André Malraux: *The Temptation of the West*   458
Jean-Paul Sartre: Introduction to *Les Temps Modernes*   464
Albert Camus: *The Myth of Sisyphus*   476

VII. A Supermarket Culture   489

Claude Lévi-Strauss: *Man and Structure*   496
Michel Foucault: *Madness and Civilization*   500
Michel Foucault: *The Order of Things*   504
Roland Barthes: *The Death of the Author*   512
Jacques Derrida: *Signatures*   517
George Steiner: *A New Meaning of Meaning*   520

VIII. It Takes All Kinds   533

Jean Dubuffet: *Asphyxiating Culture*   539
Jean Dubuffet: *A Word About the Company of Raw Art*   545
Harold Rosenberg: *Warhol: Art's Other Self*   547
John Baldessari   552
Cesare Zavattini: *A Thesis on Neo-Realism*   555
Denis Calandra: *The Antiteater of R. W. Fassbinder*   562

IX. Crosscurrents 569

Russell Baker: *Among the Puritans* 571
Hélène Cixous: *The Laugh of the Medusa* 574
Pierre Nora: *About Intellectuals* 594
Vaclav Havel: *Politics and Conscience* 606

Afterthought 619

Introduction

> If I were founding a university I would found first a smoking room; then when I had a little more money in hand I would found a dormitory; then after that, or more probably with it, a decent reading room and a library. After, if I still had more money that I couldn't use, I would hire a professor and get some textbooks.

Stephen Leacock, a humorist, wrote these words before the First World War. A hundred years later, smoking rooms are as popular as apartheid, and carry rather similar implications. Dormitories are very different from what Leacock envisaged, reading is *passé* (fortunately, libraries now are information retrieval centers). If he were founding a university in the 1990s, the first thing Leacock would have to think of would be parking facilities, the second, cafeterias. Only professors retain their place in the pecking order, for reasons I shall leave unexplored beyond mentioning that Leacock himself professed to profess Political Science and Economics at McGill University in Montreal. And textbooks continue even lowlier than professors.

That being said, let's make no bones about it. This is a textbook—quite literally, an array of texts put together for use in my own courses. Its first purpose is to reprint the most representative statements of modern systems of thought and taste whose cultural heirs and creatures we are. They make good reading and, often, good sense. Together with my own introductory essays, these selections review two centuries of cultural development: the attitudes and programs of the major artistic and literary movements of our time. From Romanticism to Poststructuralism, here are movements, currents, trends, schools, that have marked our vocabulary and affected our expectations. We read or gaze at their results, we encounter their impact as part of the history of their times, yet we no longer quite remember their origins and intentions. Even so, we hark back to them all the time, for their influence remains alive and their tenets have become part of the way we think.

While teaching my own courses in the intellectual history of nineteenth- and twentieth-century Europe, I could not help but see that the most explicit, the

1

really classic expressions of doctrines to which we ceaselessly refer are generally ignored. Some had not been translated into English, many even though translated lay dormant in books that were hard to get, or to get at, for students—and even more so for general readers. Yet these essays, relatively few in number, seem to provide the best clear, brief statements of attitude and purpose for anyone who wishes to understand the aims and peculiarities of Romantics and Futurists, Realists, Surrealists, and all the other *isms* and *ists* that have helped to make or unmake our world. The material they contain is self-explanatory, presenting the doctrines at first hand, and helps to make up for the lack of any book in English that can supply an adequate account of them all. Read in sequence, the various and varying points of view seem to fall into place of their own accord as part of a continuum, of a tradition, to which we are the heirs.

I have drawn heavily on the manifestoes of literary and artistic movements, partly because much has already been done to make available the political and philosophical thought of the time; but partly, too, because it was through literature and the arts that ideas—developed in the more rarefied air of school and study—were funneled in time to a wider public, not necessarily eager to receive them, but open to their influence and nearly always swayed in the end. The very treatment of literature and art as aids to the study of history, the interpretation of their products as documents that, when examined by competent historians, can help us to understand the spirit of an age is itself the discovery of that Romantic spirit that lies behind every other modern movement. It was the German Romantics of the eighteenth century who first suggested that literary history was a necessary part of literary criticism, that literature and art were reflections of particular societies and times, knowledge of which could help explain their nature and the ideas behind them just as the works themselves would contribute to our understanding of the age and the milieu that gave them birth. This concept was published to the world by Madame de Staël in the second decade of the nineteenth century and, even when opposed or resented, has contributed to our treatment and comprehension of every sort of work and situation.

Of course, this sort of evidence is seldom obvious or clear, in fact often misleading, and calls for careful interpretation. But so does the *Domesday Book,* so does diplomatic correspondence, so do the treaties, monuments, and inscriptions of another day, the Cretan accounts and the Dead Sea scrolls. If such artistic evidence is incapable of unbiased and objective interpretation, so is every other kind of evidence in library or court; and if the terms are used in a relative sense only, with a decent awareness of human fallibility, then the capacity for objective and unbiased interpretation rests not in the materials themselves but in those who handle them—another matter altogether. It is becoming ever more apparent that as monuments, as documents, as potential illustrations of an age, the contributions of literature and the other arts cannot be ignored. They are part of intellectual history, as much as the great political and philosophical systems, as much as the story of scientific discovery or technological development. Yet while accounts are available of all of these in their historical setting, we know little about how great and familiar movements like Realism or Surrealism were presented as doctrines to the public. There is no single book that gives us a clear and vivid impression of the shifts and currents of intellectual orientation and taste—not in terms of stylistic changes but of an ideological evolution, not as part of a specialized development but against the background of contemporary history. This is what I have tried here to provide, very briefly.

If there should be about such a panorama a certain element of confusion, the reader might remember that reality *is* confused and only becomes clear when a great mass of apparently irrelevant material has been eliminated, and what remains is embalmed in the antiseptic pages of history books. A hundred years ago, a great English writer began his account of the French Revolution with a famous description that probably holds good for every other time:

> It was the best of times, it was the worst of times; it was the age of wisdom, it was the age of foolishness; it was the epoch of belief, it was the epoch of incredulity; it was the season of light, it was the season of darkness; it was the spring of hope, it was the winter of despair; we had everything before us, we had nothing before us; we were all going direct to Heaven, we were all going direct the other way—in short, the period was so far like the present period that some of its noisiest authorities insisted on its being received, for good or for evil, in the superlative degree of comparison only.

It is worth bearing this testimony in mind.

Movements of thought are commonly regarded—like centuries, or generations—as separate, easily identifiable and limited wholes. They follow each other like companies passing before the reviewing stand, each with its fanion, its company and subordinate commanders, its disciplined, almost identical men in the ranks. According to this view, the seventeenth century which is classical, is followed by the eighteenth century which is rational, and that in turn by the nineteenth which (since we have to examine it a little more closely) appears more varied—say, romantic *and* scientific both. As far as movements or tendencies go, it is well understood that Romantics, Realists, Naturalists, Symbolists, and Expressionists are distinct species, easily distinguished. Like the companies we can tell them by their colors, like the centuries by their number, and count them off as they pass, their tracks in the dirt of the parade ground soon obliterated by the steps of those that follow, leaving behind them only the memory of the songs they sang and a glimpse of fanions bravely fluttering in the wind.

No hint in all this that movements, like centuries, are concepts of reason, not of fact, their limits imposed upon them by human agency—interpretation. No hint, either, of the living forces that cut across these theoretical limits—the simple survival of mothers or grandfathers, for instance, to teach, to influence, sometimes to dominate, another generation. Voltaire, cold, brittle, brilliant, and spurned by the Romantics, is yet carried deep into the heart of their time by reactionary gentlemen, in exile or returned from it, who could not unlearn their youth. More people still read him in the 1830's and the 1840's than read Stendhal. On the other hand, great heroes of the Realistic school like Flaubert or Courbet are still close to a Romanticism that they continue more than they oppose. Romanticism and Realism: these labels lead us to overestimate differences and oppositions that were often more formal than real. Romantic or Realist—Victor Hugo, George Sand, or Honoré de Balzac? Romantic or Naturalist—Dickens, Monet, or Zola? Naturalist or Symbolist—Dostoevsky, Huysmans, or van Gogh? Both. Either at different stages of their careers, or at the same time. And if the difference between Romanticism and Realism is fairly clear, that between Romanticism and Symbolism is less so, and that between Realism and Naturalism, between Symbolism and Expressionism, is not clear at all. It comes down to saying that these movements, which for reasons of convenience are presented as separate, which for reasons of self-identification self-consciously stress differences and ignore identities, are not really distinct, are not at all separate, can only be understood in relation to one another, their very differences and oppositions the result of evolution, not revolution, and all of them facets of the same search for truth that began in the eighteenth century with denial of universal, universally valid, and apprehensible laws, and that has not ended today.

We shall follow this search to discover reality and express it—a reality no longer general and objective after the discoveries of modern scientists and historians, the appeals of Rousseau and Goethe. We shall follow it through the subjective explorations of nature and of self of the Romantic school; the would-be objective, but no less passionate, interest in every variety of external reality shown by the "positivistic" Realists and Naturalists; the gradual disintegration of a world taken apart first for scientific experiment, then to achieve a better representation of it, and lastly for the sake of metaphysical penetration and reinterpretation. Only, as the quest continues into the twentieth century, less and less is left to hope for from the search, less is left to grasp for, and man who had begun by thinking that his task was to discover a reality external to himself, ends by concluding that reality and its laws must be of his own making, that they lie not in objective externals, as the eighteenth century believed, but in his own subjective choice than which there is no other. The Romantic overtones of such a view are hard to miss, overtones that point to the unmistakable connection between movements more itemized in tables of contents than they are in reality.

Like great currents in the sea of time they sweep along, sometimes side by side, sometimes far apart, now mingling their waters, now turning aside in different directions toward separate shores.

And yet the presentation of these movements as unique and uniquely significant is not as treacherous as it may seem. In the first place it is, quite simply, convenient. To say that all the tendencies we find below often coexisted does not dispense from the attempt severally to describe them. But, further, it is true that the literature and the living arts of every generation have always reflected the ideas and circumstances of their time—unconsciously in part, as the products must be of those who learn the idiom of their time and express themselves in it, but also deliberately, because a work of art is necessarily the expression of a point of view. The points of view may differ, but they are always there, sometimes revolutionary, sometimes reactionary, sometimes escapist or conservative, and this is what marks the character, furnishes the controversial quality of certain works. A point of view (even for a painter) implies a whole philosophy or, at least, an attitude which, if it differs from what is currently practiced or accepted, makes for trouble and debate. In this sense, the style of a work is less important than the reason for adopting it, less important sometimes than its subject. The style may be acceptable but the subject challenging, the subject may be commonplace but the style objectionable in its implications. In both cases, it is the implications that count rather than the work itself, the matter not the manner of a work that sets the public on its ears. Witness the criticisms addressed to Courbet and Flaubert less, if at all, for their style than for their "vulgar" subjects, to Impressionists and Cubists less for their subjects than for their "shocking" style.

But then, if the artists or the writers so often find themselves in conflict with their age, what is their representative quality? How, even granting their place in the van of a general march, can they be said to reflect the ideas and the circumstances of their time? In one sense, of course, they do not. Our period more than any other has seen a split between the culturally active, productive, significant minority and *society* as a whole. The very economic developments that set artist and writer free from private patronage, that emancipated them from the service of the ruling order and of its chief representatives at court, in the church, and in the aristocracy, also cut them off from the general public—a mass ever vaster, more diverse, and less interested in and connected with contemporary cultural activities. An *intelligentsia* was born, an educated class lacking the wealth, power, and position of earlier educated classes, cut off by its values and activities from the rest of society, which it feared and despised, being distrusted and despised in return or, what is worse, ignored. Freedom, for them, often meant freedom to starve—but also to rebel. And in this rebellion lies the artist's representative character, his championship of new ideas, of more advanced ideas, of counterideas, which are often those of the significant part of the younger generation and, when successful, the ideology of tomorrow.

Such works and attitudes, however, are not always theoretical to begin with. One may, and generally does, react against injustice, ugliness, deception, or pain with anger, with a statement that is less theoretical than emotive. Often the work comes first, as experiment or reaction; the theory comes later. Many of the manifestoes that follow were written not only as most prefaces tend to be written—after the book, the play, the paintings, were done—but after the vague, uncertain beginnings had become a movement, after a doctrine or a school had made its point, had won acceptance, had even perhaps begun to wane. Hugo's preface comes *after* the battle of *Hernani* had been fought and won, Courbet's statement on Realism *after* his paintings had been painted, Zola's explanation of the experimental novel *after* he was himself getting a bit sick of it all, the Symbolist manifesto *after* Rimbaud had stopped writing.

Furthermore, many of these declarations were not made by the leader of the school but by some secondary figure who had time for theorizing, sometimes even by an artist in another field. The painters, in particular, tended to leave doctrines and explanations to their more articulate literary friends, critics like Zola, novelists like Champfleury, poets like Apollinaire, professors like Ruskin. But this, in turn, points up the close relationship between theory and practice, where the scientific discoveries and the political or literary doctrines of the time, discussed in cafés, in studios, and in little reviews, excited poets, painters, and musicians alike, each helping to strike a spark from the others.

The theories these people discussed, or that their manifestoes proclaimed, were probably no more the creative inspiration of the schools whose banners they bear than their platforms are for political parties today. There is a great deal of polemical writing, redolent of bygone issues, bristling with names today forgotten, facing up to problems irrelevant today when time has refined things down to fewer personalities and clearer lines. And those who do not mind the irrelevancies may still complain of inadequacies, of too many *mots* and not enough *choses*—the reverberating echoes and explanations of great movements, but not their products. Evidently, this was a chance I had to take: the products, after all, are already known since they are the armory of our civilization. Here, however, are their theoretical expressions, statements, and clarifications of purpose, signposts for actors and spectators, and inspiration for those in search of a pattern of their own. This should warn us not to overrate the significance of the declarations that follow, more valuable as documents than they were effective as acts. It should also warn us not to underrate their importance as expressions of opinions that both affected and were affected by their times and that played a major part in forming our taste, our point of view—the cultural idiom of today.

There is a pleasant story of Stendhal in Paris during the July days of 1830. *The Red and the Black*, just delivered into the printer's hands, had to wait because all the workers had left the shop to fight on the barricades—or perhaps to see the spectacle. So the impatient author sat in his room, where he could hear the firing in the streets, and noted the progress of the uprising on the margins of the *Memorial of Santa Helena*, which he had most appropriately taken up. Stendhal's novels consciously and deliberately hold a mirror up to contemporary history, and none more so than *The Red and the Black* itself. He was a "true painter of his time," in the Baudelairian sense of "one who can make us see and understand how great and poetic we are in our cravats and varnished boots," who can represent present life very much as it is, yet without stripping it of a certain epic grandeur and worthwhileness. He was, in spite of his would-be detachment, a terribly committed artist and, in this respect at least, no exception in a time when genius habitually meddled with propaganda, when inspiration and social consciousness so often went hand in hand, when art and artists set out almost deliberately to provide us with evidence of the issues of their day and spell out the arguments as to how these issues had best be tackled.

The relationship between a time—its preoccupations and possibilities—and its art keeps piercing through in passages like those from Hugo and Chateaubriand, Morris and Marinetti, Hermann Hesse and George Orwell. There is no mistaking the impact of contemporary political concerns, of war, of industrial and social problems, of the new horizons that modern discoveries and achievements fill with excitement and with dread. But there are other, less general, questions in which the interrelation between the work of art and the potential of its time is harder to establish. We know, for instance, that from Delacroix to Seurat painters took great interest in the results of scientific research in the relationships and effects of contrasted or juxtaposed colors; we also know that many Cubists were fascinated by the possibility of constructing their works with mathematical accuracy and listened, if only with half an ear and less understanding, to the theorizing of their mathematician friends. But just what they got from all these sources is quite uncertain still.

History is the tale of what has happened, not of what might have happened; and that does a great deal to narrow our field.

There is also the possibility of misinterpreting a relationship between two developments. I cannot help feeling, for instance, that the influence of Japanese prints on the Impressionists, of African art on Expressionists and Cubists, has been exaggerated or, at least, misrepresented. Certainly the new techniques they suggested provided fresh fuel for the imagination of Western artists but, more important and more often lost from sight, they confirmed ideas and impressions that existed already. They did suggest certain technical changes, but only because these particular changes were already being sought, because the observations of a Hokusai or a Congolese carver bore out observations already made, because their answers came to meet questions that had already been asked.

How true this is can well be seen in the relationship between painting and the new invention of photography, whose influence in our time has often been discussed. It may well be, as André Malraux has suggested, that the invention of photography has been as important to the cultural evolution of mankind as that of the printing press. It is certainly, and more immediately, true that the Impressionist painters drew quite a few conclusions from looking at photographs. But what conclusions did they draw? What lessons did they learn? It is important here not to put the cart before the horse: to remember that it was photography that began by imitating the senior art. And one has only to glance at grandma's album to see that the first photographers arranged their subjects as if they had been painters' models posing in a classic group.

The camera does what the man behind it wants, and the possibilities of movement and dissymmetry seem to have been discovered by painters on the lookout for something new, whose ideas the camera (like the Japanese print) came to confirm and, eventually, aid. It was, in other words, not the greater possibilities at their command that broadened the scope of the artists and led them off in new directions, but their search for new possibilities and new approaches that brought them to use what lay at hand.

But, again, the artists characteristically used the new tool in their own way; for the exact reproductions the cameras provided were just the sort of image that was ceasing to interest the artist in the latter half of the nineteenth century. And so the existence of the new medium helped free the painter (sometimes the writer too) to pursue his quest for truth, away from visible reality, away from objective reproduction, toward the increasingly analytic and subjective treatment first of the world around him, then of his self and his perceptions. So, photography has done much less, as it were, to inspire or help modern painting and writing than to supplement them, to facilitate and justify their drift away from Realism and Naturalism by taking their places.

The hazards of hasty interpretation also appear in many attempts to explain the style and tone of a movement by its historical background alone. Thus, Surrealism has often, and rightly, been described as an angry reaction against the bloody mess of the First World War. But its kinship with prewar movements like Cubism and Futurism, particularly the latter, is also very striking. The styles are similar and so is the message of the doctrines and their products, the feeling of dynamic impatience they all manage to impart. The war alone may provide a plausible explanation of Surrealism, but one that must beg the question of influences that were at work years before the carnage began and that had very little to do with war as such. Seen from this point of view, the First World War appears as only one more step in a process of disgust and disillusion with existing society, its values and its forms, a process that can be traced back at least as far as Nietzsche, if not to the antiscientistic reaction of the 1880s; and Surrealism is part of a chain whose first link lies in the Romantic spirit, whose nearest parent is Symbolism, and whose offspring is the anti-Utopian novel or poem of recent years.

One could go on like this for a long time; but we have had warnings enough to avoid facile explanations and categorizations. There is always a tendency to stress either differences *or* similarities between things, one at the expense of the other. The tendency of our day has been to divide and subdivide the evolution of contemporary taste and thought into the largest possible number of groups and subgroups, tendencies and countertendencies. This is convenient enough, but it is also misleading and antihistorical, since it causes us to lose sight of the deep connection between them all: the historical and socioeconomic evolution of the last two hundred years, of which they are a part as we are ourselves a part.

Though some of its characteristic works belong to the eighteenth century, the Romantic spirit spread through Europe in the wake of Napoleon's armies and in the train of his conquerors. The political effects, the vast and violent changes of the revolutionary and Napoleonic Wars, filled men's minds with confused and often contradictory ideas and undermined the old order where they did not destroy it. Liberty for man and liberty for the nation, equality for citizens but not for economic agents, the decay of an old hierarchy of birth, the rise of a new hierarchy of wealth, the affirmation of the rights of reason, the affirmation of the rights of instinct and passion—these were not always easy to reconcile. Fortunately, there was no need to reconcile them: one could entertain all at once. And along with them went the discovery that authorities which secular durability had invested with a greater appearance of divinity than the arguments of Bossuet, could, after all, be brushed aside by an irate citizenry aware of its rights and determined to assert them. This was potent doctrine, and its disturbing effects would shake the structure that 1814 and 1815 in part restored, and shake it free of many a crown in years to come. By 1830, a bourgeois king, crowned by another revolution, reigned in France and styled himself monarch—not of France, as his predecessors had done implying thereby their possession of the country as if it were an estate, but of the French people, by whose will he sat in the Tuileries, and by whose will he would decamp in 1848.

But Louis-Philippe was not a king like any other: he was—his friends took pride in the fact, his critics deprecated it—a *bourgeois* king, representative of the other development, one equally profound, that changed the face of Europe no less than the superficial plotting and brawling of its politics.

In the most general terms, revolution had come to France because the aristocracy, dominant for so long, no longer served a purpose or held a place justifying the privileges and status it insisted on retaining. A new, "bourgeois" class was rising, whose wealth and control of affairs led it first to covet and then to grasp political power to match its economic position. The issue took time to settle in politics; but there was bourgeois preponderance in cultural matters as new patrons replaced the old sources of revenue from court, church, and nobles. The new public and its taste were soon reflected in new themes, clearer, simpler, less allusive—themes for a public less refined, making up in sentimentality what had been lost in rationality and in sententiousness what had been lost in sophistication.

But the appeal from forms and formalities sanctioned by aristocratic society to self-expression sanctioned by individual genius was itself aristocratic in tone. Revolutionary against the stifling old regime, it could be equally revolutionary against the stifling Napoleonic Empire and, eventually, against the even more stifling developments of the Restoration. In its apparent inconsistencies, the Romantic spirit remained true to itself: against the old aristocracy of birth, against the new aristocracy of wealth and bureaucracy, it set the claims of a truer aristocracy of individual genius, talent, and intellect, as subversive to the conformities of the new regimes as it was to the old. Ready to assert the rights of man against the pretensions of traditional elites, the Romantics were just as ready to assert them against the pretensions of the "damned compact Liberal majority," or of emerging mass society. In the process, they themselves became an elite: a new phenomenon, the *intelligentsia,* socially displaced critics of society, defined by their peculiar standards and their detached attitude, grudging, grouchy, anarchistic, suspected, but—in spite of frauds, and crackpots, and an almost insuperable tendency to *épater le bourgeois*[1]—destined to become a recognizable elite in an increasingly classless society, increasingly devoid of standards and guideposts.

I am inclined to see in the movements represented in this book variants, in social criticism and self-expression, of this rather unexpected aristocratic self-as-

---

[1]Make the bourgeois gasp.

assurance. Some are more original, some more exciting than others—but all bear the traces of the original trait. Their differences are significant, of course; but so are their similarities. Champions of the underdog in the mass or the exception, of the oppressed minority as of the oppressed majority, of beauty in distress, and of all things that strike their fancy (because they happen to strike their fancy: from the wedding-cake patterns of neo-Gothic architecture to the hieratic stiffness of Symbolism and the explosive fantasies of later artists), these people assert values that are beyond the generally accepted commonplaces of their time and that are yet, somehow, inspired by them. Even Naturalism, the most would-be positivistic and objective of the schools, does not escape the Romantic spirit: it drips through the veins of Goncourt, it courses through those of Zola—an avenging musketeer if ever there was one, wielding the pen where d'Artagnan wielded only a rapier, smacking his lips in unscientific glee over the scrumptious details he sets out for our inspection. As for the Goncourts: "Why choose these low class *milieux* (for their novels)?" asks Edmond in his *Journal* (December 3, 1871):

> Because it is at the lower levels that in the waning of a civilization the character of things, of persons, of the language is preserved. Why again? Perhaps it is that I am a well-born writer and that the people, the rabble if you like, has for me the attraction of unknown peoples, not yet discovered, something *exotic* that travellers seek, with a thousand sufferings, in faraway lands.

This is not the scientist coolly setting out on a clinical study; it is Géricault, it is Delacroix, seeking the excitement of the grimace or the picturesque, it is the lover of the odd, the rare, and the *exotic* that travelers had seldom sought for its own sake, especially at the price of sufferings, before Romanticism had made it fashionable as a source of reverie or inspiration for the sensitive soul.

But by this time a new and disturbing possibility had appeared, not entirely unfamiliar to the Romantic, but now supported by the conclusions of scientific research. "Darwin's theory contains an essentially new creative thought," the great German scientist Hermann von Helmholtz commented in 1869, ten years after the publication of the *Origin of Species*. "It shows how adaptability of structure in organisms can result from the blind rule of a law of nature without any intervention of intelligence." If that was true, if, as Darwin suggested, the development and survival of species depended only on chance variations and on environment, then man was an object, conditioned and determined by forces outside his control, perhaps beyond his understanding. Long before Freud's perturbing revelations, here was a strong suggestion that man was not, perhaps, the captain of his soul—let alone the master of his fate.

It took time for the new implications to sink in, but the reaction to them was not devoid of Romantic spirit. The new predicament, only dimly discerned before the turn of the century, was forcefully expressed by Schopenhauer, and answered by Nietzsche. To the philosophies of both we might apply the words of Egon Friedell: "the mature, rich bloom of Romanticism."

Throughout, the new attitudes continued to mirror the political and socioeconomic conditions of their times. The excitement and the ugliness of industrial development, the new significance of time in an age when *time is money,* the progressive disillusion with the possibilities of science, of politics, of social reform—all arising out of their advances, the succession of systems, standards, and styles adopted and discarded, tried and found wanting in politics, social morality, and economic behavior—all are enlisted to serve as goad or inspiration. It is against the background they provide, indeed, impose, that we should view the story told by the documents below, a story that mirrors man's changing view of himself and his condition in a world whose mysteries he plumbs ever more deeply, with ever more disgruntling results.

The Renaissance had set out to explain the world in terms of man. The nineteenth century sketched out a return to nature, and hoped to explain man in those terms. This did not work either; at least, not well enough to provide the ultimately satisfactory answers humanity has never ceased to seek even in its most relativistic moods. Partly as a result of this, the present age appears to be less interested in nature than in the *forces* of nature or its structures. The world is no longer seen in the image of man, nor man in the mirror of nature. Man is now the subject and the prey of forces accessible neither to reason nor to the naked eye, but to other and novel perceptions—unconscious, dreamlike, psychological, dynamic—which the artist must conceive, explore, and, somehow, communicate. This has, of course, always been part of the artist's domain. Today it is almost the whole of his pursuit. The world of artist and writer is no longer a *corrida,* or even a laboratory or dissecting room: it has become a séance where he, as medium and visionary, pursues his disintegrator's task, which is simply to reflect the disintegration going on around us. A perplexing world finds in him the mirror—often the distorting mirror—of its perplexities and the suggestion, ceaselessly repeated in a myriad images and tones, that while our awareness of the problems we have to face and of their complexities has increased enormously in the last two hundred years, our ability to tackle them successfully has not conspicuously improved.

I.

Romanticism

What is Romanticism? In 1925, a Belgian scholar trying to establish the nature of the movement counted a hundred and fifty definitions. Three-quarters of a century before that, one of the German founders of the school had to admit that, were he asked to give a definition of Romanticism, he could not do it. For Ludwig Tieck, there was no difference between the Romantic and the poetic. In a sense he was right—but only by implying a definition of the "poetic" in the Romantic sense, for certainly he would not have counted Boileau as a Romantic poet. At any rate, no student of the many and varied phenomena that have been called "Romantic" (at first, generally, by their critics) could hazard more than the vaguest and most inclusive answer to the question.

The so-called Romantic spirit is to some degree simply an intellectual reaction against the eighteenth-century ideals of order, discipline, and reason, and a nationalistic reaction against French predominance in the cultural, as in the political, sphere. And certainly the movement as a whole stresses freedom, inspiration, and originality in contrast to the formal rules and imitative procedure of the classic style; it replaces the somewhat detached, sometimes impersonal approach of the late eighteenth century with the lyrical expression and expansion of personality; it denies "Enlightened" universalism by its insistence upon the local, the particular, the peculiar. The sources of the Romantic movement lie in Germany and England, away from the French cultural centers, which it only begins to infiltrate after the turn of the century and to touch seriously after Waterloo, through the agency of Chateaubriand, of Madame de Staël, whose book on Germany has been called the Romantics' Bible, and through Rousseau, long deceased yet more alive than ever when 492,500 volumes of his works were being printed between 1817 and 1824 alone.

In the various aspects of the Romantic reaction to the great Enlightenment dream of a rational and rationally comprehensible world inhabited by human beings equally accessible to reason, we may find the seeds of most subsequent cultural attitudes. In the work of the two generations whose lives were marked by the three great revolutionary explosions of the 1790s, 1830, and 1848, we find a subjective approach to reality that is assumed to lie first in the particular, then in oneself; we find respect for the organic, often incalculable, in opposition to the planned that is reducible to rational formulae; we find distrust of the Cartesian tendency to see the past in terms of the present and the conviction that, on the contrary, the present has meaning and being only in terms of its particular, frequently unfathomable but inescapable, roots in the past. We also find the passionate and uneasy discomfort or anguish, the causeless melancholy, the vague aspirations, the search for something one cannot quite identify that the Germans call *Sehnsucht*—longing. It was this unfocused longing, this vague restlessness, that carried so many of Alfred de Musset's generation to escape in premature death—in duels like Pushkin or Lermontov, in war like Petöfi or Byron, by accident or illness like Keats, or Shelley, or Novalis, by their own hand like Kleist or Gérard de Nerval.

These young men were sensitive, ardent, sometimes tormented, narcissistic, in love with love, with beauty, with passion, with themselves. Just as the humanists of the Renaissance had brandished the virtues of Greece and Rome against the "Goths," their predecessors, so the young Romantic rebels resurrected the Middle Ages, when men were men and women fair ladies, to counter the formalism and the powdered wigs that to them represented the dark ages. The aristocracy itself fell prey to the new fashion: its country houses became Gothic castles, its parks became bosky dells whose shadows sheltered mysterious phantoms of another age, its would-be imitators followed suit, and enriched bankers like Salomon Rothschild built palaces whose dining rooms "looked like a cathedral's nave." The fashion in dress reflected the fashion in literature and art: women set out to dress like damsels of the Middle Ages or the Renaissance; men, at least young ones, resembled the glamorous heroes of Victor Hugo or Dumas. A Paris tailor wrote in 1834: "Mr. Hugo is a very great man: these past two weeks he has helped me sell five jackets and eight pairs of trousers. But I still prefer M. Alexandre Dumas."

But while all this made for a highly aesthetic and egocentric approach, it could also drag the dreamer out of his contemplation, his pursuit of beauty and the self, into social and political activities designed to secure freedom of expression for the bound and the oppressed, to defend art and beauty against the rude and greasy paws of ignorance, or it could simply provide a moment's amusement. Hence, very soon, we find the Romantic not only in the studio, the ivory tower, the exotic expedition in search of color and adventure, or in the protected and lofty Parnassus (whether secured by a private income or not), but down in the street and the café, contributing to propagandist papers and pamphlets, politicking in verse, in prose, and—as in Daumier's lithographs—in pictures.

While such social and political activities, the more radical the better, are natural enough exhibitions of youthful boisterousness, it is also possible to trace their inspiration back to earlier and much more abstract sources. To the thinkers of the "classic" eighteenth century, beauty was perfection made visible. Since perfection was regarded as something absolute, beauty must be universal: a concept identical for all men wherever they might be. And, as there is only one "beauty" whose definition is universally valid, there can be only one "good taste" whose science is called aesthetics. But the aesthete cannot seek his knowledge of beauty in nature, for the world is imperfect. Perfect beauty is an ideal that our conception can approach, but never attain. And, whatever else this may imply, it follows that idealism, philosophy, the products of the mind and of reason, are necessarily superior to any imitation of nature, and "realism" is thus unthinkable for the man of good taste.

Later in the eighteenth century, *philosophes* like Diderot retained this belief in the primacy of mind, but discarded the idealism of their predecessors. Beauty and truth were rational concepts all right, or, at least, they were accessible to reason, but reason itself operated not in a realm of platonic ideas but in an analysis of nature and society. The new approach was one of selective and thoughtful common sense—an idealized common sense that taught that the purpose of man was the perpetual improvement of the world and of himself. Thus beauty becomes moral, didactic, and socially conscious. Nature becomes important, too, as a model for the artist, the writer, the philosopher, but a model from which they select whatever seems most useful and inspiring for the improvement of character and society. The sentimental morality of the late eighteenth century, with its appeals to the heart, its good intentions, its often sugary pleas for civic and family virtue, was replaced during the revolutionary period by a sterner lore which drew upon the ancients for inspiring examples of Spartan or Roman virtues more appropriate to the grand emotions of the time. But it never died. Through all the changes of a long period of revolution and war, through the different styles and fashions that led from revolution in 1789 to restoration in 1815, and beyond, the anecdotal and moral tone—so well suited to the mentality of enriched shopkeepers and businessmen who were beginning to take over in western Europe—subsisted and thrived.

Writers like Diderot and Rousseau, painters like Greuze, had thought that art should teach a moral lesson. Many Romantics agreed. In 1800, in her essay on *Literature Considered in Its Relations with Social Institutions,* Madame de Staël wrote that "the truly beautiful is that which makes man better." In the early 1830s, Social Catholics like Lammenais preached that art must help regenerate society. And even a long time later confirmation of this came from an unexpected quarter: in his prize-giving speech at the Salon of 1868, Napoleon III's representative and minister of Fine Arts, Marshal Vaillant, said the same thing: "Painting must try to speak to the masses which, today more than ever, it must be the mission of art to moralize."

These references to the mission of art and the regeneration of society reflect the influence of another great figure, that of the Comte de Saint-Simon, who had died in 1825 preaching the coming of a new age and a new society in which men would be ranked according to their talents and the use they made of them. Social antagonisms, said Saint-Simon, must give way to universal association, hereditary property must disappear, the state should own all resources and allocate them according to individual talents and social needs. It was the Saint-Simonians who first launched a now-familiar slogan: "To everyone according to his capacities, to each capacity according to its works." Saint-Simon's ideas, the emphasis he laid on productivity, on the rational ordering of society, and on social justice of the most economically advantageous sort, were to leave their imprint on the whole century. More specifically, however, his theories reinforced the view that art, which is the product of its environment and hence of present society, has an important part to play in shaping the better society of the future. In Saint-Simon's scheme of world regeneration the artist is assigned an important role, almost a sacred mission: as the sculptors of the great Gothic cathedrals had interpreted the Christian message to the illiterate but hungry masses of their time, so the artist of today must become the interpreter, the prophet, of the new ideas.

Affected by these concepts, many writers and painters tried to do just that; and the Swiss-French painter Gleyre, who in 1835 met Saint-Simon's successor, Enfantin, and his disciples in Egypt, planned three great panels on the theme of Past, Present, and Future, which would represent first the old alliance of king and priest, then the bourgeois drawing the revenues of his factories and fields, and lastly the sovereign People receiving and examining the accounts of its servants. The painting did not meet much public success, and this should remind us, if a reminder be needed, that ideas of true morality and beauty varied widely between established authorities who liked the established order and enthusiastic youth eager to change it. The results of this difference of opinion were not long in appearing.

The connection between revolutionary activities in art and in politics soon became apparent both to artists, some of whom had begun by ignoring it, and to the public, which had always suspected it. Between the publication of Victor Hugo's *Cromwell* in 1827 and the battle over his next play, *Hernani,* in 1830, the political orientation of the rising generation was reflected in its publications. Historians like Thiers, Guizot, and Sismondi, the first two destined for great political careers, were publishing what looked like very revolutionary works. A greater and more romantic historian, Michelet, was presenting European history as a long struggle for freedom. Meanwhile, on the musical front, Rossini's *William Tell* and Auber's *Muette de Portici* made the same point to audiences enthused by heroes fighting cruel tyrants against heavy odds. In July 1830, it was a young musician, Hector Berlioz, who rushed through the competition in which his entry was to win the much-coveted *Prix de Rome* and left as soon as he could in search of weapons with which to fight for liberty—the same liberty that the greatest of Romantic painters, Eugène Delacroix, was to paint soon after the Revolution as leading the people forward, not in the class struggles of a later day, but in affirmation of the common rights of man.

Soon enough, and especially under the influence of contemporary reformers and theorists like Saint-Simon, a politically revolutionary attitude became a socially revolutionary one. The July Monarchy (1830–1848) was the heyday of this social romanticism which, stifled in other parts of Europe, could flourish in Paris. From Rome, where his prize had taken him, we now find Berlioz writing to a Saint-Simonian friend at home, asking what he could do to help the cause and confiding that he wants to be "musically useful." But writers could be more useful still, their products more easily accessible to the general public; and so the chief figures of the new movement were poets, critics, and novelists: Sainte-Beuve, George Sand, Victor Hugo, Lamartine. The last of these was even, for a brief while, one of the leading figures of the 1848 revolution and of the short-lived Second Republic that followed in France.

At this point labels and categories become hazy: social awareness and revolt led away from the intensely personal and lyrical attitudes of the first Romantics, toward the "realistic" choice and treatment of the subject matter that would stress the angry and pessimistic arguments of would-be reformers. What we call Realism may, in any case, have been inherent in the Romantic mentality. Jacques Barzun, whose *Romanticism and the Modern Ego* provides a sane interpretation of this ill-defined attitude, has called his heroes "comprehensive realists," because they "instinctively knew that there is more than one layer of experience and many mysteries encountered in exploring it." And, in one sense, it is in such knowledge, and the explorations that followed upon it, that the tale of modern intellectual developments consists.

Yet, though this is true enough, such awareness would just as often make for withdrawal as for some "realistic" activism. We shall see the latter tendency develop in Section II. As for the Romantics proper, especially after 1848, the increasingly widespread feeling of frustration in the face of social injustice, political ineffectiveness, inability to make themselves understood, led many back to the ivory towers of an earlier day, to a new Hermetism, an art for initiates, to the searching investigation of subjective possibilities in the imagination and the senses rather than in the marketplace, that we shall find in Symbolism and in the aesthetic ideas of "art for art's sake."

Wordsworth

William Wordsworth (1770–1850) was schooled in the little Lake District village of Hawkshead and at St. John's College, Cambridge. His education left him with an appreciation of wild nature and a sound grounding in the classics. A visit to France, 1791–1792, furnished the opportunity for a bout of Girondist republicanism and a love affair with a young French girl, Annette Vallon, who bore him a daughter. Both passions dulled after the outbreak of war between England and France and the shock of Jacobin excesses. In 1795, a legacy enabled the disillusioned young man to settle down with his sister Dorothy, who helped him find a new fulfillment in nature and in poetry. In 1798, together with Samuel Coleridge, he published the *Lyrical Ballads,* which expressed his revolt against the formal literary element in poetry, aimed at plainness and at a poetic quality drawn not from style but from the poet's own imaginative experience. He was, as he explained, out to tell the truth about simple people by using "the language of conversation in the lower and middle classes," and this meant the abandonment of the formality and the heroic couplets until then *de rigueur.* A second edition of the *Lyrical Ballads* was published in 1800, for which Wordsworth wrote a preface (revised in 1802) designed to explain "what he had proposed himself to perform."

    Though he grew older, duller, and ever more detached, the disillusioned revolutionary would continue to protest against social wrongs, to decry the unwarranted fettering of men in general and artists in particular, and to affirm his belief in man, in nature, and in the high moral purpose that had always inspired him.

Preface to the Second Edition of the *Lyrical Ballads*

The first Volume of these Poems has already been submitted to general perusal. It was published, as an experiment, which, I hoped might be of some use to ascertain, how far, by fitting to metrical arrangement a selection of the real language of men in a state of vivid sensation, that sort of pleasure and that quantity of pleasure may be imparted, which a Poet may rationally endeavour to impart.

I had formed no very inaccurate estimate of that probable effect of those Poems: I flattered myself that they who should be pleased with them would read them with more than common pleasure: and, on the other hand, I was well aware, that by those who should dislike them, they would be read with more than common dislike. The result has differed from my expectation in this only, that I have pleased a greater number than I ventured to hope I should please. . . .

Several of my Friends are anxious for the success of these Poems from a belief, that, if the views with which they were composed were indeed realised, a class of Poetry would be produced, well adapted to interest mankind permanently, and not unimportant in the multiplicity, and in the quality of its moral relations: and on this account they have advised me to prefix a systematic defence of the theory upon which the poems were written. But I was unwilling to undertake the task, because I knew that on this occasion the Reader would look coldly upon my arguments, since I might be suspected of having been principally influenced by the selfish and foolish hope of reasoning him into an approbation of these particular Poems: and I was still more unwilling to undertake the task, because, adequately to display my opinions, and fully to enforce my arguments, would require a space wholly disproportionate to the nature of a preface. For to treat the subject with the clearness and coherence of which I believe it susceptible, it would be necessary to give a full account of the present state of the public taste in this country, and to determine how far this taste is healthy or depraved; which, again, could not be determined, without pointing out, in what manner language and the human mind act and re-act on each other, and without retracing the revolutions, not of literature alone, but likewise of society itself. I have therefore altogether declined to enter regularly upon this defence; yet I am sensible, that there would be some impropriety in abruptly obtruding upon the Public, without a few words of introduction, Poems so materially different from those upon which general approbation is at present bestowed.

It is supposed, that by the act of writing in verse an Author makes a formal engagement that he will gratify certain known habits of association; that he not only thus apprises the Reader that certain classes of ideas and expressions will be found in his book, but that others will be carefully excluded. This exponent or symbol held forth by metrical language must in different areas of literature have excited very different expectations: for example, in the age of Catullus, Terence, and Lucretius, and that of Statius or Claudian; and in our own country, in the age of Shakespeare and Beaumont and Fletcher, and that of Donne and Cowley, or Dryden, or Pope. I will not take upon me to determine the exact import of the promise which by the act of writing in verse an Author, in the present day, makes to his Reader; but I am certain it

will appear to many persons that I have not fulfilled the terms of an engagement thus voluntarily contracted. They who have been accustomed to the
gaudiness and inane phraseology of many modern writers, if they persist in
reading this book to its conclusion, will no doubt, frequently have to struggle
with feelings of strangeness and awkwardness: they will look round for poetry, and will be induced to inquire by what species of courtesy these attempts
can be permitted to assume that title. I hope therefore the Reader will not
censure me, if I attempt to state what I have proposed to myself to perform;
and also (as far as the limits of a preface will permit), to explain some of the
chief reasons which have determined me in the choice of my purpose: that
at least he may be spared any unpleasant feeling of disappointment, and that
I myself may be protected from the most dishonourable accusation which can
be brought against an Author, namely, that of an indolence which prevents
him from endeavouring to ascertain what is his duty, or, when his duty is
ascertained, prevents him from performing it.

The principal object, then, which I proposed to myself in these Poems was
to choose incidents and situations from common life, and to relate or describe
them, throughout, as far as was possible, in a selection of language really
used by men, and at the same time, to throw over them a certain colouring
of imagination, whereby ordinary things should be presented to the mind in
an unusual way; and further, and above all, to make these incidents and situations interesting by tracing in them, truly though not ostentatiously, the
primary laws of our nature: chiefly, as far as regards the manner in which we
associate ideas in a state of excitement. Low and rustic life was generally
chosen, because in that condition, the essential passions of the heart find a
better soil in which they can attain their maturity, are less under restraint,
and speak a plainer and more emphatic language; because in that condition
of life our elementary feelings co-exist in a state of greater simplicity, and
consequently may be more accurately contemplated, and more forcibly communicated; because the manners of rural life germinate from those elementary feelings and, from the necessary character of rural occupations, are more
easily comprehended, and are more durable; and lastly, because in that condition the passions of men are incorporated with the beautiful and permanent
forms of nature. The language, too, of these men is adopted (purified indeed
from what appear to be its real defects, from all lasting and rational causes of
dislike or disgust) because such men hourly communicate with the best objects from which the best part of language is originally derived; and because,
from their rank in society and the sameness and narrow circle of their inter-
course, being less under the influence of social vanity, they convey their feelings and notions in simple and unelaborated expressions. Accordingly, such
a language, arising out of repeated experience and regular feelings, is a more

permanent, and a far more philosophical language, than that which is frequently substituted for it by Poets, who think that they are conferring honour upon themselves and their art, in proportion as they separate themselves from the sympathies of men, and indulge in arbitrary and capricious habits of expression, in order to furnish food for fickle tastes, and fickle appetites, of their own creation.

I cannot, however, be insensible of the present outcry against the triviality and meanness, both of thought and language, which some of my contemporaries have occasionally introduced into their metrical compositions; and I acknowledge that this defect, where it exists, is more dishonourable to the Writer's own character than false refinement or arbitrary innovation, though I should contend at the same time, that it is far less pernicious in the sum of its consequences. From such verses the Poems in these volumes will be found distinguished at least by one mark of difference, that each of them has a worthy *purpose*. Not that I mean to say, I always began to write with a distinct purpose formally conceived; but my habits of meditation have so formed my feelings, as that my descriptions of such objects as strongly excite those feelings, will be found to carry along with them a *purpose*. If in this opinion I am mistaken, I can have little right to the name of a Poet. For all good poetry is the spontaneous overflow of powerful feelings; and though this be true, Poems to which any value can be attached were never produced on any variety of subjects but by a man, who being possessed of more than usual organic sensibility, had also thought long and deeply. For our continued influxes of feeling are modified and directed by our thoughts, which are indeed the representatives of all our past feelings; and, as by contemplating the relation of these general representatives to each other, we discover what is really important to men, so by the repetition and continuance of this act, our feelings will be connected with important subjects, till at length, if we be originally possessed of much sensibility, such habits of mind will be produced, that by obeying blindly and mechanically the impulses of those habits, we shall describe objects, and utter sentiments, of such a nature, and in such connexion with each other, that the understanding of the being to whom we address ourselves, if he be in a healthful state of association, must necessarily be in some degree enlightened, and his affections ameliorated.

I have said that each of these poems has a purpose. I have also informed my Reader what this purpose will be found principally to be: namely, to illustrate the manner in which our feelings and ideas are associated in a state of excitement. But, speaking in language somewhat more appropriate, it is to follow the fluxes and refluxes of the mind when agitated by the great and simple affections of our nature. This object I have endeavoured in these short essays to attain by various means; by tracing the maternal passion through many of its more subtle windings . . . ; by accompanying the last struggles of a human being, at the approach of death, cleaving in solitude to life and society . . . ; by showing . . . the perplexity and obscurity which in childhood attend our notion of death, or rather our utter inability to admit that notion; or by displaying the strength of fraternal, or to speak more philosophically, of moral attachment when early associated with the great and beautiful objects of nature, . . . by placing my Reader in the way of receiving from ordinary moral sensations another and more salutary impression than we are accustomed to receive from them. It has also been part of my general purpose to attempt to sketch characters under the influence of less impassioned feelings. . . . Characters of which the elements are simple, belonging rather to nature than to manners, such as exist now, and will probably always exist, and which from their constitution may be distinctly and profitably contemplated. I will not abuse the indulgence of my Reader by dwelling longer upon this subject; but it is proper that I should mention one other circumstance which distinguishes these Poems from the popular Poetry of the day; it is this, that the feeling therein developed gives importance to the action and situation, and not the action and situation to the feeling. . . .

I will not suffer a sense of false modesty to prevent me from asserting, that I point my Reader's attention to this mark of distinction, far less for the sake of these particular Poems than from the general importance of the subject. The subject is indeed important! For the human mind is capable of being excited without the application of gross and violent stimulants; and he must have a very faint perception of its beauty and dignity who does not know this, and who does not further know, that one being is elevated above another, in proportion as he possesses this capability. It has therefore appeared to me, that to endeavour to produce or enlarge this capability is one of the best services in which, at any period, a Writer can be engaged; but this service, excellent at all times, is especially so at the present day. For a multitude of causes, unknown to former times, are now acting with a combined force to blunt the discriminating powers of the mind, and unfitting it for all voluntary exertion, to reduce it to a state of almost savage torpor. The most effective of these causes are the great national events which are daily taking place, and the increasing accumulation of men in cities, where the uniformity of their occupations produces a craving for extraordinary incident, which the rapid communication of intelligence hourly gratifies. To this tendency of life and manners the literature and theatrical exhibitions of the country have conformed themselves. The invaluable works of our elder writers, I had almost said the works of Shakespeare and Milton, are driven into neglect by frantic novels, sickly and stupid German Tragedies, and deluges of idle and extravagant stories in verse— When I think upon this degrading thirst after outrageous stimulation, I am almost ashamed to have spoken of the feeble effort with which I have endeavoured to counteract it; and reflecting upon the magnitude of the general evil, I should be oppressed with no dishonourable melancholy, had I not a deep impression of certain inherent and indestructible qualities of the human mind, and likewise of certain powers in the great and permanent objects that act upon it, which are equally inherent and indestructible; and did I not further add to this impression a belief, that the time is approaching when the evil will be systematically opposed, by men of greater powers, and with far more distinguished success.

Having dwelt thus long on the subjects and aim of these Poems, I shall request the Reader's permission to apprise him of a few circumstances relating to their *style,* in order, among other reasons, that I may not be censured for not having performed what I never attempted. The Reader will find that personifications of abstract ideas rarely occur in these volumes; and I hope, are utterly rejected, as an ordinary device to elevate the style, and raise it above prose. I have proposed to myself to imitate, and as far as is possible, to adopt the very language of men; and assuredly such personifications do not make any natural or regular part of that language. They are, indeed, a figure of speech occasionally prompted by passion, and I have made use of them as such; but I have endeavoured utterly to reject them as a mechanical device of style, or as a family language which Writers in metre seem to lay claim to by prescription. I have wished to keep my Reader in the company of flesh and blood, persuaded that by so doing I shall interest him. I am, however, well aware that others who pursue a different track may interest him likewise; I do not interfere with their claim, I only wish to prefer a different claim of my own. There will also be found in these Volumes little of what is usually called poetic diction; I have taken as much pains to avoid it as others ordinarily take to produce it; this I have done for the reason already alleged, to bring my language near to the language of men, and further, because the pleasure which I have proposed to myself to impart, is of a kind very different from that which is supposed by many persons to be the proper object of poetry. I do not know how, without being culpably particular, I can give my Reader a more exact notion of the style in which I wished these poems to be written, than by informing him that I have at all times endeavoured to look steadily at my subject, consequently, I hope that there is in these Poems little falsehood of description, and that my ideas are expressed in language fitted to their respective importance. Something I must have gained by this practice, as it is friendly to one property of all good poetry, namely, good sense; but it has necessarily cut me off from a large portion of phrases and figures of speech which from father to son have long been regarded as the common inheritance of Poets. I have also thought it expedient to restrict myself still further, having abstained from the use of many expressions, in themselves proper and beautiful, but which have been foolishly repeated by bad Poets, till such feelings of disgust are connected with them as it is scarcely possible by any art of association to overpower. . . .

Taking up the subject, then, upon general grounds, I ask what is meant by the word Poet? What is a Poet? To whom does he address himself? And what language is to be expected from him? He is a man speaking to men: a man, it is true, endued with more lively sensibility, more enthusiasm and tenderness, who has a greater knowledge of human nature, and a more comprehensive soul, than are supposed to be common among mankind; a man pleased with his own passions and volitions, and who rejoices more than other men in the spirit of life that is in him; delighting to contemplate similar volitions and passions as manifested in the goings-on of the Universe, and habitually impelled to create them where he does not find them. To these qualities he has added a disposition to be affected more than other men by absent things as if they were present; an ability of conjuring up in himself passions, which are indeed far from being the same as those produced by real events, yet (especially in those parts of the general sympathy which are pleasing and delightful) do more nearly resemble the passions produced by real events, than any thing which, from the motions of their own minds merely, other men are accustomed to feel in themselves; whence, and from practice, he has acquired a greater readiness and power in expressing what he thinks and feels, and especially those thoughts and feelings which, by his own choice, or from the structure of his own mind, arise in him without immediate external excitement.

But, whatever portion of this faculty we may suppose even the greatest Poet to possess, there cannot be a doubt but that the language which it will suggest to him, must, in liveliness and truth, fall far short of that which is uttered by men in real life, under the actual pressure of those passions, certain shadows of which the Poet thus produces, or feels to be produced, in himself.

However exalted a notion we would wish to cherish of the character of a Poet, it is obvious, that, while he describes and imitates passions, his situation is altogether slavish and mechanical, compared with the freedom and power of real and substantial action and suffering. So that it will be the wish of the Poet to bring his feelings near to those of the persons whose feelings he describes, nay, for short spaces of time, perhaps, to let himself slip into an entire delusion, and even confound and identify his own feelings with theirs; modifying only the language which is thus suggested to him by a consideration that he describes for a particular purpose, that of giving pleasure. Here, then, he will apply the principle on which I have so much insisted, namely, that of selection; on this he will depend for removing what would otherwise be painful or disgusting in the passion; he will feel that there is no necessity to trick out or to elevate nature: and, the more industriously he applies this principle, the deeper will be his faith that no words, which his fancy or imagination can suggest, will be to be compared with those which are the emanations of reality and truth.

But it may be said by those who do not object to the general spirit of these remarks, that as it is impossible for the Poet to produce upon all occasions language as exquisitely fitted for the passion as that which the real passion itself suggests, it is proper that he should consider himself as in the situation of a translator, who deems himself justified when he substitutes excellencies of another kind for those which are unattainable by him; and endeavours occasionally to surpass his original, in order to make some amends for the general inferiority to which he feels that he must submit. But this would be to encourage idleness and unmanly despair. Further, it is the language of men who speak of what they do not understand; who talk of Poetry as of a matter of amusement and idle pleasure; who will converse with us as gravely about a taste for Poetry, as they express it, as if it were a thing as indifferent as a taste for Rope-dancing, or Frontiniac or Sherry. Aristotle, I have been told, hath said, that Poetry is the most philosophic of all writing: it is so: its object is truth, not individual and local, but general, and operative; not standing upon external testimony, but carried alive into the heart by passion; truth which is its own testimony, which gives strength and divinity to the tribunal to which it appeals, and receives them from the same tribunal. Poetry is the image of man and nature. The obstacles which stand in the way of the fidelity of the Biographer and Historian, and of their consequent utility, are incalculably greater than those which are to be encountered by the Poet who has an adequate notion of the dignity of his art. The Poet writes under one restriction only, namely, that of the necessity of giving immediate pleasure to a human Being possessed of that information which may be expected from him, not as a lawyer, a physician, a mariner, an astronomer, or a natural philosopher, but as a Man. Except this one restriction, there is no object standing between the Poet and the image of things; between this, and the Biographer and Historian there are a thousand.

Nor let this necessity of producing immediate pleasure be considered as a degradation of the Poet's art. It is far otherwise. It is an acknowledgment of the beauty of the universe, an acknowledgment the more sincere, because it is not formal, but indirect; it is a task light and easy to him who looks at the world in the spirit of love: further, it is a homage paid to the native and naked dignity of man, to the grand elementary principle of pleasure by which he knows, and feels, and lives, and moves. We have no sympathy but what is propagated by pleasure: I would not be misunderstood; but wherever we sympathise with pain, it will be found that the sympathy is produced and carried on by subtle combinations with pleasure. We have no knowledge, that is, no general principles drawn from the contemplation of particular facts, but what has been built up by pleasure, and exists in us by pleasure alone. The Man of Science, the Chemist and Mathematician, whatever difficulties and disgusts they may have had to struggle with, know and feel this. However painful may be the objects with which the Anatomist's knowledge is connected, he feels that his knowledge is pleasure; and where he has no pleasure he has no knowledge. What then does the Poet? He considers man and the objects that surround him as acting and re-acting upon each other, so as to produce an infinite complexity of pain and pleasure; he considers man in his own nature and in his ordinary life as contemplating this with a certain quantity of immediate knowledge, with certain convictions, intuitions, and deductions, which by habit become of the nature of intuitions; he considers him as looking upon this complex scene of ideas and sensations, and finding every where objects that immediately excite in him sympathies which, from the necessities of his nature, are accompanied by an overbalance of enjoyment.

To this knowledge which all men carry about with them, and to these sympathies in which, without any other discipline than that of our daily life, we are fitted to take delight, the Poet principally directs his attention. He considers man and nature as essentially adapted to each other, and the mind of man as naturally the mirror of the fairest and most interesting qualities of nature. And thus the Poet, prompted by this feeling of pleasure which accompanies him through the whole course of his studies, converses with general nature with affections akin to those, which, through labour and length of time, the Man of Science has raised up in himself, by conversing with those particular parts of nature which are the objects of his studies. The knowledge both of the Poet and the Man of Science is pleasure; but the knowledge of the one cleaves to us as a necessary part of our existence, our natural and unalienable inheritance; the other is a personal and individual acquisition, slow to come to us, and by no habitual and direct sympathy connecting us with our fellow-beings. The Man of Science seeks truth as a remote and unknown benefactor; he cherishes and loves it in his solitude: the Poet, singing a song in which all human beings join with him, rejoices in the presence of truth as our visible friend and hourly companion. Poetry is the breath and finer spirit of all knowledge; it is the impassioned expression which is in the countenance of all Science. Emphatically may it be said of the Poet, as Shakespeare hath said of man, "that he looks before and after." He is the rock of defence of human nature; an upholder and preserver, carrying every where with him relationship and love. In spite of difference of soil and climate, of language and manners, of laws and customs, in spite of things silently gone out of mind, and things violently destroyed, the Poet binds together by passion and knowledge the vast empire of human society, as it is spread over the whole earth, and over all time. The objects of the Poet's thoughts are every where; though the eyes and senses of man are, it is true, his favourite guides, yet he will follow wheresoever he can find an atmosphere of sensation in which to move his wings. Poetry is the first and last of all knowledge—it is as immortal as the heart of man. If the labours of Men of Science should ever create any material revolution, direct or indirect, in our condition, and in the impressions which we habitually receive, the Poet will sleep then no more than at present, but he will be ready to follow the steps of the Man of Science, not only in those general indirect effects, but he will be at his side, carrying sensation into the midst of the objects of the Science itself. The remotest discoveries of the Chemist, the Botanist, or Mineralogist, will be as proper objects of the Poet's art as any upon which it can be employed, if the time should ever come when these things shall be familiar to us, and the relations under which they are contemplated by the followers of these respective Sciences shall be manifestly and palpably material to us as enjoying and suffering beings. If the time should ever come when what is now called Science, thus familiarised to men, shall be ready to put on, as it were, a form of flesh and blood, the Poet will lend his divine spirit to aid the transfiguration, and will welcome the Being thus produced, as a dear and genuine inmate of the household of man.—It is not, then, to be supposed that any one, who holds that sublime notion of Poetry which I have attempted to convey, will break in upon the sanctity and truth of his pictures by transitory and accidental ornaments, and endeavour to excite admiration of himself by arts, the necessity of which must manifestly depend upon the assumed meanness of his subject.

What I have thus far said applies to Poetry in general; but especially to those parts of composition where the Poet speaks through the mouths of his characters; and upon this point it appears to have such weight, that I will conclude, there are few persons of good sense, who would not allow that the dramatic parts of composition are defective, in proportion as they deviate from the real language of nature, and are coloured by a diction of the Poet's own, either peculiar to him as an individual Poet or belonging simply to Poets in general, to a body of men who, from the circumstance of their compositions being in metre, it is expected will employ a particular language.

It is not, then, in the dramatic parts of composition that we look for this distinction of language; but still it may be proper and necessary where the Poet speaks to us in his own person and character. To this I answer by referring my Reader to the description which I have before given of a Poet.

Among the qualities which I have enumerated as principally conducing to form a Poet, is implied nothing differing in kind from other men, but only in degree. The sum of what I have there said is, that the Poet is chiefly distinguished from other men by a great promptness to think and feel without immediate external excitement, and a greater power in expressing such thoughts and feelings as are produced in him in that manner. But these passions and thoughts and feelings are the general passions and thoughts and feelings of men. And with what are they connected? Undoubtedly with our moral sentiments and animal sensations, and with the causes which excite these; with the operations of the elements, and the appearances of the visible universe; with storm and sunshine, with the revolutions of the seasons, with cold and heat, with loss of friends and kindred, with injuries and resentments, gratitude and hope, with fear and sorrow. These, and the like, are the sensations and objects which the Poet describes, as they are the sensations of other men, and the objects which interest them. The Poet thinks and feels in the spirit of the passions of men. How, then, can his language differ in any material degree from that of all other men who feel vividly and see clearly? It might be proved that it is impossible. But supposing that this were not the case, the Poet might then be allowed to use a peculiar language when expressing his feelings for his own gratification, or that of men like himself. But Poets do not write for Poets alone, but for men. Unless therefore we are advocates for that admiration which depends upon ignorance, and that pleasure which arises from hearing what we do not understand, the Poet must descend from this supposed height, and, in order to excite rational sympathy, he must express himself as other men express themselves. To this it may be added, that while he is only selecting from the real language of men, or which amounts to the same thing, composing accurately in the spirit of such selection, he is treading upon safe ground, and we know what we are to expect from him. Our feelings are the same with respect to metre; for, as it may be proper to remind the Reader, the distinction of metre is regular and uniform, and not, like that which is produced by what is usually called poetic diction, arbitrary, and subject to infinite caprices upon which no calculation whatever can be made. In the one case, the Reader is utterly at the mercy of the Poet respecting what imagery or diction he may choose to connect with the passion, whereas, in the other, the metre obeys certain laws, to which the Poet and Reader both willingly submit because they are certain, and because no interference is made by them with the passion but such as the concurring testimony of ages has shown to heighten and improve the pleasure which co-exists with it. . . .

I have said that poetry is the spontaneous overflow of powerful feelings: it takes its origin from emotion recollected in tranquility: the emotion is contemplated till, by a species of re-action, the tranquility gradually disappears, and an emotion, kindred to that which was before the subject of contemplation, is gradually produced, and does itself actually exist in the mind. In this mood successful composition generally begins, and in a mood similar to this it is carried on; but the emotion of whatever kind, and in whatever degree, from various causes, is qualified by various pleasures, so that in describing any passions whatsoever, which are voluntarily described, the mind will, upon the whole, be in a state of enjoyment. Now, if Nature be thus cautious in preserving in a state of enjoyment a being thus employed, the Poet ought to profit by the lesson thus held forth to him, and ought especially to take care, that whatever passions he communicates to his Reader, those passions, if his Reader's mind be sound and vigorous, should always be accompanied with an overbalance of pleasure. Now the music of harmonious metrical language, the sense of difficulty overcome, and the blind association of pleasure which has been previously received from works of rhyme or metre of the same or similar construction, an indistinct perception perpetually renewed of language closely resembling that of real life, and yet, in the circumstance of metre, differing from it so widely—all these imperceptibly make up a complex feeling of delight, which is of the most important use in tempering the painful feeling which will always be found intermingled with powerful descriptions of the deeper passions. . . .

Hazlitt

William Hazlitt (1778–1830), son of a Unitarian minister, spent part of his boyhood in the newly established United States that his father admired, before returning to finish his education in his native England. Although Hazlitt set out to be a portrait painter, his friendships with Samuel Coleridge and Charles Lamb turned him toward literary interests. A brilliant essayist, his *Lectures on the English Poets* (1818) afforded a presentation, popular in its time and useful in ours, of the Lake Poets' approach and ideas by a man who knew them well and who, in his clear expositions, may have done more than the poets themselves to popularize the new concepts of beauty and art.

Wordsworth and the Lake Poets

Mr. Wordsworth is at the head of that which has been denominated the Lake school of poetry; a school which, with all my respect for it, I do not think

---

Source: From *Lectures on the English Poets,* 1818.

sacred from criticism or exempt from faults, of some of which faults I shall speak with becoming frankness; for I do not see that the liberty of the press ought to be shackled, or freedom of speech curtailed, to screen either its revolutionary or renegade extravagances. This school of poetry had its origin in the French revolution, or rather in those sentiments and opinions which produced that revolution; and which sentiments and opinions were indirectly imported into this country in translation from the German about that period. Our poetical literature had, towards the close of the last century, degenerated into the most trite, insipid, and mechanical of all things, in the hands of the followers of Pope and the old French school of poetry. It wanted something to stir it up, and it found that something in the principles and events of the French revolution. From the impulse it thus received, it rose at once from the most servile imitation and tamest common-place, to the utmost pitch of singularity and paradox. The change in the belles-lettres was as complete, and to many persons as startling, as the change in politics, with which it went hand in hand. There was a mighty ferment in the heads of statesmen and poets, kings and people. According to the prevailing notions, all was to be natural and new. Nothing that was established was to be tolerated. All the common-place figures of poetry, tropes [figures of speech], allegories, personifications, with the whole heathen mythology, were instantly discarded; a classical allusion was considered as a piece of antiquated foppery; capital letters were no more allowed in print, than letters-patent of nobility were permitted in real life; kings and queens were dethroned from their rank and station in legitimate tragedy or epic poetry, as they were decapitated elsewhere; rhyme was looked upon as a relic of the feudal system, and regular metre was abolished along with regular government. Authority and fashion, elegance or arrangement, were hooted out of countenance as pedantry and prejudice. Every one did that which was good in his own eyes. The object was to reduce all things to an absolute level; and a singularly affected and outrageous simplicity prevailed in dress and manners, in style and sentiment. A striking effect produced where it was least expected, something new and original, no matter whether good, bad, or indifferent, whether mean or lofty, extravagant or childish, was all that was aimed at, or considered as compatible with sound philosophy and an age of reason. The licentiousness grew extreme: Coryate's *Crudites* were nothing to it. The world was to be turned topsy-turvy; and poetry, by the good will of our Adam-wits, was to share its fate and begin *de novo*. It was a time of promise, a renewal of the world and of letters; and the Deucalions, who were to perform this feat of regeneration, were the present poet laureate [Robert Southey] and the two authors of the *Lyrical Ballads*. The Germans, who made heroes of robbers, and honest women of cast-off mistresses, had already exhausted the extravagant and marvellous in sentiment and situation: our native writers adopted a wonderful simplicity of style and matter. The paradox they set out with was, that all things are by nature equally fit subjects for poetry; or that if there is any preference to be given, those that are the meanest and the most unpromising are the best, as they leave the greatest scope for the unbounded stores of thought and fancy in the writer's own mind.

❦

Chateaubriand

François-René de Chateaubriand (1768–1848), who in his life span saw five kings, one emperor, two republics, and a fair selection of revolutions pass over France, was a Breton nobleman who emigrated during the Revolution and returned to France in 1800 after years of exile and hardship. He made his reputation with the *Génie du Christianisme* (The Genius of Christianity, 1802), which pleaded the Catholic case against the rationalism of the Enlightenment and appealed less to philosophical argument than to souls searching for beauty and self-expression. Enough of these were abroad to make the work a great success. The new treatment of nature as a work of God, and of religion as a thing of beauty, was a milestone in the development of Romantic literature. It was popularized in two episodes of the *Génie,* based on Chateaubriand's American travels and published separately—*Atala* (1801) and *René* (1805)—stories of unhappy love, religious experience, and a young man's quest for self-fulfillment, that sold like hotcakes.

Chateaubriand's relations with Napoleon, who had at first been enthusiastic about the young man's religious propaganda when religion appeared useful as a pillar of national order, first cooled and then broke. After the murder of the Duc d'Enghien, kidnapped and executed by Napoleon's orders to strike terror into the hearts of any who might think of plotting against him, Chateaubriand retired into private life whence he only emerged after the Bourbon restoration to become, first, Ambassador to London, then Minister of Foreign Affairs. In the latter role he was responsible for the French expedition to Spain in support of the bloated and barbarous rule of the Spanish Bourbons. One is always someone else's tyrant.

His writing has all the sensitiveness, the passion, the brilliance of style and imaginative power, the eloquence and color, that soon became characteristic of the Romantic style. The *Memoirs* from which a passage follows were written when he had grown old and were entitled *Mémoires d'outre-tombe* (Memoirs from Beyond the Tomb) because he intended them to appear only after his death. They did, in fact, appear in 1849 and 1850, and while they are hardly in their bulk and contentiousness fit to be read at one go or to provide credible historical evidence, they do make excellent bedside reading and give a good idea of the influence their writer exercised over the development of Romantic attitudes in the first half of the nineteenth century.

The *Génie du Christianisme*

What hope could I have, I with no name and no extollers, of destroying the influence of Voltaire, which had prevailed for more than half a century, of Voltaire, who had raised the huge edifice completed by the Encyclopaedists and consolidated by all the famous men in Europe? What! were the Diderots, the d'Alemberts, the Duclos, the Dupuis, the Helvetius, the Condorcets minds that carried no authority? What! was the world to return to the Golden Legend, to renounce the admiration it had acquired for masterpieces of science and reason? How could I ever win a case which Rome armed with its thunders, the clergy with its might, had been unable to save: a case defended in vain by the Archbishop of Paris, Christophe de Beaumont, supported by the decrees of the Parliament and the armed force and name of the King? Was it not as ridiculous as it was rash on the part of an unknown man to set himself against a philosophical movement so irresistible as to have produced the Revolution? It was curious to see a pygmy "toughen his little arms" to stifle the progress of a century, stop civilization, and thrust back the human race! Thank God, a word would be enough to pulverize the madman: wherefore M. Ginguené, when trouncing the *Génie du Christianisme* in the *Décade,* declared that the criticism came too late, since my tautologous production was already forgotten. He said this five or six months after the publication of a work which the attack of the whole French Academy, on the occasion of the decennial prizes, was not able to kill.

It was amid the ruins of our temples that I published the *Génie du Christianisme*. The faithful thought themselves saved: men at that time felt a need for faith, a thirsting for religious consolations, which arose from the want of those consolations experienced since long years. What supernatural strength was required to bear all the adversities undergone! How many mutilated families had to go to the Father of mankind in search of the children they had lost! How many broken hearts, how many solitary souls, were calling for a divine hand to cure them! One threw one's self into the house of God, as one enters a doctor's house on the outbreak of an infection. The victims of our disturbances (and how many different kinds of victims!) saved themselves at the altar: shipwrecked men clinging to the rock on which they seek for salvation.

Bonaparte, at that time hoping to found his power on the first basis of society, had just made arrangements with the Court of Rome: he at first raised no obstacle against the publication of a work calculated to enhance the popularity of his schemes; he had to struggle against the men about him and

---

Source: From *Memoirs,* translated by A. Teixera de Mattos, New York, 1902.

against the declared enemies of religion; he was glad therefore to be defended from the outside by the opinion called up by the *Génie du Christianisme*. Later, he repented him of his mistake; ideas of regular monarchy had sprung into being together with ideas of religion.

An episode in the *Génie du Christianisme,* which at the time caused less stir than *Atala,* fixed one of the characters of modern literature; but I may say that, if *René* did not exist, I should not now write it: if it were possible for me to destroy it, I would do so. A family of *Renés,* poets and prose-writers, has swarmed into being: we have heard nothing but mournful and desultory phrases; it has been a question of nothing but winds and storms, of unknown words directed to the clouds and the night. No scribbler fresh from college but has imagined himself the unhappiest of men; no babe of sixteen but has believed himself to have exhausted life and to be tormented by his genius, but has, in the abyss of his thoughts, abandoned himself to the "wave of his passions," struck his pale and dishevelled brow, and astonished stupefied mankind with a misfortune of which he did not know the name, nor they either.

In *René* I had laid bare one of the infirmities of my century; but it was a different madness in the novelists to try to make universal such transcendental afflictions. The general sentiments which compose the basis of humanity, paternal and maternal affection, filial piety, friendship, love, are inexhaustible; but particular ways of feelings, idiosyncrasies of mind and character, cannot be spread out and multiplied over wide and numerous scenes. The small undiscovered corners of the human heart are a narrow field; there is nothing left to gather in that field after the hand which has been the first to mow it. A malady of the soul is not a permanent nor natural state: one cannot reproduce it, make a literature of it, make use of it as of a general passion constantly modified at the will of the artists who handle it and change its form.

Be that as it may, literature became tinged with the colours of my religious paintings, even as public affairs have retained the phraseology of my writings on citizenship: the *Monarchy according to the Charter* has been the rudiment of our representative government, and my article in the *Conservateur,* on "Moral Interests and Material Interests," has bequeathed those two designations to politics.

Writers did me the honour of imitating *Atala* and *René,* in the same way that the pulpit borrowed my accounts of the missions and advantages of Christianity. The passages in which I show that, by driving the pagan divinities from the woods, our broader religion has restored nature to its solitudes; the paragraphs where I discuss the influence of our religion upon our manner of seeing a painting, where I examine the changes wrought in poetry and eloquence; the chapters which I devote to inquiries into the foreign sentiments introduced into the dramatic characters of antiquity contain the germ of the new criticism. Racine's characters, as I have said, both are and are not Greek characters: they are Christian characters; that is what no one had understood.

If the effect of the *Génie du Christianisme* had been only a reaction against doctrines to which the revolutionary misfortunes were attributed, that effect would have ceased as soon as the cause was removed; it would not have been prolonged to the time at which I am writing. But the action of the *Génie du Christianisme* upon public opinion was not confined to the momentary resurrection of a religion supposed to be in its grave: a more lasting metamorphosis was operated. If the work contained innovations of style, it also contained changes of doctrine; not only the manner, but the matter was altered; atheism and materialism were no longer the basis of the belief or unbelief of young minds; the idea of God and of the immortality of the soul resumed its empire: whence came an alteration in the chain of ideas linked one to the other. A man was no longer riveted to his place by an antireligious prejudice; he no longer thought himself obliged to remain a mummy of annihilation, wrapped in philosophical swathing-bands; he permitted himself to examine any system, however absurd it might seem to him, even though it were Christian.

Besides the faithful who returned at the sound of there shepherd's voice, there were formed, by this right of free examination, other *a priori* faithful. Lay down God as a principle, and the Word will follow. The Son proceeds necessarily from the Father.

The various abstract combinations succeed only in substituting for the Christian mysteries other mysteries still more difficult of comprehension. Pantheism, which, besides, exists in three or four shapes, and which it is the fashion nowadays to ascribe to enlightened intelligences, is the absurdest of Eastern dreams brought back to light by Spinoza. One has but to read the article by the sceptic Bayle on that Jew of Amsterdam. The positive tone in which certain people speak of all these things would be revolting, were it not that it arises from want of study; they take up words which they do not understand, and imagine themselves to be transcendental geniuses. Be assured that Abelard, that St. Bernard, that St. Thomas Aquinas and their fellows brought to bear upon the study of metaphysics a superiority of judgment which we do not approach; that the Saint-Simonian, Phalansterian, Fourieristic, Humanitarian systems were discovered and practised by the different heresies; that what is placed before us as progress and discovery is so much old lumber hawked about for fifteen centuries in the schools of Greece and the colleges of the Middle Ages. The misfortune is that the first sectaries could not succeed in founding their Neo-Platonic Republic, when Gallienus permitted Plotinus to make the experiment in Campania; later, people made the great mistake of burning the sectaries when they proposed to establish the community of goods and to pronounce prostitution holy, by urging that a woman cannot, without sin, refuse a man who asks of her a transient union in the name of Jesus Christ; all that was needed, said they, to accomplish this union was to annihilate one's soul and deposit it for a moment in the bosom of God.

The shock which the *Génie du Christianisme* gave to men's minds caused the eighteenth century to emerge from the old road and flung it for ever out of its path. People began again, or rather they began for the first time to study the sources of Christianity; on re-reading the Fathers (presuming that they had read them before) they were struck at meeting with so many curious facts, so much philosophical science, so many beauties of style of every kind, so many ideas which, by a more or less perceptible gradation, produced the transition from ancient to modern society: an unique and memorable era of humanity, in which Heaven communicates with earth through the medium of souls set in men of genius.

Beside the crumbling world of paganism there arose, in former times, as though outside society, another world, looking on at those great spectacles, poor, retiring, secluded, taking no part in the business of life except when its lessons or its succour were needed. It was a marvellous thing to see those early bishops, almost all honoured with the name of saints and martyrs, those simple priests watching over the relics and cemeteries; those monks and hermits in their convents or in their caves, laying down laws of peace, morals, charity, when all was war, corruption, barbarism; going between the tyrants of Rome and the leaders of the Tartars and Goths, to prevent the injustice of the former and the cruelty of the latter; stopping armies with a wooden cross and a peaceful word; the weakest of men, and protecting the world against Attila; placed between two universes to be the link that joined them, to console the last moments of an expiring society and support the first steps of a society in its cradle.

It was impossible but that the truths unfolded in the *Génie du Christianisme* should contribute to a change of ideas. Again, it is to this work that the present love for the buildings of the Middle Ages is due: it is I who have called upon the young century to admire the old temples. If my opinion has been misused; if it is not true that our cathedrals approach the Parthenon in beauty; if it is false that those churches teach us unknown facts in their documents of stone; if it is madness to maintain that those granite memories reveal to us things that escaped the learned Benedictines; if by dint of eternally repeating the word Gothic people grow wearied to death of it: that is not my fault. For the rest, with respect to the arts, I know the shortcomings of the *Génie du Christianisme;* that portion of my work is faulty, because, in 1800, I was not acquainted with the arts: I had not seen Italy, nor Greece, nor Egypt. Also, I did not make sufficient use of the lives of the saints and of the legends, although they offered me a number of marvellous instances: by selecting with taste, one could there reap a plentiful harvest. This field of the wealth of mediaeval imagination surpasses the *Metamorphoses* of Ovid and the Milesian fables in fruitfulness. My work, moreover, contains some scanty or false judgments, such as that which I pronounce upon Dante, to whom I have since paid a brilliant tribute. In the serious respect, I have completed the *Génie du Christianisme* in my *Études historiques,* one of my writings that has been least spoken of and most plundered.

The success of *Atala* had delighted me, because my soul was still fresh; that of the *Génie du Christianisme* was painful to me: I was obliged to sacrifice my time to a more or less useful correspondence and to irrelevant civilities. A so-called admiration did not atone to me for the vexations that await a man whose name the crowd remembers. What good can supply the place of the peace which you have lost by admitting the public to your intimacy? Add to that the restlessness with which the Muses love to afflict those who attach themselves to their cult, the worries attendant upon a compliant character, inaptitude for fortune, loss of leisure, an uncertain temper, livelier affections, unreasonable melancholy, groundless joys: who, if he had the choice, would purchase on those conditions the uncertain advantages of a reputation which you are not sure of obtaining, which will be contested during your life, which posterity will refuse to confirm, and which your death will snatch from you for ever?

The literary controversy on innovations of style which *Atala* had aroused was renewed upon the publication of the *Génie du Christianisme.*

A characteristic feature of the imperial school, and even of the republican school, must be noted: while society advanced for better or for worse, literature remained stationary; foreign to the change of the ideas, it did not belong to its own time. In comedy, the squires of the village, the Colins, the Babets, or else the intrigues of the drawing-rooms, which were no longer known, were played, as I have already remarked, before coarse and bloodthirsty men, themselves the destroyers of the manners whose picture was presented to them; in tragedy, a plebeian pit interested itself in the families of nobles and kings.

Two things kept literature at the date of the eighteenth century: the impiety which it derived from Voltaire and the Revolution, and the despotism with which Bonaparte struck it. The head of the State found a profit in those subordinate letters which he had put in barracks, which presented arms to him, which sallied forth at the command of "Turn out, the guard!" which marched in rank, and which went through their evolutions like soldiers. Any form of independence seemed a rebellion against his power; he would no more consent to a riot of words and ideas than he suffered insurrection. He suspended the Habeas Corpus for thought as well as for individual liberty. Let us also recognise that the public, weary of anarchy, was glad to submit again to the yoke of law and order.

The literature which expresses the new era did not commence to reign until forty or fifty years after the time of which it was the idiom. During that half-century, it was employed only by the opposition. It was Madame de Staël, it was Benjamin Constant, it was Lemercier, it was Bonald, it was myself, in short, who were the first to speak that language. The alteration in literature of which the nineteenth century boasts came to it from the Emigration and from exile: it was M. de Fontanes who brooded on those birds of a different species from himself, because, by going back to the seventeenth century, he had gained the strength of that fertile period and lost the barrenness of the eighteenth. One portion of the human intelligence, that which treats of transcendental matters, alone advanced with an even step with civilisation; unfortunately, the glory of knowledge was not without stain: the Laplaces, the Lagranges, the Monges, the Chaptals, the Berthollets, all the prodigies, once haughty democrats, became Napoleon's most obsequious servants. Let it be said to the honour of Letters: the new literature was free, science was servile; character did not correspond with genius, and they whose thought had sped to the uppermost sky were not able to raise their souls above the feet of Bonaparte: they pretended to have no need of God, that was why they needed a tyrant.

The Napoleonic classic was the genius of the nineteenth century dressed up in the periwig of Louis XIV, or curled as in the days of Louis XV. Bonaparte had ordained that the men of the Revolution should not appear at Court save in full dress, sword at side. One saw nothing of the France of the moment; it was not order, it was discipline. Nor could anything be more tiresome than that pale resuscitation of the literature of former days. That cold copy, that unproductive anachronism, disappeared when the new literature broke in noisily with the *Génie du Christianisme*. The death of the Duc d'Enghien had for me this advantage: that, by causing me to step aside, it left me free in my solitude to follow my own inspiration, and prevented me from enlisting in the regular infantry of old Pindus: I owed my moral to my intellectual liberty.

In the last chapter of the *Génie du Christianisme*, I discuss what would have become of the world if the Faith had not been preached at the time of the invasion of the Barbarians; in another paragraph, I speak of an important work to be undertaken on the changes which Christianity introduced in the laws after the conversion of Constantine.

Supposing religious opinion to exist in its present form, if the *Génie du*

Christianisme were yet to be written, I would compose it quite differently: instead of recalling the benefits and the institutions of our religion in the past, I would show that Christianity is the thought of the future and of human liberty; that that redeeming and Messianic thought is the only basis of social equality; that it alone can establish the latter, because it places by the side of that equality the necessity of duty, the corrective and regulator of the democratic instinct. Legality is no sufficient restraint, because it is not permanent; it derives its strength from the law: now, the law is the work of men who pass away and differ. A law is not always obligatory; it can always be changed by another law: as opposed to that, morals are constant; they have their force within themselves, because they spring from the immutable order: they alone, therefore, can ensure permanency.

I would show that, wherever Christianity has prevailed, it has changed ideas, rectified notions of justice and injustice, substituted assertion for doubt, embraced the whole of humanity in its doctrines and precepts. I would try to conjecture the distance at which we still are from the total accomplishment of the Gospel, by calculating the number of evils that have been destroyed and of improvements that have been effected in the eighteen centuries which have elapsed on this side of the Cross. Christianity acts slowly, because it acts everywhere; it does not cling to the reform of any particular society, it works upon society in general; its philanthropy is extended to all the sons of Adam: that is what it expresses with a marvellous simplicity in its commonest petitions, in its daily prayers, when it says to the crowd in the temple:

"Let us pray for every suffering thing upon earth."

What religion has ever spoken in this way? The Word was not made flesh in the man of pleasure, it became incarnate in the man of sorrow, with a view to the enfranchisement of all, to an universal brotherhood and an infinite salvation.

If the *Génie du Christianisme* had only given rise to such investigations, I should congratulate myself on having published it. It remains to be seen whether, at the time of the appearance of the book, a different *Génie du Christianisme*, raised on the new plan the outline of which I have barely indicated, would have obtained the same success. In 1803, when nothing was granted to the old religion, when it was the object of scorn, when none knew the first word of the question, would one have done well to speak of future liberty as descending from Calvary, at a time when people were still bruised from the excesses of the liberty of the passions? Would Bonaparte have suffered such a work to appear? It was perhaps useful to stimulate regrets, to interest the imagination in a cause so misjudged, to call attention to the despised object, to render it endearing before showing how serious it was, how mighty and how salutary.

Now, supposing that my name leaves some trace behind it, I shall owe this to the *Génie du Christianisme:* with no illusion as to the intrinsic value of the work, I admit that it possesses an accidental value; it came just at the right moment. For this reason it caused me to take my place in one of those historic periods which, mixing an individual with things, compel him to be remembered. If the influence of my work was not limited to the change which, in the past forty years, it has produced among the living generations; if it still served to resuscitate among latecomers a spark of the civilizing truths of the earth; if the slight symptom of life which one seems to perceive was there sustained in the generations to come, I should depart full of hope in the divine mercy. O reconciled Christian, do not forget me in thy prayers, when I am gone; my faults, perhaps, will stop me outside those gates where my charity cried on thy behalf:

"Be ye lifted up, O eternal gates!"

Hugo

Victor Marie, Count Hugo (1802–1885), son of one of Napoleon's generals, may not be much in vogue today, though many of his books still sell (in bookshops, in cinemas, and onstage), but he was one of the most virile and dynamic figures of his time. André Gide, when asked to name the greatest of French poets, had to reply "Victor Hugo, alas!" and, though the grandeur and facility of his poetic output seem more doubtful today, his contemporaries were impressed. Louis XVIII gave him a royal pension, Louis-Philippe dubbed him a peer of France, the Second Republic elected him to its Assemblies, and the Third venerated him as a national monument. Only during the Second Empire, which his liberal politics opposed, did conviction (or pride) drive him into exile, where he produced one of the great Romantic novels of social history, *Les Misérables,* and a good deal of magnificent invective.

The plays whose prefaces appear below are landmarks both in his career and in that of the French theater. *Cromwell,* published in 1827, is too long, too poorly constructed, and too far removed from historical fact to count as a good play in any sense; but the long essay in which the young poet explained his ideas became the mainfesto of the new Romantic drama. *Hernani* is something more. Coming as it did after *Amy Robsart* had been hissed off the stage in 1828 and *Marion Delorme* banned by political censorship in 1829, it marked the pitched encounter between the old Classic and the new Romantic schools, and the victory of the latter. The play itself was hardly as significant as the occasion of its triumph: grandiloquent, involved, and unlikely, it mattered not for what it said but for the way it said it, breaking the classical rules and unities, roaming wildly in time and space, and allowing "prosaic" turns of phrase to creep into a verse structure that tragedy had hitherto maintained at loftier levels.

Berlioz, Delacroix, Gautier, Gérard de Nerval, and other young men of the young generation supported Hugo in the battle over *Hernani,* which began with its debut on February 25, 1830, and went on for several weeks not only as a fight for artistic freedom, but also as a vast undergraduate rag in which the young rebels rose against their dull and established elders. When the battle had been won and Hugo's partisans had shouted down the embattled bourgeoisie, the right of the artist to use the concrete, the commonplace, the pedestrian and particular detail, had been established on the French stage, and the revolution was just as successful as that which followed a few months later to overthrow Charles X was successful—that is, as limited. For just as the July Monarchy deceived its more radical supporters, so the Romantic revolution soon turned out to be too respectable, too dull, above all too divorced from reality, for the taste of the more advanced among the young. Both Balzac and Stendhal, who had been present on the famous first night,[1] came to feel that Hugo's principles were no safe or sufficient guide in a quest that must carry the artist much further than mere technical innovations or the assertion of certain stylistic liberties. In feeling this they heralded, as did Sainte-Beuve, the next step in the artistic development of the time; a step, however, which could not have been taken before *Hernani's* tumultuous success had consolidated the victory of Romantic tragedy.

Preface to *Cromwell*

The drama contained in the following pages has nothing to commend it to the attention or the good will of the public. It has not, to attract the interest of political disputants, the advantage of the veto of the official censorship, nor even, to win for it at the outset the literary sympathy of men of taste, the honour of having been formally rejected by an infallible reading committee.

It presents itself, therefore, to the public gaze, naked and friendless, like the infirm man of the Gospel—*solus, pauper, nudus.*

Not without some hesitation, moreover, did the author determine to burden his drama with a preface. Such things are usually of very little interest to the reader. He inquires concerning the talent of a writer rather than concerning his point of view; and in determining whether a work is good or bad, it matters little to him upon what ideas it is based, or in what sort of a mind it germinated. One seldom inspects the cellars of a house after visiting its salons, and when one eats the fruit of a tree, one cares but little about its root.

On the other hand, notes and prefaces are sometimes a convenient method of adding to the weight of a book, and of magnifying, in appearance at least,

---

[1]After the first night, to which Prosper Mérimée had secured him a ticket, Stendhal had written: "Champagne and *Hernani* did not suit me at all."

Source: From *The Dramatic Works of Victor Hugo,* translated by George Burnham Ives, Vol. III, pp. 3–54. New York: The Athenaeum Society, copyright 1909 by Little, Brown and Company.

the importance of a work; as a matter of tactics this is not dissimilar to that of the general who, to make his battlefront more imposing, puts everything, even his baggage-trains, in the line. And then, while critics fall foul of the preface and scholars of the notes, it may happen that the work itself will escape them, passing uninjured between their crossfires, as an army extricates itself from a dangerous position between two skirmishes of outposts and rearguards.

These reasons, weighty as they may seem, are not those which influenced the author. This volume did not need to be *inflated,* it was already too stout by far. Furthermore, and the author does not know why it is so, his prefaces, frank and ingenuous as they are, have always served rather to compromise him with the critics than to shield him. Far from being staunch and trusty bucklers, they have played him a trick like that played in a battle by an unusual and conspicuous uniform, which, calling attention to the soldier who wears it, attracts all the blows and is proof against none.

Considerations of an altogether different sort acted upon the author. It seemed to him that, although in fact, one seldom inspects the cellars of a building for pleasure, one is not sorry sometimes to examine its foundations. He will, therefore, give himself over once more, with a preface, to the wrath of the *feuilletonists.*[1] *Che sara, sara.* He has never given much thought to the fortune of his works, and he is but little appalled by dread of the literary *what will people say.* In the discussion now raging, in which the theatre and the schools, the public and the academies, are at daggers drawn, one will hear, perhaps, not without some interest, the voice of a solitary *apprentice* of nature and truth, who has withdrawn betimes from the literary world, for pure love of letters, and who offers good faith in default of good taste, sincere conviction in default of talent, study in default of learning. . . .

This said, let us pass on.

Let us set out from a fact. The same type of civilization, or to use a more exact, although more extended expression, the same society, has not always inhabited the earth. The human race as a whole has grown, has developed, has matured, like one of ourselves. It was once a child, it was once a man; we are now looking on at its impressive old age. Before the epoch which modern society has dubbed "ancient," there was another epoch which the ancients called "fabulous," but which it would be more accurate to call "primitive." Behold then three great successive orders of things in civilization, from its origin down to our days. Now, as poetry is always superposed upon

---

[1]Newspaper critics.

society, we propose to try to demonstrate, from the form of its society, what the character of the poetry must have been in those three great ages of the world—primitive times, ancient times, modern times.

In primitive times, when man awakes in a world that is newly created, poetry awakes with him. In the face of the marvellous things that dazzle and intoxicate him, his first speech is a hymn simply. He is still so close to God that all his meditations are ecstatic, all his dreams are visions. His bosom swells, he sings as he breathes. His lyre has but three strings—God, the soul, creation; but this threefold mystery envelops everything, this threefold idea embraces everything. The earth is still almost deserted. There are families, but no nations; patriarchs, but no kings. Each race exists at its own pleasure; no property, no laws, no contentions, no wars. Everything belongs to each and to all. Society is a community. Man is restrained in nought. He leads that nomadic pastoral life with which all civilizations begin, and which is so well adapted to solitary contemplation, to fanciful reverie. He follows every suggestion, he goes hither and thither, at random. His thought, like his life, resembles a cloud that changes its shape and its direction according to the wind that drives it. Such is the first man, such is the first poet. He is young, he is cynical. Prayer is his sole religion, the ode is his only form of poetry.

This ode, this poem of primitive times, is Genesis.

By slow degrees, however, this youth of the world passes away. All the spheres progress; the family becomes a tribe, the tribe becomes a nation. Each of these groups of men camps about a common centre, and kingdoms appear. The social instinct succeeds the nomadic instinct. The camp gives place to the city, the tent to the palace, the ark to the temple. The chiefs of these nascent states are still shepherds, it is true, but shepherds of nations; the pastoral staff has already assumed the shape of a sceptre. Everything tends to become stationary and fixed. Religion takes on a definite shape; prayer is governed by rites; dogma sets bounds to worship. Thus the priest and king share the paternity of the people; thus theocratic society succeeds the patriarchal community.

Meanwhile the nations are beginning to be packed too closely on the earth's surface. They annoy and jostle one another; hence the clash of empires—war. They overflow upon another; hence, the migrations of nations—voyages. Poetry reflects these momentous events; from ideas it proceeds to things. It sings of ages, of nations, of empires. It becomes epic, it gives birth to Homer.

Homer, in truth, dominates the society of ancient times. In that society, all is simple, all is epic. Poetry is religion, religion is law. . . .

We say again, such a civilization can find its one expression only in the epic. The epic will assume diverse forms, but will never lose its specific character. Pindar is more priestlike than patriarchal, more epic than lyrical. If the chroniclers, the necessary accompaniments of this second age of the world, set about collecting traditions and began to reckon by centuries, they labour to no purpose—chronology cannot expel poesy; history remains an epic. Herodotus is a Homer.

But it is in the ancient tragedy, above all, that the epic breaks out at every turn. It mounts the Greek stage without losing aught, so to speak, of its immeasurable, gigantic proportions. Its characters are still heroes, demigods, gods; its themes are visions, oracles, fatality; its scenes are battles, funeral rites, catalogues. That which the rhapsodists formerly sang, the actors declaim—that is the whole difference.

There is something more. When the whole plot, the whole spectacle of the epic poem have passed to the stage, the Chorus takes all that remains. The Chorus annotates the tragedy, encourages the heroes, gives descriptions, summons and expels the daylight, rejoices, laments, sometimes furnishes the scenery, explains the moral bearing of the subject, flatters the listening assemblage. Now, what is the Chorus, this anomalous character standing between the spectacle and the spectator, if it be not the poet completing his epic?

The theatre of the ancients is, like their dramas, huge, pontifical, epic. It is capable of holding thirty thousand spectators; the plays are given in the open air, in bright sunlight; the performances last all day. The actors disguise their voices, wear masks, increase their stature; they make themselves gigantic, like their roles. The stage is immense. It may represent at the same moment both the interior and the exterior of a temple, a palace, a camp, a city. Upon it, vast spectacles are displayed. There is—we cite only from memory—Prometheus on his mountain; there is Antigone, at the top of a tower, seeking her brother Polynices in the hostile army *(The Phoenicians)*; there is Evadne hurling herself from a cliff into the flames where the body of Capaneus is burning (*The Suppliants* of Euripides); there is a ship sailing into port and landing fifty princesses with their retinues (*The Suppliants* of Aeschylus). Architecture, poetry, everything assumes a monumental character. In all antiquity there is nothing more solemn, more majestic. Its history and its religion are mingled on its stage. Its first actors are priests; its scenic performances are religious ceremonies, national festivals.

One last observation, which completes our demonstration of the epic character of this epoch: in the subjects which it treats, no less than in the forms it adopts, tragedy simply re-echoes the epic. All the ancient tragic authors derive their plots from Homer. The same fabulous exploits, the same catastrophes, the same heroes. One and all drink from the Homeric stream. The *Iliad* and *Odyssey* are always in evidence. Like Achilles dragging Hector at his chariot-wheel, the Greek tragedy circles about Troy.

But the age of the epic draws near its end. Like the society that it repre-

sents, this form of poetry wears itself out revolving upon itself. Rome reproduces Greece, Virgil copies Homer, and, as if to make a becoming end, epic
poetry expires in the last parturition.

It was time. Another era is about to begin, for the world and for poetry.

A spiritual religion, supplanting the material and external paganism, makes
its way to the heart of the ancient society, kills it, and deposits, in that corpse
of a decrepit civilization, the germ of modern civilization. This religion is
complete, because it is true; between its dogma and its cult, it embraces a
deep-rooted moral. And first of all, as a fundamental truth, it teaches man
that he has two lives to live, one ephemeral, the other immortal; one on earth,
the other in heaven. It shows him that he, like his destiny, is twofold: that
there is in him an animal and an intellect, a body and a soul; in a word, that
he is the point of intersection, the common link of the two chains of beings
which embrace all creation—of the chain of material beings and the chain of
incorporeal beings; the first starting from the rock to arrive at man, the second starting from man to end at God.

A portion of these truths had perhaps been suspected by certain wise men
of ancient times, but their full, broad, luminous revelation dates from the
Gospels. The pagan schools walked in darkness, feeling their way, clinging
to falsehoods as well as to truths in their haphazard journeying. Some of their
philosophers occasionally cast upon certain subjects feeble gleams which illuminated but one side and made the darkness of the other side more profound. Hence all the phantoms created by ancient philosophy. None but divine wisdom was capable of substituting an even and all-embracing light for
all those flickering rays of human wisdom. Pythagoras, Epicurus, Socrates,
Plato, are torches; Christ is the glorious light of day.

Nothing could be more material, indeed, than the ancient theogony. Far
from proposing, as Christianity does, to separate the spirit from the body, it
ascribes form and features to everything, even to impalpable essences, even
to the intelligence. In it everything is visible, tangible; fleshly. Its gods need
a cloud to conceal themselves from men's eyes. They eat, drink, and sleep.
They are wounded and their blood flows; they are maimed, and lo! they limp
forever after. That religion has gods and halves of gods. Its thunderbolts are
forged on an anvil, and among other things three rays of twisted rain *(tres
imbris torti radios)* enter into their composition. Its Jupiter suspends the
world by a golden chain; its sun rides into a four-horse chariot; its hell is a
precipice the brink of which is marked on the globe; its heaven is a mountain.

Thus paganism, which moulded all creations from the same clay, minimizes
divinity and magnifies man. Homer's heroes are of almost the same stature
as his gods. Ajax defies Jupiter, Achilles is the peer of Mars. Christianity on
the contrary, as we have seen, draws a broad line of division between spirit

and matter. It places an abyss between the soul and the body, an abyss between man and God.

At this point—to omit nothing from the sketch upon which we have ventured—we will call attention to the fact that, with Christianity, and by its means, there entered into the mind of the nations a new sentiment, unknown to the ancients and marvellously developed among moderns, a sentiment which is more than gravity and less than sadness—melancholy. In truth, might not the heart of man, hitherto deadened by religions purely hierarchical and sacerdotal, awake and feel springing to life within it some unexpected faculty, under the breath of a religion that is human because it is divine, a religion which makes of the poor man's prayer, the rich man's wealth, a religion of equality, liberty and charity? Might it not see all things in a new light, since the Gospel had shown it the soul through the senses, eternity behind life?

Moreover, at that very moment the world was undergoing so complete a revolution that it was impossible that there should not be a revolution in men's minds. Hitherto the catastrophes of empires had rarely reached the hearts of the people; it was kings who fell, majesties that vanished, nothing more. The lightning struck only in the upper regions, and, as we have already pointed out, events seemed to succeed one another with all the solemnity of the epic. In the ancient society, the individual occupied so lowly a place that, to strike him, adversity must needs descend to his family. So that he knew little of misfortune outside of domestic sorrows. It was an almost unheard-of thing that the general disasters of the state should disarrange his life. But the instant that Christian society became firmly established, the ancient continent was thrown into confusion. Everything was pulled up by the roots. Events, destined to destroy ancient Europe and to construct a new Europe, trod upon one another's heels in their ceaseless rush, and drove the nations pell-mell, some into the light, others into darkness. So much uproar ensued that it was impossible that some echoes of it should not reach the hearts of the people. It was more than an echo, it was a reflex blow. Man, withdrawing within himself in presence of these imposing vicissitudes, began to take pity upon mankind, to reflect upon the bitter disillusionments of life. Of this sentiment, which to Cato the heathen was despair, Christianity fashioned melancholy.

At the same time was born the spirit of scrutiny and curiosity. These great catastrophes were also great spectacles, impressive cataclysms. It was the North hurling itself upon the South; the Roman world changing shape; the last convulsive throes of a whole universe in the death agony. As soon as that world was dead, lo! clouds of rhetoricians, grammarians, sophists, swooped down like insects on its immense body. People saw them swarming and heard them buzzing in that seat of putrefaction. They vied with one another in scrutinizing, commenting, disputing. Each limb, each muscle, each fibre of the huge prostrate body was twisted and turned in every direction. Surely it must have been a keen satisfaction to those anatomists of the mind, to be able, at their début, to make experiments on a large scale; to have a dead society to dissect, for their first "subject."

Thus we see melancholy and meditation, the demons of analysis and controversy, appear at the same moment, and, as it were, hand-in-hand. At one extremity of this era of transition is Longinus, at the other St. Augustine. We must beware of casting a disdainful eye upon that epoch wherein all that has since borne fruit was contained in germs; upon that epoch whose least eminent writers, if we may be pardoned a vulgar but expressive phrase, made fertilizer for the harvest that was to follow. The Middle Ages were grafted on the Lower Empire.

Behold, then, a new religion, a new society; upon this twofold foundation there must inevitably spring up a new poetry. Previously—we beg pardon for setting forth a result which the reader has probably already foreseen from what has been said above—previously, following therein the course pursued by the ancient polytheism and philosophy, the purely epic muse of the ancients had studied nature in only a single aspect, casting aside without pity almost everything in art which, in the world subjected to its imitation, had not relation to a certain type of beauty. A type which was magnificent at first, but, as always happens with everything systematic, became in later times false, trivial and conventional. Christianity leads poetry to the truth. Like it, the modern muse will see things in a higher and broader light. It will realize that everything in creation is not humanly *beautiful*, that the ugly exists beside the beautiful, the unshapely beside the graceful, the grotesque on the reverse of the sublime, evil with good, darkness with light. It will ask itself if the narrow and relative sense of the artist should prevail over the infinite, absolute sense of the Creator; if it is for man to correct God; if a mutilated nature will be the more beautiful for the mutilation; if art has the right to duplicate, so to speak, man, life, creation; if things will progress better when their muscles and their vigour have been taken from them; if, in short, to be incomplete is the best way to be harmonious. Then it is that, with its eyes fixed upon events that are both laughable and redoubtable, and under the influence of that spirit of Christian melancholy and philosophical criticism which we described a moment ago, poetry will take a great step, a decisive step, a step which, like the upheaval of an earthquake, will change the whole face of the intellectual world. It will set about doing as nature does, mingling in its creations—but without confounding them—darkness and light, the grotesque and the sublime; in other words, the body and the soul, the beast and the intellect; for the starting-point of religion is always the starting-point of poetry. All things are connected.

Thus, then, we see a principle unknown to the ancients, a new type, introduced in poetry; and as an additional element in anything modifies the whole of the thing, a new form of the art is developed. This type is the grotesque; its new form is comedy.

And we beg leave to dwell upon this point; for we have now indicated the significant feature, the fundamental difference which, in our opinion, separates modern from ancient art, the present form from the defunct form; or, to use less definite but more popular terms, *romantic* literature from *classical* literature.

"At last!" exclaim the people who for some time past *have seen what we were coming at,* "at last we have you—you are caught in the act. So then you put forward the ugly as a type for imitation, you make the *grotesque* an element of art. But the graces; but good taste! Don't you know that art should correct nature? that we must *ennoble* art? that we must *select*? Did the ancients ever exhibit the ugly or the grotesque? Did they ever mingle comedy and tragedy? The example of the ancients, gentlemen! And Aristotle, too; and Boileau; and La Harpe. Upon my word!"

These arguments are sound, doubtless, and, above all, of extraordinary novelty. But it is not our place to reply to them. We are constructing no system here—God protect us from systems! We are stating a fact. We are a historian, not a critic. Whether the fact is agreeable or not matters little; it is a fact. Let us resume, therefore, and try to prove that it is of the fruitful union of the grotesque and the sublime types that modern genius is born—so complex, so diverse in its forms, so inexhaustible in its creations; and therein directly opposed to the uniform simplicity of the genius of the ancients; let us show that that is the point from which we must set out to establish the real and radical difference between the two forms of literature. . . .

In truth, in the new poetry, while the sublime represents the soul as it is, purified by Christian morality, the grotesque plays the part of the human beast. The former type, delivered of all impure alloy, has as its attributes all the charms, all the graces, all the beauties; it must be able some day to create Juliet, Desdemona, Ophelia. The latter assumes all the absurdities, all the infirmities, all the blemishes. In this partition of mankind and of creation, to it fall the passions, vices, crimes; it is sensuous, fawning, greedy, miserly, false, incoherent, hypocritical; it is, in turn, Iago, Tartuffe, Basile, Polonius, Harpagon, Bartholo, Falstaff, Scapin, Figaro. The beautiful has but one type, the ugly has a thousand. The fact is that the beautiful, humanly speaking, is merely form considered in its simplest aspect, in its most perfect symmetry, in its most entire harmony with our make-up. Thus the *ensemble* that it offers us is always complete, but restricted like ourselves. What we call the ugly, on the contrary, is a detail of a great whole which eludes us, and which is in harmony, not with man but with all creation. That is why it constantly presents itself to us in new but incomplete aspects.

It is interesting to study the first appearance and the progress of the grotesque in modern times. At first, it is an invasion, an eruption, an overflow, as of a torrent that has burst its banks. It rushes through the expiring Latin literature . . . it imposes its characteristic qualities upon that wonderful architecture which, in the Middle Ages, takes the place of all the arts. It affixes its mark on the façades of cathedrals, frames its hells and purgatories in the ogive arches of great doorways, portrays them in brilliant hues on window-glass, exhibits its monsters, its bull-dogs, its imps about capitals, along friezes, on the edges of roofs. It flaunts itself in numberless shapes on the wooden façades of houses, on the stone façades of châteaux, on the marble façades of palaces. From the arts it makes its way into the national manners, and while it stirs applause from the people for the *graciosos* of comedy, it gives to the kings court-jesters. . . . From the manners, it makes its way into the laws; numberless strange customs attest its passage through the institutions of the Middle Ages. . . . Finally, having made its way into the arts, the manners, and the laws, it enters even the Church. In every Catholic city we see it organizing some one of those curious ceremonies, those strange processions, wherein religion is attended by all varieties of superstition—the sublime attended by all the forms of the grotesque. To paint it in one stroke, so great is its vigour, its energy, its creative sap, at the dawn of letters, that it casts, at the outset, upon the threshold of modern poetry, three burlesque Homers: Ariosto in Italy, Cervantes in Spain, Rabelais in France.

It would be mere surplusage to dwell further upon the influence of the grotesque in the third civilization. Everything tends to show its close creative alliance with the beautiful in the so-called "romantic" period. Even among the simplest popular legends there are none which do not somewhere, with an admirable instinct, solve this mystery of modern art. Antiquity could not have produced *Beauty and the Beast.* . . .

We have now reached the poetic culmination of modern times. Shakespeare is the drama; and the drama, which with the same breath moulds the grotesque and the sublime, the terrible and the absurd, tragedy and comedy—the drama is the distinguishing characteristic of the third epoch of poetry, of the literature of the present day.

Thus, to sum up hurriedly the facts that we have noted thus far, poetry has three periods, each of which corresponds to an epoch of civilization: the ode, the epic, and the drama. Primitive times are lyrical, ancient times epical, modern times dramatic. The ode sings of eternity, the epic imparts solemnity to history, the drama depicts life. The characteristic of the first poetry is ingenuousness, of the second, simplicity, of the third, truth. The rhapsodists mark the transition from the lyric to the epic poets, as do the romancists that from the lyric to the dramatic poets. Historians appear in the second period, chroniclers and critics in the third. The characters of the ode are colossi—Adam, Cain, Noah; those of the epic are giants—Achilles, Atreus, Orestes; those of the drama are men—Hamlet, Macbeth, Othello. The ode lives upon the ideal, the epic upon the grandiose, the drama upon the real. Lastly, this threefold poetry flows from three great sources—The Bible, Homer, Shakespeare.

Such then—and we confine ourselves herein to noting a single result—such are the diverse aspects of thought in the different epochs of mankind and of civilization. Such are its three faces, in youth, in manhood, in old age. Whether one examines one literature by itself or all literatures *en masse,* one will always reach the same result: the lyric poets before the epic poets, the epic poets before the dramatic poets. In France, Malherbe before Chapelain, Chapelain before Corneille; in ancient Greece, Orpheus before Homer, Homer before Aeschylus; in the first of all books, *Genesis* before *Kings, Kings* before *Job;* or to come back to that monumental scale of all ages of poetry, which we ran over a moment since, The Bible before the *Iliad,* the *Iliad* before Shakespeare.

In a word, civilization begins by singing of its dreams, then narrates its doings, and, lastly, sets about describing what it thinks. It is, let us say in passing, because of this last, that the drama, combining the most opposed qualities, may be at the same time full of profundity and full of relief, philosophical and picturesque. . . .

The drama, then, is the goal to which everything in modern poetry leads. *Paradise Lost* is a drama before it is an epic. As we know, it first presented itself to the poet's imagination in the first of these forms, and as a drama it always remains in the reader's memory, so prominent is the old dramatic framework still beneath Milton's epic structure! When Dante had finished his terrible *Inferno,* when he had closed its doors and nought remained save to give his work a name, the unerring instinct of his genius showed him that that multiform poem was an emanation of the drama, not of the epic; and on the front of that gigantic monument, he wrote with his pen of bronze: *Divina Commedia.* . . .

On the day when Christianity said to man: "Thou art twofold, thou art made up of two beings, one perishable, the other immortal, one carnal, the other ethereal, one enslaved by appetites, cravings and passions, the other borne aloft on the wings of enthusiasm and reverie—in a word, the one always stooping toward the earth, its mother, the other always darting up toward heaven, its fatherland"—on that day the drama was created. Is it, in truth, anything other than that contrast of every day, that struggle of every moment, between two opposing principles which are ever face to face in life, and which dispute possession of man from the cradle to the tomb?

The poetry born of Christianity, the poetry of our time, is, therefore, the drama; the real results from the wholly natural combination of two types, the sublime and the grotesque, which meet in the drama, as they meet in life and in creation. For true poetry, complete poetry, consists in the harmony of contraries. Hence, it is time to say aloud—and it is here above all that exceptions prove the rule—that everything that exists in nature exists in art.

On taking one's stand at this point of view, to pass judgment on our petty conventional rules, to disentangle all those scholastic labyrinths, to solve all those trivial problems which the critics of the last two centuries have laboriously built up about the art, one is struck by the promptitude with which the question of the modern stage is made clear and distinct. The drama has but to take a step to break all the spiders' webs with which the militia of Lilliput have attempted to fetter its sleep.

And so, let addle-pated pedants (one does not exclude the other) claim that the deformed, the ugly, the grotesque should never be imitated in art; one replies that the grotesque is comedy, and that comedy apparently makes a part of art. Tartuffe is not handsome, Pourceaugnac is not noble, but Pourceaugnac and Tartuffe are admirable flashes of art.

If, driven back from this entrenchment to their second line of customhouses, they renew their prohibition of the grotesque coupled with the sublime, of comedy melted into tragedy, we prove to them that, in the poetry of Christian nations, the first of these two types represents the human beast, the second the soul. These two stalks of art, if we prevent their branches from mingling, if we persistently separate them, will produce by way of fruit, on the one hand abstract vices and absurdities, on the other, abstract crime, heroism and virtue. The two types, thus isolated and left to themselves, will go each its own way, leaving the real between them, at the left hand of one, at the right hand of the other. Whence it follows that after all these abstractions there will remain something to represent—man; after these tragedies and comedies, something to create—the drama.

In the drama, as it may be conceived at least, if not executed, all things are connected and follow one another as in real life. The body plays its part no less than the mind; and men and events, set in motion by this twofold agent, pass across the stage, burlesque and terrible in turn, and sometimes both at once. Thus the judge will say: "Off with his head and let us go to dinner!" Thus the Roman Senate will deliberate over Domitian's turbot. Thus Socrates, drinking the hemlock and discoursing on the immortal soul and the only God, will interrupt himself to suggest that a cock be sacrificed to Aesculapius. Thus Elizabeth will swear and talk Latin. Thus Richelieu will submit to Joseph the Capuchin, and Louis XI to his barber, Maître Olivier le Diable. Thus Cromwell will say: "I have Parliament in my bag and the King in my pocket"; or, with the hand that signed the death sentence of Charles I, smear with ink the face of a regicide who smilingly returns the compliment. Thus Caesar, in his triumphal car, will be afraid of overturning. For men of genius, however great they be, have always within them a touch of the beast which mocks at their intelligence. Therein they are akin to mankind in general, for therein they are dramatic. "It is but a step from the sublime to the ridiculous," said Napoleon, when he was convinced that he was mere man; and that outburst of a soul on fire illumines art and history at once; that cry of anguish is the resumé of the drama and of life.

It is a striking fact that all these contrasts are met with in the poets themselves, taken as men. By dint of meditating upon existence, of laying stress upon its bitter irony, of pouring floods of sarcasm and raillery upon our infirmities, the very men who make us laugh so heartily become profoundly sad. These Democrituses are Heraclituses as well. Beaumarchais was surly. Molière gloomy, Shakespeare melancholy.

The fact is, then, that the grotesque is one of the supreme beauties of the drama. It is not simply an appropriate element of it, but is oftentimes a necessity. Sometimes it appears in homogeneous masses, in entire characters, as [in] Juliet's nurse; sometimes impregnated with terror, as Richard III, ... Tartuffe, Mephistopheles; sometimes, too, with a veil of grace and refinement, as Figaro, Osric, Mercutio, Don Juan. It finds its way in everywhere; for just as the most commonplace have their occasional moments of sublimity, so the most exalted frequently pay tribute to the trivial and ridiculous. Thus, often impalpable, often imperceptible, it is always present on the stage, even when it says nothing, even when it keeps out of sight. Thanks to it, there is no thought of monotony. Sometimes it injects laughter, sometimes horror, into tragedy. It will bring Romeo face to face with the apothecary, Macbeth with the witches, Hamlet with the grave-diggers. Sometimes it may, without discord, as in the scene between King Lear and his jester, mingle its shrill voice with the most sublime, the most dismal, the dreamiest music of the soul.

That is what Shakespeare alone among all has succeeded in doing, in a fashion of his own, which it would be no less fruitless than impossible to imitate—Shakespeare, the god of the stage, in whom, as in a trinity, the three characteristic geniuses of our stage, Corneille, Molière, Beaumarchais, seem united.

We see how quickly the arbitrary distinction between the species of poetry vanishes before common sense and taste. No less easily one might demolish the alleged rule of the two unities. We say *two* and not *three* unities, because unity of plot or of *ensemble,* the only true and well-founded one, was long ago removed from the sphere of discussion.

Distinguished contemporaries, foreigners and Frenchmen, have already attacked, both in theory and in practice, that fundamental law of the pseudo-Aristotelian code. Indeed, the combat was not likely to be a long one. At the first blow it cracked, so worm-eaten was that timber of the old scholastic hovel!

The strange thing is that the slaves of routine pretend to rest their rule of the two unities on probability, whereas reality is the very thing that destroys it. Indeed, what could be more improbable and absurd than this porch or peristyle or ante-chamber—vulgar places where our tragedies are obliging enough to develop themselves; whither conspirators come, no one knows whence, to declaim against the tyrant, and the tyrant to declaim against the conspirators, each in turn, as if they had said to one another in bucolic phrase:—

Alternis cantemus; amant alterna Camenae.[2]

Where did anyone ever see a porch or peristyle of that sort? What could be more opposed—we will not say to the truth, for the scholastics hold it very cheap, but to probability? The result is that everything that is too characteristic, too intimate, too local, to happen in the ante-chamber or on the street-corner—that is to say, the whole drama—takes place in the wings. We see on the stage only the elbows of the plot, so to speak; its hands are somewhere else. Instead of scenes we have narrative; instead of tableaux, descriptions. Solemn-faced characters, placed, as in the old chorus, between the drama and ourselves, tell us what is going on in the temple, in the palace, on the public square, until we are tempted many a time to call out to them: "Indeed! then take us there! It must be very entertaining—a fine sight!" To which they would reply no doubt: "It is quite possible that it might entertain or interest you, but that isn't the question; we are the guardians of the dignity of the French Melpomene." And there you are!

"But," someone will say, "this rule that you discard is borrowed from the Greek drama." Wherein, pray, do the Greek stage and drama resemble our

---

[2] We shall sing in alternate verses; the muses enjoy alternation.

stage and drama? Moreover, we have already shown that the vast extent of the ancient stage enabled it to include a whole locality, so that the poet could, according to the exigencies of the plot, transport it at his pleasure from one part of the stage to another, which is practically equivalent to a change of stage-setting. Curious contradiction! the Greek theatre, restricted as it was to a national and religious object, was much more free than ours, whose only object is the enjoyment, and, if you please, the instruction, of the spectator. The reason is that the one obeys only the laws that are suited to it, while the other takes upon itself conditions of existence which are absolutely foreign to its essence. One is artistic, the other artificial.

People are beginning to understand in our day that exact localization is one of the first elements of reality. The speaking or acting characters are not the only ones who engrave on the minds of the spectators a faithful representation of the facts. The place where this or that catastrophe took place becomes a terrible and inseparable witness thereof; and the absence of silent characters of this sort would make the greatest scenes of history incomplete in the drama. Would the poet dare to murder Rizzio elsewhere than in Mary Stuart's chamber? to stab Henri IV elsewhere than in Rue de la Ferronerie, all blocked with drays and carriages? to burn Jeanne d'Arc elsewhere than in the Vieux-Marché? to despatch the Duc de Guise elsewhere than in that château of Blois where his ambition roused a popular assemblage to frenzy? to behead Charles I and Louis XVI elsewhere than in those ill-omened localities whence Whitehall or the Tuileries may be seen, as if their scaffolds were appurtenances of their palaces?

Unity of time rests on no firmer foundation than unity of place. A plot forcibly confined within twenty-four hours is as absurd as one confined within a peristyle. Every plot has its proper duration as well as its appropriate place. Think of administering the same dose of time to all events! of applying the same measure to everything! You would laugh at a cobbler who should attempt to put the same shoe on every foot. To cross unity of time and unity of place like the bars of a cage, and pedantically to introduce therein, in the name of Aristotle, all the deeds, all the nations, all the figures which Providence sets before us in such vast numbers in real life—to proceed thus is to mutilate men and things, to cause history to make wry faces. Let us say, rather, that everything will die in the operation, and so the dogmatic mutilaters reach their ordinary result: what was alive in the chronicles is dead in tragedy. That is why the cage of the unities often contains only a skeleton. . . .

"But," the customs-officers of thought will cry, "great geniuses have submitted to these rules which you spurn!" Unfortunately, yes. But what would those admirable men have done if they had been left to themselves? At all events they did not accept your chains without a struggle. You should have seen how Pierre Corneille, worried and harassed at his first step in the art on account of his marvellous work, *Le Cid,* struggled under Mairet, Claveret, d'Aubignac and Scudéri! How he denounced to posterity the violent attacks of those men, who, he says, made themselves "all white with Aristotle"! You should read how they said to him—and we quote from books of the time: "Young man, you must learn before you teach; and unless one is a Scaliger or a Heinsius, that is intolerable!" Thereupon Corneille rebels and asks if their purpose is to force him "much below Claveret." Here Scudéri waxes indignant at such a display of pride, and reminds the "thrice great author of *Le Cid* of the modest words in which Tasso, the greatest man of his age, began his apology for the finest of his works against the bitterest and most unjust censure perhaps that will ever be pronounced. M. Corneille," he adds, "shows in his replies that he is as far removed from that author's moderation as from his merit." The young man *so justly and gently reproved* dares to protest; thereupon Scudéri returns to the charge; he calls to his assistance the Eminent Academy: "Pronounce, O my Judges, a decree worthy of your eminence, which will give all Europe to know that *Le Cid* is not the chef-d'oeuvre of the greatest man in France, but the least judicious performance of M. Corneille himself. You are bound to do it, both for your own private renown; and for that of our people in general, who are concerned in this matter; inasmuch as foreigners who may see this precious masterpiece—they who have possessed a Tasso or a Guarini—might think that our greatest masters were no more than apprentices."

These few instructive lines contain the everlasting tactics of envious routine against growing talent—tactics which are still followed in our own day, and which, for example, added such a curious page to the youthful essays of Lord Byron. Scudéri gives us its quintessence. In like manner the earlier works of a man of genius are always preferred to the newer ones, in order to prove that he is going down instead of up—*Mélite* and *La Galérie du Palais* placed above *Le Cid.* And the names of the dead are always thrown at the heads of the living—Corneille stoned with Tasso and Guarini (Guarini!), as, later, Racine will be stoned with Corneille, Voltaire with Racine, and as to-day, everyone who shows signs of rising is stoned with Corneille, Racine and Voltaire. These tactics, as will be seen, are well-worn; but they must be effective as they are still in use. However, the poor devil of a great man still breathed. Here we cannot help but admire the way in which Scudéri, the bully of this tragic-comedy, forced to the wall, blackguards and maltreats him, how pitilessly he unmasks his classical artillery, how he shows the author of *Le Cid* "what the episodes should be, according to Aristotle, who tells us in the tenth and sixteenth chapters of his *Poetics*"; how he crushes Corneille, in the name of the same Aristotle "in the eleventh chapter of his *Art of Poetry,* wherein we find the condemnation of *Le Cid*"; in the name of Plato, "in the tenth book of his *Republic*"; in the name of Marcellinus, "as may be seen in the twenty-seventh book"; in the name of "the tragedies of Niobe and Jephthah"; in the name of the "*Ajax* of Sophocles"; in the name of "the example of Euripides"; in the name of "Heinsius, chapter six of the *Constitution of Tragedy;* and the younger Scaliger in his poems"; and finally, in the name of the Canonists and Jurisconsults, under the title "Nuptials." The first arguments were addressed to the Academy, the last one was aimed at the Cardinal. After the pin-pricks the blow with a club. A judge was needed to decide the question. Chapelain gave judgment. Corneille saw that he was doomed; the lion was muzzled, or, as was said at the time, the crow *(Corneille)* was plucked. Now comes the painful side of this grotesque performance: after he had been thus quenched at his first flash, this genius, thoroughly modern, fed upon the Middle Ages and Spain, being compelled to lie to himself and to hark back to ancient times, drew for us that Castilian Rome, which is sublime beyond question, but in which, except perhaps in *Nicomède,* which was so ridiculed by the eighteenth century for its dignified and simple colouring, we find neither the real Rome nor the true Corneille. . . .

But still the same refrain is repeated, and will be, no doubt, for a long while to come: "Follow the rules! Copy the models! It was the rules that shaped the models." One moment! In that case there are two sorts of models, those which are made according to the rules, and, prior to them, those according to which the rules were made. Now, in which of these two categories should genius seek a place for itself? Although it is always disagreeable to come in contact with pedants, is it not a thousand times better to give them lessons than to receive lessons from them? And then—copy! Is the reflection equal to the light? Is the satellite which travels unceasingly in the same circle equal to the central creative planet? With all his poetry Virgil is no more than the moon of Homer.

And whom are we to copy, I pray to know? The ancients? We have just shown that their stage has nothing in common with ours. Moreover, Voltaire, who will have none of Shakespeare, will have none of the Greeks, either. Let him tell us why: "The Greeks ventured to produce scenes no less revolting to us. Hippolyte, crushed by his fall, counts his wounds and utters doleful cries. Philoctetes falls in his paroxysms of pain; black blood flows from his wound. Oedipus, covered with the blood that still drops from the sockets of the eyes he has torn out, complains bitterly of gods and men. We hear the shrieks of Clytemnestra, murdered by her own son, and Electra, on the stage, cries: 'Strike! spare her not! she did not spare our father.' Prometheus is fastened to a rock by nails driven through his stomach and his arms. The Furies reply to Clytemnestra's bleeding shade with inarticulate roars. Art was in its infancy in the time of Aeschylus, as it was in London in Shakespeare's time."

Whom shall we copy, then? The moderns? What! Copy copies! God forbid!

"But," someone else will object, "according to your conception of the art, you seem to look for none but great poets, to count always upon genius." Art certainly does not count upon mediocrity. It prescribes no rules for it, it knows nothing of it; in fact, mediocrity has no existence so far as art is concerned; art supplies wings, not crutches. Alas! D'Aubignac followed rules. Campistron copied models. What does it matter to art? It does not build its palaces for ants. It lets them make their ant-hill, without taking the trouble to find out whether they have built their burlesque imitation of its palace upon its foundation.

The critics of the scholastic school place their poets in a strange position. On the one hand they cry incessantly: "Copy the models!" On the other hand they have a habit of declaring that "the models are inimitable"! Now, if their craftsman, by dint of hard work, succeeds in forcing through this dangerous defile some colourless tracing of the masters, these ungrateful wretches, after examining the new *refaccimiento,* exclaim sometimes: "This doesn't resemble anything!" and sometimes: "This resembles everything!" And by virtue of a logic made for the occasion each of these formulae is a criticism.

Let us then speak boldly. The time for it has come, and it would be strange if, in this age, liberty, like the light, should penetrate everywhere except to the one place where freedom is most natural—the domain of thought. Let us take the hammer to theories and poetic systems. Let us throw down the old plastering that conceals the façade of art. There are neither rules nor models; or, rather, there are no other rules than the general laws of nature, which soar above the whole field of art, and the special rules which result from the conditions appropriate to the subject of each composition. The former are of the essence, eternal, and do not change; the latter are variable, external, and are used but once. The former are the framework that supports the house; the latter the scaffolding which is used in building it, and which is made anew for each building. In a word, the former are the flesh and bones, the latter the clothing, of the drama. But these rules are not written in the treatises on poetry. Richelet has no idea of their existence. Genius, which divines rather than learns, devises for each work the general rules from the general plan of things, the special rules from the separate *ensemble* of the subject treated; not after the manner of the chemist, who lights the fire under his furnace, heats his crucible, analyzes and destroys; but after the manner of the bee, which flies on its golden wings, lights on each flower and extracts its honey, leaving it as brilliant and fragrant as before.

The poet—let us insist on this point—should take counsel therefore only of nature, truth and inspiration, which is itself both truth and nature. *"Quando he,"* says Lope de Vega:

Quando he de escrivir una comedia,
Encierro los preceptos con seis llaves.[3]

To secure these precepts "six keys" are none too many, in very truth. Let the poet beware especially of copying anything whatsoever—Shakespeare no more than Molière, Schiller no more than Corneille. If genuine talent could abdicate its own nature in this matter, and thus lay aside its original personality, to transform itself into another, it would lose everything by playing this role of its own double. It is as if a god should turn valet. We must draw our inspiration from the original sources. . . .

Let there be no misunderstanding: if some of our poets have succeeded in being great, even when copying, it is because, while forming themselves on the antique model, they have often listened to the voice of nature and to their own genius—it is because they have been themselves in some one respect. Their branches became entangled in those of the near-by tree, but their roots were buried deep in the soil of art. They were the ivy, not the mistletoe. Then came imitators of the second rank, who, having neither roots in the earth, nor genius in their souls, had to confine themselves to imitation. As Charles Nodier says: "After the school of Athens, the school of Alexandria." Then there was a deluge of mediocrity; then there came a swarm of those treatises on poetry, so annoying to true talent, so convenient for mediocrity. We were told that everything was done, and God was forbidden to create more Molières or Corneilles. Memory was put in place of imagination. Imagination itself was subjected to hard-and-fast rules, and aphorisms were made about it: "To imagine," says La Harpe, with his naive assurance, "is in substance to remember, that is all."

But nature! Nature and truth!—And here, in order to prove that, far from demolishing art, the new ideas aim only to reconstruct it more firmly and on a better foundation, let us try to point out the impassable limit which in our opinion, separates reality according to art from reality according to nature. It is careless to confuse them as some ill-informed partisans of *romanticism* do. Truth in art cannot possibly be, as several writers have claimed, *absolute* reality. Art cannot produce the thing itself. Let us imagine, for example, one of those unreflecting promoters of absolute nature, of nature viewed apart from art, at the performance of a romantic play, say *Le Cid*. "What's that?" he will ask at the first word. "The Cid speaks in verse? It isn't *natural* to speak in verse."—"How would you have him speak, pray?"—"In prose." Very good. A moment later, "How's this!" he will continue, if he is consistent; "the Cid

---

[3]When I have to write a comedy,
I enclose the precepts with six keys.

is speaking French!"—"Well?"—"Nature demands that he speak his own language; he can't speak anything but Spanish."

We shall fail entirely to understand but again—very good. You imagine that this is all? By no means: before the tenth sentence in Castilian, he is certain to rise and ask if the Cid who is speaking is the real Cid, in flesh and blood. By what right does the actor, whose name is Pierre or Jacques, take the name of the Cid? That is *false*. There is no reason why he should not go on to demand that the sun should be substituted for the footlights, *real* trees and *real* houses for those deceitful wings. For, once started on that road, logic has you by the collar, and you cannot stop.

We must admit therefore, or confess ourselves ridiculous, that the domains of art and of nature are entirely distinct. Nature and art are two things—were it not so, one or the other would not exist. Art, in addition to its idealistic side, has a terrestrial, material side. Let it do what it will, it is shut in between grammar and prosody, between Vaugelas and Richelet. For its most capricious creations, it has formulae, methods of execution, a complete apparatus to set in motion. For genius there are delicate instruments, for mediocrity, tools.

It seems to us that someone has already said that the drama is a mirror wherein nature is reflected. But if it be an ordinary mirror, a smooth and polished surface, it will give only a dull image of objects, with no relief—faithful, but colourless; everyone knows that colour and light are lost in a simple reflection. The drama, therefore, must be a concentrating mirror, which, instead of weakening, concentrates and condenses the coloured rays, which make of a mere gleam a light, and of a light a flame. Then only is the drama acknowledged by art.

The stage is an optical point. Everything that exists in the world—in history, in life, in man—should be and can be reflected therein, but under the magic wand of art. Art turns the leaves of the ages, of nature, studies chronicles, strives to reproduce actual facts (especially in respect to manners and peculiarities, which are much less exposed to doubt and contradiction than are concrete facts), restores what the chroniclers have lopped off, harmonises what they have collected, divines and supplies their omissions, fills their gaps with imaginary scenes which have the colour of the time, groups what they have left scattered about, sets in motion anew the threads of Providence which work the human marionettes, clothes the whole with a form at once poetical and natural, and imparts to it that vitality of truth and brilliancy which gives birth to illusion, that prestige of reality which arouses the enthusiasm of the spectator, and of the poet first of all, for the poet is sincere. Thus the aim of art is almost divine: to bring to life again if it is writing history, to create if it is writing poetry. . . .

It will readily be imagined that, for a work of this kind, if the poet must *choose* (and he must), he should choose, not the *beautiful,* but the *characteristic*. Not that it is advisable to "make local colour," as they say to-day; that is, to add as an afterthought a few discordant touches here and there to a work that is at best utterly conventional and false. The local colour should not be on the surface of the drama, but in its substance, in the very heart of the work, whence it spreads of itself, naturally, evenly, and, so to speak, into every corner of the drama, as the sap ascends from the root to the tree's topmost leaf. The drama should be thoroughly impregnated with this colour of the time, which should be, in some sort, in the air, so that one detects it only on entering the theatre, and that on going forth one finds one's self in a different period and atmosphere. It requires some study, some labour, to attain this end; so much the better. It is well that the avenues of art should be obstructed by those brambles from which everybody recoils except those of powerful will. Besides, it is this very study, fostered by an ardent inspiration, which will ensure the drama against a vice that kills it—the *commonplace.* To be commonplace is the failing of short-sighted, short-breathed poets. In this tableau of the stage, each figure must be held down to its most prominent, most individual, most precisely defined characteristic. Even the vulgar and the trivial should have an accent of their own. Like God, the true poet is present in every part of his work at once. Genius resembles the die which stamps the king's effigy on copper and golden coins alike. . . .

[Hugo then attacks the conventional refinement and prudery that balks at the so-called commonplace and invests everything with an artificial nobility.—Ed.]

If we were entitled to say what, in our opinion, the style of dramatic poetry should be, we would declare for a free, outspoken, sincere verse, which dares say everything without prudery, expresses its meaning without seeking for words; which passes naturally from comedy to tragedy, from the sublime to the grotesque; by turns practical and poetical, both artistic and inspired, profound and impulsive, of wide range and true; verse which is apt opportunely to displace the caesura, in order to disguise the monotony of Alexandrines; more inclined to the *enjambement* that lengthens the line, than to the inversion of phrases that confuses the sense; faithful to rhyme, that enslaved queen, that supreme charm of our poetry, that creator of our metre; verse that is inexhaustible in the verity of its turns of thought, unfathomable in its secrets of composition and of grace; assuming, like Proteus, a thousand forms without changing its type and character; avoiding long speeches; taking delight in dialogue; always hiding behind the characters of the drama; intent, before everything, on being in its place, and when it falls to its lot to be *beautiful,* being so only by chance, as it were, in spite of itself and uncon-

sciously; lyric, epic, dramatic, at need; capable of running through the whole
gamut of poetry, of skipping from high notes to low, from the most exalted
to the most trivial ideas, from the most extravagant to the most solemn, from
the most superficial to the most abstract, without ever passing beyond the
limits of a spoken scene; in a word, such verse as a man would write whom
a fairy had endowed with Corneille's mind and Molière's brain. It seems to
us that such verse would be *as fine as prose.*

There would be nothing in common between poetry of this sort and that
of which we made a *post mortem* examination just now. The distinction will
be easy to point out if a certain man of talent, to whom the author of this
book is under personal obligation, will allow us to borrow his clever phrase:
the other poetry was descriptive, this would be picturesque. . . .

(Meanwhile, the first, the indispensable merit of a dramatic writer, whether
he write in prose or verse, is correctness.) Not a mere superficial correctness,
the merit or defect of the descriptive school . . . but that intimate, deep-
rooted, deliberate correctness, which is permeated with the genius of a language, which has sounded its roots and searched its etymology; always unfettered, because it is sure of its footing, and always more in harmony with
the logic of the language. Our Lady Grammar leads the other in leading-
strings; the other holds grammar in leash. It can venture anything, can create
or invent its style; it has a right to do so. For, whatever certain men may
have said who did not think what they were saying, and among whom we
must place, notably, him who writes these lines, the French tongue is not
fixed and never will be. A language does not become fixed. The human intellect is always on the march, or, if you prefer, in movement, and languages
with it. Things are made so. When the body changes, how could the coat
not change? The French of the nineteenth century can no more be the French
of the eighteenth, than that is the French of the seventeenth, or than the
French of the seventeenth is that of the sixteenth. Montaigne's language is
not Rabelais's, Pascal's is not Montaigne's, Montesquieu's is not Pascal's.
Each of the four languages, taken by itself, is admirable because it is original.
Every age has its own ideas; it must have also words adapted to those ideas.
Languages are like the sea, they move to and fro incessantly. At certain times
they leave one shore of the world of thought and overflow another. All that
their waves thus abandon dries up and vanishes. It is in this wise that ideas
vanish, that words disappear. It is the same with human tongues as with
everything. Each age adds and takes away something. What can be done? It
is the decree of fate. In vain, therefore, should we seek to petrify the mobile
physiognomy of our idiom in a fixed form. In vain do our literary Joshuas
cry out to the language to stand still; languages and the sun do not stand

still. The day when they become *fixed,* they are dead.—That is why the French of a certain contemporary school is a dead language.

Such are, substantially, but without the more elaborate development which would make the evidence in their favour more complete, the *present* ideas of the author of this book concerning the drama. . . .

There is to-day the old literary regime as well as the old political regime. The last century still weighs upon the present one at almost every point. It is notably oppressive in the matter of criticism. For instance, you find living men who repeat to you this definition of taste let fall by Voltaire: "Taste in poetry is no different from what it is in women's clothes." Taste, then, is coquetry. Remarkable words, which depict marvellously the painted, *moucheté,*[4] powdered poetry of the eighteenth century—that literature in panniers, pompons and falbalas.[5] They give an admirable resumé of an age with which the loftiest geniuses could not come in contact without becoming petty, in one respect or another; of an age when Montesquieu was able and apt to produce *Le Temple de Gnide,* Voltaire *Le Temple du Goût,* Jean-Jacques [Rousseau] *Le Devin du Village.*

Taste is the common sense of genius. This is what will soon be demonstrated by another school of criticism; powerful, outspoken, well-informed— a school of the century which is beginning to put forth vigorous shoots under the dead and withered branches of the old school. This youthful criticism, as serious as the other is frivolous, as learned as the other is ignorant, has already established organs that are listened to, and one is sometimes surprised to find, even in the least important sheets, excellent articles emanating from it. Joining hands with all that is fearless and superior in letters, it will deliver us from two scourges: tottering *classicism,* and false *romanticism,* which has the presumption to show itself at the feet of the true. For modern genius already has its shadow, its copy, its parasite, its *classic,* which forms itself upon it, smears itself with its colours, assumes its livery, picks up its crumbs, and, like *the sorcerer's pupil,* puts in play, with words retained by the memory, elements of theatrical action of which its master many a time has much difficulty in making good. But the thing that must be destroyed first of all is the old false taste. Present-day literature must be cleansed of its rust. In vain does the rust eat into it and tarnish it. It is addressing a young, stern, vigorous generation, which does not understand it. The train of the eighteenth century is still

---

[4]An artificial beauty spot (on the face).

[5]Looped skirts, flounces, and furbelows, respectively.

dragging in the nineteenth; but we, we young men who have seen Bonaparte, are not the ones who will carry it.

We are approaching, then, the moment when we shall see the new criticism prevail, firmly established upon a broad and deep foundation. People generally will soon understand that writers should be judged, not according to rules and species, which are contrary to nature and art, but according to the immutable principles of the art of composition, and the special laws of their individual temperaments. The sound judgment of all men will be ashamed of the criticism which broke Pierre Corneille on the wheel, gagged Jean Racine, and which ridiculously rehabilitated John Milton only by virtue of the epic code of Père le Bossu. People will consent to place themselves at the author's standpoint, to view the subject with his eyes, in order to judge a work intelligently. They will lay aside—and it is M. de Chateaubriand who speaks— "the paltry criticism of defects for the noble and fruitful criticism of beauties." It is time that all acute minds should grasp the thread that frequently connects what we, following our special whim, call "defects" with what we call "beauty." Defects—at all events those which we call by that name—are often the inborn, necessary, inevitable conditions of good qualities.

Scit genius, natale comes qui temperat astrum.[6]

Who ever saw a medal without its reverse? a talent that had not some shadow with its brilliancy, some smoke with its flame? Such a blemish can be only the inseparable consequence of such beauty. This rough stroke of the brush, which offends my eye at close range, completes the effect and gives relief to the whole picture. Efface one and you efface the other. Originality is made up of such things. Genius is necessarily uneven. There are no high mountains without deep ravines. Fill up the valley with the mountain and you will have nothing but a steppe, a plateau, the plain of Les Sablons instead of the Alps, swallows and not eagles.

We must also take into account the weather, the climate, the local influences. The Bible, Homer, hurt us sometimes by their very sublimities. Who would want to part with a word of either of them? Our infirmity often takes fright at the inspired bold flights of genius, for lack of power to swoop down upon objects with such vast intelligence. And then, once again, there are *defects* which take root only in masterpieces; it is given only to certain geniuses to have certain defects. Shakespeare is blamed for his abuse of metaphysics, of wit, of redundant scenes, of obscenities, for his employment of the mythological nonsense in vogue in his time, for exaggeration, obscurity,

---

[6]"The tutelar deity knows, the companion who regulates the star of one's birth"—i.e., one's ruling spirit knows, for he is the one who controls one's fate.

bad taste, bombast, asperities of style. The oak, that giant tree which we were comparing to Shakespeare just now, and which has more than one point of resemblance to him, the oak has an unusual shape, gnarled branches, dark leaves, and hard, rough bark; but it is the oak.

And it is because of these qualities that it is the oak. If you would have a smooth trunk, straight branches, satiny leaves, apply to the pale birch, the hollow elder, the weeping willow; but leave the mighty oak in peace. Do not stone that which gives you shade. . . .

One last word. It may have been noticed that in this somewhat long journey through so many different subjects, the author has generally refrained from resting his personal views upon texts or citations of authorities. It is not, however, because he did not have them at his hand.

"If the poet establishes things that are impossible according to the rules of his art, he makes a mistake unquestionably; but it ceases to be a mistake when by this means he has reached the end that he aimed at; for he has found what he sought."—"They take for nonsense whatever the weakness of their intellects does not allow them to understand. They are especially prone to call absurd those wonderful passages in which the poet, in order the better to enforce his argument, departs, if we may so express it, from his argument. In fact, the precept which makes it a rule sometimes to disregard rules, is a mystery of the art which it is not easy to make men understand who are absolutely without taste and whom a sort of abnormality of mind renders insensible to those things which ordinarily impress men."

Who said the first? Aristotle. Who said the last? Boileau. By these two specimens you will see that the author of this drama might, as well as another, have shielded himself with proper names and taken refuge behind others' reputations. But he preferred to leave that style of argument to those who deem it unanswerable, universal and all-powerful. As for himself, he prefers reasons to authorities; he has always cared more for arms than for coats-of-arms.

October, 1827.

Preface to *Hernani*

Only a few weeks since, the Author of this drama wrote, concerning a poet who died before maturity,[1] as follows:

Source: Translated by Mrs. Newton Crosland, London, 1887.

[1]Joseph Delorme, allegedly a poet who died young, in fact a pen name for Charles Sainte-Beuve, who actually wrote the poems published under that name.

"At this moment of literary turmoil and contention, whom should we the more pity, those who die, or those who wrestle? Truly it is sad to see a poet of twenty years old pass away, to behold a broken lyre, and a future that vanishes; but, is not repose also some advantage? Are there not those around whom calumnies, injuries, hatreds, jealousies, secret wrongs, base treasons incessantly gather; true men, against whom disloyal war is waged; devoted men, who only seek to bestow on their country one sort of freedom the more, that of art and intelligence; laborious men, who peaceably pursue their conscientious work, a prey on one side to the vile stratagems of official censure, and on the other exposed too often to the ingratitude of even those for whom they toil; may not such be permitted sometimes to turn their eyes with envy towards those who have fallen behind them, and who rest in the tomb? *Invideo,* said Luther, in the cemetery of Worms, *invideo quia quiescunt.*[2]

"What does it signify? Young people, take heart. If the present be made rough for us, the future will be smooth. Romanticism, so often ill-defined, is only—and this is its true definition if we look at it from its combative side—liberalism in literature. This truth is already understood by nearly all the best minds, and the number is great; and soon, for the work is well advanced, liberalism in literature will not be less popular than in politics. Liberty in Art, liberty in Society, behold the double end towards which consistent and logical minds should tend; behold the double banner that rallies the intelligence—with but few exceptions, which will become more enlightened—of all the young who are now so strong and patient; then, with the young, and at their head the choice spirits of the generation which has preceded us, all those sagacious veterans, who, after the first moment of hesitation and examination, discovered that what their sons are doing to-day is the consequence of what they themselves have achieved, and that liberty in literature is the offspring of political liberty. This principle is that of the age, and will prevail. The *Ultras* of all sorts, classical and monarchical, will in vain help each other to restore the old system, broken to pieces, literary and social; all progresses of the country, every intellectual development, every stride of liberty will have caused their scaffolding to give way. And, indeed, their efforts at reaction will have been useful. In revolution every moment is an advance. Truth and liberty have this excellence, that all one does for and against them serves them equally well. Now, after all the great things that our fathers have done, and that we have beheld, now that we have come out of the old social form, why should there not proceed a new out of the old poetic form? For a new people, new art. In admiring the literature of Louis XIV's age, so well adapted to his monarchy, France will know well how to

---

[2] I envy those who rest.

have its own and national literature of the nineteenth century, to which Mirabeau gave its liberty, and Napoleon its power."

Let the author of this drama be pardoned for thus quoting himself. His words have so little the power of impressing, that he often needs to repeat them. Besides, at present it is perhaps not out of place to put before readers the two pages just transcribed. It is not this drama which can in any respect deserve the great name of new art or new poetry. Far from that; but it is that the principle of freedom in literature has advanced a step; it is that some progress has been made, not in art, this drama is too small a thing for that, but in the public; it is that in this respect at least one part of the predictions hazarded above has just been realized.

There is, indeed, some danger in making changes thus suddenly, and risking on the stage those tentative efforts hitherto confided to paper, which endures everything; the reading public is very different from the theatrical public, and one might dread seeing the latter reject what the former had accepted. This has not been the case. The principle of literary freedom already comprehended by the world of readers and thinkers, has not been less fully accepted by that immense crowd, eager for this pure enjoyment of art, which every night fills the theatres of Paris. This loud and powerful voice of the people, likened to the voice of God, declares that henceforth poetry shall bear the same device as politics: TOLERATION AND LIBERTY.

Now let the poet come! He has a public.

And whatever may be this freedom, the public wills that in the State it shall be reconciled with order, and in literature with art. Liberty has a wisdom of its own, without which it is not complete. That the old rules of D'Aubignac should die with the old customs of Cujas is well; that to a literature of the court should succeed a literature of the people is better still; but, above all, it is best that an inner voice should be heard from the depths of all these novelties. Let the principle of liberty work, but let it work well. In letters, as in society, not etiquette, not anarchy, but laws. Neither red heels nor red caps. . . .[3]

Baudelaire

Charles Baudelaire, who appears in his own right in another section of this book (p. 220), was born in Paris in 1821, and began his literary career as soon as he graduated from the *Collège Louis le Grand* in 1839. The poor and passionate young man (poor

---

[3]Shoes with red heels had distinguished members of the royal family; red phrygian bonnets had been worn by certain revolutionaries of 1789.

because spendthrift and ever at loggerheads with his family) began to attract public attention with his writings on art, especially his critical accounts of the Paris art exhibitions of 1845 and 1846. Part of the latter, the *Salon of 1846*,[1] is reprinted below for the gentle barbs it casts into the thick, resilient hide of that perennial enemy of the artist—the bourgeois.

Baudelaire's presence in these pages under two different labels is characteristic. The man cannot be "placed": he wrote an article on Constantin Guys, the painter of modern life, that was considered one of the clearest manifestoes of Naturalism; he defended in his *Salon* articles the rights of imagination to express itself in the best Romantic vein; he interpreted and exalted Delacroix, who considered himself a Classic and whom we consider among the greatest Romantic painters; and, as we shall see, he created a poetic style that inspired the Symbolists and their later heirs.

The Salon of 1846: To the Bourgeois

You are the majority—in number and intelligence; therefore you are the force—which is justice.

Some are scholars, others are owners; a glorious day will come when the scholars shall be owners and the owners scholars. Then your power will be complete, and no man will protest against it.

Until that supreme harmony is achieved, it is just that those who are but owners should aspire to become scholars; for knowledge is no less of an enjoyment than ownership.

The government of the city is in your hands, and that is just, for you are the force. But you must also be capable of feeling beauty; for as not one of you today can do without power, so not one of you has the right to do without poetry.

You can live three days without bread—without poetry, never! and those who say the contrary are mistaken; they are out of their minds.

The aristocrats of thought, the distributors of praise and blame, the monopolists of the things of the mind, have told you that you have no right to feel and to enjoy—they are Pharisees.

For you have in your hands the government of a city whose public is the public of the universe, and it is necessary that you should be worthy of that task.

---

[1]The exhibition opened on March 16 at the Musée Royal. Baudelaire's review appeared as a booklet on May 13.

Source: Reprinted from *The Mirror of Art* by Charles Baudelaire. Translated and edited by Jonathan Mayne, 1955, by Phaidon Press Limited, Oxford.

Enjoyment is a science, and the exercise of the five senses calls for a particular initiation which only comes about through good will and need.

Very well, you need art.

Art is an infinitely precious good, a draught both refreshing and cheering which restores the stomach and the mind to the natural equilibrium of the ideal.

You understand its function, you gentlemen of the bourgeoise—whether lawgivers or business-men—when the seventh or the eighth hour strikes and you bend your tired head towards the embers of your hearth or the cushions of your arm-chair.

That is the time when a keener desire and a more active reverie would refresh you after your daily labours.

But the monopolists have decided to keep the forbidden fruit of knowledge from you, because knowledge is their counter and their shop, and they are infinitely jealous of it. If they had merely denied you the power to create works of art or to understand the processes by which they are created, they would have asserted a truth at which you could not take offence, because public business and trade take up three-quarters of your day. And as for your leisure hours, they should be used for enjoyment and pleasure.

But the monopolists have forbidden you even to enjoy, because you do not understand the technique of the arts, as you do those of the law and of business.

And yet it is just that if two-thirds of your time are devoted to knowledge, then the remaining third should be occupied by feeling—and it is by feeling alone that art is to be understood; and it is in this way that the equilibrium of your soul's forces will be established.

Truth, for all its multiplicity, is not two-faced; and just as in your politics you have increased both rights and benefits, so in the arts you have set up a greater and more abundant communion.

You, the bourgeois—be you king, lawgiver or business-man—have founded collections, museums and galleries. Some of those which sixteen years ago were only open to the monopolists have thrown wide their doors to the multitude.

You have combined together, you have formed companies and raised loans in order to realize the idea of the future in all its varied forms—political, industrial and artistic. In no noble enterprise have you ever left the initiative to the protesting and suffering minority,[1] which anyway is the natural enemy of art.

---

[1] i.e., the Republicans.

For to allow oneself to be outstripped in art and in politics is to commit suicide; and for a majority to commit suicide is impossible.

And what you have done for France, you have done for other countries too. The Spanish Museum[2] is there to increase the volume of general ideas that you ought to possess about art; for you know perfectly well that just as a national museum is a kind of communion by whose gentle influence men's hearts are softened and their wills unbent, so a foreign museum is an international communion where two peoples, observing and studying one another more at their ease, can penetrate one another's mind and fraternize without discussion.

You are the natural friends of the arts, because you are some of you rich men and the others scholars.

When you have given to society your knowledge, your industry, your labour and your money, you claim back your payment in enjoyments of the body, the reason and the imagination. If you recover the amount of enjoyments which is needed to establish the equilibrium of all parts of your being, then you are happy, satisfied and well-disposed, as society will be satisfied, happy and well-disposed when it has found its own general and absolute equilibrium.

And so it is to you, the bourgeois, that this book is naturally dedicated; for any book which is not addressed to the majority—in number and intelligence—is a stupid book.

1st May 1846

A Romantic Painter

Eugène Delacroix (1799–1863) was the greatest, and probably the most typical, of French Romantic painters—not least so in the controversial nature of work that early met both success and persistent, almost malevolent, misunderstanding. The complex nature of the Romantic spirit, so-called, appears clearly in this man who liked to think of himself as a classicist, who preferred Mozart to Beethoven, yet who loved both Paganini and Chopin, who, Baudelaire could say, "was passionately in love with passion, and coldly determined to seek the means of expressing it in the most visible way," and whose interest in the complementary

---

[2]The Musée Espagnol of Paris contained Spanish pictures belonging to the Orléans family, which now can be seen in the Louvre.

qualities of colors led Paul Signac to write *From Eugène Delacroix to Neo-Impressionism*. The subject as well as the technique of his paintings accentuated the pathetic aspect and the conflicting emotions so dear to Romantic hearts. His vivid use of color, in part inspired by Constable's paintings, in part learned from a trip to Spain and Morocco where a diplomatic mission took him in 1832, helped him do justice to the oriental scenes he found so fascinating, whose charm he did much to introduce to the European public, but whose exoticism does not exclude the realistic treatment of exciting subjects.

Delacroix's politics were a mixed lot—élitist but nonconformist—and it is hard to tell whether he would have done as well had it not been for the protection and support of Thiers, and of Thiers's own patron, Talleyrand, whose illegitimate son he was rumored to be. In any event, after the July Revolution, and in spite of the lack of sympathy he showed for the new regime, many of Delacroix's paintings were bought by the state, although one at least ("Liberty Leading the People") was hung for a while with its face to the wall so as not to contaminate the public.

His great admirer, Charles Baudelaire, wrote a great deal about him[1]—both as critic and as memorialist. Though Delacroix expressed himself in his own *Journal* with as much richness and variety as in his paintings, it has seemed best to present him here not through his private jottings but in the manner he was presented, and his ideas explained, to the public of the time by a critic of genius.

Baudelaire

The Life and Work of Eugène Delacroix

I

What is Delacroix? What role did he come into this world to play, and what duty to perform? That is the first question that we must examine. I shall be brief, and I look for immediate conclusions. Flanders has Rubens, Italy Raphael and Veronese; France has Lebrun, David and Delacroix.

---

[1]The following article by Baudelaire, in the form of a long letter to the editor, was published in the *Opinion Nationale* in three parts (September 2 and 14, and November 22, 1863). Delacroix had died on August 13, 1863. Baudelaire also used the article as a lecture in Brussels (May 2, 1864), when he preceded it with a short passage of introduction (see Crépet's edition of *L'Art Romantique*).

Source: Reprinted from *The Mirror of Art* by Charles Baudelaire. Translated and edited by Jonathan Mayne, 1955, by Phaidon Press Limited, Oxford.

A superficial mind may well be shocked, at first glance, by the coupling of these names which represent such differing qualities and methods. But a keener mental eye will see at once that they are united by a common kinship, a kind of brotherhood or cousinage which derives from their love of the great, the national, the immense and the universal—a love which has always expressed itself in the kind of painting which is called "decorative," or in what are known as great machines.

Many others, no doubt, have painted great machines; those that I have mentioned, however, painted them in the way most suited to leave an eternal trace upon the memory of mankind. Which is the greatest of these great men who differ so much from one another? Each must decide as he pleases, according as whether his temperament urges him to prefer the prolific, radiant, almost jovial abundance of Rubens; the mild dignity and eurhythmic order of Raphael; the paradisal—one might almost say the afternoon—colour of Veronese; the austere and strained severity of David; or the dramatic and almost literary rhetoric of Lebrun.

None of these men is replaceable; aiming, all of them, at a like goal, they yet used different means, drawn from their individual natures. Delacroix, the last to come upon the scene, expressed with an admirable vehemence and fervour what the others had translated but incompletely. To the detriment of something else, perhaps, as they too had done? It may be; but that is not the question that we have to examine.

Many others apart from myself have gone out of their way to pontificate on the subject of the fatal consequences of an essentially personal genius; and it may also be quite possible, after all, that the finest expressions of genius, elsewhere than in Heaven—that is to say, on this poor earth, where perfection itself is imperfect—could only be secured at the price of an unavoidable sacrifice.

But doubtless, Sir, you will be asking what is this strange, mysterious quality which Delacroix, to the glory of our age, has interpreted better than anyone else? It is the invisible, the impalpable, the dream, the nerves, the soul; and this he has done—allow me, please, to emphasize this point—with no other means but colour and contour; he has done it better than anyone else— he has done it with the perfection of a consummate painter, with the exactitude of a subtle writer, with the eloquence of an impassioned musician. It is, moreover, one of the characteristic symptoms of the spiritual condition of our age that the arts aspire if not to take another's place, at least reciprocally to lend one another new powers.

Delacroix is the most suggestive of all painters; he is the painter whose works, even when chosen from among his secondary and inferior productions, set one thinking the most and summon to the memory the greatest number of poetic thoughts and sentiments which, although once known, one had believed to be forever buried in the dark night of the past.

The achievement of Delacroix sometimes appears to me like a kind of mnemotechny of the grandeur and the native passion of universal man. This very special and entirely new merit, which has permitted the artist to express, simply with contour, the gesture of man, no matter how violent it may be, and with colour what one might term the atmosphere of the human drama, or the state of the creator's soul—this utterly original merit has always earned him the support of all the poets; and if it were permissible to deduce a philosophical proof from a simple material manifestation, I would ask you, Sir, to observe that amongst the crowd that assembled to pay him his last honours, you could count many more men of letters than painters. To tell the blunt truth, these latter have never perfectly understood him.

II

And what is so very surprising in that, after all? Do we not know that the age of the Raphaels, the Michelangelos and the Leonardos—not to speak of the Reynoldses—is already long past, and that the general intellectual level of artists has singularly dropped? It would doubtless be unfair to look for philosophers, poets and scholars among the artists of the day; but it would seem legitimate to demand from them a little more interest in religion, poetry and science than in fact they show.

Outside of their studios, what do they know? What do they love? What ideas have they to express? Eugène Delacroix, however, at the same time as being a painter in love with his craft, was a man of general education; as opposed to the other artists of today, who for the most part are little more than illustrious or obscure daubers, sad specialists, old or young—mere artisans, possessing some the ability to manufacture academic figures, others fruit and others cattle. Eugène Delacroix loved and had the ability to paint everything, and knew also how to appreciate every kind of talent.

His was of all minds the most open to every sort of idea and impression; he was the most eclectic and the most impartial of voluptuaries.

A great reader, it is hardly necessary to mention. The reading of the poets left him full of sublime, swiftly-defined images—ready-made pictures, so to speak. However much he differed from his master Guérin both in method and in colour, he inherited from the great Republican and Imperial school a love of the poets and a strangely impulsive spirit of rivalry with the written word. David, Guérin and Girodet kindled their minds at the brazier of Homer, Virgil, Racine and Ossian. Delacroix was the soul-stirring translator of Shakespeare, Dante, Byron and Ariosto. The resemblance is important; the difference but slight.

But let us enter a little further, if you please, into what one might call the teaching of the master—a teaching which, for me, results not only from the successive contemplation of all his works, and from the simultaneous contemplation of certain of them (as we had the opportunity of enjoying at the *Exposition Universelle* of 1855), but also from many a conversation that I had with him.

III

Delacroix was passionately in love with passion, and coldly determined to seek the means of expressing it in the most visible way. In this duality of nature—let us observe in passing—we find the two signs which mark the most substantial geniuses who are scarce made to please those timorous, easily-satisfied souls who find sufficient nourishment in flabby, soft and imperfect works. An immense passion, reinforced with a formidable will—such was the man.

Now he used continually to say:

"Since I consider the impression transmitted to the artist by nature as the most important thing of all to translate, is it not essential that he should be armed in advance with all the most rapid means of translation?"

It is evident that in his eyes the imagination was the most precious gift, the most important faculty, but that this faculty remained impotent and sterile if it was not served by a resourceful skill which could follow it in its restless and tyrannical whims. He certainly had no need to stir the fire of his always-incandescent imagination; but the day was never long enough for his study of the material means of expression.

It is this never-ceasing preoccupation that seems to explain his endless investigations into colour and the quality of colours, his lively interest in matters of chemistry, and his conversations with manufacturers of colours. In that respect he comes close to Leonardo da Vinci, who was no less a victim of the same obsessions.

In spite of his admiration for the fiery phenomena of life, never will Eugène Delacroix be confounded among that herd of vulgar artists and scribblers whose myopic intelligence takes shelter behind the vague and obscure word "realism." The first time that I saw M. Delacroix—it was in 1845, I think (how the years slip by, swift and greedy!)—we chatted much about commonplaces—that is to say, about the vastest and yet the simplest questions; about Nature, for example. . . .

"Nature is but a dictionary," he kept on repeating. Properly to understand the extent of meaning implied in this sentence, you should consider the numerous ordinary usages of a dictionary. In it you look for the meaning of words, their genealogy and their etymology—in brief, you extract from it all the elements that compose a sentence or a narrative; but no one has ever thought of his dictionary as a composition, in the poetic sense of the word. Painters who are obedient to the imagination seek in their dictionary the elements which suit with their conception; in adjusting those elements, however, with more or less of art, they confer upon them a totally new physiognomy. But those who have no imagination just copy the dictionary. The result is a great vice, the vice of banality, to which those painters are particularly prone whose specialty brings them closer to what is called inanimate nature—landscape painters, for example, who generally consider it a triumph if they can contrive not to show their personalities. By dint of contemplating and copying, they forget to feel and think. . . .

A good picture, which is a faithful equivalent of the dream which has begotten it, should be brought into being like a world. Just as the creation, as we see it, is the result of several creations, in which the preceding ones are always completed by the following, so a harmoniously conducted picture consists of a series of pictures superimposed on one another, each new layer conferring greater reality upon the dream and raising it by one degree towards perfection. . . .

To be brief, I must pass over a whole crowd of corollaries resulting from my principal formula in which is contained, so to speak, the entire formulary of the true aesthetic, and which may be expressed thus: The whole visible universe is but a store-house of images and signs to which the imagination will give a relative place and value; it is a sort of pasture which the imagination must digest and transform. All the faculties of the human soul must be subordinated to the imagination, which puts them in requisition all at once. Just as a good knowledge of the dictionary does not necessarily imply a knowledge of the art of composition, and just as the art of composition does not itself imply a *universal* imagination, in the same way a *good* painter need not be a *great* painter. But a great painter is perforce a good painter, because the universal imagination embraces the understanding of all means of expression and the desire to acquire them.

As a result of the ideas which I have just been making as clear as I have been able (but there are still so many things that I should have mentioned, particularly concerning the concordant aspects of all the arts, and their similarities in method!), it is clear that the vast family of artists—that is to say, of men who have devoted themselves to the expression of beauty—can be divided into two quite distinct camps. There are those who call themselves "realists"—a word with a double meaning, whose sense has not been properly defined, and so, in order the better to characterize their effort, I propose to call them "positivists"; and *they* say, "I want to represent things as they are, or rather as they would be, supposing that I did not exist." In other words, the universe without man. The others, however—the "imaginatives"—say, "I want to illuminate things with my mind, and to project their reflection upon other minds." Although these two absolutely contrary methods could magnify or diminish any subject, from a religious scene to the most modest landscape, nevertheless the man of imagination has generally tended to express himself in religious painting and in fantasy, while landscape and the type of painting called "genre" would appear to offer enormous opportunities to those whose minds are lazy and excitable only with difficulty. . . .

The imagination of Delacroix! Never has it flinched before the arduous peaks of religion! The heavens belong to it, no less than hell, war, Olympus and love. In him you have the model of the painter-poet. He is indeed one of the rare elect, and the scope of his mind embraces religion in its domain. His imagination blazes with every flame and every shade of crimson, like the banks of glowing candles before a shrine. All that there is of anguish in the Passion impassions him; all that there is of splendour in the Church casts its glory upon him. On his inspired canvases he pours blood, light and darkness in turn. I believe that he would willingly bestow his own natural magnificence upon the majesties of the Gospel itself, out of superabundance. . . .

. . . This is the moment to recall that the great masters, whether poets or painters, Hugo or Delacroix, are always several years ahead of their timid admirers.

In relation to genius, the public is like a slow-running clock. Who among the ranks of the discerning does not understand that the master's very first picture contained all his others in embryo? But that he should be ceaselessly perfecting and diligently sharpening his natural gifts, that he should extract new effects from them and should himself drive his nature to its utmost limits—that is inevitable, foredoomed and worthy of praise. The principal characteristic of Delacroix's genius is precisely the fact that he knows not decadence; he only displays progress. The only thing is that his original qualities were so forceful and so rich, and they have left such a powerful impression upon even the most commonplace of minds, that day-to-day progress is imperceptible for the majority; it is only the dialecticians of art who can discern it clearly.

[There is a] class of heavy and boorish spirits (their number is legion) who appraise objects solely by their contour, or worse still, by their three dimensions, length, breadth and height—for all the world like savages and rustics. I have often heard people of that kind laying down a hierarchy of qualities which to me was absolutely unintelligible; I have heard them declare, for example, that the faculty that enables one man to produce an exact contour, or another a contour of a supernatural beauty, is superior to the faculty whose skill it is to make an enchanting assemblage of *colours*. According to those people, colour has no power to dream, to think, or to speak. It would seem that when I contemplate the works of one of those men who are specifically called "colourists," I am giving myself up to a pleasure whose nature is far from a noble one; they would be delighted to call me a "materialist," reserving for themselves the aristocratic title of "spiritualist."[1]

It seems not to have occurred to those superficial minds that the two faculties can never be entirely separated, and that they are both of them the result of an original seed that has been carefully cultivated. External nature does nothing more than provide the artist with a constantly renewed opportunity of cultivating that seed; it is nothing but an incoherent heap of raw materials which the artist is invited to group together and put in order—a stimulant, a kind of alarum for the slumbering faculties. Strictly speaking there is neither line nor colour in nature. It is man that creates line and colour. They are twin abstractions which derive their equal status from their common origin.

A born draughtsman (I am thinking of him as a child) observes in nature, whether at rest or in motion, certain undulations from which he derives a certain thrill of pleasure, and which he amuses himself in fixing by means of lines on paper, exaggerating or moderating their inflexions at his will. He learns thus to achieve stylishness, elegance and character in drawing. But now let us imagine a child who is destined to excel in that department of art which is called colour; it is the collision or the happy marriage of two tones, and his own pleasure resulting therefrom, that will lead him towards the infinite science of tonal combinations. In neither case has nature been other than a pure *excitant*.

Line and colour both of them have the power to set one thinking and dreaming; the pleasures which spring from them are of different natures, but of a perfect equality and absolutely independent of the subject of the picture.

A picture by Delacroix will already have quickened you with a thrill of supernatural pleasure even if it be situated too far away for you to be able to judge of its linear graces or the more or less dramatic quality of its subject. You feel as though a magical atmosphere has advanced towards you and already envelops you. This impression, which combines gloom with sweetness, light with tranquillity—this impression, which has taken its place once and for all in your memory, is certain proof of the true, the perfect colourist. And when you come closer and analyze the subject, nothing will be deducted from, or added to, that original pleasure, for its source lies elsewhere and far away from any material thought.

---

[1] In the philosophical, not the mediumistic sense.

Let me reverse my example. A well-drawn figure fills you with a pleasure which is absolutely divorced from its subject. Whether voluptuous or awe-inspiring, this figure will owe its entire charm to the arabesque which it cuts in space. So long as it is skilfully drawn, there is nothing—from the limbs of a martyr who is being flayed alive, to the body of a swooning nymph—that does not admit of a kind of pleasure in whose elements the subject-matter plays no part. If it is otherwise with you, I shall be forced to believe that you are either a butcher or a rake.

But alas! what is the good of continually repeating these idle truths?

Gautier

Théophile Gautier (1811–1872) was early fascinated by the writings of the French sixteenth and early seventeenth centuries—especially the poetic *Pléiade*—and this was reflected in his early verses and literary essays. Not yet twenty, he joined the Romantic circle dominated by Hugo and became the toughest defender of the new ideas against the fuddy-duddies of classicism. His *Histoire du Romantisme* sketches the eccentric circle of young enthusiasts, including Gérard de Nerval, Pétrus Borel, and Camille Corot, whom he led into battle wearing the pink waistcoat that has since become famous and whom he provided with a name when, in 1833, he published *Les Jeunes-France*.

Gautier's literary reputation, however, is based on his novel *Mademoiselle de Maupin* (1835), whose preface proclaims a new concept of art for art's sake, a point of view to which political and social issues were less than secondary when beauty was all and all-important. "For the poet," said Gautier, "words have in themselves and apart from the sense they express a peculiar beauty and value, like precious stones still uncut and unmounted in bracelets, necklaces and rings; they charm the *connoisseur* who gazes at them and picks them out of the little jar where they are stored like a goldsmith devising a jewel. There are diamond, sapphire, ruby, emerald words, others which gleam like phosphorus when rubbed, and it is no mean task to select them." It becomes clear in the pages that follow that Gautier selected words with devilish ingenuity, suggestiveness, and verve, to be used against the dull, the timid, and, above all, against the critics who become pincushions for the poet's poisoned darts.

There was nothing untoward in Gautier's romantic aestheticism. Yet, when taken up by Pater and Baudelaire, these ideas provided the inspiration for the aestheticism and symbolism of a later day. They echoed forward not only in Rimbaud, but in Oscar Wilde and J. K. Huysmans, and continue to suggest a symbolic language to the artists of the twentieth century.

Preface to *Mademoiselle de Maupin*

One of the most comical traits of the glorious epoch in which it is our happy lot to live is unquestionably the rehabilitation of virtue which all our newspapers—no matter of what stripe, red, green, or tri-colour—have undertaken.

Unquestionably virtue is a very respectable thing, and we have not the least intention of being rude to the good and worthy lady, Heaven help us!—We are of opinion that her eyes beam quite brightly enough through her spectacles, that her stockings have no wrinkles to speak of, that she takes her pinch of snuff from her gold box with all possible grace, that her pet dog curtsies like a dancing master. We grant all that. We even grant that, taking her age into account, she is still comely enough, and that she carries off her years undeniably well. She is a very pleasant grandmother, but a grandmother. It seems to me natural to prefer to her, especially when one is twenty years old, some little trig immorality, coquettish to a degree, easy going, her hair out of curl, her skirt short rather than long, with an ankle and a glance that draw the eye, a cheek somewhat aglow, a laugh on the lips, and her heart on her sleeve. The most monstrously virtuous journalists cannot possibly hold a different opinion, and, if they assert the contrary, it is very likely they do not think as they speak. To think one way and to write in another happens every day, especially to virtuous people.

I remember the sarcasms hurled before the Revolution (the Revolution of July, I mean) at the unfortunate and maidenlike Viscount Sosthène de la Rochefoucauld, who lengthened the skirts of the ballet-dancers at the Opera, and with his patrician hands stuck a modesty-preserving plaster just below the waist of all statues. The Viscount Sosthène de la Rochefoucauld has been left far behind. Modesty has been vastly improved upon since his day, and we indulge in refinements he would never have thought of.

For myself, as I am not in the habit of looking at certain parts of statues, I thought, as others did, the fig-leaf cut out by the scissors of the director of Fine Arts, the most ridiculous thing in the world. It seems that I am wrong and that the fig-leaf is a most meritorious institution.

I have been told—though so strange is the statement that I refused to credit it—that there are people who see nothing in Michelangelo's fresco of the *Last Judgment,* but the group of libertine prelates, and who veil their faces as they lament the abomination of desolation!

These people know only the couplet of the adder in the romance of Rodriguez. If there be, in a book or a picture, any nudity, they go straight to it

---

Source: Translated by F. C. de Sumichrast, New York, 1900.

as a pig to filth, and take no account of the blooming flowers or of the fair golden fruits which hang everywhere.

I confess that I am not virtuous enough for that sort of thing. Dorine, the bold soubrette, may freely exhibit in my presence her swelling bosom; I shall certainly not pull out my handkerchief to cover those breasts one ought not to look at. I shall look at her bosom as at her face, and, if it be white and shapely, I shall like to look at it. But I shall not feel Elmira's dress to see if the stuff be soft, and I shall not devoutly press her against the edge of the table, as that "poor chap" Tartuffe did.

The great pretence of morality which reigns nowadays would be very funny, were it not very wearisome. Every *feuilleton* is turned into a pulpit, every newspaper writer into a preacher; the tonsure and the clerical collar alone are wanting. We are having nothing but rain and homilies, and the one and the others can be avoided only by taking a carriage to go out, and regarding Pantagruel between the bottle and the pipe.

Merry on us! what excitement! what frenzy! What has bitten you? what has stung you? what the devil is the matter with you that you are yelling so loud, and what has poor Vice done to you that you are so angry with it— Vice, which is so good-natured, so easy to get on with, and which merely wants to enjoy itself and not to bore others, if this be possible? Do to Vice as Serre did to the constable: kiss and have done. Believe me, you will be the better for it. Good Heavens! what would you do but for Vice, O ye preachers? You would be reduced to poverty no later than to-morrow, if men turned virtuous to-day. The theatres would close this very evening. Where would you find material for your article? No more Opera balls to fill your columns,—no more novels to dissect; for balls, novels, and plays are the very pomps of Satan, if our Holy Mother the Church is to be believed. The actress would dismiss the man who keeps her, and could no longer afford to pay you for praising her. Your papers would have no subscribers. People would read Saint Augustine, go to church, tell their beads. Very nice, no doubt, but you would not be the gainers. What would you do with your articles on the immorality of the age, if people were virtuous? You see that Vice is of some use after all.

But it is the fashion now to be virtuous and Christian; it is a way we have. A man affects to be a Saint Jerome as formerly to be a Don Juan; he cultivates pallor and emaciation; he wears his hair of an apostolic length; he walks with clasped hands and eyes bent on the ground. He tries to look as if butter would not melt in his mouth; he keeps a Bible open on his mantelpiece and hangs a crucifix and a sprig of box, blessed by the priest above his bedstead; he eschews swearing; he smokes but little; he scarcely ever chews. Then he is a Christian; talks of the sacredness of art, of the artist's high mission, of the poetry of Catholicism, of de Lamennais, of the painters of the Angelic School, of the Council of Trent, of progressive humanity, and a thousand other fine things. Some mingle a small dose of republicanism with their religion; they are not the least peculiar. They couple Robespierre and Jesus Christ in the jolliest way, and mix, with a seriousness worthy of all praise, the Acts of the Apostles and the decrees of the sainted Convention—that is the regulation epithet. Others add, by way of final ingredient, a few of Saint-Simon's ideas. These are the finished variety; after them there is no more to be said. It is not possible for man to carry absurdity to greater lengths. . . .

Thanks to the prevailing hypocrisy, Christianity is so much in vogue that neo-Christianity itself enjoys a certain amount of favour. It is said to reckon as many as one follower, including Mr. Drouineau.

An exceedingly curious variety of the journalist properly called moral is the journalist with a family of women.

This variety carries the susceptibility of modesty almost to the point of cannibalism.

Its method of working, simple and easy at first glance, is none the less most comical and highly diverting, and I think it worthy of being preserved for the benefit of posterity,—for our ultimate descendants, as the asses of our so-called Golden Age used to say.

To begin with, in order to start as a journalist of this sort, a few trifling properties are needed as a preliminary,—two or three legitimate wives, a few mothers, as many sisters as possible, a complete assortment of daughters, and innumerable cousins. Next, any play or novel, pen, ink, paper, and a printer. An idea or two and a few subscribers might come in usefully, but with plenty of philosophy and the money of the stockholders these may be dispensed with.

When you have these things you can start out as a moral journalist. The two following recipes, suitably varied, suffice for the editorial work:—

Models of Virtuous Articles on a First Performance

"After sanguinary literature, filthy literature; after the morgue and the penitentiary, the bedroom and the house of ill fame; after the rags stained by murder, the rags soiled by debauch; after . . . etc. (according to need and space one may go on in this fashion for from six to fifty lines and more)—that is to be expected. This is the result of romantic excess and the forgetfulness of healthy doctrine; the stage has become a school of prostitution, into which one ventures to enter but hesitatingly with a respectable woman. You go to the theatre on the strength of an illustrious name, and you are compelled to withdraw at the third act with your daughter all upset and not knowing which way to look. Your wife conceals her blushes behind her fan;

your sister, your cousin, etc." (The names of relatives may be diversified at will; it is sufficient that they should be feminine.)

Note:—One of these journalists has carried morality to the point of declaring, "I shall not go to see that drama with my mistress." I admire that man; I love him; I bear him in my heart as Louis XVIII bore all France in his; for he has had the most triumphant, the most pyramidal, the most startling, the most gigantic idea which has penetrated the brain of man in this blessed nineteenth century, in which so many and so funny ideas have come into men's heads.

The mode of reviewing a book is very expeditious and within reach of all minds:—

"If you intend to read this book, lock yourself up carefully in your own room; do not let it lie about on your table. If your wife or your daughter happened to open it she would be lost. This book is dangerous; it preaches vice. It might have had much success; perchance, in Crébillon's time, in houses of ill fame, at the select suppers of duchesses; but nowadays, when morals are purer, when the hand of the people has thrown down the rotten edifice of aristocracy, etc., etc., etc., that . . . that . . . that . . . there must be in every book an idea, an idea . . . why, a moral, a religious idea that . . . a lofty, a deep view which satisfies the needs of humanity; for it is most regrettable that young writers should sacrifice the holiest things to success, and should devote their meritorious talents to libidinous descriptions that would bring a blush to the cheek of a captain of dragoons." (The maidenliness of captains of dragoons is the finest discovery made for many a year since the discovery of America.) "The novel we criticise recalls Theresa the Philosopher, Felicia, Gaffer Matthew, Grécourt's Tales."

The virtuous journalist is deeply versed in filthy novels; I should greatly like to know why.

It is appalling to reflect that in the world of newspaperdom there are many worthy artisans who have no other means of livelihood for themselves and the numerous family they employ than these two recipes.

I am apparently the most enormously immoral individual in Europe or elsewhere, for I see nothing more licentious in the novels and plays of today than in the novels and plays of a former time, and I can scarcely understand why the morals of our journalists have suddenly become so jansenistically prurient.

I do not believe that the simplest-minded journalist will venture to say that Pigault-Lebrun, Crébillon the younger, Louvet, Voisenon, Marmontel, and all other writers of novels and tales are not more immoral—since immorality is insisted upon—than the most outrageous and the freest productions of Messrs. So-and-So, whom I do not name, in order to spare their blushes.

A man would have to be perversely untruthful not to own it.

And let it not be objected that I have cited names little known. If I have not selected dazzling and splendid names, it is not because they would fail to confirm my statement by their great weight.

Voltaire's novels and tales are assuredly not, save so far as difference in merit goes, fitter to be given as prizes to the youngsters in our boarding-schools than are the immoral tales of our friend the Lycanthrope or even the moral tales of sugared Marmontel.

What do you find in the comedies of the great Molière? The holy institution of marriage (to speak like catechisms and journalists) derided and turned into ridicule in every scene.

The husband is old, ugly, and peevish; he wears his wig awry; his coat is old-fashioned; he carries a stick with a hooked head; his nose is filthy with snuff; he is short-legged; he has a corporation as big as the budget. He cannot speak distinctly, and talks nonsense; he acts as foolishly as he talks; he sees nothing, hears nothing; you can kiss his wife to his face; he has no idea of what that means, and so it goes on until he is plainly and duly made out a cuckold, to his own knowledge and that of the very much edified audience, which applauds loudly.

It is the most thorough-paced husbands in the audience who applaud most loudly.

In Molière, marriage bears the name of George Dandin or Sganarelle; adultery, that of Damis or Clitandre; there is no name too sweet or charming for it. The adulterer is always young, handsome, well-made, and a marquis at the very least. He comes in from the wings humming the latest *coranto;* he steps on to the stage in the most deliberate and victorious fashion; he scratches his ear with the rosy nail of his little finger, coquettishly stuck out; he combs out his handsome blond wig with his tortoise-shell comb; he resettles his voluminous trunk-lace; his doublet and trunk hose disappear under pointlaces and favours; his scarf is from the right makers, his gloves are perfumed with more delicate scent than benzoin and civet; his feathers have cost a louis apiece.

What a flashing eye and what a peach-like cheek! What smiling lips and white teeth! What soft and well-washed hands.

When he speaks, it is only in madrigals and perfumed gallantries of the best *précieux* style and of the bravest air; he has read novels and knows poetry; he is valiant and ready to draw; he scatters gold with a lavish hand,—so Angelica, Agnes, and Isabella can scarce refrain from throwing themselves in his arms, well-bred and great ladies though they are; and so the husband is regularly betrayed in the fifth act, and is very lucky if it is not in the first.

That is how marriage is treated by Molière, one of the loftiest and most serious geniuses that have ever existed. Does any one believe there is anything stronger in the indictments of "Indiana" and "Valentine"?

Paternity is even less respected, if it were possible. Just see Orgon, Géronte, all the fathers, how they are robbed by their sons, beaten by their valets! How, without pity for their age, their avarice, their obstinacy, their imbecility are laid bare! What pleasantries and practical jokes at their expense! How they are hustled out of life, these poor old fellows who put off dying and who will not give up their money! How the tenacity of life of parents is talked of; what arguments against heredity; and how much more convincing all this is than are the declamations of a Saint-Simon!

A father is an ogre, an Argus, a jailer, a tyrant, of no use save to delay marriage during the space of three acts until the final recognition takes place. A father is the perfectly complete ridiculous husband. Sons never are ridiculous in Molière's plays, for Molière, like all authors of all times, paid his court to the rising generation at the expense of the older.

And the Scapins, with their capes striped Neapolitan fashion, their cap cocked on one ear, their feathers waving, are they not more pious and chaste individuals, fit subjects for canonisation? Penitentiaries are full of honest people who have not done one fourth of what they have done. The villainies of Tralph are peccadilloes in comparison with theirs. And what of the Lisettes, the Martons? Nice young females truly! The street-walkers are less shameless, less ready with libidinous reply. How cleverly they can smuggle you a note!— how well keep watch during a rendezvous! On my word, they are invaluable young women, ready to oblige and full of sage counsel.

A nice company it is that lives and moves and has its being in these comedies and imbroglios! Befooled guardians, cuckold husbands, libertine maids, swindling valets, daughters crazed with love, debauched sons, adulterous wives. Are they not at least the peers of the young and handsome melancholy heroes, and of the poor, weak, oppressed, and passionate women in the dramas and novels of our popular writers?

In all this, bar the final dagger-thrust, the indispensable bowl of poison, the *dénouements* are as bright as the endings of fairy tales, and everybody, even the husband, is fully satisfied. In Molière, virtue is always kicked out and beaten; it is virtue which wears horns and is thrashed by Mascarille; it is but once that, towards the end of the play, morality puts in a brief appearance in the somewhat *bourgeois* incarnation of Loyal the constable.

It is not to take aught from Molière's glory that we have said all this. We are not crazy enough to attempt to shake this colossus of bronze with our puny arms. Our intention was merely to demonstrate to our pious newspaper writers, whom the new works of the Romantic school cause to shudder and shy, that the classics, the reading and imitation of which they daily recommend, greatly surpass these works in licentiousness and immorality.

To Molière we might easily join both Marivaux and La Fontaine, each of whom incarnates two opposite sides of the French mind, and Regnier and Rabelais and Marot and many more. But it is not our intention to deliver here, because we are discussing morality, a course on literature for the use of those virgins, our newspaper writers.

In my opinion there is no reason for making so much fuss over so slight a matter. We are fortunately no longer in the days of fair-haired Eve, and honestly, we cannot be as primitive and patriarchal as they were in the Ark. We are not little girls preparing for their first communion, and when we play at capping rimes, we do not answer *tarte à la crême*. Our ignorance is pretty learned, and our virginity has long since vanished; these are things to be possessed once only, and do what we may we cannot again have them, for nothing is swifter than disappearing virginity and vanishing illusions.

And perhaps it is no great harm, after all, and the knowledge of all things may be preferable to the ignorance of all things. That is a question the discussion of which I leave to those who are more learned than I. What is certain is that the world has got beyond the stage at which one may affect modesty and maidenly shame, and I think that the world is too old a duffer to assume to be childish and maidenly without becoming ridiculous.

Since its marriage to civilisation society has forfeited its right to be ingenuous and prudish. There is a blush which beseems the bride as she is being bedded, which would be out of place on the morrow; for the young wife mayhap remembers no more what it is to be a girl, or if she does remember it, it is very indecent, and seriously compromises the reputation of the husband.

When perchance I peruse one of those fine sermons which, in our public prints, have taken the place of literary criticism, I sometimes feel very remorseful and very apprehensive, for there lie on my conscience sundry broad jests, somewhat highly spiced, as may well be the case of a youth who is hot-blooded and high-spirited.

Compared with these Bossuets of the Café de Paris, these Bourdaloues of the dress circle at the Opera, or these penny-a-liner Catos who reprove our age so tartly, I own to being indeed the most awful scoundrel that ever trod this earth, and yet, Heaven knows, the enumeration of my sins, both mortal and venial, with the customary spaces and leads, would scarcely, even in the hands of the cleverest publishers, make more than one or two octavo volumes a day, which is not much for a man who has no idea of entering paradise in the next world, or of winning the Monthyon prize or of being crowned with roses for virginity in this.

Then when I recall that I have met under the table, and even elsewhere, a pretty good number of these paragons of virtue, I come to have a better opinion of myself, and I consider that, whatever my own defects may be,

they have one which, in my opinion, is the greatest and the worst of all—
hypocrisy.

I dare say that if we were to look closely we might find another little vice
to be added to this one, but this little vice is so hideous that, candidly, I dare
not name it. Come near, and I shall whisper its name in your ear: it is—envy.

Envy; nothing else.

Envy it is that crawls and meanders in and out of all these paternal homilies; careful though it is to conceal itself, from time to time you see glitter,
above the metaphors and the rhetorical figures, its little flat, viper head. You
catch it licking with its forked tongue its lips blue with venom; you hear it
hissing softly under some insidious epithet.

I know that it is unbearably conceited to claim that people are envious of
you, and that it is almost as sickening as a fop who brags of his successes. I
am not braggart enough to fancy that I have enemies and that men are envious of me; that is a piece of luck which does not fall to every one's share,
and it is probable that it will not fall to mine for a long while yet; therefore
I shall speak out freely and without reserve, as one who is very much disinterested in this matter.

A thing which it is easy to prove to those who have any doubt about it is
the natural antipathy of the critic towards the poet,—of the one who creates
nothing towards him who creates something,—of the hornet towards the
bee,—of the gelding towards the stallion.

A man turns critic only after he has become thoroughly convinced that he
cannot be a poet. Before he comes down to the wretched business of looking
after the overcoats, or of marker in a billiard-room or a tennis-court, he has
long courted the Muse of Poetry, he has tried to ravish her, but he proved
not vigorous enough for the task and fell, pale and panting, at the foot of the
sacred mount.

I understand the critic's hatred. It is distressful to see another man sit down
to the banquet to which one is not bidden, or lie with the woman who would
have none of you. I pity from the bottom of my heart the poor eunuch who
is compelled to witness the enjoyment of the Grand Seignior.

He is admitted into the most secret recesses of the Oda; he takes the sul-
tanas to the bath; he sees, under the silvery water of the great reservoirs, the
sheen of those fair forms streaming with pearls and smoother than agate; the
most hidden beauties are unveiled before him. Why trouble about him? He
is a eunuch. The sultan caresses his favourite in his presence, and kisses her
luscious lips. A very awkward situation for him, in truth, in which he can
scarce know which way to look.

It is the same with the critic who sees the poet wandering about the garden
of Poesy with his nine lovely odalisques and lazily disporting himself in the
shade of the great green laurels. He finds it pretty difficult to keep from pick-

ing up the stones on the highway, to throw them at him and hit him behind his wall, if he be skilful enough to do it.

The critic who has produced nothing is a coward; he is like a priest courting a layman's wife; the layman can neither fight the priest nor seduce his wife.

I am of opinion that a history of the different methods of running down a book—no matter which—since a month ago down to the present day, would form a history at least as interesting as that of Tiglath-Pileser or Gemmagog who invented pointed shoes.

There exists matter enough for fifteen or sixteen folio volumes; but we shall take pity on the reader and confine ourselves to a few lines; in return for which blessing, we ask for more than eternal gratitude. At a very distant time, lost in the mist of ages—it is quite three weeks ago—the mediaeval novel flourished in Paris and the suburbs. The blazoned surcoat was highly honoured; the Hennin head-dress was not looked down upon; party-coloured trunks were highly prized; daggers were priceless; pointed shoes adored as fetishes. Everywhere pointed arches, turrets, columns, stained-glass, cathedrals, and castles; everywhere damosels and young sirs, pages and valets, beggars and mercenaries, brave knights and fierce lords; all of which things were certainly more innocent than children's games, and did no harm to any one.

The critic did not wait for the publication of the second novel to begin his work of depreciation. As soon as the first appeared he put on his camel-hair shirt, scattered a bushel of ashes upon his head, and, lifting up his voice in loud lamentation, called—

"More Middle Ages! Nothing but Middle Ages! Who shall deliver me from the Middle Ages, from these Middle Ages which are not the Middle Ages at all?—Middle Ages of pasteboard and terra-cotta with nothing mediaeval about them but their name. Oh! the barons of iron in their armour of steel, with their hearts of steel in their iron breasts! Oh! the cathedrals with ever-blooming rose-windows, flowering stained-glass, with granite lace-work, and open-work trefoils, their serrated gables, and chasuble of stone embroidered like a bridal veil, with their tapers and chants, splendidly vested priests and kneeling congregations, deep, tremulous notes of organs, and angels hovering under the arches against which flutter their wings! How they have spoiled the Middle Ages for me,—my exquisite and richly coloured Middle Ages! They have plastered them over with coarse whitewash and crude colourings! Ah! ye ignorant daubers who fancy you are colourists because you have stuck red on blue, white on black, red on green, you have seen but the outer pellicle of the Middle Ages, you have not discovered their spirit, no blood flows in the epidermis with which you have clothed your phantoms, no heart beats beneath the steel corslets, no legs fill the cotton trunk-hose, no stomach, no breasts are underneath the blazoned tunics; these are clothes with the out-ward semblance of men,—no more. So away with the Middle Ages turned out for us by the hacks (there! the murder is out! Hacks!). The day of the Middle Ages is past; we want something else."

And the public, seeing that the writers for the press were barking at the heels of the Middle Ages, was seized with a great passion for those poor mediaeval days which the critics thought they had killed at one stroke. The Middle Ages—helped on by newspaper opposition—invaded everything: the drama, the melodrama, the song, the tale, poetry; there were even mediaeval vaudevilles, and Momus sang feudal refrains.

By the side of the mediaeval novel budded the novel of rottenness, a very delightful form of tale, greatly in request among kept women of a nervous disposition, as also among disillusioned cooks of the female persuasion.

The newspaper writers were as quickly drawn by the stench thereof as are crows by a dead body, and with the sharp nib of their pens they tore to pieces and wickedly did to death this unhappy sort of novel, that only asked to prosper and to rot in peace upon the sticky shelves of circulating libraries. The things they said, the things they wrote about it! They called it morgue literature, penitentiary literature, hangman's nightmare, drunken butcher's hallucinations, delirious jailer's literature. They gently hinted that the authors were assassins and vampires, that they had contracted the virtuous habit of murdering their father and mother, that they drank blood out of skulls, used legbones for forks, and cut their bread with a guillotine.

And yet they knew better than any one—because they had often lunched with them—that the authors of these delightful butcheries were worthy sons of good families, debonair, belonging to good society, wearing white gloves, fashionably short-sighted, feeding by preference on beefsteak rather than on human chops, and as a rule drinking claret rather than the blood of maidens or newborn babes. Having seen and fingered their manuscripts, they knew very well that they were written in ink, on English paper, and not with blood from the dripping guillotine, upon the skin of a Christian that had been flayed alive.

But no matter what they said or did, the times wanted corruption, and the charnel house was preferred to the boudoir. The reader refused to be caught save by a book baited with a small corpse in the first stage of putrefaction. This is easily understood. Bait your line with a rose, and the spiders will have time to weave their web in the crook of your elbow—you will catch not the smallest fish. But bait it with a worm or a bit of ripe cheese, and carps, barbels, pikes, and eels will leap three feet out of water to catch it. Men are not as unlike fishes as most people seem to think.

One might have thought the journalists had turned Brahmin, Quaker, or followers of Pythagoras, or bulls, so suddenly did they display a detestation of blood and of red. Never had they appeared so melting, so emollient; they were as cream and buttermilk. Two colours—sky-blue and apple-green—were alone recognized by them. They barely tolerated rose, and, had the public given them their way, they would have taken it to graze on spinach on the banks of the Lignon in company with the sheep of Amaryllis. They had exchanged their black frock-coat for the dove-coloured doublet of Celadon or Sylvander, and they had adorned their quills with Burgundy roses and favours after the manner of a shepherd's crook. They allowed their hair to grow long like children's, and by using Marion Delorme's recipe they had renewed their virginity with success equal to hers. They applied to literature the commandment of the Decalogue: Thou shall not kill. Not the tiniest of murders was allowed, and a fifth act had become an impossibility.

They looked on the poniard as excessive, on poison as monstrous, on the axe as unmentionable. They would have had the heroes of dramas reach the good old age of a Melchisedec, although it has been recognised from times immemorial that the end and aim of every tragedy is the doing to death in the last scene of some poor helpless devil of a great man, just as the end and aim of every comedy is to join together in the bonds of holy matrimony two idiots of young lovers of some threescore years each of them.

It was about that time that I burned (after having made a careful copy, in accordance with unfailing custom) two superb, magnificent mediaeval dramas, the one in verse, the other in prose, the heroes whereof were quartered and boiled on the stage, an ending most jovial in itself and possessing the merit of almost complete novelty.

To conform to the critic's ideas, I have since then written a tragedy after the antique, in five acts, named "Heliogabalus," the hero of which precipitates himself into the latrines, a wholly new situation which has the advantage of involving a setting yet unknown to the stage. I also have written a modern drama vastly superior to "Antony Arthur, or The Fated Man," in which the heaven-sent idea arrives in the shape of a Strasburg *pâté de foie gras,* which the hero consumes to the uttermost atom, after having repeatedly committed rape; a combination which, remorse being added to it, brings on a violent attack of indigestion that causes his death. A moral ending, if ever there was one, which proves that God is just, and that vice is always punished, and virtue recompensed.

As for the monster variety, you know what they have done to it, how they have treated Han d'Islande, devourer of men, Habibrah the Obeah, Quasimodo the bell-ringer, and Triboulet, a mere hunchback; all the curiously swarming race, all the huge loathsomeness which my dear neighbour[1] causes

---

[1]Victor Hugo.

to abound and to hop around in the virgin forests and the cathedrals in his novels. Neither the mighty strokes after the manner of Michelangelo, nor the peculiarities worthy of Callot, nor the effects of light and shade after the fashion of Goya, nothing, in short, found mercy at their hands. When he wrote novels they quoted his odes; when he composed dramas they sent him back to his novels; which is the customary procedure of newspaper writers, who always prefer what one has done to what one does. Happy the man, however, whose talent is acknowledged, even by the newspaper reviewers, to show in all his works, save of course the one they are reviewing, and who would merely have to write a theological treatise or a cookery-book to have his drama considered admirable.

As for the novel of the heart, the novel of fire and passion, whose father is Werther the German, and whose mother is Manon Lescaut the French-woman, we have said something, at the beginning of this preface, of the moral leprosy which strenuously attaches to it under pretext of morality and religion. The lice of criticism resemble the lice of the human body, which desert the dead for the living. Abandoning the dead mediaeval novel, the critics have fastened upon the novel of passion, which has a tough and living skin that may break their teeth.

We think, saving the respect we entertain for modern apostles, that the authors of these alleged immoral novels, though not as much married as the virtuous journalists, have usually a mother, that many have sisters, and own, too, numerous female relatives; but their mothers and sisters do not read novels, even immoral ones; they sew, embroider, and look after the house. Their stockings, as Mr. Planard might say, are spotlessly white; they can stand having their legs looked at—they are not blue; and old Chrysale, who so cordially hated learned women, would propose them as models to Philaminte.

As for these gentlemen's wives, since they have so many of them, virgin though their husbands be, it seems to me that there are certain things they are bound to know—though, after all, they may not have taught them any-thing. So I understand that they are anxious to maintain them in that pre-cious and blessed ignorance. God is great and Mahomet is his prophet! Women are inquisitive; Heaven and morality grant that they satisfy their curiosity more legitimately than did Eve, their foremother, and that they do not go asking questions of the serpent.

As for their daughters, if they have been to boarding-school, I do not see what these books could possibly teach them.

It is just as absurd to say that a man is a drunkard because he describes an orgy, or a debauchee because he tells of a debauch, as to claim that a man is virtuous because he has written a work on morality; the contrary is met with every day. It is the characters that speak, not the author; his hero is an atheist, it does not follow that he is one himself. He makes brigands speak and act like brigands, but that does not make him one. If it did, Shakespeare, Corneille, and all tragic writers would have to be sent to the scaffold; they have committed more murders than Mandrin and Cartouche; yet it has not been done, and I doubt whether it will ever be done, however virtuous and moral criticism may become. It is one of the manias of these small-brained cads to constantly put the author in the place of his work, and to have recourse to personalities in order to give some flavour of scandal to their wretched lucubrations, which, they are well aware, no one would read did they contain but their own opinions.

We scarce understand the drift of all this abuse, anger, and vituperation, why these petty Geoffreys should play the part of Don Quixotes of morality and true literary policemen, why they should arrest and club, in the name of virtue, any idea which happens to trip through a book with its cap cocked the least little bit, or its skirts raised something too much. It is very curious.

The time, no matter what, they affirm is immoral (though we doubt whether "immoral" means anything); and no better proof is needed than the number of immoral books it produces and the success they meet with. Books are the product of manners, not manners of books. The Regency produced Crébillon; it was not Crébillon who made the Regency what it was. Boucher's shepherdesses were rouged and free and easy because the marchionesses of his day were rouged and of easy manners. Pictures are made from models, not models from pictures. I forget who has said that literature and art influence manners; whoever he was he was unquestionably a great ass. It is just as if one said, "Sweet peas make the spring grow." On the contrary, sweet peas grow because it is springtime, and cherries, because it is summertime. Trees bear fruits, not fruit, trees assuredly,—a law eternal, and invariable in its variety. Centuries follow centuries, and each has its results, which are not those of the preceding age; so books are the results of manners.

By the side of the moral journalist, under that shower of homilies comparable to rain in summer in a park, there has sprung up, between the planks of the Saint-Simon staging, a band of mushrooms of a new and curious kind, the natural history of which we shall now relate.

They are the utilitarian critics,—poor wights whose nose is so diminutive that spectacles cannot stay on them, and who yet cannot see as far as the end of their nose.

When an author threw a book on their table, novel or volume of verse, these gentlemen leaned nonchalantly back in their armchair, balanced it on its hind-legs, and themselves with a capable air, swelled out and said,—

"What is the good of this book? In what way can it be applied to the moral and physical improvement of our most numerous and poorest class? Why, there is not a word in it on the needs of society, nothing civilising, nothing progressive. How comes it that men write verse and novels that lead to nothing, which do not help on our generation on the road of the future, instead of taking up the great synthesis of humanity, and following out, through the events related by history, the phases of regenerating and providential thought? How can one trouble about form, style, rime, in presence of such grave interests? What do we care for style, rime, and form? We have nothing to do with them." (No, poor foxes; they are too green!) "Society is suffering; it is torn by fierce internal convulsions." (*Id est,* no one cares to subscribe to useful papers.) "It is the poet's business to seek out the cause of this disturbance and to cure it. He will find means to do so by sympathising with his heart and soul with humanity." (Philanthropic poets!—how rare and delightful they would be!) "We are awaiting that poet, we long for him. When he shall appear, his shall be the acclaim of the crowd, the palms, the abode in the Prytaneum. . . ."

That is all right, but as we want our reader to keep awake to the end of this blessed preface, we shall not pursue further this most faithful imitation of the utilitarian style, which is essentially very soporific, and might advantageously be substituted for laudanum and academic discourses.

No, dolts, fools, and asses that you are, a book cannot be turned into gelatine soup, a novel is not a pair of seamless boots, a sonnet an automatic syringe, a drama is not a railway,—all of which things are essentially civilising and carry mankind along the road of progress.

No! by all the entrails of popes, past, present, and future, no—two thousand times no!

You cannot make a nightcap out of a metonymy, a pair of slippers out of a comparison, an umbrella out of an antithesis; unfortunately, you cannot stick on your stomach a few variegated rimes by way of waistcoat. I am firmly convinced that an ode is too light a garment for winter, and that if one put on a strophe, an antistrophe, and an epode, one would not be more fully clothed than that Cynic's wife who, history tells us, was content with her virtue for a shift, and went about naked as a new-born babe.

And yet the famous De la Calprenède once had a coat, and when asked of what stuff is was, replied, "Sylvander." *Sylvander* was a play of his which had just been successfully performed.

That sort of reasoning makes one shrug one's shoulders higher than one's head, higher than the Duke of Gloucester.

People who claim to be economists, and who propose to reconstruct society from top to bottom, gravely put forward such nonsense.

A novel is useful in two ways, the one material, the other spiritual,—if one may apply the term to a novel. The material use is, first, to the author, the few thousand francs which fall into his pocket and so ballast him that neither wind nor devil can carry him off; to the publisher, a fine blood-horse which plunges and paws the ground, when harnessed to the cabriolet of ebony and steel, as Figaro has it; to the paper-maker, another mill on some other stream, and often a means of spoiling a fine site; to the printers, a few tons of log-wood with which to colour their throats at their weekly drinking; to the circulating library, a whole lot of big pennies most vulgarly verdigrised, and a mass of grease that, were it properly collected and turned to account, would render the whale-fishery unnecessary. The spiritual use is that when one is reading novels one is asleep, instead of reading useful, virtuous, and progressive newspapers, or other indigestible and degrading drugs.

Now, then, who will deny that novels make for civilisation? And I shall not speak of the tobacconists, grocers, and dealers in potato chips, who are each and all deeply interested in this branch of literature, the paper used in it being, as a general thing, of a much better quality than that used for newspapers.

Indeed it is enough to make one laugh a horse-laugh to hear those republican or Simonian gentry talk. First and foremost I should like to know the exact meaning of that great fool of a word with which they daily fill up their empty columns, and which is to them at once a shibboleth and a consecrated expression? Usefulness,—what is that word? What is it applied to?

There are two sorts of usefulness, and the meaning of the word itself is always relative. What is useful to one man is of no use to another. You are a cobbler, and I am a poet. It is of use to me that my first line of verse should rime with my second. A dictionary of rimes is of great use to me; it would be of no use whatever to you in patching an old pair of boots, and I am bound to say that a cobbler's knife would not be of any profit to me in the writing of an ode. Of course you may reply that a cobbler is far above a poet, and that one can dispense with the latter much better than with the former. Without venturing to cast discredit upon the illustrious profession of the cobbler, which I honour as highly as the profession of constitutional monarchs, I humbly confess that I would rather have a gaping seam in my shoe than a false rime to my verse, and that I would rather do without shoes than without poems. As I rarely go out, and progress more readily with my head than with my feet, I wear out less footwear than a virtuous republican who spends his whole time rushing from one department to another to obtain the contemptuous gift of some office or other.

I am aware that there are people who prefer mills to churches, and the bread of the body to the bread of the soul. I have nothing to say to such people. They deserve to be economists in this world and in the next likewise.

Is there anything absolutely useful on this earth and in this life of ours? To begin with, there is mighty little use in our being on this earth and living. I challenge the wisest of the company to tell us what we are good for unless it be not to subscribe to the *Constitutionnel* or any other paper.

Next, admitting that, *a priori,* our being in existence is of use, what are the things really necessary to sustain that existence? Soup and meat twice a day are all that is needed to fill our stomachs in the strict sense of the word. Man, to whom a coffin six feet long and two feet wide is more than sufficient after his death, does not need much more room while alive. A hollow cube, seven to eight feet each way, with a hole for fresh air, one cell in the hive, that is all that he needs for a lodging and to keep off the rain. A blanket properly draped round his body will protect him against the cold as well as would the most stylish and well-fitting frock-coat turned out by Staub. Better, indeed.

Thus provided for he can literally live. It is said that a man can live on a shilling a day, but to barely keep from dying is not living, and I do not see in what respect a city organised on utilitarian lines would be a pleasanter residence than the cemetery of Père-Lachaise.

There is no one beautiful thing indispensable for mere living. Flowers might be suppressed without the world suffering materially from their loss, and yet who would be willing that there should be no more flowers? I would rather do without potatoes than without roses, and I believe there is but one utilitarian in the world capable of rooting up a bed of tulips and replacing them by cabbages.

What is the use of beauty in woman? Provided a woman is physically well made and capable of bearing children, she will always be good enough in the opinion of economists.

What is the use of music?—of painting? Who would be fool enough now-adays to prefer Mozart to Carrel, Michelangelo to the inventor of white mustard?

There is nothing really beautiful save what is of no possible use. Everything useful is ugly, for it expresses a need, and man's needs are low and disgusting, like his own poor, wretched nature. The most useful place in a house is the water-closet.

For my part, saving these gentry's presence, I am of those to whom super-fluities are necessaries, and I am fond of things and people in inverse ratio to the service they render me. I prefer a Chinese vase with its mandarins and dragons, which is perfectly useless to me, to a utensil which I do not use, and the particular talent of mine which I set most store by is that which enables me not to guess logographs and charades. I would very willingly renounce my rights as a Frenchman and a citizen for the sight of an un-doubted painting by Raphael, or of a beautiful nude woman,—Princess

Borghese, for instance, when she posed for Canova, or Julia Grisi when she is entering her bath. I would most willingly consent to the return of that cannibal, Charles X, if he brought me, from his residence in Bohemia, a case of Tokai or Johannisberg; and the electoral laws would be quite liberal enough, to my mind, were some of our streets broader and some other things less broad. Though I am not a dilettante, I prefer the sound of a poor fiddle and tambourines to that of the Speaker's bell. I would sell my breeches for a ring, and my bread for jam. The occupation which best befits civilised man seems to me to be idleness or analytically smoking a pipe or a cigar. I think highly of those who play skittles, and also of those who write verse. You perceive that my principles are not utilitarian, and that I shall never be the editor of a virtuous paper, unless I am converted, which would be very comical.

Instead of founding a Monthyon prize for the reward of virtue, I would rather bestow—like Sardanapalus, that great, misunderstood philosopher—a large reward to him who should invent a new pleasure; for to me enjoyment seems to be the end of life and the only useful thing on this earth. God willed it to be so, for He created women, perfumes, light, lovely flowers, good wine, spirited horses, lapdogs, and Angora cats; for He did not say to His angels, "Be virtuous," but, "Love," and gave us lips more sensitive than the rest of the skin that we might kiss women, eyes looking upward that we might behold the light, a subtile sense of smell that we might breathe in the soul of the flowers, muscular limbs that we might press the flanks of stallions and fly swift as thought without railway or steam-kettle, delicate hands that we might stroke the long heads of greyhounds, the velvety fur of cats, and the polished shoulder of not very virtuous creatures, and, finally, granted to us alone the triple and glorious privilege of drinking without being thirsty, striking fire, and making love in all seasons, whereby we are very much more distinguished from brutes than by the custom of reading newspapers and framing constitutions.

By Jupiter! what a stupid thing is that pretended perfectibility of human kind which is being constantly dinned into our ears! In truth, it would make it appear that man is a mechanism capable of improvements, and that a cogwheel more accurately engaged, a counterpoise more suitably placed, are able to make that mechanism work more commodiously and more easily. When man shall have been given two stomachs, so that he can chew the cud like an ox; eyes at the back of his head so that, like Janus, he can see those who are putting their tongues out at him behind his back, and can contemplate his posterior in a less constrained attitude than the Venus Callypige of Athens; when he shall have had wings stuck into his shoulder-blades, so that he shall not have to pay threepence to go in a 'bus, when he shall have had a new organ bestowed on him,—then, all right, the word "perfectibility" will begin to mean something.

With all these fine improvements what has been done that was not as well and better done before the Deluge? Has man succeeded in drinking more than he did in the days of ignorance and barbarism (old style)? Alexander, the equivocal friend of handsome Hephaestion, was no mean toper, though in his day there existed no *Journal of Useful Knowledge;* and I know of no utilitarian who could drain—without fear of becoming wine-stricken and swelling to a size greater than that of Lepeintre the younger, or a hippopotamus—the huge cup he called Hercules' tankard. Marshal Bassompierre, who drank a jackboot full to the health of the Thirteen Cantons, strikes me as a singularly estimable man in his way, and one very difficult to improve upon.

Where is the economist capable of enlarging our stomach so that it shall contain as many beefsteaks as could that of Milo of Croton, who ate an ox? The menu at the Café Anglais or Véfour or at such other famous restaurant as you please, seems to me very meagre and ecumenical by the side of the menu at Trimalcion's dinner. Where is the table on which you can now have served up in a single dish a wild sow and her twelve young boars? Who among us has eaten sea-eels and lampreys fed on human flesh? Do you conscientiously believe that Brillat-Savarin has improved on Apicius? Think you that fat swine Vitellius could fill his famous Minerva buckler with the brains of pheasants and peacocks, with the tongues of flamingoes and the livers of parrot-fish at Chevet's? What do your oysters at the Rocher de Cancale amount to in comparison with those of the Lucrine lake, for which special sea water was prepared? The suburban assignation-houses of the Regency marquesses are wretched drink-shops compared with the villas of Roman patricians at Baia, Capri, and Tibur. The cyclopean splendours of these mighty voluptuaries, who built enduring monuments for a day's pleasuring, should make us fall prostrate at the feet of the genius of antiquity and forever strike from our dictionaries the word "perfectibility."

Has a single additional mortal sin been invented? Unfortunately, the number of them is still seven, as of yore, the number of a just man's falls in one day—pretty small. I do not even believe that after a century of progress at the present rate, there is a single amorous man capable of repeating the thirteenth labour of Hercules. Can one make things pleasanter for one's goddess than in Solomon's time? Many very illustrious scholars and many very respectable ladies affirm the opposite, and declare that amatory energy is steadily decreasing. Then, why talk of progress? I know very well that you will say we have an upper and a lower Chamber, that universal suffrage is expected, and the number of deputies to be doubled or tripled. Do you think there is not enough bad French spoken from the national tribune, and that there are not enough deputies for the wretched job they have to do? I do not see much use in collecting two or three hundred countrymen in a wooden barracks, with a ceiling painted by Fragonard, and to set them to pottering at and spoiling I know not how many petty, absurd, or abominable laws. What matters it whether it is a sword, a holy water sprinkler, or an umbrella that rules you? It is a stick all the same, and I am amazed that progressive men should squabble over the kind of club which is to be laid across their shoulders, when it would be far more progressive and far less costly to break it and to throw the pieces away.

There is but one of you with common-sense; he is a lunatic, a great genius, an ass, a divine poet far superior to Lamartine, Hugo, and Byron. It is Charles Fourier, the phalansterian, who is all these things in himself.[2] He alone has been logical enough and bold enough to carry out consequences to their ultimate end. He affirms without hesitation that men will shortly have fifteen-foot tails with an eye at the end; which is assuredly an improvement, and enables one to do many a fine thing that was impossible before,— such as smashing an elephant's head without striking a blow, swinging from trees without having a rope-swing, as easily as does the most perfect monkey, to do without a parasol or umbrella by merely spreading one's tail over one's head like a plume, after the fashion of squirrels, which do without umbrellas with no inconvenience,—and other perogatives too numerous to mention. Several phalansterians indeed claim that they already have a bit of a tail, which would willingly grow longer if Heaven should let them live long enough.

Charles Fourier has invented as many kinds of animals as the great naturalist Cuvier. He has invented horses which are to be three times the size of elephants, dogs as huge as tigers, fishes capable of feeding more people than Jesus Christ's two fishes; a story which incredulous followers of Voltaire call a fish story, and which I call a magnificent parable. He has built cities by the side of which Rome, Babylon, and Tyre are but mole-hills; he has heaped Babels on Babels, and carried into soaring heights spirals more unending than those in all John Martin's engravings. He has invented I know not how many orders of architecture, and how many seasonings. He has planned a theatre which would strike even Romans of the Empire as grandiose, and drawn up a dinner menu which Lucius or Nomentanus would perchance have considered sufficient for a small dinner. He promises to create new pleasures, and to develop the organs and the senses. He is going to make women

---

[2]Fourier (1772–1837) was a utopian reformer who advocated the regrouping of society into self-sufficient cooperative communities called *phalanstères*.

more beautiful and more passionate, men more robust and more capable; he warrants your having children, and intends to so diminish the population of the world that everybody shall be comfortable in it; which is more sensible than to urge the proletariat to engender more inhabitants, and, when those swarm beyond reason, to sweep them off the streets with artillery, and to fire cannon-balls at them instead of giving them bread.

Only in this way is progress possible. Any other is bitter derision, a witless prank, not good enough to fool even credulous idiots.

The phalanstery is really an improvement on the abbey of Thelema, and finally disposes of the Earthly Paradise as a worn-out, old-fashioned concern. Alone the "Thousand and One Nights" and Madame d'Aubray's "Tales," can successfully compete with the phalanstery. What fertility and invention! There is enough in it to supply marvels for three thousand waggon-loads of romantic or classic poems; and our versifiers, whether of the Academy or not, are pretty small inventors in comparison with Charles Fourier, the inventor of passionate attractions. It is unquestionably a great and lofty idea to turn to use movements which hitherto it has been sought to repress.

Ah! you claim that we are progressing. If tomorrow the crater of a volcano opened at Montmartre and threw over Paris a pall of ashes and a shroud of lava, as Vesuvius did of yore over Stabiae, Pompeii, and Herculaneum, and if, some thousands of years later, the antiquarians of those days began excavations and brought to light the remains of the dead city, tell me, what monument would have remained standing to testify to the splendour of the great buried, the Gothic Notre-Dame? A pretty idea of our art would the Tuileries—touched up by M. Fontaine—give when brought to light! And how fine would be the statues of the Louis XV bridge when transported into the museums of that day! And apart from paintings of the old schools, and the statues of antiquity or of the Renaissance collected in the gallery of the Louvre, that long shapeless passage; apart from the ceiling Ingres painted, which would prevent people from believing that Paris was a camping-ground of Barbarians, a village of the Welch or the Topinambous, what might be dug up would be mighty curious. Flint-locks of the National Guard, firemen's helmets, crowns stamped with an ugly die,—that is what would be found, instead of those fine weapons, so exquisitely chased, which the Middle Ages left within the towers and the ruined tombs, of the medals which fill Etruscan vases and underlie the foundations of all Roman constructions. As for our contemptible veneered wood furniture, all those wretched boxes, so bare, so ugly, so mean, that are called commodes or desks, all those shapeless and fragile utensils, I hope that Time would have pity enough on them to destroy the very last trace of them.

We did once get it into our heads to build ourselves a grand and splendid monument. We were first obliged to borrow the plan from the old Romans; then, even before it was finished, our Pantheon began to give way below like a child with the rickets, and swayed like a dead-drunk pensioner, so that it had to be provided with stone crutches, else it would have fallen flat in sight of the whole world and would have afforded food for laughter to the nations for more than a century. We wanted to stick up an obelisk on one of our two squares; we had to go and steal it in Luxor, and it took us two years to bring it home. Ancient Egypt bordered its road with obelisks as we border ours with poplars; it carried bundles of them under its arms, as a market-gardener carries asparagus, and it cut a monolith out of the slopes of its granite mountains more easily than we cut out an ear-pick or a toothpick. Some centuries ago they had Raphael and Michelangelo; now we have M. Paul Delaroche, and all because we are progressing.

You brag of your Opera house; ten Opera houses the size of yours could dance a saraband in a Roman amphitheatre. . . . What are your benefit performances, lasting till two in the morning, compared with those games which lasted a hundred days, with those performances in which real ships fought real battles on a real sea; when thousands of men earnestly carved each other—turn pale, O heroic Franconi!—when, the sea having withdrawn, the desert appeared, with its raging tigers and lions, fearful supernumeraries that played but once; when the leading part was played by some robust Dacian or Pannonian athlete, whom it would often have been mighty difficult to recall at the close of the performance, whose leading lady was some splendid and hungry lioness of Numidia starved for three days? Do you not consider the clown elephant superior to Mlle. Georges? Do you believe Taglioni dances better than did Arbuscula, and Perrot better than Bathyllus? Admirable as is Bocage, I am convinced Roscius could have given him points. Galeria Coppiola played young girls' parts, when over one hundred years old; it is true that the oldest of our leading ladies is scarcely more than sixty, and that Mlle. Mars has not even progressed in that direction. The ancients had three or four thousand gods in whom they believed, and we have but one, in whom we scarcely believe. That is a strange sort of progress. Is not Jupiter worth a good deal more than Don Juan, and is he not a much greater seducer? By my faith, I know not what we have invented, or even wherein we have improved.

Next to the progressive journalists and by way of antithesis to them, come the disillusioned. These range in age from twenty to twenty-two; they have never gone beyond the confines of their quarter, and have lain only with their housekeeper. But everything bores them, palls on them, wearies them; they are uninterested, disillusioned, worn out, inaccessible. They know beforehand just what you are going to say; they have seen everything, felt everything, borne everything, heard everything it is possible to feel, see, hear or experience; there is no recess of the human heart so obscure that the beams of their lantern have not shone into it. They tell you with the utmost coolness: "The human heart is not like that; women are not so constituted; that character is not true to nature." Or else, "What! never anything but love and hate, men and women? Have you nothing else to talk about? Man, as a subject, is worn threadbare, and so is woman, since M. de Balzac has taken her up. Who shall deliver me from men and women? You fancy, sir, your fabulation is novel? It is as stale as stale can be; nothing staler. I read it, I forget where, when I was at nurse or something else; it has been dinned into my ears for ten years past. Moreover, know, sir, that there is nothing of which I am ignorant, that everything is stale and unprofitable to me, and that, were your idea as virginal as the Virgin Mary, I should none the less affirm that I had seen it prostitute itself at the street-corners to the veriest cads and low fellows."

It is to these journalists we owe Jocko, the Green Monster, the Lyons of Mysore and many another fine invention.

They are always complaining of having to read books and to see plays. If they have to write about a wretched vaudeville, they bring in the almond-trees in flower, the lime-trees with their perfumed bloom, the breezes of springtime, the scent of the young leafage; they set up for lovers of nature after the fashion of young Werther, though they have never set foot outside of Paris, and could not tell a cabbage from a beet. If it happens to be winter they will talk of the pleasures of the home fireside, of crackling blazes, and-irons, slippers, reverie, and dozing, and will not fail to quote the famous line from Tibullus,—

> *Quam juvat immites ventos audire cubanteum*[3]

which will allow them to assume the most charmingly naive and disillusioned air. They will pose as men insensible henceforth to the work of men, whom dramatic emotions leave cold and hard as the penknife with which they mend their pen, but they will yell, all the same, like Jean-Jacques Rousseau, "There's a periwinkle!" [i.e., Summer is coming]. They profess fierce antipathy for Gymnase colonels, American uncles, cousins of both sexes, sentimental veterans, romantic widows, and they try to cure us of our love of vaudeville by daily giving proof in their articles that the Frenchman was not born witty. As a matter of fact, we do not object to this, and, on the contrary, gladly own that the disappearance of vaudevilles and comic opera (a national genre)

---

[3]What a pleasure, when abed, to hear the furious winds.

in France would be a great blessing. But I should like to know what kind of literature these gentlemen would allow to take their place. True, it could not possibly be worse.

Others preach against bad taste, and translate Seneca, the tragic writer. Lately, by way of bringing up the rear of the procession, a new and yet unknown band of critics has been formed.

Their formula of appreciation is the most convenient, the most widely applicable, the most malleable, the most peremptory, superlative, and victorious that could ever be invented by any critic. Zoilus would certainly not have suffered by it.

Until now, when it was desired to run down a book, or to give a bad opinion of it to the ancient and artless subscriber, incorrect or perfidiously incomplete quotations were made from it; sentences were deformed, lines mutilated in such wise that the author himself would have owned his work most ridiculous. He was accused of imaginary plagiarisms; passages from his book were compared with passages from ancient or modern writers that in no wise resembled his; he was charged, in the worst of French, and with endless solecisms, with being unacquainted with his mother tongue, and with debasing the French of Racine and Voltaire; his work drove readers to anthropophagy, and his readers invariably fell victims, within a week, to cannibalism or hydrophobia. But all that sort of thing had become stale, behind the times, exploded sham, and ancient history. By dint of having dragged its slow length along the notices, reviews, and gossip columns, the charge of immortality had lost its force, and had become so utterly unserviceable that scarce any paper, save the chaste and progressive *Constitutionnel,* was desperately courageous enough to revamp it.

So the criticism of the future, prospective criticism was invented. All at once; fancy that! Is it not splendid, and does it not betoken a fine power of imagination? The recipe is simple and easily told. The book which shall be praised is the book which has not yet been published. The one that is just published is infallibly detestable. Tomorrow's will be splendid, but it never is tomorrow. This form of criticism proceeds like the barber who had on his sign in large letters,—FREE SHAVE TO-MORROW.

All the poor devils who read the sign looked forward to enjoying next day the ineffable and supreme delight of being, once in their life, shaved without money and without price, and their beard grew six inches longer with delighted anticipation during the night which preceded the happy day. But when, neck enwrapped in napkin, the barber asked whether they had any money and told them to be ready to shell out, or he would treat them as are treated the purloiners of nuts and the appropriators of apples, and he swore his biggest oath that unless they paid he would slice their throats with his razor, then the poor devils, much cast down and crestfallen, pointed to the sign and its sacrosanct inscription. "Ha! ha!" would the barber laugh; "your education has been neglected, my little ones, and you ought to go back to school. The sign says, 'To-morrow.' I am not of so foolish or fantastic humour as to give a free shave to-day; my colleagues would accuse me of ruining the business. Come back last time, or when Sunday falls in the middle of the week, and you will be all right. May I then rot to perdition if I do not shave you free, on the word of an honest barber."

Authors who read a prospective article, in which an existing work is run down, always flatter themselves that the book they are at work on will be the book of the future. So far as they are able, they try to fall in with the critic's views, and turn social, progressive, moral, palingenetic, mythic, pantheist, buchezist, believing that they shall thus escape the awful anathema; but it is with them as with the barber's customers: to-day is not to-morrow's eve. Never will that long-promised to-morrow dawn upon the world, for the trick is too useful to be soon given up. While decrying the book he is jealous of, and that he would fain destroy, the critic assumes the air of the most generous impartiality. He makes it appear that he would dearly like to approve and to praise, but he never does approve or praise. This method is unquestionably superior to that which may be called retrospective, and which consists in praising none save ancient works, which are never read nowadays, and which disturb no one, at the expense of modern works, which we are concerned with, and which more directly, wound self-love.

On entering upon this review of critics we stated that there was matter enough for fifteen or sixteen folio volumes, but that we should confine our-selves to a few lines. I begin to fear that these few lines prove to be two to three thousand yards long apiece, and resemble those pamphlets so thick that they cannot be pierced by a penknife thrust, and whose treacherous titles read, "A Few Words on the Revolution,"—or, "A Few Words on This or That." The story of the deeds, of the many loves of the diva Magdalen de Maupin would run great danger of being passed by, and it will readily be conceived that it will take at least a whole volume to sing, as they deserve to be sung, the adventures of that fair Bradamante. That is why, however desir-ous we may be, to carry still further the description of the illustrious Aris-tarchs of the day, we shall be satisfied with the brief sketch we have just given, and add a few reflections on the simplicity of our debonair fellow-poets who, with the stupidity of a pantomime Pantaloon, stand, without a murmur, the blows of Harlequin's bat and the kicks of the clown. They are like a fencing master who should, in an assault of arms, cross his arms behind his back, and let his opponent pink him in the breast without once parrying; or like speeches for the plaintiff and the defendant, of which the King's attorney's only should be heard; or like a debate in which reply was forbidden.

The critic affirms this and affirms that; he puts on airs and slashes away:—absurd, detestable, monstrous, like nothing that ever was; like everything that ever has been. A new drama is played; the critic goes to see it; it turns out that the play in no wise corresponds to the one which, on the strength of the title, the critic has evolved for himself; therefore, in his review, he substitutes his own play for the author's. He serves up his erudition in strong doses; he pours out all the knowledge he got up the day before in some library or other, and treats in heathenish fashion people at whose feet he ought to sit, and the most ignorant of whom could give points to much wiser men than he.

Authors bear this sort of thing with a magnanimity and a patience that are really incomprehensible. For, after all, who are those critics, who with their trenchant tone, their dicta, might be supposed sons of the gods? They are simply fellows who were at college with us, and who have turned their studies to less account, since they have not produced anything, and can do no more than soil and spoil the works of others, like true stymphalid vampires.

There is something to be done in the way of criticising critics; for those fine contemners who pose as being so haughty and difficult to please are far from being as infallible as the Holy Father. Such a criticism would more than fill a daily paper of large size. The blunders they make in matters historical and others, their misquotations, their bad French, their plagiarisms, their foolish babble, their threadbare jokes in most evil taste, their lack of ideas, of intelligence, of tact, their ignorance of the simplest things, which makes them mistake the Piraeus for a man, and M. Delaroche for a painter, would afford authors material enough for revenge, without their having to do more than underline the extracts and reproduce them textually; for a great writer's commission does not go along with a critic's commission, and in order to avoid errors in grammar, or of taste, it is not enough to reproach others with making them, as our critics plainly prove every day in the week. If it were men like Chateaubriand, Lamartine, and others of that sort who wrote criticisms, I could understand people going down on their knees and worshipping; but what disgusts me and furiously angers me is that Messrs. Z., K., Y., V., Q., X., or some other letter of the alphabet between Alpha and Omega, should set up as small Quinctilians and scold us in the name of morals and letters. I wish there were a police ordinance forbidding certain names to bump up against others. I know a cat may look at a king, and that even the gigantic proportions of St. Peter's at Rome cannot prevent the Transteverini filthying its base in strange fashion, but I none the less believe it would be absurd to inscribe across certain reputations, "Committ no nuisance." Charles X alone thoroughly grasped the question. He rendered a great service to arts and civilisation when he ordered the suppression of the press. Newspapers are something like brokers or horse-dealers, who intervene between the artists and the public, the king and the public. Every one knows the fine result that has followed. This perpetual barking deadens inspiration and spreads such mistrust in hearts and minds that one dare trust neither poet nor government; so that poesy and royalty, the two greatest things in the world, become impossible, to the great misfortune of the nations which sacrifice their well-being to the petty satisfaction of reading every morning a few sheets of inferior paper dirtied with bad ink and worse style. There was no art criticism under Julius II, and I have not come across any articles of the day on Daniele da Volterra, Sebastiano del Piombo, Michelangelo, Raphael, Ghiberti della Porta, or Benvenuto Cellini; and yet I am of opinion that, for people who had no newspapers and who knew nothing of the words "art" or "artistic," they had their fair share of talent and knew their trade pretty well. The reading of newspapers is a bar to the existence of real scholars and genuine artists; it is comparable to daily excess, which lands you worn out and weak on the couch of the Muses, those hard, exacting maids who will have none but lusty and virgin lovers. The newspaper kills the book as the book killed architecture, as artillery has killed courage and muscular strength. No one suspects of what numberless treasures we are robbed by the newspapers. They take the bloom off everything; they prevent our really owning anything, our having a book to our very self. At the theatre they prevent our being surprised, and reveal to us beforehand the ending of every piece. They deprive us of the delight of tittle-tattle, gossip, back-biting and slander, of inventing a piece of news, or of carting a true one for a week through all the drawing-rooms of society. Whether we will it or not, they proclaim ready-made judgments; they prejudice us against things we would like. They are the cause that dealers in matches, provided they are endowed with memory, talk as much absurd nonsense about literature as do members of provincial Academies. It is to them that we are indebted for hearing all day long, instead of artless notions or individual idiotic remarks, ill-digested scraps of newspapers that are for all the world like omelets raw on one side and burned on the other; that we are pitilessly stuffed with news three or four hours old, already familiar to babes and sucklings. They deaden our taste and reduce us to the level of those drinkers of peppered alcohol, of the swallowers of files and scrapers, who find the finest wines flavourless and miss their perfumed and flowery bouquet. I should be infinitely obliged to Louis-Philippe if he would, once for all, suppress all literary and political sheets, and I should forthwith rime for him fine wild dithyrambics in the freest of verse and alternate rimes, signed, "Your most humble and most faithful subject," etc.

And let it not be supposed that literature would cease to interest, for in the days before newspapers were, Paris was busy four days on end with a quatrain, and talked of a first performance for six months.

It is true that suppression of the press would mean the loss of advertisements and of praise at eighteen pence a line, and notoriety would be less prompt and less tremendously sudden. But I have thought of a very ingenious way of filling the place of advertisements. If between now and the publication of this glorious novel my gracious sovereign has suppressed the press, I shall most assuredly use my method, and I expect wonders from it. The great day having come, twenty-four criers on horseback, wearing the publisher's livery with his address on breast and back, bearing in their hands banners on both sides of which would be embroidered the title of the novel, and each preceded by a tambourine and by kettledrums, should go through the streets of the city, and stopping in squares and at the crossing of streets, they should proclaim in a loud and intelligible voice: "It is to-day, not yesterday or to-morrow, that is published the admirable, inimitable, divine and more than divine novel of the most famous Théophile Gautier, 'Mademoiselle de Maupin,' which Europe, and even the other parts of the world and Polynesia have been impatiently expecting for more than a year past. It is being sold at the rate of five hundred copies a minute, and new editions appear every half-hour. A picket of municipal guards is stationed at the shop door to keep back the crowd and prevent disorder in any shape." That would certainly be worth just as much as a three-line advertisement in the *Debats* and the *Courrier français,* between elastic belts, crinoline collars, patent-nipple nursing-bottles, Regnault's comfits, and recipes for toothache.

May, 1834.

Musset

Louis Charles Alfred de Musset (1810–1857), scion of a noble French family, was early nicknamed Miss Byron for his airs both languorous and passionate. Musset drifted into the restless, fashionable life of the Paris dandy of his day, drifted into an exotic romance with George Sand and out again, drifted into venereal disease, alcoholism, and the *Académie française,* and died prematurely before the age of fifty.

Most of the plays he wrote, after the failure of his first in 1830, were designed only to be read, not staged. This allowed them great freedom of movement and conception, but also reflected the tragic ineffectiveness of their author, many of whose heroes are fate-driven and fate-vanquished rebels against society and/or convention. His poetry and plays, which are sometimes maudlin but almost always very beautiful, reflect the problems of a peculiar and passionate personality; but the scene and mood described in the *Confessions of a Child of the Century* (1836) do also illustrate the circumstances of a whole generation whose liveliest members tended to feel, like Stendhal's Julien Sorel or Musset's own Fantasio, that they had been born too late—would-be young eagles, their wings clipped so that they cannot soar. Chapter II of that autobiographical novel is reprinted here.

Reflections

During the wars of the Empire, while husbands and brothers were in Germany, anxious mothers gave birth to an ardent, pale, and neurotic generation. Conceived between battles, reared amid the noises of war, thousands of children looked about them with dull eyes while testing their limp muscles. From time to time their blood-stained fathers would appear, raise them to their gold-laced bosoms, then place them on the ground and remount their horses.

The life of Europe centered in one man; men tried to fill their lungs with the air which he had breathed. Yearly France presented that man with three hundred thousand of her youth; it was the tax to Caesar; without that troop behind him, he could not follow his fortune. It was the escort he needed that he might scour the world, and then fall in a little valley on a deserted island, under weeping willows.

Never had there been so many sleepless nights as in the time of that man; never had there been seen, hanging over the ramparts of the cities, such a nation of desolate mothers; never was there such a silence about those who spoke of death. And yet there was never such joy, such life, such fanfares of war, in all hearts. Never was there such pure sunlight as that which dried all his blood. God made the sun for this man, men said; and they called it the Sun of Austerlitz. But he made this sunlight himself with his ever-booming guns that left no clouds but those which succeed the day of battle.

It was this air of the spotless sky, where shone so much glory, where glistened so many swords, that the youth of the time breathed. They well knew that they were destined to the slaughter; but they believed that Murat was invulnerable, and the Emperor had been seen to cross a bridge where so many bullets whistled that they wondered if he were mortal. And even if one must die, what did it matter? Death itself was so beautiful, so noble, so illustrious, in its battle-scarred purple! It borrowed the color of hope, it reaped so many immature harvests that it became young, and there was no more old age. All the cradles of France, as indeed all its tombs, were armed with bucklers; there were no more graybeards, there were only corpses or demi-gods.

Nevertheless the immortal Emperor stood one day on a hill watching seven nations engaged in mutual slaughter, not knowing whether he would be master of all the world or only half. Azrael passed, touched the warrior with the tip of his wing, and hurled him into the ocean. At the noise of his fall, the dying Powers sat up in their beds of pain; and stealthily advancing with furtive tread, the royal spiders made partition of Europe, and the purple of Caesar became the motley of Harlequin.

Source: Chapter II of *Confessions of a Child of the Century*. Translated by Robert Arnot, New York, 1905.

Just as the traveller, certain of his way, hastes night and day through rain and sunlight, careless of vigils or of dangers, but, safe at home and seated before the fire, is seized by extreme lassitude and can hardly drag himself to bed, so France, the widow of Caesar, suddenly felt her wound. She fell through sheer exhaustion, and lapsed into a coma so profound that her old kings, believing her dead, wrapped about her a burial shroud. The veterans, their hair whitened in service, returned exhausted, and the hearths of deserted castles sadly flickered into life.

Then the men of the Empire, who had been through so much, who had lived in such carnage, kissed their emaciated wives and spoke of their first love. They looked into the fountains of their native fields and found themselves so old, so mutilated, that they bethought themselves of their sons, in order that these might close the paternal eyes in peace. They asked where they were; the children came from the schools, and, seeing neither sabres, nor cuirasses, neither infantry nor cavalry, asked in turn where were their fathers. They were told that the war was ended, that Caesar was dead, and that the portraits of Wellington and of Blücher were suspended in the ante-chambers of the consulates and the embassies, with this legend beneath: *Salvatoribus mundi.*[1]

Then came upon a world in ruins an anxious youth. The children were drops of burning blood which had inundated the earth; they were born in the bosom of war, for war. For fifteen years they had dreamed of the snows of Moscow and of the sun of the Pyramids. They had not gone beyond their native towns; but had been told that through each gateway of these towns lay the road to a capital of Europe. They had in their heads a world; they saw the earth, the sky, the streets and the highways; but these were empty, and the bells of parish churches resounded faintly in the distance.

Pale phantoms, shrouded in black robes, slowly traversed the countryside; some knocked at the doors of houses, and, when admitted, drew from their pockets large, well-worn documents with which they evicted the tenants. From every direction came men still trembling with the fear that had seized them when they had fled twenty years before. All began to urge their claims, disputing loudly and crying for help; strange that a single death should attract so many buzzards.

The King of France was on his throne, looking here and there to see if he could perchance find a bee in the royal tapestry.[2] Some men held out their hats, and he gave them money; others extended a crucifix and he kissed it; others contented themselves with pronouncing in his ear great names of

---

[1]Saviors of the world.

[2]The bee was one of Napoleon's symbols (as the lily was that of the royal house of France).

powerful families, and he replied to these by inviting them into his *grand'* *salle,* where the echoes were more sonorous; still others showed him their old cloaks, when they had carefully effaced the bees, and to these he gave new robes.

The children saw all this, thinking that the spirit of Caesar would soon land at Cannes and breathe upon this larva; but the silence was unbroken, and they saw floating in the sky only the paleness of the lily. When these children spoke of glory, they met the answer: "Become priests"; when they spoke of hope, of love, of power, of life: "Become priests."

And yet upon the rostrum came a man who held in his hand a contract between king and people. He began by saying that glory was a beautiful thing, and ambition and war as well; but there was something still more beautiful, and it was called liberty.

The children raised their heads and remembered that thus their grandfathers had spoken. They remembered having seen in certain obscure corners of the paternal home mysterious busts with long marble hair and a Latin inscription; they remembered how their grandsires shook their heads and spoke of streams of blood more terrible than those of the Empire. Something in that word liberty made their hearts beat with the memory of a terrible past and the hope of a glorious future.

They trembled at the word; but returning to their homes they encountered in the street three coffins which were being borne to Clamart; within were three young men who had pronounced that word liberty too distinctly.

A strange smile hovered on their lips at that sad sight; but other speakers, mounted on the rostrum, began publicly to estimate what ambition had cost and how very dear was glory; they pointed out the horror of war and called the battle-losses butcheries. They spoke so often and so long that all human illusions, like the trees in autumn, fell leaf by leaf about them, and those who listened passed their hands over their foreheads as if awakening from a feverish dream.

Some said: "The Emperor has fallen because the people wished no more of him"; others added: "The people wished the king; no, liberty; no, reason; no, religion; no, the English constitution; no, absolutism"; and the last one said: "No, none of these things, but simply peace."

Three elements entered into the life which offered itself to these children: behind them a past forever destroyed, still quivering on its ruins with all the fossils of centuries of absolutism; before them the aurora of an immense horizon, the first gleams of the future; and between these two worlds—like the ocean which separates the Old World from the New—something vague and floating, a troubled sea filled with wreckage, traversed from time to time by some distant sail or some ship trailing thick clouds of smoke; the present, in a word, which separates the past from the future, which is neither the one nor the other, which resembles both, and where one cannot know whether, at each step, one treads on living matter or on dead refuse.

It was in such chaos that the choice had to be made; this was the aspect presented to children full of spirit and of audacity, sons of the Empire and grandsons of the Revolution.

As for the past, they would have none of it, they had no faith in it; the future, they loved it, but how? As Pygmalion before Galatea, it was for them a lover in marble, and they waited for the breath of life to animate that breast, for blood to color those veins.

There remained then the present, the spirit of the time, angel of the dawn which is neither night nor day; they found him seated on a lime-sack filled with bones, clad in the mantle of egoism, and shivering in terrible cold. The anguish of death entered into the soul at the sight of that spectre, half mummy and half foetus; they approached it as does the traveller who is shown at Strasburg the daughter of an old count of Sarvenden, embalmed in her bride's dress: that childish skeleton makes one shudder, for her slender and livid hand wears the wedding-ring and her head decays enwreathed in orange-blossoms.

As on the approach of a tempest there passes through the forests a terrible gust of wind which makes the trees shudder, to which profound silence succeeds, so had Napoleon, in passing, shaken the world; kings felt their crowns oscillate in the storm, and, raising hands to steady them, found only their hair, bristling with terror. The Pope had travelled three hundred leagues to bless him in the name of God and to crown him with the diadem; but Napoleon had taken it from his hands. Thus everything trembled in that dismal forest of old Europe; then silence succeeded.

It is said that when you meet a mad dog, if you keep quietly on your way without turning, the dog will merely follow you a short distance growling and showing his teeth; but if you allow yourself to be frightened into a movement of terror, if you but make a sudden step, he will leap at your throat and devour you; that when the first bite has been taken there is no escaping him.

In European history it has often happened that a sovereign has made such a movement of terror and his people have devoured him; but if one had done it, all had not done it at the same time—that is to say, one king had disappeared, but not all royal majesty. Before the sword of Napoleon majesty made this movement, this gesture which ruins everything, not only majesty but religion, nobility, all power both human and divine.

Napoleon dead, human and divine power were reestablished, but belief in them no longer existed. A terrible danger lurks in the knowledge of what is possible, for the mind always goes further. It is one thing to say: "That may be," and another thing to say: "That has been"; it is the first bite of the dog.

The fall of Napoleon was the first flicker of the lamp of despotism; it destroyed and it parodied kings as Voltaire the Holy Scripture. And after him was heard a great noise: it was the stone of St. Helena which had just fallen on the ancient world. Immediately there appeared in the heavens the cold star of reason, and its rays, like those of the goddess of the night, shedding light without heat, enveloped the world in a livid shroud.

There had been those who hated the nobles, who cried out against priests, who conspired against kings; abuses and prejudices had been attacked; but all that was not so great a novelty as to see a smiling people. If a noble or a priest or a sovereign passed, the peasants who had made war possible began to shake their heads and say: "Ah! when we saw this man in such a time and place he wore a different face." And when the throne and altar were mentioned, they replied: "They are made of four planks of wood; we have nailed them together and torn them apart." And when some one said: "People, you have recovered from the errors which led you astray; you have recalled your kings and your priests," they replied: "We have nothing to do with those prattlers." And when some one said: "People, forget the past, work and obey," they arose from their seats and a dull jangling could be heard. It was the rusty and notched sabre in the corner of the cottage chimney. Then they hastened to add: "Then keep quiet, at least; if no one harms you, do not seek to harm." Alas! they were content with that.

But youth was not content. It is certain that there are in man two occult powers engaged in a death-struggle: the one, clear-sighted and cold, is concerned with reality, calculation, weight, and judges the past; the other is athirst for the future and eager for the unknown. When passion sways man, reason follows him weeping and warning him of his danger; but when man listens to the voice of reason, when he stops at her request and says: "What a fool I am; where am I going?" passion calls to him: "Ah, must I die?"

A feeling of extreme uneasiness began to ferment in all young hearts. Condemned to inaction by the powers which governed the world, delivered to vulgar pedants of every kind, to idleness and to ennui, the youth saw the foaming billows which they had prepared to meet, subside. All these gladiators glistening with oil felt in the bottom of their souls an unbearable wretchedness. The richest became libertines; those of moderate fortune followed some profession and resigned themselves to the sword or to the church. The poorest gave themselves up with cold enthusiasm to great thoughts, plunged into the frightful sea of aimless effort. As human weakness seeks association and as men are gregarious by nature, politics became mingled with it. There were struggles with the guard on the steps of the legislative assembly; at the theatre Talma wore a wig which made him resemble Caesar; every one flocked to the burial of a Liberal deputy.

But of the members of the two parties there was not one who, upon returning home, did not bitterly realize the emptiness of his life and the feebleness of his hands.

While life outside was so colorless and so mean, the inner life of society assumed a sombre aspect of silence; hypocrisy ruled in all departments of conduct; English ideas, combining gayety with devotion, had disappeared. Perhaps Providence was already preparing new ways, perhaps the herald angel of future society was already sowing in the hearts of women the seeds of human independence. But it is certain that a strange thing suddenly happened: in all the salons of Paris the men passed on one side and the women on the other; and thus, the one clad in white like brides, and the other in black like orphans, began to take measure of one another with the eye.

Let us not be deceived: that vestment of black which the men of our time wear is a terrible symbol; before coming to this, the armor must have fallen piece by piece and the embroidery flower by flower. Human reason has overthrown all illusions; but it bears in itself sorrow, in order that it may be consoled.

The customs of students and artists, those customs so free, so beautiful, so full of youth, began to experience the universal change. Men in taking leave of women whispered the word which wounds to the death: contempt. They plunged into the dissipation of wine and courtesans. Students and artists did the same; love was treated as were glory and religion: it was an old illusion. The *grisette,* that woman so dreamy, so romantic, so tender, and so sweet in love, abandoned herself to the counting-house and to the shop. She was poor and no one loved her; she needed gowns and hats and she sold herself. Oh! misery! the young man who ought to love her, whom she loved, who used to take her to the woods of Verrières and Romainville, to the dances on the lawn, to the suppers under the trees; he who used to talk with her as she sat near the lamp in the rear of the shop on the long winter evenings; he who shared her crust of bread moistened with the sweat of her brow, and her love at once sublime and poor; he, that same man, after abandoning her, finds her after a night of orgy, pale and leaden, forever lost, with hunger on her lips and prostitution in her heart.

About this time two poets, whose genius was second only to that of Napoleon, consecrated their lives to the work of collecting the elements of anguish and of grief scattered over the universe. Goethe, the patriarch of a new literature, after painting in his *Werther* the passion which leads to suicide, traced in his *Faust* the most sombre human character which has ever represented evil and unhappiness. His writings began to pass from Germany into France. From his studio, surrounded by pictures and statues, rich, happy, and at ease, he watched with a paternal smile his gloomy creations marching in dismal procession across the frontiers of France. Byron replied to him in a cry of grief which made Greece tremble, and hung Manfred over the abyss, as if oblivion were the solution of the hideous enigma with which he enveloped him.

Pardon, great poets! who are now but ashes and who sleep in peace! Pardon, ye demigods, for I am only a child who suffers. But while I write all this I cannot but curse you. Why did you not sing of the perfume of flowers, of the voices of nature, of hope and of love, of the vine and the sun, of the azure heavens and of beauty? You must have understood life, you must have suffered; the world was crumbling to pieces about you; you wept on its ruins and you despaired; your mistresses were false; your friends calumniated, your compatriots misunderstood; your heart was empty; death was in your eyes, and you were the Colossi of grief. But tell me, noble Goethe, was there no more consoling voice in the religious murmur of your old German forests? You, for whom beautiful poesy was the sister of science, could not they find in immortal nature a healing plant for the heart of their favorite? You, who were a pantheist, and antique poet of Greece, a lover of sacred forms, could you not put a little honey in the beautiful vases you made; you who had only to smile and allow the bees to come to your lips? And thou, Byron, hadst thou not near Ravenna, under the orange-trees of Italy, under the beautiful Venetian sky, near thy Adriatic, hadst thou not thy well-beloved? Oh, God! I who speak to you, who am only a feeble child, have perhaps known sorrows that you have never suffered, and yet I believe and hope, and still bless God.

When English and German ideas had passed thus over our heads there ensued disgust and mournful silence, followed by a terrible convulsion. For to formulate general ideas is to change saltpetre into powder, and the Homeric brain of the great Goethe had sucked up, as an alembic, all the juice of the forbidden fruit. Those who did not read him, did not believe it, knew nothing of it. Poor creatures! The explosion carried them away like grains of dust into the abyss of universal doubt.

It was a denial of all heavenly and earthly facts that might be termed disenchantment, or if you will, despair; as if humanity in lethargy had been pronounced dead by those who felt its pulse. Like a soldier who is asked: "In what do you believe?" and who replied: "In myself," so the youth of France, hearing that question, replied: "In nothing."

Then formed two camps: on one side the exalted spirits, sufferers, all the expansive souls who yearned toward the infinite, bowed their heads and wept; they wrapped themselves in unhealthful dreams and nothing could be seen but broken reeds in an ocean of bitterness. On the other side the materialists remained erect, inflexible, in the midst of positive joys, and cared for nothing except to count the money they had acquired. It was but a sob and a burst of laughter, the one coming from the soul, the other from the body.

This is what the soul said:

"Alas! Alas! religion has departed; the clouds of heaven fall in rain; we have no longer either hope or expectation, not even two little pieces of black wood in the shape of a cross before which to clasp our hands. The star of the future is loath to appear; it can not rise above the horizon; it is enveloped in clouds, and like the sun in winter its disc is the color of blood, as in '93. There is no more love, no more glory. What heavy darkness over all the earth! And death will come ere the day breaks."

This is what the body said:

"Man is here below to satisfy his senses; he has more or less of white or yellow metal, by which he merits more or less esteem. To eat, to drink, and to sleep, this is life. As for the bonds which exist between men, friendship consists in loaning money; but one rarely has a friend whom he loves enough for that. Kinship determines inheritance; love is an exercise of the body; the only intellectual joy is vanity."

Like the Asiatic plague exhaled from the vapors of the Ganges, frightful despair stalked over the earth. Already Chateaubriand, prince of poesy, wrapping the horrible idol in his pilgrim's mantle, had placed it on a marble altar in the midst of perfumes and holy incense. Already the children were clenching idle hands and drinking in a bitter cup the poisoned beverage of doubt. Already things were drifting toward the abyss, when the jackals suddenly emerged from the earth. A deathly and infected literature, which had no form but that of ugliness, began to sprinkle with fetid blood all the monsters of nature.

Who will dare to recount what was passing in the colleges? Men doubted everything: the young men denied everything. The poets sang of despair; the youth came from the schools with serene brow, their faces glowing with health, and blasphemy in their mouths. Moreover, the French character, being by nature gay and open, readily assimilated English and German ideas; but hearts too light to struggle and to suffer withered like crushed flowers. Thus the seed of death descended slowly and without shock from the head to the bowels. Instead of having the enthusiasm of evil we had only the negation of the good; instead of despair, insensibility. Children of fifteen, seated listlessly under flowering shrubs, conversed for pastime on subjects which would have made shudder with terror the still thickets of Versailles. The Communion of Christ, the Host, those wafers that stand as the eternal symbol of divine love, were used to seal letters; the children spit upon the Bread of God.

Happy they who escaped those times! Happy they who passed over the abyss while looking up to Heaven. There are such, doubtless, and they will pity us.

It is unfortunately true that there is in blasphemy a certain outlet which solaces the burdened heart. When an atheist, drawing his watch, gave God a quarter of an hour in which to strike him dead, it is certain that it was a quarter of an hour of wrath and of atrocious joy. It was the paroxysm of despair, a nameless appeal to all celestial powers; it was a poor, wretched creature squirming under the foot that was crushing him; it was a loud cry of pain. Who knows? In the eyes of Him who sees all things, it was perhaps a prayer.

Thus these youths found employment for their idle powers in a fondness for despair. To scoff at glory, at religion, at love, at all the world, is a great consolation for those who do not know what to do; they mock at themselves, and in doing so prove the correctness of their view. And then it is pleasant to believe one's self unhappy when one is only idle and tired. Debauchery, moreover, the first result of the principles of death, is a terrible millstone for grinding the energies.

The rich said: "There is nothing real but riches, all else is a dream; let us enjoy and then let us die." Those of moderate fortune said: "There is nothing real but oblivion, all else is a dream; let us forget and let us die." And the poor said: "There is nothing real but unhappiness, all else is a dream; let us blaspheme and die."

Is this too black? Is it exaggerated? What do you think of it? Am I a misanthrope? Allow me to make a reflection.

In reading the history of the fall of the Roman Empire, it is impossible to overlook the evil that the Christians, so admirable when in the desert, did to the State when they were in power. "When I think," said Montesquieu, "of the profound ignorance into which the Greek clergy plunged the laity, I am obliged to compare them to the Scythians of whom Herodotus speaks, who put out the eyes of their slaves in order that nothing might distract their attention from their work. . . . No affair of State, no peace, no truce, no negotiations, no marriage could be transacted by any one but the clergy. The evils of this system were beyond belief."

Montesquieu might have added: Christianity destroyed the emperors but it saved the people. It opened to the barbarians the palaces of Constantinople, but it opened the doors of cottages to the ministering angels of Christ. It had much to do with the great ones of earth. And what is more interesting than the death-rattle of an empire corrupt to the very marrow of its bones, than the sombre galvanism under the influence of which the skeleton of tyranny danced upon the tombs of Heliogabalus and Caracalla? How beautiful that mummy of Rome, embalmed in the perfumes of Nero and swathed in the shroud of Tiberius! It had to do, my friends the politicians, with finding the poor and giving them life and peace; it had to do with allowing the worms and tumors to destroy the monuments of shame, while drawing from the ribs of this mummy a virgin as beautiful as the mother of the Redeemer, Hope, the friend of the oppressed.

That is what Christianity did; and now, after many years, what have they done who destroyed it? They saw that the poor allowed themselves to be oppressed by the rich, the feeble by the strong, because of that saying: "The rich and the strong will oppress me on earth; but when they wish to enter paradise, I shall be at the door and I will accuse them before the tribunal of God." And so, alas! they were patient.

The antagonists of Christ therefore said to the poor: "You wait patiently for the day of justice: there is no justice; you wait for the life eternal to achieve your vengeance: there is no life eternal; you gather up your tears and those of your family, the cries of children and the sobs of women, to place them at the feet of God at the hour of death: there is no God."

Then it is certain that the poor man dried his tears, that he told his wife to check her sobs, his children to come with him, and that he stood erect upon the soil with the power of a bull. He said to the rich: "Thou who oppressest me, thou art only man," and to the priest: "Thou who hast consoled me, thou hast lied." That was just what the antagonists of Christ desired. Perhaps they thought this was the way to achieve man's happiness, sending him out to the conquest of liberty.

But, if the poor man, once satisfied that the priests deceive him, that the rich rob him, that all men have rights, that all good is of this world, and that misery is impiety; if the poor man, believing in himself and in his two arms, says to himself some fine day: "War on the rich! For me, happiness here in this life, since there is no other! for me, the earth, since heaven is empty! for me and for all, since all are equal." Oh! reasoners sublime, who have led him to this, what will you say to him if he is conquered?

Doubtless you are philanthropists, doubtless you are right about the future, and the day will come when you will be blessed; but thus far, we have not blessed you. When the oppressor said: "This world for me!" the oppressed replied: "Heaven for me!" Now what can he say?

All the evils of the present come from two causes: the people who have passed through 1793 and 1814 nurse wounds in their hearts. That which was is no more; what will be, is not yet. Do not seek elsewhere the cause of our malady.

Here is a man whose house falls in ruins; he has torn it down in order to build another. The rubbish encumbers the spot, and he waits for new materials for his new home. At the moment he has prepared to cut the stone and mix the cement, while standing pick in hand with sleeves rolled up, he is informed that there is no more stone, and is advised to whiten the old material and make the best possible use of that. What can you expect this man to do who is unwilling to build his nest out of ruins? The quarry is deep, the tools too weak to hew out the stones. "Wait!" they say to him, "we will draw out the stones one by one; hope, work, advance, withdraw." What do they not tell him? And in the mean time he has lost his old house, and has not yet built the new; he does not know where to protect himself from the rain, or how to prepare his evening meal, nor where to work, nor where to sleep, nor where to die; and his children are newly born.

I am much deceived if we do not resemble that man. Oh! people of the future! when on a warm summer day you bend over your plows in the green fields of your native land; when you see in the pure sunlight, under a spotless sky, the earth, your fruitful mother, smiling in her matutinal robe on the workman, her well-beloved child; when drying on your brow the holy baptism of sweat, you cast your eye over the vast horizon, where there will not be one blade higher than another in the human harvest, but only violets and marguerites in the midst of ripening ears; oh! free men! when you thank God that you were born for that harvest, think of those who are no more, tell yourself that we have dearly purchased the repose which you enjoy; pity us more than all your fathers, for we have suffered the evil which entitled them to pity and we have lost that which consoled them.

Murger

Henri Murger (1822–1861) provides a useful illustration of the vague delineation between Romanticism and Realism. His works have been discussed in connection with both schools, and fairly so since his sentimentality, his melancholy, his delicate treatment of the passions link him with the one, whereas the scenes he describes, taken (or purporting to be taken) from real life, and the simplicity of his style, link him to the other. To many contemporary critics, *Scenes of Bohemian Life* (1849) carried the authentic if sordid note of its milieu; to others, it was romantic and sentimental. In fact, it was both—a romanticized version of often sordid reality made bearable for its denizens by youth, enthusiasm, and their own romantic illusions.

The world of the *Bohème* was itself a direct result of the artist's rejection of society—at least, pending his acceptance by it. Gautier's advocacy of art for art's sake could be adapted to the needs of artists or would-be artists struggling to make their way against an indifferent or hostile public. Henceforth, Bohemia would be the realm of art and taste arrayed against bourgeois philistinism and, while its inhabitants were often only transient, their numbers would continue to grow as, more and more, artists found themselves at variance with the tastes, the standards, the receptivity of a public they courted and, when rejected, spurned.

Preface to *The Latin Quarter*

The Bohemians described in this book have nothing in common with the Bohemians of boulevard playwrights, who have used the word as a synonym for pickpocket and murderer; nor are they recruited from the ranks of bear-leaders, sword-eaters, vendors of key-rings, inventors of "infallible systems," stock-brokers of doubtful antecedents and the followers of the thousand and one vague and mysterious callings in which the principal occupation is to have none whatever and to be ready at any time to do anything save that which is right.

The Bohemians of this book are by no means a race of today; they have existed all over the world ever since time began, and can lay claim to an illustrious descent. In the time of the ancient Greeks (not to pursue their genealogy any further) there was once a famous Bohemian who wandered about the fertile land of Ionia trusting to luck for a living, eating the bread of charity, stopping of nights by hospitable firesides where he hung the musical lyre to which the "Loves of Helen" had been sung and the "Fall of Troy."

As we descend the course of ages we find forerunners of the modern Bohemian in every epoch famous for art or letters. Bohemia continues the tradition of Homer through the Middle Ages by the means of minstrel, *improvisatori, les enfantz du gai savoir,*[1] and all the melodious vagabonds from the lowlands of Touraine; all the muses errant who wandered with a beggar's wallet and a *trouvère's* harp over the fair and level land where the eglantine of Clemence Isaure should still flourish.

In the transition period, between the Age of Chivalry and the dawn of the Renascence, the Bohemian still frequents the highways of the realm, and is even found in Paris streets. Witness Master Pierre Gringoire, for instance, friend of vagrants and sworn foe to fasting, hungry and lean as a man may well be when his life is but one long Lent; there he goes, prowling along, head in air like a dog after game, snuffing up the odours from cookshop and kitchen; staring so hard at the hams hanging from the pork-butcher's hooks, that they visibly shrink and lose weight under the covetous gaze of his glutton's eyes; while he jingles in imagination (not, alas! in his pockets) those ten crowns promised him by their worships the aldermen for a right pious and devout sotie[2] composed by him for the stage of the Salle of the Palais de Justice. And the chronicles of Bohemia can place another profile beside the

---

Source: Translated by E. Marriage and J. Selwyn, London, 1903.

[1]Improvisers, children of the gay science.

[2]Medieval farce, hence playlet.

melancholy and rueful visage of Esmeralda's lover—a companion portrait of jollier aspect and less ascetic humour. This is Master François Villon, lover of *la belle qui fut heaulmière*[3]—poet and vagabond *par excellence,* with a breadth of imagination in his poetry. A strange obsession appears in it, caused no doubt by a presentiment of a kind which the ancients attribute to their poets. Villon is haunted by the idea of the gibbet; and indeed one day he nearly wore a hempen cravat because he looked a little too closely at the colour of the king's coinage. And this same Villon, who more than once outstripped the *posse comitatus* at his heels, this roistering frequenter at the low haunts in the Rue Pierre Lescot, this smell-feast at the court of the Duke of Egypt, this Salvator Rosa of poetry, wrote verse with a ring of heartbroken sincerity in it that touches the hardest hearts, so that at the sight of his muse, her face wet with streaming tears, we forget the rogue, the vagabond and the rake.

François Villon, besides, has been honoured above all those poets whose work is little known to folk for whom French literature only begins "when Malherbe came," for he has been more plundered than any of them, and even by some of the greatest names of the modern Parnassus. There has been a rush for the poor man's field; people have struck the coin of glory for themselves out of his little hoard of treasure. Such and such a *ballade,* written in the gutter under the drip of the eaves some bitter day by the Bohemian poet, or some love-song improvised in the den where *la belle qui fut heaulmière* unclasped her girdle for all comers, now makes its appearance, transformed to suit society and scented with ambergris and musk, in albums adorned with the armorial bearings of some aristocratic Chloris.

But now begins the grand age of the Renascence. Michelangelo mounts the scaffolding in the Sistine Chapel and looks thoughtful as young Raphael goes up the staircase of the Vatican with the sketches of the Loggie under his arm. Benvenuto is planning his Perseus and Ghiberti carving the bronze gates of the Baptistery, while Donatello rears his marble on the bridge across the Arno. The city of the Medici rivals the city of Leo X and Julius II in the possession of masterpieces, while Titian and Paul Veronese adorn the city of the Doges—St. Mark competing with St. Peter.

The fever of genius suddenly broke out with the violence of an epidemic in Italy, and the splendid contagion spread through Europe. Art, the Creator's rival, became the equal of kings. Charles V stoops to pick up Titian's brush, and Francis I waits on the printer Etienne Dolet, who is busy correcting the proofs (it may be) of *Pantagruel.*

In the midst of this resurrection of the intellect the Bohemian seeks,

---

[3]The Fair Armouress (or Helmet Maker) was the heroine of two Villon ballads.

as heretofore, for the poorest shelter and pittance of food—*la pâtée et la niche,* to use Balzac's expression. Clement Marot, a familiar figure in the ante-chambers of the Louvre, is favoured by the fair Diane, who one day would be the favourite of a king, and lights three reigns with her smile; then the poet's faithless muse will pass from the boudoir of Diane de Poitiers to the chamber of Marguerite de Valois, a dangerous honour, which Marot must pay for by imprisonment. Almost at the same time another Bohemian goes to the court of Ferrara, as Marot went to the court of Francis I. This is Tasso, whose lips were kissed by the epic muse in his childhood on the shore at Sorrento. But, less fortunate than the lover of Diane and Marguerite, the author of *Gerusalemme* must pay for his audacious love of a daughter of the House of Este with the loss of his reason and his genius.

The religious wars and political storms that broke out in France with the arrival of the Medici did not stay the flight of Art. Jean Goujon, after dis-covering anew the pagan art of Pheidias, might be struck down by a bullet on the scaffolding of the Innocents; but Ronsard would find Pindar's lyre, and with the help of the *Pléiade* found the great French school of lyric poets. To this school of revival succeeded the reaction, thanks to Malherbe and his followers. They drove out all the exotic graces introduced into the language by their predecessors' efforts to acclimatise them in poetry. And a Bohemian, Mathurin Regnier, was one of the last to defend the bulwarks of lyric poetry against the assaults of the band of rhetoricians and grammarians who pro-nounced Rabelais to be a barbarian and Montaigne obscure. It was the same Mathurin Regnier, the cynic, who tied fresh knots in Horace's scourge, and made indignant outcry against his age with "Honour is an old-fashioned saint, and nobody keeps his day."

In the seventeenth century the enumeration of Bohemia includes some of the best known names in literature under Louis XIII and Louis XIV. Bohe-mia counts wits of the Hotel Rambouillet among its members and lends a hand in the weaving of the *Guirlande de Julie*. Bohemia has her *entrées* at the Palais Cardinal and writes the tragedy of *Marianne* in collaboration with the poet-minister, the Robespierre of monarchy. Bohemia strews Marion De-lorme's *ruelle* with pretty speeches and pays court to Ninon under the trees in the Place Royale, breakfasting of a morning at the *Goinfres* or the *Epée Royale,* supping of nights at the Duc de Joyeuse's table and fighting duels under the street lamps for Uranie's sonnet as against the sonnet of Job. Bo-hemia makes love and war, and even tries a hand at diplomacy; and in her old age, tired of adventures, perpetuates a metrical version of the Old and New Testaments, signing a receipt for a living on every page till at length, well fed with fat prebends, she seats herself on a bishop's seat, or in an Aca-demical armchair founded by one of her chosen children.

'Twas in the transition period between the seventeenth and eighteenth centuries that two mighty geniuses appeared, whose names are always brought forward by the nations to which they belong in any literary rivalry. Molière and Shakespeare are two famous Bohemians, with only too many resemblances in their destinies.

The most famous names in the literature of the eighteenth century are likewise to be found in the archives of Bohemia; Jean-Jacques Rousseau and d'Alembert (the foundling left on the steps of Notre-Dame) among the greatest; and, among the most obscure, Malfilâtre and Gilbert, these two much overrated persons, for the inspiration of the one was only a pale reflection of the pallid lyric fervour of Jean Baptiste Rousseau, while that of the other was a blend of incapacity and pride, with a hatred which had not even the excuse of initiative and sincerity, since it was only the paid instrument of party spirit and party rancour.

And here we bring our rapid summary of the illustrious history of Bohemia to a close. We have purposely set these prefatory remarks in the forefront of this book, so as to set the reader on his guard against any mistaken idea of the meaning of the word "Bohemian" which he might perhaps be inclined to entertain before reading it, for the class whose customs and language we have herein endeavoured to trace makes it a point of honour to differentiate itself from those strata of society to which the name of "Bohemian" has long been misapplied.

To-day, as in the past, any man who enters the path of Art, with his art as his sole means of support, is bound to pass by way of Bohemia. Those of our contemporaries who display the noblest shields in the chivalry of Art were most of them Bohemians once, and in the calm and prosperous glory of later life they often look back (perhaps with regret) to the days when they were climbing the green upward slope of youth, which no other fortune, in the sunlight of their twenty years, but courage (a young man's virtue) and hope (the riches of the poor).

For the benefit of the nervous reader, the timorous Philistine, and that section of the public which cannot have too many dots on the i's of a definition, we repeat in axiomatic form—

"Bohemia is a stage of the artist's career; it is the preface to the Academy, the Hospital or the Morgue."

Let us add that Bohemia neither exists nor can exist anywhere but in Paris.

Bohemia, like all ranks of society, comprises various shades and diverse species and subdivisions, which it may be worthwhile to enumerate and classify.

We will begin with Bohemia unknown to fame, by far the largest section of it. It is made up of the great clan of poor artists condemned by fate to preserve their incognito because for one reason or another they cannot find some little corner above the heads of the crowd, and so attest their own existence in Art and show by what they are already what they may be some day. A race of inveterate dreamers are they, for whom art is always a creed and not a craft, and enthusiasts by conviction. The bare sight of a masterpiece throws them into a fever; their loyal hearts beat high before anything beautiful; they do not ask to what school it belongs nor to what master. This Bohemia draws its recruits from among those young aspirants of whom it is said that "they give promise" as well as from those who fulfil the promise, yet by heedlessness, shyness, or ignorance of the practical, fancy that all is done when the work of art is finished and expect that fame and fortune will burst in on them by burglarious entry. These live on the outskirts of society, as it were, in loneliness and stagnation, till, fossilised in their art, they take the consecrated formulae about "the aureole round the poet's brow" as a literal statement of fact, and being persuaded that they shine in the shadow, expect people to come to look for them there. We once knew a little school of such originals, so quaint that it is hard to believe that they really existed; they called themselves disciples of "art for Art's sake." According to these simple and ingenuous beings, "art for Art's sake" consisted in starting a mutual admiration society, in refraining from helping Chance, who did not so much as know their address, and waiting for pedestals to come to place themselves under their feet.

This, as everyone sees, is carrying stoicism to the point of absurdity. Well, let us assert it once more to be believed; in the depths of unknown Bohemia there are such beings as these, whose wretchedness demands a pitying sympathy which common sense is compelled to refuse; for put it to them quietly that we are living in the nineteenth century, that the five-franc piece is Empress of the human race, and that boots do not drop down ready varnished from the sky, and they will turn their backs upon you and abuse you for a Philistine.

Still, at any rate, their mad heroism is thoroughly carried out; they make no outcry, no complaint, submitting passively to the hard and obscure fate which they bring upon themselves. And for the most part they fall victims to the complaint which decimates them, a disease which medical science does not dare to call by its right name—Want. Yet many of them, if they chose, might escape the catastrophe that suddenly cuts them off at an age when life as a rule is only beginning. They need only make one or two concessions to the hard laws of necessity, which means they should learn to live in duplicate, to keep one life for the poet in them—the dreamer that dwells on the mountain heights where choirs of inspired voices sing together—and another for the labourer that contrives to provide daily bread. But this double life, which is almost always carried on in strong and well-balanced natures—indeed, it is one of their chief characteristics—is not often to be met with in young men of this stamp; while pride, a bastard sort of pride, makes them proof against all counsels of common sense. And so they die young, now and again one of them leaving some piece of work behind him for the world to admire at a later day; and if it had been visible before, the world would no doubt have applauded it sooner.

The battle of Art is very much like war in some respects. All the fame goes to the leaders, while the rank and file share the reward of a few lines in the order of the day; and the soldiers that fall on the field are all buried where they lie—one epitaph must do duty for a score of thousands.

In the same way the crowd always gazes at the man that rises above the rest, and never looks down into the underworld, where the obscure toilers are striving; they end in obscurity, sometimes without even the consolation of smiling over a piece of work completed, and so are laid away from life in a winding-sheet of indifference.

Another section of unexplored Bohemia is made up of young men who have been misled, by themselves or others. They take a fancy for a vocation, and urged on by a suicidal mania, die victims of a chronic attack of pride, idolatrous worshippers of a chimera.

And here may we be permitted a short digression.

The ways of Art, crowded and perilous as they are, grow more and more crowded every day, in spite of the throng, in spite of the obstacles; Bohemians in consequence have never been more numerous.

Among many reasons for this affluence we might perhaps dwell upon the following one.

Plenty of young men have been found to take seriously declamations as to unhappy artists and poets. The names of Gilbert, Malfilâtre, Chatterton and Moreau have been often, with no small imprudence and most unprofitably, made to sound abroad. People have taken the tombs of these unfortunate persons for pulpits from which to preach about the martyrdom of Art and of Poetry.

> Farewell, ungenerous earth,
> Cold sunshine, sorrows that flay!
> Unseen, as a ghost in the gloom,
> And lonely, I pass on my way.

This song of despair, composed by Victor Escousse after a hollow success had filled him with pride which stifled him, is, or was at one time, the *Marseillaise* of all the volunteers of Art who went to inscribe their names on the martyr-roll of Mediocrity.

For ambitious vanity the posthumous apotheosis and requiem panegyrics possessed all the attraction that the precipice usually has for weak heads;

many fell under the charm and thought that ill-luck was one-half of genius; many dreamed of the bed in a pauper infirmary at which Gilbert died, hoped that they too might become poets for a quarter of an hour before they died, and quite believed that these were necessary stages on the way to fame.

It is impossible to deal too severely with such immoral lies and murderous paradoxes; many a man has been drawn by them out of paths where he might have met with success, only to end miserably in a career where he is blocking the way of those who, having a true vocation, alone possess the right to enter upon it.

It is the preaching of such dangerous doctrines and the uncalled-for glorification of the dead which has brought into being the ridiculous race of the "misunderstood," the lachrymose poets whose muse is always seen with red eyes and dishevelled hair, and all the mediocrities who cannot create anything and from the limbo of manuscript call the Muse a harsh stepmother and Art their executioner.

All really powerful minds have their word to say, and, as a matter of fact, say it sooner or later. Genius or talent do not come by pure accident; they are not there without reason, and for the same reason they cannot always remain in obscurity. If the crowd does not go to them, they find their way to the crowd. Genius is like the sun: everyone can see it. Talent is the diamond: it may lie out of sight in the shadow for a long while, but somebody always finds it. So it is pity thrown away to feel moved by the lamentations and twaddle talked by a class of intruders and worthless persons who thrust themselves into the domains of Art, Art itself opposing them, and who make up a section of Bohemia where idleness, debauchery, and toadyism are the general rule.

Axiom:—Unknown Bohemia is not a thoroughfare; it is a *cul-de-sac*.

In truth, it is a life which leads to nothing. It means brutalising want; intelligence is extinguished by it, as a lamp goes out for want of air; the heart is turned to stone by a savage misanthropy; the best natures become the worst. Anyone so unfortunate as to stay too long, to go too far to turn back, can never get out again; or can only escape by forcing his way out, at his peril, into a neighbouring Bohemia, whose manners and customs belong to another jurisdiction than that of the physiology of literature.

We may cite another—a singular variety. These are Bohemians who may be called amateurs. They are not the least curious kind. Bohemian life is full of attraction for their minds—to have doubts as to whether each day will provide a dinner, to sleep out of doors while the clouds shed tears of rainy nights, and to wear nankeen in December, would appear to make up the sum of human felicity. To enter that paradise they leave their home, or the study which would have brought about a sure result, turning their backs abruptly on an honourable career for the quest of adventures and a life of uncertain chances. But since the most robust can hardly cling to a mode of life which would send a Hercules into a consumption, they throw up the game before long, scamper back in hot haste to the paternal roast, marry their little cousin, set up as notaries in some town of thirty thousand inhabitants, and of an evening by the fireside they have the satisfaction of telling "what they went through in their artist days," with all the pride of a traveller's tale of his tiger hunt. Others plume themselves on holding out; but when once they have exhausted all their means of getting credit open to young men of expectations, they are worse off than genuine Bohemians, who, never having had any other resources, can, at any rate, live by their wits. We have known one of these amateurs, who, after staying three years in Bohemia and quarrelling with his family, died one fine morning and was carried in a pauper's hearse to a pauper's grave; he had an income of ten thousand francs!

Needless to say, these Bohemians have nothing whatsoever to do with Art, and they are the most obscure, amongst the most ignored, in unknown Bohemia.

Now for Bohemia proper, the subject, in part, of this book. Those of whom it is composed are really "called," and have some chance of being among the "chosen" of Art. This Bohemia, like the others, bristles with dangers; it lies between the two gulfs of Anxiety and Want. But, at any rate, there is a road between the two gulfs, and it leads to a goal which the Bohemians may behold with their eyes until they can lay their hands upon it.

This is official Bohemia, so called because its members have given evidence to the public of their existence; they have made some sign of their presence in life other than the entry on the registrar's page; in short (to use their own expression), they have "got their names up," are known in the literary and artistic market; there is a sale, at moderate prices it is true, but still a sale, for produce bearing their mark.

To arrive at this end, which is quite definitely determined, all ways are good; and the Bohemian knows how to turn everything, even the very accidents by the road, to advantage. Rain or dust, shadow or sun, nothing brings these bold adventurers to a stand. Their very faults have virtues to back them. Ambition keeps their wits always on the alert, sounds the charge, and urges them on to the assault of the future; invention never slackens, it is always grappling with necessity, always carrying a lighted fuse to blow up any obstacle so soon as it is felt to be in the way. Their very subsistence is a work of genius, a daily renewed problem, continually solved by audacious feats of mathematics. These are the men to extract a loan from Harpagon and to find truffles on the raft of the Medusa. They can, at a pinch, practise abstinence with all the virtue of an anchorite; but let a little good fortune come their way and you shall presently see them riding the most ruinous hobbies, making love to the youngest and fairest, drinking of the oldest and best. There are not windows enough for them to fling their money through. Then, when their last five-franc piece is dead and buried, they go back to dine at the common board of Chance, where a knife and fork is always laid for them; and preceded by a pack of cunning shifts, they go a-poaching in the preserves of every industry in the neighbourhood of Art, stalking from morning to evening that shyest of game known as the five-franc piece.

Bohemians go everywhere and know everything; sometimes their boots are varnished, sometimes down at heel, and their knowledge and the manner of their going varies accordingly. You may find one of them one day leaning against the chimney-piece of some fashionable drawing-room, and the next at a table in some dancing saloon. They cannot go ten paces on the boulevard but they meet a friend, nor thirty without coming across a creditor.

Bohemia has an inner language of its own, taken from studio talk, the slang of green-rooms, and debates in newspaper offices. All eclecticisms of style meet in this unparalleled idiom, where apocalyptic terms of expression jostle the cock-and-bull story and the rusticity of popular sayings is allied with high-flown periods shaped in the mould whence Cyrano drew his hectoring tirades; where paradox (that spoilt child of modern literature) treats common sense as Cassandra is treated in the pantomimes; where irony bites like the most powerful acid, and as those dead shots who can hit the bull's-eye with their eyes bandaged. 'Tis an intelligent argot, albeit unintelligible to those who have not the key to it, and audacious beyond the utmost bounds of free speech in any tongue. The vocabulary of Bohemia is the hell of rhetoric and the paradise of the neologism.

Such, in brief, is Bohemian life—little known of the social puritan, disparaged by the puritans of Art, insulted by fearful and jealous mediocrity in every form, which cannot clamour forth lies and slander enough to drown the voices and the names of those who reach success through this forecourt of fame by yoking audacity to their talent.

It is a life that needs patience and courage. No one can attempt the struggle unless he wears the stout armour of indifference, proof against fools and envious attacks; and no one can afford to lose his pride in himself for a moment; it is his staff, and without it he will stumble by the way. Delightful and terrible life, which boasts its conquerors and its martyrs, on which no one should enter unless he has made up his mind beforehand to submit to the ruthless law: *vae victis.*[4]

H.M.

---

[4]Woe to the defeated.

P.S.: Germany

There is always a danger that collections of this sort may degenerate into anthologies when anthologizing is not their purpose. Instead of printing only the major documents, an editor may be moved to include material less significant but more attractive to him because, though not a source document, it provides a touch of local color or serves to illustrate a particular atmosphere or mood. This kind of thing becomes impossible to avoid for the second half of our century, when major documents are lamentably lacking or still undiscerned by eyes unendowed with the clairvoyance of historical perspective. I have, however, done my best not to give way to the temptation to compile a survey or anthology of earlier periods and to stick as closely as possible to the most influential or characteristic expressions of the various schools. This may, incidentally, help to explain the prevalence of French spokesmen for years when Paris held the focus of the literary and artistic stage, and when most avant-garde movements were centered in that city or looking toward it. That being so, it seemed useless, merely for the sake of a fairer or more complete geographical coverage, to seek out in Italy, Russia, Germany, or elsewhere statements of views whose origins and core were to be found in France.

Such a statement does not, of course, hold good of the Romantic movement. Romanticism came late to France, partly because of the Napoleonic Wars, partly because of a native French tradition that we know the Romantics sought to challenge, and it came as we have seen from England and from the North. Nevertheless, a search for German theoretical manifestoes that could match the influence of Wordsworth's *Preface,* or of the writings of later French Romantics, produces little. The great German contribution was made in plays and poems and stories that do not come within our scope, and certainly *Werther* was more important than a dozen manifestoes. But also, we forget too easily that the West did not really awake to the importance of what went on in Germany for ten or twenty years after the turn of the century. Educated people read and spoke English or French—not, until disheartened French *émigrés* began to learn it, German. With few exceptions, the busy activity of German Romantics found no echo beyond German borders, outside the interpretations of their English and French admirers; and though they came later, the declarations of the French Romantics carried further than those of their German predecessors or contemporaries. Within Germany itself, the Romantics found little echo and the thinnest of publics until the second decade of the nineteenth century. According to Goethe himself, the German writer lived "in a desert." This is not to minimize in any way the importance of what was written in Germany, or elsewhere, but to explain why it has found so little room in these pages.

Even so, it did not seem that a section on Romanticism would be complete without German participation. Goethe (1749–1832) generally appears under this heading, but Goethe is very awkward to fit into any category. Certainly his belief that "national literature is of no great importance nowadays; the era of world literature is dawning, and everyone must do his part to hasten its arrival," goes squarely against the contemporary tendency toward a hardening of national identities. And, though his early works figure quite rightly in every anthology of Romantic literature, he himself would not and cannot be classed as anything but a universal genius. As he grew older, he viewed contemporary tendencies with a very critical eye, and his remarks to Riemer (November 25, 1808) show an uncanny foreboding of developments still to come:

> In no revolution is it possible to avoid excesses. Generally, in political revolutions, people only want to destroy a few abuses but before you notice you find yourself already deep in massacres and atrocities. In their present literary revolution the French asked no more than a freer form, but they have not stopped at that, they now reject the contents with the form. One begins by declaring that the presentation of noble thoughts and acts is a bore: one goes on to try and interpret every folly. Instead of the beautiful figures of Greek mythology one sees devils, witches, vampires, and the noble levels of the past have to give way to crooks and convicts. "They are amusing. This is what affects the public." But when the public has developed a taste for these violently spiced dishes and has got used to them, it calls for ever stronger mixtures. A fresh talent that wants to become known and influential and lacks the power to make its own way, must conform to the taste of the day, must even try to overbid its predecessors in cruelty and horrors. In this chase after external effects, all serious study, all gradual intimate development of the talent and the man, are forgotten. Nothing worse can happen to talent, but it is possible that literature, on the whole, may benefit from it.

Goethe's affinities seem rather with the humane and enlightened (though not skeptical) philosophers of the eighteenth century, especially with Diderot, than with his own Werther, or with his more mystical and passionate contemporaries. The other giant of this time, however, although his only manifestoes were his musical works, should serve our purpose much better. Here, therefore, are two letters—one about Beethoven, and one by him—which reflect some of the spirit of that very active, very passionate age.

Brentano

Elisabeth "Bettina" Brentano (1785–1859) was, like Goethe, born in Frankfurt, one of the twenty children of an immigrant Italian businessman. Bettina, as she was called, who eventually married the poet and the novelist Achim von Arnim, from her childhood moved in the company of the best-known figures of the German literary world, including Goethe, who was a good friend of her aunt, and Beethoven, whose conquest she describes below. Her lavish correspondence provided her with the raw material for a number of rather controversial books that, more or less faithfully, cite the letters she sent and received; but perhaps her chief role in the history of German Romanticism was that of a delightful, witty, and talented hostess for the poets and musicians, critics and professors, artists, philosophers, theologians, and scientists who gravitated to her Berlin *salon*.

More than a mere blue-stocking, however, and more than a dilettante, she was also an active social reformer, seeking out in their unpleasant reality the causes of poverty, violence, and disease in the Berlin slums, publishing the results of her investigations, and seeking to move to action the German public and the Prussian king. Seldom successful in her social and political efforts, she holds nevertheless an important place in the annals of social Romanticism.

Beethoven's declarations to the enthusiastic young girl who burst in upon him on a showery spring afternoon express a view of musical creation that is wholly Romantic. Before Beethoven such passion and fire had been unknown or, at least, unboasted; but now the artist affirms himself no longer a mere technician (however skilled) or entertainer (however successful). He is the carrier and interpreter of divine inspiration, an almost holy vessel of the sublime, whose creations attempt to interpret the torrential forces and revelations that possess him. Some of his words recall Alfred de Vigny's Moses, whom God had caused to live *"puissant et solitaire"*: another possessed and powerful Romantic giant, calling to his like across the wastes of puny humanity as Beethoven calls to Goethe in the letter below.

Letter to Goethe

Vienna, May 10, 1810.

When I met the man about whom I want to tell you today, the whole world disappeared for me. . . .

It was in front of Beethoven, about whom I want to talk to you, that I forgot the whole world and even yourself. I am, it is true, only a child, but I am not mistaken when I affirm (what perhaps no one will understand and

---

Source: Translated by Eugen Weber.

believe today) that he is fast advancing far ahead of human civilization—and who knows whether we shall ever catch up with him? I doubt it. May he only live until the perfect ripening of the sublime and powerful enigma he carries within him, oh! yes, may he attain his supreme goal! Surely then he will leave in our hands the key of a heavenly initiation that will carry us one degree closer to true beatitude.

I can well confess it to you: I believe in a divine magic that is an element of spiritual nature; and this magic, Beethoven exercises it in his art. All he could tell you about it is pure magic; no motive, no orientation which is not the expression of a superior existence, and Beethoven himself feels himself to be the founder of a new perceptible principle of spiritual life.

You will work out for yourself what I want to say and what is true. Who among us could replace this genius? from whom could we expect a similar achievement? All human activity is like the pendulum of a clock that comes and goes for him: he alone is free and produces of his own free will, as he wishes, the uncreated and the unexpected. What matters then his traffic with the world, to him whom the rising sun finds already engaged upon the hallowed task of every day and who hardly lifts his eyes at sunset to glance about him; he who forgets to feed his body and whom the torrent of his inspiration keeps far removed from the platitudes of daily life? He has told me himself: "From the moment when I open my eyes I begin to groan, for what I see goes against my religion, and I must despise the world which does not sense that music is a more sublime revelation than all wisdom and all philosophy; it is the wine that inspires and leads to fresh creations, and I am the Bacchus who presses for mankind this wine of magnificence, it is I who makes them spiritually drunk; and when they find themselves with an empty stomach once more, they have in their intoxication fished in all sorts of things that they bring back with them onto the dry shore. I have no friend, I have to live alone with myself; but I know well that God is closer to me in my art than to all others, and I advance with him without fear, having recognized and understood him every time. Nor do I feel anxious about my music which could have no adverse destiny: he who freely opens his mind and his feelings shall be forever exempt from all the misery in which the others drag along."

All these things Beethoven said to me when I saw him for the first time. A great sentiment of veneration took hold of me on hearing him thus reveal his thoughts to me who must have seemed to him so puny. I was the more surprised since I had been assured that he was misanthropic and would engage in conversation with no one. Nobody wanted to introduce me to him; I had to seek him out for myself. He owns three apartments in which he hides in turn: one in the country, one in town, the third in the *bastion;* it was there, in the third, that I was to find him. I went in unannounced; he was at the piano; I told him my name. He received me affectionately and asked me at once whether I would like to hear a song he had just put to music. And then he started to sing *Kennst du das Land* . . . [Knowst thou the land . . . one of Mignon's songs from Goethe's *Wilhelm Meister*] in a voice so powerful and penetrating that its melancholy took possession of me.—"Is it not beautiful?" he asked me enthusiastically. "Wonderful." "I shall sing it a second time." He rejoiced at my delighted approval. "Most humans," he said to me, "are moved by something good, but they are in no way artistic natures; artists are made of fire; they do not weep." And he began once more to sing another song of yours, which he had composed in the last few days: *Tröcknet nicht, Tränen der ewigen Liebe* . . . [Dry not, tears of everlasting love . . .] He walked me back to the house, stopping on the way and speaking so loudly that one needed some courage to listen to him: but he speaks with so much passion and says such unexpected things that one forgets one is in the street. Everyone was very surprised to see him come home with me, where we found a great company, and stay to dinner. After dinner, he sat down at the piano of his own accord, without being asked, and he played long and wonderfully; his pride fermented together with his genius. In these moments of inspiration, his genius creates the Imperceptible and his fingers shape the Impossible.

Since then, whether he comes here or I go there, we see each other every day. That is why I have abandoned social gatherings, exhibitions, shows, and even, yes, the tower of St. Stephen's [Cathedral]. Beethoven said to me: "Bah! what do you want to go and see there? I shall come to pick you up and we shall go, towards evening, strolling in the alleys of Schönbrunn." Yesterday I went with him through a splendid garden where everything was in flower; and, the greenhouses open wide, the scents were intoxicating. Beethoven stood stock still full in the sun and said: "The verses of Goethe have a great effect on me, not only through their contents, but also by their rhythm. This language that bears itself as if lifted higher and higher by some aerial spirits and which already carries within itself the secret of harmony, calls and urges me to compose. Indeed, at the incandescent moment of inspiration, I have to let the melody run over everywhere and escape me; I pursue it passionately, I attain it again, I see it fleeing, flying, disappearing, in a mass of emotions, of divers and different impulses; soon I grasp it once more and seize upon it with a new transport of passion; I can no longer separate from it, I have to develop all my very varied modulations in an ecstasy of enthusiasm, and it is only at the last moment, then, that I triumph at last over my first musical idea; you see: that is the symphony. Yes, music is the proper bond between the life of the mind and the life of the senses. I should like to talk with Goethe about all this, but will he understand me? Melody is the perceptible life of poesy. Is it not melody which translates the spiritual content of the poem into a comprehensible sentiment? is it not melody which makes us understand in the song of Mignon all the maiden's feelings? and does not this sensation awaken fresh emotions in its turn? Then the mind wants to reach out towards the boundless universal where, all in all, it becomes the channel of this great apprehension that rises from the simple and pure musical thought and which without it would remain occult, unnoticed, unsuspected. That is what harmony is, the harmony my symphonies express, in which the fusion of varied forms darts forward in one stream towards the goal. That is when one feels that there is something eternal, infinite, impossible to grasp, in all things of the spirit; and though in my works I always have a sense of success, nevertheless, I always feel an unquenchable thirst to start over again, like a child, that which only a moment before seemed finished and exhausted with the last crash of the cymbals which came to drive, like a wedge, my joy and my musical convictions into my listeners' ears. Talk to Goethe about me, tell him to go and listen to my symphonies and he will admit that I am right, that music is the sole and immaterial gate which leads to the higher world of knowledge: this world that surrounds man but which man, for his part, cannot manage to grasp.

"It is advisable to have a rhythm of the spirit in order to grasp music in its intimate essence; it gives the feeling, it carries the inspiration, of heavenly sciences; and that which the mind perceptibly draws from it is the incarnation of spiritual knowledge.—Even though minds live on music as we live on air, it is nevertheless something else again to understand music through the mind; but still, the more the soul gets of its indicated nourishment, the more the mind itself ripens upon this happy accord, when it achieves perfect harmony with it.—But rare are the chosen ones; for even as there are thousands who marry for love, and among these thousands love does not reveal itself even once (even though all follow the calling of love), so there are thousands who follow the calling of music and yet lack its revelation. It is also that music has for groundwork and foundation, like every art, the great marks of moral sentiment: every authentic sensation is a moral progress. To submit oneself to its inscrutable laws, to manage to curb one's own spirit to these laws, to lead it according to them so that it should reflect its revelations, this is the isolating principle of the art: to be dissolved into these revelations is to give oneself up to the sublime, to abandon oneself to the divinity that in the serene repose of its sublime authority masters the fury of untamed forces and thus leads imagination to the highest degree of efficacy. It is thus that art always proceeds from divinity, and that human relations with it are religion. That which we get from art we hold from God: what it tends to is the divine inspiration which fixes a goal to man's aspirations, and one such that he can attain.

"We do not know what knowledge awaits us. The almost wholly closed seed needs a damp soil, electrically warm, in order to shoot up, to conceive, to express itself; music is that electric ground in which the spirit lives, thinks, and discovers. Philosophy is a mere derivative, an echoing discharge of the electric spirit; but music is alone to fill the need, the need of all of us, to relate everything to an unique initial principle; and even though the mind should not become capable of mastering that which it had begotten, through it nevertheless it knows happiness in creation. Thus every authentic creation of the art is independent and stronger than the artist himself. By these apparitions it ever returns to its sacred source, and its only connection with man is in so far as it furnishes proof of the divine acting in him.

"Music provides the intellect its relationship with harmony. An isolated thought still carries in the mind the sense of its whole relationship, of generalization by analogy; and this is why all musical thought is an intimate and inseparable part of the general community of harmony, which is Unity. Everything of an electric nature impels the spirit to expand, to express itself, to create musically.

"I am an electric nature. . . . But I must stop expounding my not very wise wisdom, or I shall miss the rehearsal! Write to Goethe telling him about me if you have understood me; for if I cannot be responsible for what you will write, I shall on the other hand be very glad to accept his teaching."

I promised him to write you everything as well as I could. He took me to an important rehearsal of the grand orchestra, where I settled down alone in the great hall, dark and deserted. Through the cracks and the holes in the partitions there passed a few rays of light in which, as in a river, there danced here and there little glittering specks; you would have thought they were heavenly highways travelled by innumerable happy souls.

Then I saw this immense, prodigious genius conduct his company. O, Goethe! no king, no emperor, has such consciousness of his power, none emanates such forces as this very Beethoven who, only a moment before, in the garden, sought to know whence he drew them. If I understood him as well as I feel him, then I should know all things. He stood there, straight and firmly resolved, all his movements and his face expressing the complete perfection of his work; he anticipated every mistake, every slip in interpretation; not the slightest breath that came from any initiative, everything was ordered, controlled, worked up by the tremendous presence of his genius. One could easily predict that such a spirit must reappear in its next incarnation as the master of the world.

I wrote this letter yesterday evening and read it to him this morning from beginning to end; he asked "Did I say that?—Then I must have been in a trance." He reread everything again, carefully, struck out what is up above and wrote in between the lines because he expressly wants you to understand him.

Give me the joy of a prompt reply, that Beethoven should know you esteem him highly; we had always intended to talk about music, and I was fond of it myself, but now, because of Beethoven, I feel that henceforward I shall be completely incapable of it.

My address is: Erdberggasse, Birckenstock house, where your answer will find me for about two weeks.

Bettina.

Beethoven

Born in Bonn, on the Rhine, son of a court musician of Flemish descent, the young Ludwig van Beethoven (1770–1827) was trained to be an infant prodigy, his cloddish, drunken father going so far as to falsify his birthdate by three years in order to make him seem younger than he really was. The young man's talent secured for him first the patronage of his father's master, the Archbishop-Elector of Cologne, then of the musical and cultivated Viennese aristocracy; but his originality began by shocking the public, first and foremost among them fellow musicians like Haydn. Though never free of criticism, by the time Bettina Brentano sought him out the forty-year-old musician had achieved recognition. The Viennese public held him to be one of the chief ornaments of their city, and he himself claimed the rights due to his genius. By 1813, the son of a Rhenish court servant (for musicians were no more than that) would affirm the exceptional position and privileges of his superior talent, even at the expense of the Austrian Imperial family; and if the truth of the story his letter tells is not altogether certain *(si non e vero, e ben trovato),* its implications in Romantic thinking are perfectly clear. The French revolutionary and the Romantic artist both affirmed the supreme importance of personal achievement and personal endowment, which must always count for more than rank or titles. Probably the revolutionary had more concrete goals in mind than the Romantic, but, as the case of Werther shows, the two attitudes were never far apart, and Beethoven claiming priority for genius appears as revolutionary as the French mob claiming equality for men. Though this was not immediately evident, one asserted a qualitative standard where the other emphasized the quantitative; and therein lay the seeds of future misunderstanding and friction. But meanwhile, both claims—that of the rights of genius and that of the rights of men—would deeply subvert the old order of things.

Letter to Bettina Brentano

Töplitz, August 15, 1813

My good and very dear friend,

Kings and princes can turn out as many professors and privy councillors as they please, grant titles and ribbons, but they cannot produce great men, minds that rise above the human herd and whose task it is to make themselves, for which they must be regarded with respect. When two men like Goethe and myself walk together, these great lords must be shown what we hold to be great. Yesterday, as we were walking back, we met all the Imperial family, we saw them coming from afar, and Goethe let go my arm to get out of their way onto the side of the road. No good arguing with him, it was impossible to make him take another step ahead. For myself, I pulled my hat down over my eyes and bore down on the very centre of the company, hands crossed behind my back! Princes and courtiers parted and stood aside, the Archduke Rudolph took off his hat to me, the Empress was the first to salute me; their lordships *know* me. I saw, to my great amusement, the procession pass before Goethe: he stood there by the roadside, hat in hand, bowing deeply; then I told him off good and proper, allowing no excuses, and I taxed him with all his sins, especially against you, dear friend, of whom we had just been talking. God! if I had spent as much time beside you as he has, I should have produced, you may believe me, far more and greater things. A musician is also a poet, two eyes have also the power to carry him into a more beautiful world, where greater minds converse with him and impose upon him truly important duties. What did not pass through my mind when I learnt to know you in the little observatory, during that magnificent May shower which was fruitful for me too! Under your gaze, the most beautiful themes came straight to my heart, melodies which will enchant the world when Beethoven no longer conducts them. May God grant me another couple of years and I shall see you again, dear friend, as wills that voice which still and always maintains its rights within me. Minds can also love each other and mine will always seek out yours; your approval is for me the dearest thing in the whole world. I told Goethe what I thought, and how approval acts upon us others, and that one wants one's peers to understand one through the intelligence: emotional sensitivity is a woman's business (forgive me), for men the fire of music must flash out of the mind. Ah! my dearest child! it is so long since we are of one mind on everything! Nothing is so good as to have a fine intelligence, that one sees reflected in everything, and before which there is no need to

---

Source: Translated by Eugen Weber.

hide. *One must be somebody if one wants to appear somebody.*—One day the world will come round to recognizing this, it is not so unjust; but it matters little, for my aim is higher.

I hope to have a letter from you in Vienna, write me soon, very soon, and a lot, I shall be there in a week. The court leaves tomorrow; today they give one more performance. He [Goethe] has rehearsed the Empress in her role; his Duke [the Grand Duke of Saxa-Weimar, whom Goethe accompanied as privy councillor] and himself wanted me to play some of my music; I refused them both. Both of them love China porcelain, one must not hold it against them since the intelligence no longer holds the reins. But I will not play my music for their flounces and furbelows, I will have no part of these absurdities-in-common, and never with the princes who, anyway, never do a good job.

Farewell, farewell, dearest, your last letter remained all of one night upon my heart where it quickened and vivified me. Musicians permit themselves everything.

God! how I love you!

Your very loyal friend and your deaf brother,
Beethoven.

II.

The Positivistic Reaction

Realism and Naturalism

The *Concise Oxford Dictionary* defines Realism as "the practice of regarding things in their true nature and dealing with them as they are, freedom from prejudice and convention, practical views and policy; fidelity of representation, truth to nature, insistence upon details." It defines Naturalism as a "view of the world that excludes the supernatural or spiritual; realistic method, adherence to nature, in literature and art; indifference to conventions." Apart from Naturalism's exclusion of "supernatural or spiritual," there seems to be little that distinguishes the two terms. We have the choice, or course, of regarding Realism as a further stage of the Romantic interest in nature, truth, and freedom, shading off into a Naturalism that merely carries these ideas to their logical conclusion; or seeing the same movements as successive steps *away* from idealistic Romanticism, on the path of less subjective and more positive, less private and more impersonal action. There is probably some truth in both views, and Sainte-Beuve's essay of 1830 lends credence to both, but no reader of Realistic or Naturalistic writers can miss the note of imagination or passion, the frequent inaccuracies, the slipshod arguments, the vague assertions, in other words, the armory of the very Romantic school they were trying to leave behind.

135

It might be possible to go even further and argue that each of these schools continues a different Romantic tendency, that Realism was simply a more advanced aspect of social Romanticism, and that Naturalism resulted from the marriage of contemporary scientism and art for art's sake. Both schools refer to nature, as the Romantics had done, but no longer to those pure or noble aspects of it that the earlier Romantics preferred. By a natural reaction against the artificially elevated themes extolled by the Establishment and by a bourgeois morality anxious above all not to rock the boat, they select in their work, in their moralizing, not the lofty and the fine but the ugly and the low. They differ among themselves, however, as to the *kind* of ugliness that catches their eyes: Realists like Courbet, Couture, Flaubert, stress the bourgeois, the vulgar, and the commonplace; Naturalists like Degas or Zola, Lautrec or Goncourt, lean toward the extraordinary, the picturesquely peculiar, the more sensational aspects of low life. Madness, corruption, and death recur in their works and in their lives, as does the prostitute, symbol of moral and social decay. All the great Naturalist writers seem to have taken the prostitute for a model at least once: in 1876 Huysmans published *Marthe, Histoire d'une Fille;* in 1877 Edmond de Goncourt published *La Fille Elisa;* in 1880 Zola published *Nana;* in 1881 Maupassant published *La Maison Tellier,* the story of a brothel. Toulouse-Lautrec executed hundreds of paintings, drawings, and lithographs of prostitutes, and even decorated the reception room of one of his favorite brothels. Degas left a large number of scenes from their life, even though some seventy of them were destroyed by his brother after the painter's death "out of a pious feeling" for the good name of the departed.

Of course, painters have often sought their models among prostitutes. Carpaccio, Frans Hals, Caravaggio, had done as much, and so had the great Japanese— Utamaro, Haru-Nobu, Hokusai—whose prints were already in the 1860s fascinating Western artists. It seemed, however, as if a particular attraction led the Naturalists to observe the prostitute more insistently, more intimately, more sympathetically, than had ever been known. Van Gogh, Lautrec, Raffaëlli, Félicien Rops, Emile Bernard, all worked in brothels or painted their inmates with an ominous and bitter passion. So much that licentiousness and Naturalism became associated in the public mind, and what we now know as the French cancan was in its time called, quite naturally, *quadrille naturaliste.*

Respectable people had long suspected that advanced views in philosophy or art went together with lax morals and dangerous political notions. The political ideas flaunted by some of these doubtful characters merely confirmed such opinions. When Courbet declared (in the *Précurseur d'Anvers,* August 2, 1861) that "the basis of Realism is the negation of the ideal," this was bad enough. When he added that this negation of the ideal leads to "the emancipation of the individual and finally to democracy. Realism is the essentially democratic art," no further proof was needed to convince the press and the public that his work and that of painters like Couture and Jules Breton was dangerously "social-democratic" and "demagogic."

Whatever their tone and whatever their derivation, the true inspiration of both Realism and Naturalism may be found in the Positivism of the time and, specifically, in its chief contemporary manifestations, science and reform, concerns that went hand-in-hand in the nineteenth century as they had done in the eighteenth. The 1830s had seen Romantic retreats invaded by social concerns, Romantic artists and writers becoming involved in contemporary political activities. But these men and women, whom awareness of economic injustice and social imperfections ranged in the ranks of the party of Change, became persuaded that reform could and should be approached scientifically, like medicine or history. The tremendous development of the natural sciences, the vulgarization and popularization of new ideas and hypotheses, led first the writers, then the artists, to compare their methods with those of the scientist and to seek inspiration in the latter's work.[1] From Delacroix to Seurat and beyond, painters were fascinated by discoveries concerning the color composition of light and the effect of hues contrasted or juxtaposed. From Balzac to Zola and beyond, the discoveries of men who studied animals or plants intrigued writers dealing with less predictable material than that of the laboratory. In 1845 we find Balzac writing about "the naturalists of the novel"; a few years later, Flaubert recognized in Balzac "a scientific observer" out to establish "the conceptual law of ideas and of visible beings." By the late 1850s, Victor Hugo spoke of the poet or philosopher as one who tries to operate on social facts as the naturalist does on zoological facts.

All of these judgments reflect the influence of a philosopher who spent most of his life in obscurity and relative want but whose work, like that of Saint-

---

[1]Evidence of contemporary growth enthused and excited poets and artists over what scientific and industrial developments held in store for humankind. In 1794, already, we find Wordsworth writing about

> those favored souls . . .
> to whom the harmonious doors
> Of science have unbarred celestial stores,
> To whom a burning energy has given
> That other eye which darts thro' earth and heaven.

In due course the technological and industrial developments that had stirred such enthusiasm created shocking social problems. By the 1850s one Englishman in seven was a pauper, one London house in sixty was a brothel. Other countries were no better. But by then most of the articulate and politically effective public were more interested in making the best of the opportunities this situation offered than in revolting against its injustices.

Simon—whose private secretary he had been—left an indelible mark on the thinking of his time. The *Course of Positive Philosophy* that Auguste Comte (1798– 1857) propounded between 1830 and 1842, in the very midst of the Romantic revolution, set out to analyze and interpret history by scientific methods and to establish scientifically valid laws which, by extrapolating the past, would enable us to understand the present and, in a sense, to predict the future—or, at least, the lines on which the future should develop. Comte's great historical laws applied to art as to everything else. Naturally, Saint-Simon's old secretary viewed art as a function of its social and religious surroundings, affected like everything else by the nature of the great stages of historical evolution that he had outlined, stages in which humanity advances from primitive fetishism, through polytheism and monotheism, to that level where positive, i.e., scientific, knowledge alone guides man and rules his thinking and his activities. In this positive stage, the origins of art and hence its nature can be seen to lie in certain physiological tendencies or needs: like language, art begins by imitating nature, in response to instincts that drive us to express our feelings and to reproduce the sights, sounds, and objects around us. Over a long period of time, refinement and abstraction turn these crude beginnings into language, writing, style, and all the other things we connect with art and communication. From this the superficial conclusion could follow that, born of a physiological need, developed on scientifically ascertainable lines, art, like medicine, can and should proceed "like science."

At this point and over this issue Realism and Naturalism become fighting words, slogans of the great forward struggle of scientific discovery and scientific *method,* which so many in mid-nineteenth century believed would replace discredited superstitions and help to build the modern state, the modern world.

Careful, though! This scientific enthusiasm is not, at first, the dominant theme; for that is furnished by a more familiar concern already very evident in the Romantics—the desire to surprise, to shock, to cleave to reality and thumb their noses at convention, all at the same time. And the Realists express this by stressing in their works the existence and the conditions of existence of social classes that until that time had been ignored or parodied—the middle and lower middle classes, the peasants, the workers—painting their lives and deaths in dull, dreary, sometimes sordid colors that seemed to them truer to life than the fanciful or vivid Romantic tints. Moreover, and more startling, they painted them with an emphasis and on a scale that claimed for them a significance, an importance, that *society,* and society-conscious art, had never attached to them.

This was the first revolution, and it seemed bad enough to drag art down from its lofty haunts to the commonplace level of mundane, bourgeois, provincial lives. It was only in the 1860s that the scientific approach as such came into its own. In

1863 Sainte-Beuve, who had sniffed the change, described the Naturalistic tendency to introduce into everything the methods and results of science: "Themselves emancipated," he wrote, "they try to free mankind from all illusions, from vague debates and vain solutions, from idols and delusions." A year later the Goncourt brothers published *Germinie Lacerteux,* in which love is treated not as a subject for romantic description but of "clinical analysis." Zola's first Naturalistic novel, *Thérèse Raquin,* followed in 1867.

Inspired by Balzac and by Flaubert, Zola was even more strongly affected by extraliterary influences stemming from the critic and historian, Taine, and the physiologist Claude Bernard. Taine, the philosopher of Realism *par excellence,* argues that in effect psychology is a function of physiology, our destinies a function of environment and heredity, the fate of men like that of nations a matter of determinism. Taine's influence turned the novel from story and description into an investigation of humanity, the writer aspiring to the position and claiming the results of a scientific investigator. Not only the scientist's results, however, but his amoral detachment: writers and artists may investigate anything and everything, but they must do it as observers, in a controlled experiment, and not as judges. They seek causes and try to determine laws; they no more pass judgment on what they discover than does the scientist in his laboratory. "Virtue and vice," wrote Taine in 1864, "are products like vitriol and sugar." And Zola used this phrase that shocked so many as a motto for the second edition of *Thérèse Raquin.*

The theories Zola expressed in the essay on *The Experimental Novel* were born in 1865 when Claude Bernard published his *Introduction to Experimental Medicine,* in which he argued that medicine is not, and need not be, an art as it was then considered; that it was, or at least could be, a science—provided it based itself on the firm ground of physiology and the experimental method. The great physiologist's ideas spread far and fast in the next few years to become a sort of *Discourse on Method* of the exact sciences, but furnishing also and incidentally the inspiration for a new literary approach. There were new horizons here not only for literature, but for France and for humankind. By the 1870s scientism had become a creed firmly held in many intellectual—and less intellectual—quarters. The powers of science and the efficacy of scientific methods were hardly questioned; hence, when Zola affirmed that literature could do in the psychological sphere what science could do in the natural sphere, he was in tune with the times. Literature or art, from being mere sources of private delight, now became machines for social experiment and reform. Naturalism, identified with progress, was part of the dominant positive creed of those who built the Third Republic in France or, indeed, the regime of Porfirio Diaz in Mexico. Science and republican government, together, could not fail to make for a better world. In this light, Zola's famous assertion that "The Republic will be naturalistic or will not be" becomes easier to understand.

We see similar tendencies reflected in the theater, which appears for a while as one of the most effective battering rams of the new ideas, and in the plastic arts. There is something significant about the fact that the first Impressionist group show was held in 1874 in the old Paris studio of the famous photographer, Nadar. But where the daguerreotype had led young men like Champfleury away from the late-Romantic taste for the strange, the emphatic, the grotesque, to found "the school of sincerity in art" in which the writer could depict only the things he had seen with his own eyes just as he saw them, it seems to have inspired painters to explore not the regions where the photographers challenged them but rather those the photograph could not cope with.

And yet, there is in the painting of the moderns—in the realism of Courbet, in the glittering experiments of the Impressionists—the same insistence on reality: taking the subject out of the studio and into the open, shifting from classic themes into novel unorthodox areas, choosing new subjects, new classes, new perspectives, new and sketchy methods designed to capture reality *sur le vif,* refusing to group the subjects in classic order, attempting to render movement— of subjects, of light, and even of time—all this amounted to a new Realism. Contemporary observers understood this. They regarded the new movements in literature and painting as closely connected, recognizing the affinities between Flaubert and Courbet as, later, between Naturalists and Impressionists. And it could be no accident that the leading protagonist of the Naturalist school should also be one of the first defenders of Manet, Monet, and their friends. As Champfleury had defended Courbet, so Zola explained and defended Manet. Their sympathies were not based on doctrinal or personal connections alone: here too political interests ran parallel to artistic ones; reformers and revolutionaries in art played the same part in politics. Their political doctrines were often, though not always, mirrored in their works, their artistic views (or their public reception) often affected their politics, though here too there were exceptions.

For us their interest must lie first and foremost in the reflection they furnish of their time—its strong rationalistic and scientific current, its no less strong tendency toward utopian assumptions, its social consciousness. Where Romanticism had sought reality in the subjective questioning and interpretation of nature and the self, Naturalism sought it in the would-be objective "scientific" and "clinical" analysis or experiment. Naturalism, properly speaking, lasted only a short while, flourishing in the 1860s and 1870s. But it left literature, the arts, and taste itself the richer for the residue of its dreams and for its fresh awareness of the many and many-sided aspects and possibilities of modern life.

Sainte-Beuve

Charles Augustin Sainte-Beuve (1804–1869), undistinguished as poet or novelist, only moderately successful as Mme. Hugo's lover, was one of the most influential critics and literary historians of his time. It was his devotion to truth that informed his social as well as his literary criticism—an interest not in theories, not in "fictions" as he called them, but in life: "What occupies me seriously is life itself and the object of it." This preoccupation produced his great study of the Jansenist community at *Port-Royal* (1840–1848) and what is still an unrivaled guide to French literature—weekly articles written in a succession of Paris periodicals comprising the fifteen volumes of the *Causeries du lundi* and the thirteen further volumes of the *Nouveaux lundis*. It produced also his attachment to "the diocese of free thought" on whose behalf he defended freedom of thought and freedom of the press against the conservative majority and the wishes of the imperial regime, even after Napoleon III had appointed him senator in 1865.

The essay that follows was written when Sainte-Beuve was still young and unknown, not far from the Romantic circles of Hugo and Nodier, but already aware that the victories of the immediate past, both in literature and in politics, were only the beginning of a movement vaster and more complex than his more idealistic contemporaries suspected. The next step, as the young literary critic saw it, must be for art to become popular. In saying this he echoed the tendencies of the time but hardly, perhaps, those of art itself.

Hopes and Desires of the Literary and Poetic Movement after the Revolution of 1830

With every great political and social revolution, art, which is one of the main aspects of society, changes, is modified, and undergoes in its turn a revolution, not in its own internal principles which are eternal, but in its conditions of life and ways of expression, in its relationship with surrounding objects and phenomena, in the various nature of the ideas, of the sentiments, which color it, of the inspirations upon which it draws. The Revolution of 1830 found art in France at a certain stage of development that, at first, it tended to disturb and interrupt; but this perturbation could only be a passing one: the destinies of art are not an accident that another accident can cancel; they will take up their course according to a new bent and work out a new direction through a more splendid and fertile society. Yet many questions arise: will art gain from this general change, does it not run the risk of splitting, of

---

Source: Le Globe, Paris, October 11, 1830. Translated by Eugen Weber.

thinning out into a multitude of currents and channels as soon as it mixes further in this society, all industrial and democratic? And may we not also fear, if art wants to remain isolated, on a fringe apart, and choose unfrequented places to spread and to contain itself, may we not fear that it will gather in obscure, sacred, secret lakes where none will go to steep themselves? Alternately, mingling with everything, though identified with nothing, brought back in full torrent over the common ground and driven toward a vast and unknown end, reflecting harmoniously in its waters the shoals and shapes of its shores, will it henceforth become more profound, broader than ever, above all less inaccessible? We shall not attempt here to take up these mysteries of the future in all their vague extent; limiting ourselves to that which concerns the literary and poetical movement itself we shall try to show how we conceive the inevitable change art will undergo, and for which it is ripe. It will become clear in what fresh terms we think the poetic and literary question must appear to the artist as well as to the critic.

In the eighteenth century, art had fallen, as we know, into a sad state of decay or, rather, art no longer existed in and by itself, no longer led an independent life; it had no personality any more. Talent enlisted in the service of certain religious or philosophical ideas that needed it to fight and destroy others. Wit, and what was called *taste,* still survived and swarmed in plenty; but they were like flimsy flowers thrown over weapons, like spangles on the silken scabbard of a sword. Talent, most of the time, appeared only as a means to some other end; it subordinated itself to hatreds, to rantings, to certain accepted and imposed philosophical tactics; it debased itself to a commonplace task, useful enough, but simply destructive. We know the exceptions that can be brought up against us. Diderot would rise to lofty theories and attained more than once in his meditations the eternal elements of art; but he failed too often in carrying them out. Rousseau appears as an admirable and learned writer, a vigorous philosopher, rather than a great poet; Voltaire, as an artist, triumphs only in his mockery, which is a type of poetry that is antipoetic *par excellence.* Beaumarchais, more than any of them, reflected in brilliant fits the pure whim of genius. André Chenier and Bernardin de Saint-Pierre, alone, remain altogether apart: exquisite and delicate artists, poets true and chaste, loving beauty for itself, worshiping it with no aim but worship, cultivating it with delicacy, innocence, and a curious ingenuity, they surprise and console at the turns of the century like friends unexpectedly met; they guard discreetly and nurse in their breast, as the social torment approaches, the most charming gifts of the Muse.

All through the violent course of the French Revolution, art was silent; it existed less than ever apart; its personality was as if engulfed and annihilated before the incomparable events that dismayed all hearts and carried them away. It was impossible, however, for the repercussions of this social destruction not to be felt sooner or later in poetry, and that poetry should not also carry out a revolution of its own. In effect, this revolution soon began; but it developed at first a little in the margin and outside the public places of society; it was prepared on the heights and did not from the first descend onto the highways of his rejuvenated society. While France, still shaken by the blows of its religious and political revolution, was busy trying to develop or restrict its consequences and, its calm not yet recovered, tried to draw up the balance sheet of profit and error; while, seized by an intoxicating lust for battle, she hurled herself through Europe and spent her surplus energy on victories, the artistic revolution was preparing within, little understood, ignored or ridiculed to begin with, but real, swelling, irresistible. Two great talents that we like to name together and to join in equal admiration, M. de Chateaubriand and Mme. de Staël, opened the revolution from fairly distant sides and in slightly different directions only to converge and mingle in the end. Mme. de Staël, as early as 1796, had the profound and consoling sentiment of a free humanity, of a regenerate society; she was impelled toward the future by a sort of vague aspiration, confused but powerful; she retained a sad and wise memory of the past; but she did not feel the strength to cut herself off from it, to take leave of it and entrust herself to the current of things and the movement of progress. Still, all these impressions of a heart friendly to the new spirit of the times, this belief in a more realistic and human philosophy, this reconquered moral freedom, this accepted spontaneity, this confidence bestowed on the most glorious and disinterested faculties of our being, all these qualities and views of Mme. de Staël, carried into the books she wrote, gave them a unique turn, a really modern originality, treasure of warmth, of emotion and of life, a scope that was tremendous though sometimes beyond the limits of reality. The immoderate and vaguely instinctive quality of her work prevented Mme. de Staël's being understood at the time and appreciated at her worth as artist and poet. M. de Chateaubriand, a greater man and with a better idea of how to go about it, was more effective; and yet at his beginnings he was less in harmony than Mme. de Staël with the progressive spirit and the future destinies of society, but he appealed to a more actual and concrete inclination: he had made himself the brilliant spokesman of that numerous party which the reaction of 1800 carried sharply back to the memories and regrets of the past, to the splendor of religious worship, to the prestige of the old monarchy. He was thus popular up to a point, popular in the *châteaux,* in the clergy, in the pious families; his considerable fame owed much to the kind of sentimental and poetic religion which he celebrated with talent, to the brave opposition that people appreciated, to the imperial disfavor he had dared to incur. Mme. de Staël's renown was equally due to political opposition, to the persecution that caused her to appear interesting, and to the sentimental philosophy which was then the fashion in certain circles. Art had very little to do with their glory; the people were rather inclined to mock the artistic label. The revolution preparing in that direction had not yet come; it was still too much influenced by their own peculiar talents, still too artificial when compared to society. When M. de Chateaubriand, a much greater artist than Mme. de Staël, wanted to go in for pure art, he composed his poem on *The Life of the Martyrs,* which has so little in common with the world he lived in, which is so completely cut off from contemporary affections and sympathies; a true alexandrine epic, brilliant, erudite, detached; and august hymn born of leisure, imagination, study, and consecrating a fulfilled past. . . . *The Martyrs* was not understood. . . . Society, given the artificial structure it had acquired under the Empire, could not entertain the artistic revolution, and pure art could do no better than remain for yet awhile outside this society which, almost unanimously reactionary in literature, found ample entertainment in army reports, in the columns of Geoffroy, and in the sprightly verse of the Abbé Delille.

At this point the Restoration took over; the first three or four years were hardly literary; the political factions, the stormy and hostile debates, the reviving conflict between old régime and revolution, killed the frail crop of Delillean poetry; but only in 1819 does one see a new poetry arise on the heights of society, in the spots most sheltered from the popular breath, least touched by the mob. From the first, this poetry drew its inspiration from the Catholic, chivalric, and monarchist talent of M. de Chateaubriand. Aristocratic by origin and inclination, but independent by nature, loyal and haughty in the manner of Montrose and Sombreuil, it turned toward the past, worshiped it, lovingly sang it, and tried in its illusion to rediscover it and carry it into the present; the Middle Ages were its passion, it fathomed their beauties, it idealized their glories; it made the mistake of believing that they could be partly reconstructed in their best parts and here it was fooled by the fictions of divine right and of pretendedly essential aristocracy, fictions which falsely glossed over the democratic basis of modern society. And yet these young poets were not at all alien to this society whose profound and invincible tendencies they misunderstood at the time. They had contact with a certain section of society, because they appealed to passions that were still very much alive, to reactionary sympathies that an elite shared with them. The vague religious sensations and the reveries they knew how to impart, and which were like a social malady of the last few years, brought them much support from young men and from women that would not have been won

over by the feudal or monarchist coloring without the rest. All this reactionary and militant period of the poetic school known as *Romantic,* continues
until 1824 and ends after the Spanish war, at the time of M. de Chateaubriand's sudden resignation. At this time, the political ardor and the honorable illusions of the young poets were consumed; they understood that the
restored monarchy, with its miserable stock-jobbing dodges and its obscure
clerical intrigues did not in the least resemble the ideal they had imagined
and for which they would have fought; from that moment on, they withdrew
from the hurly-burly into which they had strayed and, as impartial onlookers,
no longer exasperated by the liberal spirit around them, they preferred to
seclude themselves in the pursuit of art unbiased and uncommitted: a new
period began for them, which has just ended in 1830.

In *The Oldster and the Young Man* of M. Ballanche, the young man who,
full of noble and sincere affections, begins by rejecting the present as incomplete and arid, who stands up against still uncertain social destinies and takes
despairing refuge in a utopian past—this young man, faithful portrait of
many of the tender souls of our age, ends by coming to terms with the new
society—now better understood—and by realizing, under the tutelage of the
old man, that is of philosophy and experience, that we live in a period of
crisis and renewal, that this present which shocks him is the end of a process
of demolition, a ruin being even further leveled; that the past is in the process
of dying and that the harmony he finds missing in ideas and things can only
be recaptured by going forward. It is more or less also what happened to the
poets we mentioned. Liberal in fact and in nature, even when their opinions
tended backward, men of fancy and independence, they carried within them
a ready-made and pre-existing sympathy for the future movement of society.
Only, they sought harmony; and as the society of that time was nothing less
than harmonious they laid the blame for this on the revolutionary spirit
which had disturbed it. Then, later, when they felt that this revolutionary
spirit was the very life and future of humanity, they came to terms with it
and hoped, like a lot of decent people at the time, that the restored dynasty
would in its turn come to terms with the times, that we were on the verge of
a period of peaceful progress, and that Constitutional monarchy [*La Monarchie selon la Charte*] would be more than just another poem by the illustrious author of *The Martyrs*.

They were mistaken; but their error, honorable in its principle, did not
remain sterile in its results. They secluded themselves in their art, believing
that the time had come to revolutionize it; they were filled with that enthusiasm which alone can make for greatness; and they achieved a great deal,
while thinking that they could do even more.

Thanks to them, to their theories and their works, the art which did not

yet mix in the general activities of society, acquired, at least during this withdrawal from common concerns, a deep and distinct self-consciousness; it
tried itself, learnt its worth, and steeled its weapons. I shall not attempt to
deny that there were many drawbacks to this rather absolute fashion of conceiving and practicing art, of cutting it off from the world, from contemporary political and religious passions, of making it above all unattached, amusing, colored, ingenious; that there was in this an excess of individual
preoccupation, a too-loving predilection for form. I will not deny all this,
even though its drawbacks have been much exaggerated. . . . It would,
however, be unjust to deny the memorable development of art during
these last few years, its emancipation from all servitudes, its internal kingdom
well established and recognized, its happy conquests in various areas
which had not until then been touched by reality and life, its intimate interpretation of nature, and its eagle's flight above the highest notabilities of
history.

However, let us admit it, art is not yet popular; its activity does not include
or reflect the great social movement which spreads and advances day by day.
Regretfully descended from its medieval heights, it had got too used to considering the comfortable terrace of the Restoration as a sort of royal terrace
like that at Saint-Germain en Laye, a gay and peaceful plateau where one
could dream and sing in the shade, stroll or recline at leisure, untouched by
the dust and heat of the day. It was content to see from time to time the
people, the great mass of society, milling confusedly below in the great common highway where, apart from the well-beloved name of Béranger, no
poet's name resounded.

Today that the Restoration is no more, that the laboriously built terrace
has collapsed, and [now] that people and poets will march together, a new
era opens for poetry; art is henceforth on a common footing, in the market
place with everybody, side by side with tireless humanity. Fortunately, it has
life and it has youth; it has confidence in itself and it knows that there is
room for its kingdom even in the midst of republican nations. Art remembers
the past that it loved, it understood, and from which it broke away with tears;
but it is toward the future that its wishes and its efforts henceforth tend. Sure
of itself, aware of the past, it is armed and fully equipped for its distant pilgrimage. The almost infinite destinies of regenerate society, the religious and
obscure anxieties that disturb it, the absolute emancipation toward which it
aspires, all invite art to blend closely with society, to charm it during the
journey, to sustain it against weariness by acting as the harmonious echo,
the prophetic mouthpiece, of its somber and dubious thought. The mission,
the task, of art today is really the human epic; it is to interpret, in a thousand

ways, in drama and ode, novel and *elegy*—yes, even in the elegy turned solemn and primitive once more in the midst of its personal and peculiar emotions—it is ceaselessly to reflect and *radiate* in a thousand colors the feelings and opinions of progressive humanity, to rediscover this aspect of humanity in the depths of the philosophies of the past, to reach and follow it through the ages, to encompass it and its passions in a harmonious and living nature, to give it as canopy a sovereign sky, vast and clear, where the light can always be seen through the darkness.

Champfleury

Champfleury was the pen name of Jules François Félix Husson (1821–1889), a great admirer of Courbet and Balzac. Tired of the Romantic bombast and fantasy abounding around him, he attempted a new approach, in which he would abandon the falsehoods of fantasy and "artistic" style for an almost photographic realism. The matter-of-fact reproduction of contemporary life was, he said, as artistically significant as the imaginative works of men bent on ignoring their world and their age as not being sufficiently picturesque. A sentimental Romantic himself, Champfleury never lived up to his own principles, but he did a great deal to influence and defend the development of Realism in the French novel and painting. The lower middle classes pushing forward in the social and economic field were suddenly promoted to consideration as valid subjects for literature and art. Demands for cultural recognition echoed demands for political recognition; and, certainly, the political and artistic doctrines of the new Realists could hardly be separated.

This is what was thought in Champfleury's and Courbet's own circle. One of Courbet's greatest admirers was his fellow Franc-Comtois, Pierre Joseph Proudhon (1809–1865), writer, printer, political philosopher, and as such one of the chief theorists of nineteenth-century socialism. Proudhon's comment that "property is theft" has often been repeated, but he seems to have meant it mainly insofar as one man's property deprived others of their due. What Proudhon wanted was a social revolution to bring about a regime in which men should be equal and free, unoppressed by mammoth institutions, whether political or economic. Patriotic and libertarian, he produced a small man's socialism, verging at times on Jeffersonianism and at times on anarchy, and fated to clash with the far more rigorous doctrines of Marx. This was the man whom Champfleury cites in the letter he addressed to another pillar of sentimental socialism (or, as it has been more accurately called, social Romanticism): Aurore Dupin, Baroness Dudevant (1804–1876), better known to literary history as George Sand.

Letter to Madame Sand, concerning M. Courbet

At the present moment, Madame, there can be seen, close to the Exhibition of Painting, in the avenue Montaigne, a signboard that reads as follows: RE-ALISM. *G. Courbet. Exhibition of forty paintings of his work.* It is an exhibition in the English manner. A painter whose name exploded in the public eye during the February revolution [1848] has selected the most significant canvases among all his works and had a studio built to house them.

It is an action of incredible daring, it is the subversion of the established jury practice, it is a direct appeal to the public, it is liberty, say some.

It is a scandal, it is anarchy, it is art dragged through the mud, it is the mountebank's booth, say others.

I admit, Madame, that I think like the former, like all those who demand the most complete *liberty* in all its guises. Juries, academies, competitions of every sort, have demonstrated more than once their impotence to create either men or works. If the freedom of the theater existed, we should not see a *Rouvière* forced to play *Hamlet* before an audience of peasants, in a barn, causing old Shakespeare's shade to grin and think itself, here in the nineteenth century, back in London showing his plays in some dirty City hole.

We ignore how many unknown geniuses die who do not know how to bend before the exigencies of society, who cannot tame their rudeness, and who end by committing suicide in the dungeon cells of conventionality. M. Courbet has not come to that yet: since 1848 he has shown, without interruption, in the various *Salons,* important works which always had the privilege of provoking argument. The government of the [Second] Republic even bought an important canvas, *After Dinner at Ornans,* which I have seen again beside the old masters in the Lille Museum, holding its own very well in the midst of hallowed, established works.

This year, the jury [that decides the admission or rejection of works for the *Salons*] has shown itself mean in the space it granted young painters trying to get into the Universal Exhibition: the hospitality extended to the established men of France and of foreign nations was so great that youth suffered a little. I have little time to spare for wandering around the studios, but I have seen canvases refused which, at other times, would certainly have met with legitimate success. M. Courbet, confident in the public opinion which had favored his name these last five or six years, hurt by the jury's refusal which fell upon some of his most important works, has appealed di-

---

Source: Le Réalisme, Paris, 1857. Translated by Eugen Weber.

rectly to the public. His reasoning may be summed up as follows: I am called a *Realist,* so I want to point out through a series of known paintings what I conceive *Realism* to be. Not content with building a studio and exhibiting his canvases, the painter has issued a manifesto and on the door he has inscribed: *Realism.*

If I write to you, Madame, it is because of the lively and loyal curiosity that you have shown for a doctrine which takes shape day by day and which has its representatives in all the arts. A hyper-romantic German musician, Mr. Wagner, whose works are unknown in Paris, has been very roughly handled in the musical journals by M. Fétis who accuses the new composer of being tainted by *Realism.* All those who put forward any new aspiration are called *Realists.* We shall surely see realistic doctors, realistic chemists, realistic manufacturers, realistic historians. M. Courbet is a realist, I am a realist: since the critics say so, I let them say it. But, to my great shame, I confess to having never examined the code which contains the laws according to which the first comer is able to produce realistic works.

The name horrifies me by its pedantic ending; I fear the schools like cholera and my greatest pleasure is to come across clear-cut personalities. That is what, in my eyes, makes M. Courbet a new man.

The painter himself, in his manifesto, has said some first-rate things: "The title of Realist was forced on me much as the Romantic label was imposed upon the men of 1830. *Titles have never, at any time, provided a correct idea of things; were it otherwise, works would be superfluous.*" But you, Madame, know better than anybody what a peculiar city is Paris when it comes to opinions and debates. The most intelligent city in Europe necessarily includes the greatest number of incompetents, of half- and third- and quarter-wits. Indeed, we have to desecrate this fair word of "wit" to adorn these poor babblers, these argumentative ninnies, these wretches living off the gutter press, these pryers who insinuate themselves everywhere, these impertinents that one dreads to see open their mouths, these scribblers at so much a line driven to letters by wretchedness or sloth, in short, this horde of useless people who judge, reason, applaud, contradict, praise, flatter, criticize without conviction, who are not the multitude and yet pretend to stand for it.

Given ten intelligent people, the question of *Realism* could be thoroughly explored; with this mob of ignorants, envious, impotents, critics, all one gets is words. I will not attempt to define *Realism:* I do not know whence it comes, where it goes, what it is; Homer might be a *Realist*—after all he observed and described with precision the manners of his time.

It is not sufficiently known that Homer was violently attacked as a dangerous realist. "In fact," says Cicero speaking of Homer, "all these are sheer inventions of the poet who delighted in bringing Gods *down* to human level; it would have been better to *raise* men to that of Gods." What else do they say every day in the papers?

If I needed other famous examples, I would only have to open the first volume of criticism that comes to hand, for it is fashionable these days to reprint in book form the useless stuff that the papers publish week by week. One would see, among other things, that realism it was which led poor old Gérard de Nerval to a tragic death. It is a gentleman-dilettante who has written such tosh; your country stories are tainted with realism. They contain *peasants*. There is the crime. Lately, Béranger has been accused of realism. How men can be carried away by words!

M. Courbet is seditious because, in all good faith, he has represented bourgeois, peasants, village women, in natural size. This is the first point against him. It cannot be admitted that a stone breaker is worth a prince: the aristocracy flies into a passion to see so many feet of canvas devoted to common people; only sovereigns have the right to be painted full size, with their medals, their embroideries and their public faces. What do you mean! A man of Ornans, a peasant lying in his coffin, dares to gather at his burial a large crowd—farmers, low-class people—and this display is given as much space as Largillière[1] had the right to give to magistrates attending the Mass of the Holy Ghost! If Velasquez worked on a large scale, his subjects were Spanish grandees, Infants, Infantas; at least there is a great deal of silk, much gold on the costumes, there are medals, there are feathers. Van der Helst has painted burgomasters full size, but these stout Flemings are saved by the *costume*.

It would seem that our costume does not count as *costume*; I am ashamed, Madame, to pay attention to such reasonings. The costume of every period is affected by unknown, perhaps hygienic, laws which penetrate fashion without this being realized. Every fifty years the fashion in dress is overthrown; as with physiognomies, old fashions become *historical* and as strange to examine, as peculiar to look at, as the garb of some savage people. The portraits of Gérard, dating back to 1800, which may have seemed vulgar at first, later acquire a singular aspect. That which artists call *costume,* that is a thousand knick-knacks (feathers, patches, plumes, etc.), can amuse frivolous minds for a moment; but the serious reproduction of present-day figures, the round hats, the black dress-coats, the lacquered pumps or the peasant's wooden clogs, this is much the more interesting.

I may be granted this and yet be told: your painter lacks an ideal. I shall

---

[1]Nicolas de Largillière (1656–1746) is best known as a portrait painter, but Champfleury refers to a work executed for the Church of Saint-Etienne du Mont, in Paris.

answer that in a moment, with the help of a man who has drawn very sensible conclusions from M. Courbet's work.

The forty paintings in the avenue Montaigne include landscapes, portraits, some large domestic scenes, and a work that the artist calls *Allégorie réelle*. It is possible to follow at a glance the developments that have affected the mind and the brush of M. Courbet. Above all, he is a born *painter*, which means that none can dispute his robust and powerful talent as a workman: he attacks a great piece of work undaunted, he may not seduce all eyes, some parts may be clumsy or neglected, but every one of his pictures is *painted;* and, above all others, I consider the Flemings and the Spaniards to be painters. Veronese, Rubens, will always be great painters, whatever opinion one may hold, whatever point of view one may choose. Likewise, I know no one who thinks of denying M. Courbet's quality as a painter.

M. Courbet does not overdo the *sonority* of his tones—to speak the musical language long since carried into the domain of painting. It is up to every serious work not to attract attention by useless sonorities: a sweet Haydn symphony, intimate and homely, will still live when M. Berlioz's numerous trumpets will be spoken of with derision. The uproar of brasses in music means no more than loud tonalities in painting. We clumsily call *colorists* those painters whose furibond palette bursts forth in clamorous tonalities. M. Courbet's scale is tranquil, imposing, and calm. And I was not surprised to rediscover the famous *Burial at Ornans*, henceforth forever hallowed within me, which was the first shot fired by the artist now regarded as a rebel in art. It is almost eight years since I published on M. Courbet, then unknown, phrases that foretold his destiny: I shall not quote them, I am no keener to be the first to be right than I am to wear the latest Ascot fashion. To discover men and works ten years before most people do is a question of literary *dandyism* which causes a lot of time to be wasted. In his many critical articles, Stendhal published as early as 1825 many daring truths that did him much harm. Even today he remains ahead of his time. "I bet," he writes to a friend in 1822, "that twenty years hence they will be playing a prose version of Shakespeare in France." *Thirty-three* years have already elapsed since then and pretty certainly we shall not have this pleasure in our lifetime. M. Courbet is far from being accepted today, he certainly will be in a few years. Wouldn't I be a busybody if I wrote twenty years hence that I had discovered M. Courbet? The public does not care about the asses that hooted when Rossini's music was first played in France; the witty, the amorous Rossini was as little spared on his first appearance as M. Courbet. A wealth of insult and slander was printed about his works just as it has been about that of M. Courbet.

What is the use of being right? One is never right. Two village beadles with red phiz, two winesacks, provide the theme of those literary-minded critics I mentioned above; compare them in the same painting with the charming children, the group of women, the mourners, as beautiful in their grief as all the Antigones of antiquity, it is still impossible to prove one's point.

The midday sun strikes the rocks, the grass is gay and smiles at the sunshine, the air is fresh, there is plenty of space, you recognize the essence of the mountains, you breathe in their scent; a joker comes up who, having drawn his wisdom and his wit from the funny papers, will scoff at the *Village Damsels*.

Criticism is a nasty business that paralyzes man's noblest faculties extinguishes, annihilates them: also, criticism has no real worth outside the hands of really great creators: Diderot, Goethe, Balzac, and others who prefer every morning to give vent to their enthusiastic sensibilities than to water the thistles each critic keeps on his window sill in a dirty jar.

I recognized, in the avenue Montaigne, those celebrated *Bathers,* fuller of scandal than they are of flesh. Two years have passed since the famous scandal has died down, and I see today nothing but a creature solidly painted which has the great drawback, for the friends of convention, of not recalling the Venus Anadyomenes of antiquity.

M. Proudhon, in the *Philosophy of Progress* (1853), appraised the *Bathers* quite coldly: "The image of vice like that of virtue belongs as much to the realm of painting as to that of poetry; according to the lesson the artist wants to give, every figure, handsome or ugly, can fulfill the aims of art."

Every figure, handsome or ugly, can fulfill the aims of art! And the philosopher continues: "May the people, recognizing itself in its misery, learn to blush for its cowardice and to loathe its tyrants; may the aristocracy, exposed in its fat and obscene nakedness, be whipped on every muscle for its parasitism, its insolence, and its corruption." I skip several lines and come to the conclusion: "And may each generation, leaving thus on canvas and on marble the secret of its spirit, reach posterity with no other reproach or apology than the works of its artists." Do not these few words help us forget the stupidities one ought neither to hear nor lend an ear to, but which irritate nevertheless, like the buzzing of a persistent fly?

. . . In the field of art the practice is to overwhelm the living with the dead, the new works of a master with his old. Those who, when Courbet was just starting, would have howled loudest against the *Burial* will necessarily be those who praise it most highly today. Not wanting to be confused with the nihilists, I must say that the idea of the *Burial* is impressive, clear to all, that it depicts *a* small-town funeral and yet reproduces the funerals of *all* small towns. The triumph of the artist who paints individuality is to respond to every man's intimate observations, to choose a type in such a manner that everyone thinks he has known him, and can exclaim: "That one is real: I have seen him!" The *Burial* possesses these characteristics in the highest degree: it moves, it touches, it makes one smile, it makes one think, and leaves in the spirit, despite the open grave, that supreme tranquillity which the grave-digger shares—a grand and philosophical type that the painter has been able to produce in all his beauty as a man of the people.

Since 1848 M. Courbet has been privileged to astonish the crowd. Every year we expect surprises and, up to now, the painter has answered the expectations both of enemies and friends.

In 1848, *After Dinner at Ornans,* a broad painting of private life, won a real success without too much debate. It is always this way at an artist's beginnings. Then came the successive scandals:

> First scandal—The Burial at Ornans (1850).
> Second scandal—The Village Damsels (1851).
> Third scandal—The Bathers (1852).
> Fourth scandal—Realism.—Private Exhibition.—Manifesto.—Forty paintings exhibited.—Reunion of various scandals, etc. (1855).

Now, of all these scandals, I prefer the *Burial* over other canvases because of the idea within it, because of the complete and human drama in which tears, selfishness, indifference, and the grotesque are treated with the touch of a great master. The *Burial at Ornans* is a *masterpiece;* since David's *Marat Murdered* nothing of this sort, nothing as striking, has been painted in France.

The *Bathers,* the *Wrestlers,* the *Stonebreakers,* do not contain the *ideas* they have been endowed with after the event. I would find these ideas rather in the *Village Damsels,* and in the numberless landscapes which show how closely M. Courbet is bound to his native soil, his profound nationalism, and the advantage he can derive from it.

People still repeat the old jest attributed to the painter: *Long live ugliness! Ugliness alone is lovable!* It is surprising that such nonsense is dredged up again, when thirty years ago the same rubbish was being thrown up against Victor Hugo and his school. The pattern of the old story will keep on reviving. Progress is slow, and we have not gone far in thirty years.

Hence, it is the duty of those who struggle and fight to help each other, to attract if necessary the ire of mediocrities, to be steadfast in their opinions, and not to imitate the prudence of Fontenelle grown old.

I have a handful of truths, and hasten to offer them. . . .

If there is one quality M. Courbet possesses in the highest degree, it is *conviction.* One could no more deny him this than the sun its heat. He advances in art with imperturbable steps, he proudly shows from where he started, where he has arrived, resembling in this the rich manufacturer who hung from his ceiling the wooden shoes that had carried him to Paris.

Portrait of the Author (Venetian study), he says himself in his catalog; *Head of Young Girl* (in the Florentine manner), *Imaginary Landscape* (in the Flemish manner), and lastly *Lying in Wait (L'Affût)* which the author himself jokingly entitles *Studio Landscape*—these are the wooden shoes with which he arrived from Ornans and which helped him in his pursuit of nature.

These few paintings belong to the realm of *convention;* what gigantic strides the painter has taken since that period in order to escape from this domain so dear to the heart of the fashionable painters! There is no doubt he would have found success there if he had had the indolence to stay, and he would have added to the hundred talented artists whose success is so great in the windows of the picture dealers of the rue Notre-Dame-de-Lorette. How easy to produce pretty, pleasing things, tender, stylish, precious, falsely idealized, conventional stuff for the use of demi-reps and bankers! M. Courbet has not followed this path—anyway, his temperament would have carried him away from it. M. Proudhon prophesied his fate in 1853.

The public, he said then, wants to be shown as handsome and believed to be so *(veut qu'on le fasse beau et qu'on le croie tel).* "An artist who, in the work of his studio, followed the aesthetic principles formulated above (I refer to the earlier axiom: every figure, ugly or beautiful, can fulfill the aim of art), will be treated as subversive, driven out of the competition, deprived of any State commissions, and condemned to starve to death."

This question of ugliness in relation to the *Bathers* the philosopher treated from a lofty viewpoint. Daumier, the caricaturist, saw the same thing from the grotesque point of view. The eternal bourgeois whom his pencil has immortalized and who will survive through the centuries in all their modern ugliness, cry out before one of M. Courbet's paintings, "Is it possible to paint such horrible people?" But, above the bourgeois who have been overmuch maligned, we must place a more intelligent class which has all the vices of the old aristocracy without its qualities. I refer to the sons of the bourgeoisie, a race that has made the most of the fortunes of doctors, lawyers, merchants, which has done nothing, learnt nothing, thrown itself into the gambling clubs, which has a passion for horses and elegance, which has a shot at everything, even the writing desk, which even buys a mistress and a quarter share of a Review, which wants to give orders to women and to writers. It is with this new race in mind that the philosopher Proudhon concluded his remarks on M. Courbet:

"Let the magistrate, the soldier, the merchant, the peasant, let all orders of society, seeing themselves both in the idealism of their dignity and in their vileness, learn, through glory and through shame, to rectify their ideas, to correct their manners, and to perfect their institutions."

September 1855.

Courbet

Gustave Courbet (1819–1877) was the son of a well-to-do yeoman landowner of Ornans, in Franche-Comté. During his peregrinations through various Paris studios he picked up ideas from different quarters (Corot, Delacroix, the Dutch painters of the seventeenth century) but became especially interested in a naturalistic approach that would emphasize the most commonplace themes, whereas contemporary academic painting emphasized the most elevated and affected ones. This approach was strengthened by pride in his provincial origin, by the theories—artistic and socialistic—of the "realistic" artists and writers he frequented, and by the ideas of his great friend, the anarchist philosopher Proudhon.

Diderot had waxed enthusiastic over Greuze's sickly-sweet moral anecdotes; Proudhon, more virile but no less prejudiced, picked Courbet to adore. The painter dabbled in sociology, the philosopher in art; neither knew much about the other's specialty. Proudhon saw art as a social tool in the service of science and morality, an educational force. He proposed putting the *Stonebreakers* in a church, where the painting's edifying qualities could work on the beholders' souls. As for Courbet, fascinated by Proudhon's theories, he tried to translate them in terms of paint and canvas. And, no mistake, loud-mouthed, handsome, large, vulgar, and verbose as he was, Courbet was also a great painter. To us, he presents an almost perfect type of committed artist, of the sort our own time admires: committed to the freedom of art and of artistic expression, up to and including the part he played in the Paris Commune of 1871, his subsequent arrest, his exile, and his death.

The public and the critics were shocked by the realism of Courbet's paintings, a realism that their vast size seemed to emphasize. The story of his exhibition of 1855, decided on in a fit of pique at having some of his entries rejected by the academic judges of the official exhibition, has been told by Champfleury. Although it stirred up a good deal of discussion, the venture was hardly a success; but the break with traditional academic methods, announced in the brief introduction to the exhibition's catalog and shown more strikingly in the paintings themselves, did open the way for Manet and for the Impressionists who came after.

Realism

The title of Realist was forced on me much as the Romantic label was imposed upon the men of 1830. Titles have never, at any time, provided a correct idea of things; were it otherwise, works would be superfluous.

Source: From the catalog for the *Exhibition and Sale of 38 Paintings and a Drawing, from the work of M. Gustave Courbet*. Translated by Eugen Weber.

Without going into the greater or lesser justification for an epithet that no one, I should hope, need really understand, I shall confine myself to a few words of explanation designed to put an end to present misunderstandings.

I have studied, without prejudice or theoretical views, the art of the ancients and the art of the moderns. I no more wanted to imitate the ones than to copy the others; nor did I intend to reach the idle end of *art for art's sake*. No! I simply wished to derive from a thorough acquaintance with tradition the reasoned and independent sense of my own individuality.

My purpose was to gain knowledge the better to act. To be in a position to translate and represent the ways, the ideas and the aspect of my time as I see them, to be not only a painter but also a man, in a word to practice a living art—that is my aim.

G.C.

The Goncourts

The Goncourt brothers, Edmond (1822–1896) and Jules (1830–1870), wrote always in collaboration until the younger brother's death the year of the Franco-Prussian war. Seeking to invent a new sort of novel, the two men tried to combine the analytical approach of the scientist with the manifold vision of the artist, presenting reality not as an objective and chronologically accessible whole, but as a patchwork of broken patterns and constant movement. There was in the infinite detail and varied color of their work a vision of the world not far removed from the Impressionism of Claude Monet. Like Monet, the Goncourts give no evidence, as yet, of a wish to go beyond the physical appearance of things, rich and complex enough in all conscience to keep the artist busy comprehending and presenting it. But their novels begin to scratch and pierce the surface, because the Goncourts want to produce more authentic pictures of real life. *Germinie Lacerteux,* for example, was inspired by the discovery that one of their own servants who served them long and faithfully had all the time been leading a life of debauchery and vice that brought her to a miserable end. The Goncourts' novels were supposed to be *documentary*—limited to such appearances as research revealed. Yet, even superficial appearance, when perceived through the nerves as much as through the eyes, is already subjective. The artist does not have to press beyond the surface, beyond the shifting relationships of the myriad little incidents, little moments, that comprise it; but in this ultimate recipe for objective observation lies the suggestion that a multiple reality must be shattered before it may be encompassed.

Preface to *Germinie Lacerteux*

We must beg the public's pardon for offering it this book, and give warning of what will be found therein.

The public likes untrue novels: this novel is a true one.

The public likes stories which appear to take place in society: this story comes from the street.

The public likes the slightly licentious works, memoirs of prostitutes, bedroom confessions, bits of erotic dirt, the scandal that tucks up its skirts in booksellers' shop windows: the pages it will read are severe and pure. Let it not expect a photograph of Pleasure flaunting its nakedness: the study that follows is the clinical analysis of Love.

The public still likes anodyne and consoling writings, adventures where everything ends well, inventions that spoil neither its digestion nor its peace of mind: this book, with its sad and violent disturbance, is designed to thwart its habits and spoil its well-being.

Why, then, have we written it? Is it simply in order to shock the public and scandalize its tastes?

No.

Living in the nineteenth century, in a time of universal suffrage, democracy, liberalism, we asked ourselves whether what one calls "the lower classes" have no right to the Novel; whether this society below society, the people, had to remain under the weight of literary interdict and of the scorn of writers who have, up to now, kept silence on the heart and spirit it might have. We asked ourselves whether there should still exist, be it for writer or reader in these times of equality, classes too unworthy, sufferings too low, tragedies too foulmouthed, catastrophes whose terror is not sufficiently noble. We began to wonder whether Tragedy—the conventional form of a literature once celebrated, of a society that has disappeared—whether Tragedy was, once and for all, dead; whether in a country without caste or legal aristocracy the sufferings of the poor and humble could touch our interest, our pity, our emotions, as sharply as the sufferings of the rich and mighty; whether, in a word, the tears that are shed below could make us cry as easily as those that are shed above.

These thoughts had encouraged us to write the story of *Sister Philomena* in 1861; today they lead us to publish *Germinie Lacerteux*.

Now, if this book is slandered, it matters very little. Today that the Novel broadens and grows, that it begins to be the serious, impassioned, living form

---

Source: Paris, 1864. Translated by Eugen Weber.

of literary study and social investigation, that it becomes, by means of its analytical approach and psychological research, contemporary moral history; today that the Novel has taken up the studies and the duties of science; it is entitled to claim both its liberties and its candor. Let it aim at Art and Truth; let it reveal sufferings that the fortunate of Paris should not be allowed to forget; let it show "society" that which philanthropic ladies have the courage to face, that which the Queens of yesteryear put under their children's eyes in almshouses and hospitals: that human suffering, immediate and alive, which teaches charity. Let the Novel's faith be that which the past century called by the vast and ample name of Humanity; here is scruple enough: here is its law.

Taine

Hippolyte Adolphe Taine (1828–1893), well-known critic, philosopher, and historian, was one of the chief prophets of the mid-nineteenth-century reaction against Romanticism and toward a more positivistic—that is, rational—approach that would be based on lessons learned from the biological sciences. The methods of biology could, Taine and his followers argued, be applied to history, art, literature, or psychology— all of which are ruled by fixed laws and must, therefore, be comprehensible to those who use a scientifically rigorous approach. There are moral facts that are as determined as physical ones. They can be analyzed and assessed in terms of three basic factors: race, environment, and the momentum of past cultural tradition.

The difficulty of exactly defining the power or influence of any of these, or of applying the quantitative methods of the exact sciences to highly speculative forces of this sort was not, apparently, evident either to Taine himself or to his admirers. Taine's brilliance, his intellectual sensitiveness, and his literary skill masked the theory's flaws until the turn of the century. Yet, though misleading in its claims of ultimate validity, the system provided useful pointers toward a reasonable approach to historical interpretation. While rigid determinism was soon abandoned, Taine's work still stands— grim, somber, vast, and more impressionistic than he knew, to dazzle and depress the student of French history in general and of the French Revolution in particular.

The Principles of Historical Analysis

The historian might place himself for a certain time, during several centuries or among a certain people, in the midst of the spirit of humanity.

Source: Introduction to *History of English Literature* (1864), translated by N. Van Laun, New York, 1895.

He might study, describe, relate all the events, the changes, the revolutions which took place in the inner man; and when he had reached the end, he would possess a history of the civilization of the nation and the period he selected.

—Guizot, *Civilization in Europe*, p. 25

History has been revolutionized, within a hundred years in Germany, within sixty years in France, and that by the study of their literatures.

It was perceived that a work of literature is not a mere play of imagination, a solitary caprice of a heated brain, but a transcript of contemporary manners, a type of a certain kind of mind. It was concluded that one might retrace, from the monuments of literature, the style of man's feelings and thoughts for centuries back. The attempt was made, and it succeeded.

Pondering on these modes of feeling and thought, men decided that in them were embalmed facts of the highest order. They saw that these facts bore reference to the most important occurrences, that they explained and were explained by them, that it was necessary thenceforth to give them a rank, and a most important rank, in history. This rank they have received, and from that moment history has undergone a complete change: in its subject matter, its system, its machinery, the appreciation of laws and of causes. It is this change, as it has happened and must still happen, that we shall here endeavor to exhibit.

I

What is your first remark on turning over the great, stiff leaves of a folio, the yellow sheets of a manuscript—a poem, a code of laws, a declaration of faith? This, you say, was not created alone. It is but a mold, like a fossil shell, an imprint, like one of those shapes embossed in stone by an animal which lived and perished. Under the shell there was an animal, and behind the document there was a man. Why do you study the shell, except to represent to yourself the animal? So do you study the document only in order to know the man. The shell and the document are lifeless wrecks, valuable only as a clew to the entire and living existence. We must reach back to this existence, endeavor to re-create it. It is a mistake to study the document, as if it were isolated. This were to treat things like a simple pedant, to fall into the error of the bibliomaniac. Behind all, we have neither mythology nor languages, but only men, who arrange words and imagery according to the necessities of their organs and the original bent of their intellects. A dogma is nothing in itself; look at the people who have made it—a portrait, for instance, of the sixteenth century, the stern and energetic face of an English archbishop or martyr. Nothing exists except through some individual man; it is this individual with whom we must become acquainted. When we have established the parentage of dogmas, or the classification of poems, or the progress of constitutions, or the modification of idioms, we have only cleared the soil: genuine history is brought into existence only when the historian begins to unravel, across the lapse of time, the living man, toiling, impassioned, entrenched in his customs, with his voice and features, his gestures and his dress, distinct and complete as he from whom we have just parted in the street. Let us endeavor, then, to annihilate as far as possible this great interval of time, which prevents us from seeing man with our eyes, with the eyes of our head. What have we under the fair glazed pages of a modern poem? A modern poet, who has studied and traveled, a man like Alfred de Musset, Victor Hugo, Lamartine, or Heine, in a black coat and gloves, welcomed by the ladies, and making every evening his fifty bows and his score of bon-mots in society, reading the papers in the morning, lodging as a rule on the second floor; not over gay, because he has nerves, and especially because in this dense democracy where we choke one another, the discredit of the dignities of office has exaggerated his pretensions while increasing his importance, and because the refinement of his feelings in general disposes him somewhat to believe himself a deity. This is what we take note of under modern meditations or sonnets. Even so, under a tragedy of the seventeenth century we have a poet, like Racine for instance, elegant, staid, a courtier, a fine speaker, with a majestic wig and ribboned shoes, at heart a royalist and a Christian, "having received the grace of God not to blush in any company, kings nor gospelers"; clever at entertaining the prince, and rendering for him into good French the "old French of Amyot"; very respectful to the great, always "knowing his place"; as assiduous and reserved at Marly as at Versailles, amid the regular pleasures of a polished and fastidious nature, amid the salutations, graces, airs, and fopperies of the braided lords, who rose early in the morning to obtain the promise of being appointed to some office in case of the death of the present holder, and among charming ladies who count their genealogies on their fingers in order to obtain the right of sitting down in the presence of the king or queen. On that head consult Saint-Simon and the engravings of Perelle, as for the present age you have consulted Balzac and the water-colors of Eugène Lami. Similarly, when we read a Greek tragedy, our first care should be to realize to ourselves the Greeks, that is, the men who live half naked, in the gymnasia, or in the public squares, under a glowing sky, face to face with the most noble landscapes, bent on making their bodies nimble and strong, on conversing, discussing, voting, carrying on patriotic piracies, but for the rest lazy and temperate, with three urns for their furniture, two anchovies in a jar of oil for their food, waited on by slaves, so as to give them leisure to cultivate their understanding and exercise their limbs, with no desire beyond that of having the most beautiful town, the most beautiful processions, the most beautiful ideas, the most beautiful men. On this subject, a statue such as the Meleager, or the Theseus of the Parthenon, or still more, the sight of the Mediterranean, blue and lustrous as a silken tunic, and islands arising from it like masses of marble, and added to these, twenty select phrases from Plato and Aristophanes, will teach you much more than a multitude of dissertations and commentaries. And so again, in order to understand an Indian Purana, begin by imagining to yourself the father of a family, who "having seen a son on his son's knees," retires, according to the law, into solitude, with an axe and a pitcher, under a banana tree, by the river-side, talks no more, adds fast to fast, dwells naked between four fires, and under a fifth, the terrible sun, devouring and renewing without end all things living; who step by step, for weeks at a time, fixes his imagination upon the feet of Brahma, next upon his knee, next upon his thigh, next upon his navel, and so on, until, beneath the strain of this intense meditation, hallucinations begin to appear, until all the forms of existence, mingled and transformed the one with the other, quaver before a sight dazzled and giddy, until the motionless man, catching in his breath, with fixed gaze, beholds the universe vanishing like a smoke beyond the universal and void Being into which he aspires to be absorbed. To this end a voyage to India would be the best instructor; or for want of better, the accounts of travelers, books of geography, botany, ethnology, will serve their turn. In each case the search must be the same. A language, a legislation, a catechism, is never more than an abstract thing: the complete thing is the man who acts, the man corporeal and visible, who eats, walks, fights, labors. Leave on one side the theory and the mechanism of constitutions, religions and their systems, and try to see men in their workshops, in their offices, in their fields, with their sky and earth, their houses, their dress, cultivations, meals, as you do when, landing in England or Italy, you remark faces and motions, roads and inns, a citizen taking his walk, a workman drinking. Our great care should be to supply as much as possible the want of present, personal, direct, and sensible observation which we can no longer practice; for it is the only means of knowing a thing, it must be before us; there is no experience in respect of what is absent. Doubtless this reconstruction is always incomplete: it can produce only incomplete judgments; but to that we must resign ourselves. It is better to have an imperfect knowledge than a futile or false one; and there is no other means of acquainting ourselves approximately with the events of other days, than to see approximately the men of other days.

This is the first step in history: it was made in Europe at the new birth of imagination, toward the close of the last century, by Lessing, Walter Scott; a little later in France, by Chateaubriand, Augustin Thierry, Michelet, and others. And now for the second step.

II

When you consider with your eyes the visible man, what do you look for? The man invisible. The words which enter your ears, the gestures, the motions of his head, the clothes he wears, visible acts and deeds of every kind, are expressions merely; somewhat is revealed beneath them, and that is a soul. An inner man is concealed beneath the outer man; the second does but reveal the first. You look at his house, furniture, dress; and that in order to discover in them the marks of his habits and tastes, the degree of his refinement or rusticity, his extravagance or his economy, his stupidity or his cunning. You listen to his conversation, and you note the inflections of his voice, the changes in his attitudes; and that in order to judge of his intensity, his self-forgetfulness or his gayety, his energy or his constraint. You consider his writings, his artistic productions, his business transactions or political ventures; and that in order to measure the scope and limits of his intelligence, his inventiveness, his coolness, to find out the order, the description, the general force of his ideas, the mode in which he thinks and resolves. All these externals are but avenues converging to a center; you enter them simply in order to reach that center; and that center is the genuine man, I mean that mass of faculties and feelings which are produced by the inner man. We have reached a new world, which is infinite, because every action which we see involves an infinite association of reasonings, emotions, sensations new and old, which have served to bring it to light, and which, like great rocks deep-seated in the ground, find in it their end and their level. This underworld is a new subject-matter, proper to the historian. If his critical education suffice, he can lay bare, under every detail of architecture, every stroke in a picture, every phrase in a writing, the special sensation whence detail, stroke, or phrase had issue; he is present at the drama which was enacted in the soul of artist or writer: the choice of a word, the brevity or length of a sentence, the nature of a metaphor, the accent of a verse, the development of an argument—everything is a symbol to him; while his eyes read the text, his soul and mind pursue the continuous development and the ever-changing succession of the emotions and conceptions out of which the text has sprung: in short, he unveils a psychology. If you would observe this operation, consider the originator and model of contemporary culture, Goethe, who, before writing "Iphigenia," employed day after day in designing the most finished statues, and who at last, his eyes filled with the noble forms of ancient scenery, his mind penetrated by the harmonious loveliness of antique life, succeeded in reproducing so exactly in himself the peculiarities of the Greek imagination, that he gives us almost the twin sister of the Antigone of Sophocles, and the goddesses of Phidias. This precise and proved interpretation of past sensations has given to history, in our days, a second birth; hardly anything of the sort was known to the preceding century. They thought men of every race and century were all but identical; the Greek, the barbarian, the Hindoo, the man of the Restoration, and the man of the eighteenth century, as if they had been turned out of a common mold; and all in conformity to a certain abstract conception, which served for the whole human race. They knew man, but not men; they had not penetrated to the soul; they had not seen the infinite diversity and marvelous complexity of souls; they did not know that the moral constitution of a people or an age is as particular and distinct as the physical structure of a family of plants or an order of animals. Nowadays, history, like zoology, has found its anatomy; and whatever the branch of history to which you devote yourself, philology, linguistic lore, mythology, it is by these means you must strive to produce new fruit. Amid so many writers who, since the time of Herder, Ottfried Müller, and Goethe, have continued and still improve this great method, let the reader consider only two historians and two works, Carlyle's "Cromwell," and Sainte-Beuve's "Port-Royal": he will see with what justice, exactness, depth of insight, one may discover a soul beneath its actions and its works; how behind the old general, in place of a vulgar, hypocritical schemer, we recover a man travailing with the troubling reveries of a melancholic imagination, but with definite instincts and faculties, English to the core, strange and incomprehensible to one who has not studied the climate and the race; how, with about a hundred meager letters and a score of mutilated speeches, one may follow him from his farm and team, to the general's tent and to the Protector's throne, in his transmutation and development, in his pricks of conscience and his political conclusions, until the machinery of his mind and actions becomes visible, and the inner tragedy, ever-changing and renewed, which exercised this great, darkling soul, passes, like one of Shakespeare's through the soul of the looker-on. He will see (in the other case) how, behind the squabbles of the monastery, or the contumacies of nuns, one may find a great province of human psychology; how about fifty characters, that had been buried under the uniformity of a circumspect narrative, reappear in the light of day, each with its own specialty and its countless diversities; how, beneath theological disquisitions and monotonous sermons, one can unearth the beatings of ever-living hearts, the convulsions and apathies of monastic life, the unforeseen reassertions and wavy turmoil of nature, the inroads of surrounding worldiness, the intermittent victories of grace, with such a variety of overcloudings, that the most exhaustive description and the most elastic style can hardly gather the inexhaustible harvest, which the critic has caused to spring up on this abandoned field. And so it is throughout. Germany, with its genius so pliant, so liberal, so apt for transformation, so well calculated to reproduce the most remote and anomalous conditions of human thought; England, with its intellect so precise, so well calculated to grapple closely with moral questions, to render them exact by figures, weights and measures, geography, statistics, by quotation and by common sense; France, with her Parisian culture, with her drawing-room manners, with her untiring analysis of characters and actions, her irony so ready to hit upon a weakness, her finesse so practiced in the discrimination of shades of thought; all have worked the same soil, and one begins to understand that there is no region of history where it is not imperative to fill this deep level, if one would see a serviceable harvest rise between the furrows.

This is the second step; we are in a fair way to its completion. It is the proper work of the contemporary critic. No one has done it so justly and grandly as Sainte-Beuve: in this respect we are all his pupils; his method renews, in our days, in books, and even in newspapers, every kind of literary, of philosophical and religious criticism. From it we must set out in order to begin the further development. I have more than once endeavored to indicate this development; there is here, in my mind, a new path open to history, and I will try to describe it more in detail.

III

When you have observed and noted in man one, two, three, then a multitude of sensations, does this suffice, or does your knowledge appear complete? Is a book of observations a psychology? It is no psychology, and here as elsewhere the search for causes must come after the collection of facts. No matter if the facts be physical or moral, they all have their causes; there is a cause for ambition, for courage, for truth, as there is for digestion, for muscular movement, for animal heat. Vice and virtue are products, like vitriol and sugar; and every complex phenomenon has its springs from other more simple phenomena on which it hangs. Let us then seek the simple phenomena for moral qualities, as we seek them for physical qualities; and let us take the first fact that presents itself: for example, religious music, that of a Protestant church. There is an inner cause which has turned the spirit of the faithful toward these grave and monotonous melodies, a cause broader than its effect; I mean the general idea of the true, external worship which man owes to God. It is this which has modeled the architecture of the temple, thrown down the statues, removed the pictures, destroyed the ornaments, curtailed the ceremonies, shut up the worshipers in high pews which prevent them from seeing anything, and regulated the thousand details of decoration, of posture, and the general surroundings. This itself comes from another more general cause, the idea of human conduct in all its comprehensiveness, internal and external, prayers, actions, dispositions of every kind by which man is kept face to face with God; it is this which has enthroned doctrine and grace, lowered the clergy, transformed the sacraments, suppressed various practices, and changed religion from a discipline to a morality. This second idea in its turn depends upon a third still more general, that of moral perfection, such as is met with in the perfect God, the unerring judge, the stern watcher of souls, before whom every soul is sinful, worthy of punishment, incapable of virtue or salvation, except by the crisis of conscience which He provokes, and the renewal of heart which He produces. That is the master idea, which consists in erecting duty into an absolute king of human life, and in prostrating all ideal models before a moral model. Here we track the root of man; for to explain this conception it is necessary to consider race itself, that is, the German, the Northman, the structure of his character and intelligence, his general processes of thought and feeling, the sluggishness and coldness of sensation which prevent his falling easily and headlong under the sway of pleasure, the bluntness of his taste, the irregularity and revolutions of his conception, which arrest in him the birth of fair dispositions and harmonious forms, the disdain of appearances, the desire of truth, the attachment to bare and abstract ideas, which develop in him conscience, at the expense of all else. There the search is at an end; we have arrived at a primitive disposition, as a trait proper to all sensations, to all the conceptions of a century or a race, at a particularity inseparable from all the motions of his intellect and his heart. Here lie the grand causes, present at every moment and in every case, everywhere and always acting indestructibly, and in the end infallibly supreme, since the accidents which thwart them, being limited and partial, end by yielding to the dull and incessant repetition of their force; in such a manner that the general structure of things, and the grand features of events, are their work; and religions, philosophies, poetries, industries, the framework of society and of families, are in fact only the imprints stamped by their seal.

IV

There is then a system in human sentiments and ideas; and this system has for its motive power certain general traits, certain marks of the intellect and the heart common to men of one race, age, or country. As in mineralogy the crystals, however diverse, spring from certain simple physical forms, so in history, civilizations, however diverse, are derived from certain simple spiritual forms. The ones are explained by a primitive geometrical element, as the others are by a primitive psychological element. In order to master the classification of mineralogical systems, we must first consider a regular and general solid, its sides and angles, and observe in this the numberless transformations of which it is capable. So, if you would realize the system of historical varieties, consider first a human soul generally, with its two or three fundamental faculties, and in this compendium you will perceive the principal forms which it can present. After all, this kind of ideal picture, geometrical as well as psychological, is hardly complex, and one speedily sees the limits of the outline in which civilizations, like crystals, are constrained to exist.

What do we find, at first sight, in man? Images or representations of things, something, that is, which floats within him, exists for a time, is effaced, and returns again, after he has been looking upon a tree, an animal, any sensible object. This is the subject matter, the development whereof is double, either speculative or practical, according as the representations resolve themselves into a *general conception* or an *active resolution*. Here we have the whole of man in an abridgment; and in this limited circle human diversities meet, sometimes in the womb of the primordial matter, sometimes in the twofold primordial development. However minute in their elements, they are enormous in the aggregate, and the least alteration in the factors produces vast alteration in the results. According as the representation is clear and as it were cut out by machinery or confused and faintly defined, according as it embraces a great or small number of the marks of the object, according as it is violent and accompanied by impulses, or quiet and surrounded by calm, all the operations and processes of the human machine are transformed. So, again, according as the ulterior development of the representation varies, the whole human development varies. If the general conception in which it results is a mere dry notation (in Chinese fashion), language becomes a sort of algebra, religion and poetry dwindle, philosophy is reduced to a kind of moral and practical common sense, science to a collection of formulas, classifications, utilitarian mnemonics, and the whole intellect takes a positive bent. If, on the contrary, the general representation in which the conception results is a poetical and figurative creation, a living symbol, as among the Aryan races, language becomes a sort of cloudy and colored word-stage, in which every word is a person, poetry and religion assume a magnificent and inextinguishable grandeur, metaphysics are widely and subtly developed, without regard to positive applications; the whole intellect, in spite of the inevitable deviations and shortcomings of its effort, is smitten with the beautiful and the sublime, and conceives an ideal capable by its nobleness and its harmony of rallying round it the tenderness and enthusiasm of the human race. If, again, the general conception in which the representation results is poetical but not precise; if man arrives at it not by a continuous process, but by a quick intuition; if the original operation is not a regular development, but a violent explosion—then, as with the Semitic races, metaphysics are absent, religion conceives God only as a king solitary and devouring, science cannot grow, the intellect is too rigid and complete to reproduce the delicate operations of nature, poetry can give birth only to vehement and grandiose exclamations, language cannot unfold the web of argument and of eloquence, man is reduced to a lyric enthusiasm, an unchecked passion, a fanatical and constrained action. In this interval between the particular representation and the universal conception are found the germs of the greatest human differences. Some races, as the classical, pass from the first to the second by a graduated scale of ideas, regularly arranged, and general by degrees; others, as the Germanic, traverse the same ground by leaps, without uniformity, after vague and prolonged groping. Some, like the Romans and English, halt at the first steps; others, like the Hindoos and Germans, mount to the last. If, again, after considering the passage from the representation to the idea, we consider that from the representation to the resolution, we find elementary differences of the like importance and the like order, according as the impression is sharp, as in southern climates, or dull, as in northern; according, as it results in instant action, as among barbarians, or slowly, as in civilized nations; as it is capable or not of growth, inequality, persistence, and connections. The whole network of human passions, the chances of peace and public security, the sources of toil and action, spring from hence. Other primordial differences there are: their issues embrace an entire civilization; and we may compare them to those algebraical formulas which, in a narrow limit, contain in advance the whole curve of which they form the law. Not that this law is always developed to its issue; there are perturbing forces; but when it is so, it is not that the law was false, but that its action was impeded. New elements become mingled with the old; great forces from without counteract the primitive. The race emigrates, like the Aryan, and the change of climate has altered in its case the whole economy, intelligence, and organization of society. The people has been conquered like the Saxon nation, and a new political structure has imposed on it custom, capacities, and inclinations which it had not. The nation has installed itself in the midst of a conquered people, downtrodden and threatening, like the ancient Spartans; and the necessity of living like troops in the field has violently distorted in an unique direction the whole moral and social constitution. In each case, the mechanism of human history is the same. One continually finds, as the original mainspring, some very general disposition of mind and soul, innate and appended by nature to the race, or acquired and produced by some circumstance acting upon the race. These mainsprings, once admitted, produce their effect gradually: I mean that after some centuries they bring the nation into a new condition, religious, literary, social, economic; a new condition which, combined with their renewed effort, produces another condition, sometimes good, sometimes bad, sometimes slowly, sometimes quickly, and so forth; so that we may regard the whole progress of each distinct civilization as the effect of a permanent force which, at every stage, varies its operation by modifying the circumstances of its action.

V

Three different sources contribute to produce this elementary moral state—the race, the surroundings, and the epoch. What we call the race are the innate and hereditary dispositions which man brings with him to the light, and which, as a rule, are united with the marked differences in the temperament and structure of the body. They vary with various peoples. There is a natural variety of men, as of oxen and horses, some brave and intelligent, some timid and dependent, some capable of superior conceptions and creations, some reduced to rudimentary ideas and inventions, some more specially fitted to special works, and gifted more richly with particular instincts, as we meet with species of dogs better favored than others—these for hunting, these for fighting, these for chase, these again for house-dogs or shepherds' dogs. We have here a distinct force—so distinct, that amid the vast deviations which the other two motive forces produce in him, one can recognize it still; and a race, like the old Aryans, scattered from the Ganges as far as the Hebrides, settled in every clime, spread over every grade of civilization, transformed by thirty centuries of revolutions, nevertheless manifests in its tongues, religions, literatures, philosophies, the community of blood and of intellect which to this day binds its offshoots together. Different as they are, their parentage is not obliterated; barbarism, culture and grafting, differences of sky and soil, fortunes good and bad, have labored in vain: the great marks of the original model have remained, and we find again the two or three principal lineaments of the primitive imprint underneath the secondary imprints which time has stamped above them. There is nothing astonishing in this extraordinary tenacity. Although the vastness of the distance lets us but half perceive—and by a doubtful light—the origin of species, the events of history sufficiently illumine the events anterior to history, to explain the almost immovable steadfastness of the primordial marks. When we meet with them, fifteen, twenty, thirty centuries before our era, in an Aryan, an Egyptian, a Chinese, they represent the work of several myriads of centuries. For as soon as an animal begins to exist, it has to reconcile itself with its surroundings; it breathes after a new fashion, renews itself, is differently affected according to the new changes in air, food, temperature. Different climate and situation bring it various needs, and consequently a different course of actions; and this, again, a different set of habits; and still again, a different set of aptitudes and instincts. Man, forced to accommodate himself to circumstances, contracts a temperament and a character corresponding to them; and his character, like his temperament, is so much more stable, as the exter-

nal impression is made upon him by more numerous repetitions, and is transmitted to his progeny by a more ancient descent. So that at any moment we
may consider the character of a people as an abridgement of all its preceding
actions and sensations; that is, as a quantity and as a weight, not infinite since
everything in nature is finite, but disproportioned to the rest, and almost
impossible to lift, since every moment of an almost infinite past has contributed to increase it, and because, in order to raise the scale, one must place in
the opposite scale a still greater number of actions and sensations. Such is the
first and richest source of these master faculties from which historical events
take their rise; and one sees at the outset that if it be powerful, it is because
this is no simple spring, but a kind of lake, a deep reservoir wherein other
springs have, for a multitude of centuries, discharged their several streams.

Having thus outlined the interior structure of a race, we must consider the
surroundings in which it exists. For man is not alone in the world; nature
surrounds him, and his fellow-men surround him; accidental and secondary
tendencies come to place themselves on his primitive tendencies, and physical
or social circumstances disturb or confirm the character committed to their
charge. In course of time the climate has had its effect. Though we can follow
but obscurely the Aryan peoples from their common fatherland to their final
countries, we can yet assert that the profound differences which are manifest
between the German races on the one side, and the Greek and Latin on the
other, arise for the most part from the difference between the countries in
which they are settled: some in cold moist lands, deep in black marshy forests
or on the shores of a wild ocean, caged in by melancholy or violent sensations, prone to drunkenness and gluttony, bent on a fighting, blood-spilling
life; others, again, within a lovely landscape, on a bright and laughing sea-
coast, enticed to navigation and commerce, exempt from gross cravings of
the stomach, inclined from the beginning to social ways, to a settled organization of the state, to feelings and dispositions such as develop the art of
oratory, the talent for enjoyment, the inventions of science, letters, arts.
Sometimes the state policy has been at work, as in the two Italian civilizations: the first wholly turned to action, conquest, government, legislation, by
the original site of its city of refuge, by its border-land emporium, by an
armed aristocracy, who, by inviting and drilling the strangers and the conquered, presently set face to face two hostile armies, having no escape from
its internal discords and its greedy instincts but in systematic warfare; the
other, shut out from unity and any great political ambition by the stability
of its municipal character, the cosmopolitan condition of its pope, and the
military intervention of neighboring nations, directed the whole of its magnificent, harmonious bent toward the worship of pleasure and beauty. Sometimes the social conditions have impressed their mark, as eighteen centuries

ago by Christianity, and twenty-five centuries ago by Buddhism, when around the Mediterranean, as in Hindoostan, the extreme results of Aryan conquest and civilization induced an intolerable oppression, the subjugation of the individual, utter despair, a curse upon the world, with the development of metaphysics and myth, so that man in this dungeon of misery, feeling his heart softened, begot the idea of abnegation, charity, tender love, gentleness, humility, brotherly love—there, in a notion of universal nothingness, here under the Fatherhood of God. Look around you upon the regulating instincts and faculties implanted in a race—in short, the mood of intelligence in which it thinks and acts at the present time: you will discover most often the work of some one of these prolonged situations, these surrounding circumstances, persistent and gigantic pressures, brought to bear upon an aggregate of men who, singly and together, from generation to generation, are continually molded and modeled by their action; in Spain, an eight-century crusade against the Mussulmans, protracted even beyond and until the exhaustion of the nation by the expulsion of the Moors, the spoliation of the Jews, the establishment of the Inquisition, the Catholic wars; in England, a political establishment of eight centuries, which keeps a man erect and respectful, in independence and obedience, and accustoms him to strive unitedly, under the authority of the law; in France, a Latin organization, which, imposed first upon docile barbarians, then shattered in the universal crash, is reformed from within under a lurking conspiracy of the national instincts, is developed under hereditary kings, ends in a sort of legality-republic, centralized, administrative, under dynasties exposed to revolution. These are the most efficacious of the visible causes which mold the primitive man: they are to nations what education, career, condition, abode, are to individuals; and they seem to comprehend everything, since they comprehend all external powers which shape human matter, and by which the external acts on the internal.

There is yet a third rank of causes; for, with the forces within and without, there is the work which they have already produced together, and this work itself contributes to produce that which follows. Beside the permanent impulse and the given surroundings, there is the acquired momentum. When the national character and surrounding circumstances operate, it is not upon a *tabula rasa*, but on a ground on which marks are already impressed. According as one takes the ground at one moment or another, the imprint is different; and this is the cause that the total effect is different. Consider, for instance, two epochs of a literature or an art—French tragedy under Corneille and under Voltaire, the Greek drama under Aeschylus and under Euripides, Italian painting under Da Vinci and under Guido. Truly, at either of these two extreme points the general idea has not changed; it is always the same human type which is its subject of representation or painting; the mold of verse, the structure of the drama, the form of body has endured. But among several differences there is this, that the one artist is the precursor, the other the successor; the first has no model, the second has; the first sees objects face to face, the second sees them through the first; that many great branches of art are lost, many details are perfected, that simplicity and grandeur of impression have diminished, pleasing and refined forms have increased—in short, that the first work has outlived the second. So it is with a people as with a plant; the same sap, under the same temperature, and in the same soil, produces, at different steps of its progressive development, different formations, buds, flowers, fruits, seed-vessels, in such a manner that the one which follows has always the first for its condition, and grows from its death. And if now you consider no longer a brief epoch, as our own time, but one of those wide intervals which embrace one or more centuries, like the Middle Ages, or our last classic age, the conclusion will be similar. A certain dominant idea has had sway; men, for two, for five hundred years, have taken to themselves a certain ideal model of man; in the Middle Ages, the knight and the monk; in our classic age, the courtier, the man who speaks well. This creative and universal idea is displayed over the whole field of action and thought; and after covering the world with its works, involuntarily systematic, it has faded, it has died away, and lo, a new idea springs up, destined to a like domination, and the like number of creations. And here remember that the second depends in part upon the first, and that the first, uniting its effect with those of national genius and surrounding circumstances, imposes on each new creation its bent and direction. The great historical currents are formed after this law—the long dominations of one intellectual pattern, or a master idea, such as the period of oratorical models called the Classical Age, or the series of mystical compositions called the Alexandrian and Christian eras, or the series of mythological efflorescences which we meet with in the infancy of the German people, of the Indian and the Greek. Here as elsewhere we have but a mechanical problem; the total effect is a result, depending entirely on the magnitude and direction of the producing causes. The only difference which separates these moral problems from physical ones is, that the magnitude and direction cannot be valued or computed in the first as in the second. If a need or a faculty is a quantity, capable of degrees, like a pressure or weight, this quantity is not measurable like the pressure or the weight. We cannot define it in an exact or approximative formula; we cannot have more, or give more, in respect of it, than a literary impression; we are limited to marking and quoting the salient points by which it is manifested, and which indicate approximately and roughly the part of the scale which is its position. But though the means of notation are not the same in the moral and physical sciences, yet as in both the matter is the same, equally made up of forces, magnitudes, and directions, we may say that in both the final result is produced after the same method. It is great or small, as the fundamental forces are great or small and act more or less exactly in the same sense, according as the distinct effects of race, circumstance, and epoch combine to add the one to the other, or to annul one another. Thus are explained the long impotences and the brilliant triumphs which make their appearance irregularly and without visible cause in the life of a people; they are caused by internal concords or contrarieties. There was such a concord when in the seventeenth century the sociable character and the conversational aptitude, innate in France, encountered the drawing-room manners and the epoch of oratorical analysis; when in the nineteenth century the profound and elastic genius of Germany encountered the age of philosophical compositions and of cosmopolitan criticism. There was such a contrariety when in the seventeenth century the rude and lonely English genius tried blunderingly to adopt a novel politeness; when in the sixteenth century the lucid and prosaic French spirit tried vainly to cradle a living poetry. That hidden concord of creative forces produced the finished urbanity and the noble and regular literature under Louis XIV and Bossuet, the grand metaphysics and broad critical sympathy of Hegel and Goethe. That hidden contrariety of creative forces produced the imperfect literature, the scandalous comedy, the abortive drama under Dryden and Wycherley, the vile Greek importations, the groping elaborate efforts, the scant half-graces under Ronsard and the Pleiad. So much we can say with confidence, that the unknown creations toward which the current of the centuries conducts us, will be raised up and regulated altogether by the three primordial forces; that if these forces could be measured and computed, one might deduce from them as from a formula the specialties of future civilization; and that if, in spite of the evident crudeness of our notations, and the fundamental inexactness of our measures, we try now to form some idea of our general destiny, it is upon an examination of these forces that we must ground our prophecy. For in enumerating them, we traverse the complete circle of the agencies; and when we have considered race, circumstance, and epoch, which are the internal mainsprings, the external pressure, and the acquired momentum, we have exhausted not only the whole of the actual causes, but also the whole of the possible causes of motion.

VI

It remains for us to examine how these causes, when applied to a nation or an age, produce their results. As a rivulet falling from a height spreads its streams, according to the depth of the descent, stage after stage, until it reaches the lowest level of the soil, so the disposition of intellect or soul impressed on a people by race, circumstance, or epoch, spreads in different proportions and by regular descents, down the diverse orders of facts which make up its civilization. If we arrange the map of a country, starting from the watershed, we find that below this common point the streams are divided into five or six principal basins, then each of these into several secondary basins, and so on, until the whole country with its thousand details is included in the ramifications of this network. So, if we arrange the psychological map of the events and sensations of a human civilization, we find first of all five or six well-defined provinces—religion, art, philosophy, the state, the family, the industries; then in each of these provinces natural departments; and in each of these smaller territories, until we arrive at the numberless details of life such as may be observed within and around us every day. If now we examine and compare these diverse groups of facts, we find first of all that they are made up of parts, and that all have parts in common. Let us take first the three chief works of human intelligence—religion, art, philosophy. What is a philosophy but a conception of nature and its primordial causes, under the form of abstractions and formularies? What is there at the bottom of a religion or of an art but a conception of this same nature and of these same causes, under the form of symbols more or less concise, and personages more or less marked; with this difference, that in the first we believe that they exist, in the second we believe that they do not exist? Let the reader consider a few of the great creations of the intelligence in India, Scandinavia, Persia, Rome, Greece, and he will see that, throughout, art is a kind of philosophy made sensible, religion a poem taken for true, philosophy an art and a religion dried up, and reduced to simple ideas. There is, therefore, at the core of each of these three groups, a common element, the conception of the world and its principles; and if they differ among themselves, it is because each combines with the common, a distinct element: now the power of abstraction, again the power to personify and to believe, and finally the power to personify and not believe. Let us now take the two chief works of human association, the family and the state. What forms the state but a sentiment of obedience by which the many unite under the authority of a chief? And what forms the family but the sentiment of obedience, by which wife and children act under the direction of a father and husband? The family is a natural state, primitive and restrained, as the state is an artificial family, ulterior and expanded; and among the differences arising from the number, origin, and condition of its members, we discover in the small society as in the great, a like disposition of the fundamental intelligence which assimilates and unites them. Now suppose that this element receives from circumstance, race, or epoch certain special marks, it is clear that all the groups into which it enters, will be modified proportionately. If the sentiment of obedience is merely fear, you will find, as in most Oriental states, a brutal despotism, exaggerated punishment, oppression of the subject, servility of manners, insecurity of property, an impoverished production, the slavery of women, and the customs of the harem. If the sentiment of obedience has its root in the instinct of order, sociality, and honor, you will find, as in France, a perfect military organization, a fine administrative hierarchy, a want of public spirit with occasional jerks of patriotism, ready docility of the subject with a revolutionary impatience, the cringing courtier with the counter-efforts of the genuine man, the refined sympathy between conversation and society on the one hand, and the worry at the fireside and among the family on the other, the equality of the married with the incompleteness of the married state, under the necessary constraint of the law. If, again, the sentiment of obedience has its root in the instinct of subordination and the idea of duty, you will find, as among the Germans, security and happiness in the household, a solid basis of domestic life, a tardy and incomplete development of society, an innate respect for established dignities, a superstitious reverence for the past, the keeping up of social inequalities, natural and habitual regard for the law. So in a race, according as the aptitude for general ideas varies, religion, art, and philosophy vary. If man is naturally inclined to the widest universal conceptions, and apt to disturb them at the same time by the nervous delicacy of his over-sensitive organization you will find, as in India, an astonishing abundance of gigantic religious creations, a glowing outgrowth of vast and transparent epic poems, a strange tangle of subtle and imaginative philosophies, all so well interwoven, and so penetrated with a common essence, as to be instantly recognized, by their breadth, their coloring, and their want of order, as the products of the same climate and the same intelligence. If, on the other hand, a man naturally staid and balanced in mind limits of his own accord the scope of his ideas, in order the better to define their form, you will find, as in Greece, a theology of artists and tale-tellers; distinctive gods, soon considered distinct from things, and transformed, almost at the outset, into recognized personages; the sentiment of universal unity all but effaced, and barely preserved in the vague notion of Destiny; a philosophy rather close and delicate than grand and systematic, confined to a lofty metaphysics, but incomparable for logic, sophistry, and morals; poetry and arts superior for clearness, spirits, scope, truth, and beauty to all that have ever been known. If, once more, man, reduced to narrow conceptions, and deprived of all speculative refinement, is at the same time altogether absorbed and straitened by practical occupations, you will find, as in Rome, rudimentary deities, mere hollow names, serving to designate the trivial details of agriculture, generation, household concerns, etiquettes, in fact of marriage, of the farm, producing a mythology, a philosophy, a poetry, either worth nothing or borrowed. Here, as everywhere, the law of mutual dependence comes into play. A civilization forms a body, and its parts are connected with each other like the parts of an organic body. As in an animal, instincts, teeth, limbs, osseous structure, muscular envelope, are mutually connected, so that a change in one produces a corresponding change in the rest, and a clever naturalist can by a process of reasoning reconstruct out of a few fragments almost the whole body; even so in a civilization, religion, philosophy, the organization of the family, literature, the arts, make up a system in which every local change induces a general change, so that an experienced historian, studying some particular part of it, sees in advance and predicts the character of the rest. There is nothing vague in this interdependence. In the living body the regulator is, first, its tendency to manifest a certain primary type; then its necessity for organs whereby to satisfy its wants, and for harmony with itself in order that it may live. In a civilization, the regulator is the presence, in every great human creation, of a productive element, present also in other surrounding creations—to wit, some faculty, aptitude, disposition, effective and discernible, which, being possessed of its proper character, introduces it into all the operations in which it assists, and, according to its variations, causes all the works in which it co-operates to vary also.

VII

At this point we can obtain a glimpse of the principal features of human transformations, and begin to search for the general laws which regulate, not events only, but classes of events, not such and such religion or literature, but a group of literatures or religions. If, for instance, it were admitted that a religion is a metaphysical poem, accompanied by a belief; and remarking at the same time that there are certain epochs, races, and circumstances in which belief, the poetical and metaphysical faculty, are combined with an unwonted vigor; if we consider that Christianity and Buddhism were produced at periods of grand productions, and amid such miseries as raised up the fanatics of the Cévennes; if we recognize, on the other hand, that primitive religions are born at the awakening of human reason, during the richest blossoming of human imagination, at a time of the fairest artlessness and the greatest credulity; if we consider, also, that Mohammedanism appeared with the dawning of poetic prose, and the conception of national unity, among a people destitute of science, at a period of sudden development of the intellect—we might then conclude that a religion is born, declines, is reformed and transformed according as circumstances confirm and combine with more or less exactitude and force its three generative instincts; and we should understand why it is endemic in India, amid imaginative, philosophic, eminently fanatic brains; why it blossomed forth so strangely and grandly in the Middle Ages, amid an oppressive organization, new tongues and literatures; why it was aroused in the sixteenth century with a new character and heroic enthusiasm, amid universal regeneration, and during the awakening of the German races; why it breaks out into eccentric sects amid the rude American democracy, and under the bureaucratic Russian despotism; why, in fine, it is spread, at the present day, over Europe in such different dimensions and such various characteristics, according to the differences of race and civilization. And so for every kind of human production—for literature, music, the fine arts, philosophy, science, statecraft, industries, and the rest. Each of these has for its direct cause a moral disposition, or a combination of moral dispositions: the cause given, they appear; the cause withdrawn, they vanish; the weakness or intensity of the cause measures their weakness or intensity. They are bound up with their causes, as a physical phenomenon with its condition, as the dew with the fall of the variable temperature, as dilatation with heat. There are such dualities in the moral as in the physical world, as rigorously bound together, and as universally extended in the one as in the other. Whatever in the one case produces, alters, suppresses the first term, produces, alters, suppresses the second as a necessary consequence. Whatever lowers the temperature, deposits the dew. Whatever develops credulity side by side with poetical thoughts, engenders religion. Thus phenomena have been produced; thus they will be produced. As soon as we know the sufficient and necessary condition of one of these vast occurrences, our understanding grasps the future as well as the past. We can say with confidence in what circumstances it will reappear, foresee without rashness many portions of its future history, and sketch with care some features of its ulterior development.

VIII

History is now upon, or perhaps almost upon, this footing that it must proceed after such a method of research. The question propounded nowadays is of this kind. Given a literature, philosophy, society, art, group of arts, what is the moral condition which produced it? what conditions of race, epoch, circumstance, are most fitted to produce this moral condition? There is a distinct moral condition for each of these formations, and for each of their branches; one for art in general, one for each kind of art—for architecture, painting, sculpture, music, poetry; each has its special germ in the wide field of human psychology; each has its law, and it is by virtue of this law that we see it raised, by chance, as it seems, wholly alone, amid the miscarriage of its neighbors, like painting in Flanders and Holland in the seventeenth century, poetry in England in the sixteenth, music in Germany in the eighteenth. At this moment, and in these countries, the conditions have been fulfilled for one art, not for others, and a single branch has budded in the general barrenness. For these rules of human growth must history search; with the special psychology of each special formation it must occupy itself; the finished picture of these characteristic conditions it must now labor to compose. No task is more delicate or more difficult; Montesquieu tried it, but in his time history was too new to admit of his success; they had not yet even a suspicion of the road necessary to be traveled, and hardly now do we begin to catch sight of it. Just as in its elements astronomy is a mechanical and physiology a chemical problem, so history in its elements is a psychological problem. There is a particular inner system of impressions and operations which makes an artist, a believer, a musician, a painter, a wanderer, a man of society; and of each the affiliation, the depth, the independence of ideas and emotions, are different; each has its moral history and its special structure, with some governing disposition and some dominant feature. To explain each, it would be necessary to write a chapter of esoteric analysis, and barely yet has such a method been rudely sketched. One man alone, Stendhal, with a singular bent of mind and a singular education, has undertaken it, and to this day the majority of readers find his books paradoxical and obscure: his talent and his ideas were premature; his admirable divinations were not understood, any more than his profound sayings thrown out cursorily, or the astonishing justness of his perception and of his logic. It was not perceived that, under the exterior of a conversationalist and a man of the world, he explained the most complicated of esoteric mechanisms; that he laid his finger on the mainsprings; that he introduced into the history of the heart scientific processes, the art of notation, decomposition, deduction; that he first marked the fundamental causes of nationality, climate, temperament; in short, that he treated sentiments as they should be treated—in the manner of the naturalist, namely, and of the natural philosopher, who constructs classifications and weighs forces. For this very reason he was considered dry and eccentric: he remained solitary, writing novels, voyages, notes, for which he sought and obtained a score of readers. And yet we find in his books at the present day essays the most suitable to open the path which I have endeavored to describe. No one has better taught us how to open our eyes and see, to see first the men that surround us and the life that is present, then the ancient and authentic documents, to read between the black and white lines of the pages, to recognize under the old impression, under the scribbling of a text, the precise sentiment, the movement of ideas, the state of mind in which they were written. In his writings, in Sainte-Beuve, in the German critics, the readers will see all the wealth that may be drawn from a literary work: when the work is rich, and one knows how to interpret it, we find there the psychology of a soul, frequently of an age, now and then of a race. In this light, a great poem, a fine novel, the confessions of a superior man, are more instructive than a heap of historians with their histories. I would give fifty volumes of charters and a hundred volumes of state-papers for the memoirs of Cellini, the epistles of St. Paul, the Table-talk of Luther, or the comedies of Aristophanes. In this consists the importance of literary works: they are instructive because they are beautiful; their utility grows with their perfection; and if they furnish documents, it is because they are monuments. The more a book represents visible sentiments, the more it is a work of literature; for the proper office of literature is to take note of sentiments. The more a book represents important sentiments, the higher is its place in literature; for it is by representing the mode of being of a whole nation and a whole age, that a writer rallies round him the sympathies of an entire age and an entire nation. This is why, amid the writings which set before our eyes the sentiments of preceding generations, a literature, and notably a grand literature, is incomparably the best. It resembles that admirable apparatus of extraordinary sensibility, by which physicians disentangle and measure the most recondite and delicate changes of a body. Constitutions, religions, do not approach it in importance; the articles of a code and of a catechism only show us the spirit roughly and without delicacy. If there are any writings in which politics and dogma are full of life, it is in the eloquent discourses of the pulpit and the tribune, memoirs, unrestrained confessions; and all this belongs to literature: so that, in addition to itself, it has all the advantage of other works. It is then chiefly by the study of literatures that one may construct a moral history, and advance toward the knowledge of psychological laws, from which events spring.

I am about to write the history of a literature, and to seek in it for the psychology of a people: if I have chosen this one in particular, it is not without a reason. I had to find a people with a grand and complete literature, and this is rare: there are few nations who have, during their whole existence, really thought and written. Among the ancients, the Latin literature is worth nothing at the outset, then borrowed and imitative. Among the moderns, German literature is almost wanting for two centuries. Italian literature and Spanish literature end at the middle of the seventeenth century. Only ancient Greece, modern France, and England, offer a complete series of great significant monuments. I have chosen England, because being yet alive, and subject to direct examination, it may be better studied than a destroyed civilization, of which we retain but the scraps, and because, being different from France, it has in the eyes of a Frenchman a more distinct character. Besides, there is a peculiarity in this civilization, that apart from its spontaneous development, it presents a forced deviation, it has suffered the last and most effectual of all conquests, and that the three grounds whence it has sprung, race, climate, the Norman invasion, may be observed in its remains with perfect exactness; so well, that we may examine in this history the two most powerful moving springs of human transformation, natural bent and constraining force, and we may examine them without uncertainty or gap, in a series of authentic and unmutilated memorials. I have endeavored to define these primary springs, to exhibit their gradual effects, to explain how they have ended by bringing to light great political, religious, and literary works, and by developing the recondite mechanism whereby the Saxon barbarian has been transformed into the Englishman of to-day.

Zola

Emile-Edouard-Charles-Antoine Zola (1840–1902) was educated mostly at Aix-en-Provence, where Paul Cézanne was one of his closest friends. Failing the *baccalauréat* in 1859, he had to trail from job to clerical job trying hard to make ends meet; not until the late 1860s could he subsist solely by writing. From the first, his novels, strongly affected by the theories of Taine, Flaubert, and the Goncourts, sought to portray the lives and passions of their characters in terms of "objective" factors—especially genetic, neurological, and temperamental causes. The artist, as Zola would point out in the essay *The Experimental Novel,* which did not appear until 1880, should furnish more than the documented description of contemporary life that a Realist like Champfleury was interested in. The artist could and should act as a scientific observer, setting up human "experiments" which, the data once established, must be left to work themselves out according to scientific laws.

These ideas that mirror the contemporary enthusiasm over the possibilities of scientific methods, whose signal triumphs seemed to justify their application to every realm of life—these ideas Zola sought to work out in his twenty novels, a veritable saga, of the Rougon-Macquart family, which appeared between 1871 and 1893 as the "Natural and Social History of a Family under the Second Empire." His verve was unlimited, his success was not. The ideals of scientific objectivity gave way under the lush richness of his documentation, and the experience of his characters was used not to test but to prove the original hypothesis of the author. Social and economic injustice, far from being examined with scientific detachment, were held up to horror and scorn in often propagandistic tones. But if the indictments he produced did not live up to his own theories and objective pretensions, their point was nevertheless well taken and their sometimes exaggerated realism, which provoked disgust and bitter attacks, did focus attention on labor problems *(Germinal),* prostitution *(Nana),* alcoholism and slums *(L'Assommoir),* and, to name a specific case, the bad faith of Captain Dreyfus's accusers *(J'Accuse).*

The Experimental Novel

In my literary studies I have often talked of the experimental method applied to the novel and drama. The return to nature, the naturalistic evolution that has carried our time away, gradually drives all the manifestations of human intelligence into the same scientific path. Only, for lack of precision and understanding, the idea of a literature determined by science has come as a surprise. It seems useful, therefore, to explain clearly, as I see it, just what the experimental novel involves.

All I have to do here is to adapt, for the experimental method has been established with marvelous power and clarity by Claude Bernard in his *Introduction to the Study of Experimental Medicine*. This book by a scientist whose authority is decisive will furnish me with a firm base. I shall find the whole question treated there, and will limit myself, for irrefutable arguments, to the quotations I need. So all that this will be is a collection, a compilation, of relevant passages; for I intend in every case to fall back upon Claude Bernard. Generally, it will be sufficient to replace the word "doctor" by the word "novelist," in order to make my thought clear and endow it with the precision of scientific truth.

That which determined my choice and focused it on the *Introduction* is precisely the fact that medicine, for a great many people, is still an art like the novel. All his life Claude Bernard has sought and struggled to make medicine scientific. We see here the first steps of a science gradually freeing itself from empiricism in order to establish itself in truth, thanks to the experimental method. Claude Bernard proves that this method, already applied in the study of matter, in chemistry and physics, should equally be applied in the study of living bodies, in physiology and in medicine. I shall try to prove in my turn that, if the experimental method leads to the understanding of physical life, it must also lead to the understanding of emotional and intellectual life. This is only a question of degree, in the same direction, from chemistry to physiology, then from physiology to anthropology and to sociology. At the end of this we find the experimental novel.

To make myself clearer I shall here give a brief résumé of the *Introduction*. The way in which I use its ideas will be grasped more easily if the plan of the work and its subject-matter are known. Claude Bernard, after he has declared

---

Source: The Experimental Novel (Paris, 1880). The essay is based on Claude Bernard's *Introduction to the Study of Experimental Medicine* (1865) and inspired, among others, a young man of twenty-three named Raymond Poincaré (World War I President of France, 1913–1920) to publish in 1883 in the *Revue Libérale* a study on Zola and psychological literature. Translated by Eugen Weber.

that medicine now takes the scientific road based upon physiology and thanks to the experimental method, first establishes the differences between the observational and the experimental sciences. He concludes that experiment is basically only an elicited observation. All experimental reasoning is based on doubt, for the experimenter must have no preconceived idea of nature and [must] always keep an open mind. He simply accepts the phenomena that take place when they have been proved.

Then, in the second part, Claude Bernard takes up his real subject, demonstrating that the spontaneity of living bodies does not stand in the way of the experimental method. The difference comes solely from the fact that matter exists in an external and undifferentiated environment, while the elements of higher organisms are plunged in an internal and perfected environment which is endowed with constant physico-chemical properties, like the external environment. Hence, there is an absolute determinism in the conditions of life of natural phenomena which applies to living bodies as well as matter. He calls "proximate" the cause which determines the appearance of phenomena. This proximate cause, as he calls it, is simply the physical and material condition of the existence or appearance of phenomena. The aim of the experimental method, the end of all scientific research, is therefore the same for living bodies and brute matter: it consists in finding the relations which connect a certain phenomenon to its proximate cause, or in other words to determine the necessary conditions for the manifestation of this phenomenon. Experimental science does not have to bother about the *why* of things; it explains the *how,* and no more.

Having explained the experimental considerations that are common both to matter and to living things, Claude Bernard goes on to experimental considerations peculiar to human beings. The great and unique difference there, is that in the organism of living beings we must take into consideration a harmonious whole. He then deals with the practise of experiments on living beings, of vivisection, of the preparatory anatomical conditions, of the choice of animals, of the use of computations in the study of phenomena, and lastly of the physiologist's laboratory.

In the last part of the *Introduction,* Claude Bernard gives examples of experimental physiological investigation, in order to support the ideas he has formulated. He then furnishes some examples of experimental physiological criticism. And he ends by pointing out the philosophical obstacles that experimental medicine comes across. In the first place he counts the false application of physiology to medicine, scientific ignorance, as well as certain illusions of the medical mind. Then he concludes by saying that empirical and experimental medicine not being incompatible must, on the contrary, be inseparable. The last word of the book is that experimental medicine does not correspond to any medical doctrine or any philosophical system.

This is, in very general terms, the structure of the *Introduction,* stripped of its flesh. I hope that this hasty account will be enough to fill the gaps that my method of procedure will necessarily create; for, naturally, I shall only use such quotations as are needed to define and explain the experimental novel. I repeat, that this is only a position I take, the position that is richest in every kind of argument and evidence. Experimental medicine which still fumbles can alone give us a precise idea of experimental literature which, still in gestation, has not even begun to fumble.

I

The first question we have to face is this: is experiment possible in literature where, until now, observation alone seems to have been used?

Claude Bernard writes at length on observation and experiment. There is, first of all, a clear dividing line. This is it: "We call *observer* the person who applies the techniques of simple or complex research to the study of phenomena which he does not cause to vary and which, consequently, he gathers just as nature provides them; we call *experimentalist* the man who uses simple or complex research techniques in order to vary or modify, for some given purpose, natural phenomena and cause them to appear in circumstances or conditions in which nature did not present them." Astronomy, for instance, is a science of observation, because we cannot conceive the astronomer having an effect on the stars; while chemistry is an experimental science, for the chemist acts upon nature and modifies it. Such is, according to Claude Bernard, the only really important distinction separating the experimenter from the observer.

. . . As I said before, Claude Bernard ends by concluding that the experiment is basically an elicited observation. I quote: "In the experimental method, the search for facts, that is research, is always accompanied by a theory so that normally the experimenter sets up an experiment in order to check or verify the value of an experimental idea. One may say, then, that in this case experiment is an observation elicited for the purpose of verification."

Besides this, in order to determine what the experimental novel may contain of observation and experiment, I need only the following passage:

"The observer notes purely and simply the phenomena before his eyes. . . . He must be the photographer of phenomena; his observation must represent nature exactly. . . . He listens to nature and writes what she dictates. But once the fact has been noted, the phenomenon thoroughly observed, the idea follows, reasoning intervenes, and the experimenter appears to verify the phenomenon. The experimenter is he who, by means of a more or less probable but anticipated interpretation of observed phenomena, sets up the experiment so that, in logically predictable terms, it will furnish a result which will serve to check on the hypothesis or the preconceived idea. . . . From the moment when the result of the experiment becomes apparent, the experimenter is faced with a true observation which he has elicited and which must be noted like any observation, without preconceived ideas. The experimenter must then disappear or, rather, instantly turn into an observer; and it is only after he has noted the results of the experiment exactly as he would those of ordinary observation that his mind will reassert itself in order to judge, compare, and decide whether the experimental hypothesis has been verified or invalidated by these same results." . . . All in all, we can say that observation "shows" and experiment "teaches."

Returning to the novel, we see here equally that the writer is part observer and part experimenter. In him the observer provides the facts as he has seen them, decides the point of departure, establishes the firm ground on which the characters will move and phenomena develop. Then the experimenter appears and sets up the experiment, I mean to say causes the characters to move and act in a particular story, in order to show that the succession of facts will be such as the determinism of the phenomena that are being studied demands. At this point, it is nearly always what Claude Bernard calls an experiment "to see what happens." The writer sets out in search of a truth. Take, for instance, the character of Baron Hulot in Balzac's *Cousin Bette*. The general fact observed by Balzac is the havoc which the loving passion of a man can cause in him, in his family, and in society. As soon as he had picked his subject, Balzac started from observed facts, then set up his experiment by submitting Hulot to a series of tests, passing him through certain media in order to show how the mechanism of his passion worked. Evidently, there is here not only observation but also experiment, since Balzac is not a mere photographer sticking to the gathered facts, since he intervenes directly to place his creature in situations which he continues to control. The problem is to know what a certain passion acting in certain surroundings will produce from the point of view of the individual, and from that of society; and an experimental novel, *Cousin Bette* for example, is simply the official report of the experiment that the writer now repeats before the eyes of the public. The whole operation consists of taking facts from life, then of studying their structure by acting upon them through alterations of circumstances and surroundings, without ever deviating from the laws of nature. At the end, there is knowledge of man, scientific knowledge, in its individual and social operation.

No doubt we are far from the certainties of chemistry, and even of physiology. We do not yet know the reagent that will discompose passions and allow them to be analyzed. Often, in this study, I shall have occasion to recall that the experimental novel is younger than experimental medicine, itself hardly born. But I am not concerned to note established results, I only want to expound a method clearly. If the experimental novelist still fumbles through the most obscure and complex of sciences, this does not prevent the existence of science. It cannot be denied that the naturalist novel, as we conceive it at the moment, is a true experiment that the writer carries out on man, helping himself by observation.

Besides, this is not my opinion only but also that of Claude Bernard. He says: "In the routine of life, all that men do is experiment on one another." And, more conclusively, here is all the theory of the experimental novel: "When we think over our own actions, we have a sure guide because we know what we think and what we feel. But if we want to judge the actions of another man and know the motives behind them, it is another thing altogether. No doubt we can see the movements of this man and his doings which are, we feel certain, the means of expression of his feelings and his will.

"We also admit that there is a necessary connection between actions and their causes; but what is this cause? We do not feel it in ourselves, we are not aware of it as we are when it concerns us; we have therefore to interpret it, to infer it from the movements we see and the words we hear. Then we must check the actions of this man, one against the other; we consider how he acts in given circumstances and, in a word, have recourse to the experimental method." All I suggested above is resumed in this last sentence which is that of a scientist. . . .

But we see how things begin to clear when one takes this point of view of the experimental method applied in the novel, and applied with all the scientific precision that the subject can stand today. One foolish objection brought up against us naturalist writers is that we want to be solely photographers. We can protest as much as we like that we accept character, temperament, self-expression, we are still answered by inane arguments about the impossibility of being strictly true to life, about the need to arrange facts in order to create a work of art. Well! with the application of the experimental method to the novel, there is no more cause for dispute. The idea of experiment carries with it the idea of modification. We do start with true facts, which provide our firm base; but to show the structure of facts we have to produce and direct the phenomena; that is our share of imagination and talent in the work. Thus, without having to fall back on questions of form, of style, that I shall examine later, I note right away that, when we use experimental methods in our novels, we must modify nature without departing from it. If we remember the definition: "Observation shows, experiment teaches," we can begin by claiming for our books this lofty lesson of experiment.

The writer, far from being diminished, grows here in singular fashion. An experiment, even the simplest, is always based on an idea, itself born of an observation. As Claude Bernard says: "The experimental idea is neither arbitrary nor purely imaginary; it must always have a firm base in observed reality, that is in nature." Upon this idea and upon this doubt he rests his whole method. "The appearance of the experimental idea," he writes further, "is altogether spontaneous and its nature altogether individual; it is a particular sentiment, a *quid proprium,* which makes up the originality, the inventiveness, the talent of every man." Then he comes to doubt, which he presents as the great scientific lever. "The doubter is the true scientist; he only doubts himself and his interpretations, but he believes in science; he even admits, in the experimental sciences, an absolute principle or criterion, the determinate nature of phenomena, which is absolute both in the phenomena of living bodies and in those of brute matter." Thus, instead of binding the writer within narrow limits, the experimental method leaves him free to use all his intelligence as a thinker and all his talent as a creator. He will have to see, to understand, to invent. An observed fact must generate the idea of the experiment to follow, of the novel to be written, in order to get at the complete knowledge of a truth. Then, having discussed and decided the plan of the experiment, he will always judge its results with the freedom of a man who accepts only facts consistent with the determinism of phenomena. He has started from doubt to arrive at absolute knowledge; and he only stops doubt when the structure of passion, which he has taken to pieces and put together again, functions according to the laws that nature established. There is no vaster, freer task for the human mind. We shall see below the wretchedness of the scholastics, of the systematizers, of the theoreticians of idealism, when compared to the experimenters' triumph.

I sum up this first part by repeating that naturalist writers observe and experiment, and that all their labors arise from the position of doubt they take up before little-known truths, unexplained phenomena, until suddenly, one day, an experimental idea awakes their talent and incites them to set up an experiment in order to analyze the facts and master them.

II

Such is, then, the experimental method. But it has long been denied that it can be applied to living bodies. Here is the essence of the question that I shall examine along with Claude Bernard. After that the argument will be of the simplest: if the experimental method could be carried from chemistry and physics into physiology and medicine, it can be carried from physiology into the naturalistic novel.

Cuvier, to mention only this scientist, held that experiment, suitable to matter, was not suitable to living bodies; physiology according to him had to be purely a science of anatomical observation and deduction. The vitalists further admit a vital force which, in living bodies, is supposed to be incessantly at war with the physico-chemical forces and to neutralize their activity. Claude Bernard, on the contrary, denies any mysterious force and affirms that experiment is suitable everywhere. "I propose," says he, "to establish that the science of living phenomena can have no other grounds than the science of material phenomena, and that there is in this respect no difference between the principles of the biological sciences and those of the physico-chemical sciences. In effect, the end that the experimental method proposes for itself is everywhere the same; it consists in using experiment to connect natural phenomena with their conditions of life or their proximate causes."

. . . Experiments may be conducted on living bodies as easily as on brute matter; one simply has to create the necessary conditions.

I insist on this because, as I said before, this is the crux of the matter. See what Claude Bernard writes on the subject of vitalists: "They consider life as a mysterious and supernatural influence which acts arbitrarily and is free of determinism; and they call materialists all those who make an effort to connect the phenomena of life with definite organic and physico-chemical rules. These are mistaken ideas which are difficult to demolish once they have taken up their abode in a mind; only the advance of science will cause them to disappear." And he lays down this axiom: "In living beings as well as in matter, the conditions of every phenomenon's being are determined in an absolute manner."

I stop at this point so as not to overcomplicate the argument. But here you have scientific progress. In the last century, a more exact application of the experimental method creates chemistry and physics which free themselves from the irrational and the supernatural. Profound studies lead to the discovery that there are established laws; phenomena are mastered. Then a fresh step is taken. Living bodies, in which the vitalists still admitted a mysterious influence, are in their turn reduced to the general mechanism of matter. Science proves that the conditions of life of all phenomena are the same in matter and in living bodies; hence, physiology gradually acquires the same certitude as chemistry and physics. But will we stop at that? Evidently not. When we have proved that the body of man is a machine, which we shall one day be able to take to pieces and put together again at the experimenter's will, then it will be time to pass on to the sentimental and intellectual activities of man. This means that we should enter a realm which, until now, belonged wholly to philosophy and literature; it will be the decisive victory of science over the hypotheses of philosophers and writers. We already have experimental chemistry and physics; we are going to have experimental physiology; and then, later, we shall have the experimental novel. This is a necessary progression, and one whose end can easily be foreseen today. Everything is related, one had to start from the determinism of matter to arrive at the determinism of living bodies; and since scientists like Claude Bernard now demonstrate that established laws rule the human body, one can predict without fear of being deceived the time when laws of thought and of the emotions will be formulated in their turn. The same determinism must rule the stones in the roadway and the brains of man. . . .

It follows that science already enters our domain—the domain of writers like us, who are at the moment the students of man in his private and social activities. By our observations, by our experiments, we carry forward the work of the physiologist who had continued that of physicists and chemists. In a way, we may be said to practice scientific psychology designed to complete scientific physiology; and, in order to complete this evolution, we have only to introduce into our studies of nature and of man the decisive implement that is the experimental method. We must work with the characters, the emotions, the human and social facts, as the chemist and the physicist work with matter, as the physiologist works with living bodies. Determinism dominates everything. Scientific investigation, experimental reasoning, challenge one by one the hypotheses of the idealists and replace the novel of pure imagination by novels of observation and experiment. . . . We still fumble ahead, we are the last arrivals; but this must be merely another incentive toward more exact studies. We have our tool in the experimental method, and our aim is very clear—to understand the determinism of phenomena and master them.

Without going so far as to formulate any laws, I think the question of heredity plays a great part in the intellectual and emotional activities of man. I attribute great importance to environment. One would have to touch on the theories of Darwin; but this is only a general study on the experimental method as applied to the novel, and I would lose myself if I tried to go into details. I shall merely say a word about environment. Claude Bernard attributes decisive importance to the study of the intra-organic environment, which one must bear in mind when seeking to discover the determinism of phenomena in living beings. Well! I think that the social element is equally important in the study of a family, of a group of living beings. No doubt physiology will one day explain the mechanism of thought and emotion; we shall know how the individual machine of man works, how he thinks, how he loves, how he moves from reason to passion and folly; but these phenomena, these facts of the mechanism of the organs acting under the influence of the internal environment, do not manifest themselves isolated and in a vacuum. Man is not alone, he lives in society, in a social environment and, hence, for us writers, this social environment endlessly modifies the phenomena.

Our real task, our essential study, is right there, in the reciprocal effects of society on the individual and the individual on society. For the physiologist, the external and the internal environment are purely chemical and physical, and this allows him to find their laws quite easily. We have not yet reached the point of proving that the social environment is also only chemical and physical. Yet it certainly is, or, rather, it is the variable product of a group of living beings who are absolutely subject to the chemical and physical laws that rule both matter and living bodies. Hence, we shall see that one may affect the social environment by affecting the phenomena that have been mastered in man. And this is what constitutes the experimental novel: to grasp the mechanism of phenomena in man, to show the structure of intellectual and sensual events such as physiology makes known to us, under the influence of heredity and environmental circumstances, then to show the living man in the social surroundings which he has himself created, which he modifies every day, and in the midst of which he undergoes in his turn a continuous transformation. Thus, we find support in physiology, we take isolated man from the hands of the physiologist, in order to carry forward the solution of the problem and to resolve scientifically the question of knowing how men behave in society.

These general ideas are sufficient to guide us for the moment. Later, when science has advanced further, when the experimental novel has furnished decisive results, some critic will say more precisely what I only sketched out today.

[At this point] the experimental novel is a consequence of the scientific evolution of our time; it continues and completes physiology which is itself based on chemistry and physics; it substitutes for the study of the abstract, metaphysical man the study of natural man, subject to physico-chemical laws and determined by the influence of his environment; it is, in a word, the literature of our scientific age, just as classic and romantic literature corresponded to an age of scholasticism and theology. And now I pass on to the great question of its application and its morality.

III

The aim of the experimental method in physiology and medicine is to study phenomena in order to master them. Claude Bernard harks back to this on every page of his *Introduction*. As he declares: "All natural philosophy comes down to this: knowing the laws of phenomena. The whole experimental problem comes down to this: foreseeing and directing phenomena." Further, he gives an example: "It is not enough for the experimental doctor as it is for the empirical one to know that quinine cures fever; what he really cares about is the knowledge of what fever is and the understanding of the way in which quinine cures it. All this is important to the experimental doctor because, just as soon as he learns what he wants, the fact of fever's cure by quinine becomes no longer an empirical, isolated fact but a scientific one. It may be connected to rules that in turn will relate it to other phenomena, and we shall thus be led to understand the laws of the organism and the possibility of regulating their manifestations." The example is quite striking in the case of mange. "Today that the case is known and experimentally determined, everything has become scientific and the empirical approach has disappeared. . . . Mange can be cured always and without exception when it is approached in the way that has been experimentally determined to achieve this end."

Hence this is the aim, this the morality, of experimental physiology and medicine: to master life in order to direct it. Assume that science has advanced, that the unknown has been completely conquered: the scientific age Claude Bernard saw in his dreams will come to be. The doctor will be master of all ills; he will cure without doubt, he will act upon living bodies for the happiness and vigor of the species. We shall enter a time when all-powerful man will have enslaved nature and learnt to use her laws to establish on earth the greatest possible range of justice and freedom. There is no purpose more noble, more lofty, more great. This is where our part as intelligent beings lies: we must penetrate the Why of things in order to dominate them, and reduce them to the state of obedient machinery.

Well! this dream that the physiologist and the medical experimenter dreamed is also that of the writer who applies the experimental method to the natural and social study of man. Our aims are the same. We also want to master the phenomena of intellectual and personal elements, in order to direct them. We are, in a word, experimental moralists, showing by means of experiments how passion behaves in the social environment. The day when we get hold of the mechanism of passion, we shall be able to treat and curtail it, or at least render it as harmless as possible. So this is the utility and the lofty morality of our naturalist works, which experiment on man, which take the human mind to pieces and reassemble it, to make it function under the influence of given surroundings. In time, when we have established laws, all we shall have to do if we want better social conditions will be to act upon the people and their environment. Thus, in fact, we practice practical sociology and our work helps the political and economic sciences. I repeat that I do not know a nobler work, nor a vaster relevance. To be master of good and ill, to regulate life, to regulate society, to resolve eventually all the problems of socialism, above all to furnish solid foundations for justice by solving through experiment the problems of criminality, does this not make us the most useful, the most moral, of laborers?

Compare for a moment the work of idealist writers and our own; and here the term idealist refers to writers who give up observation and experiment to base their works on the supernatural and the irrational, who admit the existence of mysterious forces outside, beyond, the determinism of phenomena. Claude Bernard will again speak for me: "The distinction between experimental and scholastic reasoning lies in the fertility of one and the sterility of the other. It is precisely scholasticism which imagines it has absolute certainty and which gets nowhere; this is understandable, for its absolute principles place it outside nature where everything is relative. On the other hand, the experimenter who always doubts and who does not think he has absolute certainty about anything, succeeds in mastering surrounding phenomena and extending his power over nature." I shall soon return to this question of the ideal, which is in fact simply the question of undeterminism. Claude Bernard says rightly: "The intellectual victory of man is won by diminishing indeterminism and driving it back in proportion to the ground he gains with the help of the experimental method in understanding determinism." Our true task, as experimental novelists, lies in proceeding from the known to the unknown in order to master nature; while the idealistic novelists remain, as a foregone conclusion, on the side of the unknown, under the stupefying pretext that the unknown is more noble and beautiful than the known. If our, sometimes cruel, works, if our terrible paintings [of reality], needed an excuse, I should once more draw the decisive argument from Claude Bernard: "We shall never reach really fruitful and luminous generalizations about vital phenomena except to the extent that we have experimented and bestirred ourselves in the hospital, the operating room, the laboratory, the rank and pulsating reality of life. . . . If I had to furnish a comparison giving my feelings on the science of life, I should say that it is a splendid parlor, glittering with light, which one can reach only by passing through a frightful kitchen."

I insist on this term that I have used, of experimental moralists, when it is applied to the naturalist writers. . . .

And now I come to the great objection with which some have thought to overwhelm naturalist writers by accusing them of fatalism. How often have people tried to prove that, since we did not accept free will, since man was for us no more than an animal machine acting under the influence of environment and heredity, we fell into a coarse fatalism, we debased humanity to the level of a herd moving under the goad of destiny! We must be clear about this: we are not fatalists, we are determinists, which is not the same thing. Claude Bernard defines the two terms very well: "We have named determinism the proximate or determining cause of phenomena. We never act upon the essence of natural phenomena, but only on their determinism and, by the mere fact that we affect it, determinism differs from fatality which cannot be affected. Fatalism assumes the necessary manifestation of a phenomenon independent of its conditions, while determinism is the necessary condition of a phenomenon whose manifestation is not obligatory. Once the research of the determinism of phenomena is granted as the fundamental principle of the experimental method, there is no more materialism, or spiritualism, or brute matter, or living matter; there are only phenomena whose conditions have to be determined—that is, the circumstances which, in relation to these phenomena, play the part of proximate causes." This is decisive. In our novels we simply apply this method and we are therefore determinists who, experimentally, seek to determine the conditions of phenomena without ever departing in our investigations from the laws of nature. As Claude Bernard says so well, since we can act and do act upon the determinism of phenomena by, for instance, modifying their surroundings, we are not fatalists.

Here, then, is a good definition of the experimental novelist's role. I have often said that we had not to draw any conclusions from our works, and this means that our works carry their conclusions in themselves. An experimenter does not have to conclude, just because the experiment furnishes his conclusions for him. He will, if necessary, repeat his experiment a hundred times before the public, explain it, but personally he does not need to approve or disapprove: such is the truth, such the mechanism of phenomena; it is up to society to continue to produce these phenomena or to produce them no longer, according to whether the result is useful or dangerous. One cannot conceive, as I said elsewhere, a scientist being angry with nitrogen because nitrogen is unfit for life; he suppresses nitrogen when it is noxious, and that is all. As our power is not the same as that of the scientist, since we are experimenters without being practitioners, we must be content to seek the determinants of social phenomena, leaving to legislators, to men of affairs, the task of sooner or later directing these phenomena so as to develop the good and curtail the bad from the point of view of human utility.

To sum up our role as experimental moralists. We show the mechanism of the useful and the hurtful, we point out the determinism of human and social phenomena, so that they may one day be mastered and directed. In one word, we work with our time at the great task which is the conquest of nature, the increase in the power of man. And see, beside our own, the work of the idealist writers who lean upon the irrational and supernatural, and whose every transport is followed by a steep drop into metaphysical chaos. It is we who have efficacy and morality on our side.

IV

. . . We are not chemists, or physicists, or physiologists; we are simply novelists taking our stand upon the sciences. True, we do not pretend to make discoveries in the physiological field that we do not practice; only, since we have to study man, we think we cannot avoid taking into account the new physiological truths. And I would add that novelists are certainly the writers who have to draw on the greatest number of sciences at once, for they touch on everything and they have to know everything, since the novel has become a general inquiry on nature and on man. This is how we have come to apply the experimental method in our work from the day when that method became the most powerful instrument of knowledge. We sum up the inquiry, we drive forward to the conquest of the ideal using all the knowledge of man as we do it.

It is, of course, understood that I speak here of the *how* of things and not of the *why*. For an experimental scientist, the ideal which he strives to subdue, the indeterminate, lies only in the *how*. He leaves the *whys*, which he has given up hope to determine ever, he leaves this other ideal to the philosophers. I believe that the experimental novelists must also pay no heed to this unknown if they do not want to lose themselves in the follies of poets and philosophers. The task is already sufficiently great, the attempt to grasp the mechanism of nature difficult enough, without worrying for the moment about its origin as well. If one day we get to know it, this will certainly be thanks to the method, and so it is best to start at the beginning with the study of phenomena, instead of hoping that a sudden revelation will furnish us the secret of the world. We are laborers, we leave to the speculators this unknown *why* with which they have battled vainly for centuries, in order to tackle the unknown *how* which every day diminishes before our inquiry. The only ideal which must exist for us, experimental writers, is that which we can conquer.

Besides, in the slow conquest of this unknown that surrounds us, we humbly acknowledge our ignorance. We begin to move forward—no more—and our only real force lies in our method. Claude Bernard, after having admitted that experimental medicine still fumbles, does not hesitate in practice to leave plenty of room for empirical medicine. "After all," he says, "empiricism— that is to say casual observation or experiment—is at the origin of every science. In the complex sciences of humanity empiricism will necessarily dominate practice far longer than in the simple sciences." And he readily admits that in dealing with the sick, when the mechanism of the pathological phenomenon has not been found, it is best to proceed empirically; which is, in any case, in the natural course of things since the empirical approach necessarily precedes the scientific account of a notion. Certainly if the doctor must rely in most cases on the empirical approach, we novelists, whose science is more complex and less well established, have even better reason to do so. It is not a question, I repeat, of setting up afresh the science of man as an individual and as a member of society; it is a question of emerging gradually, and proceeding as tentatively as may prove necessary, from the obscurity where we find ourselves, happy when in the midst of so much error we manage to establish one truth. We experiment, that is to say that we must for a long time yet use the false to get at the true.

This is the feeling of the strong and confident. Claude Bernard firmly opposes those who insist on seeing in the doctor only an artist. He knows the usual objections of those who affect to consider experimental medicine "as a theoretical conception whose practical reality is not for the moment borne out by anything, since no fact proves that one can attain in medicine the scientific precision of the physical sciences." But he does not let that bother him, he shows that "experimental medicine is only the natural expansion of medical inquiry practised and directed by a scientific mind." And this is his conclusion: "No doubt we are far from the time when medicine has become altogether scientific; but that does not prevent us from conceiving the possibility, and from making every effort to attain it by seeking to introduce right now the method that will lead us to it."

All this, I will not tire of repeating it, applies exactly to the experimental novel. Replace the word "medicine" by the word "novel" and the passage holds good.

To the rising young literary generation I would address these powerful words of Claude Bernard's. I know of none more virile. "Medicine is destined to gradually emerge from empiricism, and it will emerge like all other sciences through the experimental method. This deep conviction upholds and directs my scientific life. I am deaf to the voice of doctors who demand an experimental explanation of measles and scarlet fever, who think to draw from this an argument against the use of the experimental method. These discouraging and negative objections generally derive from systematical or lazy minds which prefer to rest on their systems or slumber in obscurity instead of working and making an effort to get out of them. The experimental direction that medicine has taken is today irreversible. In effect, this is not the result of the passing influence of some personal system; it is the result of the scientific evolution of medicine itself. It is my beliefs in this connection that I seek to impart to the young doctors who take my courses at the Collège de France. . . . Above all, young men must be imbued with the scientific spirit and initiated in the notions and tendencies of the modern sciences."

Often have I written the same words, given the same advice, and I will repeat it here. "The experimental method alone can raise the novel out of the lies and the errors in which it drags. All my literary life has been directed by this belief. I am deaf to the voice of the critics who ask me to formulate the laws of heredity in my characters and those of the influence of environment; those who raise such negative and discouraging objections do so only through laziness of mind, by stubborn adherence to tradition, through more or less conscious attachment to philosophical or religious beliefs. . . . The experimental direction of the novel is today irreversible. This is not the result of the passing influence of some personal system; it is the outcome of the scientific evolution, of the study of man itself. It is my beliefs in this connection that I try to impart to the young writers who read me, for I hold that they must, above all, be instilled with the scientific spirit and initiated in the notions and the tendencies of the modern sciences."

V

. . . I have spoken only of the experimental novel, but I am firmly persuaded that the method, having triumphed in history and criticism, will not fail to triumph everywhere—in the theater and even in poetry. The evolution is fatal. Whatever one may say, literature does not at all lie in the creator, it lies also in the nature it describes, in the man it studies. Now, if the scientists change our ideas of nature, if they discover the true mechanism of life, they force us to follow them, even to precede them, in order to play our part in the new hypothesis. Metaphysical man is dead; with physiological man our position changes. No doubt the anger of Achilles, the love of Dido, remain eternally beautiful descriptions; but now we feel the need to analyze anger and love, and see precisely how these passions operate in the human being. The point of view is new, it becomes experimental instead of being philosophical. Altogether, everything is summed up in this grand fact: the experimental method, in letters as well as in the sciences, is in the process of determining the natural phenomena, both individual and social, whose metaphysical interpretation had hitherto produced only irrational and supernatural explanations.

Impressionism

In the plastic arts the rebellion of Realism and Naturalism was continued first by Edouard Manet (1832–1883), then by the Impressionist painters (Bazille, Pissarro, Monet, Sisley, Renoir, etc.). Like Courbet, Manet believed that art should hold a mirror up to life and that too much of the art of his time was anecdotal, allegorical, or moralistic—removed from reality. Moved by similar ideas, Pre-Raphaelites in England and so-called Nazarenes in Germany had tried to remedy this lack in contemporary academic art by turning to a sort of primitivism addled by antiquarian notions of ideal beauty. This was not the way to improve matters. So, where Courbet had reacted against the prevailing idealism by shunning idealized subjects of a morally elevating kind, Manet reacted further against the still-prevalent notion of an ideal style. In doing this he completed in the 1860s the revolution begun by Courbet in the 1850s and he stands with the master of Ornans as one of the great pioneers of the modern movement.

In spite of his pioneering role in art, Manet combined to a curious degree the conformist and the unconventional. Socially conservative, he was politically progressive, a constant opponent of the Second Empire, good friend of Republican figures like Gambetta, Zola, and Jules Ferry, admirer of radicals and revolutionaries like Clemenceau and Rochefort, both of whom he painted. As a young man in 1848 he had sketched those who died for liberty on the barricades; during the Commune of 1871 he was, along with Corot, Courbet, and Daumier, elected to the Federation of Paris Artists. A few years later his offers to cover the walls of the Paris Hôtel de Ville with frescoes based on one of Zola's great social poems, *Le Ventre de Paris*—markets, streets, docks, and railway stations—remained unanswered but marked none the less the tone of his preoccupations.[1] Yet with all that, Manet always remained the gentleman, distanced by birth, taste, and social position, as well as by the limits he set to his revolutionary experiments, from most of his contemporaries.

Hence, even though the 1870s called the Impressionists *la bande à Manet*—Manet's gang—the relation between them was rather coincidental. Both played a large part in introducing the urban landscape into painting, the modern city with its railway stations, factories, canals and music halls, streets and race courses, cobbles and steam and electric light. Zola regarded Manet as a Realistic painter; in the same sense the Impressionists may be called Naturalistic. Like Naturalist writers, Impressionist painters compared nature with the work of admired and accepted masters, and found that the two did not match. They set out, therefore, to restore truth to painting by accurate, analytical observation and, further, to

---

[1]The subversive character of Manet's painting appeared evident to his contemporaries. When, in 1894, a private collector left his paintings to the French State, to be exhibited in its museums, the representatives of academic art rose in arms against the prospect of museums being sullied by the presence of such works. "This is anarchy," wrote historical painter Benjamin Constant. "A deplorable example," complained Lecomte de Nouy; while the painter Gérôme asserted, in terms familiar to our own day: "We live in a time of imbecility and decay. . . . The level of society as a whole is getting lower every day . . . Manet . . . Pissarro . . . anarchists and madmen . . . It is the end of the nation, the end of France" (*Journal des Artistes*, April 1894). Already, thirty years before, the exhibition in 1865 of Manet's *Olympia* (inspired by Titian's Venus of Urbino) had revolted the critics: "What is this yellow-bellied odalisque, this ignoble model picked up God knows where?" asked the well-known critic, Jules Clarétie. Another critic spluttered with rage: "Never has such a spectacle been seen . . . cynical effect . . . women about to become mothers, and young ladies if they are prudent, would do well to flee such a sight!"

produce *impressions* of the moment, working outdoors and catching sensation on the wing as they had seen it captured in the work of English artists.

When Turner had painted "Rain, Steam and Speed," he recognized these elusive phenomena, and their peculiar problems of movement and light, as fit subjects for painting. A later Turner, "Venice in the Twilight," was concerned not so much with Venice as with the twilight, stressing again that forms of reality existed that were rather atmospheric than objective, and that presented painters with a new challenge. Turner himself did not get far; but in the 1870s his perceptions fired the imagination of Monet, Pissarro, and Sisley, whom the Franco-Prussian War had driven to London, and of their friends when they returned to France. These men were out to seize the moment just as it is, if necessary in a sketchy manner, line being sacrificed to light and, hence, design to color—the latter being thought to render the requisite impression more effectively than any line.

In one sense, Impressionism marks the high point of materialistic and "objective" art, setting out to produce instantaneous photographs, dissecting reality the better to put it together again. Yet its very fruitfulness carried with it early disintegration. For by dissecting reality the more faithfully to reconstruct it, Impressionism opened the door to Cubism and Expressionism. Once the solid surface of reality was shattered, it became natural and relatively easy to reach through to what lay beyond.

Zola

The Realists of the Salon of 1866

I should be in despair if my readers thought for a moment that I come here as the representative of a school. To make me a Realist, a member of a party, would be to misunderstand me.

I have my own party, the party of life and truth, and that is all. I have some things in common with Diogenes who sought a man; I also seek men in art, fresh and forceful temperaments.

I do not give a hoot for Realism, in the sense that the word has no precise meaning for me. If you mean by it the need for painters to study and repre-

Source: From "The Realists of the Salon of 1866," first published in *l'Evénement*, May 11, 1866; in book form in *Mon Salon* (Paris, 1866), dedicated to Paul Cézanne. Translated by Eugen Weber.

sent true nature, there is no doubt that all artists must be realists. Painting dreams is a game for women and children; the task of men is to paint realities.

They take nature and reproduce it, they reproduce it through the medium of their particular temper. Thus, every artist will give us a different world and I shall willingly accept all these different worlds provided each of them should be the living expression of a particular temper. I admire the worlds of Delacroix and of Courbet. Given such a statement, I do not think anyone can class me in any particular school.

Only, see what happens in our time of psychological and physiological analysis. The wind blows from the quarter of science; we are driven, in spite of ourselves, toward the exact study of facts and of things. Thus, all the strong personalities that appear, affirm themselves in the direction of truthfulness. The temper of the time is certainly realistic or, rather, positivistic. I am thus forced to admire men who seem to share a certain kinship, the kinship of the time in which they live.

I am told that I praise "the painting of the future." I do not know what this term can mean. I believe that every talent is born free, and that it leaves no disciples. The painting of the future bothers me very little; it will be what the artists and the society of tomorrow make it.

The great bugbear, believe me, is not Realism—it is temperament. Every man who is not like others becomes by that very fact an object of mistrust. As soon as the crowd does not understand any more, it laughs. A whole process of education is necessary before genius can be accepted. The history of literature and art is a sort of martyrology which recounts the obloquy and hooting that met every fresh manifestation of the human spirit. . . .

. . . This is the way I interpret the development of every true artist—for instance that of Edouard Manet. Feeling that he was getting nowhere copying the old masters, painting nature seen through personalities different from his, he must have realized quite simply one fine morning that he had now to try to see nature as she is, not through the works and opinions of others. As soon as he got this idea, he took some object, a being or a thing, placed it in a corner of his studio and started to reproduce it on canvas according to his faculties of sight and understanding. He made an effort to forget everything he had studied in the galleries; he tried not to remember the advice he had received, the paintings he had looked at. All that was left there was a particular intelligence served by organs endowed in a certain manner, face to face with nature, and translating it in its own way.

Thus the artist achieved a work that was his own flesh and blood. Certainly this work belonged to the great family of human products; it had its sisters among the thousands of works that have been created; it more or less resembled some of them. But its beauty was its own, living a personal life. The different elements which made it up, taken perhaps from here and there, blended into a whole of novel flavor and particular aspect; and this whole, created for the first time, had an appearance as yet unknown to human talent. Henceforth, Edouard Manet had found his way or, more correctly, he had found himself: he saw through his own eyes, he was to give us in each of his paintings a translation of nature into that original language which he had discovered in the depths of himself. . . .

Blémont

The Impressionists

What is an Impressionist painter? We have been given no satisfactory definition, but it seems that the artists who group themselves, or who are grouped, under this name pursue a similar end through different methods of work. Their aim is to reproduce with absolute sincerity, without contrivance or palliation, by a treatment simple and broad, the impression awakened in them by the aspects of reality.

Art is not for them a minute and punctilious imitation of what was once called "the beauties of nature." They are not concerned to reproduce more or less slavishly beings and things, or laboriously to reconstruct, minor detail by minor detail, a general picture. They do not imitate; they translate, they interpret, they apply themselves to extricate the consequence of the many lines and colors that the eye perceives in a view.

They are not analysts but synthesizers, and we believe that they are right in this; for if analysis is the scientific method *par excellence,* synthesis is the true method of operation for art. They have no other law than the necessary relations of things; they think, like Diderot, that the idea of beauty rests in the perception of these relations. And, as there are perhaps no two men in the world who perceive exactly the same relations in the same object, they see no reason to change, according to this or that convention, their personal and direct sensation of things.

In principle, in theory, we believe therefore that we can approve them wholeheartedly.

In practice, it is another matter. One does not always do what one wants

---

Source: Emile Blémont in *Le Rappel,* April 9, 1876. Translated by Eugen Weber.

to do, as it should be done; one does not always attain the end one sees clearly.

Zola

Naturalism in the Salon

These last few years something very interesting and instructive has been happening under our own eyes. I refer to the independent exhibitions put on by a group of painters that have been called "the Impressionists." . . . I use this term "Impressionist" here, because a label is really wanting to name the young artists who, in the wake of Courbet and of our great landscape painters, have devoted themselves to the study of nature. . . . When we come down to it, as a working painter Courbet himself is a magnificent classic. . . . The true revolutionaries of form appear with Mr. Edouard Manet, with the Impressionists, Messrs. Claude Monet, Renoir, Pissarro, Guillaumin, and still others. These propose to get out of the studio in which painters have shut themselves up for so many centuries, and go paint in the open. In the open, the light is no longer uniform, and this means a multiplicity of impressions. . . . This study of light in its thousand decompositions and recompositions is what has been called, more or less properly, Impressionism because by it a painting becomes the impression of a moment experienced in nature. The jokers of the press have started from there to caricature the Impressionist painter catching, so to speak, his impressions on the wing in half a dozen shapeless brush strokes; and it must be admitted that certain artists have unfortunately warranted these attacks by contenting themselves with sketches that are far too rudimentary. As far as I am concerned, it is true that one has to apprehend living nature in the expression of an instant; only, this instant must be fixed on the canvas for ever by a fully considered composition. In the end, nothing solid is possible without work. . . .

The public is dumbfounded when it comes face to face with certain canvases painted in the open at specific hours; it stands gaping before blue grasses, violet-colored soils, red trees, waters running with all the motley of the rainbow. And yet the artist has been conscientious; he has, perhaps, by reaction, slightly exaggerated the new tonalities his eye has noted; but, when it comes down to it, the observation is absolutely true, nature has never

---

Source: Translated by Eugen Weber from *Le Voltaire,* June 19, 1880.

adhered to the simplified notation that the established schools use to treat it. [But it is this last to which the public is used.] Hence the laughter of the crowd faced with the Impressionist paintings, despite the good faith and the very honest, naïve efforts of the young painters.

They are taken for pranksters, humbugs, charlatans making fun of the public and drumming up publicity around their works, when they are, on the contrary, severe and principled observers. What seems to be ignored is that most of these contenders are poor men who work themselves to death, sometimes quite literally from misery and weariness. Strange humbugs, these martyrs for their beliefs!

This is, then, what the Impressionist painters have to offer: a more exact examination of the causes and effects of light, exerting its influence both on color and design. They have been justifiably accused of drawing their inspiration from Japanese prints. . . . It is certain that our dark schools of painting, the bituminous-minded work of our established schools, has been surprised and forced to rethink things when faced with the limpid horizons, the beautiful vibrant spots of the Japanese water-colorists. There was in these works a simplicity of means and an intensity of performance which struck our young artists and drove them on to this path of painting soaked in air and light—a path which all the talented newcomers take today. . . .

The great pity is that this new formula which they all bring scattered in their works, not one of the artists of the group has realized powerfully and definitively. The formula is there, endlessly divided; but nowhere, in any one of them, do we find it applied by a master. . . . Yet, while we can take objection to their personal incapacity, they remain none the less the true representatives of our time. They have plenty of gaps, their workmanship is too often slack, they are too easily satisfied, they show themselves to be incomplete, illogical, exaggerated, ineffectual. No matter: it is enough for them to apply themselves to contemporary naturalism in order to find themselves at the head of a movement and play a great part in our school of painting.

Wilde

Oscar Fingall O'Flahertie Wills Wilde (1856–1900), born in Dublin the same year as George Bernard Shaw, was one of the most brilliant and ill-fated of the many Irishmen who have graced the London stage and the British world of letters. Coming to London with a reputation for brilliance already forged at Trinity College in Dublin and at Oxford, he soon established himself as an aesthete and wit, though his poetry and the literary criticism he wrote, with far less facility than he spoke it, glittering and suggestive as they were, lacked profoundity or power. The passage that follows, gathered with other ephemera in *The Decay of Lying* (1889), offers a good example of his artistic perceptiveness and also of his trick of writing in the *soufflé* style—light, delightful, and leaving little to digest.

Wilde's aphorisms on page 217 fall into the same category: apt products of an undisciplined genius, whose commitment to beauty in an age aware of the importance of being earnest irritated the many who equate hedonism and irresponsibility, and whose shots hit the mark more strikingly and more often than most of us can manage.

The Influence of Impressionism upon the Climate

Where, if not from the Impressionists, do we get those wonderful brown fogs that come creeping down our streets, blurring the gas-lamps and changing the houses into monstrous shadows? To whom, if not to them and their master, do we owe the lovely silver mists that brood over our river, and turn to faint forms of fading grace curved bridge and swaying barge? The extraordinary change that has taken place in the climate of London during the last ten years is entirely due to a particular school of art. You smile. Consider the matter from a scientific or a metaphysical point of view, and you will find that I am right. For what is Nature? Nature is no great mother who has borne us. She is our creation. It is in our brain that she quickens to life. Things are because we see them, and what we see, and how we see it, depends on the arts that have influenced us. To look at a thing is very different from seeing a thing. One does not see anything until one sees its beauty. Then, and then only, does it come into existence. At present, people see fogs, not because there are fogs, but because poets and painters have taught them the mysterious loveliness of such effects. There may have been fogs for centuries in London. I dare say there were. But no one saw them, and so we do not know anything about them. They did not exist until Art had invented them. Now, it must be admitted, fogs are carried to excess. They have become the mere mannerism of a clique, and the exaggerated realism of their method gives dull people bronchitis. Where the cultured catch an effect, the uncultured catch cold. And so, let us be humane, and invite Art to turn her wonderful eyes elsewhere. She has done so already, indeed. That white quivering sunlight that one sees now in France, with its strange blotches of mauve, and its restless violet shadows, is her latest fancy and, on the whole, Nature reproduces it quite admirably. Where she used to give us Corots and Daubignys, she gives us now exquisite Monets and entrancing Pissarros. Indeed there are moments, rare, it is true, but still to be observed from time to time, when

------

Source: From *The Decay of Lying*, 1889.

Nature becomes absolutely modern. Of course, she is not always to be relied upon. The fact is that she is in this unfortunate position. Art creates an incomparable and unique effect, and, having done so, passes on to other things. Nature, upon the other hand, forgetting that imitation can be made the sincerest form of insult, keeps on repeating this effect until we all become absolutely wearied of it. Nobody of any real culture, for instance, ever talks nowadays about the beauty of a sunset. Sunsets are quite old-fashioned. They belong to the time when Turner was the last note in Art. To admire them is a distinct sign of provincialism of temperament. Upon the other hand they go on.

III.

Consciousness
and Confusion

The prevailing positive message of the nineteenth century trumpeted human capacity, self-sufficiency, and progress. History appeared to be the story of man's increasing control over his environment and over himself. In a vulgar sense, the world was seen as a finite place with infinite possibilities, and this vision was translated into the politics, the economics, the literature, and the education of the time.

The Positivistic followers of Auguste Comte, of Taine, of Zola, thought it possible to explain and rule the world. But a reaction against them soon developed—in England, in Germany, in France—that stressed anti-Positivistic factors such as the unknown, the mysterious, and the wonderful. The first notes of this reaction were sounded in France by Baudelaire, Verlaine, Rimbaud, and Mallarmé; in England by Walter Pater and Herbert Spencer; in Germany by Schopenhauer and Wagner, who themselves harked back to earlier Romantics like Novalis and Hölderlin. Largely ignored at first, the reaction persisted and grew through the 1870s, parallelling the rise of Naturalism and Positivism, and incurring a running fire of dissent from those dominant views.

The great white hope of Positivistic doctrine had been that mystery could be destroyed and the unknown, the source of superstition and its attendant ills, be driven out—or, at least, back. Yet even in its heyday of the 1870s the strongholds of the unknown held fast and mystery soon began to reaffirm itself, partly because science had not kept the overweening promises that had been made on its behalf, and partly because men (and women perhaps even more) are seldom content with merely rational explanations. Herbert Spencer, who had long opposed the Comtian conception of a world totally open to positive investigation and understanding, published his treatise *First Principles* in 1862, the first part of which was devoted to establishing the notion of an *Unknowable* and the argument that the power behind the visible world must remain forever unfathomable for us. The 1870s saw the *First Principles* translated into German and French, and the Spencerian Unknowable became available on the continent to reinforce Hartmann's idea of the Unconscious—an all-powerful and intractable spirit that lay behind and was the prime mover of worldly reality—and also the pessimism of Schopenhauer that was beginning to make its mark in Germany and beyond. Schopenhauer's thought was not intentionally antiscientific, but his despair over the findings of science helped supplement the growing disillusion over its "failures." Meanwhile, the internal disagreements and rival theories of the scientists themselves spread doubt of the possibility of arriving at unique positive truths, and persuaded many that the wisest attitude would be an eclectic one in which the end was experience for its own sake rather than a certainty of knowledge unattainable in any case. And the eclecticism that seems to be so dominant in the intellectual world of the time is matched by a similar, though hardly deliberately thought out, tendency in the conspicuous consumption of the bourgeois home, crowded with a mixed bag of curios, souvenirs, antiques, *objets d'art,* and cumbrous plants. The collections in the homes of Emile Zola and Anatole France, in which a medieval carving neighbored a canopic jar, an antimacassar a piece of buhl, a suit of armor a Renaissance sword, a Turkish carpet a set of antlers, not to forget the prints and photographs in ornate frames, the wonderfully camouflaged objects impersonating something else (wax fruit, paper flowers, murderous oriental daggers for opening letters, stuffed bears on which to hang coat or umbrella)—homes such as these mirrored not only a contemporary taste dominant from Balmoral to Buxtehude, but a contemporary mind increasingly cluttered and confused, decreasingly able or willing to differentiate or order.

Pessimism, eclecticism, taste for mystery, disbelief in the value of effective action—which made for the rise of such "decadent" movements as the Hydropats, the Hirsutes, the Zutistes (Phooey-ists), and Jemenfoutistes (Couldntcarelessers)—all these tendencies contributed to a strong current of metaphysical idealism. Where the dominant preoccupation of the Realists had been to inventory and investigate human society, the new thinkers wanted to pierce through this superficial shell to the secrets of life. The former were interested only in objective reality, the latter were not a bit interested in surface reality and were inclined to deny the very possibility of being objective. "Objectivity," writes the *Symbolist* review, "is nothing but vain appearance, that I may vary or transform as I wish." This is the belief of many symbolists: reality, whether present or past, is either subjective or nonexistent.

If that is so, if scientist and sociologist merely clamber precariously over an insignificant exposed part of the iceberg of reality, then our true interpreters and guides must be the poets and the artists who dive below the surface of the unknown and bring back with them snatches of a more profound truth unattainable by "positive" methods. Since these new discoveries, these new experiences, are in the domain of the senses, the emotions, the realm in which we approach closer to truth than through surface experience, the question of communication has to be reconsidered. Particularly in Wagner's operas, the poets found reason to think that their statements might borrow from song an escort of words chosen for the sake of their tone, their sonority, their evocative possibilities, and their capacity through some mysterious connection (*"correspondence,"* or "analogy," as Baudelaire called it) to evoke the desired reaction by some apparently irrelevant allusion. "The most perfect creation of the poet," Wagner had written in 1860, "must be that which in its final conclusion would be perfect music." After 1885, the *Revue Wagnérienne,* devoted to this gospel, became one of the advance posts of the Symbolist movement.

It is tempting to see all this as a neo-Romantic reaction against the incumbent over-bold and boastful positive Realism. And yet the break between the two "movements" is not so clear: just as Realism grew out of certain tendencies in the Romantic quest for reality, so what we might for simplicity's sake call Symbolism grew out of the positive investigations of Realists and Naturalists. Man had set out to grasp the mechanism of the world and discover what made it tick. He started to take everything apart, and soon realized that his powers of observation, control them as you like, were not sufficient for the task. He started, then, to take apart his problems and the various objects of his research, the better to examine and depict them in detail. And, having gone as far as he thought he could in examining the objects of his sensations, he then turned back upon himself and began to examine these sensations for their own sake, and also the possibility of communicating them in suitable terms—that is, in a language of their own.

If reality is a collection of sensations—our own feelings about the things we see—then what can evoke it better, offer a readier access to its hidden worlds, than music? Thus it was that this vague and suggestive art form triumphed over every other—musicians putting verses to music, poets wanting their verses to be nothing but music, and even painters trying to be "musical" in their works. In 1849, already, one of Murger's Bohemians had worked on a great symphony on the influence of blue on the arts. Now the tables were turned and painters like Whistler, Gauguin, Cézanne, or Odilon Redon, fascinated by the influence and the possibilities of music, adopted its terminology and tried to adapt its techniques. Redon called himself a symphonist (sic) painter, Gauguin spoke of harmonies of line and color, which he called the music of painting, Cézanne painted an *Overture to Tannhäuser*, and Whistler, when his *Young Woman in White* was refused by the Salon, accepted the suggestion that *Symphony in White* would be a better name for it and henceforth composed on canvas symphonies, nocturnes, and variations, all possessed of the evocative quality of the music he so much admired.

With the approach, the scale of apprehension also changed: notes, syllables, vowels, dots of color, acquired a significance they never had. Whereas the Renaissance and Enlightenment had sought to see the world in perspective, as a whole, modern man tried to discover its secret in its details. The next step, Expressionism, should not surprise us: it is no more than a further advance toward subjectivism. For an Expressionist painter the object is simply a perception: it is a part of the perceiver, an aspect of his emotion, and thus varies from person to person and even within a person from moment to moment. The artist is no longer interested in the object, but in himself. He does not try to reproduce an impression, but rather the expression that he, the artist, confers, as it were, upon the object of his attention. Symbolism had sought to do much the same thing, but to this end it tried to borrow from nature itself the analogies that would enable it to express the relationship between subject and object, perceiver and perceived. For the Expressionist, every sensation, every emotion, becomes complicated and enriched by a whole mass of previous, until-then-forgotten sensations and experiences. Where the Impressionists tried to reproduce a surface perception, and the Symbolists the sensations this induced, the Expressionists sought to connect these sensations with our whole psychology. The difference between Expressionism and Symbolism may well be no more than a greater awareness of perception in one than in another; it remains a difference nevertheless. Basically, however, it is more profound: where the Symbolists appealed to intelligence as well as to sensitivity, the Expressionists, abandoning reflection and style, emphasized the spontaneity of the psychiatrist's couch.

Another description of the Expressionistic approach has been furnished by theologian Paul Tillich, in his essay on *The Religious Situation*.[1]

---

[1]New York: Meridian Books, 1956, p. 87.

> The individual forms of things were dissolved, not in favor of subjective impressions but in favor of objective metaphysical expression. The Abyss of Being was to be evoked in lines, colors and plastic forms. . . . Naturally the movement turned back to older, primitive and exotic forms in which the inner expressive force of reality was still to be found untamed.

It was natural, as Tillich says, for those seeking to approach reality and find "natural" means for its expression to turn to the art of primitive societies, which they believed free or at least freer of the hobbles that artificial civilization had imposed upon us. And, once again, *pace* Tillich, it seems to have been the French who led the way, with Cézanne, with the *Fauves*—the wild beasts, and the experimental Cubists grouped round Picasso and Braque. There is, here, an attempt (as all this great disintegrating movement is itself) to reconstitute a new order upon a more complete vision and control of reality. The Cubists take the classic model of reality to pieces, displace its elements, accentuate some to the point of caricature while leaving others out, and hope thereby to provide a truer presentation of their object than traditional methods can. But not of "the object" only: Cézanne attempts to seize as closely, as directly, as possible his own sense-impression of what he beholds, his "consciousness"—and in this he is at one with poets like Mallarmé and musicians like Debussy in trying to render an inner experience or subjective feeling rather than some "objective" outer perception. Beginning with Cézanne, painting is interested mainly in those particles of nature that the painter "feels" in his own way. It is the artist who creates the interest, the meaning, the value of his subject, and the interaction between the two in a subjective universe is vastly emphasized. Once upon a time, the problem of art was the relationship between humans as a race and nature as a stable reality. Since nature is no longer stable, and since its interpreters—men and women—are subjective, fluctuating forces, this link no longer holds. An era that disregards established principles, that discovers new laws, themselves all the time subject to modification, must fall back on a view of reality that will be as we have seen, subjective, eclectic, dialectic, and eventually purely pragmatic.

This is exactly what we find in every art form represented below. The dynamic force that runs like molten metal through Futuristic veins, the absurdity, anger, and dismay of the Dada and Surrealistic world, are evident enough, and it is not difficult to connect these manifestations with their times. And yet, in spite of this, henceforth art was no longer the expression of society as it had been, to the extent it had been, in the days of Rubens, of Poussin, of Chardin, or of Courbet: it became the expression of the artist as an individual. And while it goes without saying that the artist is the creature of his time, the multiplicity of reactions to a same experience in time, reflects the great discovery that a shared situation does not ensure a shared experience, and bears witness to the vast variety of views, visions, and responses that the new ideas caused to thrive side by side on the same muck-heap.

Eclecticism and Aestheticism

Inherent in the Romantic view of reality and experience as manifold is the idea that the wise will seek to sample as many facets of them, to drink from as many different sources, as possible. If there are many truths and many sources of pleasure, it is important to taste them all. What matters now is no longer the one philosophy, work of art, or situation we encounter—for it is one of many—but our experience of it, which is unique and hence invested with a supreme value of its own. In the absence of an ultimate objective reality, the subjective experience assumes ultimate importance. From this point of view, art for art's sake meant little more than experience for experience's sake, a self-consciously subjective affirmation that appeared shocking largely because it was uttered in an age not yet aware of its underlying relativism and eclecticism.

But the knowledge that no experience is ultimate could also lead to a different reaction, the decadent aestheticism of *Axel's Castle,* in which the thought that everything deceives in the end leads to refusal of experience, to a falling back on imagination, which alone cannot disappoint, to the decision—since illusion fulfilled must end in disillusion—to avoid fulfillment and concentrate entirely on the safer realms of illusion alone. As to life, says Villiers de l'Isle Adam's *Axel* (1890): "Our servants will see to that for us."

Pater

Walter Horatio Pater (1839–1894) became a fellow of Brasenose College, Oxford, in 1864 and, with his special interest in the visual arts, soon began to influence his undergraduates and the readers of the literary and philosophical essays he contributed to London periodicals. First under the influence of Ruskin, then of the German Winckelmann, he developed an eclectic philosophy of taste that, in its irrationalism, its aestheticism, its cult of genius and of the elite, was highly redolent of an earlier Romantic spirit.

The essay on Coleridge, first written in 1865, and republished in 1889 in *Appreciations: With an Essay on Style,* appears as a bridge between the *Weltschmerz* of earlier

Romantic generations and the decadent *ennui* of the *fin de siècle*. They all sought to express themselves in terms, still uncertain in Pater's own time as in Gautier's, that we now call Symbolist; ideas whose basis for the coming generation Baudelaire was just engaged in laying, across the Channel, and which Pater himself sought to explore further in the "Conclusion" to his *Studies in the History of the Renaissance* (1868).

Concerning that essay, which follows the one on Coleridge (*Art for Art's Sake,* p. 214), it might be worth remarking that another (and better known) book of the time, Jacob Burckhardt's *Civilization of the Renaissance in Italy* (1860), presented the Italian Renaissance as a work of art. The state itself appears as an artistic creation and is so described in the title of Burckhardt's first chapter. The great artists are men of their time, forging their cities, their works, and their own lives in the fires of their individual genius. To the Swiss historian, the Italian Renaissance is dominated by *beauty:* an awareness of beauty, a quest for beauty, an elevation of beauty as an ultimate and admirable value. Machiavelli's admiration for Cesare Borgia's skill at Sinigaglia is matched by Burckhardt's admiration of a tyrant's skill in checkmating his opponents. To this pessimistic Goethean, the Renaissance marks the accession, first of Italy, then of Europe, to a new life, vivid and free, but above all individualistic. Man turns to antiquity the better to realize himself in the present, but always in beauty, for beauty is the *nec plus ultra* of values and standards. Such a world, whose heroes all "burn always with this hard, gemlike flame," comes close to that of Pater. The values of the Basel patrician approached those of the Oxford don.

There is about Pater's prose a highly intellectual and philosophical quality, but nothing very clear-cut: it is subtle, delicate, and very highly polished. The eclectic, hedonistic affirmation of decadence before its time now appears more relevant in our age than in its own.

Coleridge

Forms of intellectual and spiritual culture sometimes exercise their subtlest and most artful charm when life is already passing from them. Searching and irresistible as are the changes of the human spirit on its way to perfection, there is yet so much elasticity of temper that what must pass away sooner or later is not disengaged all at once, even from the highest order of minds. Nature, which by one law of development evolves ideas, hypotheses, modes of inward life, and represses them in turn, has in this way provided that the earlier growth should propel its fibres into the later, and so transmit the whole of its forces in an unbroken continuity of life. Then comes the spectacle of the reserve of the elder generation exquisitely refined by the antagonism of the new. That current of new life chastens them while they contend against it. Weaker minds fail to perceive the change: the clearest minds abandon

---

Source: From *Appreciations: With an Essay on Style,* 1889.

themselves to it. To feel the change everywhere, yet not abandon oneself to it, is a situation of difficulty and contention. Communicating, in this way, to the passing stage of culture, the charm of what is chastened, high-strung, athletic, they yet detach the highest minds from the past, by pressing home its difficulties and finally proving it impossible. Such has been the charm of many leaders of lost causes in philosophy and in religion. It is the special charm of Coleridge, in connexion with those older methods of philosophic inquiry, over which the empirical philosophy of our day has triumphed.

Modern thought is distinguished from ancient by its cultivation of the "relative" spirit in place of the "absolute." Ancient philosophy sought to arrest every object in an eternal outline, to fix thought in a necessary formula, and the varieties of life in a classification by "kinds," or genera. To the modern spirit nothing is, or can be rightly known, except relatively and under conditions. The philosophical conception of the relative has been developed in modern times through the influence of the sciences of observation. Those sciences reveal types of life evanescing into each other by inexpressible refinements of change. Things pass into their opposites by accumulation of undefinable quantities. The growth of those sciences consists in a continual analysis of facts of rough and general observation into groups of facts more precise and minute. The faculty for truth is recognized as a power of distinguishing and fixing delicate and fugitive detail. The moral world is ever in contact with the physical, and the relative spirit has invaded moral philosophy from the ground of the inductive sciences. There it has started a new analysis of the relations of body and mind, good and evil, freedom and necessity. Hard and abstract moralities are yielding to a more exact estimate of the subtlety and complexity of our life. Always, as an organism increases in perfection, the conditions of its life become more complex. Man is the most complex of the products of nature. Character merges into temperament: the nervous system refines itself into intellect. Man's physical organism is played upon not only by the physical conditions about it, but by remote laws of inheritance, the vibration of long-past acts reaching him in the midst of the new order of things in which he lives. When we have estimated these conditions, he is still not yet simple and isolated; for the mind of the race, the character of the age, sway him this way or that through the medium of language and current ideas. It seems as if the most opposite statements about him were alike true: he is so receptive, all the influences of nature and of society ceaselessly playing upon him, so that every hour in his life is unique, changed altogether by a stray word, or glance, or touch. It is the truth of these relations that experience gives us, not the truth of eternal outlines ascertained once for all, but a world of fine gradations and subtly linked conditions, shifting intricately as we ourselves change—and bids us, by a constant clearing of the organs of observation and perfecting of analysis, to make what we can of these. To the intellect, the critical spirit, just these subtleties of effect are more precious than anything else. What is lost in precision of form is gained in intricacy of expression. It is no vague scholastic abstraction that will satisfy the speculative instinct in our modern minds. Who would change the colour or curve of a rose-leaf for that colourless, formless, intangible, being Plato put so high? For the true illustration of the speculative temper is not the Hindoo mystic, lost to sense, understanding, individuality, but one such as Goethe, to whom every moment of life brought its contribution of experimental, individual knowledge; by whom no touch of the world of form, colour, and passion was disregarded.

Now the literary life of Coleridge was a disinterested struggle against the relative spirit. With a strong native bent towards the tracking of all questions, critical or practical, to first principles, he is ever restlessly scheming to "apprehend the absolute," to affirm it effectively, to get it acknowledged. It was an effort, surely, an effort of sickly thought, that saddened his mind, and limited the operation of his unique poetic gift.

So what the reader of our own generation will least find in Coleridge's prose writings is the excitement of the literary sense. And yet, in those grey volumes, we have the larger part of the production of one who made way ever by a charm, the charm of voice, of aspect, of language, above all by the intellectual charm of new, moving, luminous ideas. Perhaps the chief offence in Coleridge is an excess of seriousness, a seriousness arising not from any moral principle, but from a misconception of the perfect manner. There is a certain shade of unconcern, the perfect manner of the eighteenth century, which may be thought to mark complete culture in the handling of abstract questions. The humanist, the possessor of that complete culture, does not "weep" over the failure of "a theory of the quantification of the predicate," nor "shriek" over the fall of a philosophical formula. A kind of humour is, in truth, one of the conditions of the just mental attitude, in the criticism of by-past stages of thought. Humanity cannot afford to be too serious about them, any more than a man of good sense can afford to be too serious in looking back upon his own childhood. Plato, whom Coleridge claims as the first of his spiritual ancestors, Plato, as we remember him, a true humanist, holds his theories lightly, glances with a somewhat blithe and naive inconsequence from one view to another, not anticipating the burden of importance "views" will one day have for men. In reading him one feels how lately it was that Croesus thought it a paradox to say that external prosperity was not necessarily happiness. But on Coleridge lies the whole weight of the sad reflection that has since come into the world, with which for us the air is full, which the "children in the marketplace" repeat to each other. His very language is forced and broken lest some saving formula should be lost—distinctities, enucleation, pentad of operative Christianity; he has a whole armoury of these terms, and expects to turn the tide of human thought by fixing the sense of such expressions as "reason," "understanding," "idea." Again, he lacks the jealousy of a true artist in excluding all associations that have no colour, or charm, or gladness in them; and everywhere allows the impress of a somewhat inferior theological literature.

"I was driven from life in motion to life in thought and sensation": so Coleridge sums up his childhood, with its delicacy, its sensitiveness, and passion. But at twenty-five he was exercising a wonderful charm, and had already defined for himself his peculiar line of intellectual activity. He had an odd, attractive gift of conversation, or rather of monologue, as Madame de Staël observed of him, full of bizarreries, with the rapid alternations of a dream, and here or there an unexpected summons into a world strange to the hearer, abounding in images drawn from a sort of divided imperfect life, the consciousness of the opium-eater, as of one to whom the external world penetrated only in part, and, blent with all this, passages of deep obscurity, precious, if at all, only for their musical cadence, echoes in Coleridge of the eloquence of those older English writers of whom he was so ardent a lover. And all through this brilliant early manhood we may discern the power of the "Asiatic" temperament, of that voluptuousness, which is connected perhaps with his appreciation of the intimacy, the almost mystical communion of touch, between nature and man. "I am much better," he writes, "and my new and tender health is all over me like a voluptuous feeling." And whatever fame, or charm, or life-inspiring gift he has had as a speculative thinker, is the vibration of the interest he excited then, the propulsion into years which clouded his early promise of that first buoyant, irresistible self-assertion. So great is even the indirect power of a sincere effort towards the ideal life, of even a temporary escape of the spirit from routine.

In 1798 he visited Germany, then, the only half-known, "promised land," of the metaphysical, the "absolute," philosophy. A beautiful fragment of this period remains, describing a spring excursion to the Bröcken. His excitement still vibrates in it. Love, all joyful states of mind, are self-expressive: they loosen the tongue, they fill the thoughts with sensuous images, they harmonise one with the world of sight. We hear of the "rich graciousness and courtesy" of Coleridge's manner, of the white and delicate skin, the abundant black hair, the full, almost animal lips—that whole physiognomy of the dreamer, already touched with narcotism. One says, of the beginning of one of his Unitarian sermons: "His voice rose like a stream of rich, distilled perfumes"; another, "He talks like an angel, and does—nothing!"

The *Aids to Reflection, The Friend, The Biographia Literaria:* those books came from one whose vocation was in the world of the imagination, the theory and practice of poetry. And yet, perhaps, of all books that have been influential in modern times, they are furthest from artistic form—bundles of notes; the original matter inseparably mixed up with that borrowed from others; the whole, just that mere preparation for an artistic effect which the finished literary artist would be careful one day to destroy. Here, again, we have a trait profoundly characteristic of Coleridge. He sometimes attempts to reduce a phase of thought, subtle and exquisite, to conditions too rough for it. He uses a purely speculative gift for direct moral edification. Scientific truth is a thing fugitive, relative, full of fine gradations: he tries to fix it in absolute formulas. The *Aids to Reflection, The Friend,* are efforts to propagate the volatile spirit of conversation into the less ethereal fabric of a written book; and it is only here or there that the poorer matter becomes vibrant, is really lifted by the spirit.

De Quincey said of him that "he wanted better bread than can be made with wheat": Lamb, that from childhood he had "hungered for eternity." Yet the faintness, the continuous dissolution, whatever its cause, which soon supplanted the buoyancy of his first wonderful years, had its own consumptive refinements, and even brought, as to the "Beautiful Soul" in *Wilhelm Meister,* a faint religious ecstasy—that "singing in the sails" which is not of the breeze. Here again is one of his occasional notes:—

"In looking at objects of nature while I am thinking, as at yonder moon, dim-glimmering through the window-pane, I seem rather to be seeking, as it were asking, a symbolical language for something within me, that already and for ever exists, than observing anything new. Even when the latter is the case, yet still I have always an obscure feeling, as if that new phenomenon were the dim awaking of a forgotten or hidden truth of my inner nature. While I was preparing the pen to make this remark, I lost the train of thought which had led me to it."

The student of empirical science asks, Are absolute principles attainable? What are the limits of knowledge? The answer he receives from science itself is not ambiguous. What the moralist asks is, Shall we gain or lose by surrendering human life to the relative spirit? Experience answers that the dominant tendency of life is to turn ascertained truth into a dead letter, to make us all the phlegmatic servants of routine. The relative spirit, by its constant dwelling on the more fugitive conditions or circumstances of things, breaking through a thousand rough and brutal classifications, and giving elasticity to inflexible principles, begets an intellectual fitness of which the ethical result is a delicate and tender justice in the criticism of human life. Who would gain more than Coleridge by criticism in such a spirit? We know how his life has appeared when judged by absolute standards. We see him trying to "apprehend the absolute," to stereotype forms of faith and philosophy, to attain, as he says, "fixed principles" in politics, morals, and religion, to fix one mode of life as the essence of life, refusing to see the parts as parts only; and all the time his own pathetic history pleads for a more elastic moral philosophy than his, and cries out against every formula less living and flexible than life itself.

"From his childhood he hungered for eternity." There, after all, is the incontestable claim of Coleridge. The perfect flower of any elementary type of life must always be precious to humanity, and Coleridge is a true flower of the *ennuyé*, of the type of René. More than Childe Harold, more than Werther, more than René himself, Coleridge, by what he did, what he was, and what he failed to do, represents that inexhaustible discontent, languor, and homesickness, that endless regret, the chords of which ring all through our modern literature. It is to the romantic element in literature that those qualities belong. One day, perhaps, we may come to forget the distant horizon, with full knowledge of the situation, to be content with "what is here and now"; and herein is the essence of classical feeling. But by us of the present moment, certainly—by us for whom the Greek spirit, with its engaging naturalness, simple, chastened, debonair . . . is itself the Sangrail of an endless pilgrimage, Coleridge, with his passion for the absolute, for something fixed where all is moving, his faintness, his broken memory, his intellectual disquiet, may still be ranked among the interpreters of one of the constituent elements of our life.

Art for Art's Sake—The Aesthetic Approach

To regard all things and principles of things as inconstant modes of fashions has more and more become the tendency of modern thought. Let us begin with that which is without—our physical life. Fix upon it in one of its more exquisite intervals, the moment, for instance, of delicious recoil from the flood of water in summer heat. What is the whole physical life in that moment but a combination of natural elements to which science gives their names? But those elements, phosphorus and lime and delicate fibres, are present not in the human body alone: we detect them in places most remote from it. Our physical life is a perpetual motion of them—the passage of the blood, the waste and repairing of lenses of the eye, the modification of the tissues of the brain under every ray of light and sound—processes which science

Source: From *Studies in the History of the Renaissance,* Conclusion, 1868.

reduces to simpler and more elementary forces. Like the elements of which we are composed, the action of these forces extends beyond us: it rusts iron and ripens corn. Far out on every side of us those elements are broadcast, driven in many currents; and birth and gesture and death and the springing of violets from the grave are but a few out of ten thousand resultant combinations. That clear, perpetual outline of face and limb is but an image of ours, under which we group them—a design in a web, the actual threads of which pass out beyond it. This at least of flame-like our life has, that it is but the concurrence, renewed from moment to moment, of forces parting sooner or later on their ways.

Or, if we begin with the inward world of thought and feeling, the whirlpool is still more rapid, the flame more eager and devouring. There it is no longer the gradual darkening of the eye, the gradual fading of colour from the wall—movements of the shore-side, where the water flows down indeed, though in apparent rest—but the race of the mid-stream, a drift of momentary acts of sight and passion and thought. At first sight experience seems to bury us under a flood of external objects, pressing upon us with a sharp and importunate reality, calling us out of ourselves in a thousand forms of action. But when reflexion begins to play upon those objects, they are dissipated under its influence; the cohesive force seems suspended like some trick of magic; each object is loosed into a group of impressions—colour, odour, texture—in the mind of the observer. And if we continue to dwell in thought on this world, not of objects in the solidarity with which language invests them, but of impressions, unstable, flickering, inconsistent, which burn and are extinguished with our consciousness of them, it contracts still further: the whole scope of observation is dwarfed into the narrow chamber of the individual mind. Experience, already reduced to a group of impressions, is ringed round for each one of us by that thick wall of personality through which no real voice has ever pierced on its way to us, or from us to that which we can only conjecture to be without. Every one of those impressions is the impression of the individual in his isolation, each mind keeping as a solitary prisoner its own dream of a world. Analysis goes a step further still, and assures us that those impressions of the individual mind to which, for each one of us, experience dwindles down, are in perpetual flight; that each of them is limited by time, and that as time is infinitely divisible, each of them is infinitely divisible also; all that is actual in it being a single moment, gone while we try to apprehend it, of which it may ever be more truly said that it has ceased to be than that it is. To such a tremulous wisp constantly re-forming itself on the stream, to a single sharp impression, with a sense in it, a relic more or less fleeting of such moments gone by, what is real in our life fines itself down. It is with this movement, with the passage and dissolution of impressions, images, sensations, that analysis leaves off—that continual vanishing away, that strange, perpetual weaving and unweaving of ourselves.

Philosophiren, says Novalis, *ist dephlegmatisiren, vivificiren.* The service of philosophy, of speculative culture, towards the human spirit, is to rouse, to startle it to a life of constant and eager observation. Every moment some form grows perfect in hand or face; some tone on the hills or the sea is choicer than the rest; some mood of passion or insight or intellectual excitement is irresistibly real and attractive to us,—for that moment only. Not the fruit of experience, but experience itself, is the end. A counted number of pulses only is given to us of a variegated, dramatic life. How may we see in them all that is to be seen in them by the finest senses? How shall we pass most swiftly from point to point, and be present always at the focus where the greatest number of vital forces unite in their purest energy?

To burn always with this hard, gemlike flame, to maintain this ecstasy, is success in life. In a sense it might even be said that our failure is to form habits: for, after all, habit is relative to a stereotyped world, and meantime it is only the roughness of the eye that makes any two persons, things, situations, seem alike. While all melts under our feet, we may well grasp at any exquisite passion, or any contribution to knowledge that seems by a lifted horizon to set the spirit free for a moment, or any stirring of the senses, strange dyes, strange colours, and curious odours, or work of the artist's hands, or the face of one's friend. Not to discriminate every moment some passionate attitude in those about us, and in the very brilliancy of their gifts some tragic dividing of forces on their ways, is, on this short day of frost and sun, to sleep before evening. With this sense of the splendour of our experience and of its awful brevity, gathering all we are into one desperate effort to see and touch, we shall hardly have time to make theories about the things we see and touch. What we have to do is to be for ever curiously testing new opinions and courting new impressions, never acquiescing in a facile orthodoxy of Comte, or of Hegel, or of our own. Philosophical theories or ideas, as points of view, instruments of criticism, may help us to gather up what might otherwise pass unregarded by us. "Philosophy is the microscope of thought." The theory or idea or system which requires of us the sacrifice of any part of this experience, in consideration of some interest into which we cannot enter, or some abstract theory we have not identified with ourselves, or of what is only conventional, has no real claim upon us.

One of the most beautiful passages of Rousseau is that in the sixth book of the *Confessions,* where he describes the awakening in him of the literary sense. An undefinable taint of death had clung always about him, and now in early manhood he believed himself smitten by mortal disease. He asked himself how he might make as much as possible of the interval that remained;

and he was not blessed by anything in his previous life when he decided that it must be by intellectual excitement, which he found just then in the clear, fresh writings of Voltaire. Well! we are all *condamnés* as Victor Hugo says: we are all under sentence of death but with a sort of indefinite reprieve—*les hommes sont tous condamnés à mort avec des sursis indéfinis:* we have an interval, and then our place knows us no more. Some spend this interval in listlessness, some in high passions, the wisest, at least among "the children of this world," in art and song. For our one chance lies in expanding that interval, in getting as many pulsations as possible into the given time. Great passions may give us this quickened sense of life, ecstasy and sorrow of love, the various forms of enthusiastic activity, disinterested or otherwise, which come naturally to many of us. Only be sure it is passion—that it does yield you this fruit of a quickened, multiplied consciousness. Of such wisdom, the poetic passion, the desire of beauty, the love of art for its own sake, has most. For art comes to you proposing frankly to give nothing but the highest quality to your moments as they pass, and simply for those moments' sake.

1868

Wilde

Preface to *The Picture of Dorian Gray*[1]

The artist is the creator of beautiful things.

To reveal art and conceal the artist is art's aim. The critic is he who can translate into another manner or a new material his impression of beautiful things.

The highest, as the lowest, form of criticism is a mode of autobiography.

Those who find ugly meanings in beautiful things are corrupt without being charming. This is a fault.

Those who find beautiful meanings in beautiful things are cultivated. For these there is hope.

They are the elect to whom beautiful things mean only Beauty.

There is no such thing as a moral or an immoral book. Books are well written or badly written. That is all.

The nineteenth-century dislike of Realism is the rage of Caliban seeing his own face in a glass.

---

[1] 1890.

The nineteenth-century dislike of Romanticism is the rage of Caliban not seeing his own face in a glass.

The moral life of man forms part of the subject-matter of the artist, but the morality of art consists in the perfect use of an imperfect medium. No artist desires to prove anything. Even things that are true can be proved.

No artist has ethical sympathies. An ethical sympathy in an artist is an unpardonable mannerism of style.

No artist is ever morbid. The artist can express everything.

Thought and language are to the artist instruments of art.

Vice and virtue are to the artist materials for art.

From the point of view of form, the type of all the arts is the art of the musician. From the point of view of feeling, the actor's craft is the type.

All art is at once surface and symbol.

Those who go beneath the surface do so at their peril.

Those who read the symbol do so at their peril.

It is the spectator and not life that art really mirrors.

Diversity of opinion about a work of art shows that the work is new, complex, and vital.

When critics disagree, the artist is in accord with himself.

We can forgive a man for making a useful thing as long as he does not admire it. The only excuse for making a useless thing is that one admires it intensely.

All art is quite useless.

Oscar Wilde.

Symbolism

The disintegrating possibilities of the Impressionistic approach have already been mentioned. Looking back, it seems clear how the most apparently Positivistic factors of the time contributed to the rise of a new idealism, not only by their failures, but by their perfection too. Thus photography, when it provided the public with a cheap substitute for painting or sculpture, helped change the direction or, at least, the reigning emphasis of the plastic arts by minimizing the need for those illustrations that the camera could henceforth provide more quickly and cheaply, and concentrating the artist's interest increasingly upon interpretation and its problems.

Art, it soon was argued, should not try to imitate nature, but to discover the hidden meaning of things that are to the artist the signs, the symbols, of a deeper reality. Thus, the artist-explorer inquires into the hidden meaning of things and then tries to suggest what he finds to others. But he cannot do this any longer by objective presentation. Before the ideas and sensations he has discerned can be communicated, they must be transposed into terms that will reach the public's inner ear or eye, its heart not its head. The artist must, in the words of Delacroix, seek to build a bridge between his heart and that of his listeners or his beholders.

Throughout the nineteenth century these ideas spread through Germany, England, and France. By the time Moréas published his *Manifesto,* poets like Baudelaire, Verlaine, Rimbaud, painters like Puvis de Chavannes, Gustave Moreau, Odilon Redon, had produced all, or much, of their work. In opposition to the would-be objective and scientific Naturalist theories these men proposed a subjective and poetic point of view, a return to more openly Romantic values, the artist playing the part of a magician, delving into the unconscious that French and German scientists like Hartmann and Charcot were exploring about this time, and exalting its importance. Once again, the connection between scientific and artistic activities is striking. In 1885, an aspiring Viennese physician makes his first trip to Paris, there to study under the great neurologist, J. M. Charcot. Sigmund Freud would soon be thirty years old. In Glasgow, the anthropologist James Frazer, only two years older, is at this time preparing his majestic *Golden Bough* (published in 1890), in which he will reveal the connection between the magic and the poetic approach, each of which uses analogy for its own ends.[1]

What this could mean for the plastic arts appeared in 1888, when Emile Bernard, whose ideas would seriously influence Gauguin—and through Gauguin the whole of modern art—decided that since the idea is the real form of things in the imagination, the painter should paint not things but the idea of a thing in the imagination, and this idea itself simplified to its essentials and divested of all

---

[1]That very same year (1885), the unknown and unsuccessful son of a Dutch provincial minister was taking music lessons from an Eindhoven organist. Vincent van Gogh liked to compare painting and music, and tried to establish some connection between them. As his lessons went on, the haggard young man continued to seek Baudelairian parallels between notes, movements, and colors. But the organist thought him mad and, frightened, broke off the lessons. Three years later, we find van Gogh writing from Arles to his brother Theo that he wants to paint so that "everyone with eyes to see can understand," and that he thinks he can use color by itself to express some of the things he wants to convey—color, but also symbols: "To express the feelings of two lovers by a marriage of two complementary colors, their mixture and their oppositions, the mysterious vibrations of tones in each other's proximity. To express the thought behind a brow by the radiance of a bright tone against a dark ground. To express hope by some star, the ardour of a being by the radiance of a setting sun. . . ."

insignificant details. Memory, said Bernard, does not retain everything: it retains only that which it finds striking. Thus, if you paint from memory instead of from objects before your eyes, or, at least, if you let those objects filter through your imagination and then paint the result, you can rid yourself of the useless complication of shapes and shades. All you will get is a schematic presentation: "all lines back to their geometric architecture, all shades back to the primary colors of the prismatic palette." In search of simplification, one sought the origins of everything, in pure color, and in geometry that provided "the typical form of all objective forms."

This is how line and color became means of poetic allusion that enabled a Gauguin to suggest ideas and feelings pictorially and, as he put it, "clothe the idea in a form perceptible to the senses." In Germany, Wagner had long since revived the *leitmotif* as a constant and significant reminder, the musical representation and symbol, of a person or theme. In France, both Baudelaire and Rimbaud had long explored the same territory and Rimbaud had endowed vowels with color: "A black, E white, I red, O blue, U green.—I regulated the form and movement of every consonant and, with indistinctive rhythms, flattered myself that I had invented a poetical language accessible, sooner or later, to every sense." Soon after Moréas's *Symbolist Manifesto,* the connection between the ends of "decadent" poets and musicians and "Post-Impressionistic" painters became clear. They all sought a language that could express and suggest feelings that they held to be as real and more significant than the objective surface realities that had concerned their predecessors. "Drop a syllable into a state of pure consciousness," as Herbert Read once wrote, "and listen for the reverberations."

Imagination and simplification: understanding these, does one really need much more to anticipate the artistic developments of the following years? Once the artist resorts to symbols to express his perceptions and his imagination in the widest sense, there is nothing to prevent the passage from one symbol to another in search of further and more effective simplification, nothing to prevent stretching the association between origin and effect, experience and end-product, to its breaking point.

Baudelaire

Charles Baudelaire (1821–1867) early received a solid Catholic education and an initiation into the delights of the plastic arts. The one and the other haunted him for the rest of his life, a life soon afflicted with the chronic want and ill health that eventually brought him down at the age of 46. Untiring in his analysis of life and self, he soon became convinced that everything had a spiritual meaning, that every object, every gesture, every sound, was the symbol of a universal analogy—"things having always expressed themselves by a reciprocal analogy since the day when God proffered the world as a complex and indivisible totality."

Between 1846 and the year of his death, Baudelaire's ideas were embraced by a literary and artistic elite. His "journalism," his essays, lectures, and reviews, would furnish the aesthetics, the basic attitudes, of Symbolism. By 1885, Léon Daudet tells us, all the older high-school boys knew Baudelaire by heart: "he affected all educated French youth, boys and girls."

The sonnet *"Correspondances"* ("Analogies") reflects these views. It emphasizes, as Baudelaire always tried to do, the spiritual nature of reality and the responsibility of poets to be seers, driving through external appearances and communicating the deeper realities and connections that externals merely cover or, at best, represent at second hand.

Correspondances

La Nature est un temple où de vivants pilliers
Laissent parfois sortir de confuses paroles;
L'homme y passe à travers des forêts de symboles
Qui l'observent avec des regards familiers.

Comme de longs échos qui de loin se confondent
Dans une ténébreuse et profonde unité,
Vaste comme la nuit et comme la clarté,
Les parfums, les couleurs et les sons se répondent.

Il est des parfums frais comme des chairs d'enfants,
Doux comme les hautbois, verts comme les prairies;
Et d'autres, corrompus, riches et triomphants,

Analogies

A temple is nature wherein living columns
Sometimes let slip a confused utterance;
Man crosses it, with great hosts of symbols
Casting upon him a familiar glance.

Like some long echo by distance confused,
In concord obscure and profound,
Vast as the night, vast as the light,
Conversing perfumes and colors and sounds all abound.

There are perfumes as fresh as the flesh of a child,
Sweet as the oboes, green as the meadows;
And others corrupt, triumphant and rich,

Source: From *Les Fleurs du Mal*, 1857. Translated by Eugen Weber.

Ayant l'expansion des choses infinies,	Opening out like infinite things,
Comme l'ambre, le musc, le benjoin et l'encens,	Like amber, like musk, benjamin, incense
Qui chantent les transports de l'esprit et des sens.	Singing the raptures of spirit and senses.

Moréas

Jean Moréas (1856–1910) was born in Athens; he changed his given name, Yannis Papadiamantopulos, when he settled in Paris in 1879. The manifesto he published in the September 18, 1886, issue of *Le Figaro* explained that Symbolist poetry seeks to clothe the idea in a perceptible form that would not, however, be an end in itself. He and his friends had learned from Baudelaire that reality could best be apprehended by intuition rather than reason, and could best be expressed not by description but by allusion and suggestion.

Their reaction against scientific Positivism and its insistence on externals carried the Symbolists to stress subjective perception, the inner world, and its intimate association through the individual sensitiveness with a material universe now endowed with a life of its own.

A Literary Manifesto

These last two years, the Paris press has taken a great deal of interest in a school of poets and prose-writers called "decadents." M. Jean Moréas, one of the best known among these literary revolutionaries, has, at our request formulated for our readers the fundamental principles of the new artistic expression.

Symbolism

Like all the arts, literature is subject to evolution: a cyclical evolution with strictly determined turns, complicated by divers modifications brought about by the passage of time and the change of its surroundings. It would be superfluous to point out that each new evolutionary phase of the art corresponds exactly to the senile decrepitude, the unavoidable end, of the imme-

---

Source: From *Le Figaro*, September 18, 1886. Translated by Eugen Weber.

diately preceding school. Two examples will suffice: Ronsard triumphs over the impotence of Marot's last imitators,[1] Romanticism unfolds its banners over the classical ruins ill defended by Casmir Delavigne and Etienne de Jouy. The fact is that every expression of art tends fatally to become impoverished and outworn; from one copy to another, from one imitation to another, that which was once full of sap and freshness becomes dry and gnarled; that which was spontaneous and fresh becomes trite and commonplace.

Thus, Romanticism, after it had tumultuously tolled the bell of rebellion, after it had had its days of battle and glory, lost its power and its grace, abandoned its heroic daring, became sedate, skeptical, and replete with common sense. It sought a fallacious revival in the honorable and petty attempts of the Parnassian poets, and then, at last, like a monarch fallen into second childhood, it allowed itself to be deposed by Naturalism—to which one cannot seriously grant more than the value of a protest, legitimate but ill advised, against the insipidities of some then-fashionable novelists.

A new form of artistic expression was therefore awaited, necessary, inevitable. Long in the making, it has now broken forth and all the anodyne jokes of would-be funny newspapermen, all the discomfort of grave critics, all the ill-humor of a public caught short in its sheeplike indifference, all these merely affirm more strongly every day the vitality of the present evolution of French literature, the evolution which hasty judges have, by some incomprehensible contradiction in terms, labeled decadent. Note however that decadent literatures have always shown themselves to be essentially tough, stringy, timorous, and servile: all the tragedies of Voltaire, for instance, are tarred with the brush of decadence. Yet what can one reproach, what does one reproach, the new school? The abuse of pomp, the strangeness of its metaphors, a new vocabulary in which harmonies combine with lines and colors: characteristics of every *renaissance*.

We have already suggested the title of *Symbolism* as one that can most reasonably describe the present tendency of the creative spirit in art. This title can be maintained.

It was said at the beginning of this article that the evolutions of art present a cyclic character extremely complicated by divergencies; thus, to follow the exact filiation of the new school it is necessary to return to certain poems of Alfred de Vigny, to Shakespeare, to the mystics, and even further. These questions would need a volume of comment; so let us simply say that

---

[1]The poems of Clément Marot (1496–1585) were pleasantly discursive, often rondeaus or madrigals. Pierre de Ronsard (1524–1585) led poets of the Pléïade, which broke with medieval traditions in order to adopt a new classical, humanistic, and individualistic tone.

Baudelaire should be considered as the true forerunner of the present movement; M. Stéphane Malarmé endowed it with a sense of mystery, and the ineffable M. Paul Verlaine broke in its honor the cruel bonds of verses which the prestigious fingers of M. Théodore de Banville had previously softened. However, the *Supreme Enchantment* is not yet consumed: a jealous and stubborn task awaits the newcomers.

Opposed to "teaching, declamation, false sensibility, objective description," symbolic poetry seeks to clothe the Idea in a perceptible form which, nevertheless, would not be an end in itself; rather, while serving to express the idea, it would remain subject to it. The Idea, in its turn, must not let itself be deprived of the sumptuous robes of external analogies; for the essential character of symbolic art consists in never going so far as to conceive the Idea in itself. Thus, in this art, the depiction of nature, the actions of men, all the concrete phenomena, could not show themselves as such: they are concrete appearances whose purpose is to represent their esoteric affinities with primordial Ideas.

There is nothing surprising about the indictments raised against such an esthetic approach by readers who take their reading in fits and starts. But what is one to do about them? The *Pythics* of Pindarus, the *Hamlet* of Shakespeare, the *Vita Nuova* of Dante, the *Second Faust* of Goethe, Flaubert's *Temptation of Saint Anthony,* were they not also taxed with ambiguity?

For the exact translation of its synthesis, Symbolism needs an archetypal and complex style: unpolluted words, firm periods to act as buttresses and alternate with others of undulating faintness, the significant pleonasm, the mysterious ellipsis, the suspended anacoluthe, every trope daring and multiform; lastly, good French—restored and modernized—the good, brisk, luxuriant French of the days before Vaugelas and Boileau-Despréaux,[2] the speech of François Rabelais and of Philippe de Commines, of Villon, of Rutebeuf, and of so many other writers who were free and ready to hurl the sharp terms of language like Thracian archers their sinuous arrows.

RHYTHM: The old meter revived; a wisely ordered disorder; the rhyme incandescent and hammered like a shield of brass and gold, beside the rhyme made up of abstruse fluidities; the alexandrine of multiple and mobile checks; the use of certain prime numbers—seven, nine, eleven, thirteen—resolved into the different rhythm combinations of which they are the sum.

---

[2]Vaugelas (1585–1650) was a grammarian; Boileau-Despréaux (1636–1711) was a poet and critic and friend of Racine and Molière. Both played a great part in establishing set forms of "good usage" against which the Romantics struggled.

At this point I beg permission to present to you my little *Interlude,* drawn from a precious book: the *Treatise on French Poetry* in which M. Théodore de Banville, like the God of Claros, pitilessly inflicts asses' ears upon the head of many a Midas.

Pay attention!

The characters in the play are:

A DISPARAGING CRITIC OF THE SYMBOLIC SCHOOL

M. THEODORE DE BANVILLE

ERATO [one of the nine muses and patron of elegiac poetry]

FIRST SCENE

DISPARAGING CRITIC: Oh! these decadents! What emphasis! What nonsense! How right was our great Molière when he said:

> This figurative style that people pride themselves on
> Deviates from good form and from truth.

T. DE BANVILLE: Our great Molière committed these two bad verses which themselves deviate far from good form. What good form? What truth? Apparent disorder, explosive madness, passionate emphasis, these are the essential truth of lyric poetry. There is no great harm about falling into an excess of figures and color. This is not the way our literature will perish. In its worst days, when it has altogether given up hope, as for instance under the First Empire, not emphasis and overornamentation kill it, but platitude. Taste, naturalness, are beautiful things but certainly less useful to poetry than people imagine. Shakespeare's *Romeo and Juliet* is written from beginning to end in a style as affected as that of Mascarille's marquis; that of Ducis shines with the happiest and most natural simplicity.[3]

DISPARAGING CRITIC: But the *caesura,* the *caesura!* They are violating the *caesura!*

T. DE BANVILLE: In his remarkable prosody, published in 1844, M. Wilhem Tenint established that the alexandrine allows twelve different combinations, beginning with the verse whose *caesura* follows the first syllable and ending with the verse whose *caesura* follows the eleventh syllable. This amounts to saying that in effect the *caesura* can be placed after no matter which syllable

---

[3]Mascarille is the roguish type of intriguing footman who appears in so many seventeenth- and eighteenth-century comedies. Jean-François Ducis (1733–1816), like so many nonentities a member of the Académie Française, committed a prudent and pedestrian translation of Shakespeare into French.

of the alexandrine verse. In the same way, he established that verses of six, seven, eight, nine, and ten syllables admit variable and variously placed *caesuras*. Let us go further; let us dare proclaim complete freedom and say that in these complex matters the ear alone shall decide. Defeat comes always not for having dared too much but for having dared too little.

DISPARAGING CRITIC: Horrors! No respect for the alternation of rhymes! Do you know, Sir, that the decadents dare to allow themselves the hiatus! even the hi-a-tus!

T. DE BANVILLE: Once the hiatus or the diphthong were accepted as a syllable in the verse, all the other things which had been forbidden, and especially the freedom to use both masculine and feminine rhymes, provided the poet of genius with a thousand opportunities for delicate touches, ever varied, ever unexpected, inexhaustible. But in order to make use of this complicated, learned verse form, one needed genius and a musical ear while, with the established rules, provided they stick to them closely, the most mediocre writers can, alas, produce *passable verses!* Who ever gained anything from the regulation and reglementation of poetry? The mediocre poets. And they alone!

DISPARAGING CRITIC: And yet it seems to me that the romantic revolution . . .

T. DE BANVILLE: Romanticism was an incomplete revolution. What a pity that Victor Hugo, that victorious and bloody-fisted Hercules, was not a complete revolutionary, and that he let live some of the monsters whom it was his duty to exterminate with his flaming arrows.

DISPARAGING CRITIC: All innovation is folly! The salvation of French poetry lies in imitating Victor Hugo!

T. DE BANVILLE:. When Hugo had emancipated the verse, people must have thought that, inspired by his example, the poets that succeeded him would want to be free and depend only on themselves. But such is our love of bondage that the new poets endlessly copied and imitated Hugo's most common forms, combinations and turns of phrase, instead of trying to find new ones. This is how, made for the yoke, we turn from one servitude to another. After the classical commonplace, there have been romantic commonplaces, platitudes in turns, in phrases, in rhymes; and the commonplace, that is the chronic banality, is Death in poetry as in everything else. Let us, on the contrary, dare to live! And to live means to breathe the air of the open sky, not the breath of our neighbor, even if our neighbor should be a god!

SECOND SCENE

ERATO *(invisible):* Your *Short Treatise of French Poetry* is a delightful work, Master Banville. But the young poets are in blood up to their eyes struggling against the *monsters* fed by Nicolas Boileau; you are wanted on the battlefield, Master Banville, and you keep silent.

T. DE BANVILLE *(dreamily)*: Damnation! Could it be that I have failed in my duty, both as an elder and as a lyric poet!

(The author of The Exiles *sighs sadly, and* The Interlude *is over.)*

Prose—novels, stories, tales, and whimsies—evolves in a direction similar to that of poetry. Apparently heterogeneous elements help it on its way: Stendhal contributes his translucent psychology, Balzac his exorbitant vision, Flaubert the rhythms of his amply spiraled phrases, M. Edmond de Goncourt his suggestive impressionism.

The conception of the symbolic novel is polymorphous: now a single character moves through spheres deformed by his own hallucinations, by his temperament, and the only *reality* lies in these deformations. Beings with mechanical gestures, with shadowy outlines, shift and turn round the solitary character: they are mere pretexts for sensations and conjectures, while he himself is a mask of tragedy or farce, whose humanity is nevertheless perfect even though rational.—At times crowds, superficially affected by the totality of the surrounding show, move through alternating clashes and moments of stagnation toward actions which remain incomplete.—At times individual *wills* express themselves; they attract each other, conglomerate, become one, while making for an end which, whether attained or not, scatters them once more into their original elements.—Then, again, mythical phantoms, from the ancient Demogorgon to Belial, from the Kabirs to the Nigromans, appear richly attired on Caliban's rock, or pass through Titania's forest to the mixolydian strains of several kinds of lyre, whether barbiton or octocord.

Thus, scorning the puerile methods of naturalism—M. Zola himself was saved by a wonderful writer's instinct—the Symbolic-Impressionist novel will build its work of *subjective deformation,* strong in this axiom: that art can only seek in the *objective* a simple and extremely succinct starting point.

Expressionism

The years after the Franco-Prussian war were for Germany a time of violent and widespread revolution. Within one generation, the country that had been a congeries of little states and provincial capitals became a great power, a highly industrialized capitalist society, and a European cultural center. The social and psychological cost of these changes was immense, and its reflection appears in the intense and twisted products of certain artists and writers whom we group under the general, probably too general, label of Expressionism. As usual, their inspiration had come largely from France, particularly from the symbolism and inward searching of men like Gauguin and van Gogh, and also from Norway, through the work of Edward Munch (1863–1944).

Like all its contemporaries (and evidently the uneasiness and trouble were not limited to Germany alone) Expressionism is a movement of revolt. It is interesting to see, however, that the revolt first spoke out under the Naturalist label, and that it was the Naturalistic approach that Germans adopted at the turn of the century to present their social grievances and to protest against injustice. The social Realism with which young artists and writers inspired chiefly by the French depicted the sufferings of the poor was soon denounced as "socialist painting"; the influence of Impressionism was branded as un-German; the new art movement, eclectic in its interests but united in its dislikes and its antiacademic attitude, became a center for antiauthoritarian radicals. It is not too surprising that in 1908 the Director of the National Gallery in Berlin, Hugo von Tschudi, who had done so much to introduce Impressionism and Post-Impressionism to the German public, was dismissed by order of the Kaiser.

By then, however, new and as yet unsuspected sources of subversion had appeared, more effective because more insidious than the Naturalists' straightforward attacks. The year 1907 had seen the publication in Germany of Wilhelm Worringer's *Abstraction and Empathy*, which presented all art as subjective and intuition as the main creative element. The same year in France Bergson had published his *Creative Evolution*, which presented every free act as a creative one and intuition, once again, as a most important factor in human activity. Intuition, subjectivity, "free" creation—these concepts were going to furnish the basis of the reaction which, especially in Germany, would express in art the growing antimaterialistic, antirationalistic, often mystical mood of anxiety and revolt. But where the Naturalistic political and social criticism of Heinrich Mann's novels, or the early paintings of Käthe Kollwitz protested against the fat philistinism of the new society and the sordid suffering of its exploited underlings, Expressionists tried to go beyond the surface horror of any particular situation to its deeper emotional meaning. They sought to express the emotions—the hope, the dread, the love, or the horror contained in a situation or an object (whether human or not)—rather than the visible surface realities. To do this they used distortion, exaggeration that ends in caricature, and a brutal, slashing color.

For the Expressionists, every object, whether lifeless or not, had an inner meaning that only the artist could reveal. Hence their writing and their painting provide a running commentary on the contemporary mood; and the disturbance this caused within them is revealed by their ever more macabre treatment of grimacing themes. For Hermann Bahr "this whole pregnant time is one great cry of anguish," and it is this anguish, this darkness, that we find in the paintings of George Grosz and in the great German films of the twenties—*The Golem* and *The Cabinet of Dr. Caligari,* for example—all of which affirm a world disturbed, full of dark arbitrary forces that threaten man.

Kandinsky

Wassily Kandinsky (1866–1944) was born in Moscow, grew up in Florence and Odessa, studied political economy and law at the University of Moscow. In 1896, the thirty-year-old Russian economist went to Munich to study painting; he soon opened his own painting school and began to move toward nonfigurative painting, trying to rely on imagination rather than on visual experience, and asking beholders to "look at the picture as a graphic representation of a mood and not as a representation of objects." In 1912, he was one of the founders of *Der Blaue Reiter* (the Blue Rider)— a group who tried to return to the "basic" elements in painting, their approach to color and form being strongly influenced by neo-Impressionists like Gauguin and van Gogh, their chief interest being in the intellectual and universally valid contents and possibilities of art. It was in 1912 that Kandinsky's essay, the first part of which follows, and most of which had been written in 1910, was published in Munich. *Über das Geistige in der Kunst* ("Concerning the Spiritual in Art") made a great stir: the German edition was reprinted thrice within the first year, and English and Russian translations had already been published before the First World War broke out.

In 1914, Kandinsky returned to Moscow, taught there for some years, briefly after the Revolution held the directorship of the Museum for Pictorial Culture, and helped found the Russian Academy of Artistic Sciences. In 1922 he joined Gropius's *Bauhaus,* but eleven years later left Germany for Paris where he remained (at Neuilly) until his death a few months following the liberation. His epitaph, only slightly exaggerated, may be left to his wife: "Kandinsky," she wrote in 1946, "was perhaps the greatest revolutionist in the field of plastic art; by completely detaching painting from the object he gave endless possibilities to those with the gift of creation."

Concerning the Spiritual in Art

I. *Introduction*

Every work of art is the child of its time; often it is the mother of our emotions. It follows that each period of culture produces an art of its own, which

Source: From *Concerning the Spiritual in Art* No. 5 Documents of Modern Art, 1947. Reprinted by permission from Wittenborn Art Books, Inc.

cannot be repeated. Efforts to revive the art principles of the past at best produce works of art that resemble a stillborn child. For example, it is impossible for us to live and feel as did the ancient Greeks. For this reason those who follow Greek principles in sculpture reach only a similarity of form, while the work remains for all time without a soul. Such imitation resembles the antics of apes: externally a monkey resembles a human being; he will sit holding a book in front of his nose, turning over the pages with a thoughtful air, but his actions have no real significance.

But among the forms of art there is another kind of external similarity, which is founded on a fundamental necessity. When there is, as sometimes happens, a similarity of inner direction in an entire moral and spiritual milieu, a similarity of ideals, at first closely pursued but later lost to sight, a similarity of "inner mood" between one period and another, the logical consequence will be a revival of the external forms which served to express those insights in the earlier age. This may account partially for our sympathy and affinity with and our comprehension of the work of primitives. Like ourselves, these pure artists sought to express only inner[1] and essential feelings in their works; in this process they ignored as a matter of course the fortuitous.

------

[1]A work of art consists of two elements, the inner and the outer.

The inner is the emotion in the soul of the artist: this emotion has the capacity to evoke a similar emotion in the observer.

Being connected with the body, the soul is affected through the medium of the senses—the felt. Emotions are aroused and stirred by what is sensed. Thus the sensed is the bridge, i.e., the physical relation, between the immaterial (which is the artist's emotion) and the material, which results in the production of a work of art. And again, what is sensed is the bridge from the material (the artist and his work) to the immaterial (the emotion in the soul of the observer).

The sequence is: emotion (in the artist) → the art work → the sensed → emotion (in the observer).

The two emotions will be like and equivalent to the extent that the work of art is successful. In this respect painting is in no way different from a song: each is a communication. The successful singer arouses in listeners his emotions; the successful painter should do no less.

The inner element, i.e., emotion, must exist: otherwise the work of art is a sham. The inner element determines the form of the work of art.

In order that the inner element, which at first exists only as an emotion, may develop into a work of art, the second element, i.e., the outer, is used as an embodiment. Emotion is always seeking means of expression, a material form, a form that is able to stir the senses. The determining and vital element is the inner one, which controls the outer form, just as an idea in the mind determines the words we use, and not vice versa. The determination of the form of a work of art is therefore determined by the irresistible inner force: this is the only unchanging law in art. A beautiful work is the consequence of an harmonious cooperation of the inner and the outer; i.e., a painting is an intellectual organism which, like every other material organism, consists of many parts. (*This explanation by Kandinsky of the relation between internal and external, or inner and outer, is a slightly revised version of a translation by Arthur Jerome Eddy of part of an article by Kandinsky that appeared in* Der Sturm, Berlin, 1913; *cf.* Cubists and Post-Impressionists, A. C. McClurg, Chicago, 1914, pp. 119–20.)

This great point of inner contact is, in spite of its considerable importance, only one point. Only just now awakening after years of materialism, our soul is infected with the despair born of unbelief, of lack of purpose and aim. The nightmare of materialism, which turned life into an evil, senseless game, is not yet passed; it still darkens the awakening soul. Only a feeble light glimmers, a tiny point in an immense circle of darkness. This light is but a presentiment; and the mind, seeing it, trembles in doubt over whether the light is a dream and the surrounding darkness indeed reality. This doubt and the oppression of materialism separate us sharply from primitives. Our soul rings cracked when we sound it, like a precious vase, dug out of the earth, which has a flaw. For this reason, the primitive phase through which we are now passing, in its present derivative form, must be short-lived.

The two kinds of resemblance between the forms of art of today and of the past can be easily recognized as diametrically opposed. The first, since it is external, has no future. The second, being internal, contains the seed of the future. After a period of materialist temptation, to which the soul almost succumbed, and which it was able to shake off, the soul is emerging, refined by struggle and suffering. Cruder emotions, like fear, joy and grief, which belonged to this time of trial, will no longer attract the artist. He will attempt to arouse more refined emotions, as yet unnamed. Just as he will live a complicated and subtle life, so his work will give to those observers capable of feeling them emotions subtle beyond words.

The observer of today is seldom capable of feeling such vibrations. He seeks instead an imitation of nature with a practical function (for example, a portrait, in the ordinary sense) or an intuition of nature involving a certain interpretation (e.g., "impressionist" painting) or an inner feeling expressed by nature's forms (as we say, a picture of "mood"[2]). When they are true works of art, such forms fulfil their purposes and nourish the spirit. Though this remark applies to the first case, it applies more strongly to the third, in which the spectator hears an answering chord in himself. Such emotional chords cannot be superficial or without value; the feeling of such a picture can indeed deepen and purify the feeling of the spectator. The spirit at least is preserved from coarseness: such pictures tune it up, as a tuning fork does the strings of a musical instrument. But the subtilization and extension of this chord in time and space remained limited, and the potential power of art is not exhausted by it.

---

[2]Alas, this word, which in the past was used to describe the poetical aspirations of an artist's soul, has been misused and finally ridiculed. Was there ever a great word that the crowd did not try immediately to desecrate?

Imagine a building, large or small, divided into rooms; each room is covered with canvases of various sizes, perhaps thousands of them. They represent bits of nature in color—animals in sunlight or shadow, or drinking, standing in water, or lying on grass; close by, a "Crucifixion," by a painter who does not believe in Christ; then flowers, and human figures, sitting, standing, or walking, and often naked; there are many naked women foreshortened from behind; apples and silver dishes; a portrait of Mister So-and-So; sunsets; a lady in pink; a flying duck; a portrait of Lady X; flying geese; a lady in white; some cattle in shadow, flecked by brilliant sunlight; a portrait of Ambassador Y; a lady in green. All this is carefully reproduced in a book with the name of the artist and the name of the picture. Book in hand, people go from wall to wall, turning pages, reading names. Then they depart, neither richer nor poorer, again absorbed by their affairs, which have nothing to do with art. Why did they come? In every painting a whole life is mysteriously enclosed, a whole life of tortures, doubts, of hours of enthusiasm and inspiration.

What is the direction of that life? What is the cry of the artist's soul, if the soul was involved in the creation? "To send light into the darkness of men's hearts—such is the obligation of the artist," said Schumann. "A painter is a man who can draw and paint everything," said Tolstoi.

Of these two definitions we must choose the second, if we think of the exhibition just described. With more or less skill, virtuosity and vigor, objects are created on a canvas, "painted" either roughly or smoothly. To bring the whole into harmony on the canvas is what leads to a work of art. With cold eye and indifferent mind the public regards the work. Connoisseurs admire "technique," as one might admire a tight-rope walker, or enjoy the "painting quality," as one might enjoy a cake. But hungry souls go hungry away.

The public ambles through the rooms, saying "nice" or "interesting." Those who could speak have said nothing; those who could hear have heard nothing. This condition is called "art for art's sake." This annihilation of internal vibrations that constitute the life of the colors, this dwindling away of artistic force, is called "art for art's sake."

The artist seeks material rewards for his facility, inventiveness and sensitivity. His purpose becomes the satisfaction of ambition and greediness. In place of an intensive cooperation among artists, there is a battle for goods. There is excessive competition, over-production. Hatred, partisanship, cliques, jealousy, intrigues are the natural consequences of an aimless, materialist art.[3]

---

[3]A few exceptions do not affect the truth of this sad and ominous picture; even the exceptions are chiefly believers in the doctrine of art for art's sake. They serve, therefore, a higher ideal, but one which is ultimately a useless waste of their strength. External beauty is one element

The public turns away from artists who have higher ideals, who find purpose in an art without purpose.

"Comprehension" is educating the spectator to the point of view of the artist. It has been said that art is the child of its time. But such an art can only repeat artistically what is already clearly realized by the contemporary. Since it is not germinative, but only a child of the age, and unable to become a mother of the future, it is a castrated art. It is transitory; it dies morally the moment the atmosphere that nourished it alters.

There is another art capable of further developments, which also springs from contemporary feeling. Not only is it simultaneously its echo and mirror but it possesses also an awakening prophetic power which can have far-reaching and profound effect.

The spiritual life to which art belongs, and of which it is one of the mightiest agents, is a complex but definite movement above and beyond, which can be translated into simplicity. This movement is that of cognition. Although it may take different forms, it holds basically to the same internal meaning and purpose.

The causes of the necessity to move forward and upward—through sweat, suffering, evil and torments—are obscure. When a stage has been reached at which obstacles have been cleared from the way, a hidden, malevolent hand scatters new obstacles. The path often seems blocked or destroyed. But someone always comes to the rescue—someone like ourselves in everything, but with a secretly implanted power of "vision."

He sees and points out. This high gift (often a heavy burden) at times he would gladly relinquish. But he cannot. Scorned and disliked, he drags the heavy weight of resisting humanity forward and upward.

Sometimes, after his body has vanished from the earth, men try by every means to recreate it in marble, iron, bronze, or stone, and on an enormous scale. As though they were any intrinsic value in the bodily existence of such divine martyrs and servants of humanity, who despised the flesh but wanted only to serve the spirit. But raising marble is evidence that a number of men have reached the point where the one they would now honor formerly stood alone.

2. *Movement*

The life of the spirit may be graphically represented as a large acute-angled triangle, divided horizontally into unequal parts, with the narrowest segment

---

in a spiritual milieu. But beyond this positive fact (that what is beautiful is good) lies the weakness of a talent not used to the full (talent in the biblical sense).

uppermost. The lower the segment, the greater it is in breadth, depth and area.

The whole triangle moves slowly, almost invisibly forward and upward. Where the apex was today, the second segment will be tomorrow; what today can be understood only by the apex, is tomorrow the thought and feeling of the second segment.[4]

At the apex of the highest segment often stands one man. His joyful vision is the measure of his inner sorrow. Even those who are nearest to him in sympathy do not understand. Angrily they abuse him as a charlatan or madman. So in his lifetime Beethoven stood, solitary and insulted.[5] How long will it be before a larger segment of the triangle reaches the spot where he once stood? Despite memorials, are there really many who have risen to his level?[6]

There are artists in each segment of the triangle. He who can see beyond the limits of his own segment is a prophet and helps the advance. But those who are near-sighted, or who retard the movement for base reasons, are fully understood and acclaimed. The larger the segment (i.e., the lower it lies in the triangle), the greater the number of people capable of understanding the artist. Every segment hungers, consciously or unconsciously, for adequate spiritual satisfactions. These are offered by artists, and for such satisfactions the segment below will tomorrow stretch out eager hands.

This schematical presentation, however, does not exploit the entire picture of spiritual life. Among other things it does not show the dark side, a great, dead black spot. It happens too often that the spiritual "bread" becomes nourishment for many who live already in a higher segment. This bread becomes poisonous for such eaters: in smaller quantities it has the effect that the soul gradually sinks from a high segment to a lower one. When used in greater quantity, this poison casts the soul into ever lower divisions. In one of his novels, Sienkiewicz compares the spiritual life to swimming; the man who does not strive tirelessly against sinking will go under. In this strait a man's talent (again in the biblical sense) becomes a curse—not only for the

---

[4]This "today" and "tomorrow" correspond to the biblical "days" of the Creation.

[5][Carl Maria von] Weber, composer of "Der Freischütz," said of Beethoven's Seventh Symphony: "The extravagances of genius have reached the limit; Beethoven is now ripe for an asylum." On the opening phrase, a reiterated "E," the Abbé Stadler said to his neighbor: "That same old 'E' again; he's run out of ideas, the bore." (*Beethoven* by August Göllerich, p. 1 in the series, *Die Musik,* ed. by R. Strauss.)

[6]Many of our monuments are melancholy answers to the question.

artist, but also for those who partake of his poison. The artist uses his strength to flatter base needs; in an ostensibly artistic form he presents what is impure, what draws weaker elements to him, betrays them and helps them to betray themselves, while they convince themselves and others that they are spiritually thirsty, that they can quench their thirst at this spring. Such art does not help the forward movement, but hinders it, dragging back those who are striving to press onward, and spreading pestilence abroad.

During periods when art has no champion, when true spiritual food is wanting, there is retrogression in the spiritual world. Souls fall ceaselessly from the higher to the lower segments of the triangle, and the whole seems motionless, or even to move down and backwards. During these mute and blind times men attribute a special and exclusive value to external success, for they judge them by outward results, thinking of material well-being. They hail some technical advance, which can help nothing but the body. Real spiritual gains are undervalued or ignored.

The love visionaries, the hungry of soul, are ridiculed or considered mentally abnormal. But the rare souls, who cannot be lulled into lethargy and who feel dark longings for spiritual life, knowledge and advancement, sound, amid the vulgar materialistic chorus, lamentful and disconsolate. The spiritual night falls deeper and deeper around such frightened souls; and their bearers, tortured and weakened by doubt and fear, often prefer complete obliteration to this gradual darkening.

In such periods art ministers to lower needs and is used for material ends. It seeks its content in crude substance, because it knows nothing fine. Objects remaining the same, their reproduction is thought to be the aim of art. The question "what?" disappears; only the question "how?" remains. By what method are these material objects reproduced? The method becomes a rationale. Art loses its soul.

The search for the "how" continues. Art becomes specialized, comprehensible only to artists, and they complain of public indifference to their work. For, since the artist in such times has no need to say much, but only to be notorious for some small originality among a small group of patrons and connoisseurs (which incidentally is also profitable), many externally gifted and skilful people come forward, so easy does the conquest of art appear. In each "art center" there are thousands of such artists, of whom the majority seek only some new mannerism, producing millions of works of art, without enthusiasm, with cold hearts and souls asleep.

Meanwhile competition grows. The savage battle for success becomes more and more material. Small groups who have fought their way to the top entrench themselves in the territory they have won. The public, left behind, looks on bewildered, loses interest and turns away.

Despite this confusion, this chaos, this wild hunt for notoriety, the spiritual triangle moves ahead, slowly but surely, with irresistible strength moving ever forward and upward.

An invisible Moses descends from the mountain and sees the dancing around the golden calf. But he brings to man fresh stores of wisdom.

His voice, inaudible to the crowd, is first heard by the artist. Almost unwittingly artists follow the voice. In the very question "how" lies a hidden seed of renascence. Sterile though this "how" may be on the whole, there is always a possibility that the "difference" which we still call personal distinction may be able to see, in the objects about it, not only what is purely material, but also something less corporeal than was seen in the period of realism, when the universal aim was to reproduce things "as they really are," without indulging in fancies.[7]

If the emotional power of the artist can overwhelm the "how" and give free scope to his feelings, then art has started on the path by which she will not fail to find the "what" she lost, the "what" which forms the spiritual necessity of the nascent awakening. This "what" will no longer be the material, objective "what" of a stagnant period, but an artistic substance, the soul of art, without which the body (i.e., the "how") can never be healthy, whether an individual or a whole people.

This "what" is the substance which only art can comprise, which only art can clearly express by those means of expression that are proper to it.

3. *Spiritual Turning-Point*

The spiritual triangle moves slowly ahead. Today one of the largest of the lower segments has reached the point of using the first battle-cry of materialism. The inhabitants of this segment call themselves Jews, Catholics, Protestants, etc. Really they are atheists, and this a few of the boldest, or the narrowest, openly avow. "Heaven is empty," "God is dead." In politics they are liberals or progressives. The fear and hatred which yesterday they felt for these political creeds they now direct against anarchism, of which they know nothing but its dread name.

---

[7]Frequent reference is made to "material" and "non-material," and to the intermediate phrases, "more" and "less" material. Is everything material—or is *everything* spiritual? Can the distinctions we make between matter and spirit be nothing but relative modifications of one or the other? Thought, which although a product of the spirit can be defined with exact science, is matter, but of fine and not coarse substance. Is whatever cannot be *touched* spiritual? The discussion lies beyond the scope of this little book; all that matters here is that the boundaries drawn should not be too definite.

In economics these people are socialists. They sharpen the sword of justice to slay the hydra of capitalism.

Because they have never solved any problem independently, but are dragged in a cart, as it were, by the noblest of their fellow-men, who have sacrificed themselves, they know nothing of toil, which they watch from a distance. Therefore they rate it lightly, putting their trust in unexceptionable precepts and infallible cures.

The men of the segment next below are blindly dragged higher by those just described. But they cling to their old position, full of dread of the unknown and of betrayal.

The higher segments are not only atheists but justify their godlessness with strange words; for example, those of Virchow[8]—so unworthy of a scholar—"I have dissected many corpses, but never yet come upon a soul."

In politics they are generally leftists, with a knowledge of different parliamentary procedures; they read the political articles in the journals. In economics they are socialists of various shades and can support their "principles" with numerous quotations, passing from Schweitzer's *Emma* via Ricardo's *Iron Law of Wages,* to Marx's *Capital,* and still further.

In these higher segments other categories of ideas gradually begin to appear—science and art, literature and music.

In science these men are positivists, recognizing only what can be weighed and measured. Everything beyond they consider harmful nonsense, as they did yesterday the theories which are "proven" today.

In art they are realists, which means that they recognize and value the personality, individuality and temperament of the artist up to a certain definite point. This point has been fixed by others, and they believe in it without reserve.

Despite their patent and well-ordered security, despite their infallible principles, there lurks among these higher segments a hidden fear, a nervousness, a sense of insecurity like that in the minds of passengers on a large, solid, ocean-going liner on the high seas when, the continent left behind in mist, dark clouds gather, and the winds raise the water into black mountains. This is the result of their upbringing. They know that the philosophers, statesmen and artists whom they revere today were spurned as arrivistes, gangsters and frauds yesterday. The higher the segment in the triangle, the better-defined this fear, this *modern* sense of insecurity. Here and there are people with eyes

---

[8]Rudolf Virchow, 1821–1902, German physician and pathologist.

that see, minds that correlate. They ask: "If the knowledge of day before yesterday was overturned by that of yesterday, and that of yesterday by that of today, is it not possible that what we call knowledge now will be overturned by the knowledge of tomorrow?" And the bravest of them answer: "It's possible."

Then people appear who can discern matters which the science of today has not yet "explained." They ask: "Will science, if it continues on the road it has followed for so long, ever attain the solution of these questions? And if it does, will man be able to rely on its answers?" In these segments are professional men of learning who remember the time when facts now recognized by the academies as firmly established were scorned. There are also aestheticians who write about an art which was condemned yesterday. In these books they remove the barriers over which art has most recently stepped and they set up new ones. They do not notice that they are erecting barriers not in front of art, but behind it. If they do, they write fresh books and hastily set the barriers a little further on. This process will go on until it is realized that the most advanced principle of aesthetics can never be of value to the future, but only to the past. No theory can be laid down for those things that lie in the realm of the immaterial. That which has no material existence cannot be materially crystallized. That which belongs to the spirit of the future can only be realized in feeling, and the talent of the artist is the only road to feeling. Theory is the lamp which sheds light on the crystallized ideas of the past. As we rise higher in the triangle, we find that confusion increases, just as a city built on the most correct architectural plan may be shaken by the uncontrollable force of nature. Humanity is living in such a spiritual city, subject to sudden disturbances for which neither architects nor mathematicians have made allowance. In one place lies a great wall fallen down like a house of cards, in another are the ruins of a huge tower which once stretched to the sky, built on presumably immortal spiritual pillars. The abandoned churchyard quakes, forgotten graves open, and from them rise forgotten ghosts. Spots appear on the sun, and the sun grows dark; and what power is left against the dark? In this city also live men who are dulled by false knowledge, who hear no crash, who are blinded by strange wisdom, so that they say "our sun shines brighter every day, and soon even the last spots will disappear." But even these people shall hear and see.

Still higher, we no longer find bewilderment. There work is going on which boldly criticizes the pillars men have set up. There we find other professional men of learning who test matter again and again, who tremble before no problem, and who finally cast doubt on that very matter which was yesterday the foundation of everything, so that the whole universe rocks. The theory of the electrons, that is, of waves in motion, designed to replace matter completely, finds at this moment bold champions who overstep here and there the limits of caution and perish in the conquest of the new scientific fortress. They are like self-sacrificing soldiers making a desperate attack. But "no fort is unconquerable."

Thus facts are being established which the science of yesterday dubbed frauds. Even newspapers, which are the most obsequious servants of worldly success and of the masses, which trim their sails to every wind, find themselves compelled to modify their ironical judgments on the "marvels" of science, and even to abandon them. Many learned men, among them ultra-materialists, are dedicating their strength to scientific research on obscure problems, which can no longer be lied about or passed over in silence.[9]

Furthermore, the number is increasing of those men who put no trust in the methods of material science when it deals with questions which have to do with "non-matter," or matter that is not accessible to our senses. Just as art is looking for help from the primitives, so these men are turning to half-forgotten times in order to get help from half-forgotten methods. However, these methods are still alive and in use among nations whom we, from the height of our knowledge, have been accustomed to regard with pity and scorn. To such nations belong the people of India, who from time to time confront our scholars with problems which we have either passed without notice or brushed aside.[10] Madame Blavatzky was the first person, after a life of many years in India, to see a connection between these "savages" and our "civilization." In that moment rose one of the most important spiritual movements, one which numbers a great many people today, and has even assumed a material form in the Theosophical Society. This society consists of groups who seek to approach the problem of the spirit by way of *inner* knowledge.

---

[9]Zöllner, Wagner, Butleroff (Petersburg), Crookes (London), etc.; later on, C. H. Richet, C. Flammarion. The Parisian newspaper *Le Matin* published about two years ago the discoveries of the two last-named, under the title "Je le constate, mais je ne l'explique pas." Finally C. Lombroso, the inventor of the anthropological method diagnosing crime, and Eusapio Palladino have turned to occult sciences and recognized transcendental phenomena. Besides individual scholars who have dedicated themselves to such studies, whole organizations have sprung up in pursuit of similar aims (e.g., Société des Etudes Psychiques, in Paris, which has even instituted committees in France to acquaint the public with the results of its research).

[10]Frequently in such cases use is made of the word hypnotism; the same hypnotism which, in its earlier form of mesmerism, was disdainfully put aside by various learned bodies.

Their methods, in opposition to positivism, derive from an ancient wisdom, which has been formulated with relative precision.[11] The theory of Theosophy which serves as the basis of this movement was set forth by Blavatzky in the form of a catechism in which the pupil receives definite answers to his questions from the theosophical point of view.[12] Theosophy, according to Blavatzky, is synonymous with *eternal truth*. "The new torch-bearer of truth will find the minds of men prepared for his message, a language ready for him in which to clothe the new truths he brings, an organization awaiting his arrival, which will remove the merely mechanical, material obstacles and difficulties from his path." And then Blavatzky continues: "The earth will be heaven in the twenty-first century in comparison with what it is now," and with these words ends her book.

Skeptical though we may be regarding the tendency of the theosophists toward theorizing and their excessive anticipation of definite answers in lieu of immense question-marks, it remains a fundamentally spiritual movement. This movement represents a strong agent in the general atmosphere, presaging deliverance to oppressed and gloomy hearts.

When religion, science and morality are shaken (the last by the strong hand of Nietzsche) and when outer supports threaten to fall, man withdraws his gaze from externals and turns it inwards. Literature, music and art are the most sensitive spheres in which this spiritual revolution makes itself felt. They reflect the dark picture of the present time and show the importance of what was at first only a little point of light noticed by the few. Perhaps they even grow dark in their turn, but they turn away from the soulless life of the present toward those substances and ideas that give free scope to the non-material strivings of the soul.

Such a poet in the realm of literature is Maeterlinck. He takes us into a world which may be called fantastic, or more justly transcendental. "La Princesse Maleine," "Les Sept Princesses," "Les Aveugles," etc., are not people of past times like the heroes in Shakespeare. They are souls lost in fog, threatened with asphyxiation, eternally menaced by some invisible and somber force.

Spiritual darkness, the insecurity of ignorance and fear pervade the world in which they move. Maeterlinck is perhaps one of the first prophets, one of the first reporters and clairvoyants of the decadence just described. The

---

[11] See Rudolph Steiner's *Theosophy* and his article on methods of cognition in *Lucifer-Gnosis*.
[12] H. P. Blavatzky, *The Key of Theosophy*, London, 1889.

gloom of the spiritual atmosphere, the terrible but all-guiding hand, the sense of utter fear, the feeling of having strayed from the path, the absence of a guide, all these are clearly felt in his works.[13]

Maeterlinck creates his atmosphere principally by artistic means. His material machinery (gloomy mountains, moonlight, marshes, wind, the cries of owls, etc.) really plays a symbolic role and helps to give the inner note.[14] Maeterlinck's principal technical weapon is words. The word is an inner sound. It springs partly, perhaps principally, from the object denoted. But if the object is not seen, but only its name heard, the mind of the hearer receives an abstract impression only of the object dematerialized, and a corresponding vibration is immediately set up in the "heart." Thus a green, yellow, or red tree in a meadow are accidental realizations of the concept tree which we formed upon hearing the word.

The apt use of a word (in its poetical sense), its repetition, twice, three times, or even more frequently, according to the need of the poem, will not only tend to intensify the internal structure but also bring out unsuspected spiritual properties in the word itself. Further, frequent repetition of a word (a favorite game of children, forgotten in later life) deprives the word of its external reference. Similarly, the symbolic reference of a designated object tends to be forgotten and only the sound is retained. We hear this pure sound, unconsciously perhaps, in relation to the concrete or immaterial object. But in the latter case pure sound exercises a direct impression on the soul. The soul attains to an objectless vibration, even more complicated, I might say more transcendent, than the reverberations released by the sound of a bell, a stringed instrument, or a fallen board. In this direction lie great possibilities for the literature of the future. This verbal potency has already been used in an embryonic form in *Serres Chaudes*.[15] An ostensibly neutral

---

[13]In the front rank of such seers of the decadence belongs also Alfred Kubin. With irresistible force both Kubin's drawings and his novel *Die andere Seite* seem to draw us into the terrible atmosphere of harsh vacuity.

[14]When one of Maeterlinck's plays was produced in St. Petersburg under his own guidance, he himself at one of the rehearsals had a tower represented by a plain piece of hanging linen. It was of no importance to him to have elaborate scenery prepared. He did as children, the greatest imaginers of all time, always do in their games: they use a stick for a horse or create entire regiments of cavalry out of paper birds, by which a fold of the paper changes a knight into a horse (Kügelgen, *Erinnerungen eines alten Mannes*). On similar lines the imagination of the spectator plays an important part in the modern theater, especially in that of Russia. This is a notable element in the transition from the material to the spiritual in the theater of the future.

[15]*Serres Chaudes, suivies de Quinze Chansons,* by Maurice Maeterlinck, Brussels, 1899.

word in its felt quality will become somber as Maeterlinck uses it. A familiar word like "hair," used in a certain way, intensifies an atmosphere of sorrow or despair. This is Maeterlinck's method. He makes us realize that thunder, lightning and a moon behind driving clouds are external, material means, which on the stage, even more than in nature, resemble the bogey-man of childhood: imaginings.

Inner forces do not lose their strength and effect so easily.[16] A word which has two meanings, the first direct, the second indirect, is the material of po-etry and literature, which these arts alone can manipulate and through which they speak to the soul.

Something similar may be seen in the music of Wagner. His famous *Leit-motiv* is an attempt to give personality to his characters by something more than theatrical paraphernalia, makeup and light effects. His method of using a definite *motiv* is a musical method. It creates a spiritual atmosphere by means of a musical phrase which precedes the hero, which he seems to radiate from any distance.[17] The most modern musicians, like Debussy, create a spir-itual impression, often taken from nature, but embodied in purely musical form. For this reason Debussy is often classed with the impressionist paint-ers, on the ground that he resembles these painters in using natural phenom-ena for the purposes of art. Whatever truth there may be in this comparison merely accentuates the fact that the various arts of today learn from each other and often resemble each other. But it would be rash to say that this proposition is an exhaustive statement of Debussy's significance. Despite a certain similarity to the impressionists, he shows such a strong drive toward essential content that we recognize at once in his work the flawed, vocal soul of the present, with all its harassing anxiety and jangled nerves. Debussy, even in his impressionist tone-pictures, never uses the wholly material note char-acteristic of program music, but relies on the creation of an abstract impres-sion.

Russian music (Moussorgsky) has had a great influence on Debussy. So it is not surprising that he stands in close relation to the young Russian com-posers, the chief of whom is Scriabin. There is an internal affinity in the compositions of the two men, and they have identical faults, which disturb the listener. He is often snatched from a series of modern discords into the

---

[16]A comparison of the work of Poe and Maeterlinck shows the course of artistic transition from the material to the abstract.

[17]Frequent attempts have shown that such a spiritual atmosphere can belong not only to heroes but to any human being. Very sensitive people cannot, for example, abide a room in which there has been a person who is spiritually antagonistic to them, even though they know nothing of his existence.

charm of conventional beauty. He feels himself often insulted, tossed about like a ball between the internal and the external beauty. The internal beauty is achieved through necessity and renunciation of the conventionally beautiful. To those who are not accustomed to it, it appears as ugliness; humanity in general inclines to external beauty and knows nothing of internal beauty. Almost alone in abandoning conventional beauty and in sanctioning every means of expression is the Austrian composer, Arnold Schönberg. This "publicity hound," "fraud," and "dilettante" says in his *Harmonielehre:* "Every combination of notes, every advance is possible, but I am beginning to feel that there are definite rules and conditions which incline me to the use of this or that dissonance."[18]

In other words, Schönberg realizes that the greatest freedom of all, the freedom of an unfettered art, can never be absolute. Every age achieves a certain measure of this freedom, but beyond the boundaries of its freedom the mightiest genius can never go. But this measure must in each instance be exhausted, let the stubborn resist as they may. Schönberg is endeavoring to make complete use of his freedom and has already discovered mines of new beauty in his search for spiritual structure. His music leads us to where musical experience is a matter not of the ear, but of the soul—and from this point begins the music of the future.

Bahr

Hermann Bahr (1863–1934) was an Austrian novelist, journalist, essayist, and playwright whose varied career included the editorship of influential reviews in Vienna and Berlin, the directorship of the famous Vienna *Burgtheater,* and successive and intense flirtations with Naturalism, Impressionism, and Expressionism. His essay describing the latter, first published in 1914 and reproduced here, reflects the vague intensity and anguish of Expressionist ideas, but also the road along which some came to hold them.

Expressionism

This is the vital point—that man should find himself again. Schiller asks: "Can man have been destined, for any purpose whatever, to lose himself?" It

---

[18]*Die Musik,* p. 104, from the *Harmonielehre* (Verlag der Universal Edition).

Source: Translated by R. T. Gribble, London, 1925; Frank Henderson, 76, Charing Cross Road, London, W.C., pp. 83–90, 109–111.

is the inhuman attempt of our time to force this loss upon him against his own nature. We would turn him into a mere instrument; he has become the tool of his own work, and he has no more sense, since he serves the machine. It has stolen him away from his soul. And now the soul demands his return. This is the vital point. All that we experience is but the strenuous battle between the soul and the machine for the possession of man. We no longer live, we are lived; we have no freedom left, we may not decide for ourselves, we are finished, man is unsouled, nature is unmanned. A moment ago we boasted of being her lords and masters and now she has opened her wide jaws and swallowed us up. Unless a miracle happens! That is the vital point— whether a miracle can still rescue this soulless, sunken, buried humanity. Never yet has any period been so shaken by horror, by such a fear of death. Never has the world been so silent, silent as the grave. Never has man been more insignificant. Never has he felt so nervous. Never was happiness so unattainable and freedom so dead. Distress cries aloud; man cries out for his soul; this whole pregnant time is one great cry of anguish. Art too joins in, into the great darkness she too calls for help, she cries to the spirit: this is Expressionism.

Never has any period found a clearer, a stronger mode of self-expression than did the period of bourgeois dominance in Impressionistic Art. This bourgeois rule was incapable of producing original music or poetry; all the music or poetry of its day is invariably either a mere echoing of the past, or a presentiment of the future; but in Impressionistic painting it has made for itself such a perfect symbol of its nature, of its disorder, that perhaps some day when humanity is quite freed from its trammels and has attained the serene perspective of historical contemplation, it may be forgiven, because of these shining tokens. Impressionism is the falling away of man from the spirit. Impressionism is man lowered to the position of a gramophone record of the outer world. Impressionists have been taken to task for not "carrying out" their pictures; they do not even carry out their "seeing," for man of the bourgeois period never "carries out," never fulfils life. He halts, breaks off midway in the process of seeing, midway in the process of life at the very point where man's participation in life begins. Halfway in the act of seeing these Impressionists stop, just where the eye, having been challenged, should make its reply: "The ear is dumb, the mouth is deaf," says Goethe; "but the eye both perceives and speaks." The eye of the Impressionist only beholds, it does not speak; it hears the question but makes no response. Instead of eyes, Impressionists have another set of ears, but no mouth, for a man of the bourgeois period is nothing but an ear, he listens to the world but does not breathe upon it. He has no mouth, he is incapable of expressing himself, incapable of pronouncing judgment upon the world, of uttering the law of the spirit. The Expressionist, on the contrary, tears open the mouth of humanity; the time of its silence, the time of its listening is over—once more it seeks to give the spirit's reply.

Expressionism is as yet but a gesture. It is not a question of this or that Expressionist, much less of any particular work of his. Nietzsche says: "The first and foremost duty of Art should be to beautify life. . . . Thereupon she must conceal or transmute all ugliness—and only after this gigantic task has been achieved can she turn to the special so-called Art of Art-production, which is but the appendage. A man who is conscious of possessing a superfluity of these beautifying and concealing and transmuting powers, will finally seek to disburden himself of this superabundance in works of Art; the same under special conditions applies to a whole nation. But at present we generally start at the wrong end of Art, we cling to her tail and reiterate the tag, that works of Art contain the whole of Art, and that by these we may repair and transform life . . . simpletons that we are!" Under this bourgeois rule the whole of man has become an appendage. Impressionism makes a splendid tail! The Expressionist, however, does not throw out a peacock's wheel, he does not consider the single production, but seeks to restore man to his rightful position; only we have outgone Nietzsche—or, rather, we have retraced our steps and gone further back beyond him and have arrived at Goethe: Art is no longer only to "beautify" life for us and to "conceal or transmute ugliness," but Art must bring Life, produce Life from within, must fulfil the function of Life as man's most proper deed and action. Goethe says, "Painting sets before us that which a man could and should see, and which usually he does not see." If Expressionism at the moment behaves in an ungainly, violent manner, its excuse lies in the prevailing conditions it finds. These really are almost the conditions of crude and primitive humanity. People little know how near the truth they are when they jeer at these pictures and say they might be painted by savages. The bourgeois rule has turned us into savages. Barbarians, other than those feared by Rodbertus, threaten; we ourselves have to become barbarians to save the future of humanity from mankind as it now is. As primitive man, driven by fear of nature, sought refuge within himself, so we too have to adopt flight from a "civilization" which is out to devour our souls. The Savage discovered in himself the courage to become greater than the threat of nature, and in honour of this mysterious inner redeeming power of his, which, through all the alarms and terrors of storm and of ravening beasts and of unknown dangers, never deserted him, never let him give in—in honour of this he drew a circle of guardian signs around him, signs of defiance against the threat of nature, obstinate signs of demarcation to protect his possessions against the intrusion of nature and to safeguard his belief in spirit. So, brought very near the edge of destruction by "civilization," we discover in ourselves powers which cannot be destroyed. With the fear of death upon us, we muster these and use them as spells against "civilization." Expressionism is the symbol of the unknown in us in which we confide, hoping that it will save us. It is the token of the imprisoned spirit that endeavours to break out of the dungeon—a tocsin of alarm given out by all panic-stricken souls. This is what Expressionism is.

Man is, however, again reduced to one-half only of Art, though the better half. Again, he does not see completely. If Impressionism has converted the eye into a mere ear, Expressionism turns it into a mere mouth. The ear is dumb—Impressionism silenced the soul; the mouth is deaf—Expressionism cannot hear the world. Goethe says: "Everything within the subject is contained in the object, and something more as well. Everything within the object is contained in the subject, and something more as well." The Impressionist represents that something more in the Object and suppresses it in the Subject; the Expressionist knows only "something more" of the Subject and blocks out part of the Object. But even as we ourselves are "the offspring of two worlds," so also is our eye: "In it is the world mirrored from without, the man from within. The totality of the inner and the outer world is accomplished by the eye." This accomplished balance of the inner and outer is lacking both in Impressionism and Expressionism; that "vital alliance of the eye of the spirit with the eye of the body" to which Goethe constantly returns with urgent insistence, and which Expressionism in art, science, and life again fails to attain. When has it ever been attained? By one or two isolated masters in one or two special works, which have always remained incomprehensible and misunderstood. Never has a whole epoch attained this. One came near doing it—the Baroque ("only the badly informed and pretentious will have a feeling of contempt at this word," says Nietzsche of the Baroque style which, by the way, he, following Jacob Burckhardt, also misunderstood).

This period, from the Council of Trent past Teresa and Vincent de Paul to Bernini and Calderón; this period of which a glowing foreboding already tormented the hearts of the thirteenth century, which gathered up all the longing, all the hunger for the divine and for spiritual power, of fifteen centuries, and yet in itself was but a promise of greater, more far-reaching syntheses; this period comprises every variety, from stormy movement to deepest calm, it shows us divine grace brought into contact with physical action; God held by man, man becoming the dispenser of grace from above— where becoming sinks back into being, and time abuts upon eternity—but stop!

For here I am at Bernini, of whom I hold as yet only a vision, as threatening as it is enchanting, in which St. Francis stretches his bleeding hands towards the great Dominicans, Eckhart and Tauler, and beyond them to Teresa, Calderón, and Bernini, till blinded by this flood of benediction, man, staggering back into the dark, is once more illumined by a penetrating ray from Goethe. But of course this is a Goethe we can hardly yet surmise, because we have first to learn to endure his greatness.

[Goethe] does not overlook the fact that each of our powers, every faculty, capability, and virtue that we are gifted with is also, as it were, an original individual in us, which has its own particular truth, in which it tolerates no interference by its neighbours with their set of truths. In the same individual, eye-truth may differ from ear-truth; each sense has its own phase of truth, and the imagination has again its own particular phase, and so have reason and temperament and will, and when they all unite they together create an entirely new configuration of Truth, which each time they unite renews itself in a different manner, according to the way they blend; thus our earthly life is maintained and kept mobile until it has brought forth all the phases of truth that it is capable of producing; then it will cease. But however much they contradict, and even seem to confound one another, down in the ultimate depths they are all one and the same; this we realize as soon as we act. In action our inner contradictions sink into silence, and all the outer contradictions draw together for this action. We are active when we act according to our conscience, convinced of hidden, everlasting, universal Truth. Man can never know it fully or declare it, but he can show it in his actions. Wherever a dreaming mother gives her breast to her child, wherever a man draws his sword for his faith, wherever any one with a pure heart gives up his will to an inner law, there is Truth. We can never grasp or hold Truth, but we can fulfil its demands everywhere.

Even our generation may not yet be ready for Goethe in his completeness; a Goethe whom, in more than one sense, though of course also with more than one reserve, one is almost tempted to call the catholic Goethe. Yet no other period has sampled the list of human possibilities, no other has been so disillusioned by them all; we have probed everything and nothing has held firm under our test. At last, not even the test that nothing holds good remains. Even that holds good no longer; it has been conquered; it was only a side glance of Truth. We have passed through every despair until we now despair of despair itself. The nearer we believed ourselves to be to Truth, the further away we had drifted. When at last we were ready to renounce her altogether, she suddenly rose up before us with terrible certainty, in every error, in every lie we saw her distorted countenance confronting us.

So we may never wholly know her, can but acknowledge her everywhere, fulfil her always, carry her out in action. For us, naked Truth is nowhere, but everything about us is her garment. Clouded by our earthly senses, we cannot behold her, but illumined by the divine spirit we can bear witness to her. Seen with human eyes everything is error, but in everything, from everything, as soon as it has been touched by the divine breath, everlasting Truth discloses her presence. *Imple superna gratia!*[1]

Hesse

Hermann Hesse (1877–1962) was born in Germany, but lived most of his life in Switzerland. His father, who had been a missionary in India, later worked as a publisher. The son reflected his family's influence in his respect for the Pietist tradition (Hermann's first studies were in theology), his interest in Orientalism, and his employment as a bookseller and a publisher. Fascinated by art, intrigued by psychoanalysis (he received prolonged treatment from a disciple of C. G. Jung), firm Humanist and humanitarian, Hesse remained stubbornly pacifist during the First and the Second World Wars.

Hesse's first collection of poetry, a slim volume entitled *Romantische Lieder* (Romantic Songs), was published in 1899. His writing career culminated in 1946, when he was awarded both the Goethe Prize and the Nobel Prize for literature.

The essay reprinted here was written during the period when the First World War's stress coincided with psychoanalysis, and appeared in 1920 in a volume aptly entitled *Blick ins Chaos* (literally: glance, or peep, into chaos). It provides not only a statement of many characteristic Expressionist ideas, but also an indication of the particular relevance the work of Dostoevsky began to acquire for Western readers with the onset of chaos and war.

The Brothers Karamazoff, or The Downfall of Europe

It appears to me that what I call the Downfall of Europe is foretold and explained with extreme clarity in Dostoevsky's works and in the most concentrated form in "The Brothers Karamazoff."

It seems to me that European and especially German youth are destined to find their greatest writer in Dostoevsky—not in Goethe, not even in Nietzsche. In the most modern poetry, there is everywhere an approach to Dostoevsky, even though it is sometimes callow and imitative. The ideal of

---

[1]Fill with superior grace.

Source: From *In Sight of Chaos,* pp. 13–21, 25–26, 28–32, 38–39, 44–46. Translated by Stephen Hudson, Zürich, 1923; Verlag Seldwyla, Zürich & A. Zwemmer, 78, Charing Cross Road, London, W.C. 2. First published as *Blick ins Chaos,* 1915.

the Karamazoff, primeval, Asiatic, and occult, is already beginning to consume the European soul. That is what I mean by the Downfall of Europe. This downfall is a return home to the mother, a turning back to Asia, to the source, to the "Faustian Mothers" and will necessarily lead, like every death on earth, to a new birth.

We contemporaries see a "downfall" in these events in the same way as the aged who, compelled to leave the home they love, mourn a loss to them irreparable while the young think only of the future, care only for what is new.

What is that Asiatic Ideal that I find in Dostoevsky, the effect of which will be, as I see it, to overwhelm Europe?

Briefly, it is the rejection of every strongly-held Ethic and Moral in favour of a comprehensive *Laissez-faire*. This is the new and dangerous faith that Elder Zossima announced, the faith lived by Alyosha and Dmitri, a faith which was brought into clearer expression by Ivan Karamazoff. In the case of Elder Zossima, the ideal Right still reigns supreme. Good and Evil always exist for him; but he bestows his love on evildoers from choice. Alyosha already makes something far more vital of this new creed, taking the way through filth and slime with an almost amoral impartiality. He reminds us of Zarathustra's vow: *"In that day I vowed that I would renounce every aversion."* But Alyosha's brothers carry this further, they take this road with greater decision; they seem often to do so defiantly. In the voluminous book it often appears as though the relationship of the Brothers Karamazoff unfolded itself too slowly so that what at one time seems stable, at another becomes solvent. The saintly Alyosha becomes ever more worldly, the worldly brothers more saintly, and similarly the most unprincipled and unbridled of them becomes the saintliest, the most sensitive, the most spiritual prophet of a new holiness, of a new morality, of a new mankind. That is very curious. The more the tale unfolds itself, the wickeder and the more drunken, the more licentious and brutal the Karamazoffs, the more brightly the new Ideal glows through the corpus of these raw appearances, people and acts; and the more spiritual, the saintlier, they inwardly become. Compared with the drunken, murdering, violent Dmitri and the cynical, intellectual Ivan—the decent, highly respectable magistrate and the other representatives of the bourgeoisie, triumph though they may outwardly, are shabby, hollow, worthless.

It seems, then, that the "New Ideal" by which the roots of the European spirit is being sapped is an entirely amoral concept, a faculty to feel the Godlike, the significant, the fatalistic in the wickedest and in the ugliest and even to accord them veneration and worship. No less than that. The ironical exaggeration with which the Magistrate in his speech seeks to hold these Karamazoffs up to the scorn of the citizens is not really an exaggeration. It

is indeed a tame indictment. For in this speech the "Russian man" is exhibited from the conservative-bourgeois point of view. He had been till then a
cock-shy. Dangerous, emotional, irresponsible, yet conscience-haunted; soft,
dreamy, cruel, yet fundamentally childish. As such one still likes to regard the
"Russian man" today, although, I believe he has for a long time been on the
road to becoming the European man. And this is the Downfall of Europe.

Let us look at this "Russian man" a moment. He is far older than Dostoevsky, but Dostoevsky has finally shown him to the world in all his fearful
significance. The "Russian man" is Karamazoff, he is Fyodor Pavlovitch, he
is Dmitri, he is Ivan, he is Alyosha. These four, different as they may appear,
belong inseparably together. Together they are the "Russian man," together
they are the approaching, the proximate man of the European crisis. Next,
notice something very remarkable. Ivan in the course of the story turns from
a civilized man into a Karamazoff, from a European into a Russian, out of a
definitely-formed historical type into the unformed raw material of Destiny.
There is a fairy-like dream-reality about the way in which Ivan slides out of
his original psychology: out of his understanding, coolness, knowledge.
There is mystical truth in this sliding of the apparently solid brother into the
hysterical, into the Russian, into the Karamazoff-like. It is just he, the
doubter, who at the end holds speech with the devil! . . .

So the "Russian man" is not drawn as the hysterical, the drunkard, the
felon, the poet, the Saint, but as one with them all, as possessing all those
characteristics simultaneously. The "Russian man," Karamazoff, is assassin
and judge, ruffian and tenderest soul, the completest egoist and the most self-
sacrificing hero. We shall not get a grasp of him from a European, from a
hard and fast moral, ethical, dogmatic standpoint. In this man the outward
and the inward, Good and Evil, God and Satan are united.

The urgent appeal ever rings out from these Karamazoffs for the symbol
after which their spirit is striving, a God who is also a Devil. Dostoevsky's
"Russian man" is penetrated by that symbol. The God-Devil, the primeval
Demiurgus, he who was there from the beginning, who alone stands on the
other side of the forbidden, who knows neither day nor night, neither good
nor evil. He is the Nothingness and the All. He is unknowable to us, for we
have only the power to recognize prohibition, we are individual beings,
bound to day and night, to warm and to cold, we need a God and a Devil.
On the other side of that which is forbidden, in Nothingness and in The All,
only Demiurgus, the God of the Altogether, who knows neither Good nor
Evil, can live.

There would be much to say about this but what I have written must
suffice. We have seen the nature of the "Russian man." He reaches forth

beyond prohibitions, beyond natural instincts, beyond morality. He is the man who has grasped the idea of freeing himself and on the other side, beyond the veil, beyond *principium individuationis,* of turning back again. This ideal man of the Karamazoffs loves nothing and everything, fears nothing and everything, does nothing and everything. He is primeval matter, he is monstrous soul-stuff. He cannot live in this form, he can only go under, he can only pass on. Dostoevsky has conjured forth this creature of the downfall, this fearful apparition. It has often been said that it is a good thing his Karamazoffs were not developed to their last stage. Otherwise not only Russia but mankind would have been exploded into the air.

But what has been said, though the speaker has not drawn from his words their ultimate implications, can never be unsaid. That which exists, that which has been thought, that which is possible, can never again be extinguished. The "Russian man" has long existed, he exists far outside Russia, he rules half Europe, and part of the dreaded explosion has indeed in these last years been audibly evident. It shows itself in that Europe is tired, it shows itself in that Europe wants to turn homewards, in that Europe wants rest, in that Europe wants to be recreated, reborn. . . .

But quite another question is how we are to regard this Downfall. Here we are at the parting of the ways as we are of the spirit. Those who cling definitely to the past, those who venerate time-honoured cultural forms, the Knights of a treasured morality, must seek to delay this downfall and will mourn it inconsolably when it passes. For them the Downfall is the End; for the others it is the Beginning. For the first, Dostoevsky is a criminal, for the others a Saint. For the one party, Europe and its soul constitute an entity once and for all, foreordained, inviolate, a thing fixed and immutable. For the other, it is a becoming, a mutable, ever-changing thing. . . .

Every formation of humanity, every culture, every civilization, every order, is based upon an endowment of something over and above that which is allowed and that which is forbidden. Man, half-way between animal and a higher consciousness, has always a great deal within him to repress, to hide, to deny, in order to be a decent human being and to be socially possible. Man is full of animal, full of primeval being, full of the tremendous, scarcely tamed instincts of a beastly, cruel selfishness. All these dangerous instincts are there, always. But culture, super-consciousness, civilisation, have covered them over. Man does not show them, he has learnt from childhood to hide these instincts and deny them. But every one of these instincts must come sooner or later to the surface. Each instinct goes on living, not one is killed, not one is permanently and for ever changed and ennobled. And each of these instincts is in itself good, is not worse than another. But for every period and culture there is a particular instinct which it regards with special aversion or horror. Now when these instincts are again aroused, in the form of unextinguished and merely superficially though carefully restrained nature forces, when these beasts again begin roaring like slaves whose spirit, long crushed by flogging and repression, is rekindled by insurgence, then the Karamazoffs are upon us. When a culture, one of these attempts to domesticate man, gets tired and begins to decay, then men become in greater measure remarkable. They become hysterical, develop strange lusts, become like young people in puberty or like women in child-birth. Longings for which man has no name arise in the soul; longings which the old culture and morality must hold for wrong. But they announce themselves with so innocent a voice, that Good and Evil become interchangeable and every law reels.

Such people are the Brothers Karamazoff. Every law easily appears to them as a convention, every morality as philistine; they lightly adopt every licence, every caprice. With ever so great a gladness they listen to the many voices in their own hearts.

But these souls need not inevitably reap crime and turbulence from Chaos. As a new direction is given to the interrupted primeval current, so the seed is sowed of a new order, of a new morality.

With every culture it is the same. We cannot destroy the primeval current, the animal in us, for with its death we should die ourselves. But we can to a certain extent guide it, to a certain extent we can calm it down, to a certain extent make the "Good" serviceable, as one harnesses a vicious horse to a good cart. Only from time to time the lustre of this "Good" becomes old and weak, the instincts no longer believe in it, refuse any longer to be yoked to it. Then the culture breaks in pieces, slowly as a rule, so that what we call ancient takes centuries to die.

And before the old, dying culture and morality can be dissolved into a new one, in that fearful, dangerous, painful stage, mankind must look again into its own soul, must see the beast arise in itself again, must again recognize the overlordship of the primeval forces in itself, forces which are super-moral. Those who are foreordained, prepared and ripe for this event are Karamazoffs. They are hysterical and dangerous, they are as ready to be malefactors as ascetics, they believe in nothing except the utter dubiousness of every belief. . . .

And do these developments in the soul of imaginary characters of fiction really signify the Downfall of Europe? Certainly. They signify it as surely as the mind's eye perceives life and eternity in the grass-blade of spring and death in its inevitability in every falling leaf of autumn. It is possible that the whole "Downfall of Europe" will play itself out "only" inwardly, "only" in the souls of a generation, "only" in changing the meaning of worn-out symbols, in the devaluation of spiritual values. Thus, the ancient world, that first brilliant coining of European culture, did not go down under Nero. Its destruction was not due to Spartacus nor to the Germanic tribes. But "only" to a thought out of Asia, that simple, subtle thought that had been there very long, but which took the form the teacher Christ gave to it. . . .

I said Dostoevsky is not a poet, or he is a poet only in a secondary sense. I called him a prophet. It is difficult to say exactly what a prophet means. It seems to me something like this. A prophet is a sick man, like Dostoevsky who was an epileptic. A prophet is the sort of sick man who has lost the sound sense of taking care of himself, the sense which is the saving of the efficient citizen. It would not do if there were many such, for the world would go to pieces. This sort of sick man, be he called Dostoevsky or Karamazoff, has that strange, occult, godlike faculty . . . he is a seer and an oracle. A people, a period, a country, a continent has fashioned out of its corpus an organ, a sensory instrument of infinite sensitiveness, a very rare and delicate organ. Other men, thanks to their happiness and health, can never be troubled with this endowment. This sensory instrument, this mantological faculty[1] is not crudely comprehensible like some sort of telepathy or magic, although the gift can show itself even in such confusing forms. Rather is it that the sick man of this sort interprets the movements of his own soul in terms of the universal and of mankind. Every man has visions, every man has fantasies, every man has dreams. And every vision, every dream, every idea and thought of a man, on the road from the unconscious to the conscious, can have a thousand different meanings of which every one may be right. But the appearances and visions of the seer and the prophet are not his own. The nightmare of visions which oppresses him does not warn him of a personal illness, of a personal death, but of the illness, the death, of that corpus whose sensory organ he is. This corpus can be a family, a clan, a people, or it can be all mankind. In the soul of Dostoevsky a certain sickness and sensitiveness to suffering in the bosom of mankind which is otherwise called hysteria, found at once its means of expression and its barometer. Mankind is now on the point of realizing this. Already half of Europe, at all events half of Eastern Europe, is on the road to Chaos. In a state of drunken illusion she is reeling into the abyss and, as she reels, she sings a drunken hymn such as Dmitri Karamazoff sang. The insulted citizen laughs that song to scorn, the saint and the seer hear it with tears.

---

[1]Ability to prophesy.

Cubism

As part of the great campaign to break through to reality and express essentials, Paul Cézanne had developed a technique of painting in almost geometrical terms and concluded that the painter "must see in nature the cylinder, the sphere, the cone." At the same time, the influence of African sculpture on a group of young painters and poets living in Montmartre—Picasso, Braque, Max Jacob, Apollinaire, Derain, and André Salmon—suggested the potential of simplification or schematization as a means of pointing out essential features at the expense of insignificant ones. Both Cézanne and the Africans indicated the possibility of abstracting certain qualities of the subject, using lines and planes for the purpose of emphasis. But if a subject could be analyzed into a series of significant features, it became feasible (and this was the great discovery of Cubist painters) to leave the laws of perspective behind and rearrange these features in order to gain a fuller, more thorough, view of the subject. The painter could view the subject from all sides and attempt to present its various aspects all at the same time, just as they existed—simultaneously.

We have here an attempt to capture yet another aspect of reality by fusing time and space in their representation as they are fused in life, but, because the medium is still flat, the Cubists introduced what they called a new dimension—movement. Before long, however, its original purpose—the capture and more complete reproduction of still objective reality—was lost from sight. Instead, the artist soon became more interested in what had started as his means: that is, in purer and purer geometrical forms with no immediate relation to the object from which they derived, and in their increasingly abstract and arbitrary arrangement.

Cubism still sees space (and through space reality) as differentiated. Its great invention was to introduce movement into painting and use the possibilities of geometrical projection. But, in time, even these innovations yielded too concrete an approach to subjective reality and expression. As the Cubist technique was applied on ever more abstract lines, differentiation shrank and disappeared. Abstractionists see no more sections, no divisions between different segments of reality; and this is not surprising since reality has been transferred from the outside to the inside of the artist where experience is all one and everything exists on the same plane: a flower pot and a flower petal, a house and a T square, exist on the same plane, quite undifferentiated. Nothing is an island any longer, nothing (or everything) *entire of itself.*

Apollinaire

Guillaume Apollinaire (1880–1918), whose real name was Wilhelm Apollinaris de Kostrowitzki, was born in Rome of Italo-Polish extraction. His talent and his artistic activities (he earned his living for a while by preparing new editions of old French pornographic classics) mirrored a complex ancestry and a somewhat unusual education. Close to the poets and painters of the early Cubist movement, himself a poet of great originality and some distinction, he set out to introduce Cubism to the public in terms that the public, even if it should depart from its usual steadfast indifference toward marginal artistic activities, would hardly understand or appreciate; but he has left us an excellent statement of the aims and attitudes of his friends, which some contemporaries, at least, found valuable. As a banker who was being shown over the New York Armory show of 1913 commented: "Something is wrong with the world. These men know."

Wounded in the war, his health and to some extent also his mind impaired, Apollinaire succumbed to the influenza epidemic that swept Europe in 1918; but before he died he had joined Dada in 1917 and, perhaps, invented Surrealism.[1] Certainly, with its mixture of erudition and dreamlike lyricism, his poetry provided an important bridge between Symbolism and Surrealism, a bridge that many of his contemporaries crossed.

On Painting

The plastic virtues: purity, unity, and truth, keep nature in subjection.

The rainbow is bent, the seasons quiver, the crowds push on to death, science undoes and remakes what already exists, whole worlds disappear for ever from our understanding, our mobile images repeat themselves, or revive their vagueness, and the colors, the odours, and the sounds to which we are sensitive astonish us, then disappear from nature—all to no purpose.

This monster beauty is not eternal.

We know that our breath has had no beginning and will never cease, but our first conceptions are of the creation and the end of the world.

However too many painters still adore plants, stones, the sea, or men.

---

[1]Apollinaire's *Mamelles de Tirésias,* a burlesque argument in favor of fecundity in wartime, first performed on April 24, 1917, was described by him as "surrealist."

Source: The Cubist Painters, No. 1 Documents of Modern Art, 1949 trans. by Lionel Abel. Reprinted by permission from Wittenborn Art Books, Inc.

We quickly get used to the bondage of the mysterious. And servitude ends by creating real delights.

Workers are allowed to control the universe, yet gardeners have even less respect for nature than have artists.

The time has come for us to be the masters. And good will is not enough to make victory certain.

On this side of eternity dance the mortal forms of love, whose accursed discipline is summed up by the name "nature."

Flame is the symbol of painting, and the three plastic virtues burn with radiance.

Flame has a purity which tolerates nothing alien and cruelly transforms in its image whatever it touches.

Flame has a magical unity; if it is divided, each fork will be like the single flame.

Finally it has the sublime and incontestable truth of its own light.

Good Western painters of this period hold to their purity without regard to natural forces.

Purity is a forgetting after study. And for a single pure artist to die, it would be necessary for all pure artists of past ages to have never existed.

Painting purifies itself in Europe with the ideal logic which the older painters handed on to the new ones, as if giving them life.

And that is all.

This painter finds pleasure, that one pain; one squanders his inheritance, another becomes rich, and still others have nothing but life.

And that is all.

You cannot carry around on your back the corpse of your father. You leave him with the other dead. You remember him, miss him, speak of him with admiration. And if you become a father yourself, you cannot expect one of your children to be willing to split in two for the sake of your corpse.

But in vain do our feet relinquish the soil which holds the dead.

To insist on purity is to baptize instinct, to humanize art, and to deify personality.

The root, the stem and the flower of the lily, instance the development of purity to its symbolical blossoming.

All bodies stand equal before light, and their modifications are determined by this dazzling power which moulds them according to its will.

We do not know all the colors. Each of us invents new ones.

But above all, the painter must contemplate his own divinity, and the pictures which he offers to the admiration of men will confer upon them, likewise, the glory of exercising their divinity—if only for a moment. To achieve this, is it necessary to encompass in one glance the past, the present, and the future.

The canvas should present that essential unity which alone can elicit ecstasy.

Then nothing unstable will send us off half-cocked. We will not be suddenly turning back. Free spectators, we will not sacrifice our life to our curiosity. The smugglers of appearances will not be able to get their contraband past the salt statues before our customs-house of reason.

We will not go astray in the unknown future, which, severed from eternity, is but a word fated to tempt man.

We will not waste our strength on the too-fugitive present; the fashionable, for the artist, can only be the mask of death.

The picture will exist ineluctably. The vision will be entire, complete, and its infinity, instead of indicating some imperfection, will simply express the relation between a newly created thing and a new creator, nothing more. Otherwise there would be no unity, and the connection which the different points of the canvas have with various dispositions, objects, and lights, would reveal only an assemblage of odds and ends, lacking all harmony.

For while an infinite number of creatures, each testifying to its creator, can exist without any one creation encroaching on the space of the others, yet it is impossible to conceive them all at once, and death results from their juxtaposition, their union, their love.

Each god creates in his own image, and so do painters. Only photographers manufacture duplicates of nature.

Neither purity nor unity counts without truth, which cannot be compared to reality, since it is always the same, subsisting beyond the scope of nature, which strives to imprison us in that fatal order of things limiting us to the nearly animal.

Artists are above all men who want to become inhuman.

Painfully they search for traces of inhumanity, traces which are to be found nowhere in nature.

These traces are clues to truth, aside from which there is no reality we can know.

But reality will never be discovered once and for all. Truth is always new. Otherwise truth would be a system even more wretched than nature itself.

But such pitiful truths, more distant, less distinct, less real each day, would reduce painting to a sort of plastic writing, intended simply to facilitate communication between people of the same race.

In our times, a machine to reproduce such signs would be quickly invented.

Many new painters limit themselves to pictures which have no real subjects. And the titles which we find in the catalog are like proper names, which designate men without characterizing them.

There are men named Stout who are in fact quite thin, and others named White who are very dark; well now, I have seen pictures entitled *Solitude* containing many human figures.

In the cases in question, the artists even condescend at times to use vaguely explanatory words such as *Portrait, Landscape,* and *Still-life;* however, many young painters use as a title only the very general term *Painting.*

These painters, while they still look at nature, no longer imitate it, and carefully avoid any representation of natural scenes which they may have observed, and then reconstructed from preliminary studies.

Real resemblance no longer has any importance, since everything is sacrificed by the artist to truth, to the necessities of a higher nature whose existence he assumes but does not lay bare. The subject has little or no importance any more.

Generally speaking, modern art repudiates most of the techniques of pleasing devised by the great artists of the past.

While the goal of painting is today, as always, the pleasure of the eye, the art-lover is henceforth asked to expect delights other than those which looking at natural objects can easily provide.

Thus we are moving towards an entirely new art which will stand, with respect to painting as envisaged heretofore, as music stands to literature.

It will be pure painting, just as music is pure literature.

The music-lover experiences, in listening to a concert, a joy of a different order from the joy given by natural sounds, such as the murmur of the brook, uproar of a torrent, the whistling of the wind in a forest, or the harmonies of human speech based on reason rather than on esthetics.

In the same way, the new painters will provide their admirers with artistic sensations by concentrating exclusively on the problem of creating harmony with unequal lights.

Everybody knows the story told by Pliny about Apelles and Protogenes. It clearly illustrates the esthetic pleasure resulting solely from the contradictory harmonies referred to above.

Apelles landed, one day, on the isle of Rhodes, and went to see the work of Protogenes who lived there. Protogenes was not in the studio when

Apelles arrived. An old woman was there, looking after the large canvas which the painter had prepared. Instead of leaving his name, Apelles drew on the canvas a line so subtle that nothing happier could be conceived.

Returning, Protogenes saw the line, recognized the hand of Apelles, and drew on the latter's line another line of another color, one even more subtle, so that it seemed as if there were three lines.

Apelles came back the next day, and again did not find his man; the subtlety of the line which he drew this time caused Protogenes to despair. The sketch aroused for many years the admiration of connoisseurs, who contemplated it with as much pleasure as if it had depicted gods and goddesses, instead of almost invisible lines.

The secret aim of the young painters of the extremist schools is to produce pure painting. Theirs is an entirely new plastic art. It is still in its beginnings, and is not yet as abstract as it would like to be. Most of the new painters depend a good deal on mathematics, without knowing it; but they have not yet abandoned nature, which they still question patiently, hoping to learn the right answers to the questions raised by life.

A man like Picasso studies an object as a surgeon dissects a cadaver.

This art of pure painting, if it succeeds in freeing itself from the art of the past, will not necessarily cause the latter to disappear; the development of music has not brought in its train the abandonment of various genres of literature, nor has the acridity of tobacco replaced the savoriness of food.

The new artists have been violently attacked for their preoccupation with geometry. Yet geometrical figures are the essence of the drawing. Geometry, the science of space, its dimensions and relations, has always determined the norms and rules of painting.

Until now, the three dimensions of Euclid's geometry were sufficient to the restiveness felt by great artists yearning for the infinite.

The new painters do not propose, any more than did their predecessors, to be geometers. But it may be said that geometry is to the plastic arts what grammar is to the art of the writer. Today, scientists no longer limit themselves to the three dimensions of Euclid. The painters have been led, quite naturally, one might say by intuition, to preoccupy themselves, with the new possibilities of spatial measurements which, in the language of the modern studios, are designed by the term: the fourth dimension.

Regarded from the plastic point of view, the fourth dimension appears to spring from the three known dimensions: it represents the immensity of space, eternalizing itself in all dimensions at any given moment. It is space itself, the dimension of the infinite; the fourth dimension endows objects with plasticity. It gives the object its right proportions on the whole, whereas in Greek art for instance, a somewhat mechanical rhythm constantly destroys the proportions.

Greek art had a purely human conception of beauty. It took man as a measure of perfection. But the art of the new painters takes the infinite universe as its ideal, and it is to this ideal that we owe a new norm of the perfect, one which permits the painter to proportion objects in accordance with the degree of plasticity he desires them to have.

Nietzsche divined the possibility of such an art:

"Oh divine Dionysius, why pull my ears?" Ariadne asks her philosophical lover in one of the celebrated dialogues on the isle of Naxos. "I find something pleasant and delightful in your ears, Ariadne; why are they not even longer?"

Nietzsche, in relating this anecdote, puts into the mouth of Dionysius an implied condemnation of all Greek art.

Finally, I must point out that the fourth dimension—this utopian expression should be analysed and explained so that nothing more than historical interest may be attached to it—has come to stand for the aspirations and premonitions of the many young artists who contemplate Egyptian, Negro, and Oceanic sculptures, meditate on various scientific works, and live in the anticipation of a sublime art.

Wishing to attain the proportions of the ideal, to be no longer limited to the human, the young painters offer us works which are more cerebral than sensual. They discard more and more the old art of optical illusion and local proportion in order to express the grandeur of metaphysical forms. This is why contemporary art, even if it does not directly stem from specific religious beliefs, nonetheless possesses some of the characteristics of great, that is to say, religious art.

It is the social function of great poets and artists to renew continually the appearance nature has for the eyes of man.

Without poets, without artists, men would soon weary of nature's monotony. The sublime idea men have of the universe would collapse with dizzying speed. The order which we find in nature, and which is only an effect of art, would at once vanish. Everything would break up in chaos. There would be no seasons, no civilization, no thought, no humanity; even life would give way, and the impotent void would reign everywhere.

Poets and artists plot the characteristics of their epoch, and the future docilely falls in with their desires.

The general form of an Egyptian mummy is in conformity with the figures drawn by Egyptian artists, and yet the ancient Egyptians were far from being all alike. They simply conformed to the art of their time.

To create the illusion of the typical is the social role and peculiar end of art. God knows how the pictures of Monet and Renoir were abused! Very well! But one has only to glance at some photographs of the period to see how closely people and things conformed to the pictures of them by these great painters.

Since of all the plastic products of an epoch, works of art have the most energy, this illusion seems to me quite natural. The energy of art imposes itself on men, and becomes for them the plastic standard of the period. Thus, those who mock the new painters are actually laughing at their own features, for people in the future will portray the men of today to be as they are represented in the most alive, which is to say, the newest art of our time. And do not tell me there are today various other schools of painting in whose images humanity will be able to recognize itself. All the art works of an epoch end by resembling the most energetic, the most expressive, and the most typical works of the period. Dolls belong to popular art; yet they always seem to be inspired by the great art of the same epoch. This is a truth which can easily be verified. Yet who would dare to say that the dolls which were sold at bargain counters, around 1880, were shaped by a sentiment akin to what Renoir felt when he painted his portraits? No one perceived the relationship then. But this only means that Renoir's art was sufficiently energetic to take hold of our senses, even though to the general public of the epoch in which he made his début his conceptions seemed absurd and foolish.

There has been a certain amount of suspicion, notably in the case of the most recent painters, of some collective hoax or error.

But in all the history of art there is not a single instance of such general collaboration in artistic fraud or error. There are, indeed, isolated cases of mystification and blundering. But the conventional elements of which works of art are to a great extent composed guarantee the impossibility of such instances becoming general.

If the new school of painting were indeed an exception to this rule, it would be so extraordinary as to verge on the miraculous. As readily imagine all the children of a country born without heads, legs, or arms, an obvious absurdity. There are no collective errors or hoaxes in art; there are only various epochs and dissimilar schools. Even if the aims pursued by these schools are not all equally elevated or equally pure, all are equally respectable, and, according to the ideas one has of beauty, each artistic school is successively admired, despised, and admired once more.

The new school of painting is known as cubism, a name first applied to it in the fall of 1908 in a spirit of derision by Henri Matisse, who had just seen a picture of some houses whose cube-like appearance had greatly struck him.

The new esthetics was first elaborated in the mind of André Dérain, but the most important and audacious works the movement at once produced were those of a great artist, Pablo Picasso, who must also be considered one of the founders: his inventions, corroborated by the good sense of Georges Braque, who exhibited a cubist picture at the *Salon des Indépendants* as early as 1908, were envisaged in the study of Jean Metzinger, who exhibited the first cubist portrait (a portrait of myself) at the *Salon des Indépendants* in 1910, and who in the same year managed to induce the Jury of the *Salon d'Automne* to admit some cubist paintings. It was also in 1910 that pictures by Robert Delaunay, Marie Laurencin and Le Fauconnier, who all belonged to the same school, were exhibited at the *Indépendants*.

The first group exhibition of the cubists, who were becoming more numerous, took place in 1911 at the *Indépendants*. Room 41, which was devoted to their works, made a deep impression. There were the knowing and seductive works of Jean Metzinger; some landscapes, *Male Nude* and *Women with Phlox* by Albert Gleizes; *Portrait of Mme Fernande X* and *Young Girls* by Marie Laurencin; *The Tower* by Robert Delaunay, *Abundance* by Le Fauconnier, and *Landscape with Nudes* by Fernand Léger.

That same year the cubists made their first appearance outside France, in Brussels; and in the preface to the catalog of this exhibition, I accepted on behalf of the exhibitors the appellations: cubism and cubist.

Towards the end of 1911 the exhibition of the cubists at the *Salon d'Automne* made a considerable stir, and Gleizes *(The Hunt, Portrait of Jacques Nayral)*, Metzinger *(Woman with Spoon)*, and Fernand Léger, were ridiculed without mercy. A new painter, Marcel Duchamp, had joined the group, as had the sculptor-architect Duchamp-Villon.

Other group exhibitions were held in November, 1911 (at the *Galérie d'Art Contemporain*, rue Tronchet, Paris), and in 1912 (at the *Salon des Indépendants*; this show was marked by the début of Juan Gris); in May of the same year another cubist exhibition was held in Spain (Barcelona welcomed the young Frenchmen with enthusiasm); finally in June, at Rouen, an exhibition was organized by the *Société des Artistes Normands* (important for presenting Francis Picabia, who had just joined the new school).

Cubism differs from the old schools of painting in that it aims, not at an art of imitation, but at an art of conception, which tends to rise to the height of creation.

In representing conceptualized reality of creative reality, the painter can give the effect of three dimensions. He can to a certain extent cube. But not by simply rendering reality as seen, unless he indulges in *trompe l'oeil,* in fore-shortening, or in perspective, thus distorting the quality of the forms conceived or created.

I can discriminate four trends in cubism. Of these, two are pure, and along parallel lines.

Scientific cubism is one of the pure tendencies. It is the art of painting new structures out of elements borrowed not from the reality of sight, but from the reality of insight. All men have a sense of this interior reality. A man does not have to be cultivated in order to conceive, for example, of a round form.

The geometrical aspect which made such an impression on those who saw the first canvases of the scientific cubists, came from the fact that the essential reality was rendered with great purity, while visual accidents and anecdotes had been eliminated. The painters who follow this tendency are: Picasso, whose luminous art also belongs to the other pure tendency of cubism, Georges Braque, Albert Gleizes, Marie Laurencin, and Juan Gris.

Physical cubism is the art of painting new structures with elements borrowed, for the most part, from visual reality. This art, however, belongs in the cubist movement because of its constructive discipline. It has a great future as historical painting. Its social role is very clear. But it is not a pure art. It confuses what is properly the subject with images. The painter-physicist who created this trend is Le Fauconnier.

Orphic cubism is the other important trend of the new art school. It is the art of painting new structures out of elements which have not been borrowed from the visual sphere, but have been created entirely by the artist himself, and been endowed by him with fulness of reality. The work of the Orphic artist must simultaneously be a pure esthetic pleasure, a structure which is self-evident, and a sublime meaning, that is, a subject. This is pure art. The light in Picasso's paintings is based on this conception, to which Robert Delaunay's inventions have contributed much, and towards which Fernand Léger, Francis Picabia, and Marcel Duchamp are also addressing themselves.

Instinctive cubism, the art of painting new structures of elements which are not borrowed from visual reality, but are suggested to the artist by instinct and intuition, has long tended towards Orphism. The instinctive artist lacks lucidity and an esthetic doctrine; instinctive cubism includes a large number of artists. Born of French Impressionism, this movement has now spread all over Europe.

Cézanne's last paintings and his water colors belong to cubism, but Courbet is the father of the new painters; and André Derain, whom I propose to discuss some other time, was the eldest of his beloved sons, for we find him at the beginning of the fauvist movement, which was a kind of introduction to cubism, and also at the beginning of this great subjective movement; but it would be too difficult today to write discerningly of a man who so wilfully stands apart from everyone and everything.

The modern school of painting seems to me the most audacious that has ever appeared. It has posed the question of what is beautiful in itself.

It wants to visualize beauty disengaged from whatever charm man has for men, and until now, no European artist has dared attempt this. The new artists demand an ideal beauty, which will be, not merely the proud expression of the species, but the expression of the universe, to the degree that it has been humanized by light.

The new art clothes its creations with a grandiose and monumental appearance which surpasses anything else conceived by the artists of our time. Ardent in its search for beauty, it is noble and energetic, and the reality it brings us is marvellously clear. I love the art of today because above all else I love the light, for man loves light more than anything; it was he who invented fire.

Futurism

The years before 1914 witnessed a widespread revival of aggressive, nationalistic, and warlike sentiments in a younger generation excited by the growing political friction of the time and tired of the rationalism of its elders, whom it did not find particularly admirable or even successful. The mood was reflected in a new movement, young, dynamic, and eager to sing the glories of the new age—machines, steel tracks, guns, and roaring engines. Speed and power furnished the dominant *motif* of the new age, and its proponents set out to translate them into prose, verse, and the plastic arts.

Although the Futurists were all Italian, their first manifesto was published in the Paris *Figaro* (February 20, 1909), and their style was borrowed largely from Cubism. The credo was remarkably revealing as a document of its time, and it affected small groups in Russia and France, but Futurism as a movement does not seem to have had many adherents outside of Italy itself. There, its advocacy of the dangerous life and of almost frenetic action for action's sake led many of its friends to Fascism: its most accomplished painter, Severini, joined Mussolini's party, and so did the poet Marinetti, who became a Fascist senator.

There is little to add to the latter's exalted declarations; they differ little from the slogans of the future Duce, but they mirrored in their time the aspirations of many schoolboys excited by the new possibilities of flight, of the internal combustion engine, of man's tremendously increasing power of movement and production. However, there is something else too, for, clearly, what we now label Surrealism was already present in Marinetti as it was in Apollinaire. Energy, intuition, and spontaneous action had come to stay in art as in the politics of the new century.

Marinetti

Filippo Tommaso Marinetti (1876–1944) was born in the Piedmont but studied in Paris. For a while, in Milan, he edited a review called *Poesia,* but his eyes like that of all lively-minded young intellectuals of the day, remained fixed on Paris, to which he kept returning. His Futuristic manifesto, published first in the Paris *Figaro* on February 20, 1909, had been preceded by a play, *Le roi Bombance* (1900), and was soon accompanied by a novel—also in French—*Mafarka le futuriste* (1910).

Soon, Marinetti's love for France, Italy's older Latin sister, as well as the dynamic implications of Futurism, led him to advocate Italian intervention in the war. His exhortation was voiced in a book characteristically entitled *War, the Sole Hygiene of the World* (1915). For an Italian yet another step remained: Marinetti took it with his *Futurismo e Fascismo,* a 1924 essay in support of the Fascist movement at an awkward moment in Mussolini's political fortunes. Admitted to the Italian Academy a few years later, Marinetti died bespattered with honors at an almost ripe old age, having escaped the fate he predicted for himself in the manifesto that follows.

The Foundation of Futurism

We have been up all night, my friends and I, beneath mosque lamps whose copper domes, as open-worked as our souls, yet had electric hearts. And, while we trod our native sloth into opulent Persian carpets, we carried our discussion to the furthest limits of logic and covered sheets of paper with insane scrawls.

A vast pride swelled in our breasts, to feel ourselves standing alone, like

---

Source: Le Figaro, February 20, 1909. Translated by Eugen Weber.

lighthouses or advanced guards, facing the army of enemy stars that camp in heavenly bivouacs. Alone with the greasers in the infernal engine-rooms of great ships, alone with the dark phantoms that rummage in the red bellies of bewitched locomotives, alone with the drunks fluttering, battering their wings against the walls!

And unexpectedly, like festive villages that the Po in flood suddenly unsettles and uproots to sweep them off, over the falls and eddies of a deluge, to the sea, we were disturbed by the rumbling of enormous double-decker trams, passing in fits and starts, streaked with lights.

Then the silence got worse. As we listened to the exhausted prayer of the old canal and heard the grating bones of palaces moribund in their greenery whiskers, all of a sudden hungry cars roared beneath our windows.

"Come," I said, "my friends! Let us go! At last Mythology and the mystic Ideal have been surpassed. We shall witness the birth of the Centaur and, soon, we'll see the first Angels fly! We must shake the gates of life to test the hinges and the locks! . . . Let us go! This is truly the first sun that dawns above the earth! Nothing equals the splendor of our red sword battling for the first time in the millennial gloom."

We approached the three snuffling machines to stroke their breasts. I stretched out on mine like a corpse in my coffin, but suddenly awoke beneath the steering wheel—blade of a guillotine—that threatened my stomach.

The great broom of folly tore us from ourselves and swept us through the streets, precipitous and profound like dry torrent beds. Here and there, unhappy lamps in windows taught us to despise our mathematical eyes.

"The scent," I cried, "the scent suffices for wild beasts!"

And we pursued, alike to young lions, Death of the dark fur spotted with pale crosses, that slipped ahead of us in the vast mauve sky, palpable and alive.

And yet we had no ideal Mistress high as the clouds, no cruel Queen to whom to offer our corpses twisted into Byzantine rings! Nothing to die for besides the desire to rid ourselves of our too weighty courage!

We went on, crushing the watchdogs on the thresholds of houses, leaving them flattened under our tires like a collar under the iron. Cajoling Death preceded me on every curve, offering her pretty paw and, by turns, lying flat with a jarring clamp of jaws to throw me velvety looks from the depths of puddles.

"Let us abandon Wisdom like a hideous vein-stone and enter like pride-spiced fruit into the vast maw of the wind! Let us give ourselves to the Unknown to eat, not for despair, but simply to enrich the unplumbable wells of Absurdity!"

As I spoke these words, I veered suddenly upon myself with the drunken folly of poodles chasing their own tail and there, at once, were two disapproving cyclists, reeling before me like two persuasive and yet contradictory arguments. Their inane undulations scanned over my ground. . . . What a bore! Phooey! . . . I cut off sharply and, in disgust, I pitched—bang!—into a ditch. . . .

Ah! motherly ditch, half full of muddy water! Factory ditch! I tasted by mouthfuls your bracing slime that recalls the saintly black breast of my Sudanese nurse!

As I arose, a shiny, stinking gadabout,I felt the red-hot iron of joy deliciously pierce my heart.

A crowd of fishermen and gouty naturalists had gathered in terror around the prodigy. Patient and meddlesome, they raised high above great iron casting nets to fish out my car that lay like a great mired shark. It emerged slowly, leaving behind in the ditch like scales, its heavy body of common sense, and its padding of comfort.

They thought my good shark dead, but I awoke it with a single caress on its all-powerful rump and there it was, revived, running full speed ahead upon its fins.

Then, face hidden by the good factory slime, covered by metal dross, by useless sweat and heavenly soot, carrying our crushed arms in a sling, amid the plaints of prudent fishermen and distressed naturalists, we dictated our first wills to all the *living* men on earth:

Futuristic Manifesto

1. We want to sing the love of danger, the habit of danger and of temerity.

2. The essential elements of our poetry will be courage, daring, and revolt.

3. Literature having up to now magnified thoughtful immobility, ecstasy, and sleep, we want to exalt the aggressive gesture, the feverish insomnia, the athletic step, the perilous leap, the box on the ear, and the fisticuff.

4. We declare that the world's wonder has been enriched by a fresh beauty: the beauty of speed. A racing car with its trunk adorned by great exhaust pipes like snakes with an explosive breath . . . a roaring car that seems to be driving under shrapnel, is more beautiful than the *Victory of Samothrace*.

5. We want to sing the man who holds the steering wheel, whose ideal stem pierces the Earth, itself launched on the circuit of its orbit.

6. The poet must expend himself with warmth, refulgence, and prodigality, to increase the enthusiastic fervor of the primordial elements.

7. There is no more beauty except in struggle. No masterpiece without an aggressive character. Poetry must be a violent attack against the unknown forces, summoning them to lie down before man.

8. We stand on the far promontory of centuries! . . . What is the use of looking behind us, since our task is to smash the mysterious portals of the

impossible? Time and Space died yesterday. We live already in the absolute, since we have already created the eternal omnipresent speed.

9. We want to glorify war—the only hygiene of the world—militarism, patriotism, the anarchist's destructive gesture, the fine Ideas that kill, and the scorn of woman.

10. We want to demolish museums, libraries, fight against moralism, feminism, and all opportunistic and utilitarian cowardices.

11. We shall sing the great crowds tossed about by work, by pleasure, or revolt; the many-colored and polyphonic surf of revolutions in modern capitals; the nocturnal vibration of the arsenals and the yards under their violent electrical moons; the gluttonous railway stations swallowing smoky serpents; the factories hung from the clouds by the ribbons of their smoke; the bridges leaping like athletes hurled over the diabolical cutlery of sunny rivers; the adventurous steamers that sniff the horizon; the broad-chested locomotives, prancing on the rails like great steel horses curbed by long pipes, and the gliding flight of airplanes whose propellers snap like a flag in the wind, like the applause of an enthusiastic crowd.

It is in Italy that we launch this manifesto of tumbling and incendiary violence, this manifesto through which today we set up *Futurism*, because we want to deliver Italy from its gangrene of professors, of archaeologists, of guides, and of antiquarians.

Italy has been too long a great secondhand brokers' market. We want to rid it of the innumerable museums that cover it with innumerable cemeteries.

Museums, cemeteries! . . . Truly identical in the sinister jostling of bodies that do not know each other. Great public dormitories where one sleeps forever side by side with beings hated or unknown. Reciprocal ferocity of painters and of sculptors killing each other with line and color in the same gallery.

They can be visited once a year as the dead are visited once a year. . . . We can accept that much! We can even conceive that flowers may once a year be left for *la Gioconda!* . . . But we cannot admit that our sorrows, our fragile courage, our anxiety may be taken through there every day! . . . Do you want to be poisoned? Do you want to rot?

What can one find in an old painting beside the embarrassing contortions of the artist trying to break the barriers that are impassable to his desire to wholly express his dream?

To admire an old painting is to pour our sensitiveness into a funeral urn, instead of throwing it forward by violent casts of creation and action. Do you mean thus to waste the best of you in a useless admiration of the past that must necessarily leave you exhausted, lessened, trampled?

As a matter of fact the daily frequentation of museums, of libraries and of academies (those cemeteries of wasted efforts, those calvaries of crucified dreams, those catalogues of broken impulses! . . .) is for the artist what the prolonged tutelage of parents is for intelligent young men, drunk with their talent and their ambitious will.

For the dying, the invalid, the prisoner, it will do. Since the future is forbidden them, there may be a salve for their wounds in the wonderful past. . . . But we want nothing of it—we the young, the strong, the living *Futurists!*

Let the good incendiaries come with their carbonized fingers! . . . Here they are! Here they are! . . . Set the library stacks on fire! Turn the canals in their course to flood the museum vaults! . . . There go the glorious canvases, floating adrift! Take up the picks and the hammers! Undermine the foundations of the venerable cities!

The oldest among us are not yet thirty; this means that we have at least ten years to carry out our task. When we are forty, let those younger and more valiant than us kindly throw us into the waste basket like useless manuscripts! . . . They will come after us from afar, from everywhere, prancing on the light rhythm of their first poems, clawing the air with their crooked fingers, sniffing at academy gates the good scent of our rotting intellects already intended for the catacombs of libraries.

But we shall not be there. They will find us at last, on some winter night, out in the country, under a sad hangar on which the monotonous rain strums, crouching by our trembling planes, warming our hands over the miserable fire of our books of today gaily blazing under the scintillating flight of their images.

They will gather in a mob around us, panting with anguish and spite, and all exasperated by our untiring courage will bound forward to kill us with the more hatred for the love and admiration in their hearts. And Injustice, strong and wholesome, will glitter radiantly in their eyes. For art can be nothing but violence, cruelty and injustice.

The oldest among us are not yet thirty and yet we have already squandered great treasures, treasures of energy, of love, of courage and eager will, hastily, deliriously, countlessly, breathlessly, with both hands.

Look at us! We are not out of breath. . . . Our heart is not in the least tired! For it feeds on fire, on hatred, on speed! . . . You find it surprising? That is because you do not even remember having lived!—Up on the crest of the world, once more we hurl our challenge to the stars!

Your objections? Enough! Enough! I know them! Fair enough! We know well enough what our fine, false intelligence asserts.—We are only, it says, the summary and the extension of our forebears.—Perhaps! Let it be so! . . . What does it matter? . . . But we don't want to listen! Beware of repeating these infamous words! Rather, look up!

Up on the crest of the world, once more we hurl our challenge to the stars!

Dada

From 1914 to 1918, the most advanced and cultivated nations in the world devoted all their energies to slaughter. And the way in which they went about it convinced a growing proportion of the survivors that society was led not only by criminals but by lunatic muddlers as well—men who, behind a disguise of reason and logical purpose, were leading mankind to perdition, the Bible in one hand and a bloody butcher's cleaver in the other. To the absurdity of a world in which the most sensible and responsible men devoted themselves to destruction and mayhem, a small group of artists reacted by preaching salvation through nonsense. As its name indicates, Dada—developed in wartime Switzerland by a Romanian, Tristan Tzara, an Alsatian, Hans Arp, and a German, Hugo Ball—was nihilistic, anticreative, and antiartistic. Above all, it was against reason. As Hans Arp would write some years later:

> art is a fruit growing out of man like the fruit out of a plant like the child out of the mother. while the fruit of the plant grows independent forms and never resembles a balloon or a president in a cutaway suit the artistic fruit of man shows for the most part a ridiculous resemblance to the appearance of other things. reason tells man to stand above nature and to be the measure of all things. thus man thinks he is able to live and to create against the laws of nature and he creates abortions. through reason man becomes a tragic and ugly figure. i dare say he would create even his children in the form of vases with umbilical cords if he could do so. reason has cut man off from nature.

Disillusioned at the speciousness and hypocrisy of existing values, Dada set out to ridicule all values and standards, artistic, social, and intellectual. Even before the war had ended, Dada groups appeared in Germany and France led by George Grosz, Max Ernst, and Arp in the one, Apollinaire, Jacob, Breton, Aragon, and Soupault in the other. Then, in 1917, Dada appeared in New York, with Marcel Duchamp's contribution to the Independent show, a plain marble urinal entitled *Fountain*.

But Dada could neither last nor create without going against its own announced purpose. Destructive and nonsensical, it had to either triumph on its own nihilistic terms, which made propaganda itself impossible, or else give way to other inspirations that were as ready to build as to destroy.

Tzara

Dada Manifesto

The magic of a word—
DADA—which has placed the
newsmen before the
gate of an unexpected world
has for us no
importance whatever

To launch a manifesto one must wish
A.B.C.
to fulminate against 1, 2, 3,
get mad and sharpen the wings to conquer and spread big and small a,b,c, cross oneself, shout, curse, contrive prose in the shape of absolute, irrefutable evidence, demonstrate one's non plus ultra and affirm that novelty resembles life like the last appearance of a courtesan proves the essence of God. His existence has already been proved by the accordion, the landscape and the soft word. ✳✳ To impose one's A.B.C. is a natural—hence regrettable—thing. Everybody does it in the shape of crystalbluffmadonna, monetary system, pharmaceutical product, bare leg inciting to ardent and sterile Spring. The love of novelty is the congenial cross, demonstrates a naïve couldn'tcarelessness, sign without cause, passing, positive. But this need has also grown obsolete. Documenting art with supreme simplicity: novelty, one is human and real for fun, impulsive, vibrating to crucify boredom. At the crossroads of light, alert, carefully watching the years in the forest. ✳✳ I write a manifesto and I want nothing, yet I say certain things, and I am against manifestoes on principle, as I am also against principles (half-pints for the moral worth of every phrase—too easy; the approximation was invented by the Impressionists). ✳✳ I write this manifesto to show that one can do opposing actions

Source: From Tristan Tzara, *Dada III,* Zürich, 1918. Translated by Eugen Weber.

together, in one fresh breath; I am against action; in favor of continuous contradiction, also in favor of assertion, I am neither for nor against and I do not explain because I hate common sense.

DADA—here is a word that leads the chase of ideas; every bourgeois is a little dramatist, invents different words, instead of disposing the characters in a manner befitting the quality of his intelligence, chrysalids on chairs, seeks the causes or the ends (according to the psychoanalytical method he practices) in order to strengthen his plot, speaking, self-defining history. ** Every spectator is a plotter, if he tries to explain a word: *(to understand!)* From the soft-lined refuge of meandering complications he has his instincts manipulated. Hence the calamities of married life.

Explaining: Amusement of redbellies in the mills of empty skulls.

☞ DADA SIGNIFIES NOTHING

If one thinks it futile, if one wastes one's time for a word that signifies nothing. . . .

The first thought that appears in those heads is of bacteriological order: to find its etymological, historical or, at least, psychological origin. The newspapers inform us that the Krou Negroes call the tail of a holy cow: DADA. The cube and the mother in a certain part of Italy: DADA. The wooden horse, the nurse, double affirmative in Romanian and Russian: DADA. Learned journalists see in it art for babies, other saints jesuscallinglittlechildren of the day see the return to a dry and boisterous, boisterous and monotonous, primitivism. Sensitiveness cannot be built upon one word; every structure converges upon the perfection that bores, stagnant idea of a golden bog, relative human product. The work of art must not be beauty in itself, for it is dead; neither gay nor sad, neither clear nor obscure, rejoice or maltreat personalities by serving them the tarts of holy haloes or the sweat of an arched race through the atmospheres. A work of art is never beautiful by decree, objectively, for all. Criticism is therefore useless, it exists only subjectively, for each and every one, and lacks all general character. Should one believe to have found the psychic ground common to all mankind? The attempt of Jesus and the bible cover with their broad and friendly wings: dung, beasts, days. How would one order the chaos that constitutes this infinite formless variation: man? The principle "love your neighbor" is hypocrisy. "Know thyself" is Utopian, but more acceptable because it bears malice within it. No pity. The slaughter over, we are left the hope of a purified humanity. I still speak about myself for I do not wish to convince, I have not the right to carry others away in my flow, I force none to follow me and everybody fashions his art in his own manner, whether he knows the joy that darts straight for the starry skies, or that which descends into the mines that bloom with corpses and with fertile spasms. Stalactites: seek them everywhere, in the cribs broadened by pain, the eyes white like the angels' hares.

Thus was DADA born[1] of a need for independence, of suspicion for the community. Those who belong to us keep their freedom. We recognize no theory. We have enough of the cubist and futuristic academies: laboratories of formalistic ideas. Does one engage in art to earn money and stroke the pretty bourgeois? The rhymes ring with the assonance of coin, the modulation glides along the curve of a stomach seen in profile. All the groups of artists, riding on different comets, have come to this bank in the end. The door opens on the possibilities of wallowing in cushions and in food.

Here we anchor in fat ground. Here we have the right to proclaim for we have known the thrills and the awakening. Returning drunk with energy we drive the trident into the indifferent flesh. We are streams of maledictions in tropical abundance of vertiginous vegetations, resin and rain is our sweat, we bleed and burn the thirst, our blood is strength.

Cubism was born of a simple way of seeing things: Cézanne painted a cup twenty inches below his eyes, the cubists look at it from above, others complicate the appearance by taking a perpendicular section and placing it soberly beside. (I do not forget the creators, nor the great issues of the subject which they finally settled.) ✷✷ The futurist sees the same cup in successive movement of objects one beside the other and maliciously adds a few force-lines. That does not prevent the canvas being a good or bad painting destined for the investment of intellectual capital.

The new painter creates a world, whose elements are also its means, a sober and definite work without a theme. The new artist protests: he no longer paints (symbolic and illusionistic reproduction) but creates directly in stone, wood, iron, tin, it being possible to turn the rocks of locomotive organisms in every direction by the limpid wind of monetary sensation. ✷✷ All pictural or plastic work is useless; let it be a monster that scares the servile spirits, not sweetly-sick to decorate the refectories of animals in human garb, illustrations of this dismal fable of humanity.

A painting is the art of causing two geometrical lines established as being parallel to meet on a canvas, before our eyes, in a reality which transposes into a world of other conditions and possibilities. This work is neither specified nor defined in the work, it belongs in its innumerable variations to the beholder. For its creator it is without cause and without theory. *Order =*

---

[1] In 1916 in the Cabaret Voltaire in Zurich.

disorder; self = non-self; affirmation = negation: supreme illuminations of an absolute art. Absolute in purity of cosmic and orderly chaos, eternal in the globule second without duration without respiration without light without verification. ✶✶ I like an ancient work for its novelty. There is only the contrast that binds us to the past. ✶✶ The writers that teach morality and discuss or improve the psychological fundamental principle have, apart from a hidden desire for gain, a ridiculous understanding of life, which they have classified, divided, canalized; they insist on seeing the categories dance to their tune. Their readers sneer and go on: what's the use?

There is a literature that never gets to the voracious mass. Work of creators, born of a real necessity of the author and for himself. Knowledge of a supreme selfishness, before which laws waste away. ✶✶ Every page must explode, be it by the profound and heavy seriousness, the whirlwind, the intoxication, the new, the eternal, the crushing hoax, the enthusiasm of its principles, or the way in which it is printed. Here is a reeling, fleeing world, affianced to the rattle of the infernal scale; here, on the other side, are new men. Rude, capering, riding on hiccups. See a mutilated world and the literary would-be doctors sighing for improvements. I tell you: there is no beginning, and we do not tremble, we are not sentimental. We tear apart, furious gale, the rags of clouds and of prayers and prepare the great show of the disaster, the conflagration, the disintegration. Let us prepare the suppression of mourning and replace tears by sirens that stretch from one continent to the next. Standards of intense joy, bereft of the dreariness of poison. ✶✶ DADA is the token of abstraction; advertising and business are also elements of poetry.

I destroy the drawers of the brain and those of social organization: to demoralize everywhere and throw the hand of heaven into hell, the eyes of hell to heaven, reestablish the fruitful cartwheels of an universal circus in the real powers and the fantasy of every individual.

The philosophy is the question: where to begin to look at life, god, ideas, or other phantoms. All one looks at is false. I do not consider the relative result more important than the choice between cake and cherries after dinner. The way of taking a quick look at the other side of a question in order to indirectly impose one's opinion is called dialectics, that is to haggle the spirit of french fried potatoes while dancing the method around.

If I cry:

Ideal, ideal, ideal,
Knowledge, Knowledge, Knowledge,
Bangbang, bangbang, bangbang,

I have given a fair account of progress, law, morality, and all the other fine qualities that different very intelligent people have discussed in so many books, in order to conclude in the end that, all the same, everyone has danced after his own personal bangbang, and that he is right because of his bangbang, satisfaction of sickly curiosity; private chimes for unexplainable needs; bath; financial difficulties; stomach with repercussion on life; authority of the mystical baton formulated in a bouquet of phantom-orchestra with mute bows, greased by philters with a base of animal ammonia. With the blue quizzing-glass of an angel they have dug into the innards for two cents' worth of unanimous gratitude. ✳✳ If all are right, and if all pills are Pink's, let us try for once not to be right. ✳✳ People think they can explain what they write rationally, through thought. But this is very relative. Thought is a fine thing for philosophy, but it is relative. Psychoanalysis is a dangerous malady, lulls the anti-real inclinations of man and systematizes the bourgeoisie. There is no ultimate Truth. The dialectic is an amusing machine which leads us [in commonplace fashion] to opinions we should have had in any case. Do you think to have established the preciseness of these opinions by the minute refinement of logic? Logic strained by the senses is an organic illness. The philosophers like to add to this element: The power to observe. But, as a matter of fact, this magnificent quality of the mind is the proof of its impotence. We observe, we look from one or more points of view, we choose them from among the millions that exist. Experience is also a result of chance and individual faculties. ✳✳ Science disgusts me as soon as it becomes speculation-cum-system, loses its useful character—which is so useless—but at least individual. I loathe fat objectivity and harmony, this science that finds everything in its place. Carry on kids, humanity. . . . Science says that we are the servants of nature: everything is fine, make love and break your necks. Carry on kids, humanity, pretty bourgeois and virginal journalists. . . . ✳✳ I am against systems, the most acceptable of systems is that of having none on principle. ✳✳ To complete oneself, to perfect oneself in one's own pettiness until one fills the cup of one's self, the courage to fight for and against thought, mystery of the bread sudden launching of an infernal propeller in economic lilies:

DADAIST SPONTANEITY

I call couldn'tcarelessness the state of a life in which everyone keeps his own circumstances, yet is able to respect other personalities, the two-step becoming the national anthem, curiosity shop, T.S.F. wireless telephone broadcasting the fugues of Bach, luminous signs and signposting for brothels, the organ spreading pinks for God, all this together, and truly, replacing photography and the unilateral catechism.

ACTIVE SIMPLICITY.

The powerlessness to discern between different degrees of light: to lick the semi-darkness and float in the great mouth full of honey and excrement. Measured on the scale Eternity all action is vain (if we allow thought to take its chance in an adventure whose outcome would be infinitely grotesque—important notion for the understanding of human impotence). But if life is a bad joke, without aim or initial delivery, and because we think we have to extricate ourselves properly from it, like washed chrysanthemums, we have proclaimed a single ground for understanding: art. It does not matter that we, knights of the spirit, have been singing to it for centuries. Art afflicts no one and those who know how to go about it will receive caresses and a splendid opportunity to fill the country with their conversation. Art is a private thing, the artist makes it for himself; a comprehensible work is a journalist's product, and because right now I like to mix this monster with oil-paints: paper tube imitating metal that one presses and automatically squeezes out hatred, cowardice, villainy. The artist, the poet rejoices over the venom of the mass condensed in a section-head of this industry, he is happy while he is being insulted: proof of his immutability. The author, the artist praised by the press, notes the comprehensibility of his work: miserable substitute of a cloak of public utility; rags that cover brutality, piss collaborating with the heat of an animal that hatches the basest instincts; flaccid and insipid flesh that multiplies thanks to typographical germs.
We have hustled out our inclination to snivel. Every strain of this sort is pickled diarrhea. To encourage this art means to digest it. We need works that are strong straight precise and ever misunderstood. Logic is a complication. Logic is always false. It pulls the strings of notions, words, in their formal outside shape, toward the ends of illusory centers. Its chains kill, enormous myriapods stifling independence. Married to logic, art would live in incest, swallowing, devouring its own tail—always its body, fornicating with itself. Temperament would become an asphalt nightmare of protestantism, a monument, a heap of heavy grayish guts. But suppleness, enthusiasm, and even the pleasure of injustice, this little truth we innocently keep company with and that makes us beautiful: we are subtle and our fingers are malleable and glide like the branches of that insinuating and almost liquid plant; it sums up our heart, say the cynics. And that is another point of view; but happily all flowers are not holy, and the divine in us is the awakening of anti-human activity. I am talking here about a paper flower for the buttonhole of the

gentlemen who attend the ball of masked life, kitchen of grace, white cousins supple or fat. They deal in the things we have selected. Contradiction and unity of polar opposites at one stroke, can be truth. That is if one has to pronounce this commonplace, appendix of a libidinous evil-smelling morality. Morality atrophies, like every scourge that intelligence has produced. The censure of morality and logic have inflicted on us our insensibility to policemen—cause of slavery, putrid rats that fill the bellies of the bourgeoisie and who have sullied the only corridors of clear, clean glass that remained open to artists. Let everyone cry out: there is a great destructive, negative task to be accomplished. Sweep, clean. The tidiness of the individual affirms itself after the state of madness, of aggressive, utter madness of a world left in the hands of bandits who tear each other up and destroy the centuries. Without aim or purpose, without organization: untamable folly, disintegration. Those who are strong by the word or by strength will survive, for they are quick in defense, the agility of their limbs and their perceptions blaze on their dappled sides. Morality has determined charity and pity, two greasy messes that have grown like elephants, like planets, and that are called good. They have nothing of goodness. Goodness is lucid, clear, decisive, pitiless toward compromise and politics. Morality is the infusion of hot chocolate in the veins of men. And this is not done at the behest of some supernatural power but of the trust of idea-merchants and of academic monopolizers. Sentimentality: seeing a group of men engaged in quarreling and tedium, they have invented the calendar and the medicine virtue. By sticking labels, the battle of philosophers broke out (mercantilism, balance, meticulous and petty measurements) and it was understood for a second time that pity is a sentiment, like diarrhea in respect to the disgust that spoils health, the impure task of putrid carrion out to compromise the sun.

I proclaim the opposition of all the cosmic faculties to this gonorrhea of a putrid sun produced by the factories of philosophical thought, the fierce, implacable struggle, with all the means of

DADAIST DISGUST

Every product of disgust apt to become a negation of the family, is *dada;* protest with the fists of all one's being in destructive action: DADA; knowledge of all the means up to now rejected by the sex chaste with facile compromise and manners: *DADA;* abolition of logic, dance of the impotents of creation: DADA; of all hierarchy and social equation set up for the values by our valets: *DADA;* every object, all the objects, the sentiments and the obscurities, the phantoms and the precise clash of parallel lines, are means in our struggle: DADA; abolition of memory: DADA; abolition of archaeol-

ogy: DADA; abolition of prophets: DADA; abolition of the future: DADA;
absolute undisputable belief in every god that is the immediate product of
spontaneity: *DADA;* elegant and unprejudiced leap from one harmony to
the other sphere; trajectory of a word cast like an emphatic record cry; respect
of all individualities in their monetary folly: serious, timorous, timid, ardent,
forceful, decisive, enthusiastic; stripping one's church of all heavy and useless
accessories; spitting out like a luminous cascade the unkindly or loving
thought, or pampering it—with the lively satisfaction of knowing that it
doesn't matter either way—with the same intensity in the thicket, unblem-
ished by insects for the well-born blood, and gilded by bodies of archangels,
of one's soul. Liberty: DADA DADA DADA, shriek of the shriveled colors,
blending of the contraries and of all the contradictions, the grotesqueries, the
inconsistencies: LIFE.

Surrealism

A world carefully nurtured and nourished on reason, its ills treated with reasonable remedies, had by 1918 revealed itself to be deeply rotten and utterly miserable. Following upon Dada, the Surrealists sought a richer, truer reality in the
unconscious, in awarenesses and techniques above and beyond realism and logic.
Their inspiration had come in part from the grotesqueries of Alfred Jarry (1873–
1907), whose gross and obscure *Ubu Roi* had, in 1896, excited the avant-garde
and shocked the bourgeoisie. They also drew from the brilliant artificialities of
Cubism and Futurism. And Dada itself of course cannot be ignored as an important influence, though the nihilism of Dada becomes in Surrealist hands a
hopeful though destructive approach.

The Surrealist movement as such was founded by a very few young men, quite
unknown at the end of the war: André Breton (1896–1966), Jean Cocteau
(1889–1963), Philippe Soupault (1897–   ), Louis Aragon (1897–1982), and Paul
Eluard (1895–1952).

In the essay that follows, Breton, who has always remained the symbol of this
violent and multifarious school, explains both the beginnings and the aims of his
invention. Very simply, Surrealism tried to apply the lessons of Freudian psycho-
analysis in art, either by the use of automatic writing or drawing (doodling from
the hand of a sensitive artist being more authentic and significant than an orderly
scheme of things), or by the jolt that things seen or done in this manner might
administer.

The constructive, optimistic side of Surrealism led a number of its adherents, concerned with creating a new world based on a fresh view of things and eager to smash the old stifling bourgeois values, toward Communism. Both Aragon and Paul Eluard joined the Communist Party; Breton drifted very close to it. There was no explicit connection between Surrealism and Communism besides a common agreement that the old order must be destroyed before a better world could be built. Only the passing identification between Russian Communism and humanistic ideals, made possible in the 1930s by the pusillanimity of the democratic Western powers, attracted some Surrealists closer to the party, and that not for long. Others, however, fascinated by activity for activity's sake, eagerly abandoned ends for means just as the Futurists had done in Italy. Meanwhile, the nonpolitically minded, like Salvador Dali, Jean Cocteau, and Joan Miró, continued their experiments chiefly in the cinema and in the other visual arts, more plastic media than either political society or unwieldy words.

Breton
What Is Surrealism?

At the beginning of the war of 1870 (he was to die four months later, aged twenty-four), the author of the *Chants de Maldoror* and of *Poésies,* Isidore Ducasse, better known by the name of Comte de Lautréamont, whose thought has been of the very greatest help and encouragement to my friends and myself through the fifteen years during which we have succeeded in carrying on a common activity, made the following remark, among many others which were to electrify us fifty years later: "At the hour in which I write, new tremors are running through the intellectual atmosphere; it is only a matter of having the courage to face them." 1868–75: it is impossible, looking back upon the past, to perceive an epoch so *poetically* rich, so victorious, so revolutionary and so charged with distant meaning as that which stretches from the separate publication of the *Premier Chant de Maldoror* to the insertion in a letter to Ernest Delahaye of Rimbaud's last poem, *Rêve,* which has not so far been included in his Complete Works. It is not an idle hope to wish to see the works of Lautréamont and Rimbaud restored to their correct

Source: Text of André Breton, *What Is Surrealism?* translated by David Gascoyne. Criterion Miscellany No. 43. Faber and Faber, Ltd., London, 1936. Reprinted by permission of the translator [himself a distingued English poet—E.W.].

historical background: the coming and the immediate results of the war of 1870. Other and analogous cataclysms could not have failed to rise out of that military and social cataclysm whose final episode was to be the atrocious crushing of the Paris Commune; the last in date caught many of us at the very age when Lautréamont and Rimbaud found themselves thrown into the preceding one, and by way of revenge has had as its consequence—and this is the new and important fact—the triumph of the Bolshevik Revolution.

I should say that to people socially and politically uneducated as we then were—we who, on the one hand, came for the most part from the petite-bourgeoisie, and on the other, were all by vocation possessed with the desire to intervene upon the artistic plane—the days of October, which only the passing of the years and the subsequent appearance of a large number of works within the reach of all were fully to illumine, could not there and then have appeared to turn so decisive a page in history. We were, I repeat, ill-prepared and ill-informed. Above all, we were exclusively preoccupied with the campaign of systematic refusal, exasperated by the conditions under which, in such an age, we were forced to live. But our refusal did not stop there; it was insatiable and knew no bounds. Apart from the incredible stupidity of the arguments which attempted to legitimize our participation in an enterprise such as the war, whose issue left us completely indifferent, this refusal was directed—and having been brought up in such a school, we are not capable of *changing* so much that it is no longer so directed—against the whole series of intellectual, moral and social obligations that continually and from all sides weigh down upon man and crush him. Intellectually, it was vulgar rationalism and chop logic that more than anything else formed the causes of our horror and our destructive impulse; morally, it was all duties: religious, civic and of the family; socially, it was work (did not Rimbaud say: "Jamais je ne travaillerai, ô flots de feu!"[1] and also: "La main à plume vaut la main à charrue. Quel siècle à mains! Je n'aurai jamais ma main!"[2]). The more I think about it, the more certain I become that nothing was to our minds worth saving, unless it was . . . unless it was, at last, "l'amour la poésie,"[3] to take the bright and trembling title of one of Paul Eluard's books, "l'amour la poésie," considered as inseparable in their essence and as the sole good. Between the negation of this good, a negation brought to its climax by the war, and its full and total affirmation ("Poetry should be made by all, not one"),

---

[1] Never shall I toil, oh billows of fire!

[2] The hand on the pen is as good as the hand on the plough. What a century of hands! I shall never have my hand!

[3] Love poetry.

the field was not, to our minds, open to anything but a Revolution truly extended into all domains, improbably radical, to the highest degree impractical and tragically destroying within itself the whole time the feeling that it brought with it both of desirability and of absurdity. Many of you, no doubt, would put this down to a certain youthful exaltation and to the general savagery of the time; I must, however, insist on this attitude, common to particular men and manifesting itself at periods nearly half a century distant from one another. I should affirm that in ignorance of this attitude one could form no idea of what surrealism really stands for. This attitude alone can account, and very sufficiently at that, for all the excesses that may be attributed to us but which cannot be deplored unless one gratuitously supposes that we could have started from any other point. The ill-sounding remarks that are imputed to us, the so-called inconsiderate attacks, the insults, the quarrels, the scandals—all the things that we are so much reproached with—turned up on the same road as the surrealist poems. From the very beginning, the surrealist attitude has had that in common with Lautréamont and Rimbaud which once and for all binds our lot to theirs, and that is wartime *defeatism*.

I am not afraid to say that this *defeatism* seems to me more relevant than ever. "New tremors are running through the intellectual atmosphere: it is only a matter of having the courage to face them." They are, in fact, *always* running through the intellectual atmosphere: the problem of their propagation and interpretation remains the same and, as far as we are concerned, remains to be solved. But, paraphrasing Lautréamont, I cannot refrain from adding that at the hour in which I speak, old and mortal shivers are trying to substitute themselves for those which are the very shivers of knowledge and of life. They come to announce a frightful disease, a disease inevitably followed by the deprivation of all rights; it is only a matter of having the courage to face them also. This disease is called fascism.

Let us be careful today not to underestimate the peril: the shadow has greatly advanced over Europe recently. Hitler, Dollfuss and Mussolini have either drowned in blood or subjected to corporal humiliation everything that formed the effort of generations straining towards a more tolerable and more worthy form of existence. In capitalist society, hypocrisy and cynicism have now lost all sense of proportion and are becoming more outrageous every day. Without making exaggerated sacrifices to humanitarianism, which always involves impossible reconciliations and truces to the advantage of the stronger, I should say that in this atmosphere, thought cannot consider the exterior world without an immediate shudder. Everything we know about fascism shows that it is precisely the homologation of this state of affairs, aggravated to its furthest point by the lasting resignation that it seeks to obtain from those who suffer. Is not the evident role of fascism to re-establish for the time being the tottering supremacy of finance-capital? Such a role is of itself sufficient to make it worthy of all our hatred; we continue to consider this feigned resignation as one of the greatest evils that can possibly be inflicted upon beings of our kind, and those who would inflict it deserve, in our opinion, to be beaten like dogs. Yet it is impossible to conceal the fact that this immense danger is there, lurking at our doors, that it has made its appearance within our walls, and that it would be pure byzantinism to dispute too long, as in Germany, over the choice of the barrier to be set up against it, when all the while, *under several aspects,* it is creeping nearer and nearer to us. During the course of taking various steps with a view to contributing, in so far as I am capable, to the organization in Paris of the anti-fascist struggle, I have noticed that already a certain doubt has crept into the intellectual circles of the left as to the possibility of successfully combating fascism, a doubt which has unfortunately infected even those elements whom one might have thought it possible to rely on and who had come to the fore in this struggle. Some of them have even begun to make excuses for the loss of the battle already. Such dispositions seem to me to be so dismaying that I should not care to be speaking here without first having made clear my position in relation to them, or without anticipating a whole series of remarks that are to follow, affirming that today, more than ever before, *the liberation of the mind,* the express aim of surrealism, demands as primary condition, in the opinion of the surrealists, *the liberation of man,* which implies that we must struggle with our fetters with all the energy of despair; that today more than ever before the surrealists entirely rely for the bringing about of the liberation of man upon the proletarian Revolution.

I now feel free to turn to the object of this pamphlet, which is to attempt to explain what surrealism is. A certain immediate ambiguity contained in the word surrealism, is, in fact, capable of leading one to suppose that it designates I know not what transcendental attitude, while, on the contrary it expresses—and always has expressed for us—a desire to deepen the foundations of the real, to bring about an ever clearer and at the same time ever more passionate consciousness of the world perceived by the senses. The whole evolution of surrealism, from its origins to the present day, which I am about to attempt to retrace, shows that our unceasing wish, growing more and more urgent from day to day, has been at all costs to avoid considering a system of thought as a refuge, to pursue our investigations with eyes wide open to their outside consequences, and to assure ourselves that the results of these investigations would be capable of facing the *breath of the street.* At the limits, for many past years—or more exactly, since the conclusion of what one may term the purely *intuitive* epoch of surrealism (1919–25)—at the limits, I say, we have attempted to present interior reality and exterior reality as two elements in process of unification, of finally becoming *one*. This final unification is the supreme aim of surrealism: interior reality and exterior reality being, in the present form of society, in contradiction (and in this contradiction we see the very cause of man's unhappiness, but also the source of his movement), we have assigned to ourselves the task of confronting these two realities with one another on every possible occasion, of refusing to allow the preeminence of the one over the other, yet not of acting on the one and on the other *both at once,* for that would be to suppose that they are less apart from one another than they are (and I believe that those who pretend they are acting on both simultaneously are either deceiving us or are a prey to a disquieting illusion); of acting on these two realities not both at once, then, but one after the other, in a systematic manner, allowing us to observe their reciprocal attraction and interpenetration and to give to this interplay of forces all the extension necessary for the trend of these two adjoining realities to become one and the same thing.

As I have just mentioned in passing, I consider that one can distinguish two epochs in the surrealist movement, of equal duration, from its origins (1919, year of the publication of the *Champs Magnétiques*) until today: a purely *intuitive* epoch, and a *reasoning* epoch. The first can summarily be characterized by the belief expressed during this time in the all-powerfulness of thought, considered capable of freeing itself by means of its own resources. This belief witnesses to a prevailing view that I look upon today as being extremely mistaken, the view that *thought is supreme over matter.* The definition of surrealism that has passed into the dictionary, a definition taken from the *Manifesto* of 1924, takes account only of this entirely idealist disposition and (for voluntary reasons of simplification and amplification destined to influence in my mind the future of this definition) does so in terms that suggest that I deceived myself at the time in advocating the use of an automatic thought not only removed from all control exercised by the reason but also disengaged from *"all aesthetic or moral preoccupations."* It should at least have been said: *conscious* aesthetic or moral preoccupations. During the period under review, in the absence, of course, of all seriously discouraging exterior events, surrealist activity remained strictly confined to its first theoretical premises, continuing all the while to be the vehicle of that total "nonconformism" which, as we have seen, was the binding feature in the coming together of those who took part in it, and the cause, during the first few years after the war, of an uninterrupted series of adhesions. No coherent political or social attitude, however, made its appearance until 1925, that is to say (and it is important to stress this), until the outbreak of the Moroccan war, which, re-arousing in us our particular hostility to the way armed conflicts affect man, abruptly placed before us the necessity of making a public protest. This protest, which, under the title *La Révolution d'Abord et Toujours* (October 1925), joined the names of the surrealists proper to those of thirty other intellectuals, was undoubtedly rather confused ideologically; it none the less marked the breaking away from a whole way of thinking; it none the less created a precedent that was to determine the whole future direction of the movement. Surrealist activity, faced with a brutal, revolting, *unthinkable* fact, was forced to ask itself what were its proper resources and to determine their *limits;* it was forced to adopt a precise attitude, exterior to itself, in order to continue to face whatever exceeded these limits. Surrealist activity at this moment entered into its *reasoning* phase. It suddenly experienced the necessity of crossing over the gap that separates absolute idealism from dialectical materialism. This necessity made its appearance in so urgent a manner that we had to consider the problem in the clearest possible light, with the result that for some months we devoted our entire attention to the means of bringing about this change of front once and for all. If I do not today feel any retrospective embarrassment in explaining this change, that is because it seems to me quite natural that surrealist thought, before coming to rest in dialectical materialism and insisting, as today, on the *supremacy of matter over mind,* should have been condemned to pass, in a few years, through the whole historic development of modern thought. It came *normally* to Marx through Hegel, just as it came *normally* to Hegel through Berkeley and Hume. These latter influences over a certain particularity in that, contrary to certain poetic influences undergone in the same way, and accommodated to those of the French materialists of the eighteenth century, they yielded a residuum of *practical action.* To try and hide these influences would be contrary to my desire to show that surrealism has not been drawn up as an abstract system, that is to say, safeguarded against all contradictions. It is also my desire to show how surrealist activity, driven, as I have said, to ask itself what were its proper resources, had in some way or another to *reflect upon itself* its realization, in 1925, of its relative insufficiency; how surrealist activity had to cease being content with the results (automatic texts, the recital of dreams, improvised speeches, spontaneous poems, drawings and actions) which it had originally planned; and how it came to consider these first results as being simply so much *material,* starting from which the problem of knowledge inevitably arose again under quite a new form.

As a *living* movement, that is to say a movement undergoing a constant process of becoming and, what is more, solidly relying on concrete facts, surrealism has brought together and is still bringing together diverse temperaments individually obeying or resisting a variety of bents. The determinant of their enduring or short-lived adherence is not to be considered as a

blind concession to an inert stock of ideas held in common, but as a continuous sequence of acts which, propelling the doer to more or less distant
points, forces him for each fresh start to return to the same starting-line.
These exercises not being without peril, one man may break a limb or—for
which there is no precedent—his head, another may peaceably submerge
himself in a quagmire or report himself dying of fatigue. Unable as yet to
treat itself to an ambulance, surrealism simply leaves these individuals by the
wayside. Those who continue in the ranks are aware of course of the casual-
ties left behind them. But what of it? The essential is always to look ahead,
to remain sure that one has not forfeited the burning desire for beauty, truth
and justice, toilingly to go onward towards the discovery, one by one, of *fresh
landscapes,* and to continue doing so indefinitely and without coercion to the
end, that others may afterwards travel the same spiritual road, *unhindered
and in all security.* Penetration, to be sure, has not been as deep as one would
have wished. Poetically speaking, a few wild, or shall we say charming, beasts
whose cries fill the air and bar access to a domain as yet only surmised, are
still far from being exorcised. But for all that, the piercing of the thicket
would have proceeded less tortuously, and those who are doing the pioneering would have acquitted themselves with unabating tenacity in the service
of the cause, if between the beginning and the end of the spectacle which
they provide for themselves and would be glad to provide for others, a
change had not taken place.

In 193[6], more than ever before, surrealism owes it to itself to defend the
postulate of the necessity of change. It is amusing, indeed, to see how the
more spiteful and silly of our adversaries affect to triumph whenever they
stumble on some old statement we may have made and which now sounds
more or less discordantly in the midst of others intended to render comprehensible our present conduct. This insidious manoeuvre, which is calculated
to cast a doubt on our good faith, or at least on the genuineness of our
principles, can easily be defeated. The development of surrealism throughout
the decade of its existence is, we take it, a function of the unrolling of historical realities as these may be speeded up between the period of relief which
follows the conclusion of a peace and the fresh outbreak of war. It is also a
function of the process of seeking after new values in order to confirm or
invalidate existing ones. The fact that certain of the first participants in surrealist activity have thrown up the sponge and have been discarded has
brought about the retiring from circulation of some ways of thinking and the
putting into circulation of others in which there were implicit certain general
dissents on the one hand and certain general assents on the other. Hence it
is that this activity has been fashioned by events. At the present moment,
contrary to current biased rumour according to which surrealism itself is

supposed, in its cruelty of disposition, to have sacrificed nearly all the blood first vivifying it, it is heartening to be able to point out that it has never ceased to avail itself of the perfect teamwork of René Crevel, Paul Eluard, Max Ernst, Benjamin Péret, Man Ray, Tristan Tzara, and the present writer, all of whom can attest that from the inception of the movement—which is also the date of our own enlistment in it—until now, the initial principle of their covenant has never been violated. If there have occurred differences on some points, it was essentially within the rhythmic scope of the integral whole, in itself a least disputable element of objective value. The others, they whom we no longer meet, can they say as much? They cannot, for the simple reason that since they separated from us they have been incapable of achieving a single concerted action that had any definite form of its own, and they have confined themselves, instead, to a reaction against surrealism with the greatest wastage to themselves—a fate always overtaking those who go back on their past. The history of their apostasy and denials will ultimately be read into the great limbo of human failings, without profit to any observer—ideal yesterday, but real today—who, called upon to make a pronouncement, will decide whether they or ourselves have brought the more appreciable efforts to bear upon a rational solution of the many problems surrealism has propounded.

Although there can be no question here of going through the history of the surrealist movement—its history has been told many a time and sometimes told fairly well; moreover, I prefer to pass on as quickly as possible to the exposition of its present attitude—I think I ought briefly to recall, for the benefit of those of you who were unaware of the fact, that there is no doubt that before the surrealist movement properly so called, there existed among the promoters of the movement and others who later rallied round it, very active, not merely dissenting but also antagonistic dispositions which, between 1915 and 1920, were willing to align themselves under the signboard of *Dada*. Post-war disorder, a state of mind essentially anarchic that guided that cycle's many manifestations, a deliberate refusal to judge—for lack, it was said, of criteria—the actual qualifications of individuals, and, perhaps, in the last analysis, a certain spirit of negation which was making itself conspicuous, had brought about a dissolution of the group as yet inchoate, one might say, by reason of its dispersed and heterogeneous character, a group whose germinating force has nevertheless been decisive and, by the general consent of present-day critics, has greatly influenced the course of ideas. It may be proper before passing rapidly—as I must—over this period, to apportion by far the handsomest share to Marcel Duchamp (canvases and glass objects still to be seen in New York), to Francis Picabia (reviews "291" and

"391"), Jacques Vaché *(Lettres de Guerre)* and Tristan Tzara *(Twenty-five Poems, Dada Manifesto,* 1918).

Strangely enough, it was round a discovery of language that what was seeking to organize itself in 1920—as yet on a basis of confidential exchange—assumed the name of *surrealism,* a word fallen from the lips of Apollinaire, which we had diverted from the rather general and very confusing connotation he had given it. What was at first no more than a new method of poetic writing broke away after several years from the much too general theses which had come to be expounded in the *Surrealist Manifesto—Soluble Fish,* 1924, the *Second Manifesto* adding others to them, whereby the whole was raised to a vaster ideological plane; and so there had to be revision.

In an article, "Enter the Mediums," published in *Littérature,* 1922, reprinted in *Les Pas Perdus,* 1924, and subsequently in the *Surrealist Manifesto,* I explained the circumstance that had originally put us, my friends and myself, on the track of the surrealist activity we still follow and for which we are hopeful of gaining ever more numerous new adherents in order to extend it further than we have so far succeeded in doing. It reads:

"It was in 1919, in complete solitude and at the approach of sleep, that my attention was arrested by sentences more or less complete, which became perceptible to my mind without my being able to discover (even by very meticulous analysis) any possible previous volitional effort. One evening in particular, as I was about to fall asleep, I became aware of a sentence articulated clearly to a point excluding all possibility of alteration and stripped of all quality of vocal sound; a curious sort of sentence which came to me bearing—in sober truth—not a trace of any relation whatever to any incidents I may at that time have been involved in; an insistent sentence, it seemed to me, a sentence I might say, that *knocked at the window.* I was prepared to pay no further attention to it when the organic character of the sentence detained me. I was really bewildered. Unfortunately, I am unable to remember the exact sentence at this distance, but it ran approximately like this: 'A man is cut in half by the window.' What made it plainer was the fact that it was accompanied by a feeble visual representation of a man in the process of walking, but cloven, at half his height, by a window perpendicular to the axis of his body. Definitely, there was the form, re-erected against space, of a man leaning out of a window. But the window following the man's locomotion, I understood that I was dealing with an image of great rarity. Instantly the idea came to me to use it as material for poetic construction. I had no sooner invested it with that quality, than it had given place to a succession of all but intermittent sentences which left me no less astonished, but in a state, I would say, of extreme detachment.

"Preoccupied as I still was at that time with Freud, and familiar with his methods of investigation, which I had practised occasionally upon the sick during the War, I resolved to obtain from myself what one seeks to obtain from patients, namely a monologue poured out as rapidly as possible, over which the subject's critical faculty has no control—the subject himself throwing reticence to the winds—and which as much as possible represents *spoken thought*. It seemed and still seems to me that the speed of thought is no greater than that of words, and hence does not exceed the flow of either tongue or pen. It was in such circumstances that, together with Philippe Soupault, whom I had told about my first ideas on the subject, I began to cover sheets of paper with writing, feeling a praiseworthy contempt for whatever the literary result might be. Ease of achievement brought about the rest. By the end of the first day of the experiment we were able to read to one another about fifty pages obtained in this manner and to compare the results we had achieved. The likeness was on the whole striking. There were similar faults of construction, the same hesitant manner, and also, in both cases, an illusion of extraordinary verve, much emotion, a considerable assortment of images of a quality such as we should never have been able to obtain in the normal way of writing, a very special sense of the picturesque, and, here and there, a few pieces of out and out buffoonery. The only differences which our two texts presented appeared to me to be due essentially to our respective temperaments, Soupault's being less static than mine, and, if he will allow me to make this slight criticism, to his having scattered about at the top of certain pages—doubtlessly in a spirit of mystification—various words under the guise of titles. I must give him credit, on the other hand, for having always forcibly opposed the least correction of any passage that did not seem to me to be quite the thing. In that he was most certainly right.

"It is of course difficult in these cases to appreciate at their just value the various elements in the result obtained; one may even say that it is entirely impossible to appreciate them at a first reading. To you who may be writing them, these elements are, in appearance, *as strange as to anyone else,* and you are yourself naturally distrustful of them. Poetically speaking, they are distinguished chiefly by a very high degree of *immediate absurdity,* the peculiar quality of that absurdity being, on close examination, their yielding to whatever is most admissible and legitimate in the world: divulgation of a given number of facts and properties on the whole not less objectionable than the others."

The word "surrealism" having thereupon become descriptive of the *generalizable* undertaking to which we had devoted ourselves, I thought it indispensable, in 1924, to define this word once and for all:

"SURREALISM, *n.* Pure psychic automatism, by which it is intended to express, verbally, in writing, or by other means, the real process of thought. Thought's dictation, in the absence of all control exercised by the reason and outside all aesthetic or moral preoccupations.

"ENCYCL. *Philos.* Surrealism rests in the belief in the superior reality of certain forms of association neglected heretofore; in the omnipotence of the dream and in the disinterested play of thought. It tends definitely to do away with all other psychic mechanisms and to substitute itself for them in the solution of the principal problems of life. Have professed *absolute surrealism:* Messrs. Aragon, Baron, Boiffard, Breton, Carrive, Crevel, Delteil, Desnos, Eluard, Gérard, Limbour, Malkine, Morise, Naville, Noll, Péret, Picon, Soupault, Vitrac.

"These till now appear to be the only ones, and there would not have been any doubt on that score were it not for the strange case of Isidore Ducasse, of whose extra-literary career I lack all data. Were one to consider their output only superficially, a goodly number of poets might well have passed for surrealists, beginning with Dante and Shakespeare at his best. *In the course of many attempts I have made towards an analysis of what, under false pretences, is called genius, I have found nothing that could in the end be attributed to any other process than this.*"

There followed an enumeration that will gain, I think, by being clearly set out thus:

"Young's *Night Thoughts* are surrealist from cover to cover. It was unfortunately a priest who spoke; a bad priest, to be sure, yet a priest.

"Heraclitus is surrealist in dialectic.

"Lulle is surrealist in definition.

"Flamel is surrealist in the night of gold.

"Swift is surrealist in malice.

"Sade is surrealist in sadism.

"Carrière is surrealist in drowning.

"Monk Lewis is surrealist in the beauty of evil.

"Achim d'Arnim is surrealist absolutely, in space and time.

"Rabbe is surrealist in death.

"Baudelaire is surrealist in morals.

"Rimbaud is surrealist in life and elsewhere.

"Hervey Saint-Denys is surrealist in the directed dream.

"Carroll is surrealist in nonsense.

"Huysmans is surrealist in pessimism.

"Seurat is surrealist in design.

"Picasso is surrealist in cubism.

"Vaché is surrealist in myself.

"Roussel is surrealist in anecdote. Etc.

290 Consciousness and Confusion

"They were not always surrealists—on this I insist—in the sense that one can disentangle in each of them a number of preconceived notions to which—very naively!—they clung. And they clung to them so because they had not heard the *surrealist voice,* the voice that exhorts on the eve of death and in the roaring storm, and because they were unwilling to dedicate themselves to the task of no more than orchestrating the score replete with marvellous things. They were proud instruments; hence the sounds they produced were not always harmonious sounds.

"We, on the contrary, who have not given ourselves to processes of filtering, who through the medium of our work have been content to be silent receptacles of so many echoes, modest *registering machines* that are not hypnotized by the pattern that they trace, we are perhaps serving a yet much nobler cause. So we honestly give back the talent lent to us. You may talk of the 'talent' of this yard of platinum, of this mirror, of this door and of this sky, if you wish.

"We have no talent. . . ."

The *Manifesto* also contained a certain number of practical recipes, entitled: "Secrets of the Magic Surrealist Art," such as the following:

"Written Surrealist Composition or First and Last Draft.

"Having settled down in some spot most conducive to the mind's concentration upon itself, order writing material to be brought to you. Let your state of mind be as passive and receptive as possible. Forget your genius, talents, as well as the genius and talents of others. Repeat to yourself that literature is pretty well the sorriest road that leads to everywhere. Write quickly without any previously chosen subject, quickly enough not to dwell on, and not to be tempted to read over, what you have written. The first sentence will come of itself; and this is self-evidently true, because there is never a moment but some sentence alien to our conscious thought clamours for outward expression. It is rather difficult to speak of the sentence to follow, since it doubtless comes in for a share of our conscious activity and so do the other sentences, if it is conceded that the writing of the first sentence must have involved even a minimum of consciousness. But that should in the long run matter little, because therein precisely lies the greatest interest in the surrealist exercise. Punctuation of course necessarily hinders the stream of absolute continuity which preoccupies us. But you should particularly distrust the prompting whisper. If through a fault ever so trifling there is a forewarning of silence to come, a fault, let us say, of inattention, break off unhesitatingly the line that has become too lucid. After the word whose origin seems suspect you should place a letter, any letter, l for example, always the letter l, and restore the arbitrary flux by making that letter the initial of the word to follow."

I shall pass over the more or less correlated considerations which the *Manifesto* discussed in their bearing on the possibilities of plastic expression in surrealism. These considerations did not assume with me a relatively dogmatic turn until later (*Surrealism and Painting*, 1928).

I believe that the real interest of that book—there was no lack of people who were good enough to concede interest, for which no particular credit is due to me because I have no more than given expression to sentiments shared with friends, present and former—rests only subordinately on the formula above given. It is rather confirmatory of a *turn of thought* which, for good or ill, is peculiarly distinctive of our time. The defence originally attempted of that turn of thought still seems valid to me in what follows:

"We still live under the reign of logic, but the methods of logic are applied nowadays only to the resolution of problems of secondary interest. The absolute rationalism which is still the fashion does not permit consideration of any facts but those strictly relevant to our experience. Logical ends, on the other hand, escape us. Needless to say that even experience has had limits assigned to it. It revolves in a cage from which it becomes more and more difficult to release it. Even experience is dependent on immediate utility, and common sense is its keeper. Under colour of civilization, under pretext of progress, all that rightly or wrongly may be regarded as fantasy or superstition has been banished from the mind, all uncustomary searching after truth has been proscribed. It is only by what must seem sheer luck that there has recently been brought to light an aspect of mental life—to my belief by far the most important—with which it was supposed that we no longer had any concern. All credit for these discoveries must go to Freud. Based on these discoveries a current of opinion is forming that will enable the explorer of the human mind to continue his investigations, justified as he will be in taking into account more than mere summary realities. The imagination is perhaps on the point of reclaiming its rights. If the depths of our minds harbour strange forces capable of increasing those on the surface, or of successfully contending with them, then it is all in our interest to canalize them, to canalize them first in order to submit them later, if necessary, to the control of the reason. The analysts themselves have nothing to lose by such a proceeding. But it should be observed that there are no means designed *a priori* for the bringing about of such an enterprise, that until the coming of the new order it might just as well be considered the affair of poets and scientists, and that its success will not depend on the more or less capricious means that will be employed. . . .

"I am resolved to render powerless that *hatred of the marvellous* which is so rampant among certain people, that ridicule to which they are so eager to expose it. Briefly: The marvellous is always beautiful, anything that is marvellous is beautiful; indeed, nothing but the marvellous is beautiful. . . .

"The admirable thing about the fantastic is that it is no longer fantastic: there is only the real. . . .

"Interesting in a different way from the future of surrealist *technics* (theatrical, philosophical, scientific, critical) appears to me the application of surrealism to action. Whatever reservations I might be inclined to make with regard to responsibility in general, I should quite particularly like to know how the first misdemeanours whose surrealist character is indubitable will be *judged*. When surrealist methods extend from writing to action, there will certainly arise the need of a new morality to take the place of the current one, the cause of all our woes."

The *Manifesto of Surrealism* has improved on the Rimbaud principle that the poet must turn *seer*. Man in general is going to be summoned to manifest through life those *new sentiments* which the gift of vision will so suddenly have placed within his reach:

"Surrealism, as I envisage it, displays our complete *nonconformity* so clearly that there can be no question of claiming it as witness when the real world comes up for trial. On the contrary, it can but testify to the complete state of distraction to which we hope to attain here below. Kant distracted by women, Pasteur distracted by 'grapes,' Curie distracted by traffic, are profoundly symptomatic in this respect. The world is only very relatively proportionate to thought, and incidents of this kind are only the most striking episodes of a war of independence in which I glory in taking part. Surrealism is the 'invisible ray' that shall enable us one day to triumph over our enemies. 'You tremble no more, carcase.' This summer the roses are blue; the wood is made of glass. The earth wrapped in its foliage makes as little effect on me as a ghost. Living and ceasing to live are imaginary solutions. Existence is elsewhere."

Surrealism then was securing expression in all its purity and force. The freedom it possesses is a perfect freedom in the sense that it recognizes no limitations exterior to itself. As it was said on the cover of the first issue of *La Révolution Surréaliste,* "it will be necessary to draw up a new declaration of the Rights of Man." The concept of surreality, concerning which quarrels have been sought with us repeatedly and which it was attempted to turn into a metaphysical or mystic rope to be placed afterwards round our necks, lends itself no longer to misconstruction, nowhere does it declare itself opposed to the need of transforming the world which henceforth will more and more definitely yield to it.

As I said in the *Manifesto:*

"I believe in the future transmutation of those two seemingly contradictory states, dream and reality, into a sort of absolute reality, of surreality, so to speak. I am looking forward to its consummation, certain that I shall never share in it, but death would matter little to me could I but taste the joy it will yield ultimately."

Aragon expressed himself in very much the same way in *Une Vague de Rêves* (1924):

"It should be understood that the real is a relation like any other; the essence of things is by no means linked to their reality, there are other relations beside reality, which the mind is capable of grasping, and which also are primary like chance, illusion, the fantastic, the dream. These various groups are united and brought into harmony in one single order, surreality. . . . This surreality—a relation in which all notions are merged together—is the common horizon of religions, magics, poetry, intoxications, and of all life that is lowly—that trembling honeysuckle you deem sufficient to populate the sky with for us."

And René Crevel, in *L'Esprit contre Raison:*

"The poet does not put the wild animals to sleep in order to play the tamer, but, the cages wide open, the keys thrown to the winds, he journeys forth, a traveller who thinks not of himself, but of the voyage, of dream-beaches, forests of hands, soul-endowed animals, all undeniable surreality."

I was to sum up the idea in these terms in *Surrealism and Painting* (1928):

"All that I love, all that I think and feel inclines me towards a particular philosophy of immanence according to which surreality will reside in reality itself, will be neither superior nor exterior to it. And conversely, because the container shall be also the contained. One might almost say that it will be a communicating vessel placed between the container and the contained. That is to say, I resist with all my strength temptations which, in painting and literature, might have the immediate tendency to withdraw thought from life as well as place life under the aegis of thought."

After years of endeavour and perplexities, when a variety of opinions had disputed amongst themselves the direction of the craft in which a number of persons of unequal ability and varying powers of resistance had originally embarked together, the surrealist idea recovered in the *Second Manifesto* all the brilliancy of which events had vainly conspired to despoil it. It should be emphasized that the *First Manifesto* of 1924 did no more than sum up the conclusions we had drawn during what one may call the *heroic epoch* of surrealism, which stretches from 1919 to 1923. The concerted elaboration of the first automatic texts and our excited reading of them, the first results obtained by Max Ernst in the domain of "collage" and of painting, the practice of surrealist "speaking" during the hypnotic experiments introduced among us by René Crevel and repeated every evening for over a year, uncontrovertibly mark the decisive stages of surrealist exploration during this first phase. After that, up till the taking into account of the social aspect of the problem round about 1925 (though nor formally sanctioned until 1930), surrealism began to find itself a prey to characteristic wranglings. These wranglings account very clearly for the expulsion-orders and tickets-of-leave which, as we went along, we had to deal out to certain of our companions of the first and second hour. Some people have quite gratuitously concluded from this that we are apt to overestimate *personal questions*. During the last ten years, surrealism has almost unceasingly been obliged to defend itself against deviations to the right and to the left. On the one hand we have had to struggle against the will of those who would maintain surrealism on a purely speculative level and treasonably transfer it onto an artistic and literary plane. (Artaud, Desnos, Ribemont-Dessaignes, Vitrac) at the cost of all the hope for subversion we have placed in it; on the other, against the will of those who would place it on a purely practical basis, available at any moment to be sacrificed to an ill-conceived political militancy (Naville, Aragon)—at the cost, this time, of what constitutes the originality and reality of its researches, at the cost of the autonomous risk that it has to run. Agitated though it was, the epoch that separates the two *Manifestoes* was none the less a rich one, since it saw the publication of so many works in which the vital principles of surrealism were amply accounted for. It suffices to recall particularly *Le Paysan de Paris* and *Traité du Style* by Aragon, *L'Esprit contre la Raison* and *Etes-vous Fous* by René Crevel, *Deuil pour Deuil* by Desnos, *Capitale de la Douleur* and *L'Amour la Poésie* by Eluard, *La Femme 100 Têtes* by Ernst, *La Révolution et les Intellectuels* by Naville, *Le Grand Jeu* by Péret, and my own *Nadja*. The poetic activity of Tzara, although claiming until 1930 no connection with surrealism, is in perfect accord with ours.

We were forced to agree with Pierre Naville when he wrote:

"Surrealism is at the crossroads of several thought-movements. We assume that it affirms the possibility of a certain steady downward readjustment of the mind's rational (and not simply conscious) activity towards more absolutely *coherent* thought, irrespective of whatever direction that thought may take; that is to say, that it proposes or would at least like to propose a new solution of all problems, but chiefly moral. It is, indeed, in that sense that it is epoch-making. That is why one may express the essential characteristic of surrealism by saying that it seeks to calculate the quotient of the unconscious by the conscious."

It should be pointed out that in a number of declarations in *La Révolution et les Intellectuels. Que peuvent faire les surréalistes?* (1926), this same author demonstrated the utter vanity of intellectual bickerings in the face of the human exploitation which results from the wage-earning system. These declarations gave rise amongst us to considerable anxiety and, attempting for the first time to justify surrealism's social implications, I desired to put an end to it in *Légitime Défense*. This pamphlet set out to demonstrate that there is no fundamental antinomy in the basis of surrealist thought. In reality, we are faced with two problems, one of which is the problem raised, at the beginning of the twentieth century, by the discovery of the relations between the conscious and the unconscious. That was how the problem chose to present itself to us. We were the first to apply to its resolution a particular method, which we have not ceased to consider both the most suitable and the most likely to be brought to perfection; there is no reason why we should renounce it. The other problem we are faced with is that of the social action we should pursue. We consider that this action has its own method in dialectical materialism, and we can all the less afford to ignore this action since, I repeat, we hold the liberation of man to be the *sine qua non* condition of the *liberation of the mind,* and we can expect this liberation of man to result only from the proletarian Revolution. These two problems are essentially distinct and we deplore their becoming confused by not remaining so. There is good reason, then, to take up a stand against all attempts to weld them together and, more especially, against the urge to abandon all such researches as ours in order to devote ourselves to the poetry and art of propaganda. Surrealism, which has been the object of brutal and repeated summonses in this respect, now feels the need of making some kind of counter-attack. Let me recall the fact that its very definition holds that it must escape, in its written manifestations, or any others, from all *control* exercised by the reason. Apart from the puerility of wishing to bring a supposedly Marxist control to bear on the immediate aspect of such manifestations, this control cannot be envisaged in *principle.* And how ill-boding does this distrust seem, coming as it does from men who declare themselves Marxists, that is to say possessed not only of a strict line in revolutionary matters, but also of a marvellously open mind and an insatiable curiosity!

This brings us to the eve of the *Second Manifesto.* These objections had to be put an end to, and for that purpose it was indispensable that we should proceed to liquidate certain individualist elements amongst us, more or less openly hostile to one another, whose intentions did not, in the final analysis, appear as irreproachable, nor their motives as disinterested, as might have been desired. An important part of the work was devoted to a statement of the reasons which moved surrealism to dispense for the future with certain collaborators. It was attempted, on the same occasion, to complete the specific method of creation proposed six years earlier, and thoroughly to tidy up surrealist ideas.

"Whatever may have been the controversial issues raised by former or present followers of surrealism, all will admit that the drift of surrealism has always and chiefly been towards a general and emphatic *crisis in consciousness* and that it is only when this is in being or is shown to be impossible that the success or historic eclipse of the movement will be decided.

"Intellectually it was and still is a question of exposing by every available means, and to learn at all costs to identify, the factitious character of the conflicts hypocritically calculated to hinder the setting on foot of any unusual agitation to give mankind were it only a faint understanding of its latent possibilities and to inspire it to free itself from its fetters by all the means available. The horror of death, the pantomime of the beyond, the total break-down of the most beautiful intellect in dream, the tower of Babel, the mirror of inconstancies, the insuperable silver-splashed wall of the brain, all these startling images of human catastrophes are perhaps nothing but images after all. There is a hint in all this of a belief that there exists a certain spiritual plane on which life and death, the real and the imaginary, the past and the future, the communicable and the incommunicable, the high and the low, are not conceived of as opposites. It would therefore be vain to attribute to surrealism any other motive than the hope to determine that plane, as it would be absurd to ascribe to it a purely destructive or constructive character: the point at issue being precisely this, that construction and destruction should no longer be flaunted against one another. It becomes clear also that surrealism is not at all interested in taking into account what passes alongside it under the guise of art and is in fact anti-art, philosophy or anti-philosophy, all, in a word, that has not for its ultimate end the conversion of the being into a jewel, internal and unseeing, with a soul that is neither of ice nor of fire. What, indeed, do they expect of surrealism, who are still anxious about the position they may occupy *in the world?* On that mental plane from which one may for oneself alone embark on the perilous, but, we think, supreme exploit, on that plane the footfalls of those who come or go are no longer of any importance, because their echo will be repeated in a land in which, by delimitation, surrealism possesses no listening ear. It is not desirable that surrealism should be dependent on the whim of this or that person. If it declares itself capable of ransoming thought from a serfdom more and more task-driven, to bring it back to the path of complete understanding, to restore to it its pristine purity, it is indeed no more than right that it should be judged only by what it has done and by what it has still to accomplish in the fulfilment of its promise. . . .

"While surrealism undertakes particularly the critical investigation of the notions of reality and unreality, of reason and unreason, of reflection and impulse, of knowing and 'fatal' ignorance, of utility and uselessness, there is nevertheless between it and Historical Materialism this similarity in tendency, that it sets out from the 'colossal abortion' of the Hegelian system. I do not see how limits, those for instance of the economic framework, can be as-signed to the exercise of a thought which is definitely adapted to negation and the negation of negation. How allow that the dialectical method is only to be applied validly to solving social problems? It is the whole of surrealism's ambition to supply it with nowise conflicting possibilities of application in the most immediate conscious domain. I really cannot see, *pace* a few muddle-headed revolutionaries, why we should abstain from taking up the problems of love, of dreaming, of madness, of art and of religion, so long as we consider these problems from the same angle as they, and we too, consider Revolution. And I have no hesitation in saying that nothing systematic had been done in this direction before surrealism, and for us also at the point where we found it, 'the dialectical method in its Hegelian form could not be put into application.' For us also it was imperative to have done with idealism proper, and our coining of the word 'surrealism' is enough to show that this was so, as it is to show the need for us—to use Engels's example—of going beyond the childish development: 'The rose is a rose. The rose is not a rose. And yet the rose is a rose.' Nevertheless—if I may say so parenthetically—we had to set 'the rose' in a profitable movement of less innocuous contradictions, a movement in which the rose is successively the rose out of the garden, the rose which holds a singular place in a dream, the rose which it is impossible to extract from 'the optical bouquet,' the rose which may change its properties completely by passing into automatic writing, the rose which retains only what the painter has allowed it to retain of a rose in a surrealist painting, and finally the rose, quite different from itself, which goes back into the garden. That is a long way from any idealist standpoint, and we should not disclaim an idealist view if we were not continuing to suffer the attacks of an elementary materialism. These attacks emanate from those who, out of low conservatism, oppose the investigation of the relation of thought to matter, and those who, through ill-digested revolutionary sectarianism, and while ignoring the whole of what is being asked of them, confuse this materialism with the materialism which Engels distinguished as essentially different from it and defined as being primarily an *intuition of the world* which had to put itself to the test and be realized. *'In the course of the development of philosophy idealism became untenable and was contradicted by modern materialism. The latter is the negation of negation and is not simply the old materialism restored: to the enduring foundations of this old materialism it adds the whole of what has been thought in philosophy and natural science throughout an evolution of two thousand years, and adds too the product of this long history itself.'* It is also essential to the proper appreciation of our starting-point to understand that we regard philosophy as *outclassed.* In this we are, I believe, at one with all those for whom reality has more than a theoretical importance, for whom it is a question of life and death to appeal passionately, as Feuerbach insisted, to this reality: *we* so appeal by committing ourselves *entirely,* without reservation, to the principle of historical materialism; *he* so appealed by casting in the face of the astounded intellectual world the idea that 'man is what he eats' and that there would be better prospects of success for a future revolution if the people were better fed, specifically if they were given peas instead of potatoes. . . .

"It was to be expected that surrealism should make its appearance in the midst of, and perhaps thanks to, an uninterrupted succession of falterings, zigzags and defections, which constantly exact the rediscussion of its original data, i.e., it is called back to the initial principle of its activity and at the same time is subject to the interrogation of the *chancy morrow* when the heart's feeling may have waxed or waned. I have to admit that everything has not been done to bring this undertaking off, if only that we have not taken full advantage of the means which have been defined for our group nor fully tested the ways of investigation recommended when the movement was born. The problem of social action is—as I have already said and as I insist—only one form of a more general problem which surrealism finds it its duty to raise, and this problem is *the problem of human expression in all its forms.* Whoever says 'expression' says, to begin with, 'language.' It is not therefore surprising that in the beginning surrealism should have confined itself almost entirely to the plane of language, nor that it should, after some incursion or other, return to that plane as if for the pleasure of behaving there in a conquered land. Nothing, indeed, can prevent the land from being to a great extent conquered. The hordes of words which were literally unleashed and to which Dada and surrealism deliberately opened their doors, are not, whatever anyone thinks, words which withdraw vainly. They will penetrate, at leisure, but certainly, the idiotic little towns of that literature which is still taught and, easily failing to distinguish between low and lofty quarterings, they will capture a fine number of turrets. In the belief that poetry alone so far is all that has been seriously shaken by us, the inhabitants are not really on their guard: they are building here and there a few unimportant ramparts. There is a pretence that it has not been noticed how much the logical mechanism of the sentence is proving more and more impotent by itself to give man the emotive shock which really gives some value to his life. On the other hand, the productions of that spontaneous or *more* spontaneous, direct or *more* direct, activity, such as surrealism is providing in ever greater numbers, in the form of books, pictures and films—these which man first looked upon with amazement, he is now placing about the home, and it is to them that, more or less timorously, he is committing the task of revolutionizing his ways of feeling. No doubt when I say 'man,' that man is not Everyman, and he must be allowed 'time' to become Everyman. But note how admirably and perversely insinuating a small number of quite modern works have already proved, those precisely about which the least that can be said is that they are pervaded by an especially unhealthy atmosphere: Baudelaire, Rimbaud (despite the reservations I have made), Huysmans, and Lautréamont—to mention only poetry. Do not let us be afraid of making a law unto ourselves of this unhealthiness. We want it to be impossible to say that we have not done everything to annihilate that foolish illusion of happiness and *good understanding* which it will be the glory of the nineteenth century to have exposed. Truly we have not ceased to be fanatically attracted by these rays of sunshine full of miasma. But at this moment, when the public authorities in France are preparing a grotesque celebration of the centenary of Romanticism, we for our part say that this Romanticism—of which we are quite ready to appear historically today as the tail, though in that case *an excessively prehensile tail*—this Romanticism is, we say, in its very essence in 1930 the negation of these authorities and this celebration; we say that for Romanticism to be a hundred years old is for it to be young, and that what has wrongly been called its heroic period can no longer pass for anything but the pulings of a being who is now only beginning to make known its wants through us; and finally we say that if it should be held that all that was thought before this infant—all that was thought 'classically'—was good, then incontestably he is out for *the whole of evil.*"

The considerations preface the critical examination of the changes and alterations which the most typical forms of surrealist expression have undergone in the course of time. This has been, as it happens, nothing less than *a rallying back to principles:*

"It is, as I was beginning to say above, regrettable that more systematic and sustained efforts, such as surrealism has constantly called for, have not been supplied in the way of automatic writing and of accounts of dreams. In spite of the way in which we have insistently included material of this sort in surrealist publications, and the remarkable place they occupy in certain works, it has to be admitted that sometimes their interest in such a context has been slight, or that they rather give the effect of being 'bravura pieces.' The presence in these items of an evident pattern has also greatly hampered the species of conversion we had hoped to bring about through them. The excessive negligence of which most of their authors were guilty is to blame: generally these authors were content to let their pens run over paper without observing in the least what was at the time going on inside themselves—this duplication being nevertheless easier to seize and more interesting to consider than that of reflective writing—or else they put together more or less arbitrary dream-elements intended to set forth their picturesqueness rather than to make visible usefully how they had come about. Such distortion of course nullifies any benefit that might be obtained from this sort of operation. Indeed, the great value of these operations for surrealism lies in the possibility they have of yielding to the reader particular logical planes, precisely those in which the logical faculty which is exercised in everything and for everything in consciousness, does not act. What am I saying! Not only do these logical planes remain unexplored, but further, we remain as little informed as ever regarding the origin of the *voice* which it is open to each one of us to hear, and which in the most singular fashion talks to us of something different from what we believe we are thinking, sometimes becoming solemn when we are most light-hearted, or talking nonsense when we are wretched.

"Nobody expressing himself does more than take advantage of a very obscure possibility of conciliation between what he knew he had to say and what on the same subject he didn't know he had to say and yet has said. The most rigorous line of thought is unable to forgo this assistance, undesirable though it yet is from the point of view of rigour. Truly, the idea gets torpedoed in the heart of the sentence enunciating it, even when this sentence escapes having any charming liberty taken with its meaning. Dadaism aimed especially at calling attention to the torpedoing. By appealing to automatism, as is well known, surrealism sets out to prevent the torpedoing of some vessel or other: something like a phantom-ship (some people have tried to make use of this image against me, but hard-worn as it may be, I find it good, and I use it again).

"There is no need to indulge in subtleties: inspiration is familiar enough. And there can be no mistake: it is inspiration which has supplied the supreme need of expression in all times and in all places. A common remark is that inspiration either *is* or *is not,* and when it is not, nothing summoned to replace it by the human skill which interest obliterates, by the discursive intelligence, or by the talent acquired with labour, can make up in us for the lack of it. We recognize it easily by the way it completely takes possession of the mind, so that for long periods when any problem is set we are momentarily prevented from being the playthings of one rational solution rather than another; and by that kind of short-circuit which it sets up between a given idea and what answers to it (in writing, for example). Just as in the physical world, the short-circuit occurs when the two 'poles' of the machine are linked by a conductor having little or no resistance. In poetry and in painting, surrealism has done everything it could to increase the number of the short-circuits. Its dearest aim now and in the future must be the artificial reproduction of that ideal moment in which a man who is a prey to a particular emotion, is suddenly caught up by 'the stronger than himself,' and thrust, despite his bodily inertia, into immortality. If he were then lucid and awake, he would issue from that predicament in terror. The great thing is that he should not be free to come out, that he should go on talking all the time the mysterious ringing is going on: indeed, it is thanks to that whereby he ceases to belong to himself that he belongs to us. Provided the products of psychic activity which dreaming and automatic writing are, are as much as possible distracted from the will to express, as much as possible lightened of ideas of responsibility ever ready to act as brakes, and as much as possible kept independent of all that is not *the passive life of the intelligence,* these products have the following advantages: that they alone furnish the material for appreciating the grand style to the body of critics who in the artistic domain are strangely disabled; that they allow of a general reclassification of lyrical values; and that they offer a key to go on opening indefinitely that box of never-ending drawers which is called man, and so dissuade him from making an about-turn for reasons of self-preservation on those occasions in the dark when he runs into the externally closed doors of the 'beyond,' of reality, of reason, of genius, and of love. The day will be when these palpable evidences of an existence other than the one we believe ourselves to be leading will no longer be treated as cavalierly as now. It will then seem surprising that, having been so close to *truth* as we are, we in general should have taken care to provide ourselves with some literary alibi or other instead of plunging into the water though ignorant of swimming, and going into the fire though not believing in the phoenix, in order to attain this truth."

Some of you may be perhaps astonished, by the way, to find me dealing thus with automatic texts and accounts of dreams:

"If I feel I must insist so much on the value of the two operations, it is not because they seem to me to constitute in themselves alone the intellectual panacea, but because for the trained observer they lend themselves less than any others to confusion or trickery, and that further they are the best that have been found to invest man with a valid sense of his resources. It goes without saying that the conditions imposed on us by life make it impossible for such an apparently unmotivated exercise of thought to go on uninterruptedly. Those who have yielded themselves up to it unreservedly, however low some of them may later have fallen, will one day turn out not to have been quite vainly projected into such a complete *internal faerie*. In comparison with this faerie, a return to any premeditated activity of mind, however it may appeal to the majority of their contemporaries, will in their eyes provide but a poor spectacle.

"These very direct means, means which are, let us say it again, open to all, means which we persist in putting forward as soon as the question is no longer essentially to produce works of art, but to light up the unrevealed and yet revealable part of our being in which all the beauty, all the love and all the virtue with which we scarcely credit ourselves are shining intensely— these immediate means are not the only ones. Notably, it seems that now there is much to be expected of certain methods of pure deception, the application of which to art and life would have the effect of fixing attention neither on the real nor on the imaginary, but on the, so to speak, *hither side of the real.* It is easy to imagine novels which cannot end as there are problems which remain unsolved. When, however, shall we have the novel in which the characters, having been abundantly defined with a minimum of particularities, will act in an altogether foreseeable way in view of an unforeseen result; and, inversely, the novel in which psychology will not scamp its great but futile duties at the expense of the characters and events, but will really hold up (as a microscopic slide is held up) between two blades a fraction of a second, and in this will be surprised the germs of incidents; this other novel, in which the verisimilitude of the scenery will for the first time fail to hide from us the strange symbolical life which even the most definite and most common objects lead in dreams; again, the novel in which the construction will be quite simple, but in which, however, an elopement will be described with the words for fatigue, a storm described with precision, but *gaily,* etc.? Whoever believes with us that it is time to have done with the provoking insanities of 'realism' will have no difficulty in adding to these proposals for himself."

From 1930 until today the history of surrealism is that of successful efforts to restore it to its proper *becoming* by gradually removing from it every trace both of political opportunism and of artistic opportunism. The review *La Révolution Surréaliste* (12 issues) has been succeeded by another, *Le Surréalisme au Service de la Révolution* (6 issues). Owing particularly to influences brought to bear by new elements, surrealist experimenting, which had for too long been erratic, has been unreservedly resumed; its perspectives and its aims have been made perfectly clear; I may say that it has not ceased to be carried on in a continuous and enthusiastic manner. This experimenting has regained momentum under the master-impulse given to it by Salvador Dali, whose exceptional interior "boiling" has been for surrealism, during the whole of this period, an invaluable ferment. As Guy Mangeot has very rightly pointed out in his *History of Surrealism* published recently by René Henriquez, Dali has endowed surrealism with an instrument of primary importance, in particular the paranoiac-critical method, which has immediately shown itself capable of being applied with equal success to painting, poetry, the cinema, to the construction of typical surrealist objects, to fashions, to sculpture and even, if necessary, to all manner of exegesis.

He [Dali] first announced his convictions to us in *La Femme Visible* (1930):

"I believe the moment is at hand when, by a paranoiac and active advance of the mind, it will be possible (simultaneously with automatism and other passive states) to systematize confusion and thus to help to discredit completely the world of reality."

In order to cut short all possible misunderstandings, it should perhaps be said: "immediate" reality.

"Paranoia uses the external world in order to assert its dominating idea and has the disturbing characteristic of making others accept this idea's reality. The reality of the external world is used for illustration and proof, and so comes to serve the reality of our mind."

In the special "Intervention surréaliste" number of *Documents 34*, under the title *Philosophic Provocations*, Dali undertakes today to give his thought a didactic turn. All uncertainty as to his real intentions seems to me to be swept away by these definitions:

"*Paranoia:* Delirium of interpretation bearing a systematic structure.

"*Paranoiac-critical activity:* Spontaneous method of '*irrational knowledge*,' based on the critical and systematic objectivication of delirious associations and interpretations.

"*Painting:* Hand-done colour 'photography' of 'concrete irrationality' and of the imaginative world in general.

"*Sculpture:* Modelling by hand of 'concrete irrationality' and of the imaginative world in general.

"Etc. . . ."

In order to form a summary idea of Dali's undertaking, one must take into account the property of *uninterrupted becoming* of any object of paranoiac activity, in other words of the ultra-confusing activity rising out of the obsessing idea. This uninterrupted becoming allows the paranoiac who is their witness to consider the images of the exterior world as unstable and transitory, or suspect; and what is so disturbing is that he is able to make other people believe in the reality of his impressions. One aspect, for instance, of the *multiple* image occupying our attention being a putrefied donkey, the "cruel" putrefaction of the donkey can be considered as "the hard and blinding flash of new gems." Here we find ourselves confronted by a new affirmation, accompanied by formal proofs, of the *omnipotence* of desire, which has remained, since the beginnings, surrealism's sole act of faith. At the point where surrealism has taken up the problem, its only guide has been Rimbaud's sibylline pronouncement: "I say that one must be a *seer*, one must make oneself a seer." As you know, this was Rimbaud's only means of reaching "the *unknown*." Surrealism can flatter itself today that it has discovered and rendered practicable many other ways leading to the unknown. The abandonment to verbal or graphic impulses and the resort to paranoiac-critical activity are not the only ones, and one may say that, during the last four years of surrealist activity, the many others that have made their appearance allow us to affirm that the automatism from which we started and to which we have unceasingly returned does in fact constitute the *crossroads* where these various paths meet. Among those we have partly explored and on which we are only just beginning to see ahead, I should single out the simulation of mental diseases (acute mania, general paralysis, dementia prae-cox), which Paul Eluard and I practised in *The Immaculate Conception* (1930), undertaking to prove that the normal man can have access to the provisorily condemned places of the human mind; the manufacture of objects function-ing symbolically, started in 1931 by the very particular and quite new emotion aroused by Giacometti's object, "L'Heure des Traces"; the analysis of the interpenetration of the states of sleep and waking, tending to make them depend entirely upon one another and even condition one another in certain affective states, which I undertook in *The Communicating Vessels;* and finally, the taking into consideration of the recent researches of the Marburg school, to which I drew attention in an article published in *Minotaure,* "The Auto-matic Message," whose aim is to cultivate the remarkable sensorial disposi-tions of children, enabling them to change any object whatever into no mat-ter what, simply by looking at it fixedly.

Nothing more could be more coherent, more systematic or more richly yielding of results than this last phase of surrealist activity, which has seen the production of two film by Luis Bunuel and Salvador Dali, *Un Chien Andalou* and *L'Age d'Or,* the poems of René Char, *L'Homme Approximatif, Où Boivent les Loups* and *L'Antitête* by Tristan Tzara, *Le Clavecin de Diderot* and *Les Pieds dans le Plat* by René Crevel, *La Vie Immédiate* by Eluard, the very precious *visual* commentaries by Madame Valentine Hugo on the works of Arnim and Rimbaud, the most intense part of the work of Yves Tanguy, the inspired sculpture of Alberto Giacometti, the coming together of Georges Hugnet, Gui Rosey, Pierre Hoyotte, Roger Caillois, Victor Brauner and Bal-thus. Never has so precise a common will united us. I think I can most clearly express this will by saying that today it applies itself to *"bring about the state where the distinction between the subjective and the objective loses its necessity and its value."*

Surrealism, starting fifteen years ago with a discovery that seemed only to involve poetic language, has spread like wildfire, on pursuing its course, not only in art but in life. It has provoked new states of consciousness and over-thrown the walls beyond which it was immemorially supposed to be impos-sible to see; it has—as is being more and more generally recognized—modi-fied the sensibility, and taken a decisive step towards the unification of the personality, which it found threatened by an ever more profound dissocia-tion. Without attempting to judge what direction it will ultimately take, for the lands it fertilizes as it flows are those of surprise itself, I should like to draw your attention to the fact that its most recent advance is producing a *fundamental crisis of the "object."* It is essentially upon the object that surreal-ism has thrown most light in recent years. Only the very close examination of the many recent speculations to which the *object* has publicly given rise (the oneiric object, the object functioning symbolically, the real and virtual object, the moving but silent object, the phantom object, the discovered object, etc.) can give one a proper grasp of the experiments that surrealism is engaged in now. In order to continue to understand the movement, it is indispensable to focus one's attention on this point.

I must crave your indulgence for speaking so technically, *from the inside*. But there could be no question of concealing any aspect of the persuasions to which surrealism has been and is still exposed. I say that there exists a lyrical element that conditions *for one part* the psychological and moral structure of human society, that has conditioned it at all times and that will continue to condition it. This lyrical element has until now, even though in spite of them, remained the fact and *the sole fact* of specialists. In the state of extreme tension to which class antagonisms have led the society to which we belong and which we tend with all our strength to reject, it is natural and it is *fated* that this solicitation should continue, that it should assume for us a thousand faces, imploring, tempting and eager by turns. It is not within our power, it would be unworthy of our historic role to give way to this solicitation. By surrealism we intend to account for nothing less than the manner in which it is possible today to make use of the magnificent and overwhelming *spiritual legacy* that has been handed down to us. We have accepted this legacy from the past, and surrealism can well say that the use to which it has been put has been to turn it to the routing of capitalist society. I consider that for that purpose it was and is still necessary for us to stand where we are, to beware against breaking the thread of our researches and to continue these researches, not as literary men and artists, certainly, but rather as chemists and the various other kinds of technicians. To pass on to the poetry and art called (doubtless in anticipation) *proletarian:* No. The forces we have been able to bring together and which for fifteen years we have never found lacking, have arrived at a particular point of application: the question is not to know whether this point of application is the best, but simply to point out that the application of our forces at this point has given us up to an activity that has proved itself valuable and fruitful on the plane on which it was undertaken, and has also been of a kind to engage us more and more on the revolutionary plane. What it is essential to realize is that no other activity could have produced such rich results, nor could any other similar activity have been so effective in combating the present form of society. On that point we have history on our side.

A comrade, Claude Cahun, in a striking pamphlet published recently: *Les Paris Sont Ouverts,* a pamphlet that attempts to predict the future of poetry by taking account both of its own laws and of the social bases of its existence, takes Aragon to task for the lack of rigour in his present position (I do not think anyone can contest the fact that Aragon's poetry has perceptibly weakened since he abandoned surrealism and undertook to place himself *directly* at the service of the proletarian cause, which leads one to suppose that such an undertaking has defeated him and is proportionately more or less unfavourable to the Revolution). The irrefutable conclusions drawn in this pamphlet corroborate and strengthen those that I formulated in *Misère de la Poésie* (1932) with regard to the impossibility of resolving as elementarily as Aragon has tried to do the conflict between man's conscious thought and his lyrical expression, a conflict sufficient to impassion to the highest degree the poetic drama in which we are the actors. It is of particular interest that the author of *Les Paris Sont Ouverts* has taken the opportunity of expressing himself from the "historic" point of view. His appreciation is as follows:

"The most revolutionary experiment in poetry under the capitalist regime having been incontestably, for France and perhaps for Europe, the Dadaist-surrealist experiment, in that it has tended to destroy all the myths about art that for centuries have permitted the ideologic as well as economic exploitation of painting, sculpture, literature, etc. (e.g., the *frottages* of Max Ernst, which, among other things, have been able to upset the scale of values of art-critics and experts, values based chiefly on technical perfection, personal touch and the lastingness of the materials employed), this experiment can and should serve the cause of the liberation of the proletariat. It is only when the proletariat has become aware of the myths on which capitalist culture depends, when they have become aware of what these myths and this culture mean for them and have destroyed them, that they will be able to pass on to their own proper development. The positive lesson of this negating experiment, that is to say its transfusion among the proletariat, constitutes the only valid revolutionary poetic propaganda."

Surrealism could not ask for anything better. Once the cause of the movement is understood, there is perhaps some hope that, on the plane of revolutionary militantism proper, our turbulence, our small capacity for adaptation, until now, to the necessary rules of a party (which certain people have thought proper to call our "blanquism"), may be excused us. It is only too certain that an activity such as ours, owing to its particularization, cannot be pursued within the limits of any one of the existing revolutionary organizations: it would be forced to come to a halt on the very threshold of that organization. If we are agreed that such an activity has above all tended to *detach* the intellectual creator from the illusions with which bourgeois society has sought to surround him, I for my part can only see in that tendency a further reason for continuing our activity.

None the less, the right that we demand and our desire to make use of it depend, as I said at the beginning, on our remaining able to continue our investigations without having to reckon, as for the last few months we have had to do, with a sudden attack from the forces of criminal imbecility. Let it be clearly understood that for us, surrealists, the interests of thought cannot cease to go hand in hand with the interests of the working class, and that all attacks on liberty, all fetters on the emancipation of the working class and all armed attacks on it cannot fail to be considered by us as attacks on thought likewise. I repeat, the danger is far from having been slow to recognize the fact, since, on the very next day after the first fascist *coup* in France, it was they amongst the intellectual circles who had the honour of taking the initiative in sending out an *Appel à la lutte,* which appeared on February 10th, 1934, furnished with twenty-four signatures. You may rest assured, comrades, that they will not confine themselves, that already they have not confined themselves, to this single act.

The Freudian Revolution

Notwithstanding the impact of Karl Marx, the work of Sigmund Freud (1856–1939) will probably remain the greatest intellectual influence of our age. As is often the case, however, the effects of his studies were not felt at a general level until time had allowed a generation of interpreters (and misinterpreters) to make his ideas accessible to the public. Freud's *Interpretation of Dreams* was published in 1900, Planck's quantum theory was formulated in 1901, Einstein's special theory of relativity four years later; but none of these really affected the public consciousness until after the First World War. Moreover, probably none affected us as drastically as Freud's proposition that the greater part of the human mind is unconscious and that our behavior and, indeed, our interpretation of our behavior, are subject to forces that we can neither comprehend nor control.

The following essay, written in 1923, shows some of the effects that the startling new awareness had on the attitudes of the artistic and literary world. As ever, the secondhand impressions proved more immediate and more potent than the original creation. (This should in no way dispense us from going further to see what Freud himself had to say—especially in a work as brilliant and as general as *Civilization and Its Discontents,* 1930).

Rivière

Jacques Rivière (1886–1925) was born in Bordeaux, of a solid family of bourgeois patricians, and eventually married the sister of his childhood friend, the novelist Alain-Fournier. In 1909 he gave up an academic career to help André Gide, Gaston Galli-mard, Jean Schlumberger, and the future theatrical innovator, Jacques Copeau, bring out the *N.R.F. (Nouvelle Revue Française)*, of which it would be written that "no periodical so uniformly symbolized the twentieth century in Europe as it did." After four years in a German prisoner-of-war camp, the young man returned to Paris at a time when, in Gertrude Stein's words, Paris was where the twentieth century was, to become editor of the *N.R.F.* until his death of typhoid fever while still in his thirties.

Under Rivière's guidance the review became what it would remain until the fall of France in 1940—the center, yet also the vanguard, of literary and artistic activity in France and, hence, in the Western world. It seemed fitting that an account of the Freudian revolution that hit European letters in the postwar years should come from the pen of a man whose strategic position placed him in the best listening post of his time. It is reprinted from the pages of a publication that was the *N.R.F.*'s friendly English rival and, until its untimely demise, its only peer—the London *Criterion*.

Notes on a Possible Generalisation of the Theories of Freud

Freud has been accused by some, Jules Romains among them, of a certain scientific levity, i.e., a certain tendency to convert his hypotheses into laws, before he has accumulated sufficient experimental and objective data to war-rant him in doing so.

"He does not hesitate," says Jules Romains, "to link up two scientific state-ments with one of those 'brilliant views,' which certainly show proof of a great activity of thought, which we are at first inclined to rate as genuine discoveries, but which we do not, on reflection, put away in that corner of the mind where we keep good scientific money. They are fiduciary bonds, bound up with the fate of the bank that issues them."

In many passages, however, Freud exhibits a quite remarkable prudence, and even takes the trouble to indicate himself the gaps in his doctrine, and the points where observation has not yet confirmed it. "The reply to this question," he writes in the *Introduction to Psycho-analysis*, "is not, I think, urgent, and, moreover, it is not sufficiently certain to permit us to venture

---

Source: Jacques Rivière, "Notes on a Possible Generalisation of the Theories of Freud," trans-lated by F. S. Flint, *The Criterion*, London, Vol. I, No. 3, April, 1923.

on it. Let the work of scientific progress go on, and wait patiently." On the threshold of a tempting generalisation of an idea which he has just expressed, he remarks, "The psycho-analytical explanation of neurosis has, however, nothing to do with considerations of so vast a range."

He always examines very carefully the objections that are made to his theories. You will find, for instance, in the last chapter of the *Introduction to Psycho-analysis* a remarkable discussion of the idea that all the discoveries of psycho-analysis might very well be a product of suggestion exercised on the patients. When you think of the weight of this objection, and then see the masterly way in which Freud replies to it, you cannot but have a feeling of confidence both in the uprightness and the power of his mind.

Yet it must be confessed: something still remains of Jules Romain's criticism, and there are certain defects of method in Freud, of which we must be fully conscious and for which we must allow, before we follow in his footsteps.

It is evident that we are dealing with a lively and bustling imagination, and one that sometimes reacts a little too quickly to the first results of an experiment. Reading Freud, you are struck with the rapidity of certain of his conclusions. Often from a single fact he will deduce an immediately general affirmation; often, too, it is quite sufficient, if he is able to interpret a fact in accordance with his theory, for him to regard any other interpretation as excluded.

Moreover, the undeniable victory over the enigmas of nature which his leading idea represents, gives him a kind of intoxication, and leads him into a sort of imperialism. I mean to say that he seeks to annex too many phenomena to his explanation. In especial, his interpretation of dreams and daydreams, which is full of profound observations, nevertheless seems to me, taken as a whole, much more factitious and much less convincing than his theory of neurosis. And when I learn that, historically, he began by an explanation of neurotic symptoms, I wonder whether the whole of his theory of dreams and day-dreams may not be a somewhat arbitrary, or at least too systematic, extension of a just idea into a domain unfitted for it, at the very least in its textual form.

In other words, I am wondering whether the order in which Freud chose to expound his doctrine in his *Introduction to Psycho-analysis,* and which is, as is known, the following: frustrated acts, dreams, neuroses,—whether this order is not extremely specious, and calculated to mislead in regard to the real working of his mind during the course of his discoveries, and in regard to the actual value of those discoveries. Even if it seems logical to show first of all the unconscious at work in the most elementary acts of our normal daily life, this becomes an error of method, if it cannot be revealed with as much evidence in those acts as in pathological acts, if its intervention therein is more disputable, and if, in fact, it was not first of all disclosed in those acts.

I cannot help it: the theory of day-dreams and the theory of dreams appear to me as a sort of double gate constructed by Freud, as an afterthought, before the monument he had raised. He thought that this would make a more agreeable and more convincing approach to that monument; but, to my mind, he was mistaken, because, in this preliminary part, you do not receive strongly enough the impression that you are in contact with an invincible, irrefutable observation, with that observation which gave rise to the theory. You feel the subtlety of the author, but you do not feel sufficiently his justification.

For this reason, I think it necessary to keep in mind continually and principally his theory of neuroses, if you wish to seize his thought at its point of maximum intensity, and to realise all the consequences it implies, all the generalisations it is capable of bearing, its furthest reach, or, if you prefer it, its greatest explosive force.

In what follows, I desire, not to analyse in detail the Freudian doctrine, but, on the contrary, supposing it to be known to all my readers, to bring out, if I may say so, its potentialities. I desire to present the three great psychological discoveries which, it seems to me, we owe to Freud, and to reveal the wonderful light which they can project into the study of internal things, and, particularly, of the feelings. I desire, especially, to show how great is their extensibility, and how they may be made to take on a more supple, and, if I may say so, a still more generous, form than that given to them by Freud.

In the account of the facts which suggested to him the first idea of his theory, and which, as is known, are the body of manifestations of hysteria, Freud insists with especial force on the complete ignorance in which his patients were of the cause and purpose of the acts they were performing. "While she was carrying out the obsessive act," he writes, "its meaning was unknown to the patient, both as regards the origin of the act and its object. Psychic processes were therefore acting in her, of which the obsessive act was the product. She certainly perceived this product with her normal psychic organisation, but none of her psychic conditions reached her conscious mind. . . . It is situations of this kind which we have in mind when we speak of *unconscious psychic processes*." And Freud concludes: "In these symptoms of obsessional neurosis, in these ideas and impulses which spring from nowhere, as it seems, which are so refractory to any influence of normal life, and which appear to the patient himself like all-powerful guests from a foreign world, like immortals who have come to mingle in the tumult of this mortal life, how is it possible not to recognise an indication of a particular psychic region, isolated from all the rest, from all the other activities and manifestations of the inner life? These symptoms, ideas, and impulses lead infallibly to the conviction of the existence of a psychic unconsciousness."

It does not appear, at first sight, that there is in these passages any very extraordinary novelty, and it might be thought paradoxical that we should see in them one of the sublimities of the Freudian theory. The unconscious is not a discovery of Freud's. You may quote immediately names that appear to reduce to the slightest proportions his originality on this point: Leibnitz, for instance, Schopenhauer, Hartmann, Bergson, and many others.

Nevertheless, I reply:

(1) That there is a considerable difference between a metaphysical conception and a psychological conception of the Unconscious, that to admit the Unconscious as a principle, as a force, as an entity, is a far different thing from admitting it as a body of facts, as a group of phenomena.

(2) That, in reality, many contemporary psychologists, particularly Pierre Janet and his school, still refuse to admit a psychological unconsciousness.

(3) Finally, that, if we admit that a psychological unconsciousness has been recognised by everybody, as a kingdom, as a domain, Freud is the first to conceive of it:

> (a) As a well-defined domain or kingdom, which has its own geography, or, dropping the metaphor, which contains extremely precise tendencies and inclinations directed towards particular aims;
> (b) As a domain or kingdom which may be explored, starting from the consciousness, and, even, which must be explored, if the consciousness is to be understood.

Here, I recover confidence to affirm that the novelty of the theory seems to me entire, and formidably important. Remember that hitherto consciousness has been conceived as a closed chamber, wherein the objects, of a definite number, were, so to speak, entered on an inventory and had affinities only with each other, and that if it was desired to explain any incident of our psychic life, you could not go to some fact which you had previously perceived. Remember that the whole of psychology was limited to a logical explanation of our determinants. Remember the scanty causal stock it had at its disposal, and imagine its richness immediately Freud opened up to it the immense reservoir of submerged causes.

He is himself, moreover, conscious of the revolution which this mere proclamation of the definite reality of the unconscious may produce in the history of ideas, and he permits himself a touch of pride. "By attributing so much importance to the unconscious in our psychic life," he cries, "we have raised up against psycho-analysis the most ill-natured critics. . . ." And yet "the lie will be given to human megalomania by that psychological research which proposes to prove to the ego that he is not only not master in his own house, but that he is so little master there that he has to be content with rare and fragmentary information on what is going on, outside his consciousness, in his psychic life. The psycho-analysts are neither the first nor the only people who have launched this appeal for modesty and composure, but it seems to have fallen to their lot to defend this point of view with the greatest earnestness, and to produce in its support materials borrowed from observation and accessible to all."

Let us reflect a moment. Let us turn, if I may say so, against us this principle of the unconscious as the seat of definite tendencies that combine to modify the conscious, and let us confront it with our own observation. In other words: *let us think for a moment of all we do not know that we want.*

Is not our life a constant seeking after possessions, pleasures, and satisfactions that not only would we not dare to confess we desire, but that we do not know we desire, we are seeking? Is it not nearly always *a posteriori* and only when we are performing it that we are aware of the long psychic labour and of all the chain of latent feelings that led us to an act?

And again: at what moment does direct inspection of our consciousness inform us exactly on all we are experiencing and all we are capable of? Are we not in constant ignorance of the degree and even of the existence of our feelings? Are there not, even in passion, moments when we discover absolutely nothing left of that passion, when it appears to us a pure construction of our mind? And yet does not that passion exist at that very moment, in what I may be allowed to call an infinitely precise fashion, since the slightest accident that may happen to place an obstacle in its way or to postpone its object may instantly provoke a complete upheaval of our whole being, which will find expression even in our physical condition and will even influence the circulation of our blood?

In love, for example, is not a sincere lover often reduced to making experiments and almost to tricks in order to auscultate his feelings and to ascertain whether they still exist? And that too at the very moment when, if he were told that he must give up hope or that he has been deceived, he would perhaps find himself on the verge of crime.

Therefore, a first great discovery (which may perhaps be presented as a negative one, but negative discoveries are no less important than the others) must be placed to Freud's credit: it is that a considerable part of our psychic life takes place, if I may say so, outside us, and can only be disclosed and known by a patient and complicated labour of inference. In other words: we are never quite wholly available to our own minds, quite wholly objects of consciousness.

This first analysis should make clear the spirit in which I have tackled the study of Freud and how I intend to follow it up. I do not by any means profess to follow his thought step by step in all its developments. I simply seek and seize on, one by one, without troubling to point out their relations one with another, the points of his doctrine that seem to me capable of being enlarged into psychological truths of general interest. I am an outsider who egotistically pillages a treasure and carries it far away from the temple. I may be judged severely from the moral point of view; but in any case it is not, I imagine, incumbent upon me to adopt the slow and processional gait which is obligatory on the priests of Psycho-analysis.

Let us therefore proceed at once to the examination of another of Freud's ideas which seems to me of considerable importance; I mean the idea of repression, with which must be connected that of the censorship of dreams.

Its essential points are well known: basing himself on his observations as a practitioner, Freud asserts that there is in every subject who is analysed or even questioned, an instinctive resistance to any question and any effort to penetrate to the background of his thought. This resistance is moreover subject to variations of intensity. The patient is more or less hostile, more or less critical, according as the thing which the doctor is endeavouring to bring to light is more or less disagreeable.

The resistance therefore seems to be the effect of a force, of a strictly affective nature, which opposes itself to the appearance in the open consciousness, to the illumination, of certain psychic elements which it considers incongruous, as impossible to be faced.

This force which is met when you set to work to cure the patient is the very same force that has produced the malady by repressing a psychic process which tended from the unconscious towards the conscious. The tendency thus baulked has in fact transformed, disguised, itself—in order to go at any rate a little further—as a mechanical act, with no apparent meaning, but which the subject is helpless to avoid: it is the symptom: "The symptom has been substituted for that which has not been accomplished."

Freud therefore brings to light the presence in the consciousness of an activity that reduces or deforms our obscure spontaneity. He also shows it at work in our dreams, and then calls it the *censorship*. Just as the censorship, during the war, either mutilated newspaper articles, or else forced their authors to present their thought only in an approximate or veiled form, in the same way a secret power modifies and disguises our unconscious thoughts, and permits them to reach our mind only in the enigmatic forms of the dream.

"The tendencies exercising the censorship are those which the dreamer, with his waking judgment, recognises as being his own, with which he feels himself in agreement. . . . The tendencies against which the censorship of dreams is directed . . . are the reprehensible tendencies, indecent from the ethical, aesthetic, and social point of view . . . are things of which one dares not think of or of which one thinks only with horror."

The neurotic symptoms are "the effects of compromises, resulting from the interplay of two opposing tendencies, and they express both what has been repressed as well as the cause of the repression, which thus too contributed to their production. The substitution may be made for the greater benefit of one or other of these tendencies; it is seldom made for the exclusive benefit of one alone."

In the same way, the dream is a sort of composite of, or rather compromise between, the repressed tendencies, to which sleep gives strength, and the tendencies really representing the self, which continued their work by means of the distorting censorship.

In other words, neurotic symptoms and dreams correspond to an effort of our diverse sincerities to display themselves at the same moment.

The whole of this conception seems to me to be extraordinarily novel and important. It may be that Freud himself has not perceived it in all its general bearings.

The discovery in us of a deceptive principle, of a falsifying activity, may nevertheless furnish an absolutely new view of the whole of consciousness.

I shall at once exaggerate my idea: all our feelings are dreams, all our opinions are the strict equivalent of neurotic symptoms.

There is in us a constant, obstinate, inexhaustively inventive tendency that impels us to camouflage ourselves. At any cost, in every circumstance, we will ourselves to be, we construct ourselves, other than we are. Of course, the direction in which this deformation is exercised and its degree vary extraordinarily with different natures. But in all the same principle of deceit and embellishment is at work.

To start out on the study of the human heart without being informed of its existence and its activity, without being armed against its subterfuges, is like trying to discover the nature of the sea-depths without sounding apparatus and by merely inspecting the surface of the waters. Or better still, as Jules Romains says, it is like the traditional method of analysis, which "even when it searches the depths is guided by the showy indications of the surface. It suspects the presence of iron only when the rocks above are red with rust, of coal only when black dust is underfoot."

Who does not know this demon which Freud calls the censorship, and which so subtly and ceaselessly makes our moral toilet? Each instant, the whole of what we are, I mean the confused and swarming mass of our appetites, is taken in hand and tricked out by it. It slips into our lowest instincts enough of nobility to enable us to recognise them no longer. It furnishes us in abundance with the pretexts, the colours, that we need to cover up the petty turpitudes we must commit in order to live. It provides us with what we call our *bonnes raisons*. It maintains us in that state of friendship and alliance with ourselves without which we cannot live, and which is yet so completely devoid of justification that we do not understand how it can possibly take its rise.

But I feel that I am leaving Freud's idea far behind. The principle governing repression and the censorship, far from working for the triumph of our appetites, is, in his opinion, what combats them, stops them. It is the representative of the moral ideas, or, at least, of convention, so far from helping to circumvent it.

Nevertheless, there are cases in which it is beaten, partially at least: the neurotic symptom, the dream, the day-dream, correspond to relative successes over it by the lower part of ourselves. And if it is not directly an agent of hypocrisy, it becomes so in so far as it does not gain the victory.

When I maintain that all our feelings, all our opinions, are dreams or obsessive acts, I mean that they are impure, masked, hypocritical states; I mean, in fine, something that must be looked straight in the face: that hypocrisy is inherent in consciousness.

Taking Freud's idea to its logical end, I will say that to possess consciousness is to be a hypocrite. A feeling, a desire, enter the consciousness only by forcing a resistance of which they retain the deforming imprint. A feeling, a desire, enter the consciousness only on the condition that they do not appear to be what they are.

From this point of view, the chapter that Freud devotes to the processes employed by the censorship to distort the latent content of the dream and to render it unrecognisable would be worth development to a considerable extent. Several of these processes are certainly used by us in the waking state, to enable us to conceive our feelings under an acceptable form. I will cite one only as an example: the displacement, the carrying over, of the accent to an aspect of what we feel, or need to feel, peacefully, which is not the *essential aspect*. In other words, the rupture by the imagination of the centre of gravity of our sentimental complexes.

Let it be said, in passing, that if I was a little severe at the beginning regarding the Freudian theory of dreams, it was very much because I regretted to see Freud apply too minutely to a particular phenomenon an idea that seemed to me to have an infinite bearing. His analysis of the symbolism of dreams goes much too far; it reintroduces into the consciousness, the suppleness and extreme convertibility of which he has shown, something fixed, which, it seems to me, has no place there. Freud's thought must be allowed to retain, if not a certain vagueness, at least a certain generality, if its value is to be fully understood.

Before leaving this idea of the censorship, one other aspect of it, of considerable importance, must be dealt with.

When I say that hypocrisy is inherent in consciousness, I either say too much or too little. The censorship, the force that controls repression, is partly made up of external contributions; they are created chiefly by education; they represent the influence of society upon the individual. Nevertheless, they are not altogether adventitious or artificial; they finally become one with the self. Freud even represents them as the tendencies constituting the ego.

And, in fact, it would be simplifying things very much to represent our lower instincts alone as constituting our personality. That which represses them is also part of us.

But then this conclusion is inevitable: that in so far as we are moral persons, and even in so far as we are persons merely, we are condemned to hypocrisy. We will no longer say hypocrisy, if you like; but we cannot avoid another word—impurity. To live, to act, if it is to be in one sole direction and with method and in such a way as to trace an image of ourselves on the retina of others, is to be composite and impure, is to be a compromise.

Sincere comes from a Latin word which means *pure,* speaking of wine. It may be said that there is no sincerity for man in his integrity. He becomes sincere again only in decomposition. Sincerity is, therefore, the exact contrary of life. You must choose between the two.

The third point in Freud's doctrine which we can, it seems to me, though to a less extent perhaps, *enlarge,* is the theory of sexuality.

The general lines of this theory may be recalled.

Inquiring into the nature of the tendencies which are stopped by repression and which are expressed by *substitution* in the symptoms and in dreams, Freud, it will be remembered, thinks that they can all be said to be of a sexual nature.

Several *nuances* should be noted here. Freud does not say, and even denies having said, that everything appearing in our dreams is of sexual origin. Only that which appears camouflaged is of sexual origin.

Moreover, Freud does not say, and denies having said (for example, in the letter published by Professor Claparède as an appendix to the brochure on psycho-analysis), that our whole being may be reduced to sexual tendencies, or even that "the sexual instinct is the fundamental impulse of all the manifestations of psychic activity." On the contrary: "In psycho-analysis it has never been forgotten that non-sexual tendencies exist; its whole edifice has been erected on the principle of a clear and definite separation between sexual tendencies and tendencies relating to the self, and it was affirmed, before any objections had been made, that the neuroses are the products, not of sexuality, but of the conflict between the *self* and sexuality."

Nevertheless, it remains true that the body of spontaneous and unconscious tendencies of the being is considered by him as fundamentally identical with the sexual instinct.

He is careful, however, to define that instinct very broadly, distinguishing it from the procreative instinct and even from strictly genital activity. In order clearly to mark its general character, he calls it *libido*.

The *libido* conception is evidently not absolutely clear. At times it has an almost metaphysical value, and the next instant it is used simply to designate the sexual appetite, desire properly so called.

But I am wondering whether, instead of reproaching Freud with this ambiguity, instead of trying to force him to hang on to this word *libido* an absolutely distinct and limited tendency, it would not be more fitting if we were grateful to him for the vagueness in which he leaves it and for the wider play it permits him. I am wondering whether his principal discovery, in the domain we are discussing, is not indeed precisely that of one sole transformable tendency, which perhaps forms the basis of our spontaneous psychic life.

In other words, the idea that desire is the motive-power of all our activity, at least of all our expansive activity, seems to me of an admirable novelty and truth. Or, better still, the idea that we are creators, producers, only in so far as we move in the direction of desire.

But we must be careful not to betray by too great precipitation Freud's idea itself, his conception of sublimation. I resume, therefore.

Freud, by a long analysis, strongly supported by experimental observations, which fills the whole of a small brochure, entitled *Three Dissertations on the Sexual Theory,* establishes that the sexual instinct has at first neither the object nor the aim we know of it. He shows it first of all immanent, so to speak, in the body of the child, and neither seeking nor even suspecting any external satisfaction. This is the period of what he calls auto-eroticism.

He shows it at the same time irradiating confusedly and impartially into all the organs, and receiving satisfactions almost indifferently from all.

Then experience, which may, moreover, be preceded by foreign interventions, teaches the *libido* to externalise itself. But even after this leap forward it remains hesitating between several possible satisfactions, and places itself exclusively at the service of the genital act only at the moment of puberty and by a kind of very complex synthetic action, which is liable to be influenced by a crowd of accidental interferences.

This desire, which is beneath its object, and which at the same time exceeds it or even transcends it, is a conception marked with boldness and of magnificent depth.

How much it permits Freud to explain may be easily understood. If the *libido* is repressed, one of two things happens: it will either turn to a means of satisfaction which he calls pregenital, and you will have a perversion, by *fixation;* or it will produce an uneasiness which will generate neuroses.

But, on the other hand, the fact that it is not really bound up in any constitutional manner with the genital act will permit it to go beyond that act and to place itself at the service of intellectual activity, to irrigate, so to speak, our spiritual faculties. Its sublimation will consist, therefore, in this deviation of the *libido* to the advantage of the intelligence or even of morality.

The reflections inspired by this part of the Freudian theory might be presented in the following manner:

(1) It is of considerable importance, from the point of view of the psychology of creation, to have established that the source of all spiritual creation is carnal, if the word may be used. This is important, not because it degrades creation, but because it brings to light the unity of our psychic life, and because it makes clear that, all in all, we have at our disposal only one kind of energy, and all our liberty is confined to directing the use of it.

It is important because it explains aesthetic emotion before a great work, and because, whatever may be the object represented, it explains the sensual element the work always possesses when it is sincere.

It is important, even from the point of view of aesthetic criticism, because it teaches us to seek in the work, not the little smothered story which may be at its origin in the author—as has been done with too much precision, in my opinion, by those who have hitherto applied psycho-analysis to art—but the current of desire, the impulse in which it was born. And a sort of vague aesthetic criterion might be established, which would enable us to distinguish works born of an inclination from those manufactured by will, the aesthetic quality being, of course, reserved to the former.

(2) By analysing, on the one hand, all that the *libido* builds up in the subconsciousness under the shelter of repression, and, on the other hand, all that the repression of the *libido* may produce in the conscious life, Freud opens up to psychology a prodigious domain.

I do not think that the analysis of dreams, as practised by Freudian orthodoxy, can lead to much of any great interest—owing, especially, to the strange preliminary telegraphic code that imprisons interpretation.

But think of what might be discovered by a psychologist without prejudice (either Freudian or anti-Freudian), who is simply resolved not to ignore what I should like to call the sexual situation of the subjects he is studying. Think of that abyss, as yet so ill-explored, of sexual attractions, and perhaps especially of sexual hatreds. Think what an access to individual character, what a key to the whole conduct of a given subject, might be given by a knowledge of his or her sexual experiences, and especially of the consequences of and the reactions from these experiences.

The novelist hitherto, even if he did not note them down, has been careful to keep in mind, for his own guidance, the social situation, the material conditions, the business, and the parentage of each of his characters. It seems impossible to me, after Freud, that he can neglect to imagine, likewise beforehand, even if he is not to say a word about it during the course of his story (his story may even have for its object merely to suggest it), the sexual situation of each of his characters and its relation—you will understand that I am using the word in its most general sense—from the sexual point of view, with the rest.

(3) By detaching the *libido* from its object, Freud implicitly adopts a subjectivist conception of love. It is evident that this mobile, shiftable desire which he describes will need to receive nothing from the object it chooses, will even be unable to receive anything from it, and that it is from its own resources entirely that the image of the beloved object will be formed in the mind of the lover.

He speaks somewhere of the "over-estimation of the sexual object," and doubtless he intends this first of all in the physical sense, but he certainly has it in mind as well that all the moral beauties with which the lover embellishes the beloved object are the reflection of the projection on it of the *libido*. He admits, therefore, that all love is hallucinatory, and seeks in foreign beings only a pretext to fix itself. He does not admit the appeal, the attraction, of one being for another, or that love can ever be born of real, objective affinities.

We must now endeavour to embrace in one view the whole of Freud's doctrine and to appraise it.

Freud brings us two things: a new world of facts, a "new family of facts" (and here I am of an entirely different opinion from Jules Romains, who denies him this kind of discovery), and, if not a new "law" of these facts, at least a new method of exploring them, or, more vaguely, a new attitude to take regarding them.

The new world is the world of the unconscious, conceived and shown for the first time as a system of definite facts, of the same nature and the same stuff as those appearing in the consciousness, and in constant relation, in constant *exchange,* with the conscious facts.

Among these unconscious facts, Freud reveals the wonderful flora of the sexual tendencies and complexes. Even if he describes them with too much precision (this is always somewhat of a defect of his), and if he typifies them too much, it is an admirable novelty merely to have unveiled them.

Others may follow his footsteps, with more lightness and a more acute sense of the individual, into this strange garden. But he has already indicated to those others—and it is his second contribution, which is equally priceless—the attitude of approach to take up in order to make good observations.

He warns us of the force that is at work in us to deceive us about ourselves; he teaches us its ruses and the means of circumventing them.

More generally, he sketches a new introspective attitude, which may be the point of origin of an entirely new direction to psychological studies. This attitude consists in endeavouring to know oneself, if I may be permitted the expression, only by the signs. Instead of attending to the feeling or sensation itself, Freud seeks for it in its effects only, in its symptoms.

Of course, long before him, attempts had been made to observe psychic phenomena, for greater safety, indirectly, particularly in their conditions. The whole of psycho-physiology was an endeavour to obtain information about the consciousness by starting from the exterior, from something that was not of it, but which had this advantage that it could be touched, measured, and made to vary. But the error of psycho-physiology, as Bergson has so well observed, was to ignore the differences of quality in the phenomena.

Bergson's own error perhaps (I indicate it here only in the most prudent and hypothetical manner) was to plunge with too much confidence into the pure psychological flow, and too naively to expect knowledge from mere embracing contact. Can you mark the course of a river by swimming in it?

Freud escapes the error of the psycho-physiologists by accepting as information concerning the psychic life only psychic facts. He builds up an independent, autonomous psychology; and that is one of the reasons for the opposition he has met with.

But, on the other hand, he does not believe in these psychic facts; I mean, he does not accept them at face value. He regards them, *a priori*, both as deceitful and as explicable. He uses them as signs enabling him to trace back inductively to a deeper and more masked psychic reality. He strives in an opposite direction to the vital current.

And thus he gives back to the intelligence that active role, that role of mistrust and of penetration, which in all the orders of intelligence has always been the only one that permitted and favoured knowledge. There would be much to say on his complete faith in psychological determinism. But as a method, to be used as long as it is possible, determinism is unassailable. It is only by this method that you can hope to make headway, with any distinction and advantage for thought, in the chaos that our soul sends out to meet us.

IV.

Social Awareness: The Reintegration of Art

The great and bloody mess of the First World War was succeeded by a queer mood compounded of relief, exasperation, and revolt. The war had shaken the foundations of the old order, but the order still stood and the first to challenge it effectively in the West were not social or political revolutionaries, but the artists and intellectuals who questioned its moral and aesthetic assumptions rather than the imperfections of its economic system. Many of the great battles of the post-war generation seem to have been fought under the banner of free love and free thought, around issues like sexual freedom, birth control, liberty to write like D. H. Lawrence, to love like André Gide, to deny the accepted values of respectable society while remaining within it and benefiting from its economy. As the Right Honorable John Strachey, M.P., explained, his generation—the generation that was born at the beginning of this century and just missed fighting in the war—"became conscious of the break-up of our old world, not by realising that its economic foundations were shattered, but by a sudden and bewildering loss of faith in the whole moral, religious and social ideology which we had inherited." Some consequences of this revolt appeared in Dada, in Surrealism, and in the tortured developments of German Expressionism whose products seemed to reflect the maladies of contemporary society.[1]

It would be hard to say how long the trumpets of the new Joshuas would have had to blow if the walls of Jericho had not been cracked already. But four years of conflict had left them severely damaged. Millions dead; millions of acres of land ruined by the war that had rolled across the continent. It would take much time and money before the land could ever yield anything again. Homes, factories, and mines destroyed by the hundreds of thousands, railroads torn up and rolling stock worn out, foreign investments recalled to meet the mounting costs of carnage, all these could not but affect the economy of Europe and the self-assurance of its ruling classes. Threatened from too many sides at once, they gave way more easily on less essential points the better to concentrate on defending their inalienable property. This may explain the relative tolerance with which respectable people treated the revolutionary artistic movements of the 1920s: there were more dangerous revolutionary movements in other fields. Even so, in Germany, in England and, to a lesser extent, in France the middle 1920s saw national economies come dangerously close to collapse and be re-established only with difficulty. Meanwhile, in many countries, failure to cope with problems born of the war led to the rise of Fascist regimes. Italy in 1922, Spain in 1923, Poland in 1925 acquired dictators; with the exception of Czechoslovakia, every country east of Germany had some kind of authoritarian regime by 1930. By 1930 it had become clear that Germany would follow suit, and Hitler's coming to power in January, 1933, did not seem to alter the German situation very much.

Regimes like that of Mussolini in Italy, Pilsudski in Poland, and, eventually, Hitler in Germany troubled opinion in Britain and France far less than the Communist regime in Russia and the possibility of Communist revolution in other lands. For some years after the war, Communist victory in Hungary, in Germany, and elsewhere seemed threateningly close. The Bolshevik menace was very real and its specter could easily be raised, and often was, to scare Western voters into the comforting arms of the right. Combined with a sense of discomfort over the ineffective sternness of the Versailles treaty, and with Anglo-American interest in the economic recovery of central Europe, this fear of Communist Russia goes far to explain the indulgence, even the sympathy, with which Fascism and Nazism

---

[1]Whereas the previous sections represented more or less successive movements, the material that follows concerns ideas and tendencies whose development is largely contemporaneous. Thus the ideas presented below reflect not chronologically distinct phases in the thought of the mid- and later-twentieth century, but concurrent and complementary aspects of it.

were greeted in the West. The former in particular, more palatable for its freedom from racial nonsense, appeared in Western eyes as a healthy phenomenon of resurgent nationalism. Fascists stamped out Communism, increased production, revitalized national sentiment, and made the trains run on time. As for democracy, for what that was worth, it could come later. First things first: and first came the preservation of social order and vested interests.

As the 1920s drew to an end, such a tolerant position became increasingly difficult to maintain. After 1929, as factories and mines went out of production and unemployment spread over Europe, attacks once directed against the outer trappings of the capitalist system now turned against its economic foundations. When Christian apologists and liberal economists had lost their credit, that some should eat while many starved seemed gross injustice, an injustice whose evidence was all around, too widespread to forget or escape for long. To those who suffered, and even more to those who suffered at the sight of suffering, Socialism and Communism carried a message of hope.

And so, where the 1920s had been subjective, escapist, or expressionistic, the 1930s reflect a shift from individualism to social concerns and a flight from negativism to affirmation—ideology and political dogma. The pendulum swings with a vengeance from the detachment of Evelyn Waugh, the useless self-affirmation of Hemingway's characters, the ruins of the Wasteland, to commitment and a certain hopefulness. The pessimism of the twenties had often been more fun: the optimism of the thirties would generally be more stern, with the earnestness of high endeavor.

This need not appear surprising since the men of the twenties, disgusted and disoriented as they might be, had after all escaped from a holocaust that the generation of the thirties saw before them—and around them—impinging upon them with great urgency. The former, fearing or despising the society around them, held aloof from it, satirized it, invested in the esoteric, the elaborate, the erudite, the sort of thing accessible only to an educated minority, food for the elite or the undergraduate hoax. The latter abandoned isolation only to go to the other extreme. As Michael Roberts put it in his preface to *New Signatures* (1932), which presented the poems of new young men with names like Auden, Spender, Day Lewis, and Julian Bell:

> It is natural that the recognition of the importance of others should sometimes lead to what appears to be the essence of the communist attitude: the recognition that oneself is no more important than a flower in a field; that it may be good to sacrifice one's own welfare that others may benefit; to plough in this year's crop so that next year's may benefit: the return is certain, what matter who receives it.

Given first the Depression, then the Fascist threat that grew more and more ominous after Hitler's advent to power in 1933, such a shift was natural enough. The early 1930s persuaded many who had not considered the matter before that social classes were really interrelated and not separate entities, that there was no such thing, and could not be, as a completely isolated individual, that—in a quotation destined for fame—no man is an island. The would-be individualistic writer, antibourgeois, antiphilistine, aloof, and detached in his ivory tower was out because the ivory tower itself was out: it had developed a distinct list and might topple over at any moment. Faced by the unemployed of the industrial cities, by the intellectuals in the concentration camps of Germany and Italy, by the attaints against human dignity reported from all sides, the artist found himself no longer an outsider with no responsibility to aught but his work and his artistic conscience. To the embattled proletarian there was nothing to choose between him and the rest of the middle class. To the Fascist the artist's supposed revolutionary sympathies, the decadent overtones of his works, or simply the questioning and doubt inherent in every intellectual quest, were reason enough for persecution. And so, the *poète maudit,* the aesthete, the deliberate outsider of the early part of the century, became the rebellious *intellectual,* opposing Fascism, supporting the popular fronts in various countries and, eventually, the Republic in Spain. True, in his new guise, he would continue to be suspected by both sides and, still more, by himself. But now he had a purpose and the belief that even in the Wasteland, something remained to be saved—human lives, integrity, humor, trust, and generosity that had been rather lost from sight in the previous decades.

Riding the crest of this fresh interest in action—social action—certain older ideas also came into their own. Fifty years before and more, men like John Ruskin and William Morris had argued that true art was more than empty show or conspicuous consumption: that true beauty was honest and functional—a synthesis of the concerns and the social realities of its time. Gothic, for Ruskin, had been the sublime synthesis of the Middle Ages, the reflection of its social system, the product of the combined efforts of its workers and thinkers, an outgrowth of the needs and ideas of the time. Modern art should imitate not its style, in wedding-cake travesties of French cathedrals for the use of railroad hotels, but its principles; should strive to be in its turn the product and delight of the people: not a luxury for the rich, but a constant source of pleasure and edification for its true creators—the workers. William Morris carried the social thought of Ruskin into outright Socialism. But it was only half a century later that German architect Walter Gropius set out to apply the functional principles of his English predecessors, along with their insistence on honesty, to the problems of twentieth-century living.

There was, here, a revival of idealistic rationalism well-suited to the new machine age. When the French architect Le Corbusier said that a house should be "a machine for living," he was not far from the tradition of Ruskin, Eastlake, and Morris, who had tried to help people lead more reasonable lives in more reasonable surroundings and, by joining the moral and the practical, had combined aesthetic ideals and a sensible approach that appealed to many. In the 1920s and 1930s, however, the puritan "functional" style of the new architects and designers like Gropius, Le Corbusier, and Mies van der Rohe—although it appealed to intellectuals eager to be up to date and to some city planners hardly yet come into their own—did not much attract a public who identified the bare lines of the glass and concrete structures with offices and factories more to be escaped than recalled after working hours. Even architecture, the most practical of the arts and the most down to earth, had by the 1930s increased the distance separating its liveliest spirits from the man in the street (or in the house) whom it sought to serve.[2]

The workers' apartments and the urban developments that Gropius planned had to be abandoned for concerns more serious and threats more bloody than those arising directly from the Depression. Before the Fascist-Nazi threat, the democracies revealed themselves unwilling or unable to react; and in the Spanish war, many found evidence that the only power willing to fight on the side of social justice and democratic government was Soviet Russia, where heroic measures had installed Communism and allowed it to prosper.

Yet, just as the Spanish war marked the peak of an era of social commitment, it provided, too, an opportunity to measure the words of Communism against its deeds, a situation in which the difference between the one and the other soon became too evident to ignore. In the event, many for whom famine and repression in distant Russia had counted for little when weighed against shortcomings and cowardice so much closer to home, decided with Stephen Spender that there was no use "in taking sides with those politicians who seem a little nearer the truth than the others." For though they may have been a little nearer the truth than others, politicians and politics, all, were now seen to be sufficiently distant from it to dismay and disgust those who had put their hopes in them for a few busy years.

Thus, 1938 and 1939 are *par excellence* the years of *The God That Failed*—failed his believers in Spain, in the Russo-German pact, and, eventually, in the Russo-Finnish war. But they are also years of clarification. The artists and the writers

---

[2]Two score years later, architecture seemed well-established as the public enemy not just of contemporary aesthetics, but of comfort and convenience as well.

who had moved to the left in order to defend human values and self-respect, now moved away from the Communism that had seemed for a while to offer the best hope of attaining their end—but not from the end itself. George Orwell, Ignazio Silone, Stephen Spender, André Malraux, continued to fight for "man's dignity" and for his right to live in freedom—his "self-possession" as Malraux would put it. But they did it now in a spirit of disillusioned stoicism: alone once more, but no longer uncommitted.

Ruskin

John Ruskin (1819–1900) was born in London, the son of "an entirely honest wine merchant" and of a puritan mother. He received his education at home and at Oxford, his father teaching him to love literature, nature, and art, his mother inculcating in him the inhibitions and repressions of her kind. As an undergraduate at Oxford he won the Newdigate Prize for poetry but, as in the case of Charles Péguy, his poetry shows best in his prose. It was in 1843 that Ruskin first broke seriously into print with an anonymous defense of Turner's paintings, an apologia that developed over the years (1843–1860) into a series of volumes entitled *Modern Painters*. His passionate feeling that art, morality, and socioeconomic justice were interconnected and had to be treated as such was expressed at length in *The Seven Lamps of Architecture* (1849), *The Stones of Venice* (1851–1853), from which a chapter appears below, and a great number of books and articles.

Criticism of competitive industrial society, its weaknesses, hypocrisies, injustices, and dishonesties, came from Carlyle in the forties, from Dickens in the sixties, from Trollope in the seventies. Ruskin, who has an obvious place in this line of critics, argued, "The first duty of a state is to see that every child born therein shall be well housed, clothed, fed and educated, till it attains years of discretion." It was a principle that implied government intervention on a scale much vaster than anyone then dreamed. It has always been a grave vice in men of vision that they see further and more clearly than their more pragmatic contemporaries. Contrary to accepted belief, in the country of the blind the one-eyed man is not king, but a subversive influence.

As Slade professor of fine art at Oxford, Ruskin's lectures were as much concerned with sociology as with art. His firm belief that good art is essentially moral and bad art immoral—that is, bad because immoral and insincere—soon clashed with the increasingly amoral eclecticism of the late nineteenth century, but his teaching left its mark on many of his students and readers, particularly men like William Morris and Arnold Toynbee, who tried to put it into practice, but also on Marcel Proust. Not surprisingly, the same ideas were eventually revived in the purposeful atmosphere of the socially dedicated interwar years.

The Nature of Gothic

The modern English mind has this much in common with that of the Greek, that it intensely desires, in all things, the utmost completion or perfection compatible with their nature. This is a noble character in the abstract, but becomes ignoble when it causes us to forget the relative dignities of the nature itself, and to prefer the perfectness of the lower nature to the imperfection of the higher; not considering that as judged by such a rule, all the brute animals would be preferable to man, because more perfect in their functions and kind, and yet are always held inferior to him, so also in the works of man, those which are more perfect in their kind are always inferior to those which are, in their nature, liable to more faults and shortcomings. For the finer the nature, the more flaws it will show through the clearness of it; and it is a law of this universe, that the best things shall be seldomest seen in their best form. The wild grass grows well and strongly, one year with another; but the wheat is, according to the greater nobleness of its nature, liable to the bitterer blight. And therefore, while in all things that we see, or do, we are to desire perfection, and strive for it, we are nevertheless not to set the meaner thing, in its narrow accomplishment, above the nobler thing, in its mighty progress; not to esteem smooth minuteness above shattered majesty; not to prefer mean victory to honorable defeat; not to lower the level of our aim, that we may the more surely enjoy the complacency of success. But, above all, in our dealings with the souls of other men, we are to take care how we check, by severe requirement or narrow caution, efforts which might otherwise lead to a noble issue; and, still more, how we withhold our admiration from great excellences, because they are mingled with rough faults. Now, in the make and nature of every man, however rude or simple, whom we employ in manual labor, there are some powers for better things: some tardy imagination, torpid capacity of emotion, tottering steps of thought, there are even at the worst; and in most cases it is all our own fault that they are tardy or torpid. But they cannot be strengthened, unless we are content to take them in their feebleness, and unless we prize and honor them in their imperfection above the best and most perfect manual skill. And this is what we have to do with all our laborers; to look for the *thoughtful* part of them, and get that out of them, whatever we lose for it, whatever faults and errors we are obliged to take with it. For the best that is in them cannot manifest itself, but in company with much error. Understand this clearly: You can teach a man to draw a straight line, and to cut one; to strike a curved line,

---

Source: From *The Stones of Venice,* 1851–1853.

and to carve it; and to copy and carve any number of given lines of forms, with admirable speed and perfect precision; and you find his work perfect of its kind: but if you ask him to think about any of those forms, to consider if he cannot find any better in his own head, he stops; his execution becomes hesitating; he thinks, and ten to one he thinks wrong; ten to one he makes a mistake in the first touch he gives to his work as a thinking being. But you have made a man of him for all that. He was only a machine before, an animated fool.

And observe, you are put to stern choice in this matter. You must either make a tool of the creature, or a man of him. You cannot make both. Men were not intended to work with the accuracy of tools, to be precise and perfect in all their actions. If you will have that precision out of them, and make their fingers measure degrees like cog-wheels, and their arms strike curves like compasses, you must unhumanize them. All the energy of their spirits must be given to make cogs and compasses of themselves. All their attention and strength must go to the accomplishment of the mean act. The eye of the soul must be bent upon the finger-point, and the soul's force must fill all the invisible nerves that guide it, ten hours a day, that it may not err from its steely precision, and so soul and sight be worn away, and the whole human being be lost at last—a heap of sawdust, so far as its intellectual work in this world is concerned; saved only by its Heart, which cannot go into the form of cogs and compasses, but expands, after the ten hours are over into fireside humanity. On the other hand, if you will make a man of the working creature, you cannot make a tool. Let him but begin to imagine, to think, to try to do anything worth doing; and the engine-turned precision is lost at once. Out come all his roughness, all his dullness, all his incapability; shame upon shame, failure upon failure, pause after pause; but out comes the whole majesty of him also; and we know the height of it only, when we see the clouds settling upon him. And, whether the clouds be bright or dark, there will be transfiguration behind and within them.

And now, reader, look round this English room of yours, about which you have been proud so often, because the work of it was so good and strong, and the ornaments of it so finished. Examine again all those accurate mouldings, and perfect polishings, and unerring adjustments of seasoned wood and tempered steel. Many a time you have exulted over them, and thought how great England was, because her slightest work was done so thoroughly. Alas! if read rightly, these perfectnesses are signs of a slavery in our England a thousand times more bitter and more degrading than that of the scourged African, or helot Greek. Men may be beaten, chained, tormented, yoked like cattle, slaughtered like summer flies, and yet remain in one sense, and the best sense, free. But to smother their souls within them, to blight and hew into rotting pollards the suckling branches of their human intelligence, to make the flesh and skin which, after the worm's work on it, is to see God, into leathern thongs to yoke machinery with,—this it is to be slave-masters indeed; and there might be more freedom in England, though her feudal lords' lightest words were worth men's lives, and though the blood of the vexed husbandman dropped in the furrows of her fields, than there is while the animation of her multitudes is sent like fuel to feed the factory smoke, and the strength of them is given daily to be wasted into the fineness of a web, or racked into the exactness of a line.

And, on the other hand, go forth again to gaze upon the old cathedral front, where you have smiled so often at the fantastic ignorance of the old sculptors: examine once more those ugly goblins, and formless monsters, and stern statues, anatomiless and rigid; but do not mock at them, for they are signs of the life and liberty of every workman who struck the stone; a freedom of thought, and rank in scale of being, such as no laws, no charters, no charities can secure; but which it must be the first aim of all Europe at this day to regain for her children.

Let me not be thought to speak wildly or extravagantly. It is verily this degradation of the operative into a machine, which, more than any other evil of the times, is leading the mass of the nations everywhere into vain, incoherent, destructive struggling for a freedom of which they cannot explain the nature to themselves. Their universal outcry against wealth, and against nobility, is not forced from them either by the pressure of famine, of the sting of mortified pride. These do much, and have done much in all ages; but the foundations of society were never yet shaken as they are at this day. It is not that men are ill fed, but that they have no pleasure in the work by which they make their bread and therefore look to wealth as the only means of pleasure. It is not that men are pained by the scorn of the upper classes, but they cannot endure their own; for they feel that the kind of labor to which they are condemned is verily a degrading one, and makes them less than men. Never had the upper classes so much sympathy with the lower, or charity for them, as they have at this day, and yet never were they so much hated by them; for, of old, the separation between the noble and the poor was merely a wall built by law; now it is a veritable difference in level of standing, a precipice between upper and lower grounds in the field of humanity, and there is pestilential air at the bottom of it. I know not if a day is ever to come when the nature of right freedom will be understood, and when men will see that to obey another man, to labor for him, yield reverence to him or to his place is not slavery. It is often the best kind of liberty,—liberty from care. The man who says to one, Go, and he goeth, and to another, Come, and he cometh, has, in most cases, more sense of restraint and difficulty than the man who obeys him. The movements of the one are hindered by the burden on his shoulder; of the other, by the bridle on his lips: there is no way by which the burden may be lightened; but we need not suffer from the bridle if we do not champ at it. To yield reverence to another, to hold ourselves and our lives at his disposal, is not slavery; often, it is the noblest state in which a man can live in this world. There is, indeed, a reverence which is servile, that is to say, irrational or selfish: but there is also noble reverence, that is to say, reasonable and loving; and a man is never so noble as when he is reverent in this kind; nay, even if the feeling pass the bounds of mere reason, so that it be loving, a man is raised by it. Which had, in reality, most of the serf nature in him,—the Irish peasant who was lying in wait yesterday for his landlord, with his musket muzzle thrust through the ragged hedge; or that old mountain servant who, 200 years ago, at Inverkeithing, gave up his own life and the lives of his seven sons for his chief[1] and as each fell, calling forth his brother to the death, "Another for Hector!" And therefore, in all ages and all countries, reverence has been paid and sacrifice made by men to each other, not only without complaint, but rejoicingly; and famine, and peril, and sword and all evil, and all shame, have been borne willingly in the causes of masters and kings; for all these gifts of the heart ennobled the men who gave, not less than the men who received them, and nature prompted, and God rewarded the sacrifice. But to feel their souls withering within them, unthanked, to find their whole being sunk into an unrecognized abyss, to be counted off into a heap of mechanism, numbered with its wheels, and weighed with its hammer strokes;—this nature bade not,—this God blesses not,—this humanity for no long time is able to endure.

We have much studied and much perfected, of late, the great civilized invention of the division of labor; only we give it a false name. It is not, truly speaking, the labor that is divided; but the men:—Divided into mere segments of men—broken into small fragments and crumbs of life; so that all the little piece of intelligence that is left in a man is not enough to make a pin, or a nail, but exhausts itself in making the point of a pin, or the head of a nail. Now it is a good and desirable thing, truly, to make many pins in a day; but if we could only see with what crystal sand their points were polished,—sand of human soul, much to be magnified before it can be discerned for what it is,—we should think there might be some loss in it also. And the great cry that rises from all our manufacturing cities, louder than their furnace blast, is all in very deed for this,—that we manufacture everything there except men; we blanch cotton, and strengthen steel, and refine sugar, and

---

[1]Vide, Preface to "Fair Maid of Perth."

shape pottery; but to brighten, to strengthen, to refine, or to form a single living spirit, never enters into our estimate of advantages. And all the evil to which that cry is urging our myriads can be met only in one way: not by teaching nor preaching, for to teach them is but to show them their misery, and to preach to them, if we do nothing more than preach, is to mock at it. It can be met only by a right understanding, on the part of all classes, of what kinds of labor are good for men, raising them, and making them happy; by a determined sacrifice of such convenience, or beauty, or cheapness as is to be got only by the degradation of the workman; and by equally determined demand for the products and results of healthy and ennobling labor.

And how, it will be asked, are these products to be recognized, and this demand to be regulated? Easily: by the observance of three broad and simple rules:

1. Never encourage the manufacture of any article not absolutely necessary, in the production of which invention has no share.

2. Never demand an exact finish for its own sake, but only for some practical or noble end.

3. Never encourage imitation or copying of any kind, except for the sake of preserving record of great works.

The second of these principles is the only one which directly rises out of the consideration of our immediate subject; but I shall briefly explain the meaning and extent of the first also, reserving the enforcement of the third for another place.

1. Never encourage the manufacture of anything not necessary, in the production of which invention has no share.

For instance. Glass beads are utterly unnecessary, and there is no design or thought employed in their manufacture. They are formed by first drawing out the glass into rods; these rods are chopped up into fragments of the size of beads by the human hand, and the fragments are then rounded in the furnace. The men who chop up the rods sit at their work all day, their hands vibrating with a perpetual and exquisitely timed palsy, and the beads dropping beneath their vibration like hail. Neither they, nor the men who draw out the rods, or fuse the fragments, have the smallest occasion for the use of any single human faculty; and every young lady, therefore, who buys glass beads is engaged in the slave-trade, and in a much more cruel one than that which we have so long been endeavoring to put down.

But glass cups and vessels may become the subjects of exquisite invention; and if in buying these we pay for the invention, that is to say for the beautiful form, or color, or engraving, and not for mere finish of execution, we are doing good to humanity.

So, again, the cutting of precious stones, in all ordinary cases, requires little exertion of any mental faculty; some tact and judgment in avoiding flaws, and so on, but nothing to bring out the whole mind. Every person who wears cut jewels merely for the sake of their value is, therefore, a slave-driver.

But the working of the goldsmith, and the various designing of grouped jewelry and enamel-work may become the subject of the most noble human intelligence. Therefore, money spent in the purchase of well-designed plate, of precious engraved vases, cameos, or enamels, does good to humanity; and, in work of this kind, jewels may be employed to heighten its splendor; and their cutting is then a price paid for the attainment of a noble end, and thus perfectly allowable.

I shall perhaps press this law further elsewhere, but our immediate concern is chiefly with the second, namely, never to demand an exact finish, when it does not lead to a noble end. For observe, I have only dwelt upon the rudeness of Gothic, or any other kind of imperfectness, as admirable, where it was impossible to get design or thought without it. If you are to have the thought of a rough and untaught man, you must have it in a rough and untaught way; but from an educated man, who can without effort express his thoughts in an educated way, take the graceful expression, and be thankful. Only *get* the thought, and do not silence the peasant because he cannot speak good grammar, or until you have taught him his grammar. Grammar and refinement are good things, both, only be sure of the better thing first. And thus in art, delicate finish is desirable from the greatest masters, and is always given by them. In some places Michelangelo, Leonardo, Phidias, Perugino, Turner, all finished with the most exquisite care; and the finish they give always leads to the fuller accomplishment of their noble purposes. But lower men than these cannot finish, for it requires consummate knowledge to finish consummately, and then we must take their thoughts as they are able to give them. So the rule is simple: Always look for invention first, and after that, for such execution as will help the invention, and as the inventor is capable of without painful effort, and *no more*. Above all, demand no refinement of execution where there is no thought, for that is slaves' work, unredeemed. Rather choose rough work than smooth work, so only that the practical purpose be answered, and never imagine there is reason to be proud of anything that may be accomplished by patience and sandpaper.

I shall only give one example, which however will show the reader what I mean, from the manufacture already alluded to, that of glass. Our modern glass is exquisitely clear in its substance, true in its form, accurate in its cutting. We are proud of this. We ought to be ashamed of it. The old Venice glass was muddy, inaccurate in all its forms, and clumsily cut, if at all. And the old Venetian was justly proud of it. For there is this difference between the English and Venetian workman, that the former thinks only of accurately matching his patterns, and getting his curves perfectly true and his edges perfectly sharp, and becomes a mere machine for rounding curves and sharpening edges, while the old Venetian cared not a whit whether his edges were sharp or not, but he invented a new design for every glass that he made, and never moulded a handle or a lip without a new fancy in it. And therefore, though some Venetian glass is ugly and clumsy enough, when made by clumsy and uninventive workmen, other Venetian glass is so lovely in its forms that no price is too great for it; and we never see the same form in it twice. Now you cannot have the finish and the varied form too. If the workman is thinking about his edges, he cannot be thinking of his design; if of his design, he cannot think of his edges. Choose whether you will pay for the lovely form or the perfect finish, and choose at the same moment whether you will make the worker a man or a grindstone.

Nay, but the reader interrupts me,—"If the workman can design beautifully, I would not have him kept at the furnace. Let him be taken away and made a gentleman, and have a studio, and design his glass there, and I will have it blown and cut for him by common workmen, and so I will have my design and my finish too."

All ideas of this kind are founded upon two mistaken suppositions: the first, that one man's thoughts can be, or ought to be, executed by another man's hands; the second, that manual labor is a degradation, when it is governed by intellect.

On a large scale, and in work determinable by line and rule, it is indeed both possible and necessary that the thoughts of one man should be carried out by the labor of others; in this sense I have already defined the best architecture to be the expression of the mind of manhood by the hands of childhood. But on a smaller scale, and in a design which cannot be mathematically defined, one man's thoughts can never be expressed by another: and the difference between the spirit of touch of the man who is inventing, and of the man who is obeying directions, is often all the difference between a great and a common work of art. How wide the separation is between original and secondhand execution, I shall endeavor to show elsewhere; it is not so much to our purpose here as to mark the other and more fatal error of despising manual labor when governed by intellect; for it is no less fatal an error to despise it when thus regulated by intellect, than to value it for its own sake. We are always in these days endeavoring to separate the two; we want one man to be always thinking, and another to be always working, and we call one a gentleman, and the other an operative; whereas the workman ought often to be thinking, and the thinker often to be working, and both should be gentlemen, in the best sense. As it is, we make both ungentle, the one envying, the other despising, his brother; and the mass of society is made up of morbid thinkers, and miserable workers. Now it is only by labor that thought can be made healthy, and only by thought that labor can be made happy and the two cannot be separated with impunity. It would be well if all of us were good handicraftsmen in some kind, and the dishonor of manual labor done away with altogether; so that though there should still be a trenchant distinction of race between nobles and commoners, there should not, among the latter, be a trenchant distinction of employment, as between idle and working men, or between men of liberal and illiberal professions. All professions should be liberal, and there should be less pride felt in peculiarity of employment, and more in excellence of achievement. And yet more, in each several profession, no master should be too proud to do its hardest work. The painter should grind his own colors; the architect work in the mason's yard with his men; the master-manufacturer be himself a more skilful operative than any man in his mills; and the distinction between one man and another be only in experience and skill, and the authority and wealth which these must naturally and justly obtain.

I should be led far from the matter in hand, if I were to pursue this interesting subject. Enough, I trust, has been said to show the reader that the rudeness or imperfection which at first rendered the term "Gothic" one of reproach is indeed, when rightly understood, one of the most noble characters of Christian architecture, and not only a noble but an *essential* one. It seems a fantastic paradox, but it is nevertheless a most important truth, that no architecture can be truly noble which is *not* imperfect. And this is easily demonstrable. For since the architect, whom we will suppose capable of doing all in perfection, cannot execute the whole with his own hands, he must either make slaves of his workmen in the old Greek, and present English fashion, and level his work to a slave's capacities, which is to degrade it; or else he must take his workmen as he finds them, and let them show their weaknesses together with their strength, which will involve the Gothic imperfection, but render the whole work as noble as the intellect of the age can make it.

But the principle may be stated more broadly still. I have confined the illustration of it to architecture, but I must not leave it as if true of architecture only. Hitherto I have used the words imperfect and perfect merely to distinguish between work grossly unskilful, and work executed with average precision and science; and I have been pleading that any degree of unskilfulness should be admitted, so only that the laborer's mind had room for expression. But, accurately speaking, no good work whatever can be perfect, and *the demand for perfection is always a sign of misunderstanding of the ends of art.*

This for two reasons, both based on everlasting laws. The first, that no great man ever stops working till he has reached his point failure; that is to say, his mind is always far in advance of his powers of execution, and the latter will now and then give way in trying to follow it; besides that he will always give to the inferior portions of his work only such inferior attention as they require; and according to his greatness he becomes so accustomed to the feeling of dissatisfaction with the best he can do, that in moments of lassitude or anger with himself he will not care though the beholder be dissatisfied also. I believe there has only been one man who would not acknowledge this necessity, and strove always to reach perfection, Leonardo; the end of his vain effort being merely that he would take ten years to a picture, and leave it unfinished. And therefore, if we are to have great men working at all, or lesser men doing their best, the work will be imperfect, however beautiful. Of human work none but what is bad can be perfect, in its own bad way.[2]

The second reason is, that imperfection is in some sort essential to all that we know of life. It is the sign of life in a mortal body, that is to say, of a state of progress and change. Nothing that lives is, or can be, rigidly perfect; part of it is decaying, part nascent. The foxglove blossom,—a third part bud, a third part past, a third part in full bloom,—is a type of the life of this world. And in all things that live there are certain irregularities and deficiencies which are not only signs of life, but sources of beauty. No human face is exactly the same in its lines on each side, no leaf in its lobes, no branch in its symmetry. All admit irregularity as they imply change; and to banish imperfection is to destroy expression, to check exertion, to paralyse vitality. All things are literally better, lovelier, and more beloved for the imperfections which have been divinely appointed, that the law of human life may be Effort, and the law of human judgment, Mercy.

Accept this then for a universal law, that neither architecture nor any other noble work of man can be good unless it be imperfect; and let us be prepared for the otherwise strange fact, which we shall discern clearly as we approach the period of the Renaissance, that the first cause of the fall of the arts of Europe was a relentless requirement of perfection, incapable alike either of being silenced by veneration for greatness, or softened into forgiveness of simplicity.

The variety of the Gothic schools is the more healthy and beautiful, because in many cases it is entirely unstudied, and results, not from the mere love of change, but from practical necessities. For in one point of view Gothic

---

[2] The Elgin marbles are supposed by many persons to be "perfect." In the most important portions they indeed approach perfection, but only there. The draperies are unfinished, the hair and wool of the animals are unfinished, and the entire bas-reliefs of the frieze are roughly cut.

is not only the best, but the *only rational* architecture, as being that which can fit itself most easily to all services, vulgar or noble. Undefined in its slope of roof, height of shaft, breadth of arch, or disposition of ground plan, it can shrink into a turret, expand into a hall, coil into a staircase, or spring into a spire, with undegraded grace and unexhausted energy; and whenever it finds occasion for change in its form or purpose, it submits to it without the slightest sense of loss either to its unity or majesty,—subtle and flexible like a fiery serpent, but ever attentive to the voice of the charmer. And it is one of the chief virtues of the Gothic builders, that they never suffered ideas of outside symmetries and consistencies to interfere with the real use and value of what they did. If they wanted a window, they opened one; a room, they added one; a buttress, they built one; utterly regardless of any established conventionalities of external appearance, knowing (as indeed it always happened) that such daring interruptions of the formal plan would rather give additional interest to its symmetry than injure it. So that, in the best times of Gothic, a useless window would rather have been opened in an unexpected place for the sake of the surprise, than a useful one forbidden for the sake of symmetry. Every successive architect, employed upon a great work, built the pieces he added in his own way, utterly regardless of the style adopted by his predecessors; and if two towers were raised in nominal correspondence at the sides of a cathedral front, one was nearly sure to be different from the other, and in each the style at the top to be different from the style at the bottom.

. . . Rudeness, and the love of change, which we have insisted upon as the first elements of Gothic, are also elements common to all healthy schools. But here is a softer element mingled with them, peculiar to the Gothic itself. The rudeness or ignorance which would have been painfully exposed in the treatment of the human form, is still not so great as to prevent the successful rendering of the wayside herbage; and the love of change, which becomes morbid and feverish in following the haste of the hunter, and the rage of the combatant, is at once soothed and satisfied as it watches the wandering of the tendril, and the budding of the flower. Nor is this all: the new direction of mental interest marks an infinite change in means and the habits of life. The nations whose chief support was in the chase, whose chief interest was in the battle, whose chief pleasure was in the banquet, would take small care respecting the shapes of leaves and flowers; and notice little in the forms of the forest trees which sheltered them, except the signs indicative of the wood which would make the toughest lance, the closest roof, or the clearest fire. The affectionate observation of the grace and outward character of vegetation is the sure sign of a more tranquil and gentle existence, sustained by the gifts, and gladdened by the splendor, of the earth. In that careful distinction of species, and richness of delicate and undisturbed organization, which characterize the Gothic design, there is the history of rural and thoughtful life, influenced by habitual tenderness, and devoted to subtle inquiry; and every discriminating and delicate touch of the chisel, as it rounds the petal or guides the branch, is a prophecy of the development of the entire body of the natural sciences, beginning with that of medicine, of the recovery of literature, and the establishment of the most necessary principles of domestic wisdom and national peace.

I have before alluded to the strange and vain supposition, that the original conception of Gothic architecture had been derived from vegetation,—from the symmetry of avenues, and the interlacing of branches. It is a supposition which never could have existed for a moment in the mind of any person acquainted with early Gothic; but, however idle as a theory, it is most valuable as a testimony to the character of the perfected style. It is precisely because the reverse of this theory is the fact, because the Gothic did not arise out of, but develop itself into, a resemblance to vegetation, that this resemblance is so instructive as an indication of the temper of the builders. It was no chance suggestion of the form of an arch from the bending of a bough, but a gradual and continual discovery of a beauty in natural forms which could be more and more perfectly transferred into those of stone, that influenced at once the heart of the people, and the form of the edifice. The Gothic architecture arose in massy and mountainous strength, axe-hewn, and iron-bound, block heaved upon block by the monk's enthusiasm and the soldier's force; and cramped and stanchioned into such weight of grisly wall, as might bury the anchoret in darkness, and beat back the utmost storm of battle, suffering but by the same narrow crosslet the passing of the sunbeam, or of the arrow. Gradually, as that monkish enthusiasm became more thoughtful, and as the sound of war became more and more intermittent beyond the gates of the convent or the keep, the stony pillar grew slender and the vaulted roof grew light, till they had wreathed themselves into the semblance of the summer woods at their fairest, and of the dead field-flowers, long trodden down in blood, sweet monumental statues were set to bloom for ever, beneath the porch of the temple, or the canopy of the tomb.

Nor is it only as a sign of greater gentleness or refinement of mind, but as a proof of the best possible direction of this refinement, that the tendency of the Gothic to the expression of vegetative life is to be admired. That sentence of Genesis, "I have given thee every green herb for meat," like all the rest of the book, has a profound symbolical as well as a literal meaning. It is not merely the nourishment of the body, but the food of the soul, that is intended. The green herb is, of all nature, that which is most essential to the healthy spiritual life of man. Most of us do not need fine scenery; the precipice and the mountain peak are not intended to be seen by all men,—perhaps their power is greatest over those who are unaccustomed to them. But trees, and fields, and flowers were made for all, and are necessary for all. God has connected the labor which is essential to the bodily sustenance, with the pleasures which are healthiest for the heart; and while He made the ground stubborn, He made its herbage fragrant, and its blossoms fair. The proudest architecture that man can build has no higher honor than to bear the image and recall the memory of that grass of the field which is, at once, the type and the support of his existence; the goodly building is then most glorious when it is sculptured into the likeness of the leaves of Paradise; and the great Gothic spirit, as we showed it to be noble in its disquietude, is also noble in its hold of nature; it is, indeed, like the dove of Noah, in that she found no rest upon the face of the waters,—but like her in this also, "LO, IN HER MOUTH WAS AN OLIVE BRANCH, PLUCKED OFF."

The fourth essential element of the Gothic mind was above stated to be the sense of the Grotesque; but I shall defer the endeavor to define this most curious and subtle character until we have occasion to examine one of the divisions of the Renaissance schools, which was morbidly influenced by it. It is the less necessary to insist upon it here, because every reader familiar with Gothic architecture must understand what I mean, and will, I believe, have no hesitation in admitting that the tendency to delight in fantastic and ludicrous, as well as in sublime, images, is a universal instinct of the Gothic imagination.

The fifth element above named was RIGIDITY; and this character I must endeavor carefully to define, for neither the word I have used, nor any other that I can think of, will express it accurately. For I mean, not merely stable, but active rigidity; the peculiar energy which gives tension to movement, and stiffness to resistance, which makes the fiercest lightning forked rather than curved, and the stoutest oak-branch angular rather than bending, and is as much seen in the quivering of the lance as in the glittering of the icicle.

I have before had occasion to note some manifestations of this energy or fixedness; but it must be still more attentively considered here, as it shows itself throughout the whole structure and decoration of Gothic work. Egyptian and Greek buildings stand, for the most part, by their own weight and mass, one stone passively incumbent on another; but in the Gothic vaults and traceries there is a stiffness analogous to that of the bones of a limb, or fibres of a tree; an elastic tension and communication of force from part to part, and also a studious expression of this throughout every visible line of the building. And, in like manner, the Greek and Egyptian ornament is either mere surface engraving, as if the face of the wall had been stamped with a seal, or its lines are flowing, lithe, and luxuriant; in either case, there is no expression of energy in framework of the ornament itself. But the Gothic ornament stands out in prickly independence, and frosty fortitude, jutting into crockets, and freezing into pinnacles; here starting up into a monster, there germinating into a blossom; anon knitting itself into a branch, alternately thorny, bossy, and bristly, or writhed into every form of nervous entanglement; but, even when most graceful, never for an instant languid, always quickset; erring, if at all, ever on the side of brusquerie.

The feelings or habits in the workman which give rise to this character in the work, are more complicated and various than those indicated by any other sculptural expression hitherto named. There is, first, the habit of hard and rapid working; the industry of the tribes of the North, quickened by the coldness of the climate, and giving an expression of sharp energy to all they do, as opposed to the languor of the Southern tribes, however much of fire there may be in the heart of that languor, for lava itself may flow languidly. There is also the habit of finding enjoyment in the signs of cold, which is never found, I believe, in the inhabitants of countries south of the Alps. Cold is to them an unredeemed evil, to be suffered, and forgotten as soon as may be; but the long winter of the North forces the Goth (I mean the Englishman, Frenchman, Dane, or German), if he would lead a happy life at all, to find sources of happiness in foul weather as well as fair, and to rejoice in the leafless as well as in the shady forest. And this we do with all our hearts; finding perhaps nearly as much contentment by the Christmas fire as in the summer sunshine, and gaining health and strength on the ice-fields of winter, as well as among the meadows of spring. So that there is nothing adverse or painful to our feelings in the cramped and stiffened structure of vegetation checked by cold; and instead of seeking, like the Southern sculptor, to express only the softness of leafage nourished in all tenderness, and tempted into all luxuriance by warm winds and glowing rays, we find pleasure in dwelling upon the crabbed, perverse, and morose animation of plants that have known little kindness from earth or heaven, but, season after season, have had their best efforts palsied by frost, their brightest buds buried under snow, and their goodliest limbs lopped by tempest.

There are many subtle sympathies and affections which join to confirm the Gothic mind in this peculiar choice of subject; and when we add to the influence of these, the necessities consequent upon the employment of a rougher material, compelling the workman to seek for vigor of effect, rather than refinement of texture or accuracy of form, we have direct and manifest causes for much of the difference between the Northern and Southern cast of conception: but there are indirect causes holding a far more important place in the Gothic heart, though less immediate in their influence on design.

Strength of will, independence of character, resoluteness of purpose, impatience of undue control, and that general tendency to set the individual reason against authority, and the individual deed against destiny, which, in the Northern tribes, has opposed itself throughout all ages to the languid submission, in the Southern, of thought to tradition, and purpose to fatality, are all more or less traceable in the rigid lines, vigorous and various masses, and daringly projecting and independent structure of the Northern Gothic ornament: while the opposite feelings are in like manner legible in the graceful and softly guided waves and wreathed bands, in which Southern decoration is constantly disposed; in its tendency to lose its independence, and fuse itself into the surface of the masses upon which it is traced; and in the expression seen so often, in the arrangement of those masses themselves, of an abandonment of their strength to an inevitable necessity, or a listless repose.

There is virtue in the measure, and error in the excess, of both these characters of mind, and in both of the styles which they have created; the best architecture, and the best temper, are those which unite them both; and this fifth impulse of the Gothic heart is therefore that which needs most caution in its indulgence. It is more definitely Gothic than any other, but the best Gothic building is not that which is *most* Gothic: it can hardly be too frank in its confession of rudeness, hardly too rich in its changefulness, hardly too faithful in its naturalism; but it may go too far in its rigidity, and, like the great Puritan spirit in its extreme, lose itself either in frivolity of division, or perversity of purpose.[3] It actually did so in its later times; but it is gladdening to remember that in its utmost nobleness, the very temper which has been thought most adverse to it, the Protestant spirit of self-dependence and inquiry, was expressed in its every line. Faith and aspiration there were, in every Christian ecclesiastical building, from the first century to the fifteenth; but the moral habits to which England in this age owes the kind of greatness that she has,—the habits of philosophical investigation, of accurate thought, of domestic seclusion and independence, of stern self-reliance, and sincere upright searching into religious truth,—were only traceable in the features which were the distinctive creation of the Gothic schools, in the veined foliage, and thorny fret-work, and shadowy niche, and buttressed pier, and fearless height of subtle pinnacle and crested tower, sent like an "unperplexed question up to Heaven."

---

[3]See the account of the meeting at Talla Linss, in 1682, given in the fourth chapter of the "Heart of Midlothian." At length they arrived at the conclusion that "they who owned (or allowed) such names as Monday, Tuesday, January, February, etc., served themselves heirs to the same if not greater punishment than had been denounced against the idolaters of old."

Morris

William Morris (1834–1896), like Ruskin the son of a wealthy father, turned his love of beauty and his interpretation of Ruskin's views to application in craftsmanship and Socialism. Intended for holy orders like his Oxford friend Edward Burne-Jones, he applied himself to architecture instead, joined Dante Gabriel Rossetti in decorating the walls of the Oxford students' union with pre-Raphaelite frescoes, and made Ruskin's chapter on *The Nature of Gothic* his bible. In 1861, backed by a respectable private income, Morris began his career as a craftsman and producer, setting up a nineteenth-century *Bauhaus* to produce furniture, tapestries, textiles, stained glass, and all sorts of mural decorations. With amazing versatility he managed to combine his business activities with a vast output of poetry and prose—mostly inspired by the idyllic medievalism he had shared with his pre-Raphaelite friends, a nostalgia for cleaner and healthier times, different from the smug ugliness of his day—poetry and prose which, in the last age of his life, he was able to print and publish himself on his own Kelmscott Press.

Morris's hatred of nineteenth-century industrialism, which he thought divorced life from beauty, life from work, drove him to the Utopian views expressed by the Socialist League he helped to found in 1884, in novels like *A Dream of John Ball* and the more famous *News from Nowhere*, and in numerous articles and lectures. *The Aims of Art* was published as a forty-page pamphlet in 1887, at the office of the Socialist League's paper, *The Commonweal*, which Morris himself published.

In his *Rendezvous with Destiny*, Eric Goldman tells us how William Morris impressed a discontented young American, Vernon Parrington, who was completing his studies in England before returning home to teach at the University of Washington. "The flame of radicalism was making ready to leap up within me," wrote Parrington many years later. "It wanted only further fuel and William Morris came bringing that fuel. In lovely prose . . . he laid bare the evils of industrialism. . . . It was a message that stirred me to the quick and convinced me . . . that the business man's society, symbolized by the cash register and existing solely for profit, must be destroyed to make way for another and better ideal."

The Aims of Art

In considering the Aims of Art, that is, why men toilsomely cherish and practise Art, I find myself compelled to generalize from the only specimen of humanity of which I know anything; to wit, myself. Now, when I think of what it is that I desire, I find that I can give it no other name than happiness. I want to be happy while I live; I have no conception of what it means, and so cannot even bring my mind to bear upon it. I know what it is to live; I cannot even guess what it is to be dead. Well, then, I want to be happy, and even sometimes, say generally, to be merry; and I find it difficult to believe that that is not the universal desire; so that, whatever tends towards that end I cherish with all my best endeavour. Now, when I consider my life further, I find out, or seem to, that it is under the influence of two dominating moods, which for lack of better words I must call the mood of energy and the mood of idleness: these two moods are now one, now the other, always crying out in me to be satisfied. When the mood of energy is upon me, I must be doing something, or I become mopish and unhappy; when the mood of idleness is on me, I find it hard indeed if I cannot rest and let my mind wander over the various pictures, pleasant or terrible, which my own experience or my communing with the thoughts of other men, dead or alive, have fashioned in it; and if circumstances will not allow me to cultivate this mood of idleness, I find I must at the best pass through a period of pain till I can manage to stimulate my mood of energy to take its place and make me happy again. And if I have no means wherewith to rouse up that mood of energy to do its duty in making me happy, and I have to toil while the idle mood is upon me, then am I unhappy indeed, and almost wish myself dead, though I do not know what that means.

Furthermore, I find that while in the mood of idleness memory amuses me, in the mood of energy hope cheers me; which hope is sometimes big and serious, and sometimes trivial, but that without it there is no happy energy. Again, I find that while I can sometimes satisfy this mood by merely exercising it in work that has no result beyond the passing hour—in play, in short—yet that it presently wearies of that and gets languid, the hope therein being too trivial, and sometimes even scarcely real; and that on the whole, to satisfy my master the mood, I must either be making something or making believe to make it.

Well, I believe that all men's lives are compounded of these two moods in various proportions, and that this explains why they have always, with more or less of toil, cherished and practised art.

Why should they have touched it else, and so added to the labour which they could not choose but do in order to live? It must have been done for their pleasure, since it has only been in very elaborate civilizations that a man could get other men to keep him alive merely to produce works of art, whereas all men that have left any signs of their existence behind them have practised art.

I suppose, indeed, that nobody will be inclined to deny that the end proposed by a work of art is always to please the person whose senses are to be made conscious of it. It was done for some one who was to be made happier by it; his idle or restful mood was to be amused by it, so that the vacancy which is the besetting evil of that mood might give place to pleased contemplation, dreaming, or what you will; and by this means he would not so soon be driven into his workful or energetic mood: he would have more enjoyment, and better.

The restraining of restlessness, therefore, is clearly one of the essential aims of art, and few things could add to the pleasure of life more than this. There are, to my knowledge, gifted people now alive who have no other vice than this restlessness, and seemingly no other curse in their lives to make them unhappy; but that is enough; it is "the little rift within the lute." Restlessness makes them hapless men and bad citizens.

But granting, as I suppose you all will do, that this is a most important function for art to fulfil, the question next comes, at what price do we obtain it? I have admitted that the practice of art has added to the labour of mankind, though I believe in the long run it will not do so; but in adding to the labour of man has it added so far, to his pain? There always have been people who would at once say yes to that question; so that there have been and are two sets of people who dislike and contemn art as an embarrassing folly. Besides the pious ascetics, who look upon it as a worldly entanglement which prevents men from keeping their minds fixed on the chances of their individual happiness or misery in the next world; who, in short, hate art, because they think that it adds to man's earthly happiness—besides these, there are also people who, looking on the struggle of life from the most reasonable point that they know of, contemn the arts because they think that they add to man's slavery by increasing the sum of his painful labour; if this were the case, it would still, to my mind, be a question whether it might not be worth the while to endure the extra pain of labour for the sake of the extra pleasure added to rest; assuming, for the present, equality of condition among men. But it seems to me that it is not the case that the practice of art adds to painful labour; nay more, I believe that, if it did, art would never have arisen at all, would certainly not be discernible, as it is, among peoples in whom only the germs of civilization exist. In other words, I believe that art cannot be the result of external compulsion; the labour which goes to produce it is voluntary, and partly undertaken for the sake of the labour itself, partly for the sake of the hope of producing something which, when done, shall give pleasure to the user of it. Or, again, this extra labour, when it is extra, is undertaken with the aim of satisfying that mood of energy by employing it to produce something worth doing, and which, therefore, will keep before the worker a lively hope while he is working; and also by giving it work to do in which there is absolute immediate pleasure. Perhaps it is difficult to explain to the non-artistic capacity that this definite sensuous pleasure is always present in the handiwork of the deft workman when he is working successfully, and that it increases in proportion to the freedom and individuality of the work.

Also you must understand that this production of art, and consequent pleasure in work, is not confined to the production of matters which are works of art only, like pictures, statues, and so forth, but has been and should be a part of all labour in some form or other; so only will the claims of the mood of energy be satisfied.

Therefore the Aim of Art is to increase the happiness of men, by giving them beauty and interest of incident to amuse their leisure, and prevent them wearying even of rest, and by giving them hope and bodily pleasure in their work; or, shortly, to make man's work happy and his rest fruitful. Consequently, genuine art is an unmixed blessing to the race of man.

But as the word "genuine" is a large qualification, I must ask leave to attempt to draw some practical conclusions from this assertion of the Aims of Art, which will, I suppose, or indeed hope, lead us into some controversy on the subject; because it is futile indeed to expect any one to speak about art, except in the most superficial way, without encountering those social problems which all serious men are thinking of; since art is and must be, either in its abundance or its barrenness, in its sincerity or its hollowness, the expression of the society amongst which it exists.

First, then, it is clear to me that, at the present time, those who look widest at things and deepest into them are quite dissatisfied with the present state of the arts, as they are also with the present condition of society. This I say in the teeth of the supposed revivification of art which has taken place of late years: in fact, that very excitement about the arts amongst a part of the cultivated people of to-day does but show on how firm a basis the dissatisfaction above mentioned rests. Forty years ago there was much less talk about art, much less practice of it, than there is now; and that is specially true of the architectural arts, which I shall mostly have to speak about now. People have consciously striven to raise the dead in art since that time, and with some superficial success. Nevertheless, in spite of this conscious effort, I must tell you that England, to a person who can feel and understand beauty, was a less grievous place to live in then than it is now; and we who feel what art means know well, though we do not often dare to say so, that forty years hence it will be a more grievous place to us than it is now if we still follow up the road we are on. Less than forty years ago—about thirty—I first saw the city of Rouen, then still in its outward aspect a piece of the Middle Ages; no words can tell you how its mingled beauty, history, and romance took hold on me; I can only say that, looking back on my past life, I find it was the greatest pleasure I have ever had: and now it is a pleasure which no one can ever have again: it is lost to the world for ever. At that time I was an undergraduate of Oxford. Though not so astounding, so romantic, or at first sight so mediaeval as the Norman city, Oxford in those days still kept a great deal of its earlier loveliness: and the memory of its grey streets as they then were has been an abiding influence and pleasure in my life, and would be greater still if I could only forget what they are now—a matter of far more importance than the so-called learning of the place could have been to me in any case, but which, as it was, no one tried to teach me, and I did not try to learn. Since then the guardians of this beauty and romance so fertile of education, though professedly engaged in "the higher education" (as the futile system of compromises which they follow is nick-named), have ignored it utterly, have made its preservation give way to the pressure of commercial exigencies, and are determined apparently to destroy it altogether. There is another pleasure for the world gone down the wind: here, again, the beauty and romance have been uselessly, causelessly, most foolishly thrown away.

These two cases are given simply because they have been fixed in my mind; they are but types of what is going on everywhere throughout civilization: the world is everywhere growing uglier and more commonplace, in spite of the conscious and very strenuous efforts of a small group of people towards the revival of art, which are so obviously out of joint with the tendency of the age that, while the uncultivated have not even heard of them, the mass of the cultivated look upon them as a joke, and even that they are now beginning to get tired of.

Now, if it be true, as I have asserted, that genuine art is an unmixed blessing to the world, this is a serious matter; for at first sight it seems to show that there will soon be no art at all in the world, which will thus lose an unmixed blessing; it can ill afford to do that, I think.

For art, if it has to die, has worn itself out, and its aim will be a thing forgotten; and its aim was to make work happy and rest fruitful. Is all work to be unhappy, all rest unfruitful, then? Indeed, if art is to perish, that will be the case, unless something is to take its place—something at present unnamed, undreamed of.

I do not think that anything will take the place of art; not that I doubt the ingenuity of man, which seems to be boundless in the direction of making himself unhappy, but because I believe the springs of art in the human mind to be deathless, and also because it seems to me easy to see the causes of the present obliteration of the arts.

For we civilized people have not given them up consciously, or of our free will; we have been forced to give them up. Perhaps I can illustrate that by the detail of the application of machinery to the production of things in which artistic form of some sort is possible. Why does a reasonable man use a machine? Surely to save his labour. There are some things which a machine can do as well as a man's hand, plus a tool, can do them. He need not, for instance, grind his corn in a hand quern; a little trickle of water, a wheel, and a few simple contrivances will do it all perfectly well, and leave him free to smoke his pipe and think, or to carve the handle of his knife. That, so far, is unmixed gain in the use of a machine—always, mind you, supposing equality of condition among men; no art is lost, leisure or time for more pleasurable work is gained. Perhaps a perfectly reasonable and free man would stop there in his dealings with machinery; but such reason and freedom are too much to expect, so let us follow our machine-inventor a step farther. He has to weave plain cloth, and finds doing so dullish on the one hand, and on the other that a power-loom will weave the cloth nearly as well as a hand-loom: so, in order to gain more leisure or time for more pleasurable work, he uses a power-loom and foregoes the small advantage of the little extra art in the cloth. But so doing, as far as the art is concerned, he has not got a pure gain; he has made a bargain between art and labour, and got a makeshift as a consequence. I do not say that he may not be right in so doing, but that he has lost as well as gained. Now, this is as far as a man who values art and is reasonable would go in the matter of machinery as long as he was free—that is, was not forced to work for another man's profit; so long as he was living in a society that had accepted equality of condition. Carry the machine used for art a step farther, and he becomes an unreasonable man, if he values art and is free. To avoid misunderstanding, I must say that I am thinking of the modern machine, which is as it were alive, and to which the man is auxiliary, and not of the old machine, the improved tool, which is auxiliary to the man, and only works as long as his hand is thinking; though I will remark, that even this elementary form of machine has to be dropped when we come to the higher and more intricate forms of art. Well, as to the machine proper used for art, when it gets to the stage above dealing with a necessary production that has accidentally some beauty about it, a reasonable man with a feeling for art will only use it when he is forced to. If he thinks he would like ornament, for instance, and knows that the machine cannot do it properly, and does not care to spend the time to do it properly, why should he do it at all? He will not diminish his leisure for the sake of making something he does not want unless some man or band of men force him to it; so he will either go without the ornament, or sacrifice some of his leisure to have it genuine. That will be a sign that he wants it very much, and that it will be worth his trouble: in which case, again, his labour on it will not be mere trouble, but will interest and please him by satisfying the needs of his mood of energy.

This, I say, is how a reasonable man would act if he were free from man's compulsion; not being free, he acts very differently. He has long passed the stage at which machines are only used for doing work repulsive to an average man, or for doing what could be as well done by a machine as a man, and he instinctively expects a machine to be invented whenever any product of industry becomes sought after. He is the slave to machinery; the new machine must be invented, and when invented he must—I will not say use it, but be used by it, whether he likes it or not.

But why is he the slave to machinery? Because he is the slave to the system for whose existence the invention of machinery was necessary.

And now I must drop, or rather have dropped, the assumption of the equality of condition, and remind you that, though in a sense we are all the slaves of machinery, yet that some men are so directly without any metaphor at all, and that these are just those on whom the great body of arts depends— the workmen. It is necessary for the system which keeps them in their position as an inferior class that they should either be themselves machines or be the servants to machines, in no case having any interest in the work which they turn out. To their employers they are, so far as they are workmen, a part of the machinery of the workshop or the factory; to themselves they are proletarians, human beings working to live that they may live to work: their part of craftsmen, or makers of things by their own free will, is played out.

At the risk of being accused of sentimentality, I will say that since this is so, since the work which produces the things that should be matters of art is but a burden and a slavery, I exult in this at least, that it cannot produce art; that all it can do lies between stark utilitarianism and idiotic sham.

Or indeed is that merely sentimental? Rather, I think, we who have learned to see the connection between industrial slavery and the degradation of the arts have learned also to hope for a future for those arts; since the day will certainly come when men will shake off the yoke, and refuse to accept the mere artificial compulsion of the gambling market to waste their lives in ceaseless and hopeless toil, and when it does come, their instincts for beauty and imagination set free along with them, will produce such art as they need; and who can say that it will not as far surpass the art of past ages as that does the poor relics of it left us by the age of commerce?

A word or two on an objection which has often been made to me when I have been talking on this subject. It may be said, and is often. You regret the art of the Middle Ages (as indeed I do), but those who produced it were not free; they were serfs, or guild-craftsmen surrounded by brazen walls of trade restrictions; they had no political rights, and were exploited by their masters, the noble caste, most grievously. Well, I quite admit that the oppression and violence of the Middle Ages had its effect on the art of those days, its shortcomings are traceable to them; they repressed art in certain directions, I do not doubt that; and for that reason I say, that when we shake off the present oppression as we shook off the old, we may expect the art of the days of real freedom to rise above that of those old violent days. But I do say that it was possible then to have social, organic, hopeful, progressive art; whereas now such poor scraps of it as are left are the result of individual and wasteful struggle, are retrospective and pessimistic. And this hopeful art was possible amidst all the oppression of those days, because the instruments of that oppression were grossly obvious, and were external to the work of the crafts-man. They were laws and customs obviously intended to rob him, and open violence of the highway-robbery kind. In short, industrial production was not the instrument used for robbing the "lower classes"; it is now the main instrument used in that honourable profession. The mediaeval craftsman was free in his work, therefore he made it as amusing to himself as he could; and it was his pleasure and not his pain that made all things beautiful that were made, and lavished treasures of human hope and thought on everything that man made, from a cathedral to a porridge-pot. Come, let us put it in the way least respectful to the mediaeval craftsman, most polite to the modern "hand": the poor devil of the fourteenth century, his work was of so little value that he was allowed to waste it by the hour in pleasing himself—and others; but our highly-strung mechanic, his minutes are too rich with the burden of perpetual profit for him to be allowed to waste one of them on art; the present system will not allow him—cannot allow him—to produce works of art.

So that there has arisen this strange phenomenon, that there is now a class of ladies and gentlemen, very refined indeed, though not perhaps as well informed as is generally supposed, and of this refined class there are many who do really love beauty and incident—i.e., art—and would make sacrifices to get it; and these are led by artists of great manual skill and high intellect, forming altogether a large body of demand for the article. And yet the supply does not come. Yes, and moreover, this great body of enthusiastic demanders are no mere poor and helpless people, ignorant fisher-peasants, half-mad monks, scatter-brained sansculottes—none of those, in short, the expression of whose needs has shaken the world so often before, and will do yet again. No, they are of the ruling classes, the masters of men, who can live without labour, and have abundant leisure to scheme out the fulfillment of their de-sires; and yet I say they cannot have the art which they so much long for, though they hunt it about the world so hard, sentimentalizing starving pro-letarians of her towns, now that all the picturesqueness has departed from the poor devils of our own country-side, and of our own slums. Indeed, there is little of reality left them anywhere, and that little is fast fading away before the needs of the manufacturer and his ragged regiment of workers, and before the enthusiasm of the archaeological restorer of the dead past. Soon there will be nothing left except the lying dreams of history, the miserable wreckage of our museums and picture-galleries, and the carefully guarded interiors of our aesthetic drawing-rooms, unreal and foolish, fitting witnesses of the life of corruption that goes on there, so pinched and meagre and cowardly, with its concealment and ignoring, rather than restraint of, natural longings; which does not forbid the greedy indulgence in them if it can but be decently hidden.

The art then is gone, and can no more be "restored" on its old lines than a mediaeval building can be. The rich and refined cannot have it though they would, and though we will believe many of them would. And why? Because those who could give it to the rich are not allowed by the rich to do so. In one word, slavery lies between us and art.

I have said as much as that the aim of art was to destroy the curse of labour by making work the pleasurable satisfaction of our impulse towards energy, and giving to that energy hope of producing something worth its exercise.

Now, therefore, I say, that since we cannot have art by striving after its mere superficial manifestation, since we can have nothing but its sham by so doing, there yet remains for us to see how it would be if we let the shadow take care of itself and try, if we can, to lay hold of the substance. For my part I believe, that if we try to realize the aims of art without much troubling ourselves what the aspect of the art itself shall be, we shall find we shall have what we want at last: whether it is to be called art or not, it will at least be life; and, after all, that is what we want. It may lead us into new splendours and beauties of visible art; to architecture with manifold magnificence free from the curious incompleteness and failings of that which the older times have produced—to painting, uniting to the beauty which mediaeval art attained the realism which modern art aims at; to sculpture, uniting the beauty of the Greek and the expression of the Renaissance with some third quality yet undiscovered, so as to give us the images of men and women splendidly alive, yet not disqualified from making, as all true sculpture should, architectural ornament. All this it may do; or, on the other hand, it may lead us into the desert, and art may seem to be dead amidst us; or feebly and uncertainly to be struggling in a world which has utterly forgotten its old glories.

For my part, with art as it now is, I cannot bring myself to think that it much matters which of these dooms awaits it, so long as each bears with it some hope of what is to come; since here, as in other matters, there is no hope save in Revolution. The old art is no longer fertile, no longer yields us anything save elegantly poetical regrets; being barren, it has but to die, and the matter of moment now is, as to how it shall die, whether with hope or without it.

What is it, for instance, that has destroyed the Rouen, the Oxford of my elegant poetic regret? Has it perished for the benefit of the people, either slowly yielding to the growth of intelligent change and new happiness? or has it been, as it were, thunderstricken by the tragedy which mostly accompanies some great new birth? Not so. Neither phalangstere nor dynamite has swept its beauty away, its destroyers have not been either the philanthropist or the Socialist, the co-operator or the anarchist. It has been sold, and at a cheap price indeed: muddled away by the greed and incompetence of fools who do not know what life and pleasure mean, who will neither take them themselves nor let others have them. That is why the death of that beauty wounds us so: no man of sense or feeling would dare to regret such losses if they had been paid for by new life and happiness for the people. But there is the people still as it was before, still facing for its part the monster who destroyed all that beauty, and whose name is Commercial Profit.

I repeat, that every scrap of genuine art will fall by the same hands if the matter only goes on long enough, although a sham art may be left in its place, which may very well be carried on by dilettanti fine gentlemen and ladies without any help from below; and, to speak plainly, I fear that this gibbering ghost of the real thing would satisfy a great many of those who now think themselves lovers of art; though it is not difficult to see a long vista of its degradation till it shall become at last a mere laughing-stock; that is to say, if the thing were to go on: I mean, if art were to be for ever the amusement of those whom we now call ladies and gentlemen.

But for my part I do not think it will go on long enough to reach such depths as that; and yet I should be hypocritical if I were to say that I thought that the change in the basis of society, which would enfranchise labour and make men practically equal in condition, would lead us by a short road to the splendid new birth of art which I have mentioned, though I feel quite certain that it would not leave what we now call art untouched, since the aims of that revolution do include the aims of art—viz., abolishing the curse of labour.

I suppose that this is what is likely to happen; that machinery will go on developing, with the purpose of saving men labour, till the mass of the people attain real leisure enough to be able to appreciate the pleasure of life; till, in fact, they have attained such mastery over Nature that they no longer fear starvation as a penalty for not working more than enough. When they get to that point they will doubtless turn themselves and begin to find out what it is that they really want to do. They would soon find out that the less work they did (the less work unaccompanied by art, I mean), the more desirable a dwelling-place the earth would be; they would accordingly do less and less work, till the mood of energy, of which I began by speaking, urged them on afresh: but by that time Nature, relieved by the relaxation of man's work, would be recovering her ancient beauty, and be teaching men the old story of art. And as the Artificial Famine, caused by men working for the profit of a master, and which we now look upon as a matter of course, would have long disappeared, they would be free to do as they chose, and they would set aside their machines in all cases where the work seemed pleasant or desirable for handiwork; till in all crafts where production of beauty was required, the most direct communication between a man's hand and his brain would be sought for. And there would be many occupations also, as the processes of agriculture, in which the voluntary exercise of energy would be thought so delightful, that people would not dream of handing over its pleasure to the jaws of a machine.

In short, men will find out that the men of our days were wrong in first multiplying their needs, and then trying, each man of them, to evade all participation in the means and processes whereby those needs are satisfied; that this kind of division of labour is really only a new and wilful form of arrogant and slothful ignorance, far more injurious to the happiness and contentment of life than the ignorance of the processes of Nature, of what we sometimes call science, which men of the earlier days unwittingly lived in.

They will discover, or rediscover rather, that the true secret of happiness *lies in the taking a genuine interest in all the details of daily life,* in elevating them by art instead of handing the performance of them over to unregarded drudges, and ignoring them; and that in cases where it was impossible either so to elevate them and make them interesting, or to lighten them by the use of machinery, so as to make the labour of them trifling, that should be taken as a token that the supposed advantages gained by them were not worth the trouble and had better be given up. All this to my mind would be the outcome of men throwing off the burden of Artificial Famine, supposing, as I cannot help supposing, that the impulses which have from the first glimmerings of history urged men on to the practice of Art were still at work in them.

Thus and thus only can come about the new birth of Art, and I think it will come about thus. You may say it is a long process, and so it is; but I can conceive of a longer. I have given you the Socialist or Optimist view of the matter. Now for the Pessimist view.

I can conceive that the revolt against Artificial Famine or Capitalism, which is now on foot, may be vanquished. The result will be that the working class—the slaves of society—will become more and more degraded; that they will not strive against overwhelming force, but, stimulated by that love of life which Nature, always anxious about the perpetuation of the race, has implanted in us, will learn to bear everything—starvation, overwork, dirt, ignorance, brutality. All these things they will bear, as, alas! they bear them too well even now; all this rather than risk sweet life and bitter livelihood, and all sparks of hope and manliness will die out of them.

Nor will their masters be much better off: the earth's surface will be hideous everywhere, save in the uninhabitable desert; Art will utterly perish, as in the manual arts so in literature, which will become, as it is indeed speedily becoming, a mere string of orderly and calculated ineptitudes and passionless ingenuities; Science will grow more and more one-sided, more incomplete, more wordy and useless, till at last she will pile herself up into such a mass of superstition, that beside it the theologies of old time will seem mere reason and enlightenment. All will get lower and lower till the heroic struggles of the past to realize hope from year to year, from century to century, will be utterly forgotten, and man will be an indescribable being—hopeless, desireless, lifeless.

And will there be deliverance from this even? Maybe man may, after some terrible cataclysm, learn to strive towards a healthy animalism, may grow from a tolerable animal into a savage, from a savage into a barbarian, and so on; and some thousands of years hence he may be beginning once more those arts which we have now lost, and be carving interlacements like the New Zealanders, or scratching forms of animals on their cleaned blade-bones, like the pre-historic men of the drift.

But in any case, according to the Pessimist view, which looks upon revolt against Artificial Famine as impossible to succeed, we shall wearily trudge the circle again, until some accident, some unforeseen consequence of arrangement, makes an end of us altogether.

That pessimism I do not believe in, nor, on the other hand, do I suppose that it is altogether a matter of our wills as to whether we shall further human progress or human degradation; yet, since there are those who are impelled towards the Socialist or Optimistic side of things, I must conclude that there is some hope of its prevailing, that the strenuous efforts of many individuals imply a force which is thrusting them on. So that I believe that the "Aims of Art" will be realized, though I know that they cannot be, so long as we groan under the tyranny of Artificial Famine. Once again I warn you against supposing, you who may specially love art, that you will do any good by attempting to revivify art by dealing with its dead exterior. I say it is the aims of art that you must seek rather than the art itself; and in the search we may find ourselves in a world blank and bare, as the result of our caring at least this much for art, that we will not endure the shams of it.

Anyhow, I ask you to think with me that the worst which can happen to us is to endure tamely the evils that we see; that no trouble or turmoil is so bad as that; that the necessary destruction which reconstruction bears with it must be taken calmly; that everywhere—in State, in Church, in the household—we must be resolute to endure no tyranny, accept no lie, quail before no fear, although they may come before us disguised as piety, duty, or affection, as useful opportunity and good-nature, as prudence or kindness. The world's roughness, falseness, and injustice will bring about their naural consequences, and we and our lives are part of those consequences; but since we inherit also the consequences of old resistance to those curses, let us each look to it to have our fair share of that inheritance also, which, if nothing else come of it, will at least bring to us courage and hope; that is, eager life while we live, which is above all things the Aim of Art.

Bauhaus

From 1919 to the advent of Hitler in 1933, the Bauhaus school, first in Weimar, then at Dessau, was the center of a concerted attempt to adapt design to the needs and spirit of the machine age. The Bauhaus approach, laid down by the school's founder, Walter Gropius, was simple and rational, using straight lines and the materials made available by new industrial developments—such as chrome plating and tubular steel or aluminum frames. Under Gropius and later under his successor Ludvig Mies van der Rohe, the Bauhaus became famous throughout Europe as the very symbol of advanced design. It disappeared in the 1930s when many of its members left Germany for fairer climes free of the Nazi clamor. Both Gropius and Mies ended up in the United States, where Gropius became Chairman of Harvard's Department of Architectural Sciences, and Mies Director of the Department of Architecture and City Planning of the Illinois Institute of Technology. The following essay, the founder's statement of the Bauhaus's purpose, helps illuminate—in a time when art and reality, art and the public, seemed far apart—the attempts of a few men working against this background of disconnection to establish new and working connections between the way of the world and the artist's will to find relevance in comment and service.

Gropius
The New Architecture and the Bauhaus

Can the real nature and significance of the New Architecture be conveyed in words? If I am to attempt to answer this question, it must needs be in the

Source: From Walter Gropius, *Bauhaus: 1919–1928,* New York. The Museum of Modern Art, 1937; translated by P. Morton Shand. Reprinted by permission of The Museum of Modern Art.

form of an analysis of my own work, my own thoughts and discoveries. I hope, therefore, that a short account of my personal evolution as an architect will enable the reader to discern its basic characteristics for himself.

A bridge has been made with the past, which allows us to envisage new aspects of architecture corresponding to the technical civilization of the age we live in; the morphology of dead styles has been destroyed; and we are returning to honesty of thought and feeling. The general public, formerly profoundly indifferent to everything to do with building, has been shaken out of its torpor; personal interest in architecture as something that concerns every one of us in our daily lives has been very widely aroused; and the broad lines of its future development are already clearly discernible. It is now becoming widely recognized that although the outward forms of the New Architecture differ fundamentally in an organic sense from those of the old, they are not the personal whims of a handful of architects avid for innovation at all costs, but simply the inevitable logical product of the intellectual, social and technical conditions of our age. A quarter of a century's earnest and pregnant struggle preceded their eventual emergence.

But the development of the New Architecture encountered serious obstacles at a very early stage of its development. Conflicting theories and the dogmas enunciated in architects' personal manifestoes all helped to confuse the main issue. Technical difficulties were accentuated by the general economic decline that followed the war. Worst of all, "modern" architecture became fashionable in several countries; with the result that formalistic imitation and snobbery distorted the fundamental truth and simplicity on which this renascence was based.

That is why the movement must be purged from within if its original aims are to be saved from the straightjacket of materialism and false slogans inspired by plagiarism or misconception. Catchphrases like "functionalism" and "fitness for purpose = beauty" have had the effect of deflecting appreciation of the New Architecture into external channels or making it purely one-sided. This is reflected in a very general ignorance of the true motives of its founders: an ignorance that impels superficial minds, who do not perceive that the New Architecture is a bridge uniting opposite poles of thought, to relegate it to a single circumscribed province of design.

For instance rationalization, which many people imagine to be its cardinal principle, is really only its purifying agency. The liberation of architecture from a welter of ornament, the emphasis on its structural function, and the concentration on concise and economical solutions, represent the purely material side of that formalizing process on which the *practical* value of the New Architecture depends. The other, the aesthetic satisfaction of the human soul, is just as important as the material. Both find their counterpart in that unity which is life itself. What is far more important than the structural economy and its functional emphasis is the intellectual achievement which has made possible a new spatial vision. For whereas building is merely a matter of methods and materials, architecture implies a mastery of space.

For the last century the transition from manual to machine production has so preoccupied humanity that, instead of pressing forward to tackle the new problem of design postulated by this unprecedented transformation, we have remained content to borrow our styles from antiquity and perpetuate historical prototypes in decoration.

That state of affairs is over at last. A new conception of building, based on reality, has emerged; and with it has come a new conception of space. These changes, and the superior technical resources we can now command as a direct result of them, are embodied in the very different appearance of the already-numerous examples of the New Architecture.

Just think of all that modern technique has contributed to this decisive phase in the renascence of architecture, and the rapidity of its development!

Our fresh technical resources have furthered the disintegration of solid masses of masonry into slender piers, with consequent far-reaching economies in bulk, space, weight, and haulage. New synthetic substances—steel, concrete, glass—are actively superseding the traditional raw materials of construction. Their rigidity and molecular density have made it possible to erect wide-spanned and all but transparent structures, for which the skill of previous ages was manifestly inadequate. This enormous saving in structural volume was an architectural revolution in itself.

One of the outstanding achievements of the new constructional technique has been the abolition of the separating function of the wall. Instead of making the walls the element of support, as in a brick-built house, our new space-saving construction transfers the whole load of the structure to a steel or concrete framework. Thus the role of the walls becomes restricted to that of near screens stretched between the upright columns of this framework to keep out rain, cold, and noise. In order to save weight and bulk still further, these non-supporting and now merely partitioning walls are made of lightweight pumice-concrete, breeze, or other reliable synthetic materials, in the form of hollow blocks or thin slabs. Systematic technical improvement in steel and concrete, and nicer and nicer calculation of their tensile and compressive strengths, are steadily reducing the area occupied by supporting members. This, in turn, naturally leads to a progressively bolder (i.e., wider) opening up of the wall surfaces, which allows rooms to be much better lit. It is, therefore, only logical that the old type of window—a hole that had to be hollowed out of the full thickness of a supporting wall—should be giving place more and more to the continuous horizontal casement, subdivided by thin steel mullions, characteristic of the New Architecture. And as a direct result of the growing preponderance of voids over solids, glass is assuming an ever greater structural importance. Its sparkling insubstantiality, and the way it seems to float between wall and wall imponderably as the air, adds a note of gaiety to our modern homes.

In the same way the flat roof is superseding the old penthouse roof with its tiled or slated gables. For its advantages are obvious: (1) light, normally shaped top-floor rooms instead of poky attics, darkened by dormers and sloping ceilings, with their almost inutilisable corners; (2) the avoidance of timber rafters, so often the cause of fires; (3) the possibility of turning the top of the house to practical account as a sun-loggia, open-air gymnasium, or children's playground; (4) simpler structural provision for subsequent additions, whether as extra stories or new wings; (5) elimination of unnecessary surfaces presented to the action of wind and weather, and therefore less need for repairs; (6) suppression of hanging gutters, external rain-pipes, etc., that often erode rapidly. With the development of air transport the architect will have to pay as much attention to the bird's eye perspective of his houses as to their elevations. The utilisation of flat roofs as "grounds" offers us a means of reacclimatizing nature amidst the stony deserts of our great towns; for the plots from which she has been evicted to make room for buildings can be given back to her up aloft. Seen from the skies, the leafy housetops of the cities of the future will look like endless chains of hanging gardens. But the primary advantage of the flat roof is that it renders possible a much freer kind of interior planning.

Standardization

The elementary impulse of all national economies proceeds from the desire to meet the needs of the community at less cost and effort by the improvement of its productive organizations. This has led progressively to mechanization, specialized division of labor, and rationalization: seemingly irrevocable steps in industrial evolution which have the same implications for building as for every other branch of organized production. Were mechanization an end in itself it would be an unmitigated calamity, robbing life of half its fulness and variety by stunting men and women into subhuman, robot-like automatons. (Here we touch the deeper causality of the dogged resistance of the old civilization of handicrafts to the new world-order of the machine.) But in the last resort mechanization can have only one object: to abolish the individual's physical toil of providing himself with the necessities of existence in order that hand and brain may be set free for some higher order of activity.

Our age has initiated a rationalization of industry based on the kind of working partnership between manual and mechanical production we call standardization, which is already having direct repercussions on building. There can be no doubt that the systematic application of standardization to housing would effect enormous economies—so enormous, indeed, that it is impossible to estimate their extent at present.

Standardization is not an impediment to the development of civilization, but, on the contrary, one of its immediate prerequisites. A standard may be defined as that simplified practical exemplar of anything in general use which embodies a fusion of the best of its anterior forms—a fusion preceded by the elimination of the personal content of their designers and all otherwise un-generic or non-essential features. Such an impersonal standard is called a "norm," a word derived from a carpenter's square.

The fear that individuality will be crushed out by the growing "tyranny" of standardization is the sort of myth which cannot sustain the briefest examination. In all great epochs of history the existence of standards—that is the conscious adoption of type-forms—has been the criterion of a polite and well ordered society; for it is a commonplace that repetition of the same things for the same purposes exercises a settling and civilizing influence on men's minds.

As the basic cellular unit of that larger unit the street, the dwelling house represents a typical group-organism. The uniformity of the cells whose multiplication by streets forms the still larger unit of the city therefore calls for formal expression. Diversity in their sizes provides the necessary modicum of variation, which in turn promotes natural competition between dissimilar types developing side by side. The most admired cities of the past are conclusive proof that the reiteration of "typical" (i.e., typified) buildings notably enhances civic dignity and coherence. As a maturer and more final model than any of the individual prototypes merged in it, an accepted standard is always a formal common denominator of a whole period. The unification of architectural components would have the salutary effect of imparting that homogeneous character to our own towns which is the distinguishing mark of a superior urban culture. A prudent limitation of variety to a few standard types of buildings increases their quality and decreases their cost; thereby raising the social level of the population as a whole. Proper respect for tradition will find a truer echo in these than in the miscellaneous solutions of an often arbitrary and aloof individualism because the greater communal utility of the former embodies a deeper architectural significance. The concentration of essential qualities in standard types presupposes methods of unprecedented industrial potentiality, which entail capital outlay on a scale that can only be justified by mass production.

Rationalization

Building, hitherto an essentially manual trade, is already in course of transformation into an organised industry. More and more work that used to be done on the scaffolding is now carried out under factory conditions far away from the site. The dislocation which the seasonal character of building operations causes employers and employed alike—as, indeed, the community at large—is being gradually overcome. Continuous activity throughout the year will soon become the rule instead of the exception.

And just as fabricated materials have been evolved which are superior to natural ones in accuracy and uniformity, so modern practice in house construction is increasingly approximating to the successive stages of a manufacturing process. We are approaching a state of technical proficiency when it will become possible to rationalize buildings and mass-produce them in factories by resolving their structure into a number of component parts. Like boxes of toy bricks, these will be assembled in various formal compositions in a dry state: which means that building will definitely cease to be dependent on the weather. Ready-made houses of solid, fireproof construction, that can be delivered fully-equipped from stock, will ultimately become one of the principal products of industry. Before this is practicable, however, every part of the house—floor beams, wall slabs, windows, doors, staircases, and fittings—will have to be normed. The repetition of standardized parts, and the use of identical materials in different buildings, will have the same sort of coordinating and sobering effect on the aspect of our towns as uniformity of type in modern attire has in social life. But that will in no sense restrict the architect's freedom of design. For although every house and block of flats will bear the unmistakable impress of our age, there will always remain, as in the clothes we wear, sufficient scope for the individual to find expression for his own personality. The net result should be a happy architectonic combination of maximum standardization and maximum variety. Since 1910 I have consistently advocated prefabrication of houses in numerous articles and lectures; besides which I have undertaken a number of practical experiments in this field of research in conjunction with important industrial concerns.

Dry assembly offers the best prospects because (to take only one of its advantages) moisture in one form or another is the principal obstacle to economy in masonry or brick construction (mortar joints). Moisture is the direct cause of most of the weaknesses of the old methods of building. It leads to badly fitting joints, warping and staining, unforeseen piece-work, and serious loss of time and money through delays in drying. By eliminating this factor, and so assuring the perfect interlocking of all component parts, the prefabricated house makes it possible to guarantee a fixed price and a definite period of construction. Moreover the use of reliable modern materials enables the stability and insulation of the building to be increased and its weight and bulk decreased. A prefabricated house can be loaded on to a couple of lorries at the factory—walls, floors, roofs, fittings and all—conveyed to the site, and put together in next to no time regardless of the season of the year.

The outstanding concomitant advantages of rationalized construction are superior economy and an enhanced standard of living. Many of the things that are regarded as luxuries today will be standard fitments in the homes of tomorrow.

So much for technique!—but what about beauty?

The New Architecture throws open its walls like curtains to admit a plenitude of fresh air, daylight, and sunshine. Instead of anchoring buildings ponderously into the ground with massive foundations, it poises them lightly, yet firmly, upon the face of the earth; and bodies itself forth, not in stylistic imitation of ornamental frippery, but in those simple and sharply modelled designs in which every part merges naturally into the comprehensive volume of the whole. Thus its esthetic meets our material and psychological requirements alike.

For unless we choose to regard the satisfaction of those conditions which can alone animate, and so humanize, a room—spatial harmony, repose, proportion—as an ideal of some higher order, architecture cannot be limited to the fulfilment of its structural function.

We have had enough and to spare of the arbitrary reproduction of historic styles. In the progress of our advance from the vagaries of mere architectural caprice to the dictates of structural logic, we have learned to seek concrete expression of the life of our epoch in clear and crisply simplified forms.

Having briefly surveyed what the New Architecture has already achieved, and outlined the probable course of its development in the near future, I will turn back to my own part in its genesis. In 1908, when I finished my preliminary training and embarked on my career as an architect with Peter Behrens, the prevalent conceptions of architecture and architectural education were still entirely dominated by the academic stylisticism of the classical "Orders." It was Behrens who first introduced me to logical and systematical coordination in the handling of architectural problems. In the course of my active association with the important schemes on which he was then engaged, and frequent discussions with him and other prominent members of the *Deutscher Werkbund,* my own ideas began to crystallize as to what the essential nature of building ought to be. I became obsessed by the conviction that modern constructional technique could not be denied expression in architecture, and that that expression demanded the use of unprecedented forms. Dynamic as was the stimulus of Behrens's masterly teaching, I could not contain my growing impatience to start on my own account. In 1910 I set up in independent practice. Shortly afterwards I was commissioned to design the *Fagus Werke* at Alfeld-an-der-Leine in conjunction with the late Adolf Meyer. This factory, and the buildings entrusted to me for the Cologne *Werkbund* Exhibition of 1914, clearly manifested the essential characteristics of my later work.

The full consciousness of my responsibility in advancing ideas based on my own reflections only came home to me as a result of the war, in which these theoretical premises first took definite shape. After that violent interruption, which kept me, like most of my fellow architects, from work for four years, every thinking man felt the necessity for an intellectual change of front. Each in his own particular sphere of activity aspired to help in bridging the disastrous gulf between reality and idealism. It was then that the immensity of the mission of the architects of my own generation first dawned on me. I saw that an architect cannot hope to realize his ideas unless he can influence the industry of his country sufficiently for a new school of design to arise as a result; and unless that school succeeds in acquiring authoritative significance. I saw, too, that to make this possible would require a whole staff of collaborators and assistants: men who would work, not automatically as an orchestra obeys its conductor's baton, but independently, although in close cooperation, to further a common cause.

The Bauhaus

This idea of the fundamental unity underlying all branches of design was my guiding inspiration in founding the original *Bauhaus*. During the war I had been summoned to an audience with the Grand Duke of Sachsen-Weimar-Eisenach to discuss my taking over the Weimar School of Arts and Crafts from the distinguished Belgian architect, Henri van de Welde, who had himself suggested that I should be his successor. Having asked for, and been accorded, full powers in regard to reorganization I assumed control of the Weimar School of Arts and Crafts and also of the Weimar Academy of Fine Arts, in the spring of 1919. As a first step towards the realization of a much wider plan—in which my primary aim was that the principle of training the individual's natural capacities to grasp life as whole, a single cosmic entity, should form the basis of instruction throughout the school instead of in only one or two arbitrarily "specialized" classes—I amalgamated these institutions into a *Hochschule für Gestaltung,* or High School for Design, under the name of *Das Staatliche Bauhaus Weimar.*

In carrying out this scheme I tried to solve the ticklish problem of combining imaginative design and technical proficiency. That meant finding a new and hitherto nonexistent type of collaborator who could be moulded into being equally proficient in both. As a safeguard against any recrudescence of the old dilettante handicraft spirit I made every pupil (including the architectural students) bind himself to complete his full legal term of apprenticeship in a formal letter of engagement registered with the local trades council. I insisted on manual instruction, not as an end in itself, or with any idea of turning it to incidental account by actually producing handicrafts, but as providing a good all-round training for hand and eye, and being a practical first step in mastering industrial processes.

The *Bauhaus* workshops were really laboratories for working out practical new designs for present-day articles and improving models for mass production. To create type-forms that would meet all technical, esthetic and commercial demands required a picked staff. It needed a body of men of wide and general culture as thoroughly versed in the practical and mechanical side of design as in its theoretical and formal laws. Although most parts of these prototype models had naturally to be made by hand, their constructors were bound to be intimately acquainted with factory methods of production and assembly, which differ radically from the practices of handicraft. It is to its intrinsic particularity that each different type of machine owes the "genuine stamp" and "individual beauty" of its products. Senseless imitation of handmade goods by machinery infallibly bears the mark of a makeshift substitute. The *Bauhaus* represented a school of thought which believed that the difference between industry and handicraft is due far less to the nature of the tool employed in each than to the subdivision of labor in the one and undivided control by a single workman in the other. Handicrafts and industry may be regarded as opposite poles that are gradually approaching each other. The former have already begun to change their traditional nature. In the future the field of handicrafts will be found to lie mainly in the preparatory stages of evolving experimental new-type forms for mass-production.

There will, of course, always be talented craftsmen who can turn out individual designs and find a market for them. The *Bauhaus,* however, deliberately concentrated primarily on what has now become a work of paramount urgency: to avert mankind's enslavement by the machine by giving its products a content of reality and significance, and so saving the home from mechanistic anarchy. This meant evolving goods specifically designed for mass-production. Our object was to eliminate every drawback of the machine without sacrificing any one of its real advantages. We aimed at realizing standards of excellence, not creating transient novelties.

When the *Bauhaus* was four years old, and all the essentials of its organization had been definitely established, it could already look back on initial achievements that had commanded widespread attention in Germany and abroad. It was then that I decided to set forth my views. These had naturally developed considerably in the light of experience, but they had not undergone any substantial change as a result. The pages which follow are abstracted

from this essay, which was published in 1923, under the title of THE CON-
CEPTION AND REALIZATION OF THE BAUHAUS.

The art of building is contingent on the coordinated team-work of a band
of active collaborators whose orchestral cooperation symbolizes the cooperative organism we call society. Architecture and design in a general sense are
consequently matters of paramount concern to the nation at large. There is
a widespread heresy that art is just a useless luxury. This is one of our fatal
legacies from a generation which arbitrarily elevated some of its branches
above the rest of the "Fine Arts," and in so doing robbed all of their basic
identity and common life. The typical embodiment of the *l'art pour l'art* mentality, and its chosen instrument, was "the Academy." By depriving handicrafts and industry of the informing services of the artists the Academies
drained them of their vitality, and brought about the artist's complete isolation from the community. Art is not one of those things that may be imparted. Whether a design be the outcome of knack or creative impulse depends on individual propensity. But if what we call art cannot be taught or
learned, a thorough knowledge of its principles and of sureness of hand can
be. Both are as necessary for the artist of genius as for the ordinary artisan.

What actually happened was that the Academies turned out an "artistic
proletariat" foredoomed to semi-starvation. Lulled by false hopes of the rewards of genius, this soon numerous class was brought up to the "professions" of architect, painter, sculptor, etc., without the requisite training to
give it an independent artistic volition and to enable it to find its feet in the
struggle for existence. Thus such skill as it acquired was of that amateurish
studio-bred order which is innocent of realities like technical progress and
commercial demand. The besetting vice of the Academy schools was that they
were obsessed by that rare "biological sport," the commanding genius; and
forgot that their business was to teach drawing and painting to hundreds and
hundreds of minor talents, barely one in a thousand of whom could be expected to have the makings of a real architect or painter. In the vast majority
of cases this hopelessly one-sided instruction condemned its pupils to the
lifelong practice of a purely sterile art. Had these hapless drones been given
a proper practical training they could have become useful members of society.

The rise of the academies spelt the gradual decay of the spontaneous traditional art that had permeated the life of the whole people. All that remained
was a "Salon Art," entirely remote from everyday life which by the middle of
the nineteenth century had petered out into mere exercises in individual virtuosity. It was then that the revolt began. Ruskin and Morris strove to find
a means of reuniting the world of art with the world of work. Towards the
end of the century their lead was followed by Van de Welde, Olbrich, Beh-

rens and others on the Continent. This movement, which started with the building of the "Artists' Colony" at Darmstadt and culminated in the founding of the *Deutscher Werkbund* in Munich, led to the establishment of *Kunstgewerbeschulen* in the principal German towns. These were intended to give the rising generation of artists a practical training for handicrafts and industry. But the academic spirit was too firmly implanted for that "practical" training to be more than a dilettante smattering. The *projet* and the "composition" still held pride of place in the curriculums. The first attempts to get away from the old unreal art-for-art's-sake attitude failed because they were not planned on a sufficiently wide front and did not go deep enough to touch the root of the evil.

Notwithstanding, commerce, and more particularly industry, began to look towards the artist. There was a genuine ambition to supplement efficiency by beauty of shape and finish: things which the working technician was not in a position to supply. So manufacturers bought "artistic designs." But these paper aids proved broken reeds. The artist was a man, "remote from the world," at once too unpractical and too unfamiliar with technical requirements to be able to assimilate his perceptions of form to the processes of manufacture. On the other hand the businessman and the technician lacked sufficient foresight to realize that the combination of form, efficiency and economy they desired could only be obtained by recognizing painstaking cooperation with a responsible artist as part of the routine of production. Since the kind of designer to fill this gap was nonexistent, the future training of artistic talent clearly demanded a thorough practical grounding under factory conditions combined with some theoretical instruction in the laws of design.

Thus the *Bauhaus* was inaugurated with the specific object of realizing a modern architectonic art, which, like human nature, should be all-embracing in its scope. Within that sovereign federative union all the different "arts" (with the various manifestations and tendencies of each)—every branch of design, every form of technique—could be coordinated and find their appointed place. Our ultimate goal, therefore, was the composite but inseparable work of art, the great building, in which the old dividing-line between monumental and decorative elements would have disappeared for ever.

Roberts

The personality of Michael Roberts, the English poet responsible for the essay that follows, is less important than the movement his opinions reflected and which the books he edited, *New Signatures* (1932) and *New Country* (1933), represent. Their contributors—men like W. H. Auden, Cecil Day Lewis, John Lehmann, William Plomer, and Stephen Spender—were young, ardent, and extremely uncomfortable in a social system whose disintegration bestowed on them the guilt though not the comforts of their social class. All sons of the middle class, most of them graduates of Oxford or Cambridge, they were not unaware of the *Communist Manifesto*'s prediction that "in times when the class struggle nears its decisive hour the process of dissolution going on within the ruling class . . . assumes such a violent, glaring character, that a small section of the ruling class [in particular, a portion of the bourgeois ideologists] cuts itself adrift, and joins the revolutionary class, the class that holds the future in its hands." As Roberts explains, they did not necessarily accept the Communist Party's interpretation of Communist policy or historical necessity, but simply joined the side that stood for the necessary revolution and the no-less-necessary social reform. That many of these men soon (or eventually) changed their minds is not, at this point, relevant. More important is the effect of their vision on the public and, concerning that, one might repeat the comment a nineteenth-century observer (J. A. Roebuck) once made upon the work of another school, that of Jeremy Bentham's utilitarian disciples:

> They produced a much more serious effect on public opinion than superficial inquirers perceived, or interested ones would acknowledge. The important practical effect was not made evident by converting and bringing over large numbers of political partisans from one banner or class to another, or by making them renounce one appellation and adopt another; but it was shown by affecting the conclusions of all classes, and inducing them, while they retained their old distinctive names, to reason after a new fashion, and according to principles wholly different from those to which they had been previously accustomed.

Preface to *New Country*

To me, "pre-war" means only one sunny market-day at Sturminster Newton, the day I boldly bought a goat for 1s.9d. and then, shelving all transport problems (we lived thirty miles away) and postponing the announcement to my father, went out into the country and, finding a gatepost for a table, cut out from the *Express* a picture of a dozen Serbian soldiers (we spelt it Servian then) in spotless uniforms, elbow to elbow in a shallow trench, standing exactly like my own toy soldiers, the Royal West Kent Regiment (*The Buffs*), manufactured by Wm. Britain and Sons Ltd.

But there are others who have even less than a one-and-ninepenny goat for

---

Source: From *New Country* edited by Michael Roberts, published by Leonard and Virginia Woolf at the Hogarth Press, London 1933. Reprinted by permission.

their share of pre-war prosperity; Mr. Plomer is older, but most of the other contributors to this book are younger, than I. Sergeants of our school O.T.C.s, admirers of our elder brothers, we grew up under the shadow of war: we have no memory of pre-war prosperity and a settled Europe. To us, that tale is text-book history: Wolsey, Canute, Disraeli, Balfour. We remember only post-war booms which even we, poets, schoolmasters, engineers, could see were doomed to sharp extinction. Politics isn't, and hasn't been, a real activity in our time. The older generation, remembering the days when an Asquith, or a Balfour, could still claim to exert some control over the destinies of this country, may think of Baldwin and MacDonald as their natural successors. To us, that control is legendary, the history of a vanished era, the days of a favorable trade-balance and of middle-class security. To-day we have no security. Not that the world is in the grip of the Financiers, but simply that it is not in anybody's grip at all. It is not intelligence which is lacking, but control. The world is deluged with good advice, advice which is useless only because in a maze of warring interests no one can act on it. There must be conferences, and committees and delays and interim reports, and neither the public interest, nor any group of private interests, is able to control the system.

Meanwhile we see all that we believe in threatened: the efforts of the scientist and the doctor and the engineer wasted, and print, which should be the medium of the man who has something to say, turned into a daily mirror of the public mind. If our sympathies turn toward revolutionary change it is not because of our pity for the unemployed and the underpaid but because we see at last that our interests are theirs, and that a system which permits exploitation for private profit, though it may abolish poverty, must retain in the hands of certain men the power to threaten the masses with starvation and to dictate what men shall eat and drink and wear and think.

But communism is a hard-worked word, and for ten years now its ambiguities have allowed intellectuals to boggle at any definite decision. There are very many people in this country—and I think there are as many of them in the Conservative Party as there are in the Labour Party—who are being forced to realise that no party which they know will ever be able to grapple with the situation. In vicarage and golf club as in dockyard and miners' lodge, there are men who, reluctant to commit themselves to a reorientation, a reorganisation of their whole lives, still feel that they are helpless units in an organism which is dying.

Communism, in this country, is associated with hooliganism, tactlessness, inefficient propaganda, mere discontent. The Communist Party of Great Britain has produced no Lenin, no Trotsky, no Lunacharsky. But sooner or later, if we toy with this notion of revolutionary change, we make clear our politics.

If there are certain reservations which prevent us from joining a party, we must formulate them clearly and so transcend the difficulty, not cherish them as excuses for inaction. If Marxism seems to us to be tainted with its nineteenth-century origin yet nevertheless to be, in the main, true, if, in the hands of its present exponents, the doctrine seems inelastic and fails to understand a temper which is not merely bourgeois but inherently English, it is for us to prepare the way for an English Lenin by modifying and developing that doctrine. The politicians will not help us, for the percentage of men who care a tuppenny damn for poetry, for science and for their country is no higher among Communists than it is among Conservatives. The only way of ensuring that a political party shall represent our ideals is to work with it now, to help to choose its leaders and to remember always that beyond our theoretical divergences there is our practical agreement, and we must learn to settle differences in friendliness and not hostility.

If, in this book, the emphasis is laid on the anticultural aspects of the present system, if we emphasise not the physical horror of war but its disastrous effects on our activities, it is not from any lack of sympathy but from a belief that the attack on war and economic chaos will be strengthened if the intellectuals realise that all which they hold valuable is threatened. It is too late for a letter to *The Times*. . . . What is the use of isolated protests? You can't control exploitation for private profit in this piecemeal fashion, even though you bother only about the amenities of a cultured leisured class. It is time that those who would conserve something which is still valuable in England began to see that only a revolution can save their standards. It's past the stage of sentimental pity for the poor, we're all in the same boat. They can no longer hold aloof from politics as intellectuals have done since the institution of a nominal democracy. One way or another they must make up their minds. And to a revolutionary party their lingering prestige and their technical ability as organisers and propagandists can be of immense value.

It is clear that for some years the pre-war generations will continue to be the determining political factor. But what will happen when we ourselves are the middle-aged or the elder generation? A revolutionary situation in the Marxian sense may not occur in our time. Propaganda against war, measures of state capitalism, social fascism and currency reform may enable the capitalist machine to be patched up and made to jog along to a later crisis. The newspaper magnates and the industrialists may make a desperate bid to retain their power by attacking the financier. The problem of leisure may be solved, but it will not be solved as we would wish. Shall we see our lives dictated more and more by the proprietors of Guinness, the Gaumont Palaces, Harrods and the *Daily Mail*? Shall we watch our children hypnotised into mere buying-machines? These are the questions which those of us who are engaged

in engineering, teaching, law, literature, medicine are compelled to ask. Daily
we see our efforts wasted or turned against society. Our researches turn men
out of work, not into decent leisure, but into starvation. And as the competitive machine forces the lowest level of standardisation, so our attempts as
poets and teachers fail. How can you help people to become their most
kindly, intelligent, sensitive selves when it pays to purvey one form of entertainment for all, when Test Matches replace village cricket, when the whole
system forces the ordinary man to become passive, not active?

And this standardisation and the resulting centralisation breaks up all local
communities and isolates a world of poets and a world of scientists and a
world of miners. Provincial life is impoverished and the intellectual is turned
to a pettifogging squabbler in Bloomsbury drawing-rooms or a recluse "in
country houses at the end of drives." And Bloomsbury is absurd not because
of its minor affectations, but because of its impotence, because it is an ag-
glomeration of individuals wrenched out of their proper environment so that
their abilities no longer serve or give pleasure to themselves or to others. We
do not need a new moral code, we do not need new standards of criticism,
we need a social system which will bring people into contact with those who,
from their own experience, can advise and help them. But to-day, even the
strictest individualist, the man who would willingly use his abilities to gain
for himself the services of others, is finding the possibilities more and more
restricted. Free competition survives only among the huge groups and combines. We, the intellectuals and the white-collar workers, have served our
purpose in making possible the world of modern industry; are we now to
become useless survivals, pensioners of a system of which we disapprove? Or
is there still something for us to do?

I think, and the writers of this book obviously agree, that there is only one
way of life for us: to renounce that system now and to live by fighting against
it. And that not because we would sacrifice the present to the future, nor
because we imagine that the world which we shall help to make will be in
any absolute sense "better" than the present, but because there is no other
decent way of life for us, no other way of living at our best. But if you, reader,
stand for the accepted order; if you cannot envisage a state in which resources
are used to meet the needs of the community and not for individual profit,
please remember that the Union Jack, the British Grenadiers, and cricket are
not your private property. They are ours. Your proper emblem is a balance
sheet. You're a fool if you think your system will give you cricket much
longer. Haven't you realised? *Cricket doesn't pay.* If you want cricket you'd
better join us. We're out for a decent life for ourselves and our successors,
not for a paper profit. What good has all your pre-war profit-snatching done
for us? We're not appealing to you to join the poor working-classes: you'll

be forced to do that soon enough. We're asking you to help us abolish the whole class system. And as soon as each man has a decent real income, as soon as he lacks only luxuries (the things for which he won't humiliate himself), the whole class system *will* perish. Something will have to take its place; and when I talk of intellectuals I am thinking of those people who are sufficiently acute, articulate and sensitive to be properly employed in building that new world. It will not be easy for the intellectual near-communists, each with his own Utopian scheme, to submit themselves to the job in hand, to accept independence of thought, but unanimity in action. And it will not be easy for a revolutionary party to see that clear distinction between the necessary anarchy of thought and the essential dictatorship of action. Without that clarity of vision there will be waste and wanton stupidity and suffering.

But you, the readers of the *Observer, The Times:* what are you going to do? We know that you have a stake in the present scheme of things, but you know as well as we do, that the smash will come soon, before you have time to retire on your savings. You know that even if the financiers or the industrialists find a solution to the present muddle it will be by way of a violent change which will hit the little *rentier* hard. But I don't mean that you are purely mercenary, you are merely reasonably prudent, you want security for your old age and for your children, as we all do. Plainly, you love your country, even though we cannot always understand you. And you see clearly enough the symptoms of her illness. Cannot you see that they are all symptoms of the one disease? And can't you see that the only way to save England is to save the world? Just as the nation is too big a unit for some things, so it is too small for others; but instead of tackling the root problem, whose solution would remove all hindrances, you toy with your Scottish Nationalism and your League of Nations. And you do nothing, for nothing can be done now unless we attack the inhibiting bonds directly. How long will you go on talking as though your 1910 were coming back?

It is not that we are pessimists: we have indeed greater faith in England than you. The country which first developed Parliamentary government, industrialism, banking and democracy may yet be the first to advance beyond; there are signs that English industrialists are preparing to demand far-reaching changes in the money system, and that only ten years after the first appearance of heterodox money schemes. Such changes are necessary, not sufficient. They may avoid war and may avoid starvation, but they cannot prevent the slow degradation of the countryside, the steady impoverishment of our lives and the commercialisation of culture.

It is essential that the intellectuals should become part of the community, not servants of a financial machine, and to do that they must realise that all this time they have been such servants and the measure of their servitude is the measure of the difficulty which they experience in rebelling.

But how is all this to affect our writing? First, it will affect our subject-matter and our attitude to it. The novelist, since it is his business to write about people, is compelled more obviously than the poet to choosing what class he shall write about. And because his audience is predominantly middle-class, and because it was the class among which his means permitted him to live, his novels represented mainly the life and aspirations of that class. How many novels of any note have dealt with shirt-sleeve labour? But the white-collar class, with its pitiful trade-balance superiority to the manual labourer, is doomed; even its cultural superiority has vanished under the standardisation and the vulgarisation of the Press.

The novelist, therefore, must either write in a way which shows the fatuity and hopelessness of that class, or he must turn for his subject-matter to the working class, the class which is, he thinks, not utterly corrupted by capitalist spoon-feeding and contains within itself the seeds of revolution. And he will find, in the lower working class, the clearest symbols of those passions and activities he values, for they will be less confused and muddled by the intricacies of a crumbling system. And so even though he feels that his job is to arouse and clarify the vision of the class from which he sprang, he will look elsewhere for his material and in so doing he will give new life and value to his work.

I do not mean by this statement to accept the cruder Marxian evaluation which equates a work of art to its social purpose or propaganda value. That is the mode of valuation of a man who doesn't care two hoots for art and hasn't the eye for a job well done. It is the judgment of a man who, knowing nothing of the finer points of the game, wants to see his home team win. But if you know the game, whether it is poetry or football, you become so engrossed in its technicalities, so delighted by that clever piece of forward play or that ingenious use of assonance that you forget, for a moment, the names of the opposing teams. You forget whether you are for or against the player: you simply find it good to see a man doing his job better than you had imagined to be possible.

But very few of us are interested in literature in that way. Nearly all of us want one team rather than another to win. And a man doesn't play well if he is merely trying to exhibit his skill. Most people are interested only in literature which deals with their own immediate problems; historical literature which tackles problems of the past means nothing to them, and they would never think of going to see a film of a Czechoslovakian pre-war Cup Final. And I do not think that a man is likely to write well if his inspiration is purely literary. . . .

But we must not think that our own "sincerity" makes our work more "important" than that of any other generation. In the future state, the assessment of past literature by the minority who possess keen literary perception will be much the same as it is now, but except in so far as that minority influences the others, the mass judgment will be very different. And let us remember that it is not only the Thackerays and the Galsworthys and the Shaws who will be contemptuously dismissed, but also those of us who, writing before the final collapse, made our rough sketches for a new life and delivered satiric judgment on the old. There is a very real danger that we may be deluged with vague Utopian lyrics. You cannot go on writing about the new state for ever any more than you can go on writing about cows for ever. Some of us, wiser than Mr. Davies, know this. If your writing about a new world is to mean more than buttercup lyricism, you must know how that world is to come into being and precisely what sort of world it will be. Much of the verse of the sleeping-car-celandine school (we have all written it at some time in the past five years) is not "revolutionary" at all. It resulted from the shock of discovering that we felt no antithesis where we had been taught to expect one. Our poems therefore differed from those of our predecessors, who set out to master material which seemed to them, and to their readers, sordid and difficult. They achieved some fine work, but it was work quite different from that of the generation which found that seaplanes and mountains, derricks, greyhounds and jessamine, all excited in them the same lyrical enthusiasm. But that initial excitement, the shock of discovery, cannot continue, though the new objects of lyrical feeling remain. The excitement which came from the first discovery must give way to new, and these images be used not merely for themselves but incidentally, as means to an independent end. But meanwhile the reader with an eye for the finer points of the game will see that the new imagery has resulted in a new method of using poetic imagery, something quite different from the older use of metaphor. . . .

There is another way in which the writer will be influenced by his political attitude: as he sees more and more clearly that his interests are bound up with those of the working class, so will his writing clear itself from the complexity and introspection, the doubt and cynicism of recent years, and become more and more intelligible to that class and so help in the evolution of a style which, coming partly from the shirt-sleeve workers and partly from the "intellectual," will make the revolutionary movement articulate.

If those of us who believe in this new life do indeed set our faces against the old, and if we take no pains to conceal our opinions, then we must expect indifference to crystallise into opposition. And if it is true that the attitude of the original poet does hint at the attitude of the future—an attitude which his work helps to make—then it is plain that the demarcation between the old and the new will become more and more clear; for the middle-class literary world, the supporters of the old order, have no promising recruits, no young "rebels" whom they can safely advertise as they once advertised Shaw and Wells. Those of us who believe that the change must come in our time cannot accept the system, and be accepted by it, in the same way as the professional revolutionaries of an older generation.

But there are perhaps special reasons why the work of the young men, the men who were just too young to serve in the war, has taken longer than usual to attract any attention. They found themselves in a world which possessed no traditions by which they would regulate their lives. Often they respected, admired and envied their elders, but they could not take their problems, personal or social, to them, for the older generation, however kindly and wise in its own tradition, could not feel or understand the moral scruples of the younger. Therefore they were compelled to attack consciously problems which, in a stable society, would be solved by social convention. They became self-conscious, self-analytical, dubious of the wisdom of their own decisions.

There are times when it is necessary to become conscious of things which should be instinctive. You cannot change your batting style without taking thought, and spoiling, for the time being, your play. But this analysis is only a means to an end: when you have learned the new stroke then it must become conscious and habitual. There is no need to make a life study of the dynamics of cricket: it is a specialist study for those who happen to like it.

It is not easy for those who have once learned to question every thought and feeling to become again spontaneous, even when all the problems are solved—and they are not all solved yet. It is no use to rail against the intellect as D. H. Lawrence sometimes did, only time can get us back our spontaneity. But each succeeding generation follows the development of their predecessors at an accelerated pace, and for our successors it will be easier, and our growing pains will puzzle them. And we shall be envious and yet, because they do instinctively that which we did after long deliberation, because their taste in literature leaps at once to that which we selected slowly, we shall suspect them, we shall complain a little querulously that "they don't know their stuff" as we did.

That is why you will find us, in this book, satirising not only the enemy, but also our own past interests. For there are two kinds of satire: that which is directed at the known external enemy, and that which is intended to free us from our own preoccupations and indulgences so that we may stop the pitiful waste of thought and energy, which has made us as powerless and contemptible as we are.

The present book, therefore, does not pretend to be "proletarian art," it is important only in so far as it is a picture of something which is happening: it shows how some of us are finding a way out of the individualist predicament. And for those of us who, like Mr. Day Lewis, Mr. Plomer and myself, were old enough to be influenced by the immediate post-war years, the effort is necessarily violent. It is to younger men that we must look for an acceptance of a newer outlook.

Meanwhile, if we carp at dogmatic communism, we are criticising only the crude and uninformed extension of Marxian doctrine beyond its original field, and condemning only the point of view of the party propagandist who, because he does not look beyond the work of revolution, sees in the boy of fifteen a revolutionary instrument to be used as effectively, and in precisely the same way, as the man of fifty. To communism as an economic system I, for one, can see no reasonable objection. But economic communism is valuable only in so far as it removes the vested interests which by enforcing standardisation, oppose all genuine education, the full development of the individual which might be possible in a state of social communism.

And by social communism I do not mean any diminution or mystical loss of personal identity or any vague sentiment of universal brotherhood: I mean that extension of personality and consciousness which comes sometimes to a group of men when they are working together for some common purpose.

I think some men had such an experience in the war, and to them it almost seemed to justify the filth and inhumanity of war. It is something rare in our competing, individualist world, and for myself I can point to only one definite example: a fortnight of wind and heavy snowstorm in the Jura when a dozen of us, schoolboys and undergraduates, came to accept each other's faults and virtues as part of the scheme of things, natural as the weather. I don't think I had any love or personal feeling for them at all: we were, for the moment, part of something a little bigger than ourselves. Impatience and fatigue and personal delight and suffering disappeared, and I remember only, at the end of each day's work, standing at nightfall on the last spur of the ridge, counting the tiny figures moving down the slope in sight of food and warmth again: nine, ten, eleven, black dots against the snow, and knowing that again the party was complete, uninjured, tired and content.

Day Lewis

Cecil Day Lewis (1904–1972), the son of a minister, left Oxford University in 1928 to become a teacher, and left teaching some years later because the restrictions of his profession interfered with the expression of his political ideas. His first poems had appeared in 1925, his interest in Communism had arisen, as with so many of his generation, in the 1930s. By that time his essays and especially his verse had made him one of the leading spokesmen of a younger generation disgusted with the pusillanimous ineffectiveness of its elders. His bitter, beautiful, but not unhopeful verses ranged widely in style and subject, and the poems that follow are but a taste of the varied output of a man who also translated Virgil's *Georgics* and *The Aeneid* and wrote excellent detective novels under the pseudonym Nicholas Blake.

In particular, the verses commemorating "The Twentieth Anniversary of Soviet Power" (first printed in *Russia To-day,* 1937, then reprinted in *In Letters of Red,* 1938) are hardly representative poetically: a great deal of enthusiastic occasional stuff was being churned out at the time, and this is far from the poet's best work. It does nevertheless reflect, as does the beautiful "Conflict," a widespread mood that affected many young people of the middle class, uneasy with a sense of failure in meeting the challenges of Depression and Fascism, for whom in a world threatened by violence from the outside and rot from the inside Soviet Communism offered a fresh and positive pattern for hope. Certainly in 1937, with appeasement rampant in Europe and isolationism still riding high in America, anti-Fascists could find few other objects for hope.

Lewis was to serve as a professor of poetry at Oxford from 1951 to 1956, as poet laureate of Great Britain from 1968 to his death, and as a director of the London publishing house of Chatto and Windus. The man who had predicted the revolutionary dawn, "no birth-hour without blood," also enjoyed a successful career as a member of the Establishment. Obviously, as his son put it in a biography of 1980, his was a divided identity and a "divided heart."

The Conflict

I sang as one
Who on a tilting deck sings
To keep their courage up, though the wave hangs
That shall cut off their sun.

As storm-cocks sing,
Flinging their natural answer in the wind's teeth,
And care not if it is waste of breath
Or birth-carol of spring.

As ocean-flyer clings
To height, to the last drop of spirit driving on
While yet ahead is land to be won
And work for wings.

Singing I was at peace,
Above the clouds, outside the ring:

Source: Reprinted by permission of Cecil Day Lewis.

For sorrow finds a swift release in song
And pride its poise.

Yet living here,
As one between two massing powers I live
Whom neutrality cannot save
Nor occupation cheer.

None such shall be left alive:
The innocent wing is soon shot down,
And private stars fade in the blood-red dawn
Where two worlds strive.

The red advance of life
Contracts pride, calls out the common blood,
Beats song into a single blade,
Makes a depth-charge of grief.

Move then with new desires,
For where we used to build and love
Is no man's land, and only ghosts can live
Between two fires.

On the Twentieth Anniversary of Soviet Power

Twenty years ago
That iron door of history slammed in the face
Of all the proud oppressors, the men whose profit
Had turned to mankind's loss; and still, more widely,
The reverberations of that clanging hour
Like an October gale pulse through the world,
Stripping dead wood from Time's forest, and ripping
The disguise from the faces that so falsely smiled
To work us mischief.

                            We remember now
Lenin. His mind like an oxy-acetylene flame
Sheared through the crust of centuries, laid bare

Source: This poem appeared in *Russia To-day,* 1937, and was reprinted in *In Letters of Red* (Michael Joseph, Ltd., London, 1938, pp. 154–55). Reprinted here by permission of Cecil Day Lewis.

History's secret plans and the full regalia
Of man's long-exiled love. He was loved by the people.
With him, we remember those to whom his words were
"Go hungry, work illegally, be anonymous";
Who in no comfortable bed conceived
Our future, but in agony and contempt.
Today we look towards the red flag waving
Over millions, our living comrades, and over many
Whose unregarded bodies paved the way
Into a better time, whose hopes firm-rooted
Are shade and avenue for our marching feet.

Twenty years have passed
Since a cry, All Power to the Soviets! shook the world.
We have seen new cities, arts and sciences,
A real freedom, a justice that flouts not nature,
Springing like corn exuberant from the rich heart
Of a happier people. We have seen their hopes take off
From solid ground and confidently fly
Out to the mineral north, the unmapped future.
U.S.S.R.! The workers of every land
And all who believe man's virtue inexhaustible
Greet you to-day: you are their health, their home,
The vision's proof, the lifting of despair.
Red Star, be steadfast above this treacherous age!
We look to you, we salute you.

                              There are others—
Fear's evil eye, the twitching hand of reaction—
Pointed your way. And, let us now declare it,
Your republic, Soviet Russia, is not contained
Between the Arctic floes and sunny Crimea:
Rather, its frontiers run from the plains of China
Through Spain's racked heart and Bermondsey barricades
To the factory-gates of America. We say,
Wherever instinct or reason tells mankind
To pluck from its heart injustice, poverty, traitors,
Your frontiers stand; where the batteries are unmasked
Of those who would shatter Life sooner than yield it
To its natural heirs, your frontiers stand: wherever
Man cries against the oppressors "They shall not pass,"
Your frontiers stand. Be sure we shall defend them.

Koestler

Arthur Koestler (1905–1983) was born in Budapest and educated in Vienna. First his Zionist enthusiasm, then his scientific interests, his luck, and his wanderlust, took him to Palestine, made him Near East correspondent for the Ullstein newspaper chain of Berlin, and finally brought him back to Berlin as science editor of one of the Ullstein publications. There he joined the Communist Party in December, 1931, to leave it only seven years later after an adventurous *émigré* writer's career had taken him to Russia, France, and Spain—where he narrowly missed death in one of Franco's prisons. He has told his odyssey better than anybody else could tell it in *Arrow in the Blue* and *The Invisible Writing*, but his popularity rests largely on the sensitive presentation he has given us of Communist mentality in *Darkness at Noon*. The following passage, from Koestler's contribution to *The God That Failed*,[1] makes very clear the feelings and circumstances that led many intellectuals of the 1930s into the ranks of the Communist Party, though not always to stay.

An Intellectual's Conversion

A faith is not acquired by reasoning. One does not fall in love with a woman, or enter the womb of a church, as a result of logical persuasion. Reason may defend an act of faith—but only after the act has been committed, and the man committed to the act. Persuasion may play a part in a man's conversion; but only the part of bringing to its full and conscious climax a process which has been maturing in regions where no persuasion can penetrate. A faith is not acquired; it grows like a tree. Its crown points to the sky; its roots grow downward into the past and are nourished by the dark sap of the ancestral humus.

From the psychologist's point of view, there is little difference between a revolutionary and a traditionalist faith. All true faith is uncompromising, radical, purist; hence the true traditionalist is always a revolutionary zealot in conflict with pharisaian society, with lukewarm corrupters of the creed. And vice versa: the revolutionary's Utopia, which in appearance represents a complete break with the past, is always modeled on some image of the lost Par-

---

[1] *The God That Failed* is a collection of essays in which several famous writers, including André Gide, Stephen Spender, and Ignazio Silone, explain their disillusion with Communism.

Source: Excerpt from *The God That Failed* by Arthur Koestler. Copyright 1949 by Arthur Koestler. Reprinted by permission of HarperCollins Publishers.

adise, of a legendary Golden Age. The classless Communist society, according to Marx and Engels, was to be a revival, at the end of the dialectical spiral, of the primitive Communist society which stood at its beginning. Thus all true faith involves a revolt against the believer's social environment, and the projection into the future of an ideal derived from the remote past. All Utopias are fed from the sources of mythology; the social engineer's blueprints are merely revised editions of the ancient text.

Devotion to pure Utopia, and revolt against a polluted society, are thus the two poles which provide the tension of all militant creeds. To ask which of the two makes the current flow—attraction by the ideal or repulsion by the social environment—is to ask the old question about the hen and the egg. To the psychiatrist, both the craving for Utopia and the rebellion against the status quo are symptoms of social maladjustment. To the social reformer, both are symptoms of a healthy rational attitude. The psychiatrist is apt to forget that smooth adjustment to a deformed society creates deformed individuals. The reformer is equally apt to forget that hatred, even of the objectively hateful, does not produce that charity and justice on which a utopian society must be based.

Thus each of the two attitudes, the sociologist's and the psychologist's, reflects a half-truth. It is true that the case-history of most revolutionaries and reformers reveals a neurotic conflict with family or society. But this only proves, to paraphrase Marx, that a moribund society creates its own morbid gravediggers.

It is also true that in the face of revolting injustice the only honorable attitude is to revolt, and to leave introspection for better times. But if we survey history and compare the lofty aims, in the name of which revolutions were started, and the sorry end to which they came, we see again and again how a polluted civilization pollutes its own revolutionary offspring.

Fitting the two half-truths—the sociologist's and the psychologist's—together, we conclude that if on the one hand oversensitivity to social injustice and obsessional craving for Utopia are signs of neurotic maladjustment, society may, on the other hand, reach a state of decay where the neurotic rebel causes more joy in heaven than the sane executive who orders pigs to be drowned under the eyes of starving men. This in fact was the state of our civilization when, in December, 1931, at the age of twenty-six, I joined the Communist Party of Germany.

I became converted because I was ripe for it and lived in a disintegrating society thirsting for faith. But the day when I was given my Party card was merely the climax of a development which had started long before I had read about the drowned pigs or heard the names of Marx and Lenin. Its roots reach back into childhood; and though each of us, comrades of the Pink Decade, had individual roots with different twists in them, we are products of, by and large, the same generation and cultural climate. It is this unity underlying diversity which makes me hope that my story is worth telling.

I was born in 1905 in Budapest; we lived there till 1919, when we moved to Vienna. Until the First World War we were comfortably off, a typical Continental middle-middle-class family: my father was the Hungarian representative of some old-established British and German textile manufacturers. In September, 1914, this form of existence, like so many others, came to an abrupt end; my father never found his feet again. He embarked on a number of ventures which became the more fantastic the more he lost self-confidence in a changed world. He opened a factory for radioactive soap; he backed several crank-inventions (everlasting electric bulbs, self-heating bed bricks and the like); and finally lost the remains of his capital in the Austrian inflation of the early 'twenties. I left home at twenty-one, and from that day became the only financial support of my parents.

At the age of nine, when our middle-class idyl collapsed, I had suddenly become conscious of the economic Facts of Life. As an only child, I continued to be pampered by my parents; but, well aware of the family crisis, and torn by pity for my father, who was of a generous and somewhat childlike disposition, I suffered a pang of guilt whenever they bought me books or toys. This continued later on, when every suit I bought for myself meant so much less to send home. Simultaneously, I developed a strong dislike of the obviously rich; not because they could afford to buy things (envy plays a much smaller part in social conflict than is generally assumed) but because they were able to do so without a guilty conscience. Thus I projected a personal predicament onto the structure of society at large.

It was certainly a tortuous way of acquiring a social conscience. But precisely because of the intimate nature of the conflict, the faith which grew out of it became an equally intimate part of my self. It did not, for some years, crystallize into a political creed; at first it took the form of a mawkishly sentimental attitude. Every contact with people poorer than myself was unbearable—the boy at school who had no gloves and red chilblains on his fingers, the former traveling salesman of my father's reduced to cadging occasional meals—all of them were additions to the load of guilt on my back. The analyst would have no difficulty in showing that the roots of this guilt-complex go deeper than the crisis in our household budget; but if he were to dig even deeper, piercing through the individual layers of the case, he would strike the archetypal pattern which has produced millions of particular variations on the same theme—"Woe, for they chant to the sound of harps and anoint themselves, but are not grieved for the affliction of the people."

Thus sensitized by a personal conflict, I was ripe for the shock of learning that wheat was burned, fruit artificially spoiled and pigs were drowned in the depression years to keep prices up and enable fat capitalists to chant to the sound of harps, while Europe trembled under the torn boots of hunger-marchers and my father hid his frayed cuffs under the table. The frayed cuffs and drowned pigs blended into one emotional explosion, as the fuse of the archetype was touched off. We sang the "Internationale," but the words might as well have been the older ones: "Woe to the shepherds who feed themselves, but feed not their flocks."

In other respects, too, the story is more typical than it seems. A considerable portion of the middle classes in central Europe was, like ourselves, ruined by the inflation of the 'twenties. It was the beginning of Europe's decline. This disintegration of the middle strata of society started the fatal process of polarization which continues to this day. The pauperized bourgeois became rebels of the Right or Left; Schickelgruber and Djugashwili shared about equally the benefits of the social migration. Those who refused to admit that they had become déclassé, who clung to the empty shell of gentility, joined the Nazis and found comfort in blaming their fate on Versailles and the Jews. Many did not even have that consolation; they lived on pointlessly, like a great black swarm of tired winterflies crawling over the dim windows of Europe, members of a class displaced by history.

The other half turned Left, thus confirming the prophecy of the "Communist Manifesto":

> Entire sections of the ruling classes are ... precipitated into the proletariat, or are at least threatened in their conditions of existence. They ... supply the proletariat with fresh elements of enlightenment and progress.

That "fresh element of enlightenment," I discovered to my delight, was I. As long as I had been nearly starving, I had regarded myself as a temporarily displaced offspring of the bourgeoisie. In 1931, when at last I had achieved a comfortable income, I found that it was time to join the ranks of the proletariat. But the irony of this sequence only occurred to me in retrospect.

> The bourgeois family will vanish as a matter of course with the vanishing of Capital. ... The bourgeois claptrap about the family and education, about the haloed correlation of parent and child, becomes all the more disgusting the more, by the action of modern industry, all family ties among the proletarians are torn asunder. ...

Thus the "Communist Manifesto." Every page of Marx, and even more of Engels, brought a new revelation, and an intellectual delight which I had only experienced once before, at my first contact with Freud. Torn from its context, the above passage sounds ridiculous; as part of a closed system which made social philosophy fall into a lucid and comprehensive pattern, the demonstration of the historical relativity of institutions and ideals—of family, class, patriotism, bourgeois morality, sexual taboos—had the intoxicating effect of a sudden liberation from the rusty chains with which a pre-1914 middle-class childhood had cluttered one's mind. Today, when Marxist philosophy has degenerated into a Byzantine cult and virtually every single tenet of the Marxist program has become twisted round into its opposite, it is difficult to recapture that mood of emotional fervor and intellectual bliss.

I was ripe to be converted, as a result of my personal case-history; thousands of other members of the intelligentsia and the middle classes of my generation were ripe for it, by virtue of other personal case-histories; but, however much these differed from case to case, they had a common denominator: the rapid disintegration of moral values, of the pre-1914 pattern of life in postwar Europe, and the simultaneous lure of the new revelation which had come from the East.

I joined the Party (which to this day remains "the" Party for all of us who once belonged to it) in 1931, at the beginning of that short-lived period of optimism, of that abortive spiritual renaissance, later known as the Pink Decade. The stars of that treacherous dawn were Barbusse, Romain Rolland, Gide and Malraux in France; Piscator, Becher, Renn, Brecht, Eisler, Säghers in Germany; Auden, Isherwood, Spender in England; Dos Passos, Upton Sinclair, Steinbeck in the United States. (Of course, not all of them were members of the Communist Party.) The cultural atmosphere was saturated with Progressive Writers' congresses, experimental theaters, committees for peace and against Fascism, societies for cultural relations with the USSR, Russian films and avant-garde magazines. It looked indeed as if the Western world, convulsed by the aftermath of war, scourged by inflation, depression, unemployment and the absence of a faith to live for, was at last going to

> Clear from the head the massive of impressive rubbish;
> Rally the lost and trembling forces of the will,
> Gather them up and let them loose upon the earth,
> Till they construct at last a human justice.
>
> Auden

The new star of Bethlehem had risen in the East; and for a modest sum, Intourist was prepared to allow you a short and well-focused glimpse of the Promised Land.

I lived at that time in Berlin. For the last five years, I had been working for the Ullstein chain of newspapers—first as a foreign correspondent in Palestine and the Middle East, then in Paris. Finally, in 1930, I joined the editorial staff in the Berlin "House." For a better understanding of what follows, a few words have to be said about the House of Ullstein, symbol of the Weimar Republic.

Ullstein's was a kind of super-trust: the largest organization of its kind in Europe, and probably in the world. They published four daily papers in Berlin alone, among these the venerable *Vossische Zeitung,* founded in the eighteenth century, and the *B. Z. am Mittag,* an evening paper with a record circulation and a record speed in getting the news out. Apart from these, Ullstein's published more than a dozen weekly and monthly periodicals, ran their own news service, their own travel agency, etc., and were one of the leading book publishers. The firm was owned by the brothers Ullstein—they were five, like the original Rothschild brothers, and like them also, they were Jews. Their policy was liberal and democratic, and in cultural matters progressive to the point of avant-gardism. They were antimilitaristic, antichauvinistic, and it was largely due to their influence on public opinion that the policy of Franco-German rapprochement of the Briand-Stresemann era became a vogue among the progressive part of the German people. The firm of Ullstein was not only a political power in Germany, it was at the same time the embodiment of everything progressive and cosmopolitan in the Weimar Republic. The atmosphere in the "House" in the Kochstrasse was more that of a Ministry than of an editorial office.

My transfer from the Paris office to the Berlin house was due to an article I wrote on the occasion of the award of the Nobel Prize for Physics to the Prince de Broglie. My bosses decided that I had a knack for popularizing science (I had been a student of science in Vienna) and offered me the job of Science Editor of the *Vossische* and adviser on matters scientific to the rest of the Ullstein publications. I arrived in Berlin on the fateful day of September 14, 1930—the day of the Reichstag Election in which the National Socialist Party, in one mighty leap, increased the number of its deputies from 4 to 107. The Communists had also registered important gains; the democratic parties of the Center were crushed. It was the beginning of the end of Weimar; the situation was epitomized in the title of Knickerbocker's best-seller: *Germany,—Fascist or Soviet?* Obviously there was no "third alternative."

I did my job, writing about electrons, chromosomes, rocket-ships, Neanderthal men, spiral nebulae and the universe at large; but the pressure of events increased rapidly. With one-third of its wage-earners unemployed, Germany lived in a state of latent civil war, and if one wasn't prepared to be swept along as a passive victim by the approaching hurricane it became imperative to take sides. Stresemann's party was dead. The Socialists pursued a policy of opportunistic compromise. Even by a process of pure elimination, the Communists, with the mighty Soviet Union behind them, seemed the only force capable of resisting the onrush of the primitive horde with its swastika totem. But it was not by a process of elimination that I became a Communist. Tired of electrons and wave-mechanics, I began for the first time to read Marx, Engels and Lenin in earnest. By the time I had finished with *Feuerbach* and *State and Revolution,* something had clicked in my brain which shook me like a mental explosion. To say that one had "seen the light" is a poor description of the mental rapture which only the convert knows (regardless of what faith he has been converted to). The new light seems to pour from all directions across the skull; the whole universe falls into pattern like the stray pieces of a jigsaw puzzle assembled by magic at one stroke. There is now an answer to every question, doubts and conflicts are a matter of the tortured past—a past already remote, when one had lived in dismal ignorance in the tasteless, colorless world of those who *don't know.* Nothing henceforth can disturb the convert's inner peace and serenity—except the occasional fear of losing faith again, losing thereby what alone makes life worth living, and falling back into the outer darkness, where there is wailing and gnashing of teeth. This may explain how Communists, with eyes to see and brains to think with, can still act in subjective *bona fides,* anno Domini 1949. At all times and in all creeds only a minority has been capable of courting excommunication and committing emotional harakiri in the name of an abstract truth.

Silone

Because Fascism first manifested itself in Italy, Italian intellectuals were among the first to know its promises and its brutalities. They were the first, after the Black Shirts' March on Rome (1922) and the murder of the Socialist Matteotti (1924), to see that behind the massive façade of propaganda, trains running on time, marshes drained, and Communists scotched, lay the same old running sores: corruption, misery, and unemployment. Under the new regime, however, it was no longer possible even to protest against social or economic injustice. Imperfect when compared with later creations of this kind, the Fascist police, both open and secret, ensured that critics of established order would be imprisoned, killed, cowed, or exiled in short order. Of course, most artists and intellectuals, unaware of a martyr's vocation, avoided such fates by coming to terms with the regime willingly or otherwise. But some could not do this. It was in enforced residence in a southern Italian village that Carlo Levi conceived *Christ Stopped at Eboli;* it was in Switzerland, where he fled after escaping Mussolini's prisons, that Ignazio Silone (1910–1978) wrote *Bread and Wine,* several passages from which appear below.

Born in an Abruzzi village, Silone early entered the politics of a country whose workers and peasants continued to live in medieval squalor aggravated by increasingly up-to-date methods of tax collection. His will to remedy this condition took him into labor politics and then into the Communist Party, which seemed the only segment of the left unwilling to be intimidated by or to compromise with existing ills. He left the Communists, however, when he found that, fascinated by ideology and bureaucracy, they too had drifted away from real folk and real sufferings around them.

Silone's problem, like that of the Italian countryside, was that regimes and ideologies pass and the peasant remains the same—poor, exploited, overtaxed, ignorant, superstitious, and generally landless. Under king or Duce, under liberals or Communists, nothing changes for the peasant, nothing changes for the poor. And Silone concluded that what was wanted was not a new party or a new plan, but a change of heart, something that occurs only at the individual level.

Pietro Spina, the hero of *Bread and Wine,* is a Communist activist who returns from exile to fight the regime on his own home ground, the Abruzzi countryside where he was born. It is 1935, the year of the Abyssinian war: the peasants are cowed; their old resistance broken; their old illusions dead or abandoned. Spina's conversations with a former school friend, with a comrade of the days of student Socialism and, at last, with his old teacher, reflect the evolution of Silone's own thought. In the end, like his creator, Spina discovers that "it is not a matter of putting new formulas, new gestures, or shirts of a different color into circulation, but rather a matter of a new way of living. To use an old expression, it is a matter of conversion. It is a matter of becoming a new man. Perhaps it is sufficient to say that it is a matter of becoming a man, in the real sense of the word."

Bread and Wine

"Why did you come back to Italy? If you love liberty, why didn't you stay in one of the countries where there is liberty?"

"I came back here to be able to breathe," said Spina.

Sacca tried to find language that Spina would understand.

"The greatest revolutionaries," he said, "your masters, who worked for their ideals for decades and destroyed tyrants, spent their whole lives in exile. Why can't you?" Spina was familiar with this objection.

"You are perfectly right," he said. "I do not know how to spare myself in the expectation of playing a great political role. I am a very bad revolutionary. But I shall not go back into exile."

"And if they catch you?"

"There's certainly a danger of prison, but that's not enough to keep me away from my country. I'm an internationalist, but out of my country I feel

---

Source: Selections from *Bread and Wine* by Ignazio Silone. Copyright, 1937, by Harper & Brothers.

like a fish out of water. I have had enough of exile. I don't know how to wait."

"Then it is an affair that does not concern me, and I wash my hands of it," said Nunzio Sacca, going through the motions of washing his hands as he spoke.

"I'm glad to hear you express yourself in such biblical fashion," said Spina. "It's obvious that your religious education wasn't wasted."

Then he went on:

"I spent the other night in a cave on Monte della Croce. I was hungry, thirsty, feverish, and drenched to the skin. In the distance I could see the school where we spent eight years together. The flower-beds we looked after together must still be in the garden. Do you remember my geraniums? The big dormitory, where we slept with our beds so close together that we could talk nearly all night without the prefect noticing it, must still be on the second floor. Do you remember the fantastic plans we used to make? Don Benedetto expounded the symbolism of the ancient poets, Don Sillogismo expounded the laws of logic, and Don Zaccheo held forth on the texts of the Holy Fathers and the deeds and sayings of heroes and kings. During meals in the big refectory each of us in turn used to have to read aloud the life of a martyr or a saint. When we emerged from that fantastic world we found a society, a Church, a state that were very different from the world we had grown up in, and each one of us had to make his choice. Either we had to submit to it or be crushed by it, either serve it or rebel against it. Once upon a time there were middle ways. But after the war for our generation, those ways were shut. How many years have passed since then? Fifteen. Nobody, seeing us here now, would imagine that up to the age of twenty our lives ran parallel and that we dreamed the same dreams for the future."

Nunzio Sacca was embarrassed.

"It is true," he said, "that we belong to different parties now."

"Different humanities," Spina corrected him. "Between free men and slaves, in the long run, there is more than a difference of party, there is a difference of humanity. I would say a difference of race, had that word not been compromised by the Germans. I talk like this because there are no other terms for what I have to say. In a situation in which I am completely in your hands, to pretend esteem towards you and those who have conducted themselves like you would cost me an effort of which I am not capable. Besides, the day of reckoning is not yet. You may go."

Pietro Spina walked back into the empty shed and sat down on a donkey's saddle. The doctor hesitated, then went towards him and said:

"At least let me examine you. I can get you some medicine through Cardile."

Spina reluctantly bared his chest. The lined and faded parchment of his aged-looking head and face contrasted strangely with his body, which was clean, white, and graceful, like an adolescent's. The doctor bent over his sick friend and started tapping each rib of his narrow, hollow chest, to which he repeatedly applied his ear, observing the desperate hammering of his heart, trying to fathom from every side the anxious panting of his lungs. The examination exhausted Spina's strength and he slowly slid from the saddle and lay full-length on the straw-covered floor, with half-shut eyes. Nunzio Sacca was filled with a sense of warmth and good-fellowship.

"Listen, Pietro, my friend," he said. "Don't let us quarrel. You must not die." Sacca held one of his hands and talked of the illusions, the disappointments, the wretchedness, the lies, the intrigues, the nausea of his daily life.

"All our life is lived provisionally," he said. "We think that for the time being things are bad, that for the time being we must adapt ourselves, even humiliate ourselves, but that it is all just temporary, and that one day life, real life, will begin. We get ready to die, still complaining that we have never really lived. Sometimes I am obsessed with the idea that we have only one life, and spend the whole of it living provisionally, waiting for real life to begin. And thus the time passes. Nobody lives in the present. Nobody has any profit from his daily life. Nobody can say: On that day, on that occasion, my life began. Even those who enjoy all the advantages of belonging to the government party have to live by intrigue, and are thoroughly nauseated by the dominant stupidity. They too live provisionally, and spend their lives waiting."

"One must not wait," said Spina. "In exile one spends one's life waiting too. One must act. One must say: Enough! from this very day."

"But if there is no liberty?" said Nunzio Sacca.

"Liberty isn't a thing you are given as a present," said Spina. "You can be a free man under a dictatorship. It is sufficient if you struggle against it. He who thinks with his own head is a free man. He who struggles for what he believes right is a free man. Even if you live in the freest country in the world and are lazy, callous, apathetic, irresolute, you are not free but a slave, though there be no coercion and no opposition. Liberty is something you have to take for yourself. It's no use begging it from others."

Nunzio Sacca was thoughtful and troubled.

"You are our revenge," he said. "You are the better part of us. Try to be strong. Try to live. Take real care of your health."

"Nunzio," said Pietro, speaking with difficulty, "if my return to Italy achieves nothing but to have revived that voice of yours and to have regained a lost friend, it will have been worth the cost. That was how you used to speak during those nights at school, when the rest of the dormitory was asleep." . . .

Spina used the list of addresses that Romeo gave him. Next day he succeeded in finding the home of an old friend of his, Uliva, a violinist, whom he had not heard of since they had used to meet in a Socialist students' group. All he knew about Uliva was that he had spent many months in prison and had lived completely apart ever since. Spina found him on the fourth floor of a house in the Via Panisperna in the Viminal quarter. A young, pregnant woman took him to Uliva's room, and Uliva received him with indifference, without pleasure or surprise. He was a bent, bespectacled little man, wearing a dirty black suit that gave him a sad and neglected look. Even after Spina had entered the room, he remained stretched on the divan, smoking and spitting. He spat in a wide arc, right across the room, in the direction of the washstand, but more often than not he missed it; traces of yellow tobacco juice were everywhere, on the fringes of the bed-cover, on the writing desk, and on the walls.

"We haven't seen each other for a long time," said Spina. "I didn't think you would come to this."

"Did you think I'd become a state employee?"

"Is that the only alternative?"

"For us, yes," said Uliva. "There has never been any other alternative for us. Either you serve or perish. He who desires to live disinterestedly, with no other discipline than that which he imposes on himself, is outlawed by society, and the state hunts him like an enemy. Do you remember our student group? Those who didn't end up in prison or die of hunger have met a far worse fate, as state employees. After ten months' imprisonment, for shouting 'Long Live Liberty!' in the Piazza Venezia, I spent some time sleeping in the public dormitories in winter, or under the bridges of the Tiber or in some doorway or on church steps in summer, with my coat under my head for a pillow. Every now and then there was the nuisance of the police coming on their rounds, asking: 'Who are you? What is your job? What do you live on?' You should have seen how they laughed when, for lack of other identification papers, I showed my scholastic certificate and my musician's diploma! I even tried to settle in my native village in the province of Salerno. It was impossible. Our villages have not been in such a state since the Spaniards left the country."

"The time has come to emerge from isolation," Spina said. "The time has come to combine with the working-class. The time has come to convert the masses through a series of audacious acts."

"The working-masses are cowed, corrupted, intimidated, apathetic, classified, regimented, rubber-stamped, and famished," Uliva replied. "Hunger itself has been bureaucratized. There's the official kind that gives you the right to state soup, and the unofficial kind that gives you the right to throw yourself into the Tiber."

"Nevertheless, among the pulverized mass there are some living cells," said Spina. "We are in a grave situation. A man like you must not remain isolated. Isolated sacrifices are futile. Action is necessary to reawaken the masses."

"The situation is certainly grave," Uliva replied. "There is something corpse-like even about the dictatorship that stifles us. For a long time it has not been a movement, even a reactionary movement: all it is is a bureaucracy. But what is the opposition? Another bureaucracy that aspires to totalitarian domination in its turn, in the name of different ideas and on behalf of different interests. If it does conquer, as it probably will, we shall thus pass from one tyranny to another. We shall have a so-called economic revolution, thanks to which we shall have state bread, state boots and shoes, state shirts and pants, state potatoes and state green peas, just as we now have state railways, state quinine, state salt, state matches, and state tobacco. Will that be a technical advance? Certainly it will. But it will be the basis of an official, compulsory doctrine, a totalitarian orthodoxy which will use every means, from the cinema to terrorism, to extirpate heresy and tyrannize over individual thought. A Red inquisition will succeed the present inquisition, a Red censorship the present censorship. Instead of the present deportations there will be Red deportations, of which dissident revolutionaries will be the favorite victims. Our future bureaucracy will identify itself with Labor and Socialism and persecute everyone who goes on thinking with his own head, denouncing him as a paid agent of the industrialists and the landlords, just as the present bureaucracy identifies itself with patriotism and suppresses all its opponents, denouncing them as traitors bought by foreign gold."

"Uliva, you're raving," said Spina. "You have been one of us, you know us, and you know that that is not our ideal."

"It's not your ideal, but it is your destiny," Uliva answered. "There's no way out."

"Destiny is an invention of the cowardly and resigned," said Spina.

Uliva made a gesture to indicate that it was not worth while continuing the discussion. But he added:

"You are very intelligent, but you are a coward. You don't understand because you don't want to understand. You're afraid of the truth."

Spina got up to go away. Uliva remained motionless on his divan. At the door Spina turned and said:

"There is nothing in my life which gives you the right to insult me."

"Go away and don't come back," said Uliva. "I have nothing to say to any emissary of the party."

Spina opened the door to go. But he closed it again and came and sat down at the foot of the divan on which Uliva lay.

"I shall not go away," he said, "until I have discovered why you have become like this. What was it that altered you to this extent? Imprisonment, unemployment, hunger?"

"I read and studied in my privations, and sought for at least a promise of liberation," said Uliva. "I found none. Every revolution, every single one, without any exception whatever, started as a movement for liberation and finished as a tyranny. For a long time I was tortured by that fact. Why has no revolution escaped that destiny?"

"Even if that were true, the conclusion to be drawn from it would be a different one from yours," said Spina. "If it were true that all previous revolutions had miscarried, we should have to say to ourselves, our revolution must not miscarry."

"Illusions, illusions," Uliva replied. "You have not yet won, you are still an underground movement, you have already become simply a group of professional revolutionaries. The regenerating passion by which we were animated in the student group has become an ideology, a network of fixed ideas, a cobweb. That is the proof that there is no escape for you, either. And you are only at the beginning of the parabola. That is the destiny of every new idea. It is crystallized in formulas so that it may be propagated. It is intrusted to a body of interpreters so that it may be preserved. That body is prudently recruited, sometimes specifically paid for its task, and is subject to a superior authority whose duty it is to resolve doubts and suppress deviations from the line indicated by the masters. Thus every new idea invariably ends by becoming fixed, inflexible, parasitical, and reactionary. And if it becomes the official doctrine of the state, no more escape is possible. A carpenter or a laborer can perhaps adapt himself even to a regime of totalitarian orthodoxy, and eat, digest, procreate in peace; but for an intellectual there is no escape. He must either bend the knee and enter the ranks of the dominant clerks, or resign himself to hunger and defamation and be killed off at the first favorable opportunity."

Spina was overcome with anger. He seized Uliva by the lapels of his coat and cried in him face:

"But why should that be our destiny? Why should there be no way out? Are we hens shut up in a hen-coop? Why should we remain the victims of an inexorable fate, powerless to fight against it? Why condemn a regime which does not yet exist and which we wish to create in man's image?"

"Don't shout," said Uliva. "Don't act the propagandist with me. You have understood very well what I have said. You pretend not to understand, because you are afraid of the consequences."

"I am not afraid of anything," said Spina.

"But I know you," said Uliva. "I watched you when we were both in the Socialist group. Since then I have discovered that fear is what makes you a revolutionary. You force yourself to believe in progress, to be optimistic, you make valiant efforts to believe in free will, all because you are terrified of the opposite."

Spina felt a little perplexed. He made Uliva a small concession.

"It is true," he said, "that I believe in the liberty of man. I force myself to believe at least in the possibility of the liberty of man, and hence in the possibility of progress. If I did not believe in them, you are right, I should be afraid of life."

"I do not believe in progress, and I am not afraid of life," said Uliva.

"How did you reconcile yourself to it?"

"I am not reconciled to it," said Uliva. "I am not afraid of life, but I am still less afraid of death. Against a life which is dominated by pitiless laws the only weapon left to man's free will is non-life, the destruction of life, death, beautiful death."

"I see," said Spina.

He saw, and it filled him with a great sadness. Further argument would be useless.

They belonged to different worlds.

Uliva quietly whispered in Spina's ear:

"Life can control man, but man can control death—his own death, and, with a little wariness, the death of tyrants."

The young woman who had opened the door to Spina came in to fetch something. Uliva waited till she had gone and then continued:

"My father died of drink at the age of forty-nine," he said. "A few weeks before he died he sent for me one evening and told me the story of his life, his failure. First he described his father's death—that is, my grandfather's. 'I die a poor and disappointed man,' my father's father said, 'but I rely on you to realize all my hopes. May you have from life what I have not had.' When my father felt his own death approaching, he repeated my grandfather's words. 'I, too, my son, die a poor and disappointed man, but my hopes live in you. May you have from life what I have not had.' Thus illusions, like debts, are passed on from generation to generation. I am now thirty-five years old, and I am where my father and grandfather were. I, too, a failure, and my wife is expecting a child. But I am not stupid enough to believe that my son may get from life what I did not get. I know that he will not be able to escape the same destiny. He will either die of hunger or become a state employee, which is worse."

Spina rose to go.

"I do not know whether I shall return," he said.

"It's not worth the trouble," Uliva replied. . . .

He found Don Benedetto waiting on the threshold of his cottage, as if he had been expecting him to arrive at just that movement. They shook hands and greeted each other, both slightly embarrassed by the emotion they felt. The old man led the younger into the big room on the ground floor which was full of garden tools and books. He made him sit in a big armchair by the fireplace and sat down next to him on a low stool. He was bent with age and seemed much smaller than his former pupil. The younger man tried to control his emotion and appear unconcerned.

"Behold the lost lamb that returns to its shepherd of its own accord," he said with a laugh.

Don Benedetto looked with surprise at his guest's prematurely aged face. He did not laugh, but shook his head.

"Here, among us, one cannot tell who is the lost lamb," he said bitterly. "One cannot tell which of us it is who really has need of the other's pardon; which of us it is who really feels humiliated and afflicted in the other's presence. It is sad, my friend, to make certain discoveries at my age. It is not those who say Mass and call themselves the ministers of the Lord who are most faithful to Him in spirit."

Hearing the old man talk of God, as in olden times, the young man feared he might be laboring under a wrong impression that would falsify the whole encounter. Did the old man think he was still religious?

"I lost my faith in God many years ago," the young man said, and his voice changed. "It was a religious impulse that led me into the revolutionary movement, but, once within the movement, I gradually rid my heart of all religious prejudices. If any traces of religion are left in me, they are not a help, but a hindrance, to me now. Perhaps it was the religious education I received as a boy that made me a bad revolutionary, a revolutionary full of fears, uncertainties, complexities. On the other hand, should I ever have become a revolutionary without it? Should I ever have taken life seriously?"

The old man smiled.

"It does not matter," he said. "In times of conspiratorial and secret struggle the Lord is obliged to hide Himself and assume pseudonyms. Besides, and you know it, He does not attach very much importance to His name; on the contrary, at the very beginning of His Commandments He ordained that His name should not be taken in vain. Might not the ideal of social justice that animates the masses today be one of the pseudonyms the Lord is using to free Himself from the control of the churches and the banks?"

The idea of God Almighty being forced to go about under a false passport amused the younger man greatly. He looked at his old schoolmaster in astonishment, and suddenly saw him in a very different light from the image of him that he has preserved during the long years since they had last met. Certainly he was much nearer to him now, but the thought of the pains and torments the old man must have gone through, abandoned and alone, to reach this point saddened him and made him silent.

"I live here with my sister, between my garden and my books," the old man said. "For some time, now, all my letters have been opened by the censor. My books and papers arrive late or get lost on the way. I pay no visits and receive few, and most of them are disagreeable. All the same I am aware of many things that go on, and they fill me with consternation. The Church has made religion a drug for the poor people. What belongs to God is given to Caesar, and what ought to be left to Caesar is given to God. The spirit of the Lord has abandoned the Church, which has become a formal, conventional, materialistic institution, obsessed with worldly and caste worries. It was to such a Church that the Baptist spoke the words: 'O generation of vipers, who hath warned you to flee from the wrath to come?' I was summoned to Rome, to be reproved and threatened. The few days I spent there were decisive in my mental life. The impression the papal court makes upon one is of Oriental sycophancy, of manifest and pompous sovereignty. Wherever I went I was received with rudeness and irony by young prelates promoted to high rank by the influence of banker or landlord uncles. Old acquaintances refused to receive me for fear of compromising themselves. In my absence my luggage was ransacked and notebooks and papers were stolen. If I asked those prelates what they thought of the war that was about to break out between two Christian peoples, they fled as from the presence of an *agent provocateur*. If one of them, after looking carefully all about him, dared to reply at all, he would talk in sibylline words. 'From one point of view it is true that so-and-so is the case,' he would say. 'But from another point of view it is also true that such-and-such must be taken into account. . . . Nor must it be forgotten that so-and-so. . . . And it must be admitted that such-and-such. . . . From which our attitude is perfectly clear.' In the face of all this poltroonery, all this concern for miserable material advantages, I started asking myself: Where then is the Lord? Why has He abandoned us?"

"That is a very pertinent question," the young man said. "Where is the Lord? If He is not a human invention, but an objective spiritual reality, the beginning and the end of all the rest, where is He now?"

His voice was not that of an atheist, but that of a disappointed lover.

Marta, the old man's sister, came in to greet the young man. She put two glasses and a jug of red wine on the table, and went back to her room.

"There is an old story that must be called to mind every time the existence of the Lord is doubted," the old man went on. "It is written, perhaps you will remember, that at a moment of great distress Elijah asked the Lord to let him die, and the Lord summoned him to a mountain. And there arose a great and mighty wind that struck the mountain and split the rocks, but the Lord was not in the wind. And after the wind the earth was shaken by an earthquake, but the Lord was not in the earthquake. And after the earthquake there arose a great fire, but the Lord was not in the fire. But afterwards, in the silence, there was a still, small voice, like the whisper of branches moved by the evening breeze, and that still small voice, it is written, was the Lord."

Meanwhile a breeze had arisen in the garden, and the door of the room in which the two men were sitting creaked and swung open. The young man shuddered. The old man placed his hand on his shoulder and said, with a laugh, "Do not be afraid. You have nothing to fear." He got up and closed the door.

"So I asked myself: where is the Lord, and why has He abandoned us?" he went on. "The loud-speakers proclaiming the outbreak of the war in all the market-places were certainly not the Lord. The bells that rang to summon the ragged and hungry crowds round the loud-speakers were certainly not the Lord. The shelling of African villages and the bombing raids of which the papers tell us every day are certainly not the Lord. But if a poor man alone in his village, gets up at night and takes a piece of chalk or charcoal and writes on the village walls: 'Down with the war! Long live the brother-hood of all peoples! Long live liberty!' behind that poor man there is the Lord. In his contempt for the dangers that threaten him, in the secret love he nourishes for our so-called African enemies, in his love of liberty, there is an echo of the Lord. Thus, when I read in the papers of bishops being tried in court for smuggling money, and behaving before the judges like fraudulent merchants caught red-handed, and when I read in the same paper of work-men being condemned to death for having claimed the liberty of their own consciences, even if those workmen consider themselves atheists, I have no need of much reflection before deciding on which side the Lord is. Now you can imagine what it means to make such a discovery at my age, at the age of seventy-five, almost on the brink of the tomb, when a man turns back to contemplate the road he has traveled and make an audit of his past life. A barren audit! And if I then avert my gaze from myself and consider my former pupils as a whole, I have still greater reason to consider myself a failure. A tree is judged by its fruit, and a teacher by his pupils."

The reverence and admiration that the young man had always preserved for his old schoolmaster now yielded to such a lively feeling of tenderness and affection that he got up and embraced him.

"I used to console myself a little by thinking of you, but I was mistaken," the old man went on. "You have yourself reminded me that the good you have done in your life was not because of your education, but against it and in spite of it."

The young man remained a little perplexed, and then he answered:

"We have not seen each other for fifteen years, and perhaps after this we shall never see each other again. You are an old man, and I am ill and the times are hard. Let us, then, try not to waste the precious minutes left to us in mutual compliments. I am sincerely convinced that I am no better than any of my school-fellows. I am also convinced that the society in which we live has reached such a stage of putrefaction that it is bound to contaminate anyone who does not completely break with it. I have had a better fate than my school-fellows because at the right time, and helped by a series of circumstances, I broke with it. If I had remained within it I should have run the risk of ending up like them. Instead, I live outside the law. I live under a false name. In my pocket, in case I have to flee, I have a foreign passport. I certainly run risks on the material plane, the danger of prison, the possibility of torture, and, if it came to the worst, the possibility of being shot. But in exchange for that I live secure from compromise. A few days ago I saw Dr. Nunzio Sacca. He certainly used to be no worse than I, but what a wretched state he is reduced to now! We have reached a point at which it can be said that only he can save his soul who is prepared to throw it away."

"There is no other salvation than that," the old man said. "Poor Nunzio has now realized his family's fondest dreams. He was appointed director of the government hospital a few days ago. What intrigues he had to descend to, what humiliations he had to submit to, what fairytales he had to tell, to establish his political orthodoxy and eliminate the other candidates! . . . He came to me after his first encounter with you, at Aquafredda last spring. He described the internal crisis he went through, almost in the words that you have just used. He said: 'In a dictatorial regime, how can one practise a profession that depends on government good-will and remain an honest man? Spina is lucky to be out of it.' . . ."

"I often wonder what I ought to do," the old man went on. "At the age of seventy-five one can change one's ideas, but not one's habits. A retired life is the only one that suits my character. Even when I was young I lived very much apart. I always kept aloof from politics because of my repugnance to vulgarity. Taste and an aesthetic education always withheld me from action.

Besides, my aversion to the present state of things is not political. It is not as a voter but as a man that I find this society intolerable. And then I ask myself what am I to do. I look around me and see very little that I can do. Among my parishioners? Nothing. Those among them whom I know personally avoid me now and are frightened of meeting me. In the last fifty years every priest who has left the Church has done so because of some scandalous infraction of the rule of celibacy. That is sufficient to give an idea of the spiritual condition of our clergy. If the news were spread in the diocese that another priest, one Don Benedetto, of Rocca dei Marsi, had abandoned the priesthood, the first explanation that would naturally occur to the faithful would be that yet another priest had eloped with his housemaid. I may also tell you that the only reason why I go on celebrating Mass is because I respect the simple souls about me and dislike to shock people uselessly. What am I to do?"

Comparing his own mind with that of the old man, the young one found some deep harmonies between the two, the existence of which he had not suspected before. He plucked up courage, and revealed his own bewilderment, described his own disappointments, his vain efforts to find some form of action that would rouse men's minds, his discovery at Pietrasecca of the peasants' indifference to all forms of propaganda, his recent conversation with the man from Pratola, revealing the sterility of many acts of violence. What was he to do?

Both now remained silent. Pupil and master were in the same quandary. Two lives, so different, had converged.

"One must be careful not to be led astray in the heat of the struggle by the artificial, the deceptive, the abstract," the old man said. "One must be careful not to chase apparent success. The evil I see around me is deeper than politics. It is a canker. You cannot heal a putrefying corpse with warm poultices. There is the class struggle, the town and the country, but underlying all these things there is a man, a poor, weak, terrified animal. The canker has penetrated to his marrow. . . ."

The younger man was in an exceptional state of receptivity. He listened to the old man, hung on his words for a suggestion, waited for guidance and advice. The old man felt this, and suddenly his words became more cautious.

"What then is to be done?" the young man asked again.

"In different measure and in different ways I have passed through the same experiences as you," the old man said. "I tried arguing with some of my former pupils, I took the trouble of refuting point by point the ideology of the dictatorship, that obscene hash of inanities concocted out of the spurious erudition of a handful of drunken doctors and propounded in the name of the State. It took me a long time to find out that I was wasting my time, because those to whom I spoke did not take the nonsense seriously themselves. Nevertheless, they are faithful servants of the dictatorship; they compete desperately for the honors it has to bestow, and outdo each other in acts of devotion to it at every opportunity. Even in the Marsica there have been isolated acts of violence, dictated by despair. They have not, however, reanimated the weak. On the contrary, they have only made them more intimidated than ever."

The old man stopped, and the younger man waited for him to go on. He remembered his school days, when the master had given his pupils a too difficult problem and refused to help them solve it. "If you don't know, why should I know?" he had said, with pretended seriousness. But this time the master was also at a loss. The old man and the young were at the same point. What was to be done?

"What our country lacks is not the critical spirit," the old man went on. "And it is often not without anonymous acts of violence either. Perhaps what it lacks is men. There are malcontents and there are perpetrators of violence, but Men are lacking. I, too, ask myself: what is to be done? . . . I am convinced that it would be a waste of time to show a people of intimidated slaves a different manner of speaking, a different manner of gesticulating; but perhaps it would be worth while to show them a different way of living. No word and no gesture can be more persuasive than the life, and, if necessary, the death, of a man who strives to be free, loyal, just, sincere, disinterested; a man who shows what a man can be."

The old man talked of a visit he had paid to Orta, the young man's native place.

"The people there talk of you, though they do not know what you are saying or what you are doing. They think of you because you represent a different race of men, a different way of living; and, since you were born among them, you represent what every young man at Orta might become."

"Is that enough?" the young man asked. "I do not think it is enough."

"For the time being I do not see anything else," the old man said. "One must respect time. Every season has its own work. There is the season for pruning the vines, the season for spraying them, the season for preparing the barrels, the season for gathering and pressing the grapes. If in spring, when the vines are being tied to the stakes, some one passes by and says: 'It is not worth while doing that, because if the barrels are bad the wine will be spoiled; the first thing to do is attend to the barrels,' you can answer him and say: 'Every season has its own work. This is not the season for cleaning out the barrels, but for pruning the vines and tying them to the stakes. Let me, therefore, remove the useless branches from the vines, let me prune and tie them to the stakes.'"

V.

A Literature of Disillusion: Anti-Utopia

Aldous Huxley used a passage in the works of Nikolay Berdyayev to introduce his novel, *Brave New World*—a passage in which the philosopher points out that Utopias appear far more possible today than they ever did before. The issue now, says Berdyayev, is not how to *realize* Utopia, but how to *prevent* its realization— how to oppose the constant developments in directions that (until quite recently) were still considered "Utopian," how to check further advances toward a state of things that certain thinkers continue to present by means of the Utopian convention as something to be desired.

Historically speaking this is a new attitude. Until recently Utopian schemes incited approval or disapproval but seldom, if ever, did they provoke fear, or the bitter opposition that a feeling of immediate danger can beget. The Utopian form traditionally eschews the notion of reality or immediacy. Utopia had always been nowhere, or at least very far away. After the First World War, this was no longer so: Utopia is with us, or just around the corner. Its name alone generates reactions based on quite concrete hopes or fears. It is quite significant that, whereas the classic Utopia stands in a sort of never-never land, out of time and space, the anti-Utopian novel of the 1940s (and on) has been brought closer and closer to us, not so much to foster an added sense of reality in the reader, as to reflect the sense of impending doom in the writer. Koestler's *Age of Longing* (1953) was set in the 1950s and so was the Third World War that breaks out at the end of Virgil Gheorghiu's *Twentyfifth Hour* (1949). Written in 1948, Orwell's *Nineteen Eighty-Four* foreshadowed what he saw as the day after tomorrow. It is not so widely known that we have another Utopian novel dated 1984—*The Napoleon of Notting Hill* by G. K. Chesterton. But Chesterton's 1984 (published in 1904) is a fantasy; Orwell's, on the other hand, was a deliberate projection of the immediate present into what is presented as the immediate future. Even Aldous Huxley (who in 1931, had dated his *Brave New World* six hundred years hence) explained in a foreword of 1946, "Today it seems quite possible that the horror may be upon us within a single century." Accordingly, *Ape and Essence,* which he published in 1948, dealt with a period much closer to our own. And the staid *Times Literary Supplement* (London, February 28, 1958), reviewing Mervyn Jones's *On the Last Day,* which deals with the Third World War, an ICBM race, and a world poisoned by destructive radiations, commented, "This is not Science Fiction. One would feel much happier if it were."

The Utopian novel, as a literary form, has proved an excellent vehicle for concepts of "the Good Life" or "the Good Society"; or again for criticism of the existing society, by caricaturing or dissecting its practices and concepts in the sort of satire with which we are familiar through the works of Swift and Voltaire. The anti-Utopian characteristic of our own century might be considered as a subdivision of Utopian satire. Yet it is peculiar to itself and particularized by the fact that, while it sometimes attacks existing societies or systems as such, it also and just as frequently attacks Utopian ideals—or what may appear as their fulfillment.

The anti-Utopians recognize in the society that they criticize the fulfillment of the dreams of yesterday. The ideal has triumphed, and the result is the theme of *The Twentyfifth Hour.* The world no longer belongs to men—it belongs to the "process," to the "machine" that has taken over. Men are ciphers, their fates inscribed in advance on the punch-cards of a gigantic IBM computer. It is "the Procrustean world" of Aldous Huxley, "made up by scientists—if mankind does not fit, too bad for mankind!" Or the robot world of Karel Čapek, in which mankind succumbs before Rossum's Universal Robots, first created to serve them.

In this as in other respects, Utopias and anti-Utopias reflect the great debate of our time—how to reconcile direction with freedom, free enterprise with a planned society. Another controversial novel of 1948 was written by a well-known behaviorist professor of psychology at Harvard, Brutus Frederick Skinner, to describe life in a Utopian community modeled on his own principles of social engineering. *Walden II* suggested that the effort to contrast freedom and conditioning was a spurious, outdated enterprise, raising "pseudo-questions of linguistic origin." "Our members are practically always doing what they want to do," asserts the planner of *Walden II,* "but we see to it that they will want to do precisely the things which are best for themselves and for the community." The only way to achieve freedom, it seems, is by creating an illusion of freedom. According to this view, freedom does not belong in the "good society"; it is no more than a conditioned reflex.

Advances in behavioral engineering and biocontrol appeared to corroborate such arguments. Rossum's Universal Robots may have been good enough for the 1920s, but by October 1956, the National Electronics Conference in Chicago could consider the prospect of biocontrol defined as "the control of physical movements, mental processes, emotional reactions and apparent sensory perceptions . . . by means of bioelectrical signals which are injected into the central nervous system of the subject." Perhaps, as Winston Smith eventually learns to admit in *Nineteen Eighty-Four,* "Freedom IS Slavery," and perhaps biocontrolled slavery is the nearest approach to freedom that our time can expect. However, it is not surprising that, with such ominous prospects before us, with realities almost as ominous around us, and with Utopias like *Walden II* to provoke them, the anti-Utopian writers believe that they are dealing with present problems and present dangers that affect them and their readers with an immediacy that never existed before.

That is why their work reflects the kind of disillusion and fear for which there would have been no material basis in another age. Until the twentieth century no large-scale attempts had been made to carry out Utopian concepts. There was the abortive reign of the Anabaptists in Münster; there were the programs of the enlightened despots—limited in scope and even more so in achievement. But their failure was never the failure of the Utopian dream itself: no one ever defaced Cythera, because the right ship for it never sailed. And, in any case, Cythera was always somewhere else. In earlier Utopian satires the horror is localized—either in time or in space. But in 1918, an Englishman, Owen Gregory, published *Meccania—The Super-State*—the bitter caricature of a totalitarian police-state isolated from the rest of the world in concentration-camp-like horror. *Meccania,* which refers to Germany, may seem somewhat premature and its plot still allows a possibility of escape. But the sense of doom is already present: "It seemed not impossible," writes the visitor who has left Meccania, "that the nightmare I had escaped from was a doom impending over the whole world . . . I could not dismiss this doubt. . . ." Very soon, what was doubtful in Owen Gregory appears with certainty in Karel Čapek and Zamiatin. In *R.U.R.* (1920) and *We* (1924) escape is hardly conceivable; the utterness of human defeat is ensured by the heights of human ingenuity. The influence of the First World War, its high hopes, its horror, and the anxious uncertainty that followed it, are evident. A cartoon by Max Beerbohm describes "The Future as the Twentieth Century Sees It": a haggard young man with a hopeless look gazes out at a great impenetrable mist and, on the mist, a vast question mark. To Max Weber, the mist seemed less impenetrable. In one of his lectures delivered at Munich after the war he offered his opinion of the future: before Germany and mankind there lay "a polar night of icy darkness and hardship." And, late in 1918, the Austrian poet Stefan Zweig wrote to Fridericke, his wife: "In the political sphere, an infinity of horror confronts us, endless, pathless, and at the end—catastrophe!" Like Valéry, these men entertained no doubt that our civilization, like all others, was mortal—and mortally wounded.

Perhaps, after all, it is the failure of eighteenth-century rationalism and of its dreams that these men mourned, but the significant thing is that until today we could not be sure. Every partial failure, every shot at perfection that missed, merely turned the eyes of men toward another panacea, toward another pattern, toward another plan. Nor is this over. But our generation has seen so many hopes realized only to be broken, and every Utopian illusion (Russian, Nazi, British, American, technological, and psychological) has furnished its quota of disillusioned anti-Utopians. Theirs is not a romantic Utopianism, yearning back toward a golden age or toward a simpler primitive life. (The Savage in *Brave New World* is no more attractive than his more progressive contemporaries.) And, of course, they know better than to offer one more cure-all in lieu of the others that have failed. This is what makes them not just opponents of one Utopian pattern but opponents of the Utopian heresy as such. For them there can be no salvation by legislation. They point out how, in trying to make man and society perfect, the Utopian has twisted both into a gruesome shape. They see the triumph of the artificial world, which the old Utopias imagined and which their contemporary imitations enforce, as the defeat of humanity and the defeat of man. There is not even room for such elites as had atoned to some extent for the stupefaction of underprivileged masses in an earlier day. In a book of 1942, *Gardens and Streets,* Ernst Jünger complains that the situation of the individual scientist "has become similar to that of the individual worker standing behind the machine." The work has become automated and the human being more and more replaceable and dispensable. "He can be exchanged like a machine part and, even the results to which he attains, even his perceptions, are born outside of him and rather implement the process than penetrate into him. The indispensability of the human being is disappearing with his originality and, together with these, respect for him also disappears."

This is the defeat of man: a situation in which order means regimentation; content means conditioning; education means indoctrination; freedom is only a conditioned reflex. The new security and social discipline are those of the concentration camp—potential in concepts like those presented in *Walden II*, actual in works like those of Gregory, Zamiatin, and Orwell. This actualization of the potential—both of Utopia and of real life—is characteristic of anti-Utopias as it is of our times. Nowadays what Daniel Halévy has called "the acceleration of history" allows illusion to become disillusion within a very short period. So what used to be a dream (in Russia, or Germany, or America) has become a nightmare that makes the anti-Utopian afraid and, like anyone awakened from a nightmare, reluctant to return to any dreaming at all. More than mere disillusion with existing conditions and aspirations, the anti-Utopian expresses the conviction that there is no hope elsewhere, no hope in what must be only variations on the same theme. The Utopian is either a hopeful critic or a hopeful rebel, because he has an alternative to offer; and bitter Utopian satires like Jack London's *The Iron Heel* still sound a note of hope. The anti-Utopian does not believe in alternatives: it is too late for that. He is defeated before he starts. That is why we find him where disillusion can be most thoroughly experienced, where the utmost awareness might be expected of the implications and results of Utopian reforms. In Britain, for example, where brave new worlds have fizzled out too often, the late 1980s brought a crop of novels foretelling the horrors of post-Thatcherite moldering or apocalypse: social decay, environmental disasters, class warfare, race friction, bizarre diseases, spiritual malaise, nuclear holocaust.

Americans do not yet appear really disillusioned with the possibilities open to them in the political field. They have produced satires of the bitterest kind, but the dread and despair characteristic of anti-Utopia appear only in the work of the "technologists"—Bradbury, Vonnegut, Asimov, etc.—who see the machines taking over; human personality, initiative, fantasy, lost or hamstrung in a sea of gadgets; experience garnered vicariously through electronic apparatus; independence surrendered or abolished for a mess of conditioned security. The anti-Utopian novel in America is just as despairing, the defeat of the individual is just as certain, but it is achieved by different means that reflect the author's different experience. Even so, American anti-Utopias are relatively recent, rare, and significantly camouflaged behind the appropriate but conveniently protective apparatus of science fiction.

Insofar as the anti-Utopian allows us a glimmer of hope, it lies in the instincts, in fantasy, in the irrational, in the peculiarly individualistic and egotistic characteristics most likely to fracture any system or order. This accounts for the importance of basic feelings—sex, love, selfishness, fantasy—that all Utopian planners try to control and in which all anti-Utopians seem to put their faith (what they have of it). Again and again, like Ray Bradbury in his remarkable short story, "Usher II," the anti-Utopian calls on the irrational to disrupt and destroy the planned order. Nor does it matter very much what the order is: "New presbyter is but old priest writ large." The intention is to shun systems and orders altogether, to assert the lonely individual against a society too satisfied with itself, its ends, and its means.

Yet, if the anti-Utopians are eager to reassert neglected human values, we must not forget that, in a sense, the Utopia is the characteristic manifestation of the Western cultural tradition. The search for order, the drive to harness nature and eliminate the unpredictable, are eminently human and peculiarly Western. The presumption of man, always biting off more of the fruit of the tree of knowledge than he can chew, is a stock mythological situation. Just as traditionally, his pride goes before a fall: he reaches to the sky and his tower topples over; he tries to be godlike and he is chained to a rock or cast out of Eden. The Church is familiar with the heresy that man can build a paradise on earth; and it condemns over and over again the Utopian heresy—the idea that a good society can be shaped according to the concepts of human reason. Obviously, our friends are on the side of the angels—or, at least, on that of the Church: where Utopia expresses the ambitious temerity, anti-Utopia stresses the Fall. In Isaac Asimov's novel *The End of Eternity,* men have acquired control of Eternity and find themselves at last to be masters of their fate. But they cannot deny with impunity those mysterious and uncontrollable elements that make for failure: another Adam is tempted by another Eve, and man is expelled from Eternity as he was from Eden.

And so, over and over again, the anti-Utopian warns against tinkering with nature, and prophesies failure and doom for those who persist. Yet this very antithetic character of his work indicates its close connection with the thesis it attacks: to plan and to despair are both reasonable, both human. Utopia and anti-Utopia are the strophe and antistrophe of a chorus commenting the doings of man. They continue the long debate between society and the individual, order and anarchy, affirmation and denial, every one of these theses dangerous if pressed too far and needing an antithesis just as potentially violent.

It is not surprising, therefore, that an age grown disillusioned with the omnipotence of human reason and the results of Utopian presumption should produce the anti-Utopia: not simply irrationalistic denial, but deeply skeptical and aware that dreams—if pressed too far—lead either to alarming nightmares or to frustrated waking.

Valéry

Paul Valéry (1871–1945), delicate and precise poet and essayist, was born at Sète, on the coast of the Mediterranean, of a Corsican father and an Italian mother. After an uneventful provincial youth, he arrived in Paris armed with a law degree from the University of Montpellier, a great admiration for the music of Wagner, and an already well-developed talent for mathematics and poetry. He became friends with lively minded young men like André Gide and Pierre Louys, who introduced him to the Symbolist circles revolving around Mallarmé, whose friend he also became. In the 1890s Valéry published a number of poems that were well received by the young literati, and two prose pieces. He wanted to dedicate the most striking of these, *An Evening with M. Teste,* to Edgar Degas, but forbore to do so on the artist's refusal.

Over ten years of silence followed: nothing more by Valéry appeared in print until the now not-so-young man started to publish once more. His post as private secretary of the retired, but still active and influential, head of the French Information Agency, *Havas,* left him plenty of time for his own cogitations and writing, but at the same time kept him close to the affairs of the world. The selection that follows, written in 1919 and taken from one of the five volumes of collected essays Valéry published between 1924 and 1944, reflects the negative, wistful, yet hopeless mood of a clear-sighted man living through the wake of the war.

The Intellectual Crisis

We civilizations, we know now that we are mortal.

We had heard tell of worlds wholly vanished, empires that sank like a stone, with all men and equipment on board, down into the unattainable depths of time, with their gods and their laws, their academies and their pure and applied sciences, with their grammars and their dictionaries, their classics, their romantics, their symbolists, their critics and the critics of their critics. We knew perfectly well that all the visible world is made of ashes, and that the ashes stand for something. We had glimpsed, through the depths of history, the phantom shapes of vast vessels once laden with riches and knowledge. Count them we could not. But these shipwrecks, after all, were none of our business.

Elam, Nineveh, Babylon, were beautiful vague names, and the total ruin of

---

Source: From *Variété,* Paris, Editions Gallimard, 1924. Translated by Eugen Weber.

those worlds held as little significance for us as their existence itself. But *France, England, Russia* . . . would also be beautiful names, *Lusitania* is also a beautiful name. And now we see that the chasm of history is big enough to hold everybody. We sense that a civilization is as fragile as a life. The circumstances which would send the works of Keats and those of Baudelaire to join those of Menander are no longer inconceivable: they are in the papers.

This is not all. The burning admonition is even more complete: it was not enough for our generation to learn from its own experience how the most beautiful things and the oldest, the most impressive, the best ordered, may *accidentally* perish: it has seen in the realm of thought, of feeling, and of common sense, extraordinary events, paradoxes suddenly come true, the brutal distortion of the obvious.

To give only one example: the great virtues of the German peoples have begotten more evils than all the vices ever created by idleness. We have seen, seen with our own eyes, the most conscientious labor, the most solid education, the most serious discipline and diligence, adapted to frightful purposes.

So many horrors would not have been possible without so many virtues. There is no doubt that much skill was needed to kill so many men, to waste so much wealth, to annihilate so many cities in so short a time; but *moral qualities* were no less needed. Knowledge and Duty, are you then to be suspected?

Thus the spiritual Persepolis has been laid waste like the materialistic Susa. All is not lost, but all has felt itself decaying.

An extraordinary chill has run down the spine of Europe, it has felt in all its senses that it did not recognize itself any longer, that it no longer resembled itself, that it was going to lose consciousness, a consciousness acquired through centuries of bearable suffering, through thousands of first-class men, through innumerable geographical, historical, and ethnic hazards.

Then—as for a desperate defense of its being, of its psychological possessions, all its memory confusedly returned. Its great men and its great books rose again, pell-mell, to the surface. Never have people read so much and so passionately as during the war: ask the booksellers. Never have people prayed so much and so profoundly: ask the priests. One called upon all the saviors, the founders, the protectors, the martyrs, the heroes, the founding fathers, the saintly heroines, the national poets. . . .

And in the same mental disorder, under the pressure of the same anxieties, cultivated Europe saw the rapid revival of innumerable ideas: dogmas, philosophies, heterogeneous ideals; the three hundred ways of elucidating the World; the thousand and one nuances of Christianity; the two dozen assorted shades of positivism; the whole spectrum of intellectual light displayed its matchless colors, shedding a strange, contradictory glimmer over the agony of the European soul. While scientists feverishly sought in their imaginations and in the annals of the wars of yesteryear the means to be rid of barbed wire, to avoid submarines, to paralyze the flight of planes, the soul invoked all at once all the incantations that it knew, and gave serious consideration to the strangest prophecies; it sought refuges, indications, consolations, throughout the whole record of memories, of earlier activities, of ancestral attitudes. And these are the known products of anxiety, the disorderly enterprises of the brain which runs from reality to nightmare and back from nightmare to reality, distracted like a rat in a trap. . . .

The military crisis may be over. The economic crisis is obvious and going full blast; but the intellectual crisis, which is more subtle, and which, by its very nature, takes the most misleading aspects (since it takes place in the very kingdom of dissimulation), this crisis does not easily allow us to grasp its true point, the phase it has reached.

No one can tell what will tomorrow be living or dead in literature, in philosophy, in aesthetics; no one yet knows which ideas and which modes of expression will be counted as losses, and what novelties will be proclaimed.

Certainly, hope remains and softly sings:

> *Et cum vorandi vicerit libidinem*
> *Late triumphet imperator spiritus.*[1]

But hope is merely man's suspicion of the precise conjectures of his mind. It suggests that all forecast unfavorable to us *must be* an error of judgment. The facts, however, are clear and implacable: there are the thousands of young artists and writers who have died; there is the lost illusion of an European culture, and the demonstration that knowledge is powerless to save anything; there is science, mortally wounded in its moral aspirations and as if dishonored by the cruelty of its applications; there is idealism, triumphant only with difficulty, profoundly bruised, responsible for its dreams; there is realism, deceived, defeated, overwhelmed by crimes and mistakes; covetousness and renunciation equally scouted; religious beliefs confused in both camps, cross against cross, crescent against crescent; there are the skeptics themselves, baffled by events so sudden, so violent, so moving, and which play with our thoughts like a cat with a mouse: the skeptics lose their doubts,

---

[1]Certainly, hope remains
But hope is merely man's suspicion.

find them again, lose them again, no longer know how to cope with the movements of their mind.

The ship has swung so hard that the best hung lanterns have upset at last.

What makes the intellectual crisis so grave and so profound is the state in which it found the patient.

I have neither the time nor the power to define the intellectual state of Europe in 1914. And who would dare to trace a picture of that state? The subject is immense: it calls for every kind of knowledge, for an infinite amount of information. Besides, when it is a question of such a complex whole, the difficulty of reconstituting the past, even the most recent past, is quite comparable to the difficulty of building the future, even the most immediate future; or, rather, the difficulty is the same. The prophet and the historian are in the same sack. Let us leave them there.

But right now I need only the vague and general memory of what was being thought on the eve of war, of the research that went on, of the works that were being published.

Hence, if I omit all the detail and limit myself to the hasty impression, to this *natural total* provided by an instantaneous impression, I see—*nothing!*—Nothing, though it be an infinitely rich nothing.

The physicists tell us that if our eye could subsist in an incandescent oven, it would see—nothing. No luminous variation is left to distinguish points in space. Shut up, this tremendous energy ends in invisibility, in imperceptible equality. Now, an equality of this sort is nothing but perfect *disorder.*

And in what consisted the disorder of our mental Europe? In the free coexistence in all cultivated minds of the most different ideas, of the most contradictory principles of life and knowledge. That is the characteristic of a *modern* age.

I do not mind generalizing the notion of modernity and giving this name to a certain way of life, rather than use it simply as a synonym of *contemporary.* There are times and places in history into which we could enter, *we moderns,* without excessively troubling their harmony, and without appearing ourselves as infinitely odd objects, infinitely obvious—shocking, dissonant, inassimilable beings. Where our appearance would produce the least sensation, there we are almost at home. It is clear that Trajan's Rome and the Alexandria of the Ptolemies would absorb us more easily than many places nearer in time but more specialized in a single sort of *mores* and wholly devoted to one race, one culture, one way of life.

Well! the Europe of 1914 had perhaps reached the limits of this modernism. Every mind of a certain level was a crossroads for every sort of opinion; every thinker was a universal exhibition of ideas. There were works whose wealth of contrasts and of contradictory motives brought to mind the insane light effects of the capitals of the time: the eyes burn and get bored. . . . How much material, how much work and calculation and how many centuries despoiled, how many heterogeneous lives all added together were needed to make this carnival possible, to set it up as the embodiment of supreme wisdom and the triumph of humanity?

In a given book of the time—and not one of the worst—one finds, without any effort—the influence of the Russian ballets—a little of Pascal's somber style—many impressions of the Goncourt sort—something of Nietzsche—something of Rimbaud—certain things due to the frequentation of painters, and sometimes the tone of scientific publications—all this scented with a touch of something British, difficult to assess! Let it be said in passing that in every component of this mixture one would find plenty of other *bodies*. No use looking for them: it would be a repetition of what I have just said about modernism, and it would involve the whole mental history of Europe.

Today, from an immense terrace of Elsinore, that runs from Basel to Cologne, that touches on the sands of Nieuport, on the marshes of the Somme, on the chalky soil of Champagne, on the granite of Alsace—from this terrace, the European Hamlet looks upon millions of ghosts.

But he is an intellectual Hamlet. He meditates on the life and death of truths. His ghosts are all the subjects of our controversies; his remorse is derived from all our titles to glory; he is overwhelmed by the weight of discoveries, of knowledge; he cannot let himself be caught up once more in this limitless activity. He thinks of the weary task of starting the past all over again, of the folly of always wanting to innovate. He balances between two chasms, for two dangers never cease to threaten the world: order and disorder.

If he picks up a skull, it is an illustrious one.—Whose was it?—This one was *Leonardo*. He invented flying man, but flying man has not precisely carried out the inventor's intentions: we know that flying man, mounted on his great swan (*il grande ucello sopra del dosso del suo magnis ceccero*) has in our day other tasks than going to fetch snow from the mountaintops in order to throw it, on hot days, on the cobbles of our cities. . . . And this other skull is that of *Leibnitz* who dreamt of universal peace. And this one was *Kant, Kant qui genuit Hegel, qui genuit Marx, qui genuit*. . . .

Hamlet does not exactly know what to do with all these skulls. But if he abandons them! . . . Will he not cease being himself? His mind, dreadfully clear-sighted, contemplates the transition from war to peace. It is a more obscure, more dangerous transition than that from peace to war; all the peoples are troubled by it. "And I," he says to himself—"I, the European intellectual—what will become of me? . . . And what is peace? *Peace is perhaps the state of things in which the natural hostility of men expresses itself through creations, instead of through destructions as in war.* It is the time of creative competition, and of the production struggle. But I, am I not weary of producing? Have I not exhausted the yearning for extreme endeavors, have I not had too much of skillful mixtures? Must I leave aside my difficult duties and my transcendent ambitions? Must I follow the trend and imitate Polonius who now directs a big newspaper? or Laertes who is somewhere in the air force? or Rosencrantz who is doing I do not quite know what under a Russian name?

—"Farewell, phantoms! The world needs you no more. Nor does it need me. The world, which calls progress its tendency toward a fatal precision, seeks to join the advantages of death to the good things of life. A certain confusion still reigns, but wait a little while and all will become clear; we shall see appear at last the miracle of the animal society—a perfect and final ant-heap."

Huxley

Aldous Leonard Huxley (1894–1963), a scion of the great Huxley-Arnold clan, was educated at Eton and Balliol College, Oxford, and, after coming down from Oxford, wrote for London reviews until literary success (coming first in 1921 with *Crome Yellow*) set him free to produce a brilliantly witty series of social satires that impaled human foibles for his and his readers' wry amazement. A vast range of interests enriched the list of his publications, which include two very penetrating historical studies of France in the days of Cardinal Richelieu: *Grey Eminence* and *The Devils of Loudun*.

Brave New World was published in 1932. It was followed by two other novels of the same ilk—*After Many a Summer Dies the Swan* (1939) and *Ape and Essence* (1948). Many essays carried variations on the same theme—one increasingly relevant to the postwar climate of opinion and its dominant preoccupation with the destruction of man's personality if not of man himself. The essay that follows was written in 1946, as an introduction to a new, postwar edition of *Brave New World*, which had by then become a classic. Fourteen years had allowed for second thoughts, but not for many, and though Huxley's tone was still faintly hopeful, the hope seemed to be ebbing as what had once seemed merely an amusingly clever invention now looked far too real for comfort.

Preface to the 1946 Edition of *Brave New World*

Chronic remorse, as all the moralists are agreed, is a most undesirable sentiment. If you have behaved badly, repent, make what amends you can and address yourself to the task of behaving better next time. On no account brood over your wrongdoing. Rolling in the muck is not the best way of getting clean.

Art also has its morality, and many of the rules of this morality are the same as, or at least analogous to, the rules of ordinary ethics. Remorse, for example, is as undesirable in relation to our bad art as it is in relation to our bad behaviour. The badness should be hunted out, acknowledged and, if possible, avoided in the future. To pore over the literary shortcomings of twenty years ago, to attempt to patch a faulty work into the perfection it missed at its first execution, to spend one's middle age in trying to mend the artistic sins committed and bequeathed by the different person who was oneself in youth—all this is surely vain and futile. And that is why this new *Brave New World* is the same as the old one. Its defects as a work of art are considerable; but in order to correct them I should have to rewrite the book—and in the process of rewriting, as an older, other person, I should probably get rid not only of some of the faults of the story, but also of such merits as it originally possessed. And so, resisting the temptation to wallow in artistic remorse, I prefer to leave both well and ill alone and to think about something else.

In the meantime, however, it seems worth while at least to mention the most serious defect in the story, which is this. The Savage is offered only two alternatives, an insane life in Utopia, or the life of a primitive in an Indian village, a life more human in some respects, but in others hardly less queer and abnormal. At the time the book was written, this idea, that human beings are given free will in order to choose between insanity on the one hand and lunacy on the other, was one that I found amusing and regarded as quite possibly true. For the sake, however, of dramatic effect, the Savage is often permitted to speak more rationally than his upbringing among the practitioners of a religion that is half fertility cult and half *Penitente* ferocity would actually warrant. Even his acquaintance with Shakespeare would not in reality justify such utterances. And at the close, of course, he is made to retreat from sanity; his native *Penitente*-ism reasserts its authority and he ends in maniacal

---

Source: Preface from *Brave New World* by Aldous Huxley. Copyright 1932, 1960 by Aldous Huxley. Reprinted by permission of HarperCollins Publishers.

self-torture and despairing suicide. "And so they died miserably ever after"—much to the reassurance of the amused, Pyrrhonic aesthete who was the author of the fable.

Today I feel no wish to demonstrate that sanity is impossible. On the contrary, though I remain no less sadly certain than in the past that sanity is a rather rare phenomenon, I am convinced that it can be achieved and would like to see more of it. For having said so in several recent books and, above all, for having compiled an anthology of what the sane have said about sanity and the means whereby it can be achieved, I have been told by an eminent academic critic that I am a sad symptom of the failure of an intellectual class in time of crisis. The implication being, I suppose, that the professor and his colleagues are hilarious symptoms of success. The benefactors of humanity deserve due honour and commemoration. Let us build a Pantheon for professors. It should be located among the ruins of one of the gutted cities of Europe or Japan, and over the entrance to the ossuary I would inscribe, in letters six or seven feet high, the simple words: *Sacred to the Memory of the World's Educators*. SI MONUMENTUM REQUIRIS CIRCUMSPICE.

But to return to the future. . . . If I were now to rewrite the book, I would offer the Savage a third alternative. Between the utopian and the primitive horns of his dilemma would lie the possibility of sanity—a possibility already actualized, to some extent, in a community of exiles and refugees from the Brave New World, living within the borders of the Reservation. In this community economics would be decentralist and Henry-Georgian, politics Kropotkinesque co-operative. Science and technology would be used as though, like the Sabbath, they had been made for man, not (as at present and still more so in the Brave New World) as though man were to be adapted and enslaved to them. Religion would be the conscious and intelligent pursuit of man's Final End, the unitive knowledge of the immanent Tao or Logos, the transcendent Godhead or Brahman. And the prevailing philosophy of life would be a kind of Higher Utilitarianism, in which the Greatest Happiness principle would be secondary to the Final End principle—the first question to be asked and answered in every contingency of life being: "How will this thought or action contribute to, or interfere with, the achievement, by me and the greatest possible number of other individuals, of man's Final End?"

Brought up among the primitives, the Savage (in this hypothetical new version of the book) would not be transported to Utopia until he had had an opportunity of learning something at first hand about the nature of a society composed of freely co-operating individuals devoted to the pursuit of sanity. Thus altered, *Brave New World* would possess artistic and (if it is permissible to use so large a word in connection with a work of fiction) a philosophical completeness, which in its present form it evidently lacks.

But *Brave New World* is a book about the future and, whatever its artistic or philosophical qualities, a book about the future can interest us only if its prophecies look as though they might conceivably come true. From our present vantage point, fifteen years further down the inclined plane of modern history, how plausible do its prognostications seem? What has happened in the painful interval to confirm or invalidate the forecasts of 1931?

One vast and obvious failure of foresight is immediately apparent. *Brave New World* contains no reference to nuclear fission. That it does not is actually rather odd, for the possibilities of atomic energy had been a popular topic of conversation for years before the book was written. My old friend, Robert Nichols, had even written a successful play about the subject, and I recall that I myself had casually mentioned it in a novel published in the late twenties. So it seems, as I say, very odd that the rockets and helicopters of the seventh century of Our Ford should not have been powered by disintegrating nuclei. The oversight may not be excusable; but at least it can be easily explained. The theme of *Brave New World* is not the advancement of science as such; it is the advancement of science as it affects human individuals. The triumphs of physics, chemistry and engineering are tacitly taken for granted. The only scientific advances to be specifically described are those involving the application to human beings of the results of future research in biology, physiology and psychology. It is only by means of the sciences of life that the quality of life can be radically changed. The sciences of matter can be applied in such a way that they will destroy life or make the living of it impossibly complex and uncomfortable; but, unless used as instruments by the biologists and psychologists, they can do nothing to modify the natural forms and expressions of life itself. The release of atomic energy marks a great revolution in human history, but not (unless we blow ourselves to bits and so put an end to history) the final and most searching revolution.

This really revolutionary revolution is to be achieved, not in the external world, but in the souls and flesh of human beings. Living as he did in a revolutionary period, the Marquis de Sade very naturally made use of this theory of revolutions in order to rationalize his peculiar brand of insanity. Robespierre had achieved the most superficial kind of revolution, the political. Going a little deeper, Babeuf had attempted the economic revolution. Sade regarded himself as the apostle of the truly revolutionary revolution, beyond mere politics and economics—the revolution in individual men, women and children, whose bodies were henceforward to become the common sexual property of all and whose minds were to be purged of all the natural decencies, all the laboriously acquired inhibitions of traditional civilization. Between sadism and the really revolutionary revolution there is, of course, no necessary or inevitable connection. Sade was a lunatic and the more or less conscious goal of his revolution was universal chaos and destruction. The people who govern the Brave New World may not be sane (in what may be called the absolute sense of the word); but they are not madmen, and their aim is not anarchy but social stability. It is in order to achieve stability that they carry out, by scientific means, the ultimate, personal, really revolutionary revolution.

But meanwhile we are in the first phase of what is perhaps the penultimate revolution. Its next phase may be atomic warfare, in which case we do not have to bother with prophecies about the future. But it is conceivable that we may have enough sense, if not to stop fighting altogether, at least to behave as rationally as did our eighteenth-century ancestors. The unimaginable horrors of the Thirty Years' War actually taught men a lesson, and for more than a hundred years the politicians and generals of Europe consciously resisted the temptation to use their military resources to the limits of destructiveness or (in the majority of conflicts) to go on fighting until the enemy was totally annihilated. They were aggressors, of course, greedy for profit and glory; but they were also conservatives, determined at all costs to keep their world intact, as a going concern. For the last thirty years there have been no conservatives; there have been only nationalistic radicals of the right and nationalistic radicals of the left. The last conservative statesman was the fifth Marquess of Lansdowne; and when he wrote a letter to the *Times*, suggesting that the First World War should be concluded with a compromise, as most of the wars of the eighteenth century had been, the editor of that once conservative journal refused to print it. The nationalistic radicals had their way, with the consequences that we all know—Bolshevism, Fascism, inflation, depression, Hitler, the Second World War, the ruin of Europe and all but universal famine.

Assuming, then, that we are capable of learning as much from Hiroshima as our forefathers learned from Magdeburg, we may look forward to a period, not indeed of peace, but of limited and only partially ruinous warfare. During that period it may be assumed that nuclear energy will be harnessed to industrial uses. The result, pretty obviously, will be a series of economic and social changes unprecedented in rapidity and completeness. All the existing patterns of human life will be disrupted and new patterns will have to be improvised to conform with the nonhuman fact of atomic power. Procrustes in modern dress, the nuclear scientist will prepare the bed on which mankind must lie; and if mankind doesn't fit—well, that will be just too bad for mankind. There will have to be some stretching and a bit of amputation—the same sort of stretching and amputations as have been going on ever since applied science really got into its stride, only this time they will be a good deal more drastic than in the past. These far from painless operations will be directed by highly centralized totalitarian governments. Inevitably so; for the immediate future is likely to resemble the immediate past, and in the immediate past rapid technological changes, taking place in a mass-producing economy and among a population predominantly propertyless, have always tended to produce economic and social confusion. To deal with confusion, power has been centralized and government control increased. It is probable that all the world's governments will be more or less completely totalitarian even before the harnessing of atomic energy; that they will be totalitarian during and after the harnessing seems almost certain. Only a large-scale popular movement toward decentralization and self-help can arrest the present tendency toward statism. At present there is no sign that such a movement will take place.

There is, of course, no reason why the new totalitarianisms should resemble the old. Government by clubs and firing squads, by artificial famine, mass imprisonment and mass deportation, is not merely inhumane (nobody cares much about that nowadays); it is demonstrably inefficient and in an age of advanced technology, inefficiency is the sin against the Holy Ghost. A really efficient totalitarian state would be one in which the all-powerful executive of political bosses and their army of managers control a population of slaves who do not have to be coerced, because they love their servitude. To make them love it is the task assigned, in present-day totalitarian states, to ministries of propaganda, newspaper editors and schoolteachers. But their methods are still crude and unscientific. The old Jesuits' boast that, if they were given the schooling of the child, they could answer for the man's religious opinions, was a product of wishful thinking. And the modern pedagogue is probably rather less efficient at conditioning his pupils' reflexes than were the reverend fathers who educated Voltaire. The greatest triumphs of propaganda have been accomplished, not by doing something, but by refraining from doing. Great is truth, but still greater, from a practical point of view, is silence about truth. By simply not mentioning certain subjects, by lowering what Mr. Churchill calls an "iron curtain" between the masses and such facts or arguments as the local political bosses regard as undesirable, totalitarian propagandists have influenced opinion much more effectively than they could have done by the most eloquent denunciations, the most compelling of logical rebuttals. But silence is not enough. If persecution, liquidation and the other symptoms of social friction are to be avoided, the positive sides of propaganda must be made as effective as the negative. The most important Manhattan Projects of the future will be vast government-sponsored enquiries into what the politicians and the participating scientists will call "the problem of happiness"—in other words, the problem of making people love their servitude. Without economic security, the love of servitude cannot possibly come into existence; for the sake of brevity, I assume that the all-powerful executive and it managers will succeed in solving the problem of permanent security. But security tends very quickly to be taken for granted. Its achievement is merely a superficial, external revolution. The love of servitude cannot be established except as the result of a deep, personal revolution in human minds and bodies. To bring about that revolution we require, among others, the following discoveries and inventions. First, a greatly improved technique of suggestion—through infant conditioning and, later, with the aid of drugs, such as scopolamine. Second, a fully developed science of human differences, enabling government managers to assign any given individual to his or her proper place in the social and economic hierarchy. (Round pegs in square holes tend to have dangerous thoughts about the social system and to infect others with their discontents.) Third (since reality, however utopian, is something from which people feel the need of taking pretty frequent holidays), a substitute for alcohol and the other narcotics, something at once less harmful and more pleasure-giving than gin or heroin. And fourth (but this would be a long-term project, which it would take generations of totalitarian control to bring to a successful conclusion), a foolproof system of eugenics, designed to standardize the human product and so to facilitate the task of the managers. In *Brave New World* this standardization of the human product has been pushed to fantastic, though not perhaps impossible, extremes. Technically and ideologically we are still a long way from bottled babies and Bokanovsky groups of semi-morons. But by A.F. 600, who knows what may not be happening? Meanwhile the other characteristic features of that happier and more stable world—the equivalents of soma and hypnopaedia and the scientific caste system—are probably not more than three or four generations away. Nor does the sexual promiscuity of *Brave New World* seem so very distant. There are already certain American cities in which the number of divorces is equal to the number of marriages. In a few years, no doubt, marriage licenses will be sold like dog licenses, good for a period of twelve months, with no law against changing dogs or keeping more than one animal at a time. As political and economic freedom diminishes, sexual freedom tends compensatingly to increase. And the dictator (unless he needs cannon fodder and families with which to colonize empty or conquered territories) will do well to encourage that freedom. In conjunction with the freedom to daydream under the influence of dope and movies and the radio, it will help to reconcile his subjects to the servitude which is their fate.

All things considered it looks as though Utopia were far closer to us than anyone, only fifteen years ago, could have imagined. Then, I projected it six hundred years into the future. Today it seems quite possible that the horror may be upon us within a single century. That is, if we refrain from blowing ourselves to smithereens in the interval. Indeed, unless we choose to decentralize and to use applied science, not as the end to which human beings are to be made the means, but as the means to producing a race of free individuals, we have only two alternatives to choose from: either a number of national, militarized totalitarianisms, having as their root the terror of the atomic bomb and as their consequence the destruction of civilization (or, if the warfare is limited, the perpetuation of militarism); or else one supranational totalitarianism, called into existence by the social chaos resulting from rapid technological progress in general and the atomic revolution in particular, and developing, under the need for efficiency and stability, into the welfare-tyranny of Utopia. You pays your money and you takes your choice.

1946.

Orwell

George Orwell (1903–1950) was born in India, educated at Eton, which he hated, served as a police officer in Burma in the 1920s, as a dishwasher in Paris in the 1930s, as a volunteer on the Republican side during the Spanish war, and as a radio and newspaper correspondent during the Second World War. Before the war he had published several books that had met with little attention, though some of them—*The Road to Wigan Pier, Down and Out in London and Paris, Homage to Catalonia*—have come to be recognized as minor classics. His name became widely known only after *Animal Farm,* a satire on Soviet Russia, appeared in 1945.

His next book, *Nineteen Eighty-Four,* written in 1948 and published a year before his death, provides not only an ominous prophecy for the future but also a detailed analysis of the processes of mass stupefaction that Orwell considered inherent in present trends. The book is one of the most bitterly desperate interpretations of man's future that our times have produced, and the passage that follows should provide a suggestion of what Orwell thought was in store for us.

In 1984, the world is divided among three totalitarian states—Oceania, Eurasia, and Eastasia—constantly at war with each other though the alliance pattern keeps changing, ruled by omnipotent Parties whose only concern is to perpetuate their power over an animalized multitude by every possible means. Winston Smith, a minor Party member employed in the Oceanian Ministry of Truth where he is engaged in deforming facts and rewriting history, gets into trouble partly through his growing inability to believe unquestioningly the lies he helps to manufacture, and partly because of his deviationist sexual activities. Arrested by the Thought Police, he is taken to the Ministry of Love where his thinking will be readjusted to the will of the Party and to the true reality he had tried to flout. His mentor, O'Brien, an official of the

Thought Police who had played a part in leading Smith into heresy, now does his best to reeducate him and make him reaccept the principles of the Party's rule.

Nineteen Eighty-Four

"There are three stages in your reintegration," said O'Brien. "There is learning, there is understanding, and there is acceptance. It is time for you to enter upon the second stage."

As always, Winston was lying flat on his back. But of late his bonds were looser. They still held him to the bed, but he could move his knees a little and could turn his head from side to side and raise his arms from the elbow. The dial, also, had grown to be less of a terror. He could evade its pangs if he was quick-witted enough; it was chiefly when he showed stupidity that O'Brien pulled the lever. Sometimes they got through a whole session without use of the dial. He could not remember how many sessions there had been. The whole process seemed to stretch out over a long, indefinite time—weeks, possibly—and the intervals between the sessions might sometimes have been days, sometimes only an hour or two.

"As you lie there," said O'Brien, "you have often wondered—you have even asked me—why the Ministry of Love should expend so much time and trouble on you. And when you were free you were puzzled by what was essentially the same question. You could grasp the mechanics of the society you lived in, but not its underlying motives. Do you remember writing in your diary, 'I understand *how*; I do not understand *why*'? It was when you thought about 'why' that you doubted your own sanity. You have read *the book*, Goldstein's book, or parts of it, at least. Did it tell you anything that you did not know already?"

"You have read it?" said Winston.

"I wrote it. That is to say, I collaborated in writing it. No book is produced individually, as you know."

"Is it true, what it says?"

"As description, yes. The program it sets forth is nonsense. The secret accumulation of knowledge—a gradual spread of enlightenment—ultimately a proletarian rebellion—the overthrow of the Party. You foresaw yourself that that was what it would say. It is all nonsense. The proletarians will never revolt, not in a thousand years, or a million. They cannot. I do not have to tell you the reason; you know it already. If you have ever cherished any dreams of violent insurrection, you must abandon them. There is no way in which the Party can be overthrown. The rule of the Party is forever. Make that the starting point of your thoughts."

He came closer to the bed. "Forever!" he repeated. "And now let us get back to the question of 'how' and 'why.' You understand well enough *how* the Party maintains itself in power. Now tell me *why* we cling to power. What is our motive? Why should we want power? Go on, speak," he added as Winston remained silent.

Nevertheless Winston did not speak for another moment or two. A feeling of weariness had overwhelmed him. The faint, mad gleam of enthusiasm had come back into O'Brien's face. He knew in advance what O'Brien would say: that the Party did not seek power for its own ends, but only for the good of the majority. That it sought power because men in the mass were frail, cowardly creatures who could not endure liberty or face the truth, and must be ruled over and systematically deceived by others who were stronger than themselves. That the choice for mankind lay between freedom and happiness, and that, for the great bulk of mankind, happiness was better. That the Party was the eternal guardian of the weak, a dedicated sect doing evil that good might come, sacrificing its own happiness to that of others. The terrible thing, thought Winston, the terrible thing was that when O'Brien said this he would believe it. You could see it in his face. O'Brien knew everything. A thousand times better than Winston, he knew what the world was really like, in what degradation the mass of human beings lived and by what lies and barbarities the Party kept them there. He had understood it all, weighed it all, and it made no difference: all was justified by the ultimate purpose. What can you do, thought Winston, against the lunatic who is more intelligent than yourself, who gives your arguments a fair hearing and then simply persists in his lunacy?

"You are ruling over us for our own good," he said feebly. "You believe that human beings are not fit to govern themselves, and therefore—"

He started and almost cried out. A pang of pain had shot through his body. O'Brien had pushed the lever of the dial up to thirty-five.

"That was stupid, Winston, stupid!" he said. "You should know better than to say a thing like that."

He pulled the lever back and continued:

"Now I will tell you the answer to my question. It is this. The Party seeks power entirely for its own sake. We are not interested in the good of others; we are interested solely in power. Not wealth or luxury or long life or happiness; only power, pure power. What pure power means you will understand presently. We are different from all the oligarchies of the past in that we know what we are doing. All the others, even those who resembled ourselves, were cowards and hypocrites. The German Nazis and the Russian Communists came very close to us in their methods, but they never had the courage to recognize their own motives. They pretended, perhaps they even believed, that they had seized power unwillingly and for a limited time, and that just round the corner there lay a paradise where human beings would be free and equal. We are not like that. We know that no one seizes power with the intention of relinquishing it. Power is not a means; it is an end. One does not establish a dictatorship in order to safeguard a revolution; one makes the revolution in order to establish the dictatorship. The object of persecution is persecution. The object of torture is torture. The object of power is power. Now do you begin to understand me?"

Winston was struck, as he had been struck before, by the tiredness of O'Brien's face. It was strong and fleshy and brutal, it was full of intelligence and a sort of controlled passion before which he felt himself helpless; but it was tired. There were pouches under the eyes, the skin sagged from the cheekbones. O'Brien leaned over him, deliberately bringing the worn face nearer.

"You are thinking," he said, "that my face is old and tired. You are thinking that I talk of power, and yet I am not even able to prevent the decay of my own body. Can you understand, Winston, that the individual is only a cell? The weariness of the cell is the vigor of the organism. Do you die when you cut your fingernails?"

He turned away from the bed and began strolling up and down again, one hand in his pocket.

"We are the priests of power," he said. "God is power. But at present power is only a word so far as you are concerned. It is time for you to gather some idea of what power means. The first thing you must realize is that power is collective. The individual only has power in so far as he ceases to be an individual. You know the Party slogan: 'Freedom is Slavery.' Has it ever occurred to you that it is reversible? Slavery is freedom. Alone—free—the human being is always defeated. It must be so, because every human being is doomed to die, which is the greatest of all failures. But if he can make complete, utter submission, if he can escape from his identity, if he can merge himself in the Party so that he *is* the Party, then he is all-powerful and immortal. The second thing for you to realize is that power is power over human beings. Over the body—but, above all, over the mind. Power over matter—external reality, as you would call it—is not important. Already our control over matter is absolute."

For a moment Winston ignored the dial. He made a violent effort to raise himself into a sitting position, and merely succeeded in wrenching his body painfully.

"But how can you control matter?" he burst out. "You don't even control the climate, or the law of gravity. And there are disease, pain, death—"

O'Brien silenced him by a movement of his hand. "We control matter because we control the mind. Reality is inside the skull. You will learn by degrees, Winston. There is nothing that we could not do. Invisibility, levitation—anything. I could float off this floor like a soap bubble if I wished to. I do not wish to, because the Party does not wish it. You must get rid of those nineteenth-century ideas about the laws of nature. We make the laws of nature."

"But you do not! You are not even masters of this planet. What about Eurasia and Eastasia? You have not conquered them yet."

"Unimportant. We shall conquer them when it suits us. And if we did not, what difference would it make? We can shut them out of existence. Oceania is the world."

"But the world itself is only a speck of dust. And man is tiny—helpless! How long has he been in existence? For millions of years the earth was uninhabited."

"Nonsense. The earth is as old as we are, no older. How could it be older? Nothing exists except through human consciousness."

"But the rocks are full of the bones of extinct animals—mammoths and mastodons and enormous reptiles which lived here long before man was ever heard of."

"Have you ever seen those bones, Winston? Of course not. Nineteenth-century biologists invented them. Before man there was nothing. After man, if he could come to an end, there would be nothing. Outside man there is nothing."

"But the whole universe is outside us. Look at the stars! Some of them are a million light-years away. They are out of our reach forever."

"What are the stars?" said O'Brien indifferently. "They are bits of fire a few kilometers away. We could reach them if we wanted to. Or we could blot them out. The earth is the center of the universe. The sun and the stars go round it."

Winston made another convulsive movement. This time he did not say anything. O'Brien continued as though answering a spoken objection:

"For certain purposes, of course, that is not true. When we navigate the ocean, or when we predict an eclipse, we often find it convenient to assume that the earth goes round the sun and that the stars are millions upon millions of kilometers away. But what of it? Do you suppose it is beyond us to produce a dual system of astronomy? The stars can be near or distant, according as we need them. Do you suppose our mathematicians are unequal to that? Have you forgotten doublethink?"

Winston shrank back upon the bed. Whatever he said, the swift answer crushed him like a bludgeon. And yet he knew, he *knew,* that he was in the right. The belief that nothing exists outside your own mind—surely there must be some way of demonstrating that it was false. Had it not been exposed long ago as a fallacy? There was even a name for it, which he had forgotten. A faint smile twitched the corners of O'Brien's mouth as he looked down at him.

"I told you, Winston," he said, "that metaphysics is not your strong point. The word you are trying to think of is solipsism. But you are mistaken. This is not solipsism. Collective solipsism, if you like. But that is a different thing; in fact, the opposite thing. All this is a digression," he added in a different tone. "The real power, the power we have to fight for night and day, is not power over things, but over men." He paused, and for a moment assumed again his air of a schoolmaster questioning a promising pupil: "How does one man assert his power over another, Winston?"

Winston thought. "By making him suffer," he said.

"Exactly. By making him suffer. Obedience is not enough. Unless he is suffering, how can you be sure that he is obeying your will and not his own? Power is in inflicting pain and humiliation. Power is in tearing human minds to pieces and putting them together again in new shapes of your own choosing. Do you begin to see, then, what kind of world we are creating? It is the exact opposite of the stupid, hedonistic Utopias that the old reformers imagined. A world of fear and treachery and torment, a world of trampling and being trampled upon, a world which will grow not less but *more* merciless as it refines itself. Progress in our world will be progress toward more pain. The old civilizations claimed that they were founded on love or justice. Ours is founded upon hatred. In our world there will be no emotions except fear, rage, triumph, and self-abasement. Everything else we shall destroy—everything. Already we are breaking down the habits of thought which have survived from before the Revolution. We have cut the links between child and parent, and between man and man, and between man and woman. No one dares trust a wife or a child or a friend any longer. But in the future there will be no wives and no friends. Children will be taken from their mothers at birth, as one takes eggs from a hen. The sex instinct will be eradicated. Procreation will be an annual formality like the renewal of a ration card. We shall abolish the orgasm. Our neurologists are at work upon it now. There will be no loyalty, except loyalty toward the Party. There will be no love, except the love of Big Brother. There will be no laughter, except the laugh of triumph over a defeated enemy. There will be no art, no literature, no science. When we are omnipotent we shall have no more need of science. There will be no distinction between beauty and ugliness. There will be no curiosity, no enjoyment of the process of life. All competing pleasures will be destroyed. But always—do not forget this, Winston—always there will be the intoxication of power, constantly increasing and constantly growing subtler. Always, at every moment, there will be the thrill of victory, the sensation of trampling on an enemy who is helpless. If you want a picture of the future, imagine a boot stamping on a human face—forever."

He paused as though he expected Winston to speak. Winston had tried to shrink back into the surface of the bed again. He could not say anything. His heart seemed to be frozen. O'Brien went on:

"And remember that it is forever. The face will always be there to be stamped upon. The heretic, the enemy of society, will always be there, so that he can be defeated and humiliated over again. Everything that you have undergone since you have been in our hands—all that will continue, and worse. The espionage, the betrayals, the arrests, the tortures, the executions, the disappearances will never cease. It will be a world of terror as much as a world of triumph. The more the Party is powerful, the less it will be tolerant; the weaker the opposition, the tighter the despotism. Goldstein and his heresies will live forever. Every day, at every moment, they will be defeated, discredited, ridiculed, spat upon—and yet they will always survive. This drama that I have played out with you during seven years will be played out over and over again, generation after generation, always in subtler forms. Always we shall have the heretic here at our mercy, screaming with pain, broken up, contemptible—and in the end utterly penitent, saved from himself, crawling to our feet of his own accord. That is the world that we are preparing, Winston. A world of victory after victory, triumph after triumph: an endless pressing, pressing, pressing upon the nerve of power. You are beginning, I can see, to realize what that world will be like. But in the end you will do more than understand it. You will accept it, welcome it, become part of it."

[Time passed; Winston grew stronger. In his cell, they had given him a slate and a stump of pencil.] His mind grew more active. He sat down on the plank bed, his back against the wall and the slate on his knees, and set to work deliberately at the task of re-educating himself.

He had capitulated; that was agreed. In reality, as he saw now, he had been ready to capitulate long before he had taken the decision. From the moment when he was inside the Ministry of Love—and yes, even during those minutes when he and Julia had stood helpless while the iron voice from the telescreen told them what to do—he had grasped the frivolity, the shallowness of his attempt to set himself up against the power of the Party. He knew now that for seven years the Thought Police had watched him like a beetle under a magnifying glass. There was no physical act, no word spoken aloud, that they had not noticed, no train of thought that they had not been able to infer. Even the speck of whitish dust on the cover of his diary they had carefully replaced. They had played sound tracks to him, shown him photographs. Some of them were photographs of Julia and himself. Yes, even . . . He could not fight against the Party any longer. Besides, the Party was in the right. It must be so: how could the immortal, collective brain be mistaken? By what external standard could you check its judgments? Sanity was statistical. It was merely a question of learning to think as they thought. Only—!

The pencil felt thick and awkward in his fingers. He began to write down the thoughts that came into his head. He wrote first in large clumsy capitals:

FREEDOM IS SLAVERY.

Then almost without a pause he wrote beneath it:

TWO AND TWO MAKE FIVE.

But then there came a sort of check. His mind, as though shying away from something, seemed unable to concentrate. He knew that he knew what came next, but for the moment he could not recall it. When he did recall it, it was only by consciously reasoning out what it must be; it did not come of its own accord. He wrote:

GOD IS POWER.

He accepted everything. The past was alterable. The past never had been altered. Oceania was at war with Eastasia. Oceania had always been at war with Eastasia. Jones, Aaronson, and Rutherford were guilty of the crimes they were charged with. He had never seen the photograph that disproved their guilt. It had never existed; he had invented it. He remembered remembering contrary things, but those were false memories, products of self-deception. How easy it all was! Only surrender, and everything else followed. It was like swimming against a current that swept you backwards however hard you struggled, and then suddenly deciding to turn round and go with the current instead of opposing it. Nothing had changed except your own attitude; the predestined thing happened in any case. He hardly knew why he had ever rebelled. Everything was easy, except—!

Anything could be true. The so-called laws of nature were nonsense. The law of gravity was nonsense. "If I wished," O'Brien had said, "I could float off this floor like a soap bubble." Winston worked it out. "If he *thinks* he floats off the floor, and if I simultaneously *think* I see him do it, then the thing happens." Suddenly, like a lump of submerged wreckage breaking the surface of the water, the thought burst into his mind: "It doesn't really happen. We imagine it. It is hallucination." He pushed the thought under in stantly. The fallacy was obvious. It presupposed that somewhere or other, outside oneself, there was a "real" world where "real" things happened. But how could there be such a world? What knowledge have we of anything, save through our own minds? All happenings are in the mind. Whatever happens in all minds, truly happens.

He had no difficulty in disposing of the fallacy, and he was in no danger of succumbing to it. He realized, nevertheless, that it ought never to have occurred to him. The mind should develop a blind spot whenever a danger ous thought presented itself. The process should be automatic, instinctive. *Crimestop,* they called it in Newspeak.

He set to work to exercise himself in crimestop. He presented himself with propositions—"the Party says the earth is flat," "the Party says that ice is heavier than water"—and trained himself in not seeing or not understanding the arguments that contradicted them. It was not easy. It needed great powers of reasoning and improvisation. The arithmetical problems raised, for in stance, by such a statement as "two and two make five" were beyond his intellectual grasp. It needed also a sort of athleticism of mind, an ability at one moment to make the most delicate use of logic and at the next to be unconscious of the crudest logical errors. Stupidity was as necessary as intel ligence, and as difficult to attain.

Sinyavsky

Born in 1925, Andrey Sinyavsky graduated from Moscow University in 1952 and went on to write, edit, and teach literature. The mid-1950s brought a thaw to Soviet liter ature as well as to other affairs of state. But the thaw did not last. In 1958, the poet Boris Pasternak (1890–1960) was awarded the Nobel Prize for literature, in part for his novel *Doctor Zhivago*. In Russia, the award was taken as an anti-Soviet rebuke, as the book (published in eighteen languages, though not in Russian) had been de nounced as anti-revolutionary. The Nobel Prize brought a campaign of abuse against Pasternak, who was deprived of his livelihood and forced to decline the prize. Sin yavsky, who had introduced a book of Pasternak's poems, was tarred with the same brush. His publications, henceforth, had to be smuggled to the West and published there in translation, either anonymously, like the essay reprinted here, or under the pen name of Abram Tertz. A novel, *The Trial Begins* (1960), dealt with the Doctors' Plot of 1953, during which nine doctors were unjustly accused of treason and judi cially murdered. In another, *The Makepeace Experiment* (1965), a village tyrant hood winks his constituents with magic and with lies. A series of short stories explored other aspects of despotism, dissolution, and spiritual dislocation. Meanwhile,

"Socialist Realism," published in 1959, called for less conformity and more inventiveness in Soviet literature.

Arrested in 1965 and convicted of anti-Soviet propaganda, Sinyavsky was sentenced to seven years at hard labor. Released in 1971, after much domestic and international protest, he moved to Paris where, while teaching Russian literature at the Sorbonne, he was able to analyze the efforts of Marxist authorities to make over the minds of the folk under their rule.

Several years before Sinyavsky, another Marxist writer had drawn significant conclusions from the letdown of a goal attained only to be found unsatisfactory. In his *Notes to Galilei,* published after his death, Berthold Brecht (1898–1956) refers to the dreadfulness of the disappointment "when human beings realise, or thing they realise, that they have fallen victims to an illusion, that the old is stronger than the new, that the 'facts' are against them and not for them, that their time, the new time has not yet come. . . . The effort is followed by exhaustion, exaggerated hope by exaggerated hopelessness. Those who do not fall into resignation and apathy fall into worse: those who have not lost their idealistic energy now turn it against those same ideals. No reactionary is more cruel than a failed revolutionary, no elephant a more savage enemy of wild elephants than the tamed elephant."[1]

It is fitting enough that the conclusions of the wave of social awareness and hope that appeared in the previous section should be drawn at the end of the present section. What follows is not the most brilliant presentation or refutation of Socialist Realism, but it is heartfelt and informed, and it is important, too, because its author does not reject the ends Socialist Realism had been designed to serve, only the means of which Socialist Realism is one. Most particularly, he rejects the teleological use of art, which would subordinate it to a higher and self-justifying purpose—in this case, the will to bring about Communism as quickly as possible. Not that Communism is undesirable to the author or that he can think of anything better to hope for, but that it has been used to harness art and to employ it in a particularly stupid—and stupefying—way:

> So that prisons might disappear forever, we built new ones. So that frontiers between countries might vanish, we surrounded ourselves with a Chinese wall. So that work in the future might become a rest and a pleasure, we introduced forced labor. So that no one should evermore shed one drop of blood, we killed and killed and killed.

From this terrible illusion "we arise, staggering with weariness, look around the whole universe with our blood-shot eyes, and see nothing of all we hoped to find."

But read on and you find that the conclusion of all this is not the rejection of the dream—only of a method of realizing it that has been found wrong. "In losing our faith we have not lost enthusiasm. . . . Shall we perhaps invent something astonishing?"

The answer, for the moment, seems to be—nothing much. The move away from a

---

[1]Quoted by Martin Esslin, "New Light on Brecht," *Encounter,* June 1960.

naturalism that is false to nature has led back (or forward?) to other varieties of Romanticism—Hoffmann and Dostoevsky, Goya and Chagall. Isolation has kept the devotees of Socialist Realism hobbled in an artistic backwater whence even a Pasternak sounds, in Isaac Deutscher's words, like a voice from the grave. But as we have learned since 1989, even the dead awaken. . . .

Socialist Realism

I

What is socialist realism? . . .

The most exact definition of socialist realism is that given in the statute of the Union of Soviet Writers:

> Socialist realism is the fundamental method of Soviet literature and criticism: it demands of the artist a true, historically concrete representation of reality in its revolutionary development. Further, it ought to contribute to the ideological transformation and education of the workers in the spirit of socialism.[1]

This innocent formulation serves as foundation for the whole edifice of socialist realism. It defines at once the relation of realism in the Socialist era to that of the past and what distinguishes it therefrom: both aim at a representation *in conformity with the real,* but socialist realism introduces a new element, the ability to seize upon life *in its revolutionary movement,* and to form the minds of readers and spectators in function with that perspective; that is, *in the spirit of Socialism.* The earlier realists or, as they are often called, the critical realists—because they criticised bourgeois society—Balzac, Tolstoy, Chekhov, etc. . . . gave a faithful image of reality: but, not being instructed by the genius of Marx, they could not foresee the future victories of Socialism and, in any case, they had no idea of the real and concrete ways of attaining to it. Socialist realism, however, is armed with Marx's teaching: it is enriched by experience of struggles and victories and it has the Communist Party, its friend and very vigilant preceptor, to inspire it. While it is describing present reality it hears the march of history and keeps its eyes upon the future. It sees the "visible feature of Communism" invisible to the ordinary eye. It thus constitutes a clear advance upon the art of the past and attains the highest summit of the artistic evolution of humanity, the most realistic realism. . . .

Implicit in the formula in question ("true, historically concrete represen-

Source: From *Soviet Survey,* No. 29, July–September, 1959.
[1]*Report of the First Federal Congress of Soviet Writers,* 1934, p. 716.

tation of reality in its revolutionary development"), is the notion of an End, of that ideal which embraces all things and to which the *real*—a correct image of which is given—is tending in an ineluctable revolutionary movement. To seize this movement, and to help the reader, by transforming his consciousness, to approach nearer this End—that is the meaning of socialist realism, the art which in our epoch is the most clearly orientated towards a definite goal.

That End is Communism, known in its younger days as Socialism. The poet not only writes verses; by doing so he helps in the building-up of Communism. That is just as natural as to see beside him, working at the same task, the sculptor, the musician, the agronomist, engineer, labourer, policeman, lawyer, and the machines, theatres, cannon and newspapers. . . .

Like our whole culture and our whole system, our art is entirely teleological. It is subordinated to the supreme end from which it has its title of nobility. In the last analysis, all of us are living solely to hasten the coming of Communism. . . .

Science has not delivered us from the children's question "why?" Behind the relations of causality that science establishes one still sees a hidden and deformed finalism. Science declares that "man is descended from the monkey," instead of saying that "the monkey was destined to become Man." But whatever may be the origin of man, his appearance and his destiny are inseparable from God—that is, from the highest idea of the End that is accessible, if not by our understanding, at least by our desire to know that it exists. That is the aim of all that is and all that is not—an infinite—and no doubt gratuitous—End-in-itself. For what end could the End itself have? . . .

The modern mind is powerless to imagine anything more sublime and beautiful than the Communist ideal. The most it can do is to put back into circulation the old ideas of Christian love or liberty of the person. But for the moment it is not in a condition to project yet another aim.

Western liberal individualists and Russian intellectuals find themselves in almost the same situation, in face of Socialism, as were the intelligent Roman patricians in regard to the victory of Christianity. They mocked at the madmen who worshipped the cross (that Roman guillotine), at the ineptitude of the doctrines of the Trinity, etc. . . . But it was beyond their power to put up any serious arguments against the *Ideal* of the Christ in itself. They could, it is true, assert that the best elements of the Christian moral code had been taken from Plato. (Christians of today sometimes say that the Communists borrowed their noble ideal from the Gospel.) But could they declare that a God conceived as a God of love was something evil, or base, or monstrous? And can we say that the universal happiness promised us in the Communist future is an evil?

We know not how to resist the bewitching beauty of Communism. It is too soon to invent another aim, to wrench ourselves out of ourselves and set out towards the distant horizons beyond even Communism.

It was the genius of Marx that discovered and proved that the earthly paradise of which so many people had dreamt before him was the End assigned to humanity by destiny itself. . . . At one blow everything fell into place. An iron necessity, a strict hierarchy, had shaped the course of the centuries. The ape stood up on its hind legs and started its triumphal march toward Communism. The world of the primitive commune was necessary, so that slavery might come out of it; slavery was necessary before feudalism could appear; feudalism was indispensable to the coming of capitalism, and capitalism so that Communism might arise. That is all! The magnificent End is attained, the pyramid is crowned, history is completed.

A sincerely religious man relates everything to his divinity. . . . A Christian, if he wishes to be consistent, must consider the whole life of the world before the birth of Christ as the pre-history of Jesus Christ. In the eyes of a monotheist, do not pagans exist to manifest the will of the one God and, in the end, after a long preparation, to come to believe in the one God alone?

After all that, can one be surprised if, in another religious perspective, ancient Rome is regarded as an indispensable stage upon the way that leads to Communism; or if the Crusades are explained, not as ardent efforts of Christianity, but as a phase in the development of commerce and industry, in the interplay of the forces of production which is proceeding everywhere and, at the present time, is ensuring the collapse of capitalism and the triumph of the Socialist régime?

You have only to ask a Westerner why the great French Revolution was necessary, to receive a multitude of different answers. But put the same question to any Soviet schoolboy, not to speak of better-informed people, and he will give you an exact and exhaustive explanation: The great French Revolution was necessary in order to clear the way, and hasten the coming of Communism. It is a long time since men have had such a clear explanation of the world, perhaps not since the Middle Ages. Our great privilege is to have rediscovered it. . . .

Thus, the universal history of human thought has only existed, so to speak, in order to prepare the way for "historical materialism"—that is, for Marxism, the philosophy of Communism.

And here it was before us, this unique End of the Creation, as beautiful as life eternal and as obligatory as death: and we rushed towards It, breaking all barriers in the way and rejecting all that might retard us on our headlong course. We have freed ourselves without regret from the belief in another world, or in love of our neighbour, or in liberty of the person and other prejudices, now rather down-at-heel and anyway far poorer than the ideal that opened out before us. In the name of the new religion thousands of martyrs of the revolution gave their lives, showing a courage and a sanctity in their sufferings that eclipsed the exploits of the early Christians.

But it is not only our life, our blood, our body that we have given to the new God. We have sacrificed to him our snow-white soul, and spattered it with all the dirt of the world. It is good to be gentle, to have tea with jam, to plant flowers and to cultivate love, humility, non-resistance to evil and other philanthropies. But whom have they saved, what have they changed in the world, those old men and old women, those egoists of humanism who built up a quiet conscience, penny by penny, and assured themselves of a good little place in the after-death old people's home?

For our part, we wanted no salvation for ourselves, but for all humanity. And instead of sentimental sighing, personal perfection, and charity bazaars for the benefit of the hungry, we set ourselves to put the universe right according to the best model that ever existed, that of the resplendent End moving towards us.

So that prisons might disappear forever, we built new ones. So that frontiers between countries might vanish, we surrounded ourselves with a Chinese wall. So that work in the future might become a rest and a pleasure, we introduced forced labour. So that no one should evermore shed one drop of blood, we killed and killed and killed.

In the name of the End, we had to sacrifice all that we had in reserve and resort to the same means as our enemies employed; to proclaim the omnipotence of Russia, write lies in *Pravda*,[2] put a Tsar on the now empty throne, epaulettes on the officers, and re-institute torture. Sometimes it seemed that for its complete triumph, Communism needed only one final holocaust—to give up Communism.

Lord, Lord, forgive us our sins! . . .

The results are never the same as the End one proposed at first. . . . The fires of the Inquisition helped to consolidate the Gospel, but then what was left of it? Nevertheless, both the fires of the Inquisition and the Gospel, both the night of St. Bartholomew and St. Bartholomew himself, add up to one single great Christian culture.

Yes, we are living in Communism. It no more resembles what we were seeking than the Middle Ages were like Christ, or than contemporary Western man is like a free superman, or man like God. All the same, there is a certain likeness, is there not?

Yes? It consists in the subordination of all our actions, thoughts, and in-

---

[2]*Pravda*, name of the leading Soviet newspaper, means "truth."

tentions, to this one End, which perhaps has long been a word empty of meaning but continues to have a hypnotic influence over us, and still propels us forward none knows whither. Obviously, then, art and literature could not fail to find themselves gripped in the vice of that system and becoming transformed, as Lenin foresaw, into "wheels" and "screws" of the great machine of State. . . . "Our reviews, whether scientific or artistic, cannot be non-political. . . . The strength of Soviet literature, the most progressive literature in the world, is due to its being a literature which has not, and cannot have, any other interests than those of the people, those of the State."[3]

In reading that statement in a decree of the Communist Party it is absolutely necessary to remember that, by the interests of the people and the interests of the State—which completely coincide from the State's point of view—one means no other thing than this same Communism which penetrates and absorbs everything. "Literature and art are integral parts of the struggle of the whole people for Communism . . . the highest function of literature and art is to mobilise the people for the winning of new victories in the building-up of Communism."[4]

When certain Western writers deplore the lack of freedom to create, to speak out, etc., they start from their own faith in the freedom of the person, which is the basis of their culture but is organically alien to communist culture. A convinced Soviet writer, a true Marxist, not only cannot accept such reproaches, he quite simply cannot understand them. What liberty can a religious man require of his God? Liberty to praise him still more? . . . For a believer in Communism, as N. S. Khrushchev has justly remarked in one of his latest declarations upon questions of art, "for an artist who faithfully serves his people, the question does not arise whether he is free or not in his creative work. The question does not even arise: such an artist knows perfectly how to approach the phenomena of reality; he has no need to 'conform' or to force himself. Faithfully to represent reality according to his Communist convictions is a requirement of his soul: he hold firmly to his position; he affirms and defends them in his works."

These are the aesthetic and psychological principles it is indispensable to know before one can enter into the secret of Socialist Realism.

II

The works of socialist realism are various in style and subject. But in every one of them, either literally or figuratively, explicitly or covertly, the End is

---

[3]From a decree of the Central Committee of the Communist Party dated 14 August 1946.
[4]*Report of Soviet Writers' Congress.*

present. Either it is a panegyric of Communism and everything connected therewith, or a satire upon its numerous enemies, or else it is a picture of life "in its revolutionary development"—that is, once again, in its movement towards Communism.

Thus, every production of socialist realism is sure, even before it appears, of a happy ending: the end may be sad for the hero, who runs every possible risk in battling for Communism, but it is always happy from the point of view of the End which transcends the individual; and the author, in his own name or in the words of the dying hero, never forgets to make a declaration of faith in our final victory. The lost illusions, broken hopes, and unrealised dreams so characteristic of the literature of other epochs and other systems, are absent from socialist realism. Even in the case of a tragedy, it will be an "Optimist Tragedy"—to use the title that Vs. Vishnevsky gave to one of his works.[5] (The heroine perishes at the end, but Communism triumphs.)

One has only to compare a few titles from Western literature with those of Soviet literature to be convinced of this. On the one hand: *Journey to the End of Night* (Céline); *Death in the Afternoon* and *For Whom the Bell Tolls* (Hemingway); *Everyone Dies Alone* (Fallada); *A Time to Live and a Time to Die* (Remarque); *The Death of a Hero* (Aldington) . . . and on the other hand, in the major key: *Happiness* (Pavlenko); *The First Joys* (Fedin); *It is Good* (Mayakovsky); *The Fulfilment of Desires* (Kaverin); *Light Over the Earth* (Babaevsky); *The Conquerors* (Bagritsky); *The Conqueror* (Simonov); *The Conquerors* (Chirikov); *Springtime in Victory* (Gribachev), etc. . . .

That admirable End towards which the action tends is sometimes evoked directly, at the end of the work: Mayakovsky, for instance, brilliantly terminated all his important work written after the Revolution with some statement on Communism or with imaginary scenes in the life of the future and in the Communist State. Gorki, too, who under the Soviet régime wrote chiefly about the pre-revolutionary period, concluded the majority of his novels and plays with a vision of the Revolution triumphant, which was the immediate goal on the way to Communism and the final goal of the old world.

Even when the writer does not lead up to so grandiose a conclusion, it exists implicitly, symbolically . . . for example, many of our novels and romances hinge upon work in a factory, the construction of a power-station, the administration of agricultural reforms, etc. . . . . The economic question to be resolved . . . is presented as a necessary stage on the way to the supreme End. Seen from such a definite standpoint even technical processes can take on a dramatic tension and provide interest. The reader gradually learns that,

---

[5]*La Tragédie optimiste* was published in *Esprit* (Paris) in February and March 1951.

in spite of all breakdowns, the machine-tool will be set to work, or that the kolkhoz "Victory," despite wet weather, is amassing a rich harvest of maize; and he closes the book with a sigh of relief, feeling that we have taken one more step towards Communism.

Since Communism, in our view, must be the inevitable issue of the historical process, the motive force in many novels is provided by the impetuous march of time working for us . . . our literature is often concerned with history, past or contemporary,and its episodes (civil war, collectivisation, etc.) are also so many stages upon the road we have chosen. For the more distant epochs, the ascent towards Communism is unfortunately a little harder to show. However, even in the remotest times, a perspicuous writer will know how to give prominence to the "progressive" phenomena . . . and as for the "progressive" men of the past—Peter the Great, Ivan the Terrible, or Stenka Razin—they were well aware, without even knowing the word "communism," that a luminous future was awaiting us, and are incessantly trumpeting about it in our historical novels, rejoicing the readers' hearts by their astonishing perspicacity.

A good deal of Soviet literature consists of edifying fiction depicting the metamorphosis of individuals or of whole communities into Communists. Many books, indeed, are centred upon the psychological and moral revolution which is to produce the ideal man of the future. Gorki's *The Mother* exemplified this—a case of the transformation of an ignorant and passive woman into a conscious revolutionary (written in 1906, this is regarded as the first model of socialist realism). The *Pedagogic Poem* of Makarenko is another example (showing how young criminals are converted to the life of honest work), and yet another is the novel of N. Ostrovski which tells *How the Steel Was Tempered,* i.e., how our youth was tempered in the fire of the civil war and then in the cold of the first industrial works of Communism.

As soon as the character is re-educated enough to become completely re-orientated and to be conscious of it, he can enter into the privileged caste, held in general respect, which is that of the "Positive Heroes." This is the Holy of Holies of socialism realism, its touchstone and its highest realisation.

The positive hero is not just a good man: he is a hero illuminated by the light of the ideal of all ideals: he is a model worthy of imitation by all, a "peak of humanity from whose height one can see the future," according to Leonid Leonov. He has no faults, or, if he has, only in small doses (he may, to a slight degree, lose his temper now and then), just enough to preserve some verisimilitude, and also in order to have something to eliminate while he is rising to ever higher political and moral heights. However, these faults must not be important, and above all must never take away from his fundamental qualities. These qualities of the positive hero are very difficult to enumerate:

ideological conviction, audacity, intelligence, strength of will, patriotism, respect for women, readiness to sacrifice himself, etc. . . . The most essential, of course, are the clearness and definiteness with which he sees the End and strives towards it. Hence the surprising precision of all his actions, his tastes, thoughts, feelings and judgments. He knows, unshakably, what is good and what is bad, he is either "for" or "against," and never mixes up black with white. Interior doubts, hesitations, insoluble questions or unfathomable secrets do not exist for him; and in the most entangled problem he finds the solution quite easily, by going straight for the End.

When he appeared for the first time, with Gorki, between 1900 and 1910, and when he publicly proclaimed that "one must always say yes or no," many people were struck by his assurance and the decisive firmness of his statements, by his tendency to preach to those around him and pronounce pompous monologues about his own virtue. Chekhov, who had managed to read *The Petty-Bourgeois,* raised an embarrassed eyebrow and advised Gorki to tone down the shriller declarations of his hero. Chekhov feared pretentiousness like the plague, and he thought that all these high-sounding phrases were signs of a boastfulness foreign to the Russian nature.

But Gorki took no notice. . . . He understood that this was the man of the future, and that "they only would come through, the men pitilessly straight and firm like swords" (*The Petty-Bourgeois,* 1901).

A long time has passed since then and many things have changed. . . . It was during the thirties that Soviet writers gave up their groups and renounced diversity of literary currents to adopt, almost unanimously, the best and most progressive current of all—socialist realism. . . . That is why we have seen novels and plays where everything goes on as smoothly as on wheels; if there is any conflict between the heroes it is only between the progressives and the super-progressives, between the good and the still better. Their authors (Babaevsky, Surkov, Sofronov, Virta, Gribachev, etc.) were lauded to the skies and held up as examples. It is true that since the twentieth CPSU Congress—one hardly knows why—there has been a slight change of attitude towards them, a tendency to look down on them for having made a "literature without conflict" . . . which is very unjust.

Wishing not to lose face before the West, we sometimes cease to be logical with ourselves, and throw out grand declarations about the diversity of personalities and the plurality of interests in our society, and therefore about the numerous possibilities of conflict and contradiction that literature is supposed to reflect.

Of course we are different from one another by age, sex, nationality, and even intelligence. But anyone who follows the Party line knows very well that these are only variations within the limits of monotony, discords within the framework of unanimity, conflicts in the absence of conflict.

We have one single aim—Communism; one single philosophy, Marxism; one single art, socialist realism. As it has been well put by a Soviet writer of rather second-rate talent, but on the other hand irreproachable for his political views, "Russia has chosen her own path, that of unanimity. For thousands of years men have suffered from not thinking the same thing. We Sovietists, for the first time, have understood each other: we speak a single language, universally understandable, we think in an identical way about the principal things in life. We are strong in that intellectual unanimity. Therein lies our superiority over other men, rent and dislocated by plurality of thinking ..." (V. Ilenkov, *The Great Way* (1949), a novel that won the Stalin prize).

Can we, in such circumstances, reproach certain writers for having overemphasised this harmony? If they withdrew from the actual conflicts of life, it was only to take a long view of the future—in other words, to discharge as well as possible what they owe, as writers, to Soviet realism. Babaevsky and Surkov have not deviated from the sacred principles of our art; they have, on the contrary, developed it logically and organically. . . .

· If positive heroes have multiplied incredibly, and have far surpassed, in quantity, the other characters whom they overshadow and often replace altogether, this extension is also qualitative: the virtues of the heroes have become extraordinarily developed. As the hero approaches the End, he becomes more and more positive, beautiful, and grand. And, similarly, the sense of his own dignity grows within him, especially when he compares himself with a Western man and persuades himself of his own incomparable excellence. ". . . But the Soviet man is a hundred cubits above the Occidental. He is nearing the summit whilst the other is still marking time at the foot of the mountain." (This a sample of the language allotted to simple peasants in our novels.) . . . We never had heroes of this kind before. . . . During the last century the hero who was in fashion belonged to quite another type, and all Russian literature lived and thought in quite another style. Compared with the religious fanaticism of our epoch, the nineteenth century was atheistic, tolerant, and without definite orientation. It was soft, flabby, feminine, and melancholic, full of doubts and internal contradictions, of remorseful conscience. In the whole of that century, it was perhaps only Chernyshevsky and Pobedonostsev who really believed in God, apart from an indefinite number of peasant men and women who were true believers; but these were not yet makers of history and culture. Culture was made by a handful of melancholy sceptics who had a thirst for God simply because they had no God. . . .

The nineteenth century was altogether one of searchings, of wanderings, of aspirations ardent or otherwise, without the power or the will to find a settled place under the sun—torn by uncertainty and dualism. Dostoevsky, who was sorry Russia was so wide—it needed to be made narrower!—made orthodoxy co-exist with nihilism and found room in his soul for all the Karamazovs at once, Alyosha, Mitya, Fedor (some say even Smerdyakov), and no one knows yet which of them predominated. Breadth excludes faith— it was not for nothing that we narrowed ourselves down to Marxism, so realising Dostoevsky's wish—and Dostoevsky well understood that sacrilege; which is why he was forever arguing with himself and longing passionately to put an end to a discussion so offensive to the one God.

Thirst for God, the desire to believe, springs up in desert places. It is not yet faith, and if the desire precedes the faith (Blessed are they who thirst!) it is rather in the way that hunger precedes a meal. . . . It was the hunger of the nineteenth century, perhaps, that made us in Russia pounce with such gluttony upon the nourishment provided by Marx, and swallow it before we had time to distinguish its taste, odour—and consequences. But the hunger itself was due to a calamitous lack of nourishment; it was hunger for God. That is why it was so exhausting and seemed to us unbearable: it forced us to go to the people, to stagger from radicalism into the ranks of renegades and back again, and yet to remember that we too, in spite of everything, are Christians. . . .

The universal Pushkin underlined this oscillation in *The Prisoner of the Caucasus* and other poems of his youth, before developing all its implications in *Eugene Onegin*. The theme of *Eugene Onegin* is simple, anecdotal: whilst she loves and is ready to belong to him, he is indifferent, but as soon as she is married to another, he loves her passionately and without hope. That commonplace story includes all the contradictions that Russian literature maundered about ever afterwards right up to Chekhov and Blok. . . .

The "useless man" is the name usually given to the central hero of this literature—Onegin, Pechorin, Beltov, Rudin, Lavretsky[6] and many others— because, for all the noble impulses stirring within him, this hero is incapable of finding a meaning in his life, and sets a deplorable example of the man without a purpose; he is necessary to no one. He is generally of a meditative disposition, prone to introspection and self-flagellation. His life is full of unrealised projects, his fate is sad, slightly ridiculous. The fateful role in his life is usually played by a woman.

If only he were a low fellow, incapable of elevated sentiments. But no! this is a worthy man, and the most charming of women bravely gives him her heart and her hand. But instead of rejoicing in this, and looking on the bright side of life, he begins to take unconsidered action and, against his own

---

[6]The references are to Pechorin, in the novel *A Hero of our Time*, by Lermontov (1839); Beltov, in Herzen's novel *Whose Fault Is It?* (1847); Turgenev's *Rudin* (1856); and Lavretsky, the hero of Turgenev's *A Nest of Gentlefolk* (1859).

wishes, he does everything to ensure that the woman who loves him shall never be his. . . . As for the women, all the innumerable Tatianas, Lisas, Natalias, Bellas, Ninas, they are as resplendent as the intact and inaccessible ideal cherished by the Onegins and Pechorins who love them so clumsily and always without success. It was they who in Russian literature were synonymous with the ideal, who stood for the supreme End: their ephemeral nature lent itself to this very well. . . .

In Blok's poem *The Twelve*—a work on the frontier between two hostile or mutually exclusive cultures—one episode puts the full stop to the development of the sentimental theme of the nineteenth century. The Red Guard, Petka, carried away by a fit of anger, accidentally kills his well-beloved, Katka the prostitute. This crime, and the suffering caused by the loss of the loved one, resuscitate the old drama repeated ever since Lermontov's *The Devil, Masquerade,* etc., of which there are numerous variants in Blok's own work. But whereas the earlier heroes, after having turned their empty souls inside out, became stuck in a state of inescapable remorse, Petka, who at first follows in their traces, does not end like them. His more [socially] conscious comrades push him forward and re-educate him:

> —Sure, he was going to show us
> His soul inside out. Get on!
> —Keep your dignity!
> —Control yourself!
> And Petrushka slows down
> His hurried pace . . .
> He lifts up his head,
> He's recovered his gaiety. . . .

That is how the new hero is born, such a hero as has never been seen. In the bloody struggle against the enemy, in the sufferings and the labours of the new epoch, he cures himself of sterile reflections and useless twinges of conscience. Proudly "throwing his head back" and noticeably more cheerful under the flag of the new God whom Blok by force of habit calls Jesus Christ, he marches into Soviet literature.

The useless man of the nineteenth century, who became still more useless in the twentieth, was alien and incomprehensible to the positive hero of the new epoch. . . . "Who is not for us is against us" was the attitude of the new culture. Where it still paid any attention to this type of ineffectual man, it was to show him that he was by no means useless, but harmful, dangerous, negative. . . .

This revaluation of the useless man, and his rapid transformation into a negative character, were in full swing during the twenties, the time when the positive hero was shaped. When the two were put side by side, everyone saw clearly that there could be no aimless hero, there were only people for or against; and that the useless man was, all things considered, only an enemy in disguise, a vile traitor to be unmasked and punished without delay. That is what Gorki wrote in *The Life of Klim Samgin,* Fadeyev in *The Nineteen,* and many others elsewhere. K. Fedin, in *The Towns and the Years,* emptied his heart of the last drops of pity for the formerly enchanting hero. The one discordant note was, perhaps, *Quiet Flow the Don,* in which Sholokhov portrays the tragic destiny of a useless man, Grigori Melekhov, and bids him a fully sympathetic farewell. But because Melekhov was a man of the people and not of the intelligentsia, people winked at this. Nowadays, this novel is regarded as a model of socialist realism—one which, of course, has no imitators.

Meanwhile, the other useless men who wanted to save their lives renounced their past and were rapidly re-educated into positive heroes. As one of them said lately: "There is nothing in the world more hateful than neutrality. . . . Yes, yes, I am Red! Red, devil take you!" (K. Fedin *An Extraordinary Being,* 1949.) The malediction is not now aimed at the Reds, of course, but at the Whites.

Thus did the hero of ninteenth-century Russian literature perish ingloriously.

In content, in spirit, and in the hero it praises, socialist realism is much nearer to the eighteenth than to the nineteenth century. The eighteenth century had, like us, the idea of the integral State, the feeling of its own superiority, the certainty that God was for it. . . . Like the socialist system, the eighteenth century imagined itself to be the centre of creation and, dazzled by the excellence of its own virtues, "putting itself on a pedestal and resplendent with its self-praise," it proposed itself as an example to all times and all peoples. This religious conviction was so strong that Derzhavin,[7] in *The Portrait of Felitsa* . . . eulogising the ideal reign of Catherine II, prayed that:

> . . . the distant savages
> Covered with hair or even scales,
> Attired in foliage or bark,
> Crowned with the feathers of winged birds,
> Incline before the august throne
> And hear the voice of the laws;
> While down their sunburnt face
> Tears flow in torrents . . .
> Thrilled through with happiness,
> May they forget their equality
> And all submit to Her.

---

[7]Derzhavin (1743–1816), a great Russian poet of the classical school.

The literature of the eighteenth century created a positive hero who has many features in common with the hero of our literature: he is "friend to the common good," he "strives in his spirit to surpass all others"—that is, continuing to raise his moral and political status; he has all the virtues; he indoctrinates everyone, etc. . . . That literature knew nothing of "useless men." It was equally ignorant of the destructive laughter which was the chronic malady of Russian literature from Pushkin to Blok and, after having tinged all the nineteenth century with irony, attained its maximum in the decadence. ". . . Outbursts of exhausting laughter which begin with a smile of diabolical and provocative mockery and end in revolt and sacrilege" (A. Blok's *Irony*, 1908). . . .

Thus returning to the eighteenth century, we have become severe and serious. Not that we have forgotten how to laugh, but our laughter has ceased to be shameless and disrespectful. . . . It is laughter with a severe face and uplifted forefinger: "This or that is not done; it ought not to be so!" Laughter wholly cleansed of ironical acidity. Instead of irony has come pathos: the positive hero is bathed in that element. We have ceased to be afraid of the grand word, the resounding phrase. The solemn and swelling style of the ode is what we like. . . . We represent life as we would wish it to be and as it must become when it has bent us to the logic of Marxism. That is why socialist realism might more aptly be called "socialist classicism."

In their theoretical works and articles, Soviet writers sometimes use the terms "romanticism" or "revolutionary romanticism." Gorki said a good deal about the fusion of realism with romanticism; he always had a nostalgia for "the exalted illusion that uplifts," and maintained that the artist had a right to embellish life by painting it better than it is. These appeals were not fruitless, although . . . obviously, one cannot frankly avow that what one wants is a beautiful falsehood. No, no, God forbid! We are against illusion, against idealisation; we want nothing but the truth, but besides that, we depict life "in its revolutionary development" . . . we do not want to prettify life; it has no need of that to be beautiful. We do not mean to prettify it but only to show the seed of the future that it contains. Revolutionary romanticism—which is equivalent to this "seed of the future," this "revolutionary development," is actually inherent in this life that we represent truthfully, and which is romantic in the highest degree. . . .

Truth to tell, romanticism is much to our taste, and Gorki knew it: he tends towards the ideal, he makes wishes pass for realities, loves pretty knick-knacks, is not afraid of fulsome phrases, etc. . . . That is why he has always had a certain success among us. Yet romanticism . . . for all the status he has conferred on it, has occupied a much less important place in our art than might have been expected. It makes itself felt chiefly in the beginning of socialist realism; and in its maturity, during the last thirty years, the romantic tinge grows rather faint.

Romanticism is intimately linked with the *Sturm and Drang* period of Soviet literature—the first five years of the Revolution when life and art were
dominated by unbridled passions, and when the ardours of that surge towards a happy future had not become strictly regulated by governmental
policy. . . . Both by those who took part in the Revolution and by those born
after it, its memories are cherished as sacredly as those of a dead mother. It
is easier for us to allow that everything since then is a betrayal of it than to
speak of the Revolution itself with reproach or suspicion. . . .

We are living between the past and the future, between the Revolution and
Communism. . . . We have had the Revolution; how could we dare disavow
it or blaspheme it? We are psychologically "jammed" between the two. And
if—supposing it imaginable—our enemies overcame us and made us go back
to the prerevolutionary style of life (or join in Western democracy—it matters
little), I am persuaded that we should start all over again from the previous
point of departure—the Revolution.

While working at this article I have many times found myself dropping
into irony—that literary indecency! But at the same time I was trying to avoid
such expressions as "Soviet power"! I preferred to replace them by syn-
onyms—"our State," "the socialist system," etc. . . . For it is enough, for me,
to pronounce the words "power of the Soviets" immediately to imagine the
Revolution, the storming of the Winter Palace, the crepitating ribbons of the
machine guns, the bread cards, the siege, etc.; and to speak of all that with
disrespect would make me sick. If I have something against the socialist
State—and not so very much, either—I have nothing whatever against the
Soviets. Is that odd? Perhaps; that is just where the romanticism comes in.

Yes, we are all romantics about our past. And yet, the further we get away
from it and the nearer to Communism, the weaker is the romantic glamour
that the Revolution imparts to our art. That is understandable; romanticism
corresponds to only a part of our nature, and sometimes is even opposed to
it. "The madness of the brave, that is the wisdom of life," wrote the young
Gorki. It is quite true that, just when the Revolution was happening, madmen were necessary. But can one call a five year plan "the madness of the
brave"? Or the leadership of the Party—or even, for that matter, a Communism arriving inevitably by the logical march of history? When every point is
thought out, reasonably foreseen, and divided into corresponding paragraphs? A queer madness. H'm; you hadn't read your Marx, comrade Gorki!

When it sets up an ideal, romanticism had not enough sense of the obligatory: it takes its wishes for reality. That is not bad, but it smacks of the
arbitrary, of the subjective. What we desire is real, because things ought to
be so. Our life is beautiful, not only because we wish it so, but because it
must be—it has no choice.

All these arguments, unspoken and unconscious though they are, have led, little by little, to a drying-up of the ardent current of romanticism. The stream of art has congealed under the ice of a classicism which, being more definite, rational, finally more teleological, has supplanted romanticism. As early as 1922, A. Effros, in *The Messenger on the Threshold,* declared that "The classical spirit has already come in upon us from all sides. Everyone is breathing it, but people either know not how to distinguish it, or what to call it, or they are quite simply afraid to speak of it." . . .

The first heroes of Soviet literature marched to the assault of capitalist fortresses in shoes of bark worn to shreds, their mouths full of oaths. They were coarse and natural. . . . Now they have an air of correctness, they have good manners and are neatly dressed. If they sometimes lack taste, that only denotes the national and social character of our classicism, born of the Russian democracy. But neither the authors nor their heroes have any doubts about it; they do their very best to be handsome, polite, cultivated, and they want to do "the done thing" down to the smallest detail.

> Under the white ceiling, the ornamental lustre twinkled with its pendants of transparent glass threaded like beads of ice. The tall silvered columns sustained a dazzlingly white dome, spangled with festoons of electric lights.

What is this? A palace of the Tsars? No, it is an ordinary club in a little provincial town.

> On the platform, near the gleaming wing of the piano, stood Rakitin, dressed in a dark suit, his necktie flowing like a blue river down his chest. . . .

You think this is a singer, some fashionable tenor? Not at all; he is a worker for the Party. Now let us look at the people. They are not swearing, fighting, or drinking like fish. That was all right formerly. Nowadays, if they drink, it is at a wedding breakfast around a table loaded with delicate viands, and then in response to a toast:

> Casting a glance around at the guests, Terenti coughed discreetly into his hand, and smoothed with trembling fingers the silvery waves of his beard.
> —First of all, let us congratulate the young couple and drink to their health; may they beautify the earth!
> The guests assented with a friendly hubbub, and a crystal clinking of little glasses.
> —May they honour their parents!
> —May they have children with good health!
> —May they be a credit to the kolkhoz!

The novel from which these quotations are taken, E. Maltsev's *With All His Heart* (1949), is similar to dozens and hundreds of others. It is a sample of classical prose of mediocre literary quality. These banalities have long pervaded our literature, passing from one author to another without much change. . . .

For this contradiction between the victory of socialist realism and the feeble quality of literary production, socialist realism is often blamed, from a belief that great art is impossible within its limitations, that it is deadly to art in general. Mayakovsky, first of all, enables us to refute this. . . . Art does not fear dictatorship, nor severity nor repression, not even conservatism and the cliché. Art, when it has to be so, can be strictly religious, or stupidly official, or without individuality and still be great art. We enthuse before the style of Ancient Egypt, or Russian iconography, or folklore. Art is fluid enough to fit into the Procrustean bed that history offers it. But there is one thing it cannot endure—eclecticism.

Our misery is that we are not sufficiently convinced of socialist realism: that, after having obeyed its cruel laws, we fear to go on right to the end of the road we ourselves have traced out. Were we only less cultivated, no doubt it might be easier for us to attain the degree of integrity indispensable to the artist. But we have been to school, we have read various books and learnt all too well that there were remarkable writers before us—Balzac, Maupassant, Tolstoy . . . and one other; let us see, who was that? Ah, yes! Chekhov! . . . *That* has undone us. We wanted to become famous, to write like Chekhov at the first attempt. From that unnatural liaison proceeded monsters.

In the very term "socialist realism" there is a manifest, insurmountable contradiction. An art that is socialist—which means religious, orientated to a unique End—cannot be created by the literary means called "realist" in the nineteenth century. A picture perfectly true to the real, including all the details of everyday life, the psychological analyses, the landscapes, portraits, etc., does not lend itself to depiction in a language of teleological speculation. If socialist realism really wants to rise to the level of the great world-cultures and create its "Communiada" there is only one way—to have done with realism; to renounce its pitiful, and anyway futile efforts to create a socialist *Anna Karenina* or *Cherry Orchard*. When once it no longer wants to conform to a reality that is non-existent for it, it will be able to express the grandiose, unbelievable meaning of our epoch.

Unfortunately, that development is hardly likely. The events of the last few years have driven our art along a road of half-measures and half-truths. The death of Stalin dealt a mortal blow to our system of religious aesthetic, and to replace this by reviving the worship of Lenin is difficult. Lenin is too much like an ordinary man, he has too realistic an aspect—small, bald, and in civil-ian garb. Stalin, now, he had been specially created for the hyperbole that awaited him. Mysterious, omniscient, omnipotent, he was the living monument of our epoch and only lacked one quality to become God—immortality.

Ah, if only we had been more intelligent; if only we had surrounded his death with miracles! We should have given it out on the radio that he was not dead but had gone up into heaven, whence he was still looking at us, silently, over his mystical moustache. His relics would have cured paralytics and people possessed with devils. And children, before going to bed, would have been praying by their windows, with their eyes turned towards the bright stars of the celestial Kremlin.

But we did not listen to the voice of conscience. Instead of betaking ourselves to prayer, we set to work to unmask the "cult of personality" that we had created. We ourselves have blown up the foundations of that classical masterpiece which, had we waited but a little longer, might have rivalled the pyramids of Cheops or the Apollo Belvedere, in the treasure house of universal art. . . .

The strength of a theological system consists in its permanence, its harmony, its order. Once you allow that God has carelessly sinned with Eve and that, jealous of Adam, he sent that unhappy husband away to labour at land reclamation, then the whole conception of the creation of the world is done for, and it is impossible to revive the faith. . . .

VI.

A New Individualism

It is possible, in one of those facile dichotomies so dear to the hearts of interpreters, to divide historical epochs into those when an absolute is not in question and those dominated by a relativistic and skeptical point of view. In the same generalizing vein, one might take medieval Christendom as an instance of the one and post-1917 Europe as an instance of the other. But every such period contains its opposite: the absolutistic, its Abélards; the relativistic, its desperate seekers after ultimate truth.

These last can be of two kinds: those who find their absolute in God, in Nature, or in the laws of history, and henceforth assert and act upon their revelation; or those who do not, but nevertheless assert *something*. Such men are a very modern phenomenon (not necessarily their existence, but certainly their public significance). Malraux is one of them, and so are Jean-Paul Sartre and Albert Camus.

To those too young to fight in the First World War, the 1920s were a time of disorientation and vague anxieties through which they roamed in search of a spiritual home. "I roam in my heart," wrote the future playwright Armand Salacrou in a passage reminiscent of Alfred de Musset's *Fantasio,* "lost on the tracks of a bankrupt intelligence, without fire or passion, in search of an unfaked idea that is worth what I am worth." This in 1925, the year of the Treaty of Locarno; and two years later, "Man can only live happy in a world that has clarified the mystery of life." It was the old quest all over again, but this time with fewer illusions and less hope than a century before in the day of *Fantasio* and Musset. Salacrou's despairing anxiety paralleled that of Malraux and announced that of Sartre: "Nothing has any meaning any more," he wrote, "except solitude and death." And meantime his German contemporaries called for *"ein Menschendäm-merung, ein jauchzendes Vernichten"*—an end of men, a yawning annihilation.

Sartre escaped this nihilistic despair by inventing freedom, Malraux by adopt-ing an ethic of action and adapting it to his needs. In an early essay on *European Youth* (1921) he concluded that the great problem is to restore the unanimity of man—to reconcile man and his ideas—but (with foresight) "without forcing man to conform to an idea given *a priori*."

This last temptation was only too great. A generation that feels the ground tremble beneath its feet seeks the solid reassurance of an absolute; and when the absolute is either missing or just not absolute enough to be entirely convincing, action is the best way to still one's doubts and those of others—action that may readily be confused, sometimes even by the actor himself, with conviction. In England this problem did not arise too acutely for a while; but in Italy, Germany, and France, where it was hard to tell whether the continuing tremors were the last of the past cataclysm or the first of a new one, young men turned to the cult of action—heroic action—to still their fears.

The need to do something was met by revolutionary activities and interests, whether Fascist or Communist, and many young men like Pierre Drieu la Ro-chelle were tossed about during this time between the two extremes, interested less in the rival doctrines than in their promises of faith, of change, of action. Malraux himself might well have ended on the right with contemporaries like Drieu and Henry de Montherlant, whose individualistic nihilism led them toward aristocratic, or would-be aristocratic, eclecticism. There was much in Monther-lant's declaration of 1941 which, even at late as that, Malraux could have accepted. "What do we want?" Montherlant was to write in the wake of his country's de-feat: "Someone who has both blood and intellect. His blood drives him to strug-gle, his intellect postulates unbelief. Struggle without faith is the formula to which we necessarily come."

For yet awhile, however, there would be both: the 1930s brought heroism back into fashion, in Nüremberg rallies, in the enthusiasms of English intellectuals, even in a revival of interest in the "heroic" Corneille. The reviews, whether Cath-olic, Marxist, or Fascist, turned toward "professors of energy" like Nietzsche and Péguy who had been played down for a while. And Bergson helped emphasize the positive tendencies of the time by publishing his long-considered *Two Sources of Morality and Religion* in 1932:

> Mankind groans [wrote Bergson], half crushed by the weight of its prog-ress. It does not realize sufficiently that its future depends on itself. It is up to mankind to decide in the first place whether it wants to go on living. It is up to it to consider next whether it merely wants to live, or

to provide besides the effort that is needed to accomplish, even on our stubborn planet, the essential function of the universe that is a machine for the creation of gods.

The 1935 International Congress of Revolutionary Writers reflected this mood in the new concern for the transcendence of the human condition, of man's sentence of death in an absurd universe. When André Gide told the congress that literature must show man affirming his Promethean powers, he called like Bergson for something that would give our lives meaning and promise survival.[1] This was when Malraux's *Man's Fate* (1933) won the *Prix Goncourt* for trying to do just that;[2] soon, in *Man's Hope* (1937), expressive of his Spanish experience, he found the hope and faith Montherlant lacked in the heroic action and self-affirmation Montherlant had seen as only a poor alternative to fulfillment.

A few years later, in a wartime manuscript—*The Walnut Trees of Altenburg*—this valiant pessimism no longer seems enough. The futility of war and struggle, the vanity of man's attempts to forge or affect history, have become too evident. Man still is what he makes, but he must concentrate on something he really *can* make, where he may still be master. Adventure has been tried, struggle and revolution have all been found wanting: what is left now is artistic creation. "The greatest mystery," declares the hero of *Altenburg,* "is not that we should be cast by chance between the profusion of matter and that of the stars; it is that, in this prison, we draw from ourselves images powerful enough to deny our nothingness." So, art now becomes the assertion of man's will to be free, his reply to the dumb, crushing challenge of the universe that surrounds him. All art, to Malraux, is an attempt of the spirit to create an autonomous, original order—to substitute "a world that man governs for the world that man endures."

This, indeed, seems to have been one of the prime aims of that "abstract art" so characteristic of our times, that Jacques Villon has defined as a dramatic exchange between reality on one hand and, on the other, a man out to recreate it

---

[1]Altogether, the religious theme has become more important in contemporary literature. However, a discussion of the revived religious interest that provided one of the most striking developments of the last decade would take too long and add little to our story. As Professor Walter Kaufmann has pointed out, Christian Existentialism is not a novelty but a reaffirmation of fundamental Christian doctrine. As for Social Christianity, when it does not repeat the themes of nineteenth-century reformers, it emphasizes the social role of the Church over its spiritual message. The religious ferment of our time appears in our context as one more reflection of man's desperate search for an ultimate authority, this time and not surprisingly in a familiar direction.

[2]But see the contemporary criticism, like that of François Mauriac, that discerns the work's profound despair.

on another plane: hence, in the first place, to abstract it. But the reality of the "abstract" artist partakes little of the appearances that surround us and him. The world we live in and perceive is either illusory or rotten. The artist either pierces the facade, or pulls down the old, ruined, untidy structures (including accepted art forms) in order to clear the way for something purer, truer, better—a transcendent reality expressed in terms of pure forms. Thus, while sensitive literary analysts warn men against thoughtless acceptance of ready-made commonplaces, against the easy espousal of prefabricated forms and norms, artists begin to move in the same direction, to abandon existing forms and try to make a fresh start with the nearest they could get to an ideal untainted by previous associations: geometrical forms, lines, squares, circles, preferably in the simplest, purest, of color schemes. Like Proust, these artists knew that all that had to be done had to be done by themselves. The artist stood alone and realized once more that he stood at the beginning of the world.

And so, concurrent with the limitation of choice inherent in the growth of all-powerful political and economic structures and reflected in the moth-like despair of many trapped anti-Utopians, we discover a philosophy of self-determination, the assertion that choice is not only possible but necessary and, indeed, inevitable.

The same experience and the same concerns inform the Existentialist writers properly speaking. And, although Malraux appears very much as a predecessor, his significance from this point of view only becomes more apparent, like that of Dostoevsky or Saint-Exupéry, in the light of a later more widespread experience that reproduced for many of this postwar generation the feelings of a relatively select few in the 1920s. As with Malraux's, in Camus' words, "the tragedy of our generation is to have seen a false hope." As Malraux might have said and as Camus concludes: "Beyond nihilism, all of us, among the ruins, prepare a renaissance. But few know it." But for this generation the ruins were more real, faith in a renaissance both more difficult to achieve and more ardently desired, than for the earlier ones.

In this situation where hope seems impossible in a world whose purpose is either lacking or unfathomable (which comes to the same thing), Sartre and Camus offered a limited hope for people in restricted circumstances. To Sartre, our very sense of *lack* was a good, healthy sign: the fundamental purpose of man is to bring about the synthesis of being and consciousness, and in this pursuit he creates values and beliefs that *are* the only real values and beliefs and that endow him with meaning and purpose. In effect man, as Sartre saw him, is out to do what Bergson suggested—create gods; more correctly, to turn himself into a god.

Where for Sartre our very limits promised unlimited possibilities, for Camus they seemed rather to teach the lesson of a defiant stoicism. There is, Camus explains in *The Rebel* (1951)—there is for man a possibility of thought and action *at his own level,* provided he does not aim too far beyond it, reach for the stars, try to create an absolute. "How," he asks, "can society define an absolute? Perhaps everyone seeks this absolute for all. But the task of society and politics is simply so to order the affairs of all that everyone will have the leisure and the freedom for this common quest. History can no longer be set up as an object of worship. It is simply an opportunity that must be fertilized by vigilant revolt. . . . No wisdom, today, can pretend to offer more. Revolt stumbles endlessly over evil, and can only start all over again. Man can master in himself all that must be mastered. He must mend in creation all that can be mended. After which, children will continue to die unjustly, even in the perfect society. In his greatest effort man can only try to diminish the world's pain in arithmetical terms. But injustice and suffering will remain and, however limited, they will never cease to cause disgust and indignation. The 'Why' of Dimitri Karamazov will continue to ring; art and revolt will die only with the last man."

In Malraux, in Sartre, in Camus, man transcends his limited condition. Bound to his rock like Prometheus, or rolling it like Sisyphus, always hobbled, always frustrated, he learns to triumph over his fate. As Malraux told the UNESCO after the war: "God is dead: fair enough. The problem we must face today is to know whether *man* is dead or not."

Nietzsche

Friedrich Nietzsche (1844–1900) was one of the most original, perhaps *the* most original, thinkers of his time. Son of a Saxon pastor, brought up by women and in the Spartan conditions of a crack boarding school, he became professor of classical philology at the University of Basel at the age of twenty-four. Resigning ten years later because of ill health, he still had ten years for his work. In January, 1889, he collapsed on the streets of Turin; he was to spend the last twelve years of his life in hopeless insanity.

More than that of most philosophers, his work has suffered from misinterpretation and misrepresentation, and while the oracular quality of his utterances did little to facilitate a clear understanding of his meaning, confusion has been confounded by a great deal of quotation out of context. Certainly, as Nietzsche himself pointed out, his ideas could not be grasped from any brief or superficial reading, and to this extent, the passages that follow may merely accentuate the confusion. Even so, they will have served their purpose if they provide an idea of the impression they would create when tossed, like firecrackers, into the self-satisfied and podgy-minded climate of late-nineteenth-century Europe.

In the last generation, Nietzsche was regarded as a prophet of totalitarianism and race hatred. Today, however, we can see him for what he was—the rebel against society whose complacent mediocrity he abhorred, and against democratic conformity he despised. "The philosopher," as he wrote in his attack on Wagner, "has to be the bad conscience of his age. What does a philosopher firstly and lastly require of himself? To overcome the spirit of his own age embodied in him, to become 'timeless.'" Thus, Nietzsche's will to power appears as the aspiration to power over oneself. And his insistence on individualism, self-assertion, and self-transcendence reveals him as a forerunner, and not the least important, of contemporary Existentialist thought.

Loneliness and Its Possibilities

It is not pride that has sealed my lips so long, but rather the humility of a sufferer who is ashamed to betray how much he suffers. An animal when it is sick creeps away into a dark cellar, and so likewise does the philosophic beast. . . . I am alone, absurdly alone, and in my unflinching and arduous struggle against all that men have hitherto valued and reverenced, I have become a sort of dark cellar myself . . . something hidden and mysterious, that is not to be found even when it is sought. . . . Yet, between you and me, it is not impossible that I am the greatest philosopher of the century, perhaps even more than that. I am a decisive and fateful link between two thousand centuries.

(Letter, 1888)

Our present-day Europe, the scene of a precipitate, senseless attempt to blend thoroughly both classes and races, is therefore sceptical in all the heights and depths of its being; sometimes with the nimble scepticism which springs impatiently and wantonly from branch to branch; sometimes gloomily, like a cloud overcharged with interrogative signs;—and often sick unto death of its will! Paralysis of the will: where does one fail to find this cripple sitting at present? And yet how bedecked often! How seductively decked out! There are the finest parade dresses and disguises for this disease; and that, for example, most of what is at present exhibited in the show cases as "objectivity," "the scientific spirit," "*l'art pour l'art*," "pure, voluntary knowing," etc., is merely decked-out scepticism and paralysis of will.—I will answer for this diagnosis of the European disease.—The disease of the will is diffused un-

Source: The first six selections are from *Nietzsche*, compiled and translated by Thomas Common, London, 1901. The last is from *The Portable Nietzsche*, edited and translated by Walter Kaufmann. Copyright 1954 by The Viking Press, Inc. Copyright renewed © 1982 by Viking Penguin, Inc. Reprinted by permission of Viking Penguin, a division of Penguin Books USA Inc.

equally over Europe; it shows itself most extensively and multifariously where civilization has longest been indigenous, it decreases in proportion as "the barbarian" still—or again—asserts his rights under the loose robe of western culture.

(*Beyond Good and Evil,* 1886)

The greatest modern event—that God is dead, that the belief in the Christian God has become unworthy of belief—has now begun to cast its first shadows over Europe. To the few, at least, whose eye, whose suspecting glance is strong enough and subtle enough for the spectacle, a sun seems to have set to them, some old profound truth seems to have changed into doubt; our ancient world must every day seem to them "older," stranger, more unreliable, more vespertine. In the main, however, one may say that the event itself is far too great, too much beyond the power of apprehension of many people, for even the report of it to have reached them, to say nothing of their capacity for knowing what is really involved and what must all collapse, now that this belief has been undermined—by being built thereon, by being buttressed thereby, by being engrafted therein; for example, our entire European morality. The prolonged excess and continuation of demolition, ruin, and overthrow which is now impending—who has yet understood it sufficiently to be obliged to stand up as the teacher and herald of such tremendously frightful logic, as the prophet of such an overshadowing, of such a solar eclipse as has probably never happened on earth before? Even we, the born riddle-readers, who as it were wait on the mountains, posted betwixt to-day and to-morrow, and engirt by the contradiction between to-day and to-morrow, we, the firstlings and premature births of the coming century, to whom especially the shadows which must forthwith envelop Europe *should* already have come in sight—how is it that even we, without genuine sympathy for this overshadowing, contemplate its advent without personal solicitude or fear? Are we still perhaps too much under the *immediate effects* of the event—and are these effects, especially as regards *ourselves,* perhaps the reverse of what was to be expected—not at all sad and depressing, but rather like a new and difficultly describable variety of light, happiness, alleviation, enlivenment, encouragement, and rosy dawn? In fact, we philosophers and "free spirits" feel ourselves irradiated as by a new rosy dawn by the report that "the old God is dead"; our hearts thereby overflow with gratitude, astonishment, presentiment, and expectation. At last the horizon seems once more unobstructed, granting even that it is not bright; our ships can at last start on their voyages once more, in face of every danger; every risk is again permitted to the knowing ones; the sea, our sea, again lies open before us; perhaps there never was such an open sea. . . .

When Buddha was dead, his shadow still continued to be seen for centuries afterwards in a cave—an immense, frightful shadow. God is dead, but as the human race is constituted, there will perhaps be caves for millenniums in which his shadow will be seen. And we—we have still to get the better of his shadow!

Let us be on our guard against thinking that the world is a living being. Where could it extend itself? On what could it nourish itself? How could it grow and augment? We know approximately what the organic is; and we were meant, were we, to reinterpret the inexpressibly derivative, tardy, rare and casual which we perceive only on the crust of the earth, as the essential, universal and eternal, like those who call the universe an organism? That disgusts me.—Let us be on our guard against believing that the universe is a machine; it is assuredly not constructed for one end; we invest it with far too high an honor with the word "machine."—Let us be on our guard against supposing that anything so methodical as the cyclic motions of our neighboring stars obtains generally and everywhere throughout the universe; indeed, a glance at the Milky-way induces a doubt as to whether there are not many cruder and more conflicting motions, stars with eternal rectilineal gravitating orbits, and the like. The astral arrangement in which we live is an exception, and the relatively long duration which is determined by it, has again made possible the exception of exceptions, the formation of the organic. The collective character of the world, however, is to all eternity chaos—not in the sense of the absence of necessity, but of the absence of arrangement, organisation, method, beauty, wisdom, and whatever else our aesthetic humanities are called. Judged by our reason, the unlucky casts are far oftenest the rule, nor are the exceptions the result of a hidden purpose; and the whole music-box repeats eternally its air, which can never be called a melody—and moreover the very expression "unlucky cast" is in itself an anthropomorphising which involves blame; but how could we blame or praise the universe?—Let us be on our guard against ascribing to it heartlessness and irrationality, or their opposites; it is neither perfect, nor beautiful, nor noble, nor does it seek to be anything of the kind; it does not at all attempt to imitate man. It is altogether unaffected by any of our aesthetic or moral judgments! It is also destitute of self-preservative instinct, and in general of all instinct; it likewise knows no law!—Let us be on our guard against saying that there are laws in nature. There are only necessities; there is no one who commands, no one who obeys, no one who trangresses. When you know that there is no final goal, you know also that there is no chance, for it is only in a world with final goals that the word "chance" has a meaning.—Let us be on our guard against saying that death is the contrary of life. The living being is only a species of the dead being, and a very rare species.—Let us be on our guard against thinking that the world produces eternally that which is new. There are no eternally enduring substances; matter is just an error similar to the God of the Eleatics.—But when shall we be at an end with our cautions and precautions? When will all these shadows of God cease to obscure us? When shall we have nature completely undeified? When shall we be permitted to commence *naturalising* ourselves with pure, newly-discovered, newly redeemed nature? . . .

It would be a question whether Schopenhauer with his Pessimism, *i.e.*, the problem of the *worth of existence,* was necessarily only a German? I think not. The event *after* which this problem was to be expected with certainty, so that an astronomer of the soul could have calculated the day and the hour for it— the decline of the belief in the Christian God, the victory of scientific athe-ism,—was a collective European event in which all races are supposed to have had their share of service and honor. . . . Schopenhauer was the first avowed and inflexible atheist we Germans have had; his hostility to Hegel had its ultimate motive here. The non-divinity of existence was regarded by him as something given, tangible, indiscussable; he always lost his philosophical composure and got into a passion when he saw any one hesitate and make circumlocutions here.

It is at this point that his thorough uprightness of character comes in; unconditional, honest atheism is precisely the prerequisite of his raising the problem, as a final and hard-won victory of the European conscience, as the most portentous act of two thousand years' discipline to truth, which in the end no longer tolerates the *lie* of the belief in God. . . . When we have thrust away from us the Christian interpretation of things and condemned its "significance" as a forgery, we are immediately confronted in a striking manner with the *Schopenhauerian question:* Has existence, then, *a significance at all?*—the question which will require a couple of centuries even to be com-pletely heard in all its profundity. That which Schopenhauer himself an-swered with regard to this question was—forgive me for saying so—some-what premature, somewhat juvenile, only a compromise,—a persistence in and adhesion to the very same Christian-ascetic, moral perspectives, the belief in which had got warning to quit along with the belief in God. But he *raised* the question—as we have said, as a good European, and not as a German.

(*The Gay Science,* 1882)

We who hold a belief which is different [from that of democrats, socialists and anarchists]—we who regard the democratic movement not only as a de-generating form of political organisation, but as equivalent to a degenerating, waning, type of man, as involving his mediocrising and depreciation—where have *we* to fix our hopes? *In new philosophers:* there is no other alternative; in minds strong and original enough to induce opposed estimates of value, to transvalue and subvert "eternal valuations"; in forerunners, in men of the future, who in the present shall fix the constraints and fasten the knots which will compel the will of millenniums to take *new* paths. To teach man the future of humanity as *volition*, as depending on human will, and to make preparation for vast hazardous enterprises and collective attempts in rearing and educating; in order thereby to put an end to the frightful rule of folly and chance which has hitherto gone by the name of "history" (the folly of the "greatest number" is only its latest form): for that purpose a new type of philosophers and leaders will be needed some time or other, at the very idea of which everything that has existed in the way of occult, terrible, and benevolent beings might look pale and dwarfed. The image of such leaders hovers before *our* eyes: is it lawful for me to say it aloud, ye free spirits? The conditions which one would partly have to create and partly to utilise for their genesis: the presumptive methods and tests by virtue of which a soul would grow up to such an elevation and power as to feel a *constraint* to these problems; a transvaluation of values, under the new pressure and hammer of which a conscience would be steeled and a heart transformed into brass, so as to bear the weight of such responsibility; and, on the other hand, the necessity for such leaders, the dreadful danger that they might be lacking, or miscarry and degenerate—there are *our real* anxieties and glooms, ye know it well, ye free spirits! These are the heavy, distant thoughts and storms that sweep across the heaven of *our* life.

(*Beyond Good and Evil*)

Natural death is death destitute of rationality, it is really *irrational* death, in which the pitiable substance of the shell determines how long the kernel is to endure; in which, consequently, the pining, sick, sottish prison-warden is the authority who designates the hour when his noble prisoner is to die. Natural death is the suicide of nature, that is to say, the annihilation of the most rational part by the most irrational, which is united with it. Only under religious illumination can it appear the reverse; because then, as is only fair, the higher reason (God) gives the command, to which the lower reason has to adjust itself. Apart from religion, natural death is not worthy of any glorification.—The enlightened regulation and control of death belongs to the morality of the future—at present quite intangible and seemingly immoral, the appearance of the rosy dawn of which, however, must cause indescribable happiness.

(*The Wanderer and His Shadow*, 1880)

Forward then on wisdom's road, with firm step and good confidence! Whatever be your state, serve as a source of experience to yourself! Cast away dissatisfaction with your nature, pardon yourself on account of your own *ego*, for in any case you have in yourself a ladder with a hundred rungs, on which you can ascend to knowledge. The age into the midst of which you regretfully feel yourself cast, counts you happy for such good fortune; it calls out to you that at present experiences still fall to your lot which men of later times must perhaps dispense with. Do not despise it to have been religious; understand thoroughly that you have had thereby a genuine access to art. Can you not, precisely by these experiences, follow more intelligently immense stretches of the path of earlier humanity? Is it not precisely on the *very soil* which occasionally displeases you so much, the soil of inaccurate thinking, that many of the most splendid fruits of ancient civilisation have grown? One must have loved religion and art as mother and nurse—otherwise one cannot become wise. But one must see beyond them, one must be able to outgrow them; if one remains under their spell one does not understand them. In like manner must history be familiar to you, and the cautious game with the scales: "on the one hand—on the other hand." Wander back, treading in the footsteps by which humanity has made its great, suffering journey through the desert of the past: you will thus learn most surely where it is that future humanity cannot, or should not, walk again. And when you seek, with all your power, to discover how the knot of the future has to be tied, your own life acquires the value of an instrument and expedient of knowledge. It is in your power to make all your experiences—your trials and errors, mistakes, illusions and passions, your love and your hope—to make all these subserve your aim. Your aim is to become yourself a chain of necessary culture-links, and from their necessity to infer the necessity in the process of general culture. When your glance has become strong enough to make out the bottom of the dark well of your being and experience, the distant constellations of future civilisations will also perhaps become visible to you in that mirror. Do you think that such a life, with such an aim, is too painful, too devoid of charms? Then you have not yet learned that no honey is sweeter than that of knowledge, and that the lowering clouds of tribulation must yet serve you as udders out of which you will milk the milk for your refreshment. When age comes, then only will you rightly perceive how you have obeyed the voice of nature, that nature which rules the whole world by means of delight: the same life which has its apex in age has also its apex in wisdom, in the soft, solar radiance of a constant intellectual cheerfulness; you meet both, age and wisdom, on the same mountain ridge of life—thus has nature willed it. It is then the time—and no occasion for displeasure—for the mist of death to approach. Towards the light—your last movement; an exultation of experience—your last sound.

(*Human, All-Too-Human*, 1878)

Behind the glorification of "work" and the tireless talk of the "blessings of work" I find the same thought as behind the praise of impersonal activity for the public benefit: the fear of everything individual. At bottom, one now feels when confronted with work—and what is invariably meant is relentless industry from early till late—that such work is the best policy, that it keeps everybody in harness and powerfully obstructs the development of reason, of covetousness, of the desire for independence. For it uses up a tremendous amount of nervous energy and takes it away from reflection, brooding, dreaming, worry, love, and hatred; it always sets a small goal before one's eyes and permits easy and regular satisfactions. In that way a society in which the members continually work hard will have more security; and security is now adored as the supreme goddess. And now—horrors!—it is precisely the "worker" who has become dangerous. "Dangerous individuals are swarming all around." And behind them, the danger of dangers: the individual. . . .

The madman. Have you not heard of that madman who lit a lantern in the bright morning hours, ran to the market place, and cried incessantly, "I seek God! I seek God!" As many of those who do not believe in God were standing around just then, he provoked much laughter. Why, did he get lost? said one. Did he lose his way like a child? said another. Or is he hiding? Is he afraid of us? Has he gone on a voyage? or emigrated? Thus they yelled and laughed. The madman jumped into their midst and pierced them with his glances.

"Whither is God?" he cried. "I shall tell you. *We have killed him*—you and I. All of us are his murderers. But how have we done this? How were we able to drink up the sea? Who gave us the sponge to wipe away the entire horizon? What did we do when we unchained this earth from its sun? Whither is it moving now? Away from all suns? Are we not plunging continually? Backward, sideward, forward, in all directions? Is there any up or down left? Are we not straying as through an infinite nothing? Do we not feel the breath of empty space? Has it not become colder? Is not night and more night coming on all the while? Must not lanterns be lit in the morning? Do we not hear anything yet of the noise of the grave-diggers who are burying God? Do we not smell anything yet of God's decomposition? Gods too decompose. God is dead. God remains dead. And we have killed him. How shall we, the murderers of all murderers, comfort ourselves? What was holiest and most powerful of all that the world has yet owned has bled to death under our knives. Who will wipe this blood off us? What water is there for us to clean ourselves? What festivals of atonement, what sacred games shall we have to invent? Is not the greatness of this deed too great for us? Must not we ourselves become gods simply to seem worthy of it? There has never been a greater deed; and whoever will be born after us—for the sake of this deed he will be part of a higher history than all history hitherto."

Here the madman fell silent and looked again at his listeners; and they too were silent and stared at him in astonishment. At last he threw his lantern on the ground, and it broke and went out. "I come too early," he said then; "my time has not come yet. This tremendous event is still on its way, still wandering—it has not yet reached the ears of man. Lightning and thunder require time, the light of the stars requires time, deeds require time even after they are done, before they can be seen and heard. This deed is still more distant from them than the most distant stars—*and yet they have done it themselves.*"

It has been related further that on that same day the madman entered divers churches and there sang his *requiem aeternam deo.* Led out and called to account, he is said to have relied each time, "What are the churches now if they are not the tombs and sepulchers of God?" . . .

Preparatory men. I welcome all signs that a more manly, a warlike, age is about to begin, an age which, above all, will give honor to valor once again. For this age shall prepare the way for one yet higher, and it shall gather the strength which this higher age will need one day—this age which is to carry heroism into the pursuit of knowledge and *wage wars* for the sake of thoughts and their consequences. To this end we now need many preparatory valorous men who cannot leap into being out of nothing—any more than out of the sand and slime of our present civilization and metropolitanism; men who are bent on seeking for that aspect in all things which must be *overcome;* men characterized by cheerfulness, patience, unpretentiousness, and contempt for all great vanities, as well as by magnanimity in victory and forbearance regarding the small vanities of the vanquished; men possessed of keen and free judgment concerning all victors and the share of chance in every victory and every fame; men who have their own festivals, their own weekdays, their own periods of mourning, who are accustomed to command with assurance and are no less ready to obey when necessary, in both cases equally proud and serving their own cause; men who are in greater danger more fruitful, and happier! For, believe me, the secret of the greatest fruitfulness and the greatest enjoyment of existence is: to *live dangerously!* Build your cities under Vesuvius! Send your ships into uncharted seas! Live at war with your peers and with yourselves! Be robbers and conquerors, as long as you cannot be rulers and owners, you lovers of knowledge! Soon the age will be past when you could be satisfied to live like shy deer, hidden in the woods! At long last the pursuit of knowledge will reach out for its due; it will want to *rule* and *own,* and you with it! . . .

One thing is needful. "Giving style" to one's character—a great and rare art! It is exercized by those who see all the strengths and weaknesses of their own natures and then comprehend them in an artistic plan until everything appears as art and reason and even weakness delights the eye. Here a large mass of second nature has been added; there a piece of original nature has been removed: both by long practice and daily labor. Here the ugly which could not be removed is hidden; there it has been reinterpreted and made sublime. . . . It will be the strong and domineering natures who enjoy their finest gaiety in such compulsion, in such constraint and perfection under a law of their own; the passion of their tremendous will relents when confronted with stylized, conquered, and serving nature; even when they have to build palaces, and lay out gardens, they demur at giving nature a free hand. Conversely, it is the weak characters without power over themselves, who *hate* the constraint of style. . . . They become slaves as soon as they serve; they hate to serve. Such spirits—and they may be of the first rank—are always out to interpret themselves and their environment as *free nature*—wild, arbitrary, fantastic, disorderly, astonishing; and they will do well because only in this way do they please themselves. For one thing is needful: that a human being attain his satisfaction with himself—whether it be by this or by that poetry and art; only then is a human being at all tolerable to behold. Whoever is dissatisfied with himself is always ready to revenge himself therefor; we others will be his victims, if only by always having to stand his ugly sight. For the sight of the ugly makes men bad and gloomy.

(*The Eulogists of Work*)

Gide

André Gide (1869–1951) published *Les Nourritures Terrestres* in 1897, when he was still in his twenties and literature, as he would later explain, was redolent of closeness and falsity—in need of a renewal. Stifled by his Protestant upbringing, bogged down in the traditions that a formal literary education instilled in him and his likes, the young man broke with both, vividly expressed the joy of liberation, and called on others to follow. His lush style was in an older tradition; the individualistic self-assertion was also familiar and yet also new: hedonism carried further than ever now that God was dead.

The influence of Gide's claim for man's right to express and "make" himself without false embarrassment or shame was tremendous; henceforth, it seemed, no justification was needed beside one's own will—indeed, one's own whim. In the absence of all authority but oneself, acts were necessarily "gratuitous" since they could hardly be referred to anything in particular. If God was dead, man's wish was the only authority left, and between such wishes the differences would be rather of intensity than of "reason" in a world where no basis for reason remained.

Les Nourritures Terrestres is a potpourri of counsel in prose and verse addressed to a young man, Nathaniel, who is exhorted to live in and for the moment, to let impulse and desire justify all actions, to hold himself open to all experience and sensation, to avoid choice that risks limiting the range of choices, to walk on both sides of the street, not on one alone. A joyous hedonism for those who could afford it.

Advice to Nathaniel

To act without *judging* whether the action is good or bad. To love without worrying whether it is good or evil.

Nathaniel, I shall teach you fervor.

A pathetic existence, Nathaniel, rather than tranquillity. I wish for no rest other than the sleep of death. I fear that any desire, any energy, I have left unsatisfied during my life may torment me for their survival. *I hope,* having expressed on this earth all that waited in me, satisfied, to die completely *desperate. . . .*

Nathaniel, I shall teach you fervor.

Our acts cling to us as to phosphorus its glow. They eat us up, it is true, but they make our brilliance.

And if our spirit has meant anything, it is because it has burnt more ardently than some others. . . .

There are strange possibilities in every man. The present would be full of all possible futures, if the past had not already projected a pattern upon it. But, alas! a unique past proposes a unique future—projects it ahead of us, like an infinite bridge over space.

One is certain always to do only what one is incapable of understanding. To understand, is to feel oneself capable of doing. TO ASSUME THE GREATEST DEGREE OF HUMANITY, there is the right formula.

Diverse forms of life; you all seemed beautiful to me. . . .

I sincerely hope that I have known all the passions and all the vices; at least, I have favored them. All my being has precipitated itself toward all beliefs; and there have been evenings when I was so crazed that I almost believed in my soul, to such an extent did I feel it ready to escape from my body. . . .

And our life shall have been before us like a glass full of ice-cold water, a damp glass held in the hands of a feverish man who wants to drink, and who drinks it all in one gulp, knowing well that he should wait but unable to thrust away the glass delicious to his lips, so fresh is the water, so thirsty does the searing fever make him. . . .

Source: Translated by Eugen Weber.

Nathaniel, it is only God that one cannot await. To wait for God, Nathaniel, is not to understand that you possess him already. Do not distinguish between God and happiness, and set all your happiness in the moment. . . .

Nathaniel, oh! satisfy your pleasure when your soul is still smiling—and your desire for love when your lips are still beautiful to kiss and your embrace is merry.

For you will think, you will say: "The fruits were there; their weight bent the branches, already wearied them; my mouth was there and it was filled with desires; but my mouth remained shut, and my hands could not stretch out for they remained joined in prayer; and my heart and my flesh have remained desperately thirsty. Their hour has desperately gone by. . . .

Now, Nathaniel, throw away my book. Free yourself from it. Leave me. . . . When have I said I wanted you to be like me? It is because you differ from me that I love you; I love in you only that which differs from me. To educate! Whom would I educate, but myself? Shall I tell you, Nathaniel? I have interminably educated myself. I continue. I value myself only in that which I may do.

Nathaniel, throw away my book; do not be satisfied with it. Do not believe that *your* truth could be found by someone else; more than anything, be ashamed of that. . . .

Throw away my book; understand that there is only *one* of the thousand stands one can take before life. Seek your own. That which another could do as well as you, do not do it. That which another could say as well as you, do not say it, could write as well, do not write it. Fasten only onto that part of yourself which you feel exists nowhere else but in yourself and make of yourself, impatiently or patiently, oh! the most irreplaceable of beings.

Malraux

André Malraux (1901–1976) started out as a student of archaeology and oriental lore. His interests (and an unusually enterprising nature) took him first to Indochina and then to China, the ensuing experiences furnishing the local color of his first great novels—*The Conquerors* (1928), *The Royal Road* (1930), and *Man's Fate* (1933), the last of which brought him the much-coveted Goncourt Prize and a fame that increased over the years, as the plight of his characters was seen ever more clearly to match that of modern man. The title of *Man's Fate—La Condition humaine*—was taken from Pascal:

> Let us imagine a number of men in chains, and all condemned to death, and some of these men having their throats cut every day in sight of their

fellows, and those who remain recognizing their own fate in that of their companions and, as they wait their turn, staring at each other full of anguish and without hope. Such is the picture of man's fate.

This novel was probably the first of the long series of Existentialist stories and novels, which other Frenchmen have done so much to develop. The views it expressed in 1933, however, had been foreshadowed in an earlier essay of 1926, *La Tentation de l'Occident*, which has not been reprinted since, and parts of which follow. The discussion appears as an exchange of letters between a young Frenchman traveling in China and a Chinese living in France, each of whom in his new environment discovers in a fresh light both the alien culture and his own self.

Following the early 1930s, Malraux's "existential individualism" expressed itself in a tremendously active and adventurous life, in war, revolution, resistance, and mere politics; he was DeGaulle's Minister of Cultural Affairs from 1959 to 1969. Withal he also found time to establish a solid and well-deserved reputation as one of the great writers and art historians of our time.

The Temptation of the West

Ling to A.D.   Paris

It seems to me that you attribute too much importance to what an almost general convention calls reality. The world created by this convention, a world you accept because its denial would call for great courage on the part of him who would attempt it, weighs heavily upon you. Passion, in your social order, appears as a cunning fissure. Whatever our race, we know that we live in prepared worlds, but a sort of fierce joy grips us all when the call of our deepest wants show us their arbitrariness. The passionate man is at variance with the world he has conceived, as with the one that he endures, and it makes no difference that he has foreseen passion. The man who wants to love wants to escape, and that is little; but the man or the woman who wants to be loved, who wants to cause another being to give up, for their sake, his compliance with this convention, seems to me to obey a necessity so powerful that I find in it convincing proof of this: *at the center of European man, dominating the great motions of his life, there is an essential absurdity*. Do not you think so?

Source: La Tentation de l'Occident (perhaps more fitly translated as *The Predicament of the West*), Paris, Editions Bernard Grasset, 1926. Translated by Eugen Weber.

Ling to A.D.   Paris

Whoever allows himself to be ruled by the mind will come to live only for and through it. There is no more inauspicious garb. We [Chinese] want to avoid being conscious of ourselves as individuals. The purpose of our mind is to experience clearly our fragmentary quality, and to derive from this sensation a sense of the universe. . . .

This notion of the world that you do not find in yourselves you want to replace by structures. You want a coherent world. You create it and draw from it a peculiar sensibility encompassed with extreme delicacy. Who can say what it owes to your mind? . . .

I too have walked in your incomparable gardens, where the statues mingle with the declining sun their great shadows, royal or divine. Their open hands seem then to raise a heavy offering of memories and glory. Your heart can discern in the union of these slowly lengthening shadows a long-awaited law. Ah! what lament would be worthy of a race which, to rediscover its highest thoughts, knows only to entreat its faithless dead. Despite its fixed power, the European twilight is mournful and empty, empty as the heart of a conqueror. Among the most vain and tragic actions of man none has ever seemed to me more tragic and more vain than that by which you consult your illustrious shades—race dedicated to power, desperate race. . . .

A.D. to Ling   Canton

I have been watching China for nearly two years. The first thing it has changed in me is the Western idea of Man. I can no longer conceive Man independent of his intensity. It suffices to read a psychological work to feel how our most penetrating general ideas go wrong when we want to apply them to the understanding of our actions. Their value disappears as our scrutiny advances and, always, we run up against the incomprehensible, the absurd, that is the highest degree of the particular.

Is not the key of this irrational in the ever different intensity which follows life? It is affected by our willing, conscious life, and our more secret life, made up of dreams and secret feelings reaching out in absolute freedom. That a man dreams of being king or fortunate lover has no effect on his everyday actions; but let a passion or a shock disable him: how easily somebody else's actions will resound in him, weakly or strongly according to whether he is exalted or depressed. . . . Werther is the suggestion of death, but still the suggestion is only accepted by certain people at a certain moment. And love—the love that must be differentiated from the mere will to win a woman, the love that is shared, is it not also a strange forest where, beneath

our actions and our wills, our feelings operate and suffer freely and, sometimes, draw us apart as if, *saturated by our feelings,* we can no longer endure
them? For they alter through their life even more surely than they do through
events. Profound life: triumph of uncertainty, fatal creation, ever resumed, of
a singular chance. . . .

Ling to A.D.   Paris
    Who would dream of denying that all this rests on what you call an act of
faith? You say that such an act is arbitrary. True. But, then, what is it that
permits you to live with other men and understand them? Whence comes
your strength? And what is your perception of reality, if it is not approval,
compliance? Just because you survey your civilization with some suspicion
do you imagine yourself free of your dead, of your needs, and of this tragic
peril that slumbers at the very heart of your life? . . . The intensity that your
ideas create in you now seems to me to explain your life better than the ideas
themselves. Absolute reality has been for you first God, then man; but *man
is dead,* after God, and you seek with anguish the one to whom you could
entrust his strange inheritance. Your petty attempts to construct a moderate
nihilism do not seem to me to be fated to live very long.
    What kind of knowledge can you have of this universe upon which you
have settled and that you call reality? That of a discrepancy. The total perception of the world is: death, and you have understood this. But all you know
of it is orderly, and consequently rational. Poor prop this—a reflection in
rippling water. . . . The history of the psychological life of Europeans, of the
new Europe, is that of the invasion of the understanding by feelings confused
by their equal intensity. The sight of all these men laboring to maintain the
Man who permits them to overcome thought and to live, while the world
over which he reigns becomes every day more irrelevant to them, this is, no
doubt, the last vision I shall take with me from the West.

A.D. to Ling   Tien-Tsin
    For whoever wants to live outside his immediate quest, only a strong opin-
ion can regulate the world. The worlds of facts, of thoughts, of deeds, are
not too kind to certitude; and our lagging hearts do not seem to me able to
enjoy as they should the disintegration of a Universe and a Man to the construction of which so many well-meaning characters applied themselves.
    Authority evades man twice. First it escapes its creator, then its would-be
captor. In the service of a senseless force, the elements of Western power
oppose and fight each other despite temporary human arrangements, and the
direction of the world they steer without even meaning to escapes them as

much as it does the reader of a story. The unforeseeable reverberations of deeds sway these very deeds; the powers able to change facts seize upon them so swiftly that intelligence knows it cannot exert itself upon any reality, that it cannot create the necessary connection between itself and the certitude that justifies it. She hardly attempts to divert herself in apprehending the manner of the illusion. But what does the capture of a few contrivances matter to him who is certain of their number and their power? More or less clear, the idea of the impossibility of grasping any reality dominates Europe. The power, plain even to its weakness, of pope and king would today be mere vanity; there is no longer authority sufficiently high to carry the conscience with it. Hence a profound transformation of man, far less important in terms of the cries that proclaim it than because of the breach in those barriers which, for a thousand years, had sealed and fortified the world of outer life. There is so much pleasure, my friend, for an anxious mind in the examination of an anarchic reality, the handmaid of force, in which to think is often to become conscious of an inferiority.

Waning reality allies itself to myths, and prefers those which are born of the mind. What does the vision of imperceptible powers invoke, powers that slowly raise once more the old effigy of fate, in our civilization whose magnificent and perhaps mortal law is that all temptation resolves itself in knowledge?

There is at the heart of the Western world, however we see it, a hopeless conflict: that of man and his creation. Conflict of the thinker and his thought, of the European and his civilization or his reality, conflict of our indiscriminate consciousness and of its expression in the common world in worldly terms. I find it in all the qualms and the quakes of the modern world. Swamping both the facts and itself, it teaches consciousness to disappear and prepares us for the metallic realms of absurdity.

The development of the self which aims at the conquest of power is not sustained by an assertion, but by a sort of opportunism, by constant adaptation, adjustment, or by the acceptance of the dogma of a party. Now, since the weakening of birthright aristocracies, the feeling of caste has attained a strange power. The will to be distinct from others cannot rest upon illusion alone; apart from the fact that it is no longer in our power to escape reality, we always tend to solicit caste consciousness when we think it apt to please us; it is the realm of our attempts at vindication. You can easily see our caste spirit, buttressed by our need for novelty, in the one token: fashion, a sign surely more obvious than the quality of sensitiveness to which you cling. For fashion—and I mean the change of clothes, of attitudes, of tastes, of words— peculiar to Europe and the countries it has touched, is the external mark round which a temporary aristocracy tries to form, an aristocracy whose degrees subside in proportion to the time it takes to reach them. To affirm oneself in a world that is common to all is to distinguish oneself, is to establish a difference between things of the same kind. In our psychological life, in our personal world, it is to establish a difference that is essential. One of these tendencies makes for justification, the other for the absolute uselessness of that justification. They draw further and further apart, and we perceive this separation. What irony in this twin motion, in this closed man whom only elements of discord may enter from the world outside.

Some young men apply themselves to changing the world that grows within them. This provides them with the difference that their mind needs to live. The mind becomes the servant of this purpose and has no longer any use but to show them the movements of a world without connection, a world which a passion, a gesture, a thought, force to yield—the mind becomes a trained animal, expert in unknown fancies, and thus revealing them; for thought, when it becomes its own object, attacks the world much more than passion does. The murderer of a life, or of other more secret things that the rude arm of the law ignores, can find himself affected, pervaded by his crime, *or* by the new universe it forces upon him. Strange faces are discovered in the mirror of wars. Do we change ourselves, or is it the world that changes when passion ebbs, like the sea, from the passionate act that opposed us to it?

Even more than that of the young Chinese, our thought is laid bare. . . . With a calm distress we realize the basic opposition between our actions and our profound life. This last—intensity—cannot concern the mind; the mind knows it, and spins without effect, a handsome machine stained by a few drops of blood. For this profound life of ours is also the most inchoate; and its force, which exhibits the arbitrary rule of the mind, can do nothing to deliver us from it. It tells the mind: "You are a lie and the stuff of lies, creator of realities. . . ." And the mind replies: "Yes. But it has always been true that where the daylight ends men have thought to see riches in the gloom, and yours are only the last reflections of the day that has gone."

To destroy God, and after his destruction, the European mind abolished all that could resist man: now, having attained the limit of its efforts, it finds only death. Its vision attained at last, it discovers that it can no longer summon up the old passion for it. And never was a discovery more disquieting.

There is no ideal to which we can sacrifice ourselves for we know the lies of each, we who do not know what is truth. The earthly shadow that lengthens behind the marble gods is sufficient to make us turn aside from them. How tightly man has bound himself to himself! Fatherland, justice, greatness, truth, which of the statues does not bear such traces of human hands that it arouses in us the same sad irony that old faces do that we loved once upon a time? Understanding does not permit every folly. And yet, what sacrifices, what unjustified heroism, slumber within us. . . .

Certainly, there is a higher faith: that proposed by all the village crosses and by the crosses, too, that watch over our dead. It is love, and it carries peace. I shall never accept it; I shall not demean myself to ask of it the peace to which my weakness calls me. Europe, great cemetery where only dead conquerors sleep and whose melancholy becomes more profound when adorned by their illustrious names, you leave around me only a naked horizon and the mirror of despair, old master of solitude. Perhaps it too will die, of its own life. Far away, in the harbor, a foghorn wails like a dog without a master. Voice of the cowardice I have defeated. . . . I contemplate my image.

Changing image of myself, I have no love for you. Like a great, badly healed wound, you are my dead glory and my living pain. I have given you all; and yet I know that I shall never love you. Without giving in, I shall bring you each day an offering of peace. Hungry lucidity, I still burn before you, a straight and lonely flame in this heavy night where the yellow wind howls, as in all those strange nights when the ocean wind rehearsed around me the proud clamor of the sterile sea. . . .

1921–1925

Sartre

The best-known exponent of Existentialist ideas in the West was probably Jean-Paul Sartre (1905–1980), leader of the French school of atheistic Existentialists, university teacher, novelist, playwright, and critic. In a lecture he delivered in Paris in 1945, Sartre explained that one belief all Existentialists share is that existence precedes essence—that, in effect, it is always necessary to start from subjectivity. He went on to explain: "Man begins by existing, finds himself, appears in the world, and then defines himself. If man, as the Existentialist conceives him, cannot be defined, this is because he is nothing to begin with. He will only *be* later, and he will be such as he has made himself. It follows that there is no such thing as a human nature, because there is no God to conceive it. Man simply is; not only as he conceives himself, but as he wills himself, and as he conceives himself after he has begun by existing."

After 1945, Sartre came to feel that this and other explanations put forward in the lecture failed to give a true or complete view of his thought, which may be found more fully expressed in works like *Being and Nothingness,* or in the essays collected under the title of *Situations.* Many of these views also appear very clearly in the statement below, which was written in 1945 to introduce the first number of the periodical

Les Temps Modernes, which Sartre edited until his death and in which many of his most interesting works were first presented to the public. Here we have not only the Existentialist doctrine itself, pithily expressed, but the suggestion of how it may be applied by men living in society and wanting to be effective as artists, as writers, or, quite simply, as human beings.

Like many of his generation, Sartre was offended by the negative aspects of capitalist society, fascinated by the prospect of the more just and classless society that seemed to be abuilding in Soviet Russia. Marxism provided the "unsurpassable horizon of our time." In Russia, he declared after a visit in 1954, "the freedom to think and criticize is total"—this, seven years after the revelation of Soviet work camps and other murderous aberrations, which he either denied or rationalized. Sartre regretted Krushchev's 1956 report of Stalin's crimes, because it came before workers in the West had matured sufficiently in their views to digest its horrors. For the rest of his life, Sartre remained true to his existential choice. In 1964, he was awarded the Nobel Prize for literature but refused to accept it. Believing that "commitment is an act, not a word," he kept busy promoting the necessary revolution by selling left-wing publications in the streets, fomenting and taking part in riots, and putting himself on the line whenever he could. He was engaged in a massive study of Flaubert. But when the radical bourgeois writer of the twentieth century analyzed the archetypal bourgeois writer of the nineteenth century, published results were so formidably dense that only bourgeois intellectuals could hope to penetrate them.

The blindness that overtook Sartre in the last years of his life was ironically symbolic of the experience of numerous intelligent men and women whose love of liberty and hatred of bourgeois society led them to celebrate the fantasy of a radically different, presumably better, world they thought to find elsewhere.

Introduction to *Les Temps Modernes*

Any writer of bourgeois origin has faced the temptation of irresponsibility. It has been a tradition in the career of letters for more than a century. The author rarely connects his work with the payment for it. On the one hand, he writes, he sings, he sighs; on the other hand, he is given money. They are two facts with no apparent relation; the best he can do is to tell himself that he is paid for sighing. So he considers himself more like a student who has been granted a scholarship than a worker who receives the price of his toil. The theoreticians of the Aesthetic and Realist schools confirmed him in this opinion. Has it been noticed that they have the same aims and the same origin? The main concern of the author who follows the principles of the former is to write useless works. Provided they are gratuitous, absolutely rootless, he is not far from thinking that they are beautiful. Thus, he puts

---

Source: From *Les Temps Modernes,* Vol. 1, No. 1, 1945; translated by Françoise Ehrmann.

himself outside of society, or rather he agrees to belong to it only as a consumer, precisely like the scholar. The Realist, too, likes to consume. As for
producing, it is another story. He has been told that science does not care
about the useful and he aims at the sterile impartiality of the scientist. How
many times have we been told that he "bent" his attention to the milieus he
wanted to describe! He bent his attention! Where was he then? Up in the
air? The truth is that, uncertain about his social position, too timid to stand
against the bourgeoisie who pay him, too lucid to accept it without restrictions, he chose to judge his century and convinced himself through this
means that he remained outside of it, as the experimentalist is outside of the
experimental system. Thus the indifference of pure science comes near the
gratuity of Art for Art's Sake. It is not by chance that Flaubert is at the same
time a pure stylist, reverent of form, and the father of naturalism; it is not by
chance that the Goncourts pride themselves at the same time on their keen
observation and on their artistic writing.

This inherited irresponsibility troubles many minds. They suffer from a
literary bad conscience and no longer know whether writing is admirable or
grotesque. The poet used to take himself for a prophet, it was honorable;
later, he became an accursed social outcast, it was still all right. But today he
has fallen into the ranks of specialists, and it is not without a certain uneasiness that he mentions the profession of *homme de lettres* after his name when
he signs in a hotel. *Homme de lettres:* this association of words is enough, by
itself, to cause anyone to shun writing; one thinks of an Ariel, a Vestal, an
enfant terrible; also of a harmless maniac, related to weight-lifters or numis-
matists. All this is rather ridiculous. The man of letters writes while the others
fight. One day, he is proud of it, he feels like the scholar guarding ideal
values; the next day, he is ashamed of it, he finds that literature is very much
like a kind of special affectation. With the bourgeois who read him, he is
aware of his dignity; but in front of the workers, who do not read him, he
suffers from an inferiority complex, as it has been seen in 1936, at the *Maison
de la Culture*. This complex is undoubtedly at the origin of what Paulhan
calls *terrorism*. It led the Surrealists to scorn the literature on which they lived.
After the First World War, it produced a particular lyricism. The best writers,
the purest, publicly confessed what might humiliate them most and were
satisfied when they had brought bourgeois disapproval upon themselves.
They had written something which somewhat resembled an act because of
its consequences. These isolated experiments could not prevent words from
depreciating more and more. There was a crisis in rhetoric, then a crisis in
language. Just before the Second World War, most literary men had resigned
themselves to be only nightingales. Some authors went to extremes in their
disgust for writing: outdoing their elders, they judged that it would not be

enough to publish a merely useless book, they maintained that the secret aim of literature is to destroy language, and that the only way to attain it was to speak without saying anything. This unending silence was the fashion for a time, and the distribution service of *Hachette* sent condensed silence in the form of bulky novels to the station libraries. Today, things have gone so far that some writers, blamed or punished for renting their pen to the Germans, are seen to show painful surprise. "What," they say, "does what you write commit you?"

We do not want to be ashamed of writing and we do not feel like speaking to say nothing. Besides, should we wish it, we would not succeed. No one can succeed in this. Anything written has a meaning, even if this meaning is very far from the one intended by the author. For us, the writer is neither a Vestal nor an Ariel. He is "in it," whatever he does marked, compromised, even in the farthest refuge. If at certain times he applies his art to forging trifles of sonorous inanity, it is a sign. It is because there is a crisis in letters, and probably in society, or because the power classes have directed him towards an activity of luxury without his knowing it, for fear he might join revolutionary troops. Who is Flaubert for us but a talented coupon-clipper, he who has been so violent against the bourgeois and thought he had withdrawn from the social machine? And does his minute art not imply the comfort of Croisset, the tender care of a mother or a niece, an orderly life, a successful business, dividends to cash regularly? It takes only a few years for a book to become a social fact that one questions like an institution or lists in statistics like a thing; it takes little time for it to blend with the furniture of a certain time, with its clothes, its hats, its means of transportation and its food. A historian will say about us: "They ate this, read that, dressed thus." The first railways, cholera, the Canuts rebellion, the novels of Balzac, the rapid growth of industry, equally contribute in characterizing the *Monarchie de Juillet*. All this has been said over and over again since Hegel. We want to draw from it practical conclusions. Since the writer has no means to escape, we want him tightly to embrace his time; it is his unique chance: it made itself for him and he is made for it. One regrets Balzac's indifference to the 1848 Revolution, Flaubert's frightened incomprehension of the Commune. One regrets it for *them*. There is something there that they missed forever. We do not want to miss anything in our time. There may be some more beautiful, but this one is our own. We have only *this* life to live, in the middle of *this* war, of *this* revolution perhaps. Let us not draw the conclusion that we speak for a kind of populism. It is quite the contrary. Populism is the child of old parents, the dull offspring of the last Realists. It is another attempt to get out of the game unharmed. We are convinced, on the contrary, that one *cannot* get out of the game unharmed. Should we be mute and quiet as stones, our very passitivity would be an action. The abstention of the man who would devote his life to writing novels about the Hittites would be, in itself, taking up a position. The writer is *situated* in his time. Every word has consequences. Every silence, too. I hold Flaubert and Goncourt responsible for the repression which followed the Commune because they did not write one line to prevent it. One might say that it was not their business. But was the Calas trial Voltaire's business? Dreyfus' condemnation Zola's? the administration of the Congo, Gide's? Each of these authors, in a special circumstance of his life, measured his responsibility as a writer. The Occupation taught us ours. Since we act on our time by our very existence, we decide that this action will be deliberate. Still we have to make it more precise. A writer ordinarily wants to make his modest contribution to prepare the future. But there is a vague and conceptual future which concerns all humanity and about which we know nothing: Will history have an end? Will the sun go out? What will be the condition of man in the socialist regime of the year 3000? We leave these dreams to the writers of science fiction. It is the future of *our* time that we must care about: a limited future, hardly to be distinguished from it—for a time, like a man, is first a future. It is made of its works in process, its enterprises, its immediate or long-range plans, its rebellions, its fights, its hopes. When will the war end? How will the country be re-equipped? How will international relations be handled? What will social reforms be? Will reactionary forces triumph? Will there be a revolution and which will it be? We make this future ours and we do not want any other. Certainly, some authors care less about the present and have shorter views. They wander among us as if they were absent. Where are they then? With their grand-nephews, they turn back to appreciate this dead era that was ours, of which they are the only survivors. But their idea is bad. Posthumous glory is always based on a misunderstanding. What do they know of these grandnephews who will dig them out! Immortality is a terrible alibi. It is not easy to live with one foot on this side of the grave and the other on the other side. How to deal with current matters when one looks at them from so far away! How to get excited about a fight, how to enjoy the victory! All is equivalent. They look at us without seeing us. We are already dead for them—and they go back to the novel they write for people whom they will never see. They let immortality steal their lives from them. We write for our contemporaries, we do not want to look at our world with our future eyes—it would be the surest way to kill it—but with our living eyes, our real, perishable eyes. We do not wish to win our case on appeal and we have no use for a rehabilitation after our death. It is here and while we are still living that cases are won or lost.

However, we do not think of setting up a literary relativism. We care little about the purely historical. Besides, does the purely historical exist except in M. Seignobos' books? Each time discovers an aspect of human fate; in each time man chooses himself when confronted with others, with love, death, the world; and when parties argue over the disarmament of the *F.F.I.* [resistance forces] or the aid to the Spanish Republicans, it is this metaphysical choice, this singular and absolute project which is involved. Thus, by taking sides in the singularity of our time, we finally reach eternity, and it is our duty as writers to make one aware of the eternal values implied in these social and political debates. But we do not want to look for them in an intelligible heaven: they are only interesting in their present manifestations. Far from being relativists, we highly proclaim that man is an absolute. But he is so in his time, his milieu, on his earth. What is absolute, what a thousand years of history cannot destroy, is *this* irreplaceable, incomparable decision he makes at this moment about these circumstances. Descartes is the absolute, the man who escapes us because he is dead, who lived in his time, who thought it out day after day with the only means he had, who formed his doctrine from a certain state of sciences, who knew Gassendi, Caterus and Mersenne, who loved a cross-eyed girl when he was a youth, who fought in war and who got a servant with child, who attacked not the principle of authority in general, but Aristotle's authority in particular, and who stands in his time, disarmed but not defeated, like a milestone. Cartesianism is the relative, this strolling philosophy passing from one century to another in which everyone finds what he puts in it. It is not by running after immortality that we shall become eternal: we shall not be absolutes for reflecting in our work some skinny principles, empty and worthless enough to pass through the centuries, but for passionately fighting in our time, for passionately loving it, and for electing to die entirely with it.

To sum it up, our intention is to participate in bringing forth certain changes in our society. By this, we do not mean a change in the souls: we gladly leave the direction of souls to authors who have a specialised *clientèle*. We who, without being materialist, have never differentiated the soul from the body and who only know an indecomposable reality: human reality, we side with those who want to change both the social condition of man and his conception of himself. Therefore, *à propos* of the coming social and political events, our review will take a stand in each case. It will not do it *politically,* that is to say it will not serve any party; but it will strive to isolate the conception of man on which the theses involved will be based, and it will give its opinion according to the conception it upholds. If we are able to keep to our intentions, if we are able to make some readers share our views, we will not feel over-proud; we simply will be glad to have regained a professional good conscience and to know that, at least for us, literature will have become again what it should never have ceased to be: a social function.

And, one will ask, what is this conception of man that you pretend to reveal to us? We will answer that it is a very common one and that we do not pretend to reveal it, but only to help in defining it. I will call this conception totalitarian. But, as the word may seem unfortunate, as it has been very unpopular lately, as it has been used to designate a type of oppressive and antidemocratic State and not the human person, some explanations ought to be given.

The bourgeois class, it seems to me, may intellectually be defined by its use of the analytic turn of mind, the initial postulate of which is that compounds necessarily are only a pattern of simple elements. In its hands, this postulate once was an offensive weapon which was used to dismantle the bulwarks of the *Ancien Régime*. Everything was analysed; in the same way, one reduced air and water to their elements, the mind to the sum of the impressions that compose it, society to the sum of the individuals who constitute it. The wholes vanished: they became abstract summations due to the chance of combinations. Reality took refuge in the ultimate terms of decomposition. These unvaryingly retain their essential properties—it is the second postulate of the analysis—whether they are one component in a compound or they exist in the free state. There was an immutable nature of oxygen, hydrogen, nitrogen, of the elementary impressions which make up our mind, there was an immutable nature of man. Man was man as a circle is a circle: once and for all; the individual, whether on the throne or in utter poverty, remained absolutely identical with himself because he was conceived after the pattern of an oxygen atom, which can combine with hydrogen to become water, with nitrogen to become air, without changing its inner structure. These principles presided over the Declaration of the Rights of Man. In the society conceived by the analytical mind, the individual, a solid and permanent particle, a vehicle of human nature, lives like one pea in a can of peas: he is all round, closed within himself, incommunicable. All men are *equal:* they all participate equally of the essence of man. All men are *brothers:* fraternity is a passive link between distinct molecules, instead of a solidarity of class or action that the analytical turn of mind cannot even conceive. It is a relation entirely external and purely sentimental which hides the simple juxtaposition of the individuals in the analytical society. All men are *free:* free to *be men,* of course. Which means that the action of the politician must be negative: he has nothing to do with human nature; his task is to remove any obstacle to its thriving. Thus, wishing to destroy the divine law, the right of birth and blood, birthright, all these rights based on the idea that there are differences in nature between people, the bourgeoisie blended its causes with the cause of analysis and built up the myth of the universal for its own use. Unlike the contemporary revolutionaries, it carried out its claims only by shedding its class conscience; the members of the Third Estate at the Constituent Assembly were bourgeois insofar as they looked at themselves simply as men.

After a hundred and fifty years, the analytical turn of mind remains the official doctrine of the bourgeois democracy, only it has become a defensive weapon. The interest of the bourgeoisie is still to deceive itself about classes as it used to about the synthetic reality of the institutions of the old régime. It persists in seeing only men, in proclaiming the identity of human nature through all the varieties of situation; but it is against the proletariat that it proclaims it. For it, a worker is first a man—a man like the others. If the Constitution grants to this man the right to vote and the freedom of opinion, he manifests his human nature as much as a bourgeois. A controversial literature too often has represented the bourgeois as a scheming and gloomy mind whose only care is to protect his privileges. In fact, one *becomes bourgeois* by choosing, once and for all, a certain vision of the analytical world, that one tries to impose upon every man and which blinds one from collective realities. Thus, the bourgeois defense is permanent in a way and is one with the bourgeoisie itself; but it does not reveal itself by scheming; within the world it has built for itself, there is room for virtues of lightheartedness, altruism, even generosity; only, bourgeois good deeds are individual acts addressed to universal human nature as embodied in an individual. In this sense, they are as efficient as a shrewd propaganda, for the beneficiary is forced to receive these marks of kindness as they are offered to him; that is to say, as a human being alone in front of another human being. Bourgeois charity fosters the myth of fraternity.

But there is another propaganda in which we are more particularly interested here, since we are writers, and writers are unwittingly the agents of it. This legend of the poet's irresponsibility that we denounced a moment ago, springs from the analytical mind. Since the bourgeois authors consider themselves as peas in a can, the solidarity which unites them with other people seems strictly mechanical to them, i.e., a mere juxtaposition. Even if they feel strongly about their literary mission, they think they have done enough when they have described their own nature or that of their friends. Since all men are alike, they will have helped all of them by enlightening everyone about himself. And as they start from the same postulate as analysis, it seems very simple to them to use the analytical method to know themselves. Such is the origin of intellectualist psychology, the perfect example of which we find in Proust's works. A paederast, Proust thought he could use his homosexual experience to describe Swann's love for Odette; a bourgeois, he presents this sentiment of a rich, idle bourgeois for a kept woman as the prototype of love. It is then that he believes in the existence of universal passions, the mechanism of which does not vary much when one modifies the sexual characters, the social condition, the nation or the time of the individuals who feel them. After thus "isolating" these unalterable affections, he will be able to start converting them, in their turn, into elementary particles. Abiding by the postulates of the analytical mind, he does not even think that there may be a dialectic in sentiments, but only a mechanism. Thus social atomism, the position of retreat for the contemporary bourgeoisie, brings about psychological atomism. Proust has *chosen to be a bourgeois,* he has made himself the accomplice of the bourgeois propaganda, since his work contributes in spreading the myth of human nature.

We are convinced that the analytical approach is dead and that its unique role today is to trouble the revolutionary conscience and isolate men in favor of the privileged classes. We do not believe any more in the intellectualist psychology of Proust and we consider it harmful. Since we chose his analysis of passionate love as an example, we will probably enlighten the reader by mentioning the essential points on which we disagree with him entirely.

First, we do not accept *a priori* the idea that passionate love is an affection constitutive of the human mind. It could very well have, as Denis de Rougemont suggested, a historical origin related to Christian ideology. More generally, we think that a sentiment is always the expression of a certain way of life and a certain conception of the world, common to a whole class or time, and that its evolution is not caused by I know not what inner mechanism but by these historical and social factors.

Secondly, we cannot admit that a human affection is composed of molecular elements which juxtapose without modifying one another. We consider it to be not a well-adjusted machine but an organised form. We do not conceive the possibility of *analysing* love because the evolution of this sentiment, as of all others, is *dialectic*.

Thirdly, we refuse to believe that a homosexual's love has the same characters as a heterosexual's. The secret, forbidden character of the former, its aspect of black magic, the existence of a homosexual free-masonry, and this damnation to which the invert is aware of dragging his partner with him; it seems to us that all these facts influence the whole sentiment to the very details of its evolution. We maintain that a person's various sentiments are not juxtaposed but that there is a synthetic unity of emotional functions and that each individual moves within an emotional world which is his own.

Fourthly, we deny the individual's origin, class, milieu, nation, to be mere concurrents in his sentimental life. On the contrary, we think that every affection, as any other form of his psychic life, *manifests* his social situation.

This worker, who gets a salary, who does not own his working tools, who is isolated by his work from the substance of his material, and who protects himself from being oppressed by becoming conscious of his class, would not feel, under any circumstances, like this analytical-minded bourgeois, who, because of his profession, entertains polite relations with other bourgeois.

So, against the analytical mind, we turn to a synthetic conception of reality, the principle of which is that a whole, whatever it is, is different, by nature, for the sum of its parts. For us, what men have in common is not a nature, it is a metaphysical condition; and by this, we mean all the constraints which limit them *a priori*, the necessity of being born and dying, of being *finite*, and existing in the world among other men. For the rest, they constitute inde-composable wholes, whose ideas, moods and acts are secondary and dependent structures, and whose essential character is to be *situated*, and they differ from each other as their situations differ. The unity of these significant wholes is the meaning they manifest. Whether he writes or works on a production line, whether he chooses a wife or a tie, man always manifests; he manifests his professional milieu, his family, class, and finally, as he is situated in relation to the whole world, it is the world he manifests. A man is the whole earth. He is present everywhere, he acts everywhere, he is responsible for everything, and it is everywhere, in Paris, Potsdam, Vladivostok, that his destiny is at stake. We adhere to these views because they seem true, because they seem socially useful at the present time, and because most people seem to anticipate and call for them. Our review would like to contribute, for its modest part, to the constitution of a synthetic anthropology. But we repeat, we do not want only to prepare a progress in the field of pure knowledge; the distant purpose we give ourselves is a *liberation*. Since man is a whole, it is not enough to give him the right to vote, without touching the other factors which constitute him: he must free himself entirely, that is to say become *other*, by working on his biological constitution as well as on his economical conditioning, on his sexual complexes as well as on the political data of his situation.

However, this synthetic view is very dangerous; if the individual is an arbitrary selection made by the analytical mind, don't we risk substituting the reign of collective conscience for the reign of the person, by giving up the analytical conceptions? One does not give the proper share to the synthetic approach. While hardly born, the *total-man* is going to disappear, engulfed by the class; only the class exists, it alone should be freed. But, one will say, by freeing the class, do you not free the men who belong to it? Not necessarily: would the triumph of Hitlerian Germany have been the triumph of each German? Besides, where will the synthesis stop? Tomorrow we will be told that the class is a secondary structure, depending on a bigger whole which will be, for instance, the nation. If Nazism attracted some people from the left, it is probably because it carried the totalitarian conception to the absolute; its theoreticians, too, denounced the harm done by analysis, the abstract character of democratic liberties; also, its propaganda promised to forge a new man, it retained the words Revolution and Liberation: only, for the class proletariat, a proletariat of nations was substituted. The individuals became only functions depending on the class; classes became only functions depending on the nation; the nations became only functions depending on the European continent. If, in the occupied countries, the working class fought against the invaders, it was certainly because it felt itself wounded in its revolutionary yearnings, but also because it was invincibly reluctant to let the person be dissolved in the collectivity.

Thus the contemporary conscience seems to be torn by an antinomy. Those who are attached, above all, to the dignity of the human person, his liberty, his imprescriptible rights, tend because of this to think according to the analytical mind which conceives individuals out of their real conditions of existence, which grants them an immutable and abstract nature, which isolates them and deceives itself about their solidarity. Those who strongly feel that man is rooted in collectivity and who want to stress the importance of economical, technical and historical factors, turn to the synthetical mind which, unconcerned with persons, sees only groups. This antinomy is found, for instance, in the widespread belief that socialism is completely averse to individual freedom. Thus, those who believe in the person's autonomy would be condemned to a capitalist liberalism, which we know to be harmful. Those who want a socialist organisation of the economy should turn for it I know not to what totalitarian authoritarianism. The present uneasiness springs from the fact that no one can accept the extreme consequences of these principles: there is a "synthetic" component in democrats of good will; there is an analytical component in the socialists. Remember, for instance, what the Radical Party was in France. One of its theoreticians published a book entitled: *The Citizen Against the Powers*. This title well shows how he conceived politics; everything would be better if the isolated citizen, a molecular representative of human nature, controlled his elected officials and, if need be, used his free judgment against them. But precisely, the Radicals had to admit their failure; this great party had no longer, in 1939, either will, program or ideology; it fell into opportunism: this because it wanted to solve politically problems which could not have a political solution. The best minds seemed surprised by this: if man is a political animal, how come his fate has not been settled once and for all by giving him political freedom? How come the free play of parliamentary institutions did not succeed in suppressing poverty, unemployment, the oppression of the trusts? How come there is a class conflict beyond the parties' brotherly oppositions? One did not have to go much further to see the limits of the analytical approach. The fact that radicalism constantly sought the alliance of parties of the Left clearly shows the trend it wanted to take because of its sympathies and confused aspirations, but it lacked the intellectual technique which would have enabled it not only to solve, but also to formulate the problems it felt obscurely.

On the other side, there is no less uneasiness. The working class has inherited the democratic traditions. It is in the name of democracy that it claims its liberation. Now, we saw that the democratic ideal historically takes the form of a social contract between free individuals. Thus, Rousseau's analytical claims often interfere in people's consciences with the synthetic claims of Marxism. Besides, the worker's technical education develops in him an analytical mind. Like the scientist, he must solve the problems of matter by analysis. If he turns towards persons, he tends, in order to understand them, to appeal to the way of thinking he uses in his work; thus, he applies to human behavior an analytical psychology similar to the one of the French seventeenth century.

The simultaneous existence of these two types of explanation reveals a certain hesitation; this constant use of "as if . . ." clearly shows that Marxism has not yet at its disposal a synthetic psychology fit for its totalitarian conception of the class.

As for us, we refuse to let ourselves be torn between thesis and antithesis. We conceive with no difficulty that a man may be a center of irreducible indetermination, although his situation conditions him totally. This unforeseen area which stands out of the social field, is what we call freedom and the person is nothing else but his freedom. This freedom should not be considered as a metaphysical power of human "nature"; neither is it the license to do everything we want, nor is it a kind of inner refuge which we could enjoy even while enchained. We do not do what we want; however, we are responsible for what we are: this is the fact. Man, simultaneously explained by so many causes, is still alone to bear the burden of himself. In this sense, freedom could be considered as a curse, it is a curse. But it also is the unique source of human grandeur. On this fact, the Marxists will agree with us in spirit if not in the letter, because they do not hesitate, as far as I know, to express moral condemnations. It remains to explain it: but it is the philosophers' business, not ours. We will only point out that, if society makes the person, the person, by a process similar to what Auguste Comte called the passage to subjectivity, makes society. Without its future, a society is only a heap of material, but its future is only the self-projects made, beyond the present state of things, by the millions of men who compose it. Man is only a situation: a worker is not *free* to think or to feel like a bourgeois; but in order that this situation should become *a man,* a whole man, it should be lived and left behind on the way towards a particular aim. In itself, it remains indifferent as long as a human freedom does not give it a meaning: it is neither tolerable nor unbearable as long as a freedom does not accept it, does not rebel against it, that is to say as long as a man does not choose himself in it, by choosing its significance. Then only, within this free choice, it becomes determinant because it is over-determined. No, a worker cannot live as a bourgeois; in the social organization of today, he must suffer to the end his condition of salaried worker; no escape is possible, there is nothing to do about it. But a man does not exist in the same way as a tree or a stone: he must *make himself* a worker. Totally conditioned by his class, his salary, the nature of his work, conditioned even to his feelings, his thoughts, he is the one to decide the meaning of his condition and that of his companions, he is the one who, freely, gives to the proletariat a future of endless humiliation or of conquest and victory, whether he chooses himself to be resigned or revolutionary. And he is responsible for this choice. Not free not to choose: he is committed, he must wager, abstention is a choice. But free to choose, by one and the same decision, his destiny, the destiny of all men, and the value to attribute to mankind. Thus, he chooses himself to be both worker and man, while giving a meaning to the proletariat. Such is man as we conceive him: a total man. Totally committed and totally free. However, it is this free man who must be *delivered,* by widening his possibilities of choice. In certain situations, there is only room for one alternative, one term of which is death. It must be so that man can choose life, in any circumstances.

Camus

Albert Camus, born in Algeria in 1913, was awarded the Nobel Prize for literature in 1957, and died in an automobile accident in January 1960. His works may survive less in terms of intrinsic literary value than as reflections of the problems that concerned his time—which is also our own. If it is a poet's task to reveal to his readers their own concerns and to clarify ideas that they only sense confusedly, then Camus appears as one of the great poets of a troubled generation—what a commentator on the night of his death called *un maître à sentir.* Refusing all dogmas and doctrines, Camus combined a strong sense of the absurdity of life, its unexplainable character, with an unyielding humanism that affirmed the importance of morality, however artificial (indeed, inevitably artificial, but no less essential for all that), and of happiness. From this position derived his appeal to a postwar youth, aware of the tragic inconsequence of life, unable to find theoretical panaceas for its confusion, yet insisting on happiness and some sort of viable, but not dishonest or merely pretended, values. His novels *The Stranger* and *The Plague* both reflect Existentialist man's isolation in an alien world, meaningless but for the meaning he introduces into it.

In *The Myth of Sisyphus,* Camus considers the problem of suicide (if life is pointless, why not end it?) and builds a Promethean justification for living. Friedrich Nietzsche in his last work, *Ecce Homo,* had written that the man who perfects himself and transcends his mere animal nature of "object" can achieve happiness no matter what the condition or "justification" of the world may be. This kind of man, wrote Nietzsche, "affirms the world . . . in all eternity." He learns "not only to bear the necessary, even less to conceal it . . . but to *love* it." In a sense, this may be said to be also the judgment reached by Camus and, from this point of view, it should be possible, as Camus concludes, to "imagine Sisyphus happy."

The Myth of Sisyphus

An Absurd Reasoning—Absurdity and Suicide

There is but one truly serious philosophical problem, and that is suicide. Judging whether life is or is not worth living amounts to answering the fundamental question of philosophy. All the rest—whether or not the world has three dimensions, whether the mind has nine or twelve categories—comes afterwards. These are games; one must first answer. And if it is true, as Nietzsche claims, that a philosopher, to deserve our respect, must preach by example, you can appreciate the importance of that reply, for it will precede the definitive act. These are facts the heart can feel; yet they call for careful study before they become clear to the intellect.

If I ask myself how to judge that this question is more urgent than that, I reply that one judges by the actions it entails. I have never seen anyone die for the ontological argument. Galileo, who held a scientific truth of great importance, abjured it with the greatest ease as soon as it endangered his life. In a certain sense, he did right.[1] That truth was not worth the stake. Whether the earth or the sun revolves around the other is a matter of profound indifference. To tell the truth, it is a futile question. On the other hand, I see many people die because they judge that life is not worth living. I see others paradoxically getting killed for the ideas or illusions that give them a reason for living (what is called a reason for living is also an excellent reason for dying). I therefore conclude that the meaning of life is the most urgent of

---

Source: From *The Myth of Sisyphus and Other Essays* by Albert Camus, Translated by J. O'Brien. Copyright © 1955 by Alfred A. Knopf, Inc. Reprinted by permission of the publisher.

[1]From the point of view of the relative value of truth. On the other hand, from the point of view of virile behavior, this scholar's fragility may well make us smile.

questions. How to answer it? On all essential problems (I mean thereby those that run the risk of leading to death or those that intensify the passion of living) there are probably but two methods of thought: the method of La Palisse and the method of Don Quixote. Solely the balance between evidence and lyricism can allow us to achieve simultaneously emotion and lucidity. In a subject at once so humble and so heavy with emotion, the learned and classical dialectic must yield, one can see, to a more modest attitude of mind deriving at one and the same time from common sense and understanding.

Suicide has never been dealt with except as a social phenomenon. On the contrary, we are concerned here, at the outset, with the relationship between individual thought and suicide. An act like this is prepared within the silence of the heart, as is a great work of art. The man himself is ignorant of it. One evening he pulls the trigger or jumps. Of an apartment-building manager who had killed himself I was told that he had lost his daughter five years before, that he had changed greatly since, and that that experience had "undermined" him. A more exact word cannot be imagined. Beginning to think is beginning to be undermined. Society has but little connection with such beginnings. The worm is in man's heart. That is where it must be sought. One must follow and understand this fatal game that leads from lucidity in the face of existence to flight from light.

There are many causes for a suicide, and generally the most obvious ones were not the most powerful. Rarely is suicide committed (yet the hypothesis is not excluded) through reflection. What sets off the crisis is almost always unverifiable. Newspapers often speak of "personal sorrows" or of "incurable illness." These explanations are plausible. But one would have to know whether a friend of the desperate man had not that very day addressed him indifferently. He is the guilty one. For that is enough to precipitate all the rancors and all the boredom still in suspension.[2]

But if it is hard to fix the precise instant, the subtle step when the mind opted for death, it is easier to deduce from the act itself the consequences it implies. In a sense, and as in melodrama, killing yourself amounts to confessing. It is confessing that life is too much for you or that you do not understand it. Let's not go too far in such analogies, however, but rather return to everyday words. It is merely confessing that that "is not worth the trouble." Living, naturally, is never easy. You continue making the gestures commanded by existence for many reasons, the first of which is habit. Dying voluntarily implies that you have recognized, even instinctively, the ridicu-

---

[2]Let us not miss this opportunity to point out the relative character of this essay. Suicide may indeed be related to much more honorable considerations—for example, the political suicides of protest, as they were called, during the Chinese revolution.

lous character of that habit, the absence of any profound reason for living, the insane character of that daily agitation, and the uselessness of suffering.

What, then, is that incalculable feeling that deprives the mind of the sleep necessary to life? A world that can be explained even with bad reasons is a familiar world. But, on the other hand, in a universe suddenly divested of illusions and lights, man feels an alien, a stranger. His exile is without remedy since he is deprived of the memory of a lost home or the hope of a promised land. This divorce between man and his life, the actor and his setting, is properly the feeling of absurdity.

All great deeds and all great thoughts have a ridiculous beginning. Great works are often born on a streetcorner or in a restaurant's revolving door. So it is with absurdity. The absurd world more than others derives its nobility from that abject birth. In certain situations, replying "nothing" when asked what one is thinking about may be pretense in a man. Those who are loved are well aware of this. But if that reply is sincere, if it symbolizes that odd state of soul in which the void becomes eloquent, in which the chain of daily gestures is broken, in which the heart vainly seeks the link that will connect it again, then it is as it were the first sign of absurdity.

It happens that the stage sets collapse. Rising, streetcar, four hours in the office or the factory, meal, streetcar, four hours of work, meal, sleep, and Monday Tuesday Wednesday Thursday Friday and Saturday according to the same rhythm—this path is easily followed most of the time. But one day the "why" arises and everything begins in that weariness tinged with amazement. "Begins"—this is important. Weariness comes at the end of the acts of a mechanical life, but at the same time it inaugurates the impulse of consciousness. It awakens consciousness and provokes what follows. What follows is the gradual return into the chain or it is the definitive awakening. At the end of the awakening comes, in time, the consequence: suicide or recovery. In itself weariness has something sickening about it. Here, I must conclude that it is good. For everything begins with consciousness and nothing is worth anything except through it. There is nothing original about these remarks. But they are obvious; that is enough for a while, during a sketchy reconnaissance in the origins of the absurd. Mere "anxiety," as Heidegger says, is at the source of everything.

Likewise and during every day of an unillustrious life, time carries us. But a moment always comes when we have to carry it. We live on the future; "tomorrow," "later on," "when you have made your way," "you will understand when you are old enough." Such irrelevancies are wonderful, for, after all, it's a matter of dying. Yet a day comes when a man notices or says that he is thirty. Thus he asserts his youth. But simultaneously he situates himself in relation to time. He takes his place in it. He admits that he stands at a certain point on a curve that he acknowledges having to travel to its end. He belongs to time, and by the horror that seizes him, he recognizes his worst enemy. Tomorrow, he was longing for tomorrow, whereas everything in him ought to reject it. That revolt of the flesh is the absurd.[3]

A step lower and strangeness creeps in: perceiving that the world is "dense," sensing to what a degree a stone is foreign and irreducible to us, with what intensity nature or a landscape can negate us. At the heart of all beauty lies something inhuman, and these hills, the softness of the sky, the outline of these trees at this very minute lost the illusory meaning with which we had clothed them, henceforth more remote than a lost paradise. The primitive hostility of the world rises up to face us across millennia. For a second we cease to understand it because for centuries we have understood in it solely the images and designs that we had attributed to it beforehand, because henceforth we lack the power to make use of that artifice. The world evades us because it becomes itself again. That stage scenery masked by habit becomes again what it is. It withdraws at a distance from us. Just as there are days when under the familiar face of a woman, we see as a stranger her whom we had loved months or years ago, perhaps we shall come even to desire what suddenly leaves us so alone. But the time has not yet come. Just one thing: that denseness and that strangeness of the world is the absurd.

Men, too, secrete the inhuman. At certain moments of lucidity, the mechanical aspect of their gestures, their meaningless pantomime makes silly everything that surrounds them. A man is talking on the telephone behind a glass partition; you cannot hear him, but you see his incomprehensible dumb show; you wonder why he is alive. This discomfort in the face of man's own inhumanity, this incalculable tumble before the image of what we are, this "nausea," as a writer of today calls it, is also the absurd. Likewise the stranger who at certain seconds comes to meet us in a mirror, the familiar and yet alarming brother we encounter in our own photographs is also the absurd.

I come at last to death and to the attitude we have toward it. On this point everything has been said and it is only proper to avoid pathos. Yet one will never be sufficiently surprised that everyone lives as if no one "knew." This is because in reality there is no experience of death. Properly speaking, nothing has been experienced but what has been lived and made conscious. Here, it is barely possible to speak of the experience of others' deaths. It is a substitute, an illusion, and it never quite convinces us. That melancholy conven-

---

[3]But not in the proper sense. This is not a definition, but rather an *enumeration* of the feelings that may admit of the absurd. Still, the enumeration finished, the absurd has nevertheless not been exhausted.

tion cannot be persuasive. The horror comes in reality from the mathematical aspect of the event. If time frightens us, this is because it works out the problem and the solution comes afterward. All the pretty speeches about the soul will have their contrary convincingly proved, at least for a time. From this inert body on which a slap makes no mark the soul has disappeared. This elementary and definitive aspect of the adventure constitute the absurd feeling. Under the fatal lighting of that destiny, its uselessness becomes evident. No code of ethics and no effort are justifiable *a priori* in the face of the cruel mathematics that command our condition.

Let me repeat: all this has been said over and over. I am limiting myself here to making a rapid classification and to pointing out these obvious themes. They run through all literatures and all philosophies. Everyday conversation feeds on them. There is no question of re-inventing them. But it is essential to be sure of these facts in order to be able to question oneself subsequently on the primordial question. I am interested—let me repeat again—not so much in absurd discoveries as in their consequences. If one is assured of these facts, what is one to conclude, how far is one to go to elude nothing? Is one to die voluntarily or to hope in spite of everything? Beforehand, it is necessary to take the same rapid inventory on the plane of the intelligence.

The mind's first step is to distinguish what is true from what is false. However, as soon as thought reflects on itself, what it first discovers is a contradiction. Useless to strive to be convincing in this case. Over the centuries no one has furnished a clearer and more elegant demonstration of the business than Aristotle: "The often ridiculed consequence of these opinions is that they destroy themselves. For by asserting that all is true we assert the truth of the contrary assertion and consequently the falsity of our own thesis (for the contrary assertion does not admit that it can be true). And if one says that all is false, that assertion is itself false. If we declare that solely the assertion opposed to ours is false or else that solely ours is not false, we are nevertheless forced to admit an infinite number of true or false judgments. For the one who expresses a true assertion proclaims simultaneously that it is true, and so on *ad infinitum*.

This vicious circle is but the first of a series in which the mind that studies itself gets lost in a giddy whirling. The very simplicity of these paradoxes makes them irreducible. Whatever may be the plays on words and the acrobatics of logic, to understand is, above all, to unify. The mind's deepest desire, even in its most elaborate operations, parallels man's unconscious feeling in the face of his universe; it is an insistence upon familiarity, and an appetite for clarity. Understanding the world for a man is reducing it to the human, stamping it with his seal. The cat's universe is not the universe of the anthill.

The truism "All thought is anthropomorphic" has no other meaning. Like-wise, the mind that aims to understand reality can consider itself satisfied only by reducing it to terms of thought. If man realized that the universe like him can love and suffer, he would be reconciled. If thought discovered in the shimmering mirrors of phenomena eternal relations capable of summing them up and summing themselves up in a single principle, then would be seen an intellectual joy of which the myth of the blessed would be but a ridiculous imitation. That nostalgia for unity, that appetite for the absolute illustrates the essential impulse of the human drama. But the fact of that nostalgia's existence does not imply that it is to be immediately satisfied. For if, bridging the gulf that separates desire from conquest, we assert with Par-menides the reality of the One (whatever it may be), we fall into the ridicu-lous contradiction of a mind that asserts total unity and proves by its very assertion its own difference and the diversity it claimed to resolve. This other vicious circle is enough to stifle our hopes.

These are again truisms. I shall again repeat that they are not interesting in themselves but in the consequences that can be deduced from them. I know another truism: it tells me that man is mortal. One can nevertheless count the minds that have deduced the extreme conclusions from it. It is essential to consider as a constant point of reference in this essay the regular hiatus between what we fancy we know and what we really know, practical assent and simulated ignorance which allows us to live with ideas which, if we truly put them to the test, ought to upset our whole life. Faced with this inextric-able contradiction of the mind, we shall fully grasp the divorce separating us from our own creations. So long as the mind keeps silent in the motionless world of its hopes, everything is reflected and arranged in the unity of its nostalgia. But with its first move this world cracks and tumbles; an infinite number of shimmering fragments is offered to the understanding. We must despair of ever reconstructing the familiar, calm surface which would give us peace of heart. After so many centuries of inquiries, so many abdications among thinkers, we are well aware that this is true for all our knowledge. With the exception of professional rationalists, today people despair of true knowledge. If the only significant history of human thought were to be writ-ten, it would have to be the history of its successive regrets and its impo-tences.

Yet all the knowledge on earth will give me nothing to assure me that this world is mine. You describe it to me and you teach me to classify it. You enumerate its laws and in my thirst for knowledge I admit that they are true. You take apart its mechanism and my hope increases. At the final stage you teach me that this wondrous and multicolored universe can be reduced to the atom and the atom itself can be reduced to the electron. All this is good and I wait for you to continue. But you tell me of an invisible planetary system in which electrons gravitate around a nucleus. You explain this world to me with an image. I realize then that you have been reduced to poetry: I shall never know. Have I the time to become indignant? You have already changed theories. So that science that was to teach me everything ends us in a hypothesis, that lucidity founders in metaphor, that uncertainty is resolved in a work of art. What need had I of so many efforts? The soft lines of these hills and the hand of evening on this troubled heart teach me much more. I have returned to my beginning. I realize that if through science I can seize phenomena and enumerate them, I cannot, for all that, apprehend the world. Were I to trace its entire relief with my finger, I should not know any more. And you give me the choice between a description that is sure but that teaches me nothing and hypotheses that claim to teach me but that are not sure. A stranger to myself and to the world, armed solely with a thought that negates itself as soon as it asserts, what is this condition in which I can have peace only by refusing to know and to live, in which the appetite for conquest bumps into walls that defy its assaults? To will is to stir up paradoxes. Everything is ordered in such a way as to bring into being that poisoned peace produced by thoughtlessness, lack of heart, or fatal renunciations.

Hence the intelligence, too, tells me in its way that this world is absurd. Its contrary, blind reason, may well claim that all is clear; I was waiting for proof and longing for it to be right. But despite so many pretentious centuries and over the heads of so many eloquent and persuasive men, I know that is false. On this plane, at least, there is no happiness if I cannot know. That universal reason, practical or ethical, that determinism, those categories that explain everything are enough to make a decent man laugh. They have nothing to do with the mind. They negate its profound truth, which is to be enchained. In this unintelligible and limited universe, man's fate henceforth assumes its meaning. A horde of irrationals has sprung up and surrounds him until his ultimate end. In his recovered and now studied lucidity, the feeling of the absurd becomes clear and definite. I said that the world is absurd, but I was too hasty. This world in itself is not reasonable, that is all that can be said. But what is absurd is the confrontation of this irrational and the wild longing for clarity whose call echoes in the human heart. The absurd depends as much on man as on the world. For the moment it is all that links them together. It binds them one to the other as only hatred can weld two creatures together. This is all I can discern clearly in this measureless universe where my adventure takes place. Let us pause here. If I hold to be true that absurdity that determines my relationship with life, if I become thoroughly imbued with that sentiment that seizes me in face of the world's scenes, with that lucidity imposed on me by the pursuit of a science, I must sacrifice everything to these certainties and I must see them squarely to be able to maintain them. Above all, I must adapt my behavior to them and pursue them in all their consequences. I am speaking here of decency. But I want to know beforehand if thought can live in those deserts.

The feeling of the absurd is not, for all that, the notion of the absurd. It lays the foundations for it, and that is all. It is not limited to that notion, except in the brief moment when it passes judgment on the universe. Subsequently it has a chance of going further. It is alive; in other words, it must die or else reverberate. So it is with the themes we have gathered together. But there again what interests me is not works or minds, criticism of which would call for another form and another place, but the discovery of what their conclusions have in common. Never, perhaps, have minds been so different. And yet we recognize as identical the spiritual landscapes in which they get under way. Likewise, despite such dissimilar zones of knowledge, the cry that terminates their itinerary rings out in the same way. It is evident that the thinkers we have just recalled have a common climate. To say that that climate is deadly scarcely amounts to playing on words. Living under that stifling sky forces one to get away or to stay. The important thing is to find out how people get away in the first case and why people stay in the second case. This is how I define the problem of suicide and the possible interest in the conclusions of existential philosophy.

But first I want to detour from the direct path. Up to now we have managed to circumscribe the absurd from the outside. One can, however, wonder how much is clear in that notion and by direct analysis try to discover its meaning on the one hand and, on the other, the consequences it involves.

If I accuse an innocent man of a monstrous crime, if I tell a virtuous man that he has coveted his own sister, he will reply that this is absurd. His indignation has its comical aspect. But it also has its fundamental reason. The virtuous man illustrates by that reply the definitive antinomy existing between the deed I am attributing to him and his lifelong principles. "It's absurd" means "It's impossible" but also "It's contradictory." If I see a man armed only with a sword attack a group of machine guns, I shall consider his act to be absurd. But it is so solely by virtue of the disproportion between his intention and the reality he will encounter, of the contradiction I notice between his true strength and the aim he has in view. Likewise we shall deem a verdict absurd when we contrast it with the verdict the facts apparently dictated. And, similarly, a demonstration by the absurd is achieved by comparing the consequences of such a reasoning with the logical reality one wants to set up. In all these cases, from the simplest to the most complex, the magnitude of the absurdity will be in direct ratio to the distance between the two terms of my comparison. There are absurd marriages, challenges, rancors, silences, wars, and even peace treaties. For each of them the absurdity springs from a comparison. I am thus justified in saying that the feeling of absurdity does not spring from the mere scrutiny of a fact or an impression, but that it bursts from the comparison between a bare fact and a certain reality, between an action and the world that transcends it. The absurd is essentially a divorce. It lies in neither of the elements compared; it is born of their confrontation.

In this particular case and on the plane of intelligence, I can therefore say that the Absurd is not in man (if such a metaphor could have a meaning) nor in the world, but in their presence together. For the moment it is the only bond uniting them. If I wish to limit myself to facts, I know what man wants, I know what the world offers him, and now I can say that I also know what links them. I have no need to dig deeper. A single certainty is enough for the seeker. He simply has to derive all the consequences from it.

The immediate consequence is also a rule of method. The odd trinity brought to light in this way is certainly not a startling discovery. But it resembles the data of experience in that it is both infinitely simple and infinitely complicated. Its first distinguishing feature in this regard is that it cannot be divided. To destroy one of its terms is to destroy the whole. There can be no absurd outside the human mind. Thus, like everything else, the absurd ends with death. But there can be no absurd outside this world either. And it is by this elementary criterion that I judge the notion of the absurd to be essential and consider that it can stand as the first of my truths. The rule of method alluded to above appears here. If I judge that a thing is true, I must preserve it. If I attempt to solve a problem, at least I must not by that very solution conjure away one of the terms of the problem. For me the sole datum is the absurd. The first and, after all, the only condition of my inquiry is to preserve the very thing that crushes me, consequently to respect what I consider essential in it. I have just defined it as a confrontation and an unceasing struggle.

And carrying this absurd logic to its conclusion, I must admit that that struggle implies a total absence of hope (which has nothing to do with despair), a continual rejection (which must not be confused with renunciation), and a conscious dissatisfaction (which must not be compared to immature unrest). Everything that destroys, conjures away, or exorcises these requirements (and, to begin with, consent which overthrows divorce) ruins the absurd and devaluates the attitude that may then be proposed. The absurd has meaning only in so far as it is not agreed to.

The Myth of Sisyphus

The gods had condemned Sisyphus to ceaselessly rolling a rock to the top of a mountain, whence the stone would fall back of its own weight. They had thought with some reason that there is no more dreadful punishment than futile and hopeless labor.

If one believes Homer, Sisyphus was the wisest and most prudent of mortals. According to another tradition, however, he was disposed to practice the profession of highwayman. I see no contradiction in this. Opinions differ as to the reasons why he became the futile laborer of the underworld. To begin with, he is accused of a certain levity in regard to the gods. He stole their secrets. Aegina, the daughter of Aesopus, was carried off by Jupiter. The father was shocked by that disappearance and complained to Sisyphus. He, who knew of the abduction, offered to tell about it on condition that Aesopus would give water to the citadel of Corinth. To the celestial thunderbolts he preferred the benediction of water. He was punished for this in the underworld. Homer tells us also that Sisyphus had put Death in chains. Pluto could not endure the sight of his deserted, silent empire. He dispatched the god of war, who liberated Death from the hands of her conqueror.

It is said also that Sisyphus, being near to death, rashly wanted to test his wife's love. He ordered her to cast his unburied body into the middle of the public square. Sisyphus woke up in the underworld. And there, annoyed by an obedience so contrary to human love, he obtained from Pluto permission to return to earth in order to chastise his wife. But when he had seen again the face of this world, enjoyed water and sun, warm stones and the sea, he no longer wanted to go back to the infernal darkness. Recalls, signs of anger, warnings were of no avail. Many years more he lived facing the curve of the gulf, the sparkling sea, and the smiles of earth. A decree of the gods was necessary. Mercury came and seized the impudent man by the collar and, snatching him from his joys, led him forcibly back to the underworld, where his rock was ready for him.

You have already grasped that Sisyphus is the absurd hero. He *is*, as much through his passions as through his torture. His scorn of the gods, his hatred of death, and his passion for life won him that unspeakable penalty in which the whole being is exerted toward accomplishing nothing. This is the price that must be paid for the passions of this earth. Nothing is told us about Sisyphus in the underworld. Myths are made for the imagination to breathe life into them. As for this myth, one sees merely the whole effort of a body straining to raise the huge stone, to roll it and push it up a slope a hundred times over; one sees the face screwed up, the cheek right against the stone, the shoulder bracing the clay-covered mass, the foot wedging it, the fresh start with arms outstretched, the wholly human security of two earth-clotted hands. At the very end of his long effort measured by skyless space and time without depth, the purpose is achieved. Then Sisyphus watches the stone rush down in a few moments toward that lower world whence he will have to push it up again toward the summit. He goes back down to the plain.

It is during that return, that pause, that Sisyphus interests me. A face that toils so close to stones is already stone itself! I see that man going back down with a heavy yet measured step toward the torment of which he will never know the end. That hour like a breathing-space which returns as surely as his suffering, that is the hour of consciousness. At each of those moments when he leaves the heights and gradually sinks toward the lairs of the gods, he is superior to his fate. He is stronger than his rock.

If this myth is tragic, that is because its hero is conscious. Where would his torture be, indeed, if at every step the hope of succeeding upheld him? The workman of today works every day in his life at the same tasks, and this fate is no less absurd. But it is tragic only at the rare moments when it becomes conscious. Sisyphus, proletarian of the gods, powerless and rebellious, knows the whole extent of wretched condition: it is what he thinks of during his descent. The lucidity that was to constitute his torture at the same time crowns his victory. There is no fate that cannot be surmounted by scorn.

If the descent is thus sometimes performed in sorrow, it can also take place in joy. This word is not too much. Again I fancy Sisyphus returning toward his rock, and the sorrow was in the beginning. When the images of earth cling too tightly to memory, when the call of happiness becomes too insistent, it happens that melancholy rises in man's heart: this is the rock's victory, this is the rock itself. The boundless grief is too heavy to bear. These are our nights of Gethsemane. But crushing truths perish from being acknowledged. Thus, Oedipus at the outset obeys fate without knowing it. But from the moment he knows, his tragedy begins. Yet at the same moment, blind and desperate, he realizes that the only bond linking him to the world is the cool hand of a girl. Then a tremendous remark rings out: "Despite so many ordeals, my advanced age and the nobility of my soul make me conclude that all is well." Sophocles' Oedipus, like Dostoevsky's Kirilov, thus gives the recipe for the absurd victory. Ancient wisdom confirms modern heroism.

One does not discover the absurd without being tempted to write a manual of happiness. "What! by such narrow ways—?" There is but one world, however. Happiness and the absurd are two sons of the same earth. They are inseparable. It would be a mistake to say that happiness necessarily springs from the absurd discovery. It happens as well that the feeling of the absurd springs from happiness. "I conclude that all is well," says Oedipus, and that remark is sacred. It echoes in the wild and limited universe of man. It teaches that all is not, has not been, exhausted. It drives out of this world a god who had come into it with dissatisfaction and a preference *for* futile suffering. It makes of fate a human matter, which must be settled among men.

All Sisyphus' silent joy is contained therein. His fate belongs to him. His rock is his thing. Likewise, the absurd man, when he contemplates his torment, silences all the idols. In the universe suddenly restored to its silence, the myriad wondering little voices of the earth rise up. Unconscious, secret calls, invitations from all the faces, they are the necessary reverse and price of victory. There is no sun without shadow, and it is essential to know the night. The absurd man says yes and his effort will henceforth be unceasing. If there is a personal fate, there is no higher destiny, or at least there is but one which he concludes is inevitable and despicable. For the rest, he knows himself to be the master of his days. At that subtle moment when man glances backward over his life, Sisyphus returning toward his rock, in that slight pivoting he contemplates that series of unrelated actions which becomes his fate, created by him, combined under his memory's eye and soon sealed by his death. Thus, convinced of the wholly human origin of all that is human, a blind man eager to see who knows that the night has no end, he is still on the go. The rock is still rolling.

I leave Sisyphus at the foot of the mountain! One always finds one's burden again. But Sisyphus teaches the higher fidelity that negates the gods and raises rocks. He too concludes that all is well. This universe henceforth without a master seems to him neither sterile nor futile. Each atom of that stone, each mineral flake of that night-filled mountain, in itself forms a world. The struggle itself toward the heights is enough to fill a man's heart. One must imagine Sisyphus happy.

VII.

A Supermarket Culture

The 1950s had seen the culmination of the affirmation of the self against an absurd world—something we recognize most clearly in Existentialism. It was then that Malraux pointedly asked whether, following the death of God, man was still alive. Beginning in the 1960s, first a trickle, then a flood of intellectuals—mostly French or French-inspired—began to answer his question, in the negative.

In the late 1940s already, a French social anthropologist, Claude Lévi-Strauss (1908–), distressed by the confusing mass of information about cultural systems, had set out to reduce culture to its essentials. He would reveal the formal relationships among their elements or, as his first major work put it in 1949, *The Elementary Structures of Kinship*. Lévi-Strauss defined cultures as systems of communication. The minds of men and women, and their creations, could be represented and resumed in models based on structural linguistics, information theory, and cybernetics. Man is a structure among others, and his civilizations are complicated mechanisms best interpreted as structures too. Under his poetic pen, human history was reified, flesh and blood turned into instrumental components, subjects obliterated by structures.

Lévi-Strauss's method had been developed in the service of a humane and humanistic philosophy. Its implications would be annexed by more agnostic minds. The unmanned, depersonalized man foreshadowed in the writings of Lévi-Strauss was to be explicitly brushed off by Michel Foucault (1926–1984), a Structuralist philosopher fascinated by the conceptions and codes that make society

Kojere

work, above all by those "principles of exclusion" (like the distinction between sane and insane) in terms of which a society defines itself.

Humans define themselves by defining "man." But this, like every other definition, depends on the global system of knowledge of a particular place and time: conventions, language, cultural and scientific structure: its *épistémè*. Man, declared Foucault with characteristic clarity, "had been a figure occurring between two modes of language, or, rather, he was constituted only when language, having been situated with representation and, as it were, dissolved in it, freed itself from that situation only at the cost of its own fragmentation: man composed his own figure in the interstices of that fragmented language." More simply put, man is a construct. A self-construct. And the time has come to dispense with such devious inventions. By 1966, man, who never existed, was declared dead. With him there died, or were pronounced deceased, other artificial constructs too general to hold water, like "the rights of man," equally arbitrary and equally "exclusive."

There is no "man." All men are products of an *épistémè:* of specific factors or situations, historically, sociologically, psychologically conditioned. So are our ideas. Justice, for example, is also an arbitrary construct. "The idea of justice in itself," declared Foucault, "is an idea which . . . has been invented and put to work . . . as an instrument of a certain political and economic power." Since 1966, a multitude of rhetorical decrees have declared the inexistence of nature, the State, madness, woman, man and other animals, time, politics, power, sexuality, rationality, truth, error. The more the merrier. The more I abolish, the more my philosophical stature grows. In the end I abolish a century or two of trivial and pernicious beliefs in the positive conclusions of experience, and I abolish experience, too. Our eyes are opening at last. We have learned to doubt the misleading and tempting realities of the material world. And the same is true of truth.

> We live in a society which in good part runs on "truth." I mean, which produces and circulates discourses that function as truth, passing for it and thereby holding specific powers. The establishment of "true" discourses (which as a matter of fact change all the time) is one of the fundamental problems of the West. The history of *vérité* is still to be tackled.[1]

Foucault's preferred method of tackling the problem of truth was by way of that very reason through which mankind sought to attain it, and whose triumphs the modern age was widely believed to illustrate. For Foucault, reason is no more

---

[1]From an interview with Foucault that appeared in the *Nouvel Observateur,* March 12, 1977, p. 93.

than reasoning, ratiocination, rationalization. And modern reason is quite the contrary of the liberating Enlightenment it is alleged to have brought about: the negation and expulsion of everything that does not fit allegedly universal norms that are actually specific-interest-group-related.

For Foucault, the exercise of reason and the application of reasonable order constitute progress only in appearance. Reasonable and orderly progress is probably regression, certainly repression. He demonstrates this view by telling the story of how modern society rejected the irrational (denounced as madness) in the name of rationality established as the norm. But madness, judged only in relation to official reason, was itself the product of a reason that designated as mad that which did not fit its image of itself.

Abolish the norms and you solve—indeed, dissolve—the problems norms created. If folly is the product of reason (as crime is the creation of the laws it breaks), abolish the norms of reason, reinstall madfolk in global society, and all will be healed. Western culture is based on the definition of man as a reasonable being. But our culture, like its definitions, is merely the front for a stifling apparatus of power and repression. Power is evil, sterile, monotonous, dead. Conversely, that upon which power is exercised is good, rich, alive. In the works of the likes of Goya, Sade, and Nietzsche, the Western world can find the inspiration to master reason by exploding its obfuscations and its thralldom. "Behind madhouse walls, the spontaneity of madness; behind penal repression, the generous fever of delinquency; beyond sexual repressions, the freshness of desire."

Here was a message of reductive excess well suited to its time. The intelligentsia of the 1960s looked less and less to Sartre with his ideas of neo-responsibility and self-discipline, more and more to Structuralists and Deconstructionists, all of whom denied the reality of alleged "facts" and of alleged necessities: production, organization, bureaucracy, technology, all of which they rejected in the name of clearer-sighted revelations. The impressive/oppressive emperor's clothes were an illusion. A closer look would show authority naked, repression groundless. "Under the flagstones, the beach."

As facts and necessities crumbled before such assaults, hierarchies of value (better/worse) gave way to the feeling that differences mattered little, that what had been taught as norms were no more than authoritarian constructs. "Be realistic: ask for the impossible." As norms dissolved, neo-nihilism undermined the legitimacy, hence the order of institutions, as of persons and objects. Order could be refused not in the name of a better order, but in the name of refusal: "It is forbidden to forbid." "Prohibition is prohibited."

Slogans of this sort, which reflected a complex philosophy or no philosophy at all, were pithy, witty, sometimes convincing. They exploded into public prominence in 1968. The youth rebellions of that year and subsequent years, and their radical affirmations, were directed against an oppressive bourgeois society; but even more against the boredom of irresponsible adolescence prolonged in teaching institutions whose curricula, faculties, and facilities had not kept up with the tide of students. The radical slogans of 1968, however, had been preceded in their bitter-joyous anarchy by a small group of intellectuals whose critiques of modern society had been flaunted in crudely poetic slogans ever since the fifties, and whose philosophy, closely related to Dada, contributed not just to the spirit of 1968, but also to that of Johnny Rotten's Sex Pistols—the English band that strongly affected the tone of pop and punk music after 1976.

The Situationists, as they called themselves, denounced boredom as counter-revolutionary and recommended vigorous exercise of the imagination. It was they who suggested new objectives for revolt: against impoverished language, against love as a commodity, and against happiness as a mass of commodities, against rises in the standard of living that went hand in hand with rises in the level of boredom, against all forms of social and political organization, *and* against all those who tried to change them. It was the Situationists who coined the aphorism, "I take my desire for reality because I believe in the reality of my desires." And it was their example that inspired many graffiti of 1968:

> Here one spontanizes.
>
> The dream is reality.
>
> Exaggeration is the beginning of invention.
>
> Alienation ends where yours begins.
>
> Don't liberate me, I'll do it myself.
>
> Two plus two no longer add up to 4.

And of course,

> I'm a Marxist, of the Groucho variety.

When 1968 petered out, the rejection of existing society, values, and politics that the Situationists represented turned destructive and self-destructive: action for action's sake, indifference to the results of action. Guy Debord, the best-known of their number, insisted that victory now would go to "those who know how to create disorder without loving it." Intellectual evolution was to prove him right. Glum destructiveness followed playful mayhem.

One thing that happened after 1968 (or thereabouts) was the spreading sense that life could change without society or state changing first. Individualistic, egoistic rebelliousness turned to hedonistic self-indulgence and self-affirmation, indifferent to public affairs. Yet even as public society became (or seemed to become) less accessible or less inviting to private initiative, the ego-sphere was turning into a self-service supermarket, with personal taste the order of the day.

The rebellions of 1968 and after had been precipitated by prosperity, not want. The sixties were an era of relative affluence. If the seventies proved less so, this was compensated by the generalized use of credit cards, a more revolutionary novelty than any doctrine. Credit cards sapped the traditional values that we describe as bourgeois—work, responsibility, self-control, thrift—and replaced delayed gratification by immediate satisfactions of desire. It used to be that, in order to buy, most people had to save. With credit cards all they had to do was want, and satisfy their wants. Hedonism, the doctrine that pleasure is the chief good, had been an indulgence of the privileged and amoral. It now became a mainstay of the economy, hence almost a new morality.

Yet, as new pleasure principles and traditional moral principles clashed, there was unease and mental discomfort. Personal responsibility, whether for one's acts or one's situation, often proved discomforting, hence it was shifted to society, biology, and psychology, which purged morality of responsibility and judgment of standards. Criminals were as much victims of society (or nature) as those they preyed upon. Or else they were the victims of social fictions like law, racism, justice, or property. Individuals and their actions became indifferent and interchangeable: aggressors and aggressed, predators and their prey, were acting out a script, operating in structures over which they exercised no control. The conscience was a fiction. Only pleasure and pain were real, and the abdication of conscience, of responsibility, contributed to the multiplication of pleasure and the diminution of pain. If nothing has clear value, if all standards are relative, if all values can be exploded and explained away, anything goes. Where there is no accepted morality, there is no immorality either.

What followed (we have lived it) was exacerbated hedonism, revolt, countercultures, the vogue of drugs, sexual liberation, dirty and yet dirtier speech movements, the porno-pop tide, a desperate overbidding of violence and sadomasochism. By certain philosophical standards, there is no way of describing these as either good or bad. But their advance, and the increasingly commonplace acceptance with which they were met, marked the new affirmation of limitless individual rights—at least in theory. Yet, when self-affirmation is all, awareness of other selves shrinks, dialogue with other entities becomes less relevant, the tact designed to spare others the injuries we fear ourselves dissolves, empathy atrophies, manners wither. Diversity and difference, which add spice to life and enrich experience, become irrelevant. Discrimination makes no (or little) sense. Intellectual life suffers because conventions matter. As Vaclav Havel stressed, "Where everything is allowed, nothing has the power to surprise."

Is this simply a result of relentless overbidding in a market where novelty becomes habitual, the unconventional conventional, the unusual usual? Where innovation appears a disposable commodity, like toilet tissue, novelty is banal. But there is more. The invigorating relativism of yesteryear has turned to sagging self-indulgence. Explanations, comparisons, analyses, were supposed to liberate; now they undercut the sense of freedom and, with it, the will to act. If there is no truth, there are no serious things to be taken seriously. There are only words, carrying the meaning that we give them, with which we can play games, changing the rules as we go along. A playful philosophy, but a hollow one.

For Existentialists, the world was absurd. For Postexistentialists, it is incoherent. Any structure or sense that we attribute to it are denounced as arbitrary, hence questionable. The Existentialist used will to shape the world and endow it with moral consistency. Postexistentialists use the critical faculty to explain how absurd such exercises must be. The image of minds ordering a chaos of atomized experience is replaced by the chaos of minds deluded by superficial perceptions into believing that false consciousness can be true. Not an invigorating message, but a self-fulfilling one.

Deprived of a center of gravity that can establish (or at least suggest) priorities between impulses and inclinations, *will* weakens. Free association, creative spontaneity, nondirective instruction, stimulate dispersion at the expense of concentration, stress the ephemeral against persevering constancy, dispensability against preservation, availability, receptivity, fluidity, diversity without structure. If Jell-O is better than granite, this contradicts the idea of a distinct personality, however subjective, especially subjective. In the old view, a personality with its own autonomous will cannot be reduced to a mere object. The new view of personality (what personality?) is that of an object. The subjective self, my own like that of others, turns into a sort of gadget: capable of intriguing tricks, but empty of substance.

In this continuous flux where experience of self as of others is diffuse and unreliable, considerations like equality, inequality, justice, or right become irrelevant, discrimination senseless; choice is as casual and unconstrained as it is trivial. *Epistémè* used to be cumulative, continuous, incremental. Now it is a kind of overdrawn account, dwindling, then pulverized. And epistemology, the theory of the method or grounds of knowledge, which also stressed continuity—treating human knowledge as a sort of family fortune—now focuses on discontinuity. There is no society, there are only societies; there is no history, there are only histories—better still, stories; there is no individual, only a multifaceted non-entity, sparkling with reflected light. Avoiding cause-effect relations, avoiding historical reference (geological or seismological), the new philosophy turns actions and events into miracles unrelated to explicable factors.

In the realm of the accidental, unforeseeable, contingent, no rational explanations are possible. With subjectivism in question, individuality itself is denied. And, of course, like interpretation or comprehension, experience too is an illusion. So paintings jettison the point of view; novels abandon the linear progress of a story before they abandon story itself; writer and character, artist and subject, dissolve; and so does the culture that once nurtured them. First, as with Barthes, the author dies and is removed from our equations. Then with Lévi-Strauss, all individualities follow suit. And Foucault underscores this when he proclaims the death of man. After that holocaust, only abstractions remain: not institutions or activities but frames and patterns, not speech but grammar, not hands but gestures, not thought but tectonics.

Movement is its own end: its meaning is that it is. Literature and art are not even ends, just means revealed as trivial. French philosopher Jean-Francois Lyotard explained in 1984 that writing is no more than sublimation. Since we write to please ourselves, writing is simply a form of sublimated masturbation. The same masturbator insists, in an essay entitled "The Intellectual's Tomb" (images of death proliferate, as you can see) that, since Humanism is an obstacle to understanding, philosophy must become *in*-human. But how can anything become inhuman, when man and humanity have been argued away? And how can one understand anything, when understanding is a snare and a delusion? Lyotard's school has been teaching that the authority of authors is specious. All authority is specious. So are interpretations (except, perhaps, their own?). There is no objectivity, no distance, no perspective. We are conditioned whatever we do, even when we affirm our conditioned state. "A Cretan said: all Cretans are liars." What shall we make of that? Logic suggests (but does logic still apply?) that either all are capable of being objective, or none can be so—including critics like Lyotard.

The new critics prefer to address not ideas but their authors, or the circumstances of their authoring. Their social psychoanalysis seldom asks what one is saying, rather "Who are you to say it?" Where do you come from, in terms of psychology, ethnicity, gender, the conditioning, prejudices, interests, by which what you say can be explained and, thus, explained away. But theirs? What about what they say? Critical activists, terrorists, Deconstructionists, show little inclination to consider the factors that lead them to deconstruct the statements of others, the prejudices that sharpen their sense of others' prejudices, the standards even on which their criticism is based. The new criticism is about radical doubt, but criticism is about values. In a world allegedly without values, what can criticism be about? The answer, one must guess, is—presumably—about itself and its own valuelessness. Hence the paradox of an activity that denounces itself, and of an old order condemned to be replaced not by some new order, but simply by disorder.

And yet, despite the impression that the new philosophies leave, old-fashioned social psychology still appears to work. The Structuralist vogue reflected the long struggle to qualify "social sciences" as sciences. Poststructuralism, Deconstructionism, and so on, represent more than the exhaustion of criticism. They coincide with the high point of self-destructing fashion, the establishment of a social space buttressed exclusively in the present. An ephemeral, volatile, mutable, provisional, capricious age has generated an impermanent, shifty philosophy that stresses the infatuation and inconstancy that color our culture: illusion over reality, delusion over tangibility, imponderables over empiricals. In an age of evanescent fashion, the new philosophies allegorize the indeterminacy of a present for which the past carries no lessons and the future no relevance. In an age of novelty, the new philosophies reflect the fluctuating norms, ever brought up to date, that socialize us and rationalize our behavior. So, the new philosophies are right? Right for our time, it seems, or, at least, appropriate. Until time comes for a change.

The middle-aged mutant intellectuals who appear in the section that follows are often brilliant and sometimes perceptive. But they are also pretentious, perverse, obscure, convoluted, and too often simply boring. Ideologists who do not believe in ideology, hence not in their own ideology, they fight all the more eloquently to impose it. We may recognize here the most recent manifestation of an old tradition: that of imposing liberty, if need be by constraint.

Lévi-Strauss

Philosopher and social anthropologist, Claude Lévi-Strauss (1908–   ) has been the leading exponent of Structuralism, a powerful but controversial approach to the understanding of human cultures.

Inspired by the anthropological research he conducted among Indian tribes of Brazil, Lévi-Strauss set out to reveal the essentials of culture systems by reference to semiotics—that is, the study of signs and sign-using behavior, including the use not only of words, but also of voice tone, body language, and every other means of face-to-face communication. The master and inventor of semiotics was Ferdinand de Saussure (1857–1913), who presented language as an arbitrary system of signs, a structure whose parts could be understood only in terms of each other and of the system as a whole. Cultures, like languages, were structures of communication, dependent on conventions and codes that regulated marriage, kinship ties, myths, and speech. Viewing societies as structural systems of symbols (not unlike music or mathematics) would reveal analogies between different aspects of life—and of society. All cultural phenomena—folktales, detective stories, laws, or menus—are products of the accepted code or "system of signification" by which a culture interprets and orders the elements of reality. Just as grammar defines the rules that give language meaning, so Structuralism tries to identify the constraints that shape culture and community.

Lévi-Strauss used his insights to codify and synthesize first *The Elementary Structures of Kinship* (1949), and then the way in which the human mind uses myth and "manners" to order the chaotic world around. Those who drew the conclusions of his anthropological studies used them to relativize the literary or philosophical canon. Works of literature, in this view, did not reflect a given or temporal reality or a unique authorial personality. They instead simply reflected the ruling conventions of the culture that produced them. What Lévi-Strauss had envisaged as a new method to synthesize knowledge turned abruptly into an explosive that could be used to destabilize knowledge. A humanistic, universalizing enterprise eventually challenged the basic assumptions of Humanism, which had focused on man, his reason, and his freedom to use it. The personal worth of individuals, their quest for truth, the value of their initiatives and innovations were now declared to be mere illusions, generated by pre-existing structures more accessible to study than they were to our control.

Man and Structure

As he moves forward within his environment, Man takes with him all the positions that he has occupied in the past, and all those that he will occupy in the future. He is everywhere at the same time, a crowd which, in the act of moving forward, yet recapitulates at every instant every step that it has ever taken in the past. For we live in several worlds, each more true than the one within it, and each false in relation to that within which it is itself enveloped. Some of these worlds may be apprehended in action, others exist because we have them in our thoughts: but the apparent contradictoriness of their co-existence is resolved by the fact that we are constrained to accord meaning to those worlds which are nearer to us, and to refuse it to those more distant. Truth lies rather in the progressive expansion of meaning: but an expansion conducted inwards from without and pushed home to explosion-point.

Source: From *Tristes Tropiques* by Claude Lévi-Strauss, translated by John Russell, 1972, Atheneum Publishers. Reprinted by permission of Georges Borchardt, Inc.

As an anthropologist I am no longer, therefore, the only person to suffer from a contradiction which is proper to humanity as a whole and bears within itself the reason for its existence. Only when I isolate the two extremes does the contradiction still persist: for what is the use of action, if the thinking which guides that action leads to the discovery of meaninglessness? But that discovery cannot be made immediately: it must be thought, and I cannot think it all at once. There may be twelve stages, as in the Boddhi [Buddhism: enlightenment]; but whether they are fewer, or more numerous, they exist as a single whole, and if I am to get to the end of them, I shall be called upon continually to live through situations, each of which demands something of me: I owe myself to mankind, just as much as to knowledge. History, politics, the social and economic universe, the physical world, even the sky—all surround me in concentric circles, and I can only escape from those circles in thought if I concede to each of them some part of my being. Like the pebble which marks the surface of the wave with circles as it passes through it, I must throw myself into the water if I am to plumb the depths.

The world began without the human race and it will end without it. The institutions, manners, and customs which I shall have spent my life in cataloguing and trying to understand are an ephemeral efflorescence of a creative process in relation to which they are meaningless, unless it be that they allow humanity to play its destined role. That role does not, however, assign to our race a position of independence. Nor, even if Man himself is condemned, are his vain efforts directed towards the arresting of a universal process of decline. Far from it: his role is itself a machine, brought perhaps to a greater point of perfection than any other, whose activity hastens the disintegration of an initial order and precipitates a powerfully organized Matter towards a condition of inertia which grows ever greater and will one day prove definitive. From the day when he first learned how to breathe and how to keep himself alive, through the discovery of fire and right up to the invention of the atomic and thermonuclear devices of the present day, Man has never—save only when he reproduces himself—done other than cheerfully dismantle million upon million of structures and reduce their elements to a state in which they can no longer be reintegrated. No doubt he has built cities and brought the soil to fruition; but if we examine these activities closely we shall find that they also are inertia-producing machines, whose scale and speed of action are infinitely greater than the amount of organization implied in them. As for the creations of the human mind, they are meaningful only in relation to that mind and will fall into nothingness as soon as it ceases to exist. Taken as a whole, therefore, civilization can be described as a prodigiously complicated mechanism: tempting as it would be to regard it as our universe's best hope of survival, its true function is to produce what physicists call entropy: inertia, that is to say. Every scrap of conversation, every line set up in type, establishes a communication between two interlocutors, levelling what had previously existed on two different planes and had had, for that reason, a greater degree of organization. "Entropology," not anthropology, should be the word for the discipline that devotes itself to the study of this process of disintegration in its most highly evolved forms.

And yet I exist. Not in any way, admittedly, as an individual: for what am I, in that respect, but a constantly renewed stake in the struggle between the society, formed by the several million nerve-cells which take shelter in the anthill of the brain, and my body, which serves that society as a robot? Neither psychology, nor metaphysics, nor art can provide me with a refuge; for one and all are myths subject, within and without, to that new kind of sociology which will arise one day and treat them as severely as has our earlier one. Not merely is the first person singular detestable: there is no room for it between "ourselves" and "nothing." And if, in the end, I opt for "ourselves," although it is no more than an appearance, it is because unless I destroy myself—an act which would wipe out the conditions of the decision I have to make—there is really only one choice to be made: between that appearance and nothing. But no sooner have I chosen than, by that very choice, I take on myself, unreservedly, my condition as a man. Thus liberated from an intellectual pride whose futility is only equalled by that of its object, I also agree to subordinate its claims to the objective will-to-emancipation of that multitude of human beings who are still denied the means of choosing their own destiny.

Man is not alone in the universe, any more than the individual is alone in the group, or any one society alone among other societies. Even if the rainbow of human cultures should go down forever into the abyss which we are so insanely creating, there will still remain open to us—provided we are alive and the world is in existence—a precarious arch that points towards the inaccessible. The road which it indicates to us is one that leads directly away from our present serfdom: and even if we cannot set off along it, merely to contemplate it will procure us the only grace that we know how to deserve. The grace to call a halt, that is to say: to check the impulse which prompts Man always to block up, one after another, such fissures as may be open in the blank wall of necessity and to round off his achievement by slamming shut the doors of his own prison. This is the grace for which every society longs, irrespective of its beliefs, its political regime, its level of civilization. It stands, in every case, for leisure, and recreation, and freedom, and peace of body and mind. On this opportunity, this chance of for once detaching oneself from the implacable process, life itself depends. Farewell to savages, then, farewell to journeying! And instead, during the brief intervals in which humanity can bear to interrupt its hive-like labours, let us grasp the essence of what our species has been and still is, beyond thought and beneath society: an essence that may be vouchsafed to us in a mineral more beautiful than any work of Man; in the scent, more subtly evolved than our books, that lingers in the heart of a lily; or in the wink of an eye, heavy with patience, serenity, and mutual forgiveness, that sometimes, though an involuntary understanding, one can exchange with a cat.

Foucault

Michel Foucault (1926–1984) is best known outside France for *Madness and Civilization,* which he published in 1961. A philosopher by training, his writings fall largely into the realm of social and cultural history, where he explicitly explored the past the better to understand the present and where, in fact, he rewrote the past in versions that fitted his views of the present. *Madness and Civilization* provides a good example of this. The book is about the relation of modern society to insanity or, better, about the way in which a particular society defined and confined as insane those actions and persons that did not conform to its views of reason and reasonable behavior. The preface to the book, which is reprinted here, outlines the author's argument. The gist of it is that the seventeenth century marked a turning point in Western attitudes toward deviance, which would henceforth be more thoroughly excluded, more rigorously policed, disciplined, and punished, as a matter of self-definition.

Yet mental hospitals, which had existed since the Middle Ages, really developed not after 1657, as Foucault would have it, but after 1800, in the wake of that French Revolution that we associate with a new degree of liberty. London's Bedlam (the Bethlehem Royal Hospital), founded in 1247, was thoroughly reformed only after 1815. In the France of 1660, about 2,000 mad inmates were confined in institutions. By 1800, that figure had risen to 5,000; by 1914, to 100,000. As these dates suggest, the reasons for confinement relate less to the seventeenth-century introduction of Cartesian rationalism than to the nineteenth-century advance of democracy. Modern societies do not exclude outsiders, if they can help it, but seek to integrate them because they believe people to be fundamentally similar and equal. In the inequalitarian, hierarchical societies of predemocratic days, radical differences (like those between sane and insane) posed no particular problem. The mad could be tolerated because differences between humans were taken for granted. In equalitarian societies, where we expect all folk to be like other folk, radical differences do pose a problem. Before equality, village idiots could be mocked or left to themselves. In equalitarian societies, the mad are a menace because they are too like us to be ignored: they have to be protected, tended, cured. In the new enlightened, increasingly democratic age that dawned after 1800, not only the insane, but deaf, dumb, blind, idiots—and criminals too—qualified for special attention and education meant to reintegrate them into the communities of which they would henceforth be considered a part.

It may therefore be argued that prisons and mental institutions represent not repressive but progressive aspects of modern attitudes. Mistaken perhaps, but hardly malevolent exercises of power, they regard deviance as temporary, remediable and, with luck, curable. This may be unrealistic, but it is well-intentioned, and about as restrictive and exclusive in principle as schools.

Yet, whatever criticism may be levied against Foucault's history, his message was suggestive and relevant. For Foucault was less interested in accurate description of the past than in the emancipating revelation of our repressive present. Societies to him were interesting in terms of their crises, in terms of the radical changes they effected to resolve these crises, in terms of the ruptures that occurred when old ways of thinking gave way to new discourses and new *épistémès*—new ways of looking at things and comprehending them. A fresh look at the social crises of the past would, Foucault hoped, suggest a solution to that social crisis of the present that was his real concern.

It is in this light that we should read Foucault's discussion of *The Order of Things*, the second of his prefaces reprinted here. The book's original French title, *Les Mots et les Choses* (literally: words and things) reminds us of the arbitrary and "unreasonable" nature of all cultural constructs and assumptions, not least of "truth." Truth is a sociopolitical construct like others, "a thing of this world, produced only by multiple forms of constraint."

> Each society has its own regime of truth, its "general politics" of truth:
> that is, the types of discourse which it accepts and makes function as true;
> the mechanisms and instances which enable one to distinguish true and
> false statements, the means by which each is sanctioned; the techniques
> and procedures accorded value in the acquisition of truth, the status of
> those who are charged with saying what is true.[1]

Madness and Civilization

Pascal: "Men are so necessarily mad, that not to be mad would amount to another form of madness." And Dostoievsky, in his *Diary of a Writer:* "It is not by confining one's neighbor that one is convinced of one's own sanity."

We have yet to write the history of that other form of madness, by which men, in an act of sovereign reason, confine their neighbors, and communicate and recognize each other through the merciless language of non-madness; to define the moment of this conspiracy before it was permanently established in the realm of truth, before it was revived by the lyricism of protest. We

---

[1]"Truth and Power," in *The Foucault Reader,* Paul Rabinow, ed. (New York: Pantheon Books, 1984), p. 73.

Source: From *Madness and Civilization: A History of Insanity in the Age of Reason* by Michel Foucault, translated by Richard Howard. Copyright © 1965 by Random House, Inc. Reprinted by permission of Pantheon Books, a division of Random House, Inc.

must try to return, in history, to that zero point in the course of madness at which madness is an undifferentiated experience, a not yet divided experience of division itself. We must describe, from the start of its trajectory, that "other form" which relegates Reason and Madness to one side or the other of its action as things henceforth external, deaf to all exchange, and as though dead to one another.

This is doubtless an uncomfortable region. To explore it we must renounce the convenience of terminal truths, and never let ourselves be guided by what we may know of madness. None of the concepts of psychopathology, even and especially in the implicit process of retrospections, can play an organizing role. What is constitutive is the action that divides madness, and not the science elaborated once this division is made and calm restored. What is originative is the caesura that established the distance between reason and non-reason; reason's subjugation of non-reason, wresting from it its truth as madness, crime, or disease, derives explicitly from this point. Hence we must speak of that initial dispute without assuming a victory, or the right to a victory; we must speak of those actions re-examined in history, leaving in abeyance all that may figure as a conclusion, as a refuge in truth; we shall have to speak of this act of scission, of this distance set, of this void instituted between reason and what is not reason, without ever relying upon the fulfillment of what it claims to be.

Then, and then only, can we determine the realm in which the man of madness and the man of reason, moving apart, are not yet disjunct; and in an incipient and very crude language, antedating that of science, begin the dialogue of their breach, testifying in a fugitive way that they still speak to each other. Here madness and non-madness, reason and non-reason are inextricably involved: inseparable at the moment when they do not yet exist, and existing for each other, in relation to each other, in the exchange which separates them.

In the serene world of mental illness, modern man no longer communicates with the madman: on one hand, the man of reason delegates the physician to madness, thereby authorizing a relation only through the abstract universality of disease; on the other, the man of madness communicates with society only by the intermediary of an equally abstract reason which is order, physical and moral constraint, the anonymous pressure of the group, the requirements of conformity. As for a common language, there is no such thing; or rather, there is no such thing any longer; the constitution of madness as a mental illness, at the end of the eighteenth century, affords the evidence of a broken dialogue, posits the separation as already effected, and thrusts into oblivion all those stammered, imperfect words without fixed syntax in which the exchange between madness and reason was made. The language of psychiatry, which is a monologue of reason about madness, has been established only on the basis of such a silence.

I have not tried to write the history of that language, but rather the archaeology of that silence.

The Greeks had a relation to something that they called *hubris* [pride; arrogance]. This relation was not merely one of condemnation; the existence of Thrasymachus or of Callicles suffices to prove it, even if their language has reached us already enveloped in the reassuring dialectic of Socrates. But the Greek Logos had no contrary.

European man, since the beginning of the Middle Ages, has had a relation to something he calls, indiscriminately, Madness, Dementia, Insanity. Perhaps it is to this obscure presence that Western reason owes something of its depth, as the *sophrosyne* [moderation; self-control] of the Socratic reasoners owes something to the threat of *hubris*. In any case, the Reason-Madness nexus constitutes for Western culture one of the dimensions of its originality; it already accompanied that culture long before Hieronymus Bosch, and will follow it long after Nietzsche and Artaud.

What, then, is this confrontation beneath the language of reason? Where can an interrogation lead us which does not follow reason in its horizontal course, but seeks to retrace in time that constant verticality which confronts European culture with what it is not, establishes its range by its own derangement? What realm do we enter which is neither the history of knowledge, nor history itself; which is controlled by neither the teleology of truth nor the rational sequence of causes, since causes have value and meaning only beyond the division? A realm, no doubt, where what is in question is the limits rather than the identity of a culture.

The classical period—from Willis to Pinel, from the frenzies of Racine's Oreste to Sade's Juliette and the Quinta del Sordo of Goya—covers precisely that epoch in which the exchange between madness and reason modifies its language, and in a radical manner. In the history of madness, two events indicate this change with a singular clarity: 1657, the creation of the Hôpital Général and the "great confinement" of the poor; 1794, the liberation of the chained inmates of Bicêtre. Between these two unique and symmetrical events, something happens whose ambiguity has left the historians of medicine at a loss: blind repression in an absolutist regime, according to some; but according to others, the gradual discovery by science and philanthropy of madness in its positive truth. As a matter of fact, beneath these reversible meanings, a structure is forming which does not resolve the ambiguity but determines it. It is this structure which accounts for the transition from the medieval and humanist experience of madness to our own experience, which confines insanity within mental illness. In the Middle Ages and until the Renaissance, man's dispute with madness was a dramatic debate in which he confronted the secret powers of the world; the experience of madness was clouded by images of the Fall and the Will of God, of the Beast and the Metamorphosis, and of all the marvelous secrets of Knowledge. In our era, the experience of madness remains silent in the composure of a knowledge which, knowing too much about madness, forgets it. But from one of these experiences to the other, the shift has been made by a world without images, without positive character, in a kind of silent transparency which reveals—as mute institution, act without commentary, immediate knowledge—a great motionless structure; this structure is one of neither drama nor knowledge; it is the point where history is immobilized in the tragic category which both establishes and impugns it.

The Order of Things

This book arose out of a passage in Borges, out of the laughter that shattered, as I read the passage, all the familiar landmarks of my thought—*our* thought, the thought that bears the stamp of our age and our geography—breaking up all the ordered surfaces and all the planes with which we are accustomed to tame the wild profusion of existing things, and continuing long afterwards to disturb and threaten with collapse our age-old distinction between the Same and the Other. This passage quotes a "certain Chinese encyclopaedia" in which it is written that "animals are divided into: (a) belonging to the Emperor, (b) embalmed, (c) tame, (d) sucking pigs, (e) sirens, (f) fabulous, (g) stray dogs, (h) included in the present classification, (i) frenzied, (j) innumerable, (k) drawn with a very fine camelhair brush, (l) *et cetera*, (m) having just broken the water pitcher, (n) that [which] from a long way off looks like flies." In the wonderment of this taxonomy, the thing we apprehend in one great leap, the thing that, by means of the fable, is demonstrated as the exotic charm of another system of thought, is the limitation of our own, the stark impossibility of thinking *that*.

But what is impossible to think, and what kind of impossibility are we faced with here? Each of these strange categories can be assigned a precise meaning and a demonstrable content; some of them do certainly involve fantastic entities—fabulous animals or sirens—but, precisely because it puts them into categories of their own, the Chinese encyclopaedia localizes their powers of contagion; it distinguishes carefully between the very real animals (those that are frenzied or have just broken the water pitcher) and those that reside solely in the realm of imagination. The possibility of dangerous mixtures has been exorcized, heraldry and fable have been relegated to their own exalted peaks: no inconceivable amphibious maidens, no clawed wings, no disgusting, squamous epidermis, none of those polymorphous and demoniacal faces, no creatures breathing fire. The quality of monstrosity here does not affect any real body, nor does it produce modifications of any kind in the bestiary of the imagination; it does not lurk in the depths of any strange power. It would not even be present at all in this classification had it not insinuated itself into the empty space, the interstitial blanks *separating* all these entities from one another. It is not the "fabulous" animals that are impossible, since they are designated as such, but the narrowness of the distance separating them from (and juxtaposing them to) the stray dogs, or the animals that from a long way off look like flies. What transgresses the boundaries of all imagination, of all possible thought, is simply that alphabetical series (a, b, c, d) which links each of those categories to all the others.

Moreover, it is not simply the oddity of unusual juxtapositions that we are faced with here. We are all familiar with the disconcerting effect of the proximity of extremes, or, quite simply, with the sudden vicinity of things that have no relation to each other; the mere act of enumeration that heaps them all together has a power of enchantment all its own: "I am no longer hungry," Eusthenes said. "Until the morrow, safe from my saliva all the following shall be: Aspics, Acalephs, Acanthocephalates, Amoebocytes, Ammonites, Axolotls, Ambystomas, Aphislions, Anacondas, Ascarids, Amphisbaenas, Angleworms, Amphipods, Anaerobes, Annelids, Anthozoans. . . ." But all these worms and snakes, all these creatures redolent of decay and slime are slithering, like the syllables which designate them, in Eusthenes' saliva: that is where they all have their common locus, like the umbrella and the sewing-machine on the operating table; startling though their propinquity may be, it is nevertheless warranted by that *and*, by that *in*, by than *on* whose solidity provides proof of the possibility of juxtaposition. It was certainly improbable that arachnids, ammonites, and annelids should one day mingle on Eusthenes' tongue, but, after all, that welcoming and voracious mouth certainly provided them with a feasible lodging, a roof under which to coexist.

The monstrous quality that runs through Borges's enumeration consists, on the contrary, in the fact that the common ground on which such meetings are possible has itself been destroyed. What is impossible is not the propinquity of the things listed, but the very site on which their propinquity would be possible. The animals "(i) frenzied, (j) innumerable, (k) drawn with a very fine camelhair brush"—where could they ever meet, except in the immaterial sound of the voice pronouncing their enumeration, or on the page transcribing it? Where else could they be juxtaposed except in the non-place of language? Yet, though language can spread them before us, it can do so only in an unthinkable space. The central category of animals "included in the present classification," with its explicit reference to paradoxes we are familiar with, is indication enough that we shall never succeed in defining a stable relation of contained to container between each of these categories and that which includes them all: if all the animals divided up here can be placed without exception in one of the divisions of this list, then aren't all the other divisions to be found in that one division too? And then again, in what space would that single, inclusive division have its existence? Absurdity destroys the *and* of the enumeration by making impossible the *in* where the things enumerated would be divided up. Borges adds no figure to the atlas of the impossible; nowhere does he strike the spark of poetic confrontation; he simply dispenses with the least obvious, but most compelling, of necessities; he does away with the *site,* the mute ground upon which it is possible for entities to be juxtaposed. A vanishing trick that is masked or, rather, laughably indicated by our alphabetical order, which is to be taken as the clue (the only visible one) to the enumerations of a Chinese encyclopaedia. . . . What has been removed, in short, is the famous "operating table"; and rendering to Roussel[1] a small part of what is still his due, I use that word "table" in two superimposed senses: the sun devouring all shadow—the table where, for an instant, perhaps forever, the umbrella encounters the sewing-machine; and also a table, a *tabula,* that enables thought to operate upon the entities of our world, to put them in order, to divide them into classes, to group them according to the similarities and differences upon which, since the beginning of time, language has intersected space.

That passage from Borges kept me laughing a long time, though not without a certain uneasiness that I found hard to shake off. Perhaps because there arose in its wake the suspicion that there is a worse kind of disorder than that of the *incongruous,* the linking together of things that are inappropriate; I mean the disorder in which fragments of a large number of possible orders glitter separately in the dimension, without law or geometry, of the *heteroclite,* and that word should be taken in its most literal, etymological sense: in such a state, things are "laid," "placed," "arranged" in sites so very different from one another that it is impossible to find a place of residence for them, to define a *common locus* beneath them all. *Utopias* afford consolation: although they have no real locality there is nevertheless a fantastic, untroubled

---

[1]Raymond Roussel (1877–1933), French novelist and forerunner of the Surrealists. Cf. Michel Foucault's *Raymond Roussel* (Paris, 1963). [Translator's note]

region in which they are able to unfold; they open up cities with vast avenues, superbly planted gardens, countries where life is easy, even though the road to them is chimerical. *Heterotopias* are disturbing, probably because they secretly undermine language, because they make it impossible to name this *and* that, because they shatter or tangle common names, because they destroy "syntax" in advance, and not only the syntax which causes words and things (next to and also opposite one another) to "hold together." This is why utopias permit fables and discourse: they run with the very grain of language and are part of the fundamental dimension of the *fabula*; heterotopias (such as those to be found so often in Borges) desiccate speech, stop words in their tracks, contest the very possibility of grammar at its source; they dissolve our myths and sterilize the lyricism of our sentences.

It appears that certain aphasiacs,[2] when shown various differently coloured skeins of wool on a table top, are consistently unable to arrange them into any coherent pattern; as though that simple rectangle were unable to serve in their case as a homogeneous and neutral space in which things could be placed so as to display at the same time the continuous order of their identities or differences as well as the semantic field of their denomination. Within this simple space in which things are normally arranged and given names, the aphasiac will create a multiplicity of tiny, fragmented regions in which nameless resemblances agglutinate things into unconnected islets; in one corner, they will place the lightest-coloured skeins, in another the red ones, somewhere else those that are softest in texture, in yet another place the longest, or those that have a tinge of purple or those that have been wound up into a ball. But no sooner have they been adumbrated than all these groupings dissolve again, for the field of identity that sustains them, however limited it may be, is still too wide not to be unstable; and so the sick mind continues to infinity, creating groups then dispersing them again, heaping up diverse similarities, destroying those that seem clearest, splitting up things that are identical, superimposing different criteria, frenziedly beginning all over again, becoming more and more disturbed, and teetering finally on the brink of anxiety.

The uneasiness that makes us laugh when we read Borges is certainly related to the profound distress of those whose language has been destroyed; loss of what is "common" to place and name. Atopia, aphasia. Yet our text from Borges proceeds in another direction; the mythical homeland Borges assigns to that distortion of classification that prevents us from applying it,

---

[2]Aphasia is a speech disorder. Foucault refers to a related perceptual disorder more specifically described as *agnosia*.

to that picture that lacks all spatial coherence, is a precise region whose name alone constitutes for the West a vast reservoir of utopias. In our dreamworld, is not China precisely this privileged *site* of *space*? In our traditional imagery, the Chinese culture is the most meticulous, the most rigidly ordered, the one most deaf to temporal events, most attached to the pure delineation of space; we think of it as a civilization of dikes and dams beneath the eternal face of the sky; we see it, spread and frozen, over the entire surface of a continent surrounded by walls. Even its writing does not reproduce the fugitive flight of the voice in horizontal lines; it erects the motionless and still-recognizeable images of things themselves in vertical columns. So much so that the Chinese encyclopaedia quoted by Borges, and the taxonomy it proposes, lead to a kind of thought without space, to words and categories that lack all life and place, but are rooted in a ceremonial space, overburdened with complex figures, with tangled paths, strange places, secret passages, and unexpected communications. There would appear to be, then, at the other extremity of the earth we inhabit, a culture entirely devoted to the ordering of space, but one that does not distribute the multiplicity of existing things into any of the categories that make it possible for us to name, speak, and think.

When we establish a considered classification, when we say that a cat and a dog resemble each other less than two greyhounds do, even if both are tame or embalmed, even if both are frenzied, even if both have just broken the water pitcher, what is the ground on which we are able to establish the validity of this classification with complete certainty? On what "table," according to what grid of identities, similtudes, analogies, have we become accustomed to sort out so many different and similar things? What is this coherence—which, as is immediately apparent, is neither determined by an *a priori* and necessary concatenation, nor imposed on us by immediately perceptible contents? For it is not a question of linking consequences, but of grouping and isolating, of analysing, of matching and pigeon-holing concrete contents; there is nothing more tentative, nothing more empirical (superficially, at least) than the process of establishing an order among things; nothing that demands a sharper eye or a surer, better-articulated language; nothing that more insistently requires that one allow oneself to be carried along by the proliferation of qualities and forms. And yet an eye not consciously prepared might well group together certain similar figures and distinguish between others on the basis of such and such a difference: in fact, there is no similitude and no distinction, even for the wholly untrained perception, that is not the result of a precise operation and of the application of a preliminary criterion. A "system of elements"—a definition of the segments by which the resemblances and differences can be shown, the types of variation by which those segments can be affected, and, lastly, the threshold above which there is a difference and below which there is a similitude—is indispensable for the establishment of even the simplest form of order. Order is, at one and the same time, that which is given in things as their inner law, the hidden network that determines the way they confront one another, and also that which has no existence except in the grid created by a glance, an examination, a language; and it is only in the blank spaces of this grid that order manifests itself in depth as though already there, waiting in silence for the moment of its expression.

The fundamental codes of a culture—those governing its language, its schemas of perception, its exchanges, its techniques, its values, the hierarchy of its practices—establish for every man, from the very first, the empirical orders with which he will be dealing and within which he will be at home. At the other extremity of thought, there are the scientific theories or the philosophical interpretations which explain why order exists in general, what universal law it obeys, what principle can account for it, and why this particular order has been established and not some other. But between these two regions, so distant from one another, lies a domain which, even though its role is mainly an intermediary one, is nonetheless fundamental: it is more confused, more obscure, and probably less easy to analyse. It is here that a culture, imperceptibly deviating from the empirical orders prescribed for it by its primary codes, instituting an initial separation from them, causes them to lose their original transparency, relinquishes its immediate and invisible powers, frees itself sufficiently to discover that these orders are perhaps not the only possible ones or the best ones; this culture then finds itself faced with the stark fact that there exist, below the level of its spontaneous orders, things that are in themselves capable of being ordered, that belong to a certain unspoken order; the fact, in short, that order *exists*. As though emancipating itself to some extent from its linguistic, perceptual, and practical grids, the culture superimposed on them another kind of grid which neutralized them, which by this superimposition both revealed and excluded them at the same time, so that the culture, by this very process, came face to face with order in its primary state. It is on the basis of this newly perceived order that the codes of language, perception, and practice are criticized and rendered partially invalid. It is on the basis of this order, taken as a firm foundation, that general theories as to the ordering of things, and the interpretation that such an ordering involves, will be constructed. Thus, between the already "encoded" eye and reflexive knowledge there is a middle region which liberates order itself: it is here that it appears, according to the culture and the age in question, continuous and graduated or discontinuous and piecemeal, linked to space or constituted anew at each instant by the driving force of time, related to a series of variables or defined by separate systems of coher-

ences, composed of resemblances which are either successive or corresponding, organized around increasing differences, etc. This middle region, then,
in so far as it makes manifest the modes of being of order, can be posited as
the most fundamental of all: anterior to words, perceptions, and gestures,
which are then taken to be more or less exact, more or less happy, expressions
of it (which is why this experience of order in its pure primary state always
plays a critical role); more solid, more archaic, less dubious, always more
"true" than the theories that attempt to give those expressions explicit form,
exhaustive application, or philosophical foundation. Thus, in every culture,
between the use of what one might call the ordering codes and reflections
upon order itself, there is the pure experience of order and its modes of being.

The present study is an attempt to analyse that experience. I am concerned
to show its developments, since the sixteenth century, in the mainstream of
a culture such as ours: in what way, as one traces—against the current, as it
were—language as it has been spoken, natural creatures as they have been
perceived and grouped together, and exchanges as they have been practised;
in what way, then, our culture has made manifest the existence of order, and
how, to the modalities of that order, the exchanges owed their laws, the living
beings their constants, the words their sequence and their representative
value; what modalities of order have been recognized, posited, linked with
space and time, in order to create the positive basis of knowledge as we find
it employed in grammar and philology, in natural history and biology, in the
study of wealth and political economy. Quite obviously, such an analysis does
not belong to the history of ideas or of science: it is rather an inquiry whose
aim is to rediscover on what basis knowledge and theory became possible;
within what space of order knowledge was constituted; on the basis of what
historical *a priori*, and in the element of what positivity, ideas could appear,
sciences be established, experience be reflected in philosophies, be formed,
only, perhaps, to dissolve and vanish soon afterwards. I am not concerned,
therefore, to describe the progress of knowledge towards an objectivity in
which today's science can finally be recognized; what I am attempting to
bring to light is the epistemological field, the *épistémè* in which knowledge,
envisaged apart from all criteria having reference to its rational value or to its
objective forms, grounds its positivity and thereby manifests a history which
is not that of its growing perfection, but rather that of its conditions of possibility; in this account, what should appear are those configurations within
the *space* of knowledge which have given rise to the diverse forms of empirical
science. Such an enterprise is not so much history, in the traditional meaning
of that word, as an "archaeology."

Now, this archaeological inquiry has revealed two great discontinuities in
the *épistémè* of Western culture: the first inaugurates the Classical age

(roughly half-way through the seventeenth century) and the second, at the beginning of the nineteenth century, marks the beginning of the Modern age. The order on the basis of which we think today does not have the same mode of being as that of the Classical thinkers. Despite the impression we may have of an almost uninterrupted development of the European *ratio* from the Renaissance to our own day, despite our possible belief that the classifications of Linnaeus, modified to a greater or lesser degree, can still lay claim to some sort of validity, that Condillac's theory of value can be recognized to some extent in nineteenth-century marginalism, that Keynes was well aware of the affinities between his own analyses and those of Cantillon, that the language of *general grammar* (as exemplified in the authors of Port-Royal or in Bauzée) is not so very far removed from our own—all this quasi-continuity on the level of ideas and themes is doubtless only a surface appearance; on the archaeological level, we see that the system of positivities was transformed in a wholesale fashion at the end of the eighteenth and beginning of the nineteenth century. Not that reason made any progress: it was simply that the mode of being of things, and of the order that divided them up before presenting them to the understanding, was profoundly altered. If the natural history of Tournefort, Linnaeus, and Buffon can be related to anything at all other than itself, it is not to biology, to Cuvier's comparative anatomy, or to Darwin's theory of evolution, but to Bauzée's general grammar, to the analysis of money and wealth as found in the works of Law, or Véron de Fortbonnais, or Turgot. Perhaps knowledge succeeds in engendering knowledge, ideas in transforming themselves and actively modifying one another (but how?—historians have not yet enlightened us on this point); one thing, in any case, is certain: archaeology, addressing itself to the general space of knowledge, to its configurations, and to the mode of being of the things that appear in it, defines systems of simultaneity, as well as the series of mutations necessary and sufficient to circumscribe the threshold of a new positivity.

   In this way, analysis has been able to show the coherence that existed, throughout the Classical age, between the theory of representation and the theories of language, of the natural orders, and of wealth and value. It is this configuration that, from the nineteenth century onward, changes entirely; the theory of representation disappears as the universal foundation of all possible orders; language as the spontaneous *tabula*, the primary grid of things, as an indispensable link between representation and things, is eclipsed in its turn; a profound historicity penetrates into the heart of things, isolates and defines them in their own coherence, imposes upon them the forms of order implied by the continuity of time; the analysis of exchange and money gives way to the study of production, that of the organism takes precedence over the search for taxonomic characteristics, and, above all, language loses its privileged position and becomes, in its turn, a historical form coherent with the density of its own past. But as things become increasingly reflexive, seeking the principle of their intelligibility only in their own development, and abandoning the space of representation, man enters in his turn, and for the first time, the field of Western knowledge. Strangely enough, man—the study of whom is supposed by the naïve to be the oldest investigation since Socrates—is probably no more than a kind of rift in the order of things, or, in any case, a configuration whose outlines are determined by the new position he has so recently taken up in the field of knowledge. Whence all the chimeras of the new humanisms, all the facile solutions of an "anthropology" understood as a universal reflection on man, half-empirical, half-philosophical. It is comforting, however, and a source of profound relief to think that man is only a recent invention, a figure not yet two centuries old, a new wrinkle in our knowledge, and that he will disappear again as soon as that knowledge has discovered a new form.

Barthes

Classicist and philologist by training, Roland Barthes (1915–1980) held the chair of semiology at the Collège de France, where Lévi-Strauss and Foucault also taught, from 1976 to his death in an automobile accident.

In 1953, his first book, *Writing Degree Zero,* translated into English when he had become well known thirteen years later, denounced the arbitrariness of linguistic constructs. Later works picked to pieces the symbols and attitudes of bourgeois culture. The theories he launched provided much of the inspiration for the antinovelists of the *nouveau roman* produced since the sixties by writers like Natalie Sarraute, Marguerite Duras, and Alain Robbe-Grillet. In the wake of Barthes, these new novelists rejected the traditional novel and its illusion of order and significance that reality contradicts. They dispensed with omniscient narrators, jettisoned particular interpretations, and refused to organize events in a way that might endow them with particular significance; they affirmed instead irrelevance, inconsequence, and uncertainty.

Structuralism had been intent on discovering the hidden orders and codes that affected literary and artistic products as well as socio-ideological ones. By the 1970s, Barthes had gone beyond Structuralism to argue that the complete analysis this called for was in effect unachievable or, at the very least, unreadable. He came close to proving his point.

The Poststructuralist writings of Barthes were devoted largely to denial. Works (for example, of literature) were reduced to texts, authors to obstacles, and the experience of reading in order to share the visions, experiences, characters of others was denounced as mere *plaisir* (pleasure), incomparable to the higher, bitter, but more intense, satisfaction of *jouissance* (joy, or orgasm) that only Deconstructionist lucidity can provide.

The Death of the Author

In his story *Sarrasine,* Balzac, describing a castrato disguised as a woman, writes the following sentence: "This was woman herself, with her sudden fears, her irrational whims, her instinctive worries, her impetuous boldness, her fussings, and her delicious sensibility." Who is speaking thus? Is it the hero of the story bent on remaining ignorant of the castrato hidden beneath the woman? Is it Balzac the individual, furnished by his personal experience with a philosophy of Woman? Is it Balzac the author professing "literary" ideas on femininity? Is it universal wisdom? Romantic psychology? We shall never know, for the good reason that writing is the destruction of every voice, of every point of origin. Writing is that neutral, composite, oblique space where our subject slips away, the negative where all identity is lost, starting with the very identity of the body writing.

No doubt it has always been that way. As soon as a fact is *narrated* no longer with a view to acting directly on reality but intransitively, that is to say, finally outside of any function other than that of the very practice of the symbol itself, this disconnection occurs, the voice loses its origin, the author enters into his own death, writing begins. The sense of this phenomenon, however, has varied; in ethnographic societies the responsibility for a narrative is never assumed by a person but by a mediator, shaman or relator whose "performance"—the mastery of the narrative code—may possibly be admired but never his "genius." The author is a modern figure, a product of our society insofar as, emerging from the Middle Ages with English empiricism, French rationalism and the personal faith of the Reformation, it discovered the prestige of the individual, of, as it is more nobly put, the "human person." It is thus logical that in literature it should be this positivism, the epitome and culmination of capitalist ideology, which has attached the greatest importance to the "person" of the author. The *author* still reigns in histories of literature, biographies of writers, interviews, magazines, as in the very consciousness of men of letters anxious to unite their person and their work through diaries and memoirs. The image of literature to be found in ordinary culture is tyrannically centered on the author, his person, his life, his tastes, his passions, while criticism still consists for the most part in saying that

---

Source: From *Image Music Text* by Roland Barthes and translated by Stephen Heath, 1977, pp. 142–148.

Baudelaire's work is the failure of Baudelaire the man, van Gogh's his madness, Tchaikovsky's his vice. The *explanation* of a work is always sought in the man or woman who produced it, as if it were always in the end, through the more or less transparent allegory of the fiction, the voice of a single person, the *author* "confiding" in us.

Though the sway of the Author remains powerful (the new criticism has often done no more than consolidate it), it goes without saying that certain writers have long since attempted to loosen it. In France, Mallarmé was doubtless the first to see and to foresee in its full extent the necessity to substitute language itself for the person who until then had been supposed to be its owner. For him, for us too, it is language which speaks, not the author; to write is, through a prerequisite impersonality (not at all to be confused with the castrating objectivity of the realist novelist), to reach that point where only language acts, "performs," and not "me." Mallarmé's entire poetics consists in suppressing the author in the interests of writing (which is, as will be seen, to restore the place of the reader). Valéry, encumbered by a psychology of the Ego, considerably diluted Mallarmé's theory but, his taste for classicism leading him to turn to the lessons of rhetoric, he never stopped calling into question and deriding the Author; he stressed the linguistic and, as it were, "hazardous" nature of his activity, and throughout his prose works he militated in favour of the essentially verbal condition of literature, in the face of which all recourse to writer's interiority seemed to him pure superstition. Proust himself, despite the apparently psychological character of what are called his *analyses,* was visibly concerned with the task of inexorably blurring, by an extreme subtilization, the relation between the writer and his characters; by making of the narrator not he who has seen and felt nor even he who is writing, but he who *is going to write* (the young man in the novel—but, in fact, how old is he and who is he?—wants to write but cannot; the novel ends when writing at last becomes possible), Proust gave modern writing its epic. By a radical reversal, instead of putting his life into his novel, as is so often maintained, he made of his very life a work for which his own book was the model; so that it is clear to us that Charlus does not imitate Montesquiou but Montesquiou—in his anecdotal, historical reality—is no more than a secondary fragment, derived from Charlus. Lastly, to go no further than this prehistory of modernity, Surrealism, though unable to accord language a supreme place (language being system and the aim of the movement being, romantically, a direct subversion of codes—itself moreover illusory; a code cannot be destroyed, only "played off"), contributed to the desacrilization of the image of the author by ceaselessly recommending the abrupt disappointment of expectations of meaning (the famous surrealist "jolt"), by entrusting the hand with the task of writing as quickly as possible what the head itself is unaware of (automatic writing), by accepting the principle and the experience of several people writing together. Leaving aside literature itself (such distinctions really becoming invalid), linguistics has recently provided the destruction of the Author with a valuable analytical tool by showing that the whole of the enunciation is an empty process, functioning perfectly without there being any need for it to be filled with the person of the interlocutors. Linguistically, the author is never more than the instance writing, just as "I" is nothing other than the instance saying "I"; language knows a "subject," not a "person," and this subject, empty outside of the very enunciation which defines it, suffices to make language "hold together," suffices, that it is to say, to exhaust it.

The removal of the Author (one could talk here with Brecht of a veritable "distancing," the Author diminishing like a figurine at the far end of the literary stage) is not merely an historical fact or an act of writing; it utterly transforms the modern text (or—which is the same thing—the text is henceforth made and read in such a way that at all its levels the author is absent). The temporality is different. The Author, when believed in, is always conceived of as the past of his own book: book and author stand automatically on a single line divided into a *before* and an *after*. The Author is thought to *nourish* the book, which is to say that he exists before it, thinks, suffers, lives for it, is in the same relation of antecedence to his work as a father to his child. In complete contrast, the modern scriptor is born simultaneously with the text, is in no way equipped with a being preceding or exceeding the writing, is not the subject with the book as predicate; there is no other time than that of the enunciation and every text is eternally written *here and now*. The fact is (or, it follows) that *writing* can no longer designate an operation of recording, notation, representation, "depiction" (as the Classicists would say); rather, it designates exactly what linguists, referring to Oxford philosophy, call a performative, a rare verbal form (exclusively given in the first person and in the present tense) in which the enunciation has no other content (contains no other proposition) than the act by which it is uttered—something like the *I declare* of kings or the *I sing* of very ancient poets. Having buried the Author, the modern scriptor can thus no longer believe, as according to the pathetic view of his predecessors, that his hand is too slow for his thought or passion and that consequently, making a law of necessity, he must emphasize this delay and indefinitely "polish" his form. For him, on the contrary, the hand, cut off from any voice, borne by a pure gesture of inscription (and not of expression), traces a field without origin—or which, at least, has no other origin than language itself, language which ceaselessly calls into question all origins.

We know now that a text is not a line of words releasing a single "theological" meaning (the "message" of the Author-God) but a multi-dimensional space in which a variety of writings, none of them original, blend and clash. The text is a tissue of quotations drawn from the innumerable centres of culture. Similar to Bouvard and Pécuchet, those eternal copyists, at once sublime and comic and whose profound ridiculousness indicates precisely the truth of writing, the writer can only imitate a gesture that is always anterior, never original. His only power is to mix writings, to counter the ones with the others, in such a way as never to rest on any one of them. Did he wish to *express himself,* he ought at least to know that the inner "thing" he thinks to "translate" is itself only a ready-formed dictionary, its words only explainable through other words, and so on indefinitely; something experienced in exemplary fashion by the young Thomas de Quincey, he who was so good at Greek that in order to translate absolutely modern ideas and images into that dead language, he had, so Baudelaire tells us (in *Paradis Artificiels*), "created for himself an unfailing dictionary, vastly more extensive and complex than those resulting from the ordinary patience of purely literary themes." Succeeding the Author, the scriptor no longer bears within him passions, humours, feelings, impressions, but rather this immense dictionary from which he draws a writing that can know no halt: life never does more than imitate the book, and the book itself is only a tissue of signs, an imitation that is lost, infinitely deferred.

Once the Author is removed, the claim to decipher a text becomes quite futile. To give a text an Author is to impose a limit on that text, to furnish it with a final signified, to close the writing. Such a conception suits criticism very well, the latter then allotting itself the important task of discovering the Author (or its hypostases: society, history, psyche, liberty) beneath the work: when the Author has been found, the text is "explained"—victory to the critic. Hence there is no surprise in the fact that, historically, the reign of the Author has also been that of the Critic, nor again in the fact that criticism (be it new) is today undermined along with the Author. In the multiplicity of writing, everything is to be *disentangled,* nothing *deciphered,* the structure can be followed, "run" (like the thread of a stocking) at every point and at every level, but there is nothing beneath: the space of writing is to be ranged over, not pierced; writing ceaselessly posits meaning ceaselessly to evaporate it, carrying out a systematic exemption of meaning. In precisely this way literature (it would be better from now on to say *writing*), by refusing to assign a "secret," an ultimate meaning, to the text (and to the world as text), liberates what may be called an anti-theological activity, an activity that is truly revolutionary since to refuse to fix meaning is, in the end, to refuse God and his hypostases—reason, science, law.

Let us come back to the Balzac sentence. No one, no "person," says it: its source, its voice, is not the true place of the writing, which is reading. Another—very precise—example will help to make this clear: recent research has demonstrated the constitutively ambiguous nature of Greek tragedy, its texts being woven from words with double meanings that each character understands unilaterally (this perpetual misunderstanding is exactly the "tragic"); there is, however, someone who understands each word in its duplicity and who, in addition, hears the very deafness of the characters speaking in front of him—this someone being precisely the reader (or here the listener). Thus is revealed the total existence of writing: a text is made of multiple writings, drawn from many cultures and entering into mutual relations of dialogue, parody, contestation, but there is one place where this multiplicity is focused and that place is the reader, not, as was hitherto said, the Author. The reader is the space on which all the quotations that make up a writing are inscribed without any of them being lost; a text's unity lies not in its origin but in its destination. Yet this destination cannot any longer be personal: the reader is without history, biography, psychology; he is simply that *someone* who holds together in a single field all the traces by which the written text is constituted. Which is why it is derisory to condemn the new writing in the name of a humanism hypocritically turned champion of the reader's rights. Classic criticism has never paid any attention to the reader; for it, the writer is the only person in literature. We are now beginning to let ourselves be fooled no longer by the arrogant antiphrastical recriminations of good society in favour of the very thing it sets aside, ignores, smothers, or destroys; we know that to give writing its future, it is necessary to overthrow the myth: the birth of the reader must be at the cost of the death of the Author.

Derrida

More extreme than Barthes and more influential in our time is Jacques Derrida (1930–   ), whose career has been based on a radical critique of Structuralist faith in the stability of linguistic structures. Though polemical pirouettes, verbal fireworks, and linguistic acrobatics make it hard to determine, Derrida's central argument turns on the limits of argument, the defects of expression and understanding. Thought must be framed in language, but language is fluid, ambiguous, and unreliable. Semiotics are a dubious guide. Signs have meaning only in a context. They have to be quotable, repeatable, reproducible, like names or words; otherwise, they have no value as a sign. Yet, if signs can be reproduced (which is their purpose), they can also be forged, counterfeited, or falsified. Bereft of its original meaning, the sign is then deprived of value. Every word, every text, inevitably undermines its own claims to represent something specific, to communicate a particular meaning. Or does it? Is meaning only what the reader assumes it to be? These are the questions Derrida poses in the essay on "Signatures" reproduced here.

Like Barthes, Derrida is an intellectual agnostic who argues like an atheist. He doubts that language can make sense, when the sense it seeks to express is condemned to remain incomplete, contradictory, or else incomprehensibly complex. As with reading Barthes, reading Derrida tends to prove his point. To some, however, the reading itself works to expose the "illusions" on which Western culture has been based. The great generalities of our discourse are analyzed away as illusory metaphors and concepts. Better still, the concept of structure itself is discarded as one more misleading metaphor. Interpreting myths, as Lévi-Strauss has done, is as far from the truth of things as forging myths has been shown to be, and is as open to reinterpretation.

Derrida denounces such delusion. The task today, he says (if one can understand what he says), is to try to pass "beyond man and humanism." In fact, Derrida echoes Nietzsche in his ultimate purpose: to replace Hegel's progressive dialectical history with something else—undefined, untranscended, open. Derrida affirms crisis as Camus affirmed Sisyphus happy. He revels in the intellectual shindig, he awaits the transvaluation of devalued values, he is the opaque prophet of a flickering doom.

Signatures

By definition, a written signature implies the actual or empirical nonpresence of the signer. But, it will be said, it also marks and retains his having-been present in a past now, which will remain a future now, and therefore in a now in general, in the transcendental form of nowness *(maintenance)*. This general *maintenance* is somehow inscribed, stapled to present punctuality, always evident and always singular, in the form of the signature. This is the enigmatic originality of every paraph. For the attachment to the source to occur, the absolute singularity of an event of the signature and of a form of the signature must be retained: the pure reproducibility of a pure event.

Is there such a thing? Does the absolute singularity of an event of the signature ever occur? Are there signatures?

Yes, of course, every day. The effects of signature are the most ordinary thing in the world. The condition of possibility for these effects is simultaneously, once again, the condition of their impossibility, of the impossibility of their rigorous purity. In order to function, that is, in order to be legible, a signature must have a repeatable, iterable, imitable form; it must be able to

---

Source: From *Margins of Philosophy* by Jacques Derrida and translated by Alan Bass, 1972. Reprinted by permission of The University of Chicago Press.

detach itself from the present and singular intention of its production. It is its sameness, which, in altering its identity and singularity, divides the seal. I have already indicated the principle of the analysis above.

To conclude this very dry discourse:

1. As writing, communication, if one insists upon maintaining the word, is not the means of transport of sense, the exchange of intentions and meanings, the discourse and "communication of consciousnesses." We are not witnessing an end of writing which, to follow McLuhan's ideological representation, would restore a transparency or immediacy of social relations; but indeed a more and more powerful historical unfolding of a general writing of which the system of speech, consciousness, meaning, presence, truth, etc., would only be an effect, to be analyzed as such. It is this questioned effect that I have elsewhere called *logocentrism*.

2. The semantic horizon which habitually governs the notion of communication is exceeded or punctured by the intervention of writing, that is of a *dissemination* which cannot be reduced to a *polysemia*. Writing is read, and "in the last analysis" does not give rise to a hermeneutic deciphering, to the decoding of a meaning or truth.

3. Despite the general displacement of the classical, "philosophical," Western, etc., concept of writing, it appears necessary, provisionally and strategically, to conserve the *old name*. This implies an entire logic of *paleonymy* which I do not wish to elaborate here. Very schematically: an opposition of metaphysical concepts (for example, speech/writing, presence/absence, etc.) is never the face-to-face for two terms, but a hierarchy and an order of subordination. Deconstruction cannot limit itself or proceed immediately to a neutralization: it must, by means of a double gesture, a double science, a double writing, practice an *overturning* of the classical opposition *and* a general *displacement* of the system. It is only on this condition that deconstruction will provide itself the means with which to *intervene* in the field of oppositions that it criticizes, which is also a field of nondiscursive forces. Each concept, moreover, belongs to a systematic chain, and itself constitutes a system of predicates. There is no metaphysical concept in and of itself. There is a work—metaphysical or not—on conceptual systems. Deconstruction does not consist in passing from one concept to another, but in overturning and displacing a conceptual order, as well as the nonconceptual order with which the conceptual order is articulated. For example, writing, as a classical concept, carries with it predicates which have been subordinated, excluded, or held in reserve by forces and according to necessities to be analyzed. It is these predicates (I have mentioned some) whose force of generality, generalization, and generativity find themselves liberated, grafted onto a "new" concept of writing which also corresponds to whatever always has *resisted* the

former organization of forces, which always has constituted the *remainder* irreducible to the dominant force which organized the—to say it quickly—logocentric hierarchy. To leave to this new concept the old name of writing is to maintain the structure of the graft, the transition and indispensable adherence to an effective *intervention* in the constituted historic field. And it is also to give their chance and their force, their power of *communication,* to everything played out in the operations of deconstruction.

But what goes without saying will quickly have been understood, especially in a philosophical colloquius: as a disseminating operation *separated* from presence (of Being) according to all its modifications, writing, if there is any, perhaps communicates, but does not exist, surely. Or barely, hereby, in the form of the most improbable signature.

(*Remark:* the—written—text of this—oral—communication was to have been addressed to the *Association of French Speaking Societies of Philosophies* [1971] before the meeting. Such a missive therefore had to be signed. Which I did, and counterfeit here. Where? There. J.D.)

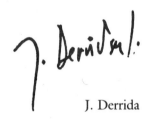

                                        J. Derrida

Steiner

Born in Paris, educated in France, England, and the United States, George Steiner (1929–   ) teaches and writes in Cambridge and Geneva. Critic and philosopher, his writings, dense and difficult at times, exhibit a rich cosmopolitan culture. His wide-ranging criticism reflects the belief that twentieth-century horrors have dealt a grievous blow to Humanism and, notably, to enlightened claims for the humanizing influence of literature. Yet even this disenchanted sceptic rears at the ultimate scepticism that Poststructuralists display. The essay reprinted here represents a partial text of the Leslie Stephen Memorial Lecture that Steiner delivered at Cambridge University in 1985.

It may not be irrelevant to mention that Sir Leslie Stephen (1832–1904), who edited the *British Dictionary of National Biography* and in whose honor these lectures were instituted, was himself a critic of distinction, an intellectual leader as influential as he was industrious. Stephen was also a sceptic, but one who never abandoned belief in positive values.

A New Meaning of Meaning

The act and art of serious reading comport two principal motions of spirit: that of interpretation (hermeneutics) and that of valuation (criticism, aesthetic judgment). The two are strictly inseparable. To interpret is to judge. No decipherment, however philological, however textual in the most technical sense, is value-free. Correspondingly, no critical assessment, no aesthetic commentary is not, at the same time, interpretative. The very word "interpretation," encompassing as it does concepts of explication, of translation and of enactment (as in the interpretation of a dramatic part or musical score) tells of this manifold interplay.

The relativity, the arbitrariness of *all* aesthetic propositions, of *all* value-judgments is inherent in human consciousness and in human speech. Anything can be said about anything. The assertion that Shakespeare's *King Lear* "is beneath serious criticism" (Tolstoy), the finding that Mozart composes mere trivia, are totally irrefutable. They can be falsified neither on formal (logical) grounds, nor in existential substance. Aesthetic philosophies, critical theories, constructs of the "classic" or the "canonic" can never be anything but more or less persuasive, more or less comprehensive, more or less consequent descriptions of this or that process of preference. A critical theory, an aesthetic, is a politics of taste. It seeks to systematize, to make visibly applicable and pedagogic, an intuitive "set," a bent of sensibility, the conservative or radical bias of a master perceiver or an alliance of opinions. There can be neither proof nor disproof. Aristotle's reading and Pope's, Coleridge's and Sainte-Beuve's, T. S. Eliot's and Croce's, do not constitute a science of judgment and disproof, of experimental advance and confirmation or falsification. They constitute the metamorphic play and counter-play of individual response of (to borrow Quine's teasing phrase) "blameless intuition." The difference between the judgment of a great critic and that of a semi-literate or censorious fool lies in the range of inferred or cited reference, in the lucidity and rhetorical strength of articulation (the critic's style) or in the accidental addendum which is that of the critic who is also a creator in his own right. But it is not a scientifically or logically demonstrable difference. No aesthetic proposition can be termed either "right" or "wrong." The sole appropriate response is personal assent or dissent.

How, in actual practice, do we handle the anarchic nature of value-judgments, the formal and pragmatic equality of all critical findings? We count

---

Source: From the *Times Literary Supplement* by George Steiner, November 8, 1985, pp. 1262, 1275–76. Reprinted by permission of Times Newspapers Ltd.

heads and, in particular, what we take to be qualified and laurelled heads. We observe that, over the centuries, a great majority of writers, critics, professors and honourable men have judged Shakespeare to be a poet and dramatist of genius and have found Mozart's music to be both emotionally enriching and technically inspired. Reciprocally, we observe that those who judge otherwise are in a tiny, literally eccentric, minority, that their critiques carry little weight and that the motives we make out behind their dissent are psychologically suspect (Jeffrey on Keats, Hanslick on Wagner, Tolstoy on Shakespeare). After which perfectly valid observations we get on with the business of literate commentary and appreciation.

Now and again, as out of an irritant twilight, we sense the partial circularity and the contingency of the whole argument. We realize that there can be no ballot on aesthetic values, that a majority vote, however constant and massive, can never refute, can never disprove the refusal, the abstention, the counter-statement of the solitary denier. We realize, more or less clearly, the degree to which "literate common sense," the acceptable limits of debate, the transmission of the generally agreed syllabus of major texts and works of art and of music, is an ideological process, a reflection of power-relations within a culture and society. The literate person is one who concurs with the reflexes of approval and aesthetic enjoyment which have been suggested and exemplified by the dominant legacy. But we dismiss such worries. We accept as inevitable and as adequate the merely statistical weight of "institutional consensus," of common-sense authority. How else could we marshal our cultural choices and be at home in our pleasures?

It is at this precise juncture that a distinction has, traditionally, been drawn between aesthetic criticism on the one hand and interpretation or analysis strictly considered on the other. The ontological indeterminancy of all value-judgments, the impossibility of any probative, logically consistent "decision procedure" as between conflicting aesthetic views, have been conceded. *De gustibus non disputandum*. The determination of a true or most probable meaning in a text has, in contrast, been held to be the reasonable aim and merit of informed reading or philology.

Linguistic, formal, historical factors may impede such determination and documented analysis. The context in which the poem or fable was composed may elude us. The stylistic conventions may have become esoteric. We may, simply, not have the requisite critical density of information, of controlling comparisons, needed to arrive at a secure choice between variant readings, between differing glosses and *explications du texte*. But these are accidental, empirical problems. In the case of ancient writings, new lexical, grammatical or contextual material may come to light. Where the inhibitions to understanding are more modern, further biographical or referential data may turn up and help elucidate the author's intentions and field of assumed echo. Unlike criticism and aesthetic valuation, which are always synchronic (Aristotle's Oedipus is not negated or made obsolete by Hölderlin's, Hölderlin's is neither impoverished nor cancelled out by Freud's), the process of textual interpretation is cumulative. Our readings become better informed, evidence progresses, substantiation grows. Ideally—though not, to be sure, in actual practice—the corpus of lexical knowledge, of grammatical analysis, of semantic and contextual matter of historical and biographical fact, will finally suffice to arrive at a demonstrable determination of what the passage means. This determination need not claim exhaustiveness; it will know itself to be susceptible to amendment, to revision, even to rejection as fresh knowledge becomes available, as linguistic or stylistic insights are sharpened. But at any given point in the long history of disciplined understanding, a decision as to the better reading, as to the more plausible paraphrase, as to the more reasonable grasp of the author's purpose, will be a rational and demonstrable one. At the end of the philological road, now or tomorrow, there *is* a best reading, there is a meaning or constellation of meanings to be perceived, analysed and chosen over others. In its authentic sense, philology is, indeed, the working passage, via the arts of scrupulous observance and trust *(philein)*, from the uncertainties of the word to the stability of the *Logos*.

It is the rational credibility and practice of this passage, of this cumulative advance towards textual understanding, which is today in sharp doubt. Let me contract, and thus radicalize, the claims of the new semantics. The poststructuralist, the deconstructionist remind us (justly) that there is no difference in substance between primary text and commentary, between the poem and the explication or critique. All propositions and enunciations, be they primary, secondary or tertiary (the commentary on the commentary; the interpretation of previous interpretations, the criticism of criticism, so familiar to our current byzantine culture), are part of an encompassing *intertextuality*. They are equivalent as *écriture*. It follows in a profoundly challenging play on words (and is not all discourse and writing a play on words?) that a primary text and each and every text it gives rise or occasion to is no more and no less than a *pre-text*. It happens to come before, temporally, by accident of chronology. It is the occasion, more or less contingent, more or less random, of the commentary, critique, variant on, pastiche, parody, citation of itself. It has no privilege of canonic originality—if only because language always precedes its user and always imposes on his usage rules, conventions, opacities for which he is not responsible and over which his control is minimal. No sentence spoken or composed in any intelligible language is, in the rigorous sense of the concept, original. It is merely one among the formally unbounded set of transformational possibilities within a rule-bound grammar. The poem or play or novel is, strictly considered, anonymous. It belongs to the topological space of the underlying grammatical and lexical structures and availabilities. We do not need to know the name of the poet to read the poem. The very name, moreover, is a naive and obtrusive ascription of identity where, in the philosophic and logical sense, there is no demonstrable identity. The ego, the *moi*, after Freud, Foucault or Lacan, is not only, as in Rimbaud *un autre,* but a kind of Magellanic cloud of interactive and changing energies, partial introspections, moments of compacted consciousness, mobile, unstable, as it were, around an even more indeterminate central region or black hole of the subconscious, of the unconscious or the pre-conscious. The notion that we can grasp an author's intentionality, that we should attend to what he would tell us of his own purpose in or understanding of his text, is utterly naive. What does he know of the meanings hidden by or projected from the interplay of semantic potentialities which he has momentarily circumscribed and formalized? Why should we trust in his own self-delusions, in the suppressions of the psychic impulses, which most likely have impelled him to produce a "textuality" in the first place? The adage had it: "Do not trust the teller but the tale." Deconstruction asks: Why trust either? Confidence is not the relevant hermeneutic note.

Invoking the commonplace but cardinal verity that in all interpretation, in all statements of understanding, language is simply being used about language in an infinitely self-multiplying series (the mirror arcade), the deconstructive reader defines the act of reading as follows. The ascription of sense, the preference of one possible reading over another, the choice of this explication and paraphrase and not that, is no more than the playful, unstable, undemonstrable option or fiction of a subjective scanner who constructs and deconstructs purely semiotic markers as his own momentary pleasures, politics, psychic needs or self-deceptions bid him do. There are no rational or falsifiable decision-procedures as between a multitude of differing interpretations or "constructs of proposal." At best, we will select (for a time, at least) the one which strikes us as the more ingenious, the richer in surprise, the more powerfully decompositional and re-creative of the original or *pre-text*. Derrida on Rousseau is richer *fun* than, say, an old literalist and historicist such as Lanson. Why labour through philological-historical exegeses of the Lurianic Kabbala when one can read the constructs of semioticians at Yale? No *auctoritas* external to the game can legislate between these alternatives. *Gaudeamus igitur.*

Let me say at once that I do not perceive any adequate logical or epistemological refutation of deconstructive semiotics. It is evident that the playful abolition of the stable subject contains a logical circularity, for it is an ego which observes or intends its own dissolution. And there is an infinite regress of intentionality in the mere denial of intent. But these formal fallacies or petitions of principle do not really cripple the deconstructive language-game or the fundamental claim that there are no valid procedures of decision between competing and even antithetical ascriptions of meaning.

The common-sense (but what, challenges the deconstructionist, is "a common sense"?) and liberal move is one of more or less unworried circumvention. The carnival and saturnalia of poststructuralism of Barthe's *jouissance*, or Lacan's and Derrida's endless punning and wilful etymologizing, will pass as have so many other rhetorics of reading. "Fashion," as Leopardi reassures us, "is the mother of death." The "common reader," Virginia Woolf's positive rubric, the serious scholar, editor and critic will get on, as they always have, with the work in hand. They will elucidate what is taken to be an authentic— though often polysemic and even ambiguous—sense, and will enunciate what are taken to be informed, rationally arguable, though always provisional and self-questioning, preferences and value-judgments. Across the millennia, a decisive majority of informed receivers has not only arrived at a manifold but broadly coherent view of what the *Iliad*, or *King Lear* or *The Marriage of Figaro*, is about (the meanings of their meaning), but have concurred in judging Homer, Shakespeare and Mozart to be supreme artists in a hierarchy of recognitions which extends from the classical summits to the trivial and mendacious. This broad concordance, with its undeniable residue of dissent, of hermeneutic and critical disputes, with its margins of uncertainty and altering "placement" (F. R. Leavis's word), constitutes an "institutional consensus," a syllabus of agreed reference and exemplariness, across the ages. This general concurrence provides culture with its energies of remembrance, and furnishes the "touchstones" (Matthew Arnold) whereby to test new literature, new art, new music.

So robust and fertile a pragmatism is seductive. It allows one, indeed it authorizes one, to "get on with the job." It bids one acknowledge, as out of the corner of a clear eye, that all determinations of textual meaning are probabilistic, that all critical assessments are ultimately uncertain; but to draw confident reinsurance from the cumulative—that is to say statistical—weight of historical agreement and practical persuasion. The bark and ironies of deconstruction resound in the night but the caravan of "good sense" passes on.

I know that this praxis of liberal consensus satisfies most readers. I know that it is the general guarantor of our literacies and common pursuits of understanding. Nevertheless, the current "crisis of sense," the current equation of text and pre-text, the abolitions of *auctoritas*, seem to me so radical as to challenge a response other than pragmatic, statistical or professional (as in the protectionism of the academy). If counter-moves are worth exploring, they will be of an order no less radical than are those of the anarchic and even "terrorist" grammatologists and masters of mirrors. The summons of nihilism demands an answer.

The initial move is one away from the autistic echo-chambers of deconstruction, from a theory and practice of games which—this is the very point and *ingenium* of the thing—subvert and alter their own rules in the course of play. It is a move palpably indebted to the Kierkegaardian triad of the aesthetic, the ethical and the religious. But the resort to certain ethical postulates or categories in respect of our interpretations and valuations of literature and the arts is older than Kierkegaard. The belief that the moral imagination relates to the analytic and the critical imaginations is at least as ancient as the poetics of Aristotle. These are, themselves, attempts to refute Plato's dissociation between aesthetics and morality. A move towards the ethical rejoins the hermeneutics of Aquinas and Dante and the aesthetics of disinterestedness in Kant (himself an obligatory and representative target of recent deconstruction). It is, I think, the abandonment of this high and rigorous ground, in the name of nineteenth-century positivism and twentieth-century secular psychology, which has brought on much of the (intensely stimulating) anarchy in which we now find ourselves.

If we wish to transcend the merely pragmatic, if we wish to meet the challenge of autistic textuality or, more accurately, "anti-textuality" on grounds as radical as its own, we must bring to bear on the act of meaning, on the understanding of meaning, the full force of moral intuition. The vitally concentrated agencies are those of tact, of courtesy of heart, of good taste, in a sense not decorous or civil, but inward and ethical. Such focus and agencies cannot be logically formalized. They are existential modes. Their underwriting is, as we shall be compelled to propose, of a transcendent kind. This makes them utterly vulnerable. But also "of the essence," that is, essential.

I take the ethical inference to entail the following, to make the following *morally*, not logically, not empirically, self-evident. The poem comes before the commentary. The primary text is first not only temporally. It is not a pre-text, an occasion for subsequent exegetic or metamorphic treatment. Its priority is one of essence, of ontological need and self-sufficiency. Even the greatest critique, or commentary, be it that of a writer or painter or composer on his own work, is *accidental* (the cardinal Aristotelian distinction). It is dependent, secondary, contingent. The poem embodies and bodies forth through a singular enactment its own *raison d'être*. The secondary text does not contain an imperative of being. Again the Aristotelian and Thomist differentiations between essence and accident are clarifying. The poem *is*, the commentary *signifies*. Meaning is an attribute of being. Both phenomenologies are, in the nature of the case, "textual." But to equate and confound their respective textualities is to confound *poiesis*, the act of creation, of bringing into autonomous being, with the derivative, secondary *ratio* of interpretation or adaptation. (We know that the violinist, however gifted and penetrating, "interprets" the Beethoven sonata; he does not compose it. To keep our knowledge of this difference at risk, we do remind ourselves that the existential status of an unperformed work, an unread text, an unseen painting is philosophically and psychologically problematic.)

It follows from these intuitive and ethical postulates that the present-day inflation of commentary and criticism, that the equalities of weight and force which deconstruction assigns to the primary and the secondary texts, are spurious. They represent that reversal in the natural order of values and interest which characterize an Alexandrine or Byzantine period in the history of the arts and of thought. It follows also that the statement propounded by an academic leader of the new semantics—"It is more interesting to read Derrida on Rousseau than to read Rousseau"—is a perversion not only of the calling of the teacher, but of common sense where common sense is a lucid, concentrated expression of moral imagining. Such a perversion of values and receptive practice, however playful, is not only wasteful and confusing *per se:* it is potentially corrosive of the strengths of creation, of true invention in literature and the arts. The current crisis of meaning does appear to coincide with a spell of enervation and profound self-doubt. Where cats are sovereign, tigers do not burn.

But liberating as I believe it to be, the ethical inference does not engage finality. It does not confront in immediacy the nihilistic supposition. It is formally conceivable and arguable that every discourse and text is idiolectic, that is to say that it is a "one-time" cryptogram whose rules of usage and decipherment are non-repeatable. If Saul Kripke is right, this would be the strong version of Wittgenstein's view of rules and language. "There can be no such thing as meaning anything by the word. Each new application we make is a leap in the dark; any present criterion could be interpreted so as to accord with anything we may choose to do. So there can be neither accord nor conflict."

Equally, it is conceivable and arguable that every assignment and experience of value is not only undemonstrable, is not only susceptible to statistical derision (on a free vote, mankind will choose bingo over Aeschylus), but is empty, is meaningless in the logical positivist use of the concept. We know of Descartes's axiomatic solution to such possibility. He postulates the *sine qua non* that God will not systematically confuse or falsify our perception and understanding of the world, that he will not arbitrarily alter the rules of reality (as these govern nature and as these are accessible to rational deduction and application). Without some such fundamental presupposition in regard to the existence of sense and value, there can be no responsible response, no answering answerability to either the act of speech or that ordering of and selections from this act which we call the text. Without some axiomatic leap towards a postulate of *meaningfulness,* there can be no striving towards intelligibility or value-judgment however provisional (and note the part of "vision" in the provisional). Where it elides the "radical"—the etymological and conceptual root—of the *Logos,* logic is indeed vacant play.

We must read *as if.*

We must read as if the text before us had meaning. This will not be a single meaning if the text is a serious one, if it makes us answerable to its force of life. It will not be a meaning or *figura* (structure, complex) of meanings isolated from the transformative and reinterpretative pressures of historical and cultural change. It will not be a meaning arrived at by any determinant or automatic process of cumulation and consensus. The true understanding(s) of the text or music or painting may, during a briefer or longer time spell, be in the custody of a few, indeed of one witness and respondent. Above all, the meaning striven towards will never be one which exegesis, commentary, translation, paraphrase, psychoanalytic or sociological decoding, can ever exhaust, can ever define as total. Only weak poems can be exhaustively interpreted or understood. Only in trivial or opportunistic texts is the sum of significance that of the parts.

We must read as if the temporal and executive setting of a text do matter. The historical surroundings, the cultural and formal circumstances, the biographical stratum, what we can construe or conjecture of an author's intentions, constitute vulnerable aids. We know that they ought to be studied with stringent irony and examined for what there is in them of subjective hazard. They matter none the less. They enrich levels of awareness and enjoyment; they generate constraints on the complacencies and licence of interpretative anarchy.

This "as if," this axiomatic conditionality, is our Cartesian-Kantian wager, our leap into sense. Without it, literacy becomes transient narcissism. But this wager is itself in need of a clear foundation. Let me spell out summarily the risks of finality, the assumptions of transcendence which, at the first and at the last, underlie the reading of the words as I conceive it. Where we read truly, where the experience is to be that of meaning, we do so as if the text (the piece of music, the work of art) incarnates (the notion is grounded in the sacramental) a real presence of significant being. This real presence, as in an icon, as in the enacted metaphor of the sacramental bread and wine, is, finally, irreducible to any other formal articulation, to any analytic deconstruction or paraphrase. It is a singularity in which concept and form constitute a tautology, coincide point to point, energy to energy, in that excess of significance over all discrete elements and codes of meaning which we call the symbol or the agency of transparence.

These are not occult notions. They are of the immensity of the common-place. They are perfectly pragmatic, experiential, repetitive, each and every time a poem, a passage of prose seizes upon our thought and feelings, enters into the sinews of our remembrance and sense of the future, each and every time a painting transmutes the landscapes of our previous perceptions (pop-lars are on fire after van Gogh, viaducts walk after Klee). To be "indwelt" by music, art, literature, to be made responsible, answerable to such habitation as a host is to a guest—perhaps unknown, unexpected—at evening, is to experience the commonplace mystery of a real presence. Not many of us feel compelled to, have the expressive means to, register the mastering quality of this experience—as does Proust when he crystallizes the sense of the world and of the word in the little yellow spot which is the real presence of a riv-erside door in Vermeer's "View of Delft" or as does Thomas Mann when he enacts in word and metaphor the coming over us, the "overcoming of us," in Beethoven's op. III. No matter. The experience itself is one we are thor-oughly at home with—an informing idiom—each and every time we live a text, sonata, a painting.

Moreover, though we have largely forgotten it, this experience of, this underwriting by, a real presence is the source of the history, methods and practice of hermeneutics and criticism, of interpretation and value-judgment in the Western inheritance. The disciplines of reading, the very idea of close commentary and interpretation, textual criticism as we know it, derive from the study of Holy Scripture, or, more accurately, from the incorporation and development in that study of older practices of Hellenistic grammar, recen-sion and rhetoric. Our grammars, our explications, our criticisms of texts, our endeavours to pass from letter to spirit, are the immediate heirs to the textualities of Western Judaeo-Christian theology and biblical-patristic exe-getics. What we have done since the masked scepticism of Spinoza, since the critiques of the rationalist Enlightenment and since the positivism of the nineteenth century, is to borrow vital currency, vital investments and con-tracts of trust from the bank or treasure-house of theology. It is from there that we have borrowed our theories of the symbol, our use of the iconic, our idiom of poetic creation and aura. It is loans of terminology and reference from the reserves of theology which provide the master readers in our times (such as Walter Benjamin and Martin Heidegger) with their licence to practise. We have borrowed, traded upon, made small change of the reserves of tran-scendent authority. Very few of us have made any return deposit. At its key points of discourse and inference, hermeneutics and aesthetics in our secular, agnostic civilization are a more or less conscious, more or less embarrassed act of larceny (it is this embarrassment which makes resonant and tensely illuminating Benjamin on Kafka or Heidegger on Trakl and on Sophocles).

What would it mean to acknowledge, indeed to repay these massive loans?

For Plato, the rhapsode is one possessed by the god. Inspiration is literal; the *daimon* enters into the artist, mastering and overreaching the bounds of his natural person. Seeking a reinsurance for the imperious obscurity, for the great burst into the inordinate of his poems, Gerard Manley Hopkins reckoned neither on the perception of a few elect spirits nor on the pedagogic authority of time. He did not know whether his language and prosody would ever be understood by other men and women. But such understanding was not of the essence. Reception and validation, said Hopkins, lay with Christ, "the only true critic." As set out in *Clio,* Péguy's analysis and description of the complete act of reading, or the *lecture bien faite,* remains the most incisive, the most indispensable we have. Here is the classic statement of the symbiosis between writer and reader, of the collaborative and organic generation of textual meaning of the dynamics of necessity and hope which knit discourse to the life-giving response of the reader and "remembrancer." In Péguy, the pre-emptions and logic of the argument are explicitly religious; the mystery of poetic, artistic creation and that of vital reception are never wholly secular. A dread sense of blasphemy in regard to the primal act of creation, of illegitimacy in the face of God, inhabits every motion of spirit and of composition in Kafka's work. The breath of inspiration, against which the true artist would seek to close his terrified lips, is that of the paradoxically animate winds which blow from "the nether regions of death" in the final sentence of Kafka's "The Hunter Gracchus." They too are not of secular, rational provenance.

In the main, Western art, music and literature have, from the time of Homer and Pindar to that of Eliot's *Four Quartets,* of Pasternak's *Doctor Zhivago* or the poetry of Paul Celan, spoken immediately either to the presence or absence of God. Often, that address has been agonistic and polemic. The great artist has had Jacob for his patron, wrestling with the terrible precedent and power of original creation. The poem, the symphony, the Sistine ceiling are acts of counter-creation. "I am God," said Matisse when he completed painting the chapel at Vence. "God, the other craftsman," said Picasso, in open rivalry. Indeed it may well be that Modernism can best be defined as that form of music, literature and art which no longer experiences God as a competitor, a predecessor, an antagonist in the long night (that of St. John of the Cross which is every true poet's). There may well be in atonal or aleatory music, in non-representational art, in certain modes of Surrealist, automatic or concrete writing, a sort of shadow-boxing. The adversary is now the form itself. Shadow-boxing can be technically dazzling and educative. But like so much of modern art it remains solipsistic. The sovereign challenger is gone. And much of the audience.

I do not imagine that He can be summoned back to our agnostic and positivist condition. I do not suppose that a theory of hermeneutics and of criticism whose underwriting is theological, or a practice of poetry and the arts which implies, which implicates the real presence of the transcendent or its "substantive absence" from a new solitude of man, can command general assent. What I have wanted to make clear is the spiritual and existential duplicity in so much of our current models of meaning and of aesthetic value. Consciously or not, with embarrassment or indifference, these models draw upon, they metaphorize crucially, the abandoned, the unpaid-for idiom, imaginings and guarantees of a theology or, at the least, of a transcendent metaphysics. The astute trivializations, the playful nihilism of deconstruction have the merits of their honesty. They instruct us that "nothing shall come of nothing."

Personally, I do not see how a secular, statistically based theory of meaning and of value can, over time, withstand either the deconstructionist challenge or its own fragmentation into liberal eclecticism. I cannot arrive at any rigorous conception of a possible determination of either sense or stature which does not wager on a transcendence, on a real presence, in the act and product of serious art, be it verbal, musical, or that of material forms.

Such a conviction leads to logical suppositions which are exceedingly difficult to express clearly, let alone to demonstrate. But the possible confusion and, in our present climate of approved sentiment, the inevitable embarrassment which must accompany any public avowal of mystery, seem to me preferable to the slippery evasions and conceptual deficits in contemporary hermeneutics and criticism. It is these which strike me as false to common experience, as incapable of bearing witness to such manifest phenomena as the creation of a literary persona who will endure far beyond the life of the creator (Flaubert's dying cry against "that whore Emma Bovary"), as incapable of insight into the invention of melody or the evident transmutations of our experiences of space, of light, of the planes and volumes of our own being, brought about by a Mantegna, a Turner or a Cézanne.

It may be the case that nothing more is available to us than the absence of God. Wholly felt and lived, that absence is an agency and *mysterium tremendum* (without which a Racine, a Dostoevsky, a Kafka are, indeed, nonsense or food for deconstruction). To infer such terms of reference, to apprehend something of the cost one must be prepared to pay in declaring them, is to be left naked to unknowing. I believe that one must take the risk if one is to have the right to strive towards the perennial, never-fully-to-be-realized ideal of all interpretation and valuation: which is that, one day, Orpheus will not turn around, and that the truth of the poem will return to the light of understanding, whole, inviolate, life-giving, even out of the dark of omission and of death.

VIII.

It Takes All Kinds

For Baudelaire, beauty was inseparably linked to modernity, contingency, actuality, fashion. Around the turn of the century, one avant-garde after another incorporated this view in its philosophy, articulated or not. Art, henceforth, would be devoted to the destruction of established forms, spaces, syntaxes, concerned with opposing official and academic rule and rules, shattering old windows to let in fresh air. One is tempted to comment that innovation had existed in all times. But in our time—over the last century, and especially the last half-century—change has turned to revolution, attempting a deliberate break between before and after. Modernism is less interested in new variation on old forms than in breaking the continuity that binds us to the past, for the sake of something radically new.

Fin-de-siècle Modernism and its twentieth-century offspring are about breaking with tradition, the cult of the new, the unprecedented, the extraordinary, and the rejection of transcendent norms. No more psychology or probability: music freed of tonal constructions, painting freed of perspective and objectivity, literature freed of chronology. After 1930, Postmodernism exaggerates this: renewal of substance gives way to renewal for its own sake, novelty self-generates until the production of novelty loses all novelty. By now the pretension to innovate, revolutionize, liberate, is old stuff. So are its interpretations. Compensation, evasion, legitimization, consumption, idealization: we have theorized them all, not from the outside, not after the event, but from within the times and societies the explanations serve.

The quest for modernity ever more modern tends to disqualify and discard one modern work after another. Almost as soon as they have been turned out, avant-garde works are consigned to the rearguard of the *déja-vu* or *déja-lu*. "Modernity," says Octavio Paz, "is a sort of creative self-destruction," forced to perpetual invention, prohibited from standing still or savoring anything it has achieved.

It follows that Modernism has no time for manifestos, no opportunity for statements that would be outdated before they got into print. It defines itself largely by negation. A paradoxical "tradition of the new" discards, devalues everything it forges: novelty turns to anachronism, then to fossil; continuous change provides the only steadfast principle of art, as it does of fashion. A new look is the categorical imperative of artistic expression.

It should not be surprising that, at this rate, innovation falters as innovators run out of breath, negation loses its creative power, the drive to generate ever different works ends (as with Andy Warhol et al.) in ritual repetition and in stereotyping. If it was not for its old-fashioned, socio-political inspirations or, at least, references, modern art would have collapsed long ago. In the late nineteenth century, what was then modern art reflected and resisted the industrial and bourgeois order around it. In the later twentieth century it has little to do with postindustrial society—except for the tricks and techniques, acrylic paints or neon tubes, it borrows from it. But the original inspiration still holds, the original stereotypes continue to be repeated. Criticism of social institutions and conventions, of bourgeois rationalism and moderation, of hypocrisy and exploitation, grows ever sharper. The romantic glorification of the spontaneous self, of authenticity, of imagination, passion, and intensity has not been dampened. Providers of toys for a society of mass consumption, purveyors of entertainment for semi-cultivated masses, artists resent their role as strongly as they did when they provided decorations and diversions for the privileged few.

Their reactions to frustrations, which are probably inseparable from the free artist's relation to an open society, are not very different from those the nineteenth century had witnessed. There are, for example, the political attacks against capitalism, its lackeys and its values, that we find in Jean Dubuffet (1901–1985), author of essays like *Anticultural Positions* and *Asphyxiating Culture* (excerpts below), inventor of "raw art" *(art brut),* and one of the leading figures of the Paris school of the 1960s and 1970s. Dubuffet was fascinated by the vitality of art works produced by children and the insane. His apparently crude productions incorporate materials such as tar, gravel, cinders, and ash. They also, and soon, came to fetch very high prices: testimony that bourgeois society and bourgeois values can now be challenged with high profit and at little risk.

Dubuffet repudiated artistic intelligence, insisted on the values and vision of the ordinary man, and advocated anonymity in art—which he reconciled with maximum personal publicity. His works, allegedly dedicated to aesthetic subversion, started as doodles with colored ballpoint pens and ended by looking much like subway graffiti. By the 1970s, one of his handsomest sculptures, the *Four Trees,* paid for by a prosperous bank, had been set up at Chase Manhattan Plaza, in the heart of New York's financial district. Witness, as art critic Harold Rosenberg put it, to "the pseudo-radical philosophies of anti-elitism which have been bringing art into accord with the aesthetics of big business and the mass media."

A lesser artist than Dubuffet, Andy Warhol (1927–1988) was nevertheless a better businessman and self-publicist. The Pop Art movement that he launched in the 1960s glorified and gloried in the banality and tawdriness of commercial culture. Warhol's artist is an impersonal, largely passive agent of mechanical processes and products, like soup cans and Brillo boxes, which he handles with repetitive insipidity. His silk-screens, great fun before they became hackneyed, were easily assimilated by the culture that they clowned. The essay on Warhol reprinted here was written by one of America's most acute critics, Harold Rosenberg (1906–1978). It was Rosenberg who, in 1952, had announced the appearance of a brash new kind of painting that was to affirm American preponderance in Western art as in Western economy. Action painters like Jackson Pollock, Willem de Kooning, Mark Rothko—or Abstract Expressionists as Rosenberg dubbed them—abandoned traditional aesthetic and social values for free, spontaneous personal experience: "the irreducible human residue in a situation where all superstructures are shaky." Different from each other in method or inspiration, painters like Pollock and de Kooning nevertheless "shared a concept of creation based on the intuition that there is nothing worth painting. No object, but also no idea. The activity of the artist became, in their opinion, primary."

If subject is out, one can also do without drawing, color, composition, texture, or traditional art materials. All that matters is the action of painting, and the psychic state or tension of the artist carrying out the action. "What matters always is the revelation contained in the act. . . . The innovation of Action Painting was to dispense with the *representation* of the state in favor of *enacting* it in physical movement. The action on the canvas became its own representation." Entertainers like Warhol drew the logical conclusions of de-definitions that made artistic enterprise and its products self-defining affairs. Art, which used to be about works of art, focused instead on artists, their personalities, their doings, until it replaced the artist by entrepreneurs and media figures. That was one trend.

Other artists prefer to opt out of the worldly hurly-burly. John Baldessari, for example, moves away from traditional artistic production, toward "conceptual" spheres where concept is as good as accomplishment. A decisive step toward such conceptualization had been taken by the Minimalist artists of the sixties and seventies, many of whose works still exist only on paper. New York's Guggenheim Museum recently sold paintings by Vassily Kandinsky, Marc Chagall, and Amedeo Modigliani in order to buy a collection of Minimalist art, part of which consists of plans and sketches, "not physical objects, but Conceptual sculptures to be constructed from site to site."

Reacting against what they described as the individualism and romanticism of their Abstract Expressionist predecessors (but what can be more romantic than to regard conception as completion?), Minimalists rejected the notion of art as a unique personal creation. They also rejected museums, galleries, walls, frames, and traditional exhibition space, which artificialize and constrict. Handmade objects, too, they argued, represented an obsolete tradition. Minimalists prefer simple geometric forms made of industrial materials like plywood or steel, and drafted so that the art work itself can be fabricated by others. As one of their number, Bruce Naumann, remarks, "Most of my pieces can be adjusted quite a bit and still meet the point of the piece." Adjustable commodities for a flexible market. *The New York Times* (June 12, 1990) quotes Michael Govan, deputy director of the Guggenheim, as saying that "[their] work poses deep philosophical problems and esthetic issues that will not soon be resolved." Quite.

Minimalist art reflects surrounding society, economy, technology. But modern(ist) art resembles its surroundings in other ways as well. Democratic equalitarian societies, which oppose selection and discrimination, have spawned views of art that are appropriately equalitarian and undiscriminating. They freed aesthetics of trammeling rules, they legitimized all subjects. In contemporary art, all approaches are free and equal. An antinomian art goes hand in hand with an antinomian society, rejecting the claims and obligations of moral law, asserting that there are no binding laws or canons, no firm ground for judgment except that adopted by one person at one time. Sauce for the social goose is just as tasty when served with an artistic gander. It was in this context that structures gave way to metaphors of structures, then to metaphors of destructuration. Books were put together and then burnt, as by the German artist Anselm Kiefer (1945–   ), who commemorated Nazi destructiveness in this way. He also exhibits dresses encrusted with ash: transparent references to the clothes discovered near the deathtraps of Auschwitz and Buchenwald—more powerful as symbols than when worn or painted.[1]

----

[1]"Performance" photographs made early in Kiefer's career show him giving the Hitler salute

The more objective, technological, scientific, the infrastructure, the more sub-jective the artistic superstructure. The more utilitarian the society, the more art and culture have aimed at gratuitousness. The more massively homogenized the society, the more personal and nonconformist art tries to be. And yet, in order to achieve the desired shock effect, even nonconformists have to adopt the idioms of those they seek to provoke. Noise, graphic signs, colored shapes, words turned to sound, designs turned to words, disgruntling to begin with, soon joined the range of marketable commodities. In a world of volume, exasperation, anxiety, and confusion, the obtrusive, exasperated anxiety and confusion of art works fitted very well. Like crusty crumpets dipped in milk, aggression turned soggy. Daring transgression became commonplace—conventional, familiar, expected, conformist even to its claims of nonconformity. The bourgeois capitalist society that artists lash assimilates them all. Inventiveness is coopted by conspicuous con-sumption and, not least, by consumption's adjunct: advertising. One avant-garde after another breaks with conformity. One after another is absorbed by the mar-ket, adopted by the establishment against which it rebelled. The history of cinema provides vivid examples of this doom.

The most original and innovative art form of our time has been the cinema, the twentieth-century art par excellence. The aftermath of the Second World War provided it with new breath and inspiration. In France, Alexandre Astruc an-nounced a new age of cinema, in which writers and directors would use the camera as a pen *(caméra-stylo)*, "to become a means of writing just as flexible and subtle as written language." Italian filmmakers were going to show that it could be not only as flexible but more impressive, too. The neo-Realists wanted to examine contemporary folk facing contemporary problems in contemporary so-ciety: not illusion, but lived reality. Roberto Rossellini's *Rome, Open City* (1945) and *Paisà* (1946), Vittorio de Sica's *Sciuscia* (*Shoeshine,* 1946) and *Bicycle Thieves* (1948), provided the models and the classics of the genre. Their inspiration was less aesthetic than moral and political: revolt against the rhetoric of power, against the hypocrisy of society, against the misery of the many and the bloated indifference of the few.

Political liberation after 1944, they said, had to march hand in hand with social and economic liberation. The camera looking straight at things as they really are could help to emancipate people—poor people, *the* people—from lies, oppressive illusions, lovelessness, alienation. The popular masses, familiar with their own

---

in various silly settings. The message is as ambiguous as in that of his much later sculpture, "The High Priestess," which consists of gigantic iron shelves stacked with books made of lead, each of which takes two men to lift. Statement, whimsy, or sheer futility? Only the artist knows. Or perhaps he doesn't.

deprivation, unemployment, poverty, and rotten housing, were not impressed; they appreciated mostly those neo-Realist films associated with melodrama, like De Santis's *Riso amaro* (*Bitter Rice,* 1948). But the social criticism that displayed widespread Italian misery for all the world to see upset the Italian government and offended the Catholic Church. Their hostile reactions provided useful publicity and spurred support from intellectuals at home and abroad.

One of the major personalities attracted by the neo-Realist enterprise was the young writer and cartoonist Federico Fellini (1920–   ), who worked with Rossellini on *Rome* and on *Paisà* before beginning to make his own films. Fellini's productions freed neo-Realism from conventional limits and showed that social criticism could be couched in terms of fantasy, illusion, distortion, and symbolism. *La Dolce Vita* (1960) and *8½* (1963) juggled realism and symbolism. The ethical offensive of the mid-forties had become detached, and detached from its moorings. In the work of Fellini, as in that of other deserters from the neo-Realist camp like Visconti and Antonioni, the artistic culmination of social commitment emphasized the dramatic solitude of individuals in a shattered world.

The original message of neo-Realism remains nevertheless important. It inspired great filmmaking in Italy; it inspired the "new wave" generation of Chabrol, Truffaut, Godard in France; and it continues to stand for a significant, if flagging, preoccupation. Neo-Realist directors expressed their ethico-political ideas in their films. The chief theoretical exponent of the school was Cesare Zavattini, who wrote many of their film scripts. The pages by Zavattini quoted below are excerpted from three of his articles, published between 1952 and 1954.

Alienation, which neo-Realists treated as curable and Fellini as a private matter, becomes total and aggressive in the work of Rainer Werner Fassbinder (1946–1982). Fassbinder dropped out of school at sixteen to become involved with avant-garde theater. In 1967, at twenty-one, he helped set up the *Antiteater,* and continued with one foot in theatre and the other in cinema until his death. His films and plays criticized middle-class societal values and middle-class sexual mores, using the shock tactics that he hoped would attract attention and provoke public reaction. Under the German's pen, description and whimsy became grotesque destructiveness, well-intentioned reformism became nihilist intimidation. But Fassbinder's self-induced death at thirty-six did more to generate public interest in his films than his excesses ever accomplished. For Astruc the fundamental problem of cinema had been how to express thought. Two score years after Astruc, his successors and those of Rossellini, Fellini, and Fassbinder would rediscover the secret of film's early success: the possibility not of expressing but of suppressing thought or, at least, dispensing with it.

By now, art, including cinematic art, is little more than show. It had set out to denigrate society, to instruct, to disgust, to inspire; now it entertains. Consumer society promotes consumer art; and art producers are treated like other entertainers, other media and media-created personalities, stars, idols. Their lives, hits, incomes, and ideas about society, politics, or ecology become as relevant (that is, as irrelevant) as those of other rich and famous insiders.

And, while the artist is quoted on society pages and on TV, the work of art is quoted on the stock exchange, its fluctuations commented on in the financial pages. Artists and art works have become creators and creations in the sense that dresses and dress-designers are. Products and producers of evanescent, trivial happenings. To what can they contribute beside fashion? What statement can they make? They cannot even aspire to express nonsense (as Dada did) in a society bereft of sense. It is when art represents nothing, says nothing, formulates nothing, that it truly represents the society in which it works and for which it produces exasperating music, incoherent poetry, impenetrable scholarship, vacuous literature, and dispensable inanities.

This is not to say that contemporary art cannot be amusing, entertaining, or titillating. Postmodern art is often most of these; indeed, that would be the best description of most Postmodern art. When existence is experienced as above all fluid, attempts to describe, address, or comment on it will mirror its essential inconsequence. The art of our time is an exhibition of *collages* that everyone may paste up for himself, a pile of scenarios that anyone may write and everyone (re)interpret. Do-it-yourself art, harmlessly exhilarating, disposable, dispensable, and, ultimately, quite a lot of fun.

Dubuffet
Asphyxiating Culture

The indoctrination process has now reached the point that it is rare to meet anyone who admits to having little esteem for a tragedy by Racine or a painting by Raphaël. This is true both among intellectuals as well as among others. Surprisingly, it is more among the others, those who have never read a line of Racine nor seen a painting by Raphaël, that the most militant defenders of these mythical values are to be found. Intellectuals would in some cases

Source: From *Asphyxiating Culture and Other Writings* by Jean Dubuffet. Translated by Carol Volk, 1986. Reprinted by permission of Four Walls Eight Windows.

consider questioning these values, but they do not dare, fearing that their authority can no longer be maintained once the prestige of these myths has fallen. They deceive themselves, and in order to close their eyes to the truth, kid themselves into believing they are touched by such outdated classical works; yet they are works with which they have little dealings. As a result of all their efforts, in the end they manage as best they can to be moved—or to convince themselves that they are.

In matters of furnishings, recourse to antique styles takes the place of good taste. The provincial bourgeois pride themselves in their Louis XIV, Louis XV, and Louis XVI armchairs. They learn to distinguish one from the other, becoming distressed when the silk upholstery is not from the right period; they are convinced that this proves them to be artists. They are able to recognize mullion windows, and the late gothic and early Renaissance styles. They are convinced that this fashionable knowledge legitimizes the preservation of their caste. They work at persuading the lower classes of this, at convincing some of them of the necessity to safeguard art, that is to say armchairs, that is to say the bourgeois who know with which silk it is proper to upholster these armchairs.

The first ministry of information was instituted in England during the war, at a time when it seemed necessary to spread false information. The available supply of genuine information has suffered as a result. The first ministry of culture was instituted in France a few years ago, and it will have and already has had the same effect, the desired effect: that of replacing free culture with a falsified substitute, which acts like an antibiotic, occupying the totality of space without leaving the slightest patch where anything else might prosper.

The word "culture" is used in two different senses, sometimes meaning the knowledge of works of the past (in addition, let's not forget that this notion of "works of the past" is entirely illusory: what has been preserved represents only a very specious, limited selection based on trends that won acceptance in the minds of scholars) and sometimes more generally the activity of the mind and the creation of art. This ambiguity is used to persuade the public that the knowledge of works of the past (at least of those works which the scholars retained) and creative activity of the mind are one and the same thing.

Intellectuals are recruited from the ranks of the dominant class, or from among those who aspire to fit in with this class. The title given the intellectual or the artist puts him on equal terms with members of the dominant caste. Molière dines with the king. The artist is invited to the home of the duchess, as is the priest. I wonder in what disastrous proportion the number of artists would drop if this prerogative were eliminated. Just look at the care that artists take (with their vestimentary disguises and their individualistic behavior) to be known as such and clearly distinguish themselves from the common people.

Even as the bourgeois caste seeks to convince itself and others that its so-called culture (the cheap finery it gives this name) legitimizes its preservation, so the Western world also legitimizes its imperalist appetite by the urgent need to introduce Africans to Shakespeare and Molière.

Culture tends to take the place formerly occupied by religion. Like religion, it now has its priests, its prophets, its saints, and its colleges of dignitaries. The conqueror who seeks consecration presents himself to the people no longer flanked by the bishop, but by the Nobel prize. To be absolved, the unjust lord no longer founds an abbey, but a museum. It is now in the name of culture that we are mobilized, that we preach crusades. It has come to play the role of "opiate of the people."

The myth of culture survived revolutions undoubtedly because it is so well accredited. The revolutionary states, whom we would have expected to denounce a myth so intimately associated with the bourgeois caste and Western imperialism, instead preserve it, and use it to their benefit. They are wrong, it seems, for sooner or later, this myth cannot help but return the Western bourgeois caste that forged it to power. We can only rid ourselves of the Western bourgeois caste by unmasking and demystifying its phony culture. It serves everywhere as this caste's weapon and Trojan Horse.

The State's directors mean to give culture the same hierarchic form as the Church of olden days, that is, a well-structured pyramid, a *vertical* arrangement. On the contrary, creative thought would gain strength and health in the form of *horizontal* proliferation, in an infinitely diversified expansion. There is no worse obstacle to this proliferation than the prestige of a few showoffs among the ranks of high dignitaries, the importance of whom has been drilled into the public. There is nothing more sterilizing than this, nothing more apt to dissuade the common man from thinking for himself, nothing more likely to make him lose all confidence in his own capacities. Also nothing is more apt to disgust him with art, which he will come to believe is only an impostor at the service of the State, in other words, of the police.

I am an individualist, that is to say that I consider it my role as an individual to oppose all constraints brought about by the interest of the social good. The interests of the individual are opposed to those of the social good. Wanting to serve both at once can only lead to hypocrisy and confusion. It is for the State to look out for the social good, and for me to look out for the good of the individual. The State has but one face for me: that of the police. To my eyes, all of the State's ministries have this single face, and I cannot imagine the ministry of culture other than as the police of culture, with its prefect and commissioners. Such a face is extremely hostile and repulsive to me. . . .

The community has now, by an almost unanimous consensus, adopted professors as its intellectual leaders. The idea is that professors, who have long been granted the leisure to examine the art of the past, are more informed than others as to what art is and what is to remain. Now, the essence of art's creation is innovation, at which professors will be all the less apt as they will have long sucked the milk of works of the past. It would be interesting to compare the number of professors currently involved in either literary activity, the press, or the diffusion and publicity of arts and letters, with the number thirty years ago. Professors, who have so much authority, hardly received any respect back then.

Professors are grown-up schoolchildren, schoolchildren who, once their school days were over, left school through one door only to return through another, like military men who reenlist. They are schoolchildren who, instead of aspiring to an adult life, that is to say a creative life, cling to this school-child's stance, a stance which is passively receptive, like a sponge. The creative spirit is as opposed as possible to that of the professor. Artistic (or literary) creation has more in common with all other forms of creation (in the most common domains of business, the crafts or any type of work, manual or otherwise) than it has with the purely confirmational attitude of the professor, who is by definition animated by no creative taste and must give his praise indifferently to all that won acceptance in the long developments of the past. The professor is the expert who indexes, who endorses, who confirms all that won acceptance, from wherever and whenever these works originated. Renaissance architects scorned the gothic style, and the architects of Art Nouveau scorned those of the Renaissance; but the professor celebrates them all at once in his impassioned discourse, for his heart is filled with enchantment for the accepted, with eagerness to applaud the accepted wherever it may be seen. . . .

It is time we face up, not to the real, precise significance of the word culture—that of an ensemble of works taken to be exemplary—but to the particular coloration currently given to this word which has succeeded in transforming not only the word, but the notion itself in the mind of the public. The word "culture" no longer signifies an ensemble of works of the past proposed as references, it signifies something else. It is associated with a militancy, an indoctrination. It is associated with an entire mechanism of intimidation and pressure. It mobilizes good citizenship and patriotism. It tends to establish a type of religion, a state religion. It makes enormous use of publicity, to the point that even the most insipid, the most vulgar advertisements are so involved with the production of art that a shift occurs in the public's mind. Instead of revering the works, the public is invited to revere the media's image of certain artists. They do not think to inquire about the works, but only about the advertising channels that spread them. . . .

There is a very tight, a very intimate collusion between business and culture; they pat each other's backs and strengthen one another; there is never one without the other; each one steps in for the other. We can only be free of the pernicious weight of culture by eliminating the notion of the value of mental productions, and to begin with, by eliminating their price, which is the sign of this value. Business senses this fact very strongly, and therefore works at propping up the myth of culture and seconding its authority. . . .

Culture is motivated by two incentives; first, by the notion of value, and second, by that of conservation. To put an end to culture, which for millenniums has been running rampant, we must first destroy its supporting idea: the idea of attributing a value to the production of art. I am using the word "value" here both in its economic and in its ethical or esthetic sense—one implies the other, in any case. We can only abolish the commercial value by abolishing the esthetic value; the latter is much more pernicious than the commercial value, and much more strongly anchored as well. The notion of conservation is also linked to the idea of value. Obviously, we conserve objects to which a value is attributed, and the desire to conserve would no longer make sense once the idea of value were abolished.

The role of the cultural body is to attribute values to productions. This prerogative, this power, brings it great pride and is what pushes so many people to join its ranks. It plays the role of an appraiser; its judgments will determine the distribution of prestige and profit. We must, moreover, bear in mind that high prices are the result of prestige and prestige results from high prices; so that there is an intimate collusion between the cultural body and commercial body. Culture and commerce walk hand in hand. We cannot destroy one without destroying the other.

Once the despicable notion of *value* has been abolished, once it has been replaced by the idea that whims and personal reasons suffice to legitimate the attraction felt for an artistic production, with the notions of justification, fairness, etc., out of the picture, then spontaneous inclination will reappear fully liberated, in all innocence. Exchanges may, and probably will reappear, a painting bought for the price of a sheep or even of a cow, but it is absolutely certain that once the commercial value has been separated from the mythical esthetic value, the prices of these sorts of transactions will be limited to small sums, and this will not be a bad thing. For, contrary to what bad philosophers tend to think, there is a great difference between small sums and large sums; it changes everything. . . .

In terms of art, the first step toward deconditioning will consist in distancing oneself from all that is traditionally expected—for example, from a painting—and in recognizing the fallacious nature of the episodic fancies dominating the manner in which this object is treated, whether this treatment tends, according to the times, toward a geometric one; and whether it makes use of impersonal means of execution or else, on the contrary, strongly personal ones. After which we will come to realize the deceptively cultural nature of the idea of the painting itself, no matter what type of treatment it has received. Indeed, there is no doubt that having infinitely modified the ideas we expect a painting to conjure up and the types of treatment available for this purpose, we will realize that the very principle of painting, inscribed in a rectangle limited by a frame, is extremely misleading and remains in all cases intimately linked to a cultural convention. Such a procedure is currently under way, and it is quite probable that soon the *painting,* a rectangle hung with a nail on the wall, will become an outdated and ridiculous object—a fruit fallen from the tree of culture and henceforth considered an antique. The field will then be open for forms of art liberated from this constraining mode of the rectangle, the nail, and the wall, but it will not be long before the detective of cultural conditioning discerns that such conditioning, though disguised under new forms, has not in the least loosened its grip. Indeed, this grip will only be released when the notion of art, and not only that of the painting, will have ceased to be conceived of and perceived, when the mind will have ceased to project art as a notion to be gazed upon, and art will be integrated in such a manner that thought, instead of facing it, will be inside it; at which point, it will cease to be among the things apt to be named. Strictly speaking, it is not art that constitutes culture's poison, but its name. What has been revealed about the painting with its frame is, of course, also valid for the statue with its pedestal, for the theater with its stage, and for the poem, the novel, and all types of literary genres. . . .

The time is right to found institutes of deculturation, kinds of nihilist gymnasiums, in which especially lucid monitors would teach deconditioning and demystification over a period of several years, so as to endow the nation with a body of solidly trained negators who would keep protestation alive, at least in small, isolated and exceptional circles, in the midst of the great and widespread waves of cultural accord. We claim that kings of days gone by used to tolerate a person qualified as a *jester* in their presence, who would laugh at all their institutions; we also say that the triumphal processions for great Roman conquerors included a character whose role it was to insult the victor. Our society of today said to be so sure of its firm grasp on culture and in a position to incorporate all types of subversion within this culture, should therefore easily be able to tolerate these gymnasiums and this body of specialists, and even, who knows? subsidize them. Perhaps this total contestation would also be incorporated into culture. This is not so sure. It is worth trying. In these colleges one would be taught to question all accepted ideas, all revered values; all our thought mechanisms which involve cultural conditioning without our being aware of it would be denounced; in this way we would clean the machinery of the mind until it was thoroughly scoured. We would empty our heads of all the masses cluttering it; with suitable exercises we would methodically develop the invigorating faculty of forgetting.

A Word About the Company of Raw Art

A non-profit and non-commercial association has been formed in Paris under the name The Company of Raw Art. The founders of this organization are Messieurs André Breton, Jean Dubuffet, Jean Paulhan, Charles Ratton, Henri-Pierre Roche and Michel Tapie.

Works Considered

We are seeking artistic works such as paintings, drawings, statues and statuettes, all types of objects, owing nothing (or as little as possible) to the imitation of works of art seen in museums, salons and galleries. On the contrary, these artistic works should put human originality to use, along with the most spontaneous and personal inventiveness; they should be productions which the creator drew (both the invention and the means of expression) from deep within, the result of his own inclinations and moods, free from the habitual means of creation, and regardless of the conventions currently in use. We are interested in these types of works even if they are sketchy and poorly made. We place little importance on manual aptitude; it is most often an aptitude at imitating the works of others, and conceals the creator instead of revealing him, as calligraphy disguises handwriting. We are seeking works that exhibit the abilities of invention and of creation in a very direct fashion, without masks or constraints. We believe these abilities exist (at least at times) in every man.

Point of View

The habitual art, pompously displayed in salons and galleries, has succeeded in passing for the only art, to the exclusion of all others, in most people's eyes. This art seems to us quite poor in content, reduced to endless repetitions and imitations, and almost devoid of personal creativity. We take it to

---

Source: From *Asphyxiating Culture and Other Writings* by Jean Dubuffet. Translated by Carol Volk, 1986. Reprinted by permission of Four Walls Eight Windows.

be a parasitic substitute which merely mimics artistic creation; having none at its source, it replaces this creation with arbitrary words and useless theoretical systems. We believe the time is near, if it has not already come, when the public will realize the enormous misunderstanding upon which the overpowering college of professional "artists" is built, with their pseudo "art critics" and their art dealers. Soon, the emptiness of these academic works, the inappropriateness of the commercial activity to which they give rise, the absurdity of the commentaries surrounding them, and the overall lack of true creativity, will become apparent. True art, in our opinion, lies elsewhere.

The Home of Raw Art

We opened our Home to the public in November 1947, in two rooms which M. René Drouin obligingly put at our disposal in the basement of his Paris gallery, and this Home was in operation for the whole of last winter and spring. We have just transferred it to a spacious pavilion that M. Gaston Gallimard was kind enough to lend us. This new locale, in the garden of the Editions Gallimard, 17 Rue de L'Université, in Paris, was opened to the public the 7th of September 1948. The current exhibition, a collection of approximately one hundred works by various artists, most of whom are unknown or anonymous, gives an idea of the general orientation of our tastes. This first exhibition will be followed shortly by a presentation of works by the late Adolf Wölfli, after which other exhibitions will take place without interruption.

Our Search

The works that interest us are almost always created by very isolated individuals, whose activities are known only by their immediate entourage. We are, therefore, in desperate need of help in our search, and would appreciate it if those who are close to these obscure artists we wish to reach would put us in contact with them.

Call to Psychiatrists

Among the most interesting works we have seen, certain were done by people considered to be mentally ill and interned in psychiatric asylums. It is only natural that people deprived of an occupation and of pleasure would be more inclined than others (as are prisoners, in fact) to create some form of joy for themselves by means of artistic activity. The clear-cut idea that we have of sanity and of insanity often seems to be based on very arbitrary distinctions. The reasons for which a man is judged unfit for life in society are irrelevant to us. Consequently, we mean to consider in the same light the works of all people, whether they are judged to be healthy or sick, and without making special categories.

Rosenberg
Warhol: Art's Other Self

The innovation of Andy Warhol consists not in his paintings but in his version of the comedy of the artist as a public figure. "Andy" (the first name was one of his means of establishing himself as a household word) has carried the ongoing de-definition of art to the point at which nothing is left of art but the fiction of the artist. "Why is *The Chelsea Girls* art?" he inquired, referring to one of his movies. "Well, first of all, it was made by an artist, and, second, that would come out as art." To this, one is given the choice of replying either "Amen!" or "Oh, yeah?" Though Warhol's retrospective, at the Whitney, was loaded with some two hundred and forty items, many of them huge, he had succeeded in approximating the performance of the painter who does not paint. Twenty years ago, the late Barnett Newman said to Rauschenberg that if the artist's aim is to produce empty canvases he ought to do it with pigment. Warhol lives up to this injunction, but with modifications. His Campbell's Soup cans, Brillo boxes, portraits of public figures, tabloid horror photographs, and flowers are for the most part images silk-screened on canvas in numerous replicas. A capsule biography in *Art in America* records, under 1961–62, when he was emerging as an artist out of commercial design, that "Warhol rejects hand-painting canvases." His performance goes beyond that of Marcel Duchamp, who for almost half a century was a dominant presence in the art world without publicly producing a work. Warhol does produce, and in profusion; even after his "retirement" he was represented at the Los Angeles County Museum exhibition of "Art and Technology" by an "environment" of "hundreds of three-dimensional daisy images, made by Cowles Communications' Xography process, seen through fluctuating sheets of sparkling artificial rain." Warhol is not an anti-artist, since to be one implies acknowledgment of the presence of art. He blandly takes his fertility for granted, but depletes his creations of any quality that might separate them from products of the conveyor belt or the machine. Within a year after his début, he set up his studio as the Factory, from which his imprinted Brillo boxes, Marilyn Monroes, and electric chairs streamed in required quantities. Instead of the nonworks of Duchamp, Warhol supplied near-nonworks–Andythings. He has shown the drawings of flowers and butterflies, the gold-paper shoes, the greeting cards, and the souvenirs he did in the thirteen years

---

Source: Reprinted with permission of Macmillan Publishing Company from *Art on the Edge* by Harold Rosenberg. Copyright © 1975 by Harold Rosenberg.

before he declared himself an artist. These exhibits are art *ex post facto*—objects elevated retroactively into the realm of aesthetic significance. Or, if one prefers, Warhol's pre-art products of whim and drudgery blend with his art-world output in that all are extensions, or relics, of the Warhol-figure; he could, if he chose, include his old sneakers or his mother's recipes.

By underwriting as art objects available in hardware stores, Duchamp demonstrated that art lay in the artist, not in the art object. The Action painters repudiated picture-making in favor of acts of discovery and self-transformation. Warhol interprets literally the overshadowing of the artwork by the artist; that is, he sees it strictly in terms of the art market. His mass production of paintings and his dramatization of himself are a radical reflection of the values that came to the fore in the art world toward the end of the 1950s. The new, expanded art public—and its representatives among dealers, collectors, and curators—had little taste for the enigmas and the exhausting bouts with the experience of Gorky, Pollock, de Kooning, Guston. It preferred images taken in at a glance and "glamourous" colors translatable into dress patterns. Above all, it admired reputations. Warhol not only understood this public but had the wit to draw practical conclusions from his encounter with it. "We fixed it like this," he said to Grace Glueck, of the *Times,* about his Whitney exhibition, "so people could catch the show in a minute and leave." Warhol was aware that whether or not visitors actually left in a minute (that might depend on the presence of free drinks) they would devote only a minute to the paintings. For the great majority of the avant-garde audience, art was not something to look at; it had become, in the newly popular phrase, an "environment." It was not necessary to scrutinize an exhibition; one needed only to know that it was there; one apprehended it with one's back. Warhol put his painting where the spectator wanted it—behind him. I once asked Leo Castelli, Warhol's dealer, about an exhibition of silk-screened flowers that was to open at his gallery. "No need to see it," said Castelli. "The pictures are the same as the announcement I sent you." Warhol had something for everyone: for gallery-goers easy art, for collectors a signature.

Warhol's practice constitutes an extremist appraisal of the status of art in present-day America; by comparison, any political or sociological pronouncement he might have made would have been superficial. A painting is a picture, *any* picture (since any can be reproduced), with a respected signature. Art is a cliché given renown by a name; this applies to the *Mona Lisa* as well as to a Rauschenberg, and to Warhol's silk-screenings of the *Mona Lisa* as well as to a photograph of Rauschenberg. Art history, which determines what shall be identified as art, devotes itself to authenticating attributions and to supplying signatures when they are missing. Greatness in an artist consists in his high worth as a label; early on, Warhol declared to a friend that he wanted "to be Matisse," but there is no evidence that he was ever interested in Matisse's paintings. Duchamp's bottle rack and bicycle wheel are in museums, but they got there through fortuitous and unpredictable developments. With Duchamp for a precedent, and with the example of Duchamp's emulators of the 1950s, such as Rauschenberg and Johns, Warhol could avoid the difficulties both of painting, on the one hand, and of overcoming the anonymity of found objects, on the other. By mechanical duplication, he could adjust supply to demand without being subjected to the hardships and uncertainties of creation; his duplications would even arouse critical admiration as a contribution to "serial imagery." At one swoop—his first New York exhibition, at the Stable Gallery, in 1962, of painted and silkscreened soup cans, "celebrities," and do-it-yourself pictures—Warhol demonstrated that art-world evaluation of the objects presented to it could be programmed by mustering attention around the artist. The power to make one's signature count is acquired through a fiction launched upon the public; no less than the President of the United States, the artist gains his authority through marketing an alter ego. The bottle rack of Duchamp, the bronzed flashlight of Johns possess formal resemblances to treasures of the museum; Warhol swept aside these academic subtleties. His undistinguished art needed only the support of a distinctive Warhol.

It was in conceiving the creator of his works that Warhol proved genuinely creative, and penetrating to the point of subversion. The archetype of the modern artist has been the Dandy, Baudelaire's detached and intellectually tormented "hero of modern life." This figure survived in a variety of versions to the threshold of the sixties. Duchamp, in his refusal of art, was a resurrection of the lone Dandy in his discipline of pride and estrangement. The "accursed" artist was emulated by Gorky with du Maurier exaggeration, refurbished by Pollock as a cowboy riproarer, reenacted by de Kooning in dungarees and workman's jacket, and, recently, by Rauschenberg as a Leatherstocking. Despite cosmetic modifications, the elegant stranger engaged in a mysterious and probably hopeless mission, equally resigned to failure and success, persisted as the model of the artist in our time.

Warhol buried the Dandy under an avalanche of soup cans. His sensibility distinguishes him not only from artists of the fifties but from other Pop artists as well. With Oldenburg, Segal, Wesselmann, Lichtenstein, America's visual banalities are suspended at the edge of the imagination; in different degrees, the 7-Up bottles and the gasoline pumps seem about to change into something else. In contrast, Warhol purged art-making of every residue of subjectivity. He externalized himself and his creations into an identity as devoid of individual references as a rubber stamp. "If you want to know all about Andy Warhol," he declared, "just look at the surface of my paintings and films and me, and there I am. There's nothing behind it." Of course, this facade—or billboard—personality is a fiction. The all-surface poker face is derived from the gunfighter of the Westerns; before Warhol moved upstage, the long, flat countenance of Jasper Johns recalled that of William S. Hart. The deadpan of the prairies and the mining-town card table is secretly in love with his horse—or with money. Something similar is true of Warhol. And although he hasn't shot anyone, he has been shot. Warhol's mask is a bit too awry to be a face. The interesting question is why the art world has been so eager to be taken in by it. The answer is that for the new collectors, critics, and curators *art* has "nothing behind it." Warhol has been the personification of their experience of art, with a fidelity that has earned him the title of St. Andy—though his self-negation is less that of saintliness than of capital accumulation.

As the fabricator of silk-screened clichés in enamel makeup, Warhol presented himself as the made-up artist. His philosophy might be summed up as "I am recognized, therefore I am." For him, the artist is eliminated from the art object except as the supplier of a trademark. In the year of his initial success, he adopted a costume of black leather jacket and silver-sprayed hair and a mask of bewildered non-commitment; the ensemble gave him a faint resemblance to the silver-topped de Kooning, then the Champ of American art. This effigy and the Factory are the initiators of Warhol items, and Warhol united the two by lining his studio with silver foil in reiteration of the emblem of his hair. The creative efforts unexpended on his painting were invested in making the public aware of their source. By 1966, he was in a position to trumpet his triumph and the limitlessness of his art-making capacity by advertising in a newspaper that he would sign anything brought to him, including (without being guilty of megalomania) currency, the value of which he now had the power to increase.

Warhol replaced the Dandy with the non-person, the demiurge of the Factory. As the originator of his all-surface nonworks, he has meticulously constructed the figure of the artist as nobody, though a nobody with a resounding signature. His performance has featured an elusiveness of identity centered on the nucleus of his name. "I'd prefer to remain a mystery," he explained in an interview. "I never give my background, and anyway, I make it all up different every time I'm asked." In keeping with this principle of self-substitution is his origination of the artist's stand-in—friends sent to impersonate him at openings and at lectures. Testing whether he will be recognized is an aspect of his passion for fame and perhaps of a genuine doubt about who he is. Part organization man (he is president of Andy Warhol Films, Inc.), part cult-gang leader, he moves surrounded by a company that participates in the execution of his works. He boasts that his taste is that of the man in the street: "The artificial fascinates me, the bright and shiny." This is as good an explanation as any of his fondness for lavenders, oranges, greens, and pinks in his paintings. He might have added that horrors fascinate him—criminals, "celebrities," and erotica. Like other tabloid readers, he has snapped up images ranging from bleeding demonstrators to weekend supermarket specials in a single gulp, and he has marketed them with the color devices of product packaging without altering their psychic blankness.

In demonstrating that art today is a commodity of the art market, comparable to commodities of other specialized markets, Warhol has liquidated the century-old tension between the serious artist and the majority culture. His art is, essentially, an art for the masses—a fact not altered by its "élitist" price tag. By way of the popular media, he has reawakened the 1930s idea of the artist as mass man, though "mass boy" would be more accurate in regard to his style, which is related to motorcycle bands and acid-rock crowds. His patrons have been mass men with money who, in a momentous development, have overcome the traditional American deference before the culture of Europe and its masterpieces. Warhol marks the point in Western culture after which art is destined to contend for its survival against the flux of the popular media.

Another significant Warhol innovation is the artist who has a limited engagement with art. He has not abandoned painting, but from the start he has manifested a readiness to depart. Though Duchamp publicly repudiated creation, he remained permanently attached to the art world as the normal habitat of the man of imagination. In contrast, Warhol sees no privilege in art as an activity, and, as we have learned, for him the artist is devoid of individual attributes. After five years, he terminated his career in the art galleries and transferred himself and his "apparatus" to the milieu of the discothèque and the movies. The Whitney Museum retrospective took its form from Warhol's refusal to present a continuity related to the inner continuity of an individual. At his insistence, the exhibition was limited to five themes, repeated as on sheets of postage stamps: soup cans, Brillo boxes, portraits, tabloid catastrophes, and flowers.

A retrospective is a résumé of an artist's development. Instead of development, which both he and his work lack, Warhol presented a career of five separate "acts," any one of which could have been the last. This amounts to an assertion that for the contemporary artist art lacks necessity and is dispensable; art today is what one can make of it. It possesses no intrinsic qualities that invite devotion. For de Kooning, art has been "a way of living"; for Warhol, it is part of one's self-projection or something to do for gain. By the force of his indifference, Warhol strips painting and sculpture of any shreds of transcendence left over from their religious and metaphysical past. He is the prophet of the Minimalist art of the sixties that sought to allude to nothing beyond itself. But he gives dramatic clarification to Minimalism by minimalizing the artist, too, and the world he inhabits. The thoroughness of his anti-illusionism, his systematic "I-am-what-I-seem," make Warhol the hero of art of the period that followed Abstract Expressionism.

John Baldessari

One of the most influential artists to have emerged since the 1960s, Los Angeles artist John Baldessari (1931–   ) has played a significant role in the international development of conceptual art. Utilizing photography and language often drawn directly from popular culture, Baldessari questions how meaning is made and challenges the conventions of painting, sculpture, and photography. Through his work Baldessari has substantially affected the character of contemporary art and the role of the artist in its making. . . .

Central to Baldessari's work is the use of appropriated images and text. Many of the photographic images incorporated into his compositions are taken from popular media sources such as magazines, newspapers, film, and television. Sources for textual elements include literary works, writings on art, movie scripts, and overheard conversations and phrases. Baldessari's diverse use of appropriation challenges long-held notions of originality in art, and his coupling of images with text—some of which may, at times, seem disparate—provides narratives that are simultaneously straightforward and oblique.

In planning a composition, the artist establishes an often complex situation in which formal elements are selected randomly (by chance) and/or carefully (by choice). By regularly employing one or both of these two strategies in his process of making art, Baldessari is able to realize a separate theoretical or thematic goal for each work.

Although a variety of subject matter is addressed by Baldessari, much recent work falls within the realm of universal themes, such as duality, violence, anxiety, human relationships, and transformation. Such themes are realized in both individual works and in series.

In the early 1960s Baldessari began experimenting with non-traditional means of artmaking, going from making paintings to composing segments of discarded billboard posters he accumulated. In the mid to late 1960s he continued to move away from traditional painting methods, and began to

---

Source: Text from *John Baldessari,* originally published in the brochure accompanying the exhibition "John Baldessari" at the Museum of Contemporary Art, Los Angeles, March 25–June 17, 1990. Reprinted by permission.

produce works containing texts and photographic images from art books, instruction manuals, and the popular media. Canvases were constructed and primed by someone else, and a sign painter was hired to do the lettering for statements that he provided, allowing Baldessari to remove himself from direct intervention in the creation of the work. Works such as *Pure Beauty* and *A Work With Only One Property* (both 1967–68), which contain only their titles painted on the canvas, and *Econo-O-Wash* (1967–68), which consists of a photograph of a laundromat above its lettered address, are invested with pure informational content.

Further suggesting Baldessari's interest in the primacy of idea, or concept, over execution is *A Painting That Is Its Own Documentation* (1968–Present). Comprised solely of text printed on the canvas, the work serves as a record of its own exhibition history. In this way, Baldessari furnishes the concept of a work of art with more importance than the physical object itself.

Another ultimately "conceptualist" work is *Commissioned Paintings* (1969). For this project, Baldessari visited amateur art exhibitions and selected fourteen artists, whom he commissioned to paint specific images of banal objects that Baldessari had photographed. The resultant paintings were grouped and exhibited together to teach viewers interested in modern art how to practice connoisseurship.

Inextricably linked to Baldessari's desire to expunge from his art the associations of traditional modes of painting, in 1970 he burned all of his artwork produced prior to 1967. This act liberated the artist from what he felt were the "suffocating" ideas from which he had been working, and literally cleared his studio of a large body of painting. It is documented by a film and the work *Cremation Project* (1970), consisting of a bronze plaque, an urn containing ashes, six color photographs, and text.

In the 1970s Baldessari continued to juxtapose photographic images with text, but stopped using canvases. Mounting his work on board to complete the move away from painting, he continued to pursue his fascination with language and linguistics. Reading Wittgenstein, Saussure, Barthes, Derrida, and others stimulated his examination of language and the potential of fragmented text to function as imagery and narrative. . . .

A common working method engaged by Baldessari to avoid compositional and aesthetic decisions was chance and accident. He often set up situations whereby the outcome of the work was unknown until the last moment, thereby keeping the artist and the viewer "off-balance." *Choosing Rhubarb* (1972) and a book from the same series, *Choosing: Green Beans* (1972), utilize photographs of objects—rhubarb, green beans, etc.—that were taken based upon selections made by the artist and a participant in a complicated "game."

An even more complex set of improvisational conditions and structures was employed by Baldessari in such later works as those in the *Blasted Allegories* series (1978). Although the "game" here is described on each work, the system by which they were created is perhaps not immediately apparent to the viewer, their difficulty demonstrating an idiosyncratic and thoroughly ambiguous narrative.

In the mid 1970s Baldessari became interested in more existential themes, such as polar opposition and reconciliation. This is evident in such groups of work as *Binary Code Series* (1974), in which dualisms such as yes/no, male/female are counterpoised. In *Binary Code Series: Lily (Yes/No),* the flower's stamen in the left-hand photograph points up to indicate yes while the right-hand photograph shows a downward pointed stamen for no. *Repair Retouch Series: An Allegory About Wholeness (Plate and Man with Crutches)* (1976) addresses another theme—of transformation. In these sets of photographs, Baldessari juxtaposed a broken plate and a legless man with their restored counterparts. This idea of putting the pieces back together may also be likened to the idea of how artists compose artworks.

Baldessari's work of the 1980s may be characterized by a movement from the cerebral towards the emotional. Technical and aesthetic changes occurred in his work as composition, scale, and color supplemented wide-ranging experimentation. The artist's role in the artmaking process transformed from one of neutrality and intellectual analyses to more profound explorations of personal emotions, psychology, and psychoanalytic therapy.

In works such as *Baudelaire Meets Poe* (1980)—a three-part installation—a much larger sense of scale emerges, along with a more poetic and complex use of visual narrative. The work is Baldessari's interpretation of a mythical meeting between Charles Baudelaire and Edgar Allan Poe and is his visual equivalent of the mental outburst that Baudelaire must have experienced upon reading Poe for the first time. . . .

In his works of the 1980s Baldessari remained the storyteller, allowing his potent images to collide, and challenging the viewer's interpretation of meaning. Often blotting out the faces of the people photographed, as in *Civic Piece* (1986), *Bloody Sunday* (1987), and the book *The Telephone Book (With Pearls)* (1988), Baldessari turned individuals into generic types. Shifting the attention from the people's faces to the details of the elements around them, new questions about the relationships of the various images arise. In *Banquet* (1987), for example, viewers see tables laden with dishes and food, but see only the hands or torsos of the people eating it. Viewers are led to question the hierarchy of the images, which picture food and dirty dishes rather than people, and to examine the idea of eating as ritual. Stacking the photographs in an architectural composition akin to stacking dishes, Baldessari suggests the sense of order versus chaos that is visually represented.

Throughout his career Baldessari has broken with tradition and grappled with contradiction. There is no doubt that the paradoxes and questions he has raised will be a part of his continuing dialogue with viewers into the 1990s and beyond.

Zavattini
A Thesis on Neo-Realism

There is no doubt that our first, and most superficial, reaction to daily existence is boredom. Reality seems deprived of all interest as long as we cannot succeed in surmounting and overcoming our moral and intellectual sloth. It is, therefore, not surprising that the cinema has always felt the "natural" and practically inevitable necessity of inserting a story into reality in order to make it thrilling and spectacular. It is evident that in this manner one could spontaneously escape from reality; it is as if nothing could be done to prevent the interference of the imagination.

The most important characteristic of neo-realism, i.e., its essential innovation, is for me, the discovery that this need to use a story was just an unconscious means of masking human defeat in the face of reality; imagination, in its own manner of functioning, merely superimposes death schemes onto living events and situations.

Yet, in fact, we are now aware that reality is extremely rich. We simply had to learn how to look at it. The task of the artist—the neo-realist artist at least—does not consist in bringing the audience to tears and indignation by means of transference, but, on the contrary, it consists in bringing them to reflect (and *then,* if you will, to stir up emotions and indignation) upon what they are doing and upon what others are doing; that is, to think about reality precisely as it is.

From a profound and unconscious lack of confidence in confronting reality, from an illusory and ambiguous evasion, we have gone on to an unlimited confidence in things, events, and in men.

Naturally, this taking of sides requires us to dig deeply, to give reality the power and faculty of communication, the radiance, which, up until the time of neo-realism, we didn't believe it could possess.

It has often been written that the war was the keystone for neo-realism.

Source: From David Overbey, ed., *Springtime in Italy* (Archon Books: Hawden, Conn., 1979), pp. 67–77. Translated by David Overbey.

This overwhelming event upset men's souls; film directors, each in his own way, tried to transpose this overwhelming emotion onto the screen. As we saw absolutely no reason for participating in it, the war seemed particularly monstrous for us Italians. We had far more reasons for not becoming involved. This rebellion, however, was not limited to that particular war; it went much further. It was the absolute—I would even say the eternal—revelation that war always violates those fundamental human needs and values which are so dear to us. This revelation was, in my opinion, the starting point of a vast human uprising.

You might reply that this revelation was not the distinction of Italy alone. I would tend to agree. Nonetheless, those very qualities which many take to be the faults of our people, but which are actually our essential virtues—extreme individualism, a lack of overweening social pride, and so on—urge us towards a full and passionate reaction against the supreme evil of war. It was not "historical man" who acted—that abstract character in novels which follows a course of action that is unrelated to a specific time and deals with dates of past, present and future wars indiscriminately—on the contrary, it was the real, deep thinking, hidden man who acted. You might object by pointing out that "historical man" and the man without a label exist side by side. That is true enough, except that they co-exist *usefully* only when, by the principle of clear channels of communication, they find a common level and merge; that is to say that the former, with his awareness, and the latter, with his profoundly original drive to live, must be in real contact. The need to live, when it is rich and happy, can transcend its limits more easily when, as in this case, it inspires and enlightens an entire fallen people who seemingly could no longer make the smallest contribution to humanity.

I dare to think that *other* peoples, even after the war, have shown that they continued to consider man as a historical *subject*, as historical material, with determined, almost inevitable, actions. This is why they, unlike the Italians, did not give the cinema its freedom. For them, everything continued; for us, everything began. For them the war had been just another war; for us, it had been the last war. What were the discoveries and the consequences of this rush of post-war pioneers, which were new, not because they had never before been known, but because they had never been felt in such a collective and tenacious manner? The results were the endless possibility of studying man that we see opening before us, a non-abstract and concrete study of man, as concrete as the men who provoked and underwent the war. We needed to know and to see how these terrible events could have occurred. The cinema was the most direct and immediate way of making this sort of study. It was preferable to other art forms which did not possess a language which would readily express our reactions against the lies of those old, generalized ideas in which we found ourselves clothed at the outbreak of the war, and which had prevented us from attempting the smallest rebellion.

This powerful desire of the cinema to see and to analyse, this hunger for reality, for truth, is a kind of concrete homage to other people, that is, to all who exist. This, among other things, is what distinguishes neo-realism from the American cinema. In effect, the American position is diametrically opposed to our own: whereas we are attracted by the truth, by the reality which touches us and which we want to know and understand directly and thoroughly, the Americans continue to satisfy themselves with a sweetened version of truth produced through transpositions.

That is why the Americans are undergoing a crisis; they have no idea what subjects to use. This is not possible in Italy, for here, there can never be a lack of truth. Every hour of the day, every place, every person, can be portrayed if they are shown in a manner which reveals and emphasizes the collective elements which continually shape them.

This is why one cannot speak of a crisis of subjects (facts), but only of the possibility, as the case may be, of a crisis of content (the interpretation of facts).

This essential difference was very clearly expressed by an American producer who told me:

> In America, the scene of a plane passing over is shown in this sequence:
> a plane passes, machine-gun fire opens, the plane falls. In Italy: a plane
> passes, it passes again, and then again.

It is the absolute truth. But it is still not enough. It is not enough to have the plane pass by three times; it must pass by twenty times. We work, therefore, to extricate ourselves from abstractions.

In a novel, the protagonists were heroes; the shoes of the hero were special shoes. We, on the other hand, are trying to find out what our characters have in common; in my shoes, in his, in those of the rich, in those of the poor, we find the same elements: the same labour of man.

Let us move on to style. How can we express this reality (truth) in the cinema? First, I would like to repeat what I have often said: The contents always engender their own expression, their own technique. Imagination, therefore, is allowed, but only on the condition that it exercise itself within reality and not on the periphery. Let me be clear: I do not intend to give the impression that only "news items" matter to me. I have tried to concentrate on these with the intention of putting them together again in the most faithful way, using a bit of imagination, which comes from a perfect understanding of the event, situation, or fact itself. Obviously, it would be more coherent for the camera to catch them at the moment they develop. This is what I intend to do when I make my film on Italy. It should never be forgotten, of course, that any relationship with an idea one wishes to express implies a choice which is part of the creative act, but that choice must be made in relationship with the subject on the spot rather than the subject being a reconstruction following an imaginative choice. This is what I call the "cinema of encounter." This method of working should lead logically to two results: first, from an ethical point of view, directors would leave the studio in search of direct contact with reality. Therefore, we will create a system of production which will bring with it the freshness of collective awareness. The number of films we make also plays an important part. If we make one hundred films a year which are inspired by these criteria, we would change the very conditions of production; if we only make three, we will have to submit to the conditions of production as they exist today.

This awareness of reality, which constitutes neo-realism, has two consequences in terms of narrative construction:

(1) Whereas in the past, cinema portrayed a situation from which a second was derived, and then a third from that, and so on, each scene being created only to be forgotten the next moment, today, when we imagine a scene, we feel the need to "stay" there inside it; we now know that it has within itself all the potential of being reborn and of having important effects. We can calmly say: give us an ordinary situation and from it we will make a spectacle. Centrifugal force which constituted (both from a technical and a moral point of view) the fundamental aspects of traditional cinema has now transformed itself into centripetal force.

(2) Whereas the cinema always told of life's external aspects, today neo-realism affirms that we should not be content with illusion, but should move toward analysis, or better, should move towards a synthesis within analysis.

For example: let us take two people who are looking for an apartment. In the past, the film-maker would have made that the starting point, using it as a simple and external pretext to base something else on. Today, one can use that simple situation of hunting for an apartment as the entire subject of the film. It must be understood, of course, that this is true only if the situation is always emphasized with all the echoes, reflections, and reverberations which are present in it.

We are, we recognize, still far from that necessary and true analysis. Now we can only speak of analysis simply in opposition to the vulgar artificiality of current production. For the time being we have only an analytic "attitude," but this attitude brings with it a powerful movement towards facts, a desire for comprehension, for adhesion, for participation, and for co-existence.

This principle of analysis arises in the consideration of style, in the most narrow sense, and is opposed to bourgeois synthesis. In the bourgeois cinema, directors choose the most representative aspects of a situation of well-being and privilege of a part of Italian culture. To understand critically the range of neo-realism, one must stress the role played by Italian culture. Given the increasingly important collaboration of writers in the creation of the cinema, it could not be otherwise. But this collaboration cannot limit itself to the furnishing of novels as a basis for film; writers should rather contribute to the enrichment of cinematic expression, an expression rich with as much potential as literary language. If writers can involve themselves in a less tentative way than they usually do, they can bring great progress to the cinema and involve the whole of Italian culture.

It should, therefore, be clear that contrary to what was done before the war, the neo-realist movement recognized that the cinema should take as its subject the daily existence and condition of the Italian people, without introducing the coloration of the imagination, and thereby, force itself to analyze it for whatever human, historical, determining and definite factors it encompasses.

I believe that the world continues to evolve towards evil because we do not know the truth: we remain unaware of reality. The most necessary task for a man today consists in attempting to resolve, as best he can, the problem of this knowledge and lack of awareness. That is why the most urgent need of our times is social contact, social awareness. But no matter how artistically successful it may be, moral allegory is no longer enough. This awareness and contact must be direct. A hungry man, a downtrodden man, must be shown as he is, with his own first and last names. A story should never be constructed in which the hungry and the oppressed merely appear, for then everything changes, becomes less effective, and far less moral.

The true function of the arts has always been that of expressing the needs of the times; it is towards this function that we should redirect them. No other means of expression has the potential which the cinema possesses for making things known directly, for making contact immediately, to the largest number of people. It was, of course, natural that even those who understood such things were still obliged, for all sorts of reasons—some valid, others not—to compose stories invented according to tradition, and even more natural that they sought to add to the stories some elements of what they themselves had discovered.

In effect, this is what neo-realism is currently in Italy.

Roma città aperta, Paisà, Sciuscià, Ladri di biciclette, and *La terra trema* are films which contain passages of great significance. They were inspired by the possibility of telling everything, but, in a certain sense, they still involve translation because they tell stories and do not apply the documentary spirit simply and fully. In films like *Umberto D,* the analytical fact is much more evident, but the analysis is set within the framework of traditional narrative. We have not yet come to real neo-realism.

The neo-realism of today is like an army prepared to march. The soldiers are prepared: Rossellini, De Sica, Visconti. They must lead the assault; it is the only way the war can be won. The important fact is that the movement has begun; now either we go forward to the very end, or we will have missed a great opportunity. Ahead of neo-realism vast perspectives are opening, perspectives beyond our imagination. We must grasp our chance. It will not be easy. Transforming every day situations into spectacle is not an easy thing to do; intensity of vision is required from both the director and the audience. It is a dialogue in which one must give life, reality, its historical importance, which exists in each instant. . . .

We have the illusion—call it that if you like—that with us something completely different and new is beginning. Today a man who suffers before my eyes is absolutely different from a man who suffered a hundred years ago. I must concentrate all my attention on the man of today. The historical baggage that I carry within myself, and from which, by the way, I neither can nor want to free myself, must not prevent me from being what I wish to be, nor from using the means I have at hand to deliver this man from his pain. This man—and this is one of my basic and fixed ideas—has a first name and a last name. He is part of society in a way that concerns us, make no mistake about that. I feel his fascination. I must feel it in such a way that I am urgently obliged to speak to him or of him, but not as a character of my imagination's invention; it is exactly at that moment one must beware, for it is then that the imagination attempts to come between reality and the self.

I have often had to explain that I do not wish to prohibit actors from playing in films. Of course actors have a place in films, it is simply that they have very little to do with neo-realistic cinema. The neo-realistic cinema does not ask those men in whom it is interested to have the talents of actors; their professional aptitudes have to do with the profession of being men. They need to be made aware of this, of course, which is the responsibility of the cinema. It is evident that this awareness can only be created or reinforced through the knowledge we give them of themselves, knowledge which we will attain through neo-realistic cinema.

How, then, does the imagination, the creative act, enter neo-realism? It is, of course, a very particular sort of imagination, and the creative act is a very new method of using that imagination.

For example: a woman goes to a shoe store to buy shoes for her son. The shoes cost 7,000 lire. The woman bargains to get them cheaper. The scene lasts ten minutes, whereas I have to make a film two hours long (we will discuss the commercial "rules" of distribution and exhibition which dictated that a film be of a certain length at another time). What then do I do? I analyze all the elements which go to make up the situation, what happened beforehand, what will come afterwards, and what is really happening while the situation exists. The woman buys the shoes, but what is happening to her son at the moment? What is happening in India which might be related to this particular pair of shoes? The shoes cost 7,000 lire. How did the woman get that money? What pain have they cost her? What do they represent for her? And the shoe shop owner who sells them: who is he? What relationship is created between these two people? There might be two other sons also there eating and chattering. Would you like to hear their conversation? Here they are. And it goes on.

It is the act of getting to the bottom of things, of showing the relationships between the situations and the process through which the situations come into being. If we analyze the purchase of a pair of shoes, we see before us a complex and vast world, rich in scope and possibilities, rich in practical, social, economic and psychological motifs. The banal disappears, for it never really existed.

I am against exceptional persons, heroes. I have always felt an instinctive hate towards them. I feel offended by their presence, excluded from their world as are millions of others like me. We are all characters. Heroes create inferiority complexes throughout an audience. The time has come to tell each member of the audience that he is the true protagonist of life. The result would be a constant emphasis on the responsibility and dignity of every human being. This is exactly the ambition of neo-realism: to strengthen everyone, and to give everyone the proper awareness of a human being.

The term neo-realism, in its larger sense, implies the elimination of technical-professional collaboration, including that of the screen writer. Manuals, grammars, syntax no longer have any meaning, no more than the terms "first take," "reaction shot" and all the rest. Each of us will "direct" in his own way, "compose a scenario" in his own way. Neo-realism shatters all schemes, shuns all dogmas. There can be no "first takes" nor "reaction shots" *a priori*. The subject, the adaptation, the direction cannot, in neo-realism, be three distinct phases of the same work. It is true that they are so today, but this is an anomaly. In neo-realism, the screen writer and the writer of dialogue disappear; there will be no scenario written beforehand, and no dialogue to adapt.

We must come to terms with the unique *auteur*, the director, but he will, in the long run, have little in common with either the theatre or cinema directors of today.

Everything is in flux. Everything is moving. Someone makes his film: everything is continually possible and everything is full of infinite potentiality, not only during the shooting, but during the editing, the mixing, throughout the entire process as well.

I have been working in the Italian cinema since 1934. I know that I have contributed to the destruction of a few of the usual and traditional schemes. If I place myself among those who believe that neo-realism is one of the most powerful forces to which we can address ourselves, it is not by any lack of imagination. On the contrary, I must constantly pull myself to a halt with both hands so as to refuse my imagination entrance into my work. I have enough imagination in the traditional sense of the word to sell and resell, but neo-realism requires us to allow our imagination to exercise itself only *in loco* and through reality, for the situations increase their natural imaginative force when they are studies in depth. It is only then that they can become dramatic spectacles, because it is then that they become revelations.

I know very well that one can make marvelous films like those of Charlie Chaplin, and that they are not neo-realist works. I know very well that there are Americans, Russians, Frenchmen, and so forth, who have made masterpieces which bring honour to humanity. They have certainly not wasted film. And God knows how many distinguished works they will continue to produce, depending upon their genius, using stars, studios, and the adaptations of novels. But the men of the Italian cinema, in order to continue to search for and to conserve their own style and inspiration, having once courageously set ajar the doors of reality and truth, must now open them wide.

Calandra

The Antiteater of R. W. Fassbinder

Rainer Werner Fassbinder began his work in the theatre in the late sixties, as a twenty-two-year-old. He acted, directed, (loosely) adapted classics by Büchner, Goethe, Sophocles, Goldoni and others, wrote several of his own plays, and in a few years emerged as the leader of a group of performers who would work with him, intensively at first, then off and on until his death in 1982. The opposition spirit of the era, however vaguely understood, pervaded the activities of the most diverse independent German theatres. Fassbinder joined the Action-Theater, some of whose members then formed what was to become "his" antiteater: the groups' names tell a story in themselves. The

Source: Copyright © 1985 by Denis Calandra. From the introduction to *Rainer Werner Fassbinder: Plays, 1985.* Reprinted by permission of PAJ Publications.

title of one of Handke's earliest plays, *Offending the Audience,* is another typical indicator. Fassbinder's place in the line of haters of traditional theatre can be seen in his affinity with early Brecht. He played the title role in Volker Schlöndorff's 1969 TV film of *Baal;* the focus on raw power-struggles in city-jungles which eat up their inhabitants connects the young anarchic Brecht with his fellow Bavarian and self-advertised enfant-terrible, Fassbinder. (Responding to Fassbinder's death, Werner Herzog said he wasn't German at all, but a "wild" Bavarian.) Fassbinder also shared in and encouraged the revival of the realistic and folk play tradition associated with Odön von Horváth, and especially Marieluise Fleisser. Besides adapting and directing Fleisser's work, his own *Katzelmacher,* dedicated to her, shares the attention to crippling small town mentality as embedded in working-class and lower-middle-class ordinary speech.

Regardless of material, the antiteater productions came to be greeted with certain expectations. Their style apparently had less to do with particular methods, or sets of exercises, than it did with an atmosphere largely created by the theatre's leader. In his book *Fassbinder: Film Maker,* Ronald Hayman writes that Fassbinder "was a creative artist in the plural: the shared work that gave him insight into his own experience gave them excited insight into theirs." German theatre critic Peter Iden described the feel of an antiteater performance in these terms:

> A great spontaneity in the playing, the tendency to explain the choice of material as arbitrary; random and irrational factors in the handling of the productions . . . but also vehemently passionate acting, and a light, nonchalant kind of aggressiveness.

Fassbinder's choice of an English title for *Pre-Paradise Sorry Now* places it firmly in its era. It was anti-Living Theatre, the direct reference being to the American group's *Paradise Now.* Though Action-Theater and antiteater seemed to share, theoretically at least, the ethos of collective creation and a vague yearning for anarchic freedom, Fassbinder's play clearly mocks the idea of ever achieving paradise, now *or* later. The central plot material has to do with an actual case, the famous English moors murders, committed by Ian Brady and Myra Hindley. Brady teaches Hindley to "enjoy submission"; together they prepare for *their* future paradise, when "inferior creatures" will learn from the master race that "death means happiness." Intercut with this material are a series of neo-realist vignettes demonstrating "the fascistoid underpinnings of everyday life," and a series of Christian liturgical passages which reveal their basis in cannibalism. The vignettes cover familiar Fassbinder territory: whores and pimps; landlords and tenants; pupils and teachers; children and parents—all to do with oppression. The play has an interesting formal structure, in that Fassbinder designated only the Brady/Hindley story to proceed in a set order. The rest can be, and has been, arranged however the production team sees fit. The result is that the beginning, middle and end of the Brady/Hindley plot drives towards a murderous conclusion propelled by the other two structures in the play.

The other Fassbinder play based on a historical event is *Bremen Freedom,* which was written specifically for that city. The play's subject matter is in the realist tradition: a nineteenth-century woman systematically eliminates the men and women who would keep her in her proper place. Her own demise is as expected as the repetition of the song she sings with each murder: "World farewell! of thee I'm tired. . . ." At the end she murders her friend Luisa in order to save her "from the kind of life you're having to lead." Even in this most conventional play, a black comedy, preserved on film as Fassbinder directed it, hopelessness outruns freedom. The round-dance of courtships and cheerful murders by which Geesche ("in the end a businesswoman") apparently rids herself of her oppressors, leads only to isolation and execution, rather than to liberation. In the film, Margit Carstensen's role as Geesche makes her seem as though she had just stepped off the last pages of *Miss Julie,* on the way to *her* inevitable suicide, into Fassbinder's landscape. Her apparent somnambulism declares her to be in the grip of some unseen force. (Fassbinder had long wanted to, and while with Frankfurt's Theater Am Turm [TAT] eventually did, play the part of Jean in Strindberg's play.)

So it is for the majority of Fassbinder's dramatic characters, whether it be embodied in the routine violence perpetrated on Jorgos the Greek laborer in *Katzelmacher* or the serial misery demonstrated in the generations of daughters and lovers in *The Bitter Tears of Petra von Kant.* In *Petra,* and later in the film *Querelle,* however, though the outcome is the same as for heterosexual characters, his treatment of homosexual relations, as a given, without any need of rationalization, marks an important feature of his work. Even here, though, there has been some dispute over the net result of the picture of homosexuality he paints.

The program cover for the 1971 antiteater production of *Blood On the Cat's Neck* features a picture of Fassbinder, seated, wearing an ascot to cover his throat. On his lap sits an oversize white kitten, obviously a cut-out, spewing liquid from its mouth. The Nuremberg subtitle for the play, in French, is "Marilyn Monroe vs. the Vampires." Who exactly the Kitty is, and who is sucking whose blood isn't worth worrying about, though the vampire motif carries over into the play. (The joke could easily have been an in-group reference to Fassbinder's relationship with his actors. Considerable space is given in the various published memoirs to the ways in which Fassbinder and his group "fed" and "fed on" each other.)

Phoebe Zeitgeist, well known from the cartoon strip, is the main character who eventually goes for everyone's jugular. Sent from a foreign planet to study human democracy, she has trouble interacting, because although she has learned the words, she never really seems to understand human language. She listens to familiar Fassbinder monologues about betrayal, about brutality of loved ones and children, worker exploitation, *etc.;* then she witnesses a series of vignettes in the style of *Pre-Paradise Sorry Now* and picks up isolated gestures and phrases. The comedy ensues when she utters the phrases without knowing the right context, or combines them with the wrong gestures. The rest of the characters, as she sinks her teeth into them one by one, descend into a state of torpor. The joke that she may have understood humanity only too well, is capped with her last lines, an extended quotation from Immanuel Kant on the faculty of human understanding.

The alienation is absolute. In his preliminary notes for a film he never made, *Cocaine,* Fassbinder said he wanted to allow his audience, without any help from him, to make the choice between a short, fulfilled life, or a longer existence, which would for the most part be "alienated" and lived outside a "fully conscious" state. His plays, like the films, are about varieties of alienation, and there seem to be no ways out for him short of the desperate, "fulfilling" gestures. The images Fassbinder created for the stage, and in films, linger as grotesque and brutal, possessing a strange, improbable truth.

Fassbinder's Last Play: *Garbage, The City and Death*

Fassbinder's major efforts at writing for the theatre ended during the 1974–75 season when he left his position as artistic director of Frankfurt's Theater am Turm in the storm of controversy which surrounded his last play, *Garbage, The City and Death.* As Fassbinder told the story, a group of actors had been trying to put together material on the topic of property speculation and political corruption in Frankfurt. When they foundered, he stepped in to shape the script, which owes some of its features to Gerhard Zwerenz's 1973 novel, *The Earth is Uninhabitable—Like the Moon.* "The play openly displays its weaknesses," Fassbinder wrote, adding that he didn't want "to hide behind any protective form." He felt a writer must be able to explore his themes using methods which are "dangerous, and maybe leave him open to attack." The city of Frankfurt halted production plans before rehearsals could even start, and eventually Suhrkamp, which had published the play, withdrew it from print. These actions were largely due to pressure exerted by the Jewish community, who accused Fassbinder of anti-semitism.

Joachim Fest writing in the *Frankfurter Allgemeine Zeitung* was especially critical: the play was an example of "left-wing fascism"; the writer was using anti-semitism as a "radical chic tactic"; "the leftists" needed a new "suggestive enemy-figure" and found him in Fassbinder's real-estate speculator, The Rich Jew (called Abraham in the Zwerenz novel). Fassbinder, not exactly endeared to the German left, seemed shocked by the extent of the reaction, pointing out the consistent defense of minorities in his other work, and explaining that his Rich Jew, besides being the only one who can feel and express love in the play, is simply doing business, making use of conditions which he did not create. According to Fassbinder, it was a repetition, on a different plane, of developments in the eighteenth century when Jews were the only ones who could be involved in the money market. The Rich Jew, the only main character in the play without a proper name, does act unscrupulously, exploiting bad conscience among other things to make a profit.

There are definite anti-semitic remarks and speeches by characters in the play. Dr. E. L. Ehrlich of B'nai B'rith objected to the central focus Fassbinder gave The Rich Jew, when corrupt business practice is not limited to any single group in Frankfurt. His letter to Suhrkamp dismissed the script as "a botched piece of work," an example of "political pornography," in which "a disgusting anti-semitic tirade in the mouth of a fascist [is] found among similar anti-semitic remarks spread through the play." When playwright Heiner Müller responded to the affair several years later he suggested thematic reasons for the play's focus: "Fassbinder's *Garbage, The City and Death* uses a victim's revenge to describe the devastation of a city in huge, harsh images. The city is Frankfurt. The means of revenge is real estate speculation and its consequences. The perversion of human relationships through their commodity character demonstrates a Biblical piece of wisdom: that the first fratricide, Cain, was also the first to establish a city. Fassbinder said it all in 1976 when he responded in *Theater Heute* to accusations of anti-semitism in the play: 'There are anti-semites in this play. But then they exist in other places too—in Frankfurt for instance.'"

The affair didn't die with Fassbinder. In August, 1984, Frankfurt officials once again stopped a production, this one planned to take place in a subway station under construction near the Old Opera House, the management of which had already contracted a director and a company of actors. Fassbinder's former wife, Ingrid Caven, was one of those engaged. The general manager of the Old Opera House was fired as a result of the controversy. With all the references to "B-level," or "subway people," in *Garbage, The City and Death*—those who literally and metaphorically live a secondary, underground existence in Frankfurt—the planned setting couldn't have been more appropriate. Even the association with opera made sense, for in his play Fassbinder had concocted an "entertainment" porridge out of kitschy music, ballads, sleazy drag routines, fifties rock and roll, and numbers from the great romantic tradition—duets from *La Traviata,* the *Liebestod,* etc. Petty rivalries between the municipal theatre system, originally set to act as co-producer, and the recently renovated Old Opera House, added fuel to the controversy.

However, anti-semitism on the one hand, and imputed infringement of the Bundesrepublik's guarantee (under the *Grundgesetz,* or Basic Law) of free expression on the other, were the chief issues. They are *always* the underlying issues, and rumors of behind the scenes financial pressures to keep the play from opening only intensified the situation. The Nazis had murdered or driven out Frankfurt's substantial Jewish cultural community, and there has been no replacement. This particular absence, in the context of Frankfurt's contribution to the crimes against the Jews, of course limited the debate. *Theater Heute* described the vicious circle that exists, claiming there were Jewish people, among them Israeli citizens, whose dubious business practices reaped for them substantial profits in immediate post-war Frankfurt. Fassbinder had specified that *Garbage, The City and Death* was to be produced in Frankfurt, in a foreign country, or not at all. Bochum and Cologne were both turned down in bids for production rights.

Aspects of the *Garbage* affair were not new to Fassbinder. He was certainly conscious that external circumstances would have an important role in the play's reception, though he couldn't predict what it would be. He could exploit *Garbage*'s event-status in Frankfurt, where the Zwerenz novel had already caused a stir. The entire tenure of Fassbinder at TAT was not a happy one for any of the parties involved. *Garbage* would be a way to rub salt into the eyes of his middle-class theatre audience as well as gleefully bite the (subsidized) hand that fed him at TAT. Thomas Elseasser's incisive analysis of Fassbinder's immersion in his films simultaneously as works of art, events, speculative commodities, etc., bears quoting in this context:

> Fassbinder's films have been made with "real" money, that is, funds that materialize from the dizzyingly complicated profit-and-loss calculations, the write-offs, deferred and refinancing policies, the ceaseless and now wholly self-evident logic of unlimited speculation. This is the most abstract, intangible form of value and exchange known; its manifestations are "everywhere to be felt, but nowhere to be seen"—a phrase that once referred to the creator of the universe.

Periodically throughout history, as Hannah Arendt has pointed out in *The Origins of Totalitarianism*, the phrase has also been applied to God's enemies, and often enough was skewed to refer to "the Jew in general," the "Jew everywhere and nowhere." Probably the strongest argument against *Garbage* is that it may unwittingly subscribe to the syllogism Jew = Finance = Exploitation: Jew as someone who will put his people's status as victim to work for him in the marketplace. But is that in fact what one would carry away with him from a production of this play, unless one were already predisposed to do so, and would it be the same in New York, say, as in Frankfurt? There are no easy answers.

Portraying The Rich Jew as someone who makes the holocaust turn a quick profit is a consistent, if abhorrent, expression of Fassbinder's view of human relationships. "All evens out in the end," says The Rich Jew in *Garbage*. The Jewish author Jean Améry, who fled Germany in 1938 and was incarcerated in a concentration camp by the Nazis, thought Fassbinder's play "would not be worth bothering with were it not for the figure of The Rich Jew as anti-hero." Fassbinder could be counted on to choose taboo material, and to treat it in an aggressively extreme manner, giving rise to the most disparate responses.

Fassbinder repeatedly explored the idea of power as the determining factor in human relationships. Whether as raw violence or in its subtler forms, parents, lovers, teachers—everyone—seems condemned to exert control, even if they desperately want to do otherwise. Petra von Kant's description of what she wanted with her husband is typical: "We didn't want that stuffy sort of marriage which grinds along in the same old routine. We wanted always to be fully conscious, always to decide for ourselves anew. . . ." That relationship failed, as does her love affair with Karin, because Petra "just wanted to possess her," not really share a love with her.

Fassbinder didn't fail to implicate himself, as is evident in the roles he chose for himself in his films. The most notorious example is Fassbinder as Fassbinder in *Germany in Autumn,* in which he victimizes his lover and browbeats his mother. In the film version of *Garbage, The City and Death* (*Shadow of Angels* by Daniel Schmid, 1975) Fassbinder played the victimizer/victim, Roma's brutal pimp Franz B. (Raoul in the film), who becomes the *object* of grotesque sexual abuse: the sort of erotics—"Let me discover humility"— Fassbinder further probed in *Querelle.*

Fassbinder's own shameless manipulation of feeling, as if emotional exploitation were the only option, has been well documented. As a drama student, in his earliest contact with theatre, he claims to have paid less attention to learning the craft than to observing the sado-masochism built into the training sessions. In his book on the artist, Ronald Hayman quotes a 1973 remark about Fassbinder's methods with actors: "Rainer solved a great deal simply through terror. . . . This tension between the people in the group, it was like a drug."

Fassbinder understood his artistic investment in human misery. In *Garbage,* Roma B. remarks to another prostitute, "Despair—call it by its proper name, that'll raise you capital." In a way, Fassbinder made a career out of despair—selling his own and others' misery in endless variations, operating according to a system he did not create.

IX.

Crosscurrents

The late twentieth century is littered with punctured illusions. Humanism discarded, Liberalism discredited, Communism wilting into perestroika, then into catastroika, tend to be treated as clichés of a vanishing era. When they do not self-destruct, principles are redefined simply as beliefs that do not correspond to facts. Poststructuralist denunciation of our categories of experience as creatures of either historical contingency, internal psychological drives, or external material forces, works as a moral and political narcotic. Postindustrial prosperity for the many increases choice and withers discrimination.[1] History itself is increasingly perceived not as understandable—something that might be planned for and controlled—but as a string of consequences not quite intended and hardly foreseen, of acts carried out for reasons other than what the actors thought. In the kingdom of contingency, whim rules the roost. Much of public life is about inessentials, issues tend to be transient, ephemeral, fugacious. The first selection in this final section, frivolous at first glance but profoundly revealing, represents this aspect of our age.

More significant challenges and more durable issues are raised by contemporary Feminists, whose literary and polemical productions have had a strong impact on the contemporary West. In the context of this collection, I have chosen to reprint an essay that illustrates the proximity of some Feminist criticism to

---

[1]"I call people rich," wrote Henry James in his novel *Portrait of a Lady* (1881), "when they are able to meet the demands of their own imagination." The demands of most contemporary imaginations are so limited that the majority may be defined as rich.

several thinkers who appeared in a previous section. More important, though, than her sympathies for Derrida and such, Hélène Cixous's essay reflects certain major preoccupations of literary Feminists: how men write about women, how women write (or should write) about men and about themselves, how both read what each writes, and how their styles differ. Difficult, poetic, metaphorical, Cixous uses words like rapiers and, even more, like foils, relishing the flourish before she drives in the point. Like every other contemporary system, Feminism is often excessive and aggressive in expression, and Cixous is an eloquent representative of this combative style. It may be, though, that only loud, shrill tones can hope to be heard, let alone to make an impact, amid the surrounding din.

As important as the explosive affirmation and incomplete emancipation of womankind in the West has been the collapse of that Marxist myth that, for three score years and more, held sway over much of the Western intelligentsia. The bicentennial year of the French Revolution, 1989, also marked the liberation, however partial, of East Europeans from Communist bondage. But the late seventies and eighties had already witnessed the liberation of many Western intellectuals from stultifying Marxist stereotypes. To provide just one example of how these stereotypes operated, Michel Foucault, a penetrating mind that was not Marxist, seems to have felt compelled from his "progressive" stance to attack the open, "capitalist" societies he knew, while sparing the Communist prison societies he only knew about. Foucault describes liberal societies as based on the shutting up of children in schools, soldiers in barracks, delinquents in prisons, madfolk in asylums. Would-be democratic societies were revealed in his pages as truly totalitarian, and this at the very time when most of the tendencies that he described, and exaggerated, in the West were at their most exacerbated in the East—in those Communist societies that really knew how to discipline and punish. There, ironically, while the West became more open, the imprisonment of deviants in psychiatric clinics had become a policy, the innocent in labor camps was a long-established practice, the citizenry deprived of the right to travel was a commonplace.

Bad faith of this order had prevailed for many years. In 1980, it prompted a French editor and historian to launch a new magazine, *Le Débat,* to attempt to counter it. Pierre Nora's introduction to the first issue of his periodical is reprinted below because it reflects the moral and intellectual problems thoughtful French men and women faced in the penultimate decade of our century. At the other end of Europe, bad faith in the saddle had more deadly effects, and the difference between good faith and bad proved more than an intellectual problem: a matter of life or death. That is what makes Vaclav Havel's meditation, reprinted here, so poignant.

To this highly cultivated offspring of an industrial society that was occupied by its own scum, old-fashioned values do not appear anachronistic: honor, loyalty, respect, contempt, tradition, even justice and personal responsibility—these are not empty words. Rules and norms are acknowledged even when all about are breaking them. Especially when they are being broken or ignored. Politics is neither indifferent nor superficial: it is about the lessons of history, and it may be about sacrifice, not profit. Havel is shocked by the young French leftist who extols the Gulag "as a tax paid for the ideals of socialism." He knows that such misperceptions are not just venial errors and matters of opinion; but he knows too that his interlocutor will not understand this until he finds himself incarcerated in a Soviet-style jail near his hometown, Toulouse. Havel himself spent several years in a Soviet-style jail near Prague, so he realizes that politics is no joke, and that opinions are more than intellectual acrobatics. And he knows that apparently naive words may be the only ones that adequately or inadequately express concrete and difficult experience; may even affect it. "A reaffirmed human responsibility," Havel declares, "is the most natural barrier to all irresponsibility." Honor, responsibility, forgotten words, forgotten notions. We should do well to relearn them.

Baker

The optimist proclaims that we live in the best of all possible worlds. The pessimist fears that is true. Both are right. The late-twentieth-century West is the wealthiest, most democratic, freest, best equipped, fed, sheltered, medicated, corner of the globe, and of history. It shows little satisfaction with its situation. It produces more self-criticism than self-approval, its cultural products attest to this deflation, its cultural tone is less triumphant than it is dubious.

The individual used to be modeled by institutions; our institutions allegedly respond to individual needs. Coercion and self-discipline have given way to the cult of authenticity, social conformity to self-fulfillment, austerity to hedonism and free expression, uniformity to diversity, tragedy to maladjustment. Accumulation of wealth gives way to its enjoyment, and inculcation of social identity to self-discovery. Identity, now, is no longer social but individual. Affirming it, on the other hand, becomes a socially-conformist gesture. Far from applauding such mellowing, observers deplore it. They decry relaxation as apathy, self-expression as narcissism. Social controls, in this version, have simply become less explicit, intolerance more spongy and absorbent.

It does not matter whether such critics are right, since they are representative. Like surveys and statistics, commentaries of this sort do not claim to represent what is true, but what most believe, or feel, or guess. What most people want or think they want, like or think they like, matters while it lasts. Ours is the age of fads, fashion, caprice: playful, volatile, erratic.

In 1967 Martin Luther King pleaded for a change from a thing-oriented society to a person-oriented society. Twenty years later, things sit as firmly on the throne as they ever did. Whether counterculturing, ecologizing, opposing war or threats of war, asserting race or gender, success feels too much like failure to satisfy. The person-oriented society has spawned the me-generation, persuaded that no cause matters as much as myself, but willing to give any cause a try just as one tries new diets. The nature of fads is that they represent a mini-subversion of existing expectations, just like a miniskirt. But the craze they set off disturbs no institution, challenges no value, overturns no style. Offering change in continuity, whim without risk, fads do not perturb; they tranquilize. We function in a present that has become indifferent to the past. Naturally, it follows that our norms fluctuate, our judgments are as inconstant as our standards, our only consistency lies in our steadfast inconsistency.

Neutralized and banalized, the high questions of 1968 have been discarded in favor of jogging, ecology, and clean living. Postmodernism has given up causes for fads. In the 1990s, Futurism would be impossible, because the future is now. The essay that follows, by Russell Baker (1925–   ), is a testimony to that self-important trivialization, and to one more passing fad. Poet, biographer, social commentator, and winner of two Pulitzer Prizes, Baker is also a columnist for *The New York Times*.

Among the Puritans

It was a wedding reception. I was at the bar working on my third glass of ginger ale and gnawing a piece of carrot. At the buffet I had already eaten three pieces of celery and had switched to the carrot to be on the safe side.

You never know when you'll pick up a newspaper and find science has discovered celery causes cancer. A carrot is better anyhow if you're going to the bar. It's sort of like a cigarette, only orange and thicker, and what good is a bar without a cigarette?

Also you cannot look like a man with savoir-faire while eating celery at a bar.

I was drinking ginger ale because they say ginger ale has no caffeine. I don't know why caffeine is bad. America won World War II on caffeine. Also on cigarettes and hard whisky. All of which are now forbidden.

Standing at the bar, I wondered:

"Suppose Hitler had been born 50 years later: Would we now be Nazis because we're too health-conscious to ride the caffeine, whisky and cigarettes to victory the way we did in World War II?"

Source: Text by Russell Baker, "Among the Puritans," June 6, 1990. Copyright © 1990 by The New York Times Company. Reprinted by permission.

"Or," I wondered, "could we maybe have won without caffeine, tobacco and whisky? Not likely. America has since given up these vices and now needs 10 or 15 years just to get a new warplane off the drawing board, and even then you can't be sure it'll fly."

It felt wrong to be wondering like this at the bar. Bars are for brooding, or used to be when I was a child. In those days there were movies in which people sat in bars brooding so beautifully that I could hardly wait to become 21 so I could frequent bars and brood the years away.

Yes, shameful to say, I yearned to brood in bars just as young men today yearn to own German automobiles.

To the ginger-ale drinker beside me I said: "Did you ever think we'd live to see a day when American lads would rather own German cars than brood in bars?"

Instead of replying civilly he said: "You sound melancholy. Are you aware that you could be seriously depressed? You'd better see a psychiatrist."

This was the first indication I'd had that my being depressed might annoy people. I had deliberately decided to be melancholy because it seemed like something you could still get away with.

I hate to annoy people, and recently it had become harder and harder to avoid doing so. More and more, it seemed that people were going out of their way to find things to be annoyed about. More and more, they seemed eager to hop all over you and pummel you because they were annoyed by something you did every day of your life, or said, or wore, or thought.

"Look," I said to my companion in ginger ale, "I am attending a lavish wedding reception where no expense has been spared to provide gaiety. . . ."

"Exactly," said he. "Be happy."

". . . no expense spared to provide gaiety," I persisted. "Yet I cannot have a martini or two."

"I should hope not," he said.

"I cannot smoke."

"Socially reprehensible," he said. "In fact, it might provoke decent, right-thinking people to throw you out."

"I cannot eat the rich meats, the delicious cheeses or the thick creamy pastries available, but must instead gnaw on this rabbit food."

"Shows you're not one of those self-indulgent swine who inflate the national health-care bill by stuffing on killer foods."

"No caffeine."

"No civilized person uses such artificial stimulants anymore."

"Look around you," I said to him. "The room is filled with women of infinite beauty and great desirability, but I must refuse to look at them."

"And rightly so," he said. "Sex is over."

"So you see," I explained, "I have decided to be depressed. Until this very moment I'd thought that being depressed was the one thing a man could still do without having the full weight of American civilization crush him until he joins the Puritan movement."

"It won't do," said he, ordering another ginger ale. "It just won't do."

"I can't even be depressed?"

"If it really made you miserable, it might be permitted," he said, "but you are obviously enjoying it. The enjoyable is forbidden."

I have been very happy since and eat many carrots.

Cixous

The struggle for the emancipation of women goes back to the eighteenth century, when a few of the Enlightenment philosophers spoke out in favor of female emancipation: equal rights for women, equal status with men, freedom to decide what their own lives and careers should be like. But the French Revolution, which spurred a woman, Olympe de Gouges, to write a *Declaration of the Rights of Women,* was conducted by men. The revolutionaries looked to ancient Greece and Rome—both patriarchal societies—for inspiration. No less than existing prejudices, therefore, the laws that such models inspired restricted rather than liberated women. Nor did Romantic glorification improve their position. Milk-white lamb that bleats for man's protection, or dangerous, deceitful seductress, woman was a creature of feeling, not thought, of passion, not reason.

Through the nineteenth century, and especially after 1848, nascent Feminist movements in Europe and America made intermittent efforts to achieve equal rights and equal suffrage with men. But ruling stereotypes were too strong, even for most women. In 1898, Julia Daudet, widow of a well-known literary figure and a writer in her own right, glorified the French woman in an open letter to another writer, Juliette Adam, in which she trotted out many stereotypes that remained current until the day before yesterday. Woman was "serious and seductive, less educated than intuitive and sensitive, less mystical than traditional." Let her be served "a little more of the wine of science," and it will fuddle rather than fortify her. Study may be appropriate for a few specialists; it can only harm the majority, "for woman has her own task and end, which is to bring up children."

> Science is useless to women unless, exceptionally, they incline to male careers, and that's always a pity. . . . Women need not lead for all to give way before them. They guide and rule by the grace of their talent and their smiles. I cannot associate myself with feminist demands that I don't understand. Apart from the just concern of the workingwoman to control her earnings, and that of the mother to ensure the moral and material future of her children, everything else—excessive independence of ideas, pursuit of liberal careers, usurpation and intrusion of hospitals and courts

as intern or lawyer, all these seem like the fantasies and ambitions of women without heart, without household or children, who do not stop to think that, beyond their simple and useful tasks, they remain free to develop even their higher faculties.

By 1898, the date of Mme. Daudet's declarations, the movement for women's suffrage was forging ahead in England. The First World War brought gains to the cause there, in Germany, and in the United States (French women did not get the vote until 1944). It also acquired a notable recruit in the person of Virginia Woolf, daughter of Sir Leslie Stephen (see p. 520), whose essay *A Room of One's Own* (1929) became a classic of the Feminist movement. But the true emancipation of women did not begin until the 1970s, although its iconic manifestation appeared as early as 1949, in Simone de Beauvoir's *The Second Sex*. Like Jean-Paul Sartre, whose longtime intimate companion she was, Beauvoir affirmed the duty to accept the burdens of our existential freedom, and to treat our fellow-humans as personalities, not objects. She pointed out that the patriarchy that governs Western culture deals with women not as persons in their own right, but as Others: projections of male fantasies and needs, subject to male norms. Patriarchal culture denies freedom and responsibility to women, refuses to treat them as persons, deprives them of responsibility for their own personality and lives. Much has been written by and about women since *The Second Sex,* but Beauvoir articulated what still stands as the gist of Feminist argument.

The 1970s were to see Feminism take off, especially in English-speaking countries, inspiring a broad swathe of women's politics, studies, and criticism, raising the public's consciousness of female and male stereotypes, of the relations between prejudice and politics, between writing and gender, and helping to advance women's participation in all areas of life.

One aspect of this efflorescence has been the development of vested interests not only in Feminist enterprise as such (which would be normal), but also in particular variants of Feminism. Asserting the universality of women's struggle, for example, as a replay of other historical rebellions against dispossession threatens those organizations and groups, programs and departments of women's studies that have met masculine exclusion with a counter-exclusion of their own, refused to give in to "masculine rationality," and affirmed the uniqueness (and separateness) of womankind. Debatable and debated though this stance may be on philosophical grounds, regrettable though it may be from the point of view of men deprived of women's alliance in many a common cause, it fits well in the mood of a generation that seems to favor interest-group politics over more general ones (spurned as mere interest-group politics in disguise), and single-cause enterprises over wider ones. Sophisticated misopatry joins primitive misogyny in the arsenal of exclusionary tricks designed to present the Other as mysterious and threatening.

Hélène Cixous (1937–   ), who teaches and writes in Paris, is one of the most audible representatives of Feminist criticism in the autonomous vein. Cixous, who established the Center for Research in Feminine Studies in 1974, is fascinated by subversion and excess. She uses both to break through cultural stereotypes, brandishing poetry and politics intertwined as weapons of social liberation. Her *Laugh of the*

Medusa is a major manifesto of French Feminism. Cixous's essay, although of interest as part of the Poststructuralist debate, should be read, above all, in the context of ongoing discussions about whether "feminine" and "masculine" writing can be identified, whether masculine or feminine styles exist or provide a valid explanation of anything. For Cixous, standard and stereotyped polarizations like feminine-masculine are both wrongheaded and antifemale. It is not quite clear what she proposes instead, but, whatever it is, it is forcefully (and brilliantly) argued.

The Laugh of the Medusa

I shall speak about women's writing: about *what it will do*. Woman must write her self: must write about women and bring women to writing, from which they have been driven away as violently as from their bodies—for the same reasons, by the same law, with the same fatal goal. Woman must put herself into the text—as into the world and into history—by her own movement.

The future must no longer be determined by the past. I do not deny that the effects of the past are still with us. But I refuse to strengthen them by repeating them, to confer upon them an irremovability the equivalent of destiny, to confuse the biological and the cultural. Anticipation is imperative.

Since these reflections are taking shape in an area just on the point of being discovered, they necessarily bear the mark of our time—a time during which the new breaks away from the old, and, more precisely, the (feminine) new from the old *(la nouvelle de l'ancien)*. Thus, as there are no grounds for establishing a discourse, but rather an arid millennial ground to break, what I say has at least two sides and two aims: to break up, to destroy; and to foresee the unforeseeable, to project.

I write this as a woman, toward women. When I say "woman," I'm speaking of woman in her inevitable struggle against conventional man, and of a universal woman subject who must bring women to their senses and to their meaning in history. But first it must be said that in spite of the enormity of the repression that has kept them in the "dark"—that dark which people have been trying to make them accept as their attribute—there is, at this time, no general woman, no one typical woman. What they have *in common* I will say. But what strikes me is the infinite richness of their individual constitutions: you can't talk about *a* female sexuality, uniform, homogeneous, classifiable into codes—any more than you can talk about one unconscious resembling another. Women's imaginary is inexhaustible, like music, painting, writing: their stream of phantasms is incredible.

Source: From *Signs,* I, 4, Summer 1976, translated by K. Cohen and P. Cohen. Reprinted by permission of The University of Chicago Press.

I have been amazed more than once by a description a woman gave me of a world all her own which she had been secretly haunting since early childhood. A world of searching, the elaboration of a knowledge, on the basis of a systematic experimentation with the bodily functions, a passionate and precise interrogation of her erotogeneity. This practice, extraordinarily rich and inventive, in particular as concerns masturbation, is prolonged or accompanied by a production of forms, a veritable aesthetic activity, each stage of rapture inscribing a resonant vision, a composition, something beautiful. Beauty will no longer be forbidden.

I wished that that woman would write and proclaim this unique empire so that other women, other unacknowledged sovereigns, might exclaim: I, too, overflow; my desires have invented new desires, my body knows unheard-of songs. Time and again I, too, have felt so full of luminous torrents that I could burst—burst with forms much more beautiful than those which are put up in frames and sold for a stinking fortune. And I, too, said nothing, showed nothing; I didn't open my mouth, I didn't repaint my half of the world. I was ashamed. I was afraid, and I swallowed my shame and my fear. I said to myself: You are mad! What's the meaning of these waves, these floods, these outbursts? Where is the ebullient, infinite woman who, immersed as she was in her naiveté, kept in the dark about herself, led into self-disdain by the great arm of parental-conjugal phallocentrism, hasn't been ashamed of her strength? Who, surprised and horrified by the fantastic tumult of her drives (for she was made to believe that a well-adjusted normal woman has a . . . divine composure), hasn't accused herself of being a monster? Who, feeling a funny desire stirring inside her (to sing, to write, to dare to speak, in short, to bring out something new), hasn't thought she was sick? Well, her shameful sickness is that she resists death, that she makes trouble.

And why don't you write? Write! Writing is for you, you are for you; your body is yours, take it. I know why you haven't written. (And why I didn't write before the age of twenty-seven.) Because writing is at once too high, too great for you, it's reserved for the great—that is, for "great men"; and it's "silly." Besides, you've written a little, but in secret. And it wasn't good, because it was in secret, and because you punished yourself for writing, because you didn't go all the way; or because you wrote, irresistibly, as when we would masturbate in secret, not to go further, but to attenuate the tension a bit, just enough to take the edge off. And then as soon as we come, we go and make ourselves feel guilty—so as to be forgiven; or to forget, to bury it until the next time.

Write, let no one hold you back, let nothing stop you: not man; not the imbecilic capitalist machinery, in which publishing houses are the crafty, obsequious relayers of imperatives handed down by an economy that works against us and off our backs; and not *yourself.* Smug-faced readers, managing editors, and big bosses don't like the true texts of women—female-sexed texts. That kind scares them.

I write woman: woman must write woman. And man, man. So only an oblique consideration will be found here of man; it's up to him to say where his masculinity and femininity are at: this will concern us once men have opened their eyes and seen themselves clearly.[1]

Now women return from afar, from always: from "without," from the heath where witches are kept alive; from below, from beyond "culture"; from their childhood which men have been trying desperately to make them forget, condemning it to "eternal rest." The little girls and their "ill-mannered" bodies immured, well-preserved, intact unto themselves, in the mirror. Frigidified. But are they ever seething underneath! What an effort it takes—there's no end to it—for the sex cops to bar their threatening return. Such a display of forces on both sides that the struggle has for centuries been immobilized in the trembling equilibrium of a deadlock.

Here they are, returning, arriving over and again, because the unconscious is impregnable. They have wandered around in circles, confined to the narrow room in which they've been given a deadly brainwashing. You can incarcerate them, slow them down, get away with the old Apartheid routine, but for a time only. As soon as they begin to speak, at the same time as they're taught their name, they can be taught that their territory is black: because you are Africa, you are black. Your continent is dark. Dark is dangerous. You can't see anything in the dark, you're afraid. Don't move, you might fall. Most of all, don't go into the forest. And so we have internalized this horror of the dark.

Men have committed the greatest crime against women. Insidiously, violently, they have led them to hate women, to be their own enemies, to mobilize their immense strength against themselves, to be the executants of their virile needs. They have made for women an antinarcissism! A narcissism

---

[1]Men still have everything to say about their sexuality, and everything to write. For what they have said so far, for the most part, stems from the opposition activity/passivity, from the power relation between a fantasized obligatory virility meant to invade, to colonize, and the consequential phantasm of woman as a "dark continent" to penetrate and to "pacify." (We know what "pacify" means in terms of scotomizing the other and misrecognizing the self.) Conquering her, they've made haste to depart from her borders, to get out of sight, out of body. The way man has of getting out of himself and into her whom he takes not for the other but for his own, deprives him, he knows, of his own bodily territory. One can understand how man, confusing himself with his penis and rushing in for the attack, might feel resentment and fear of being "taken" by the woman, of being lost in her, absorbed, or alone.

which loves itself only to be loved for what women haven't got! They have constructed the infamous logic of antilove.

We the precocious, we the repressed of culture, our lovely mouths gagged with pollen, our wind knocked out of us, we the labyrinths, the ladders, the trampled spaces, the bevies—we are black and we are beautiful. . . .

From now on, who, if we say so, can say no to us? We've come back from always.

It is time to liberate the New Woman from the Old by coming to know her—by loving her for getting by, for getting beyond the Old without delay, by going out ahead of what the New Woman will be, as an arrow quits the bow with a movement that gathers and separates the vibrations musically, in order to be more than her self.

I say that we must, for, with a few rare exceptions, there has not yet been any writing that inscribes femininity; exceptions so rare, in fact, that, after plowing through literature across languages, cultures, and ages,[2] one can only be startled at this vain scouting mission. It is well known that the number of women writers (while having increased very slightly from the nineteenth century on) has always been ridiculously small. This is a useless and deceptive fact unless from their species of female writers we do not first deduct the immense majority whose workmanship is in no way different from male writing, and which either obscures women or reproduces the classic representations of women (as sensitive—intuitive—dreamy, etc.).[3]

Let me insert here a parenthetical remark. I mean it when I speak of male writing. I maintain unequivocally that there is such a thing as *marked* writing; that, until now, far more extensively and repressively than is ever suspected or admitted, writing has been run by a libidinal and cultural—hence political, typically masculine—economy; that this is a locus where the repression of women has been perpetuated, over and over, more or less consciously, and in a manner that's frightening since it's often hidden or adorned with the mystifying charms of fiction; that this locus has grossly exaggerated all the signs of sexual opposition (and not sexual difference), where woman has never *her* turn to speak—this being all the more serious and unpardonable in that writing is precisely *the very possibility of change,* the space that can serve

---

[2] I am speaking here only of the place "reserved" for women by the Western world.

[3] Which works, then, might be called feminine? I'll just point out some examples: one would have to give them full readings to bring out what is pervasively feminine in their significance. Which I shall do elsewhere. In France (have you noted our infinite poverty in this field?—the Anglo-Saxon countries have shown resources of distinctly greater consequence), leafing through what's come out of the twentieth century—and it's not much—the only inscriptions of femininity that I have seen were by Colette, Marguerite Duras, . . . and Jean Genêt.

as a springboard for subversive thought, the precursory movement of a transformation of social and cultural structures.

Nearly the entire history of writing is confounded with the history of reason, of which it is at once the effect, the support, and one of the privileged
alibis. It has been one with the phallocentric tradition. It is indeed that same
self-admiring, self-stimulating, self-congratulatory phallocentrism.

With some exceptions, for there have been failures—and if it weren't for
them, I wouldn't be writing (I-woman, escapee)—in that enormous machine
that has been operating and turning out its "truth" for centuries. There have
been poets who would go to any lengths to slip something by at odds with
tradition—men capable of loving love and hence capable of loving others and
of wanting them, of imagining the woman who would hold out against
oppression and constitute herself as a superb, equal, hence "impossible" subject, untenable in a real social framework. Such a woman the poet could
desire only by breaking the codes that negate her. Her appearance would
necessarily bring on, if not revolution—for the bastion was supposed to be
immutable—at least harrowing explosions. . . .

But only the poets—not the novelists, allies of representationalism. Because poetry involves gaining strength through the unconscious and because
the unconscious, that other limitless country, is the place where the repressed
manage to survive: women, or as Hoffmann would say, fairies.

She must write her self, because this is the invention of a *new insurgent*
writing which, when the moment of her liberation has come, will allow her
to carry out the indispensable ruptures and transformations in her history,
first at two levels that cannot be separated.

a) Individually. By writing her self, woman will return to the body which
has been more than confiscated from her, which has been turned into the
uncanny stranger on display—the ailing or dead figure, which so often turns
out to be the nasty companion, the cause and location of inhibitions. Censor
the body and you censor breath and speech at the same time.

Write your self. Your body must be heard. Only then will the immense
resources of the unconscious spring forth. Our naphtha will spread, throughout the world, without dollars—black or gold—nonassessed values that will
change the rules of the old game.

To write. An act which will not only "realize" the decensored relation of
woman to her sexuality, to her womanly being, giving her access to her native
strength; it will give her back her goods, her pleasures, her organs, her immense bodily territories which have been kept under seal; it will tear her away
from the superegoized structure in which she has always occupied the place

reserved for the guilty (guilty of everything, guilty at every turn: for having desires, for not having any; for being frigid, for being "too hot"; for not being both at once; for being too motherly and not enough; for having children and for not having any; for nursing and for not nursing . . .)—tear her away by means of this research, this job of analysis and illumination, this emancipation of the marvelous text of her self that she must urgently learn to speak. A woman without a body, dumb, blind, can't possibly be a good fighter. She is reduced to being the servant of the militant male, his shadow. We must kill the false woman who is preventing the live one from breathing. Inscribe the breath of the whole woman.

b) An act that will also be marked by woman's *seizing* the occasion to *speak*, hence her shattering entry into history, which has always been based *on her suppression*. To write and thus to forge for herself the antilogos weapon. To become *at will* the taker and initiator, for her own right, in every symbolic system, in every political process.

It is time for women to start scoring their feats in written and oral language.

Every woman has known the torment of getting up to speak. Her heart racing, at times entirely lost for words, ground and language slipping away— that's how daring a feat, how great a transgression it is for a woman to speak—even just open her mouth—in public. A double distress, for even if she transgresses, her words fall almost always upon the deaf male ear, which hears in language only that which speaks in the masculine.

It is by writing, from and toward women, and by taking up the challenge of speech which has been governed by the phallus, that women will confirm women in a place other than that which is reserved in and by the symbolic, that is, in a place other than silence. Women should break out of the snare of silence. They shouldn't be conned into accepting a domain which is the margin or the harem.

Listen to a woman speak at a public gathering (if she hasn't painfully lost her wind). She doesn't "speak," she throws her trembling body forward; she lets go of herself, she flies; all of her passes into her voice, and it's with her body that she vitally supports the "logic" of her speech. Her flesh speaks true. She lays herself bare. In fact, she physically materializes what she's thinking; she signifies it with her body. In a certain way she *inscribes* what she's saying, because she doesn't deny her drives the intractable and impassioned part they have in speaking. Her speech, even when "theoretical" or political, is never simple or linear or "objectified," generalized: she draws her story into history.

There is not that scission, that division made by the common man between the logic of oral speech and the logic of the text, bound as he is by his antiquated relation—servile, calculating—to mastery. From which proceeds the niggardly lip service which engages only the tiniest part of the body, plus the mask.

In women's speech, as in their writing, that element which never stops resonating, which, once we've been permeated by it, profoundly and imperceptibly touched by it, retains the power of moving us—that element is the song: first music from the first voice of love which is alive in every woman. Why this privileged relationship with the voice? Because no woman stockpiles as many defenses for countering the drives as does a man. You don't build walls around yourself, you don't forego pleasure as "wisely" as he. Even if phallic mystification has generally contaminated good relationships, a woman is never far from "mother" (I mean outside her role functions: the "mother" as nonname and as source of goods). There is always within her at least a little of that good mother's milk. She writes in white ink.

Woman for women.—There always remains in woman that force which produces/is produced by the other—in particular, the other woman. *In* her, matrix, cradler; herself giver as her mother and child; she is her own sister-daughter. You might object, "What about she who is the hysterical offspring of a bad mother?" Everything will be changed once woman gives woman to the other woman. There is hidden and always ready in woman the source; the locus for the other. The mother, too, is a metaphor. It is necessary and sufficient that the best of herself be given to woman by another woman for her to be able to love herself and return in love the body that was "born" to her. Touch me, caress me, you the living no-name, give me my self as myself. The relation to the "mother," in terms of intense pleasure and violence, is curtailed no more than the relation to childhood (the child that she was, that she is, that she makes, remakes, undoes, there at the point where, the same, she others herself). Text: my body—shot through with streams of song; I don't mean the overbearing, clutchy "mother" but, rather, what touches you, the equivoice that affects you, fills your breast with an urge to come to language and launches your force; the rhythm that laughs you; the intimate recipient who makes all metaphors possible and desirable; body (body? bodies?), no more describable than god, the soul, or the Other; that part of you that leaves a space between yourself and urges you to inscribe in language your woman's style. In women there is always more or less of the mother who makes everything all right, who nourishes, and who stands up against separation; a force that will not be cut off but will knock the wind out of the codes. We will rethink womankind beginning with every form and every period of her body. The Americans remind us, "We are all Lesbians"; that is, don't denigrate woman, don't make of her what men have made of you.

Because the "economy" of her drives is prodigious, she cannot fail, in seizing the occasion to speak, to transform directly and indirectly *all* systems of exchange based on masculine thrift. Her libido will produce far more radical effects of political and social change than some might like to think.

Because she arrives, vibrant, over and again, we are at the beginning of a new history, or rather of a process of becoming in which several histories intersect with one another. As subject for history, woman always occurs simultaneously in several places. Woman un-thinks[4] the unifying, regulating history that homogenizes and channels forces, herding contradictions into a single battlefield. In woman, personal history blends together with the history of all women, as well as national and world history. As a militant, she is an integral part of all liberations. She must be farsighted, not limited to a blow-by-blow interaction. She foresees that her liberation will do more than modify power relations or toss the ball over to the other camp; she will bring about a mutation in human relations, in thought, in all praxis: hers is not simply a class struggle, which she carries forward into a much vaster movement. Not that in order to be a woman-in-struggle(s) you have to leave the class struggle or repudiate it; but you have to split it open, spread it out, push it forward, fill it with the fundamental struggle so as to prevent the class struggle, or any other struggle for the liberation of a class or people, from operating as a form of repression, pretext for postponing the inevitable, the staggering alteration in power relations and in the production of individualities. This alteration is already upon us—in the United States, for example, where millions of night crawlers are in the process of undermining the family and disintegrating the whole of American sociality.

The new history is coming; it's not a dream, though it does extend beyond men's imagination, and for good reason. It's going to deprive them of their conceptual orthopedics, beginning with the destruction of their enticement machine.

It is impossible to *define* a feminine practice of writing, and this is an impossibility that will remain, for this practice can never be theorized, enclosed, coded—which doesn't mean that it doesn't exist. But it will always surpass the discourse that regulates the phallocentric system; it does and will take place in areas other than those subordinated to philosophico-theoretical domination. It will be conceived of only by subjects who are breakers of automatisms, by peripheral figures that no authority can ever subjugate.

---

[4]"*Dé-pense*," a neologism formed on the verb *penser*, hence "unthinks," but also "spends" (from *dépenser*) [translator's note].

Hence the necessity to affirm the flourishes of this writing, to give form to its movement, its near and distant byways. Bear in mind to begin with (1) that sexual opposition, which has always worked for man's profit to the point of reducing writing, too, to his laws, is only a historico-cultural limit. There is, there will be more and more rapidly pervasive now, a fiction that produces irreducible effects of femininity. (2) That it is through ignorance that most readers, critics, and writers of both sexes hesitate to admit or deny outright the possibility or the pertinence of a distinction between feminine and masculine writing. It will usually be said, thus disposing of sexual difference: either that all writing, to the extent that it materializes, is feminine; or, inversely—but it comes to the same thing—that the act of writing is equivalent to masculine masturbation (and so the woman who writes cuts herself out a paper penis); or that writing is bisexual, hence neuter, which again does away with differentiation. To admit that writing is precisely working [in] the in-between, inspecting the process of the same and of the other without which nothing can live, undoing the work of death—to admit this is first to want the two, as well as both, the ensemble of the one and the other, not fixed in sequences of struggle and expulsion or some other form of death but infinitely dynamized by an incessant process of exchange from one subject to another. A process of different subjects knowing one another and beginning one another anew only from the living boundaries of the other: a multiple and inexhaustible course with millions of encounters and transformations of the same into the other and into the in-between, from which woman takes her forms (and man, in his turn; but that's his other history).

In saying "bisexual, hence neuter," I am referring to the classic conception of bisexuality, which, squashed under the emblem of castration fear and along with the fantasy of a "total" being (though composed of two halves), would do away with the difference experienced as an operation incurring loss, as the mark of dreaded sectility.

To this self-effacing, merger-type bisexuality, which would conjure away castration (the writer who puts up his sign: "bisexual written here, come and see," when the odds are good that it's neither one nor the other), I oppose the *other bisexuality* on which every subject not enclosed in the false theater of phallocentric representationalism has founded his/her erotic universe. Bisexuality: that is, each one's location in self (*repérage en soi*) of the presence—variously manifest and insistent according to each person, male or female—of both sexes, nonexclusion either of the difference or of one sex, and, from this "self-permission," multiplication of the effects of the inscription of desire, over all parts of my body and the other body.

Now it happens that at present, for historico-cultural reasons, it is women who are opening up to and benefiting from this vatic bisexuality which doesn't annul differences but stirs them up, pursues them, increases their number. In a certain way, "woman is bisexual"; man—it's a secret to no one—being poised to keep glorious phallic monosexuality in view. By virtue of affirming the primacy of the phallus and of bringing it into play, phallocratic ideology has claimed more than one victim. As a woman, I've been clouded over by the great shadow of the scepter and been told: idolize it, that which you cannot brandish. But at the same time, man has been handed that grotesque and scarcely enviable destiny (just imagine) of being reduced to a single idol with clay balls. And consumed, as Freud and his followers note, by a fear of being a woman! For, if psychoanalysis was constituted from woman, to repress femininity (and not so successful a repression at that—men have made it clear), its account of masculine sexuality is now hardly refutable; as with all the "human" sciences, it reproduces the masculine view, of which it is one of the effects.

Here we encounter the inevitable man-with-rock, standing erect in his old Freudian realm, in the way that, to take the figure back to the point where linguistics is conceptualizing it "anew," Lacan preserves it in the sanctuary of the phallos (φ) "sheltered" from *castration's lack!* Their "symbolic" exists, it holds power—we, the sowers of disorder, know it only too well. But we are in no way obliged to deposit our lives in their banks of lack, to consider the constitution of the subject in terms of a drama manglingly restaged, to reinstate again and again the religion of the father. Because we don't want that. We don't fawn around the supreme hole. We have no womanly reason to pledge allegiance to the negative. The feminine (as the poets suspected) affirms: ". . . And yes," says Molly, carrying *Ulysses* off beyond any book and toward the new writing; "I said yes, I will Yes."

The Dark Continent is neither dark nor unexplorable.—It is still unexplored only because we've been made to believe that it was too dark to be explorable. And because they want to make us believe that what interests us is the white continent, with its monuments to Lack. And we believed. They riveted us between two horrifying myths: between the Medusa and the abyss. That would be enough to set half the world laughing, except that it's still going on. For the phallologocentric sublation[5] is with us, and it's militant, regenerating the old patterns, anchored in the dogma of castration. They haven't changed a thing: they've theorized their desire for reality! Let the priests tremble, we're going to show them our sexts!

Too bad for them if they fall apart upon discovering that women aren't men, or that the mother doesn't have one. But isn't this fear convenient for

---

[5]Standard English term for the Hegelian *Aufhebung,* the French *la relève.*

them? Wouldn't the worst be, isn't the worst, in truth, that women aren't castrated, that they have only to stop listening to the Sirens (for the Sirens were men) for history to change its meaning? You only have to look at the Medusa straight on to see her. And she's not deadly. She's beautiful and she's laughing.

Men say that there are two unrepresentable things: death and the feminine sex. That's because they need femininity to be associated with death; it's the jitters that gives them a hard-on! for themselves! They need to be afraid of us. Look at the trembling Perseuses moving backward toward us, clad in apotropes. What lovely backs! Not another minute to lose. Let's get out of here.

Let's hurry: the continent is not impenetrably dark. I've been there often, I was overjoyed one day to run into Jean Genêt. It was in *Pompes funèbres*.[6] He had come there led by his Jean. There are some men (all too few) who aren't afraid of femininity.

Almost everything is yet to be written by women about femininity: about their sexuality, that is, its infinite and mobile complexity, about their eroticization, sudden turn-ons of a certain miniscule-immense area of their bodies; not about destiny, but about the adventure of such and such a drive, about trips, crossings, trudges, abrupt and gradual awakenings, discoveries of a zone at one time timorous and soon to be forthright. A woman's body, with its thousand and one thresholds of ardor—once, by smashing yokes and censors, she lets it articulate the profusion of meanings that run through it in every direction—will make the old single-grooved mother tongue reverberate with more than one language.

We've been turned away from our bodies, shamefully taught to ignore them, to strike them with that stupid sexual modesty; we've been made victims of the old fool's game: each one will love the other sex. I'll give you your body and you'll give me mine. But who are the men who give women the body that women blindly yield to them? Why so few texts? Because so few women have as yet won back their body. Women must write through their bodies, they must invent the impregnable language that will wreck partitions, classes, and rhetorics, regulations and codes, they must submerge, cut through, get beyond the ultimate reserve-discourse, including the one that laughs at the very idea of pronouncing the word "silence," the one that, aiming for the impossible, stops short before the word "impossible" and writes it as "the end."

Such is the strength of women that, sweeping away syntax, breaking that famous thread (just a tiny little thread, they say) which acts for men as a

---

[6]Jean Genêt, *Pompes funèbres* (Paris, 1948), p. 185.

surrogate umbilical cord, assuring them—otherwise they couldn't come—
that the old lady is always right behind them, watching them make phallus,
women will go right up to the impossible.

When the "repressed" of their culture and their society return, it's an explosive, *utterly* destructive, staggering return, with a force never yet unleashed and equal to the most forbidding of suppressions. For when the Phallic period comes to an end, women will have been either annihilated or borne
up to the highest and most violent incandescence. Muffled throughout their
history, they have lived in dreams, in bodies (though muted), in silences, in
aphonic revolts.

And with such force in their fragility; a fragility, a vulnerability, equal to
their incomparable intensity. Fortunately, they haven't sublimated; they've
saved their skin, their energy. They haven't worked at liquidating the impasse
of lives without futures. They have furiously inhabited these sumptuous bodies: admirable hysterics who made Freud succumb to many voluptuous moments impossible to confess, bombarding his Mosaic statue with their carnal
and passionate body words, haunting him with their inaudible and thunder-
ing denunciations, dazzling, more than naked underneath the seven veils of
modesty. Those who, with a single word of the body, have inscribed the
vertiginous immensity of a history which is sprung like an arrow from the
whole history of men and from biblico-capitalist society, are the women,
the supplicants of yesterday, who come as forebears of the new women, after
whom no intersubjective relation will ever be the same. You, Dora, you the
indomitable, the poetic body, you are the true "mistress" of the Signifier.
Before long your efficacity will be seen at work when your speech is no longer
suppressed, its point turned in against your breast, but written out over
against the other.

In body.—More so than men who are coaxed toward social success, toward
sublimation, women are body. More body, hence more writing. For a long
time it has been in body that women have responded to persecution, to the
familial-conjugal enterprise of domestication, to the repeated attempts at castrating them. Those who have turned their tongues 10,000 times seven times
before not speaking are either dead from it or more familiar with their
tongues and their mouths than anyone else. Now, I-woman am going to
blow up the Law: an explosion henceforth possible and ineluctable; let it be
done, right now, *in* language.

Let us not be trapped by an analysis still encumbered with the old automatisms. It's not to be feared that language conceals an invincible adversary,
because it's the language of men and their grammar. We mustn't leave them
a single place that's any more theirs alone than we are.

If woman has always functioned "within" the discourse of man, a signifier that has always referred back to the opposite signifier which annihilates its specific energy and diminishes or stifles its very different sounds, it is time for her to dislocate this "within," to explode it, turn it around, and seize it; to make it hers, containing it, taking it in her own mouth, biting that tongue with her very own teeth to invent for herself a language to get inside of. And you'll see what ease she will spring forth from that "within"—the "within" where once she so drowsily crouched—to overflow at the lips she will cover the foam.

Nor is the point to appropriate their instruments, their concepts, their places, or to begrudge them their position of mastery. Just because there's a risk of identification doesn't mean that we'll succumb. Let's leave it to the worriers, to masculine anxiety and its obsession with how to dominate the way things work—knowing "how it works" in order to "make it work." For us the point is not to take possession in order to internalize or manipulate, but rather to dash through and to "fly."[7]

Flying is woman's gesture—flying in language and making it fly. We have all learned the art of flying and its numerous techniques; for centuries we've been able to possess anything only by flying; we've lived in flight, stealing away, finding, when desired, narrow passageways, hidden crossovers. It's no accident that *voler* has a double meaning, that it plays on each of them and thus throws off the agents of sense. It's no accident: women take after birds and robbers just as robbers take after women and birds. They *(illes)*[8] go by, fly the coop, take pleasure in jumbling the order of space, in disorienting it, in changing around the furniture, dislocating things and values, breaking them all up, emptying structures, and turning propriety upside down.

What woman hasn't flown/stolen? Who hasn't felt, dreamt, performed the gesture that jams sociality? Who hasn't crumbled, held up to ridicule, the bar of separation? Who hasn't inscribed with her body the differential, punctured the system of couples and opposition? Who, by some act of transgression, hasn't overthrown successiveness, connection, the wall of circumfusion?

A feminine text cannot fail to be more than subversive. It is volcanic; as it is written it brings about an upheaval of the old property crust, carrier of masculine investments; there's no other way. There's no room for her if she's not a he. If she's a her-she, it's in order to smash everything, to shatter the framework of institutions, to blow up the law, to break up the "truth" with laughter.

---

[7]Also, "to steal." Both meanings of the verb *voler* are played on, as the text itself explains in the following paragraph [translator's note].

[8]*Illes* is a fusion of the masculine pronoun *ils,* which refers back to birds and robbers, with the feminine pronoun *elles,* which refers to women [translator's note].

For once she blazes *her* trail in the symbolic, she cannot fail to make of it the chaosmos of the "personal"—in her pronouns, her nouns, and her clique of referents. And for good reason. There will have been the long history of gynocide. This is known by the colonized peoples of yesterday, the workers, the nations, the species off whose backs the history of men has made its gold; those who have known the ignominy of persecution derive from it an obstinate future desire for grandeur; those who are locked up know better than their jailers the taste of free air. Thanks to their history, women today know (how to do and want) what men will be able to conceive of only much later. I say woman overturns the "personal," for if, by means of laws, lies, blackmail, and marriage, her right to herself has been extorted at the same time as her name, she has been able, through the very movement of mortal alienation, to see more closely the inanity of "propriety," the reductive stinginess of the masculine-conjugal subjective economy, which she doubly resists. On the one hand she has constituted herself necessarily as that "person" capable of losing a part of herself without losing her integrity. But secretly, silently, deep down inside, she grows and multiplies, for, on the other hand, she knows far more about living and about the relation between the economy of the drives and the management of the ego than any man. Unlike man, who holds so dearly to his title and his titles, his pouches of value, his cap, crown, and everything connected with his head, woman couldn't care less about the fear of decapitation (or castration), adventuring, without the masculine temerity, into anonymity, which she can merge with without annihilating herself: because she's a giver.

I shall have a great deal to say about the whole deceptive problematic of the gift. Woman is obviously not that woman Nietzsche dreamed of who gives only in order to.[9] Who could ever think of the gift as a gift-that-takes? Who else but man, precisely the one who would like to take everything?

If there is a "propriety of woman," it is paradoxically her capacity to depropriate unselfishly: body without end, without appendage, without principal "parts." If she is a whole, it's a whole composed of parts that are wholes, not simple partial objects but a moving, limitlessly changing ensemble, a cosmos tirelessly traversed by Eros, an immense astral space not organized around any one sun that's any more of a star than the others. . . .

. . . She alone dares and wishes to know from within, where she, the out-

---

[9]Reread Derrida's text, "Le Style de la femme," in *Nietzsche aujourd'hui* (Paris: Union Générale d'Editions, Coll. 10/18), where the philosopher can be seen operating an *Aufhebung* of all philosophy in its systematic reducing of woman to the place of seduction: she appears as the one who is taken for; the bait in person, all veils unfurled, the one who doesn't give but who gives only in order to (take).

cast, has never ceased to hear the resonance of fore-language. She lets the other language speak—the language of 1,000 tongues which knows neither enclosure nor death. To life she refuses nothing. Her language does not contain, it carries; it does not hold back, it makes possible. When id is ambiguously uttered—the wonder of being several—she doesn't defend herself against these unknown women whom she's surprised at becoming, but derives pleasure from this gift of alterability. I am spacious, singing flesh, on which is grafted no one knows which I, more or less human, but alive because of transformation.

Write! and your self-seeking text will know itself better than flesh and blood, rising, insurrectionary dough kneading itself, with sonorous, perfumed ingredients, a lively combination of flying colors, leaves, and rivers plunging into the sea we feed. "Ah, there's her sea," he will say as he holds out to me a basin full of water from the little phallic mother from whom he's inseparable. But look, our seas are what we make of them, full of fish or not, opaque or transparent, red or black, high or smooth, narrow or bankless; and we are ourselves sea, sand, coral, seaweed, beaches, tides, swimmers, children, waves. . . . More or less wavily sea, earth, sky—what matter would rebuff us? We know how to speak them all.

Heterogeneous, yes. For her joyous benefit she is erogenous; she is the erotogeneity of the heterogeneous: airborne swimmer, in flight, she does not cling to herself; she is dispersible, prodigious, stunning, desirous and capable of others, of the other woman that she will be, of the other woman she isn't, of him, of you.

Woman be unafraid of any other place, of any same, or any other. My eyes, my tongue, my ears, my nose, my skin, my mouth, my body-for-(the)-other—not that I long for it in order to fill up a hole, to provide against some defect of mine, or because, as fate would have it, I'm spurred on by feminine "jealousy"; not because I've been dragged into the whole chain of substitutions that brings that which is substituted back to its ultimate object. That sort of thing you would expect to come straight out of "Tom Thumb," out of the *Penisneid* whispered to us by old grandmother ogresses, servants to their father-sons. If they believe, in order to muster up some self-importance, if they really need to believe that we're dying of desire, that we are this hole fringed with desire for their penis—that's their immemorial business. Undeniably (we verify it at our own expense—but also to our amusement), it's their business to let us know they're getting a hard-on, so that we'll assure them (we the maternal mistresses of their little pocket signifier) that they still can, that it's still there—that men structure themselves only by being fitted with a feather. In the child it's not the penis that the woman desires, it's not that famous bit of skin around which every man gravitates. Pregnancy cannot be traced back, except within the historical limits of the ancients, to some form of fate, to those mechanical substitutions brought about by the unconscious of some eternal "jealous woman"; not to penis envies; and not to narcissism or to some sort of homosexuality linked to the ever-present mother! Begetting a child doesn't mean that the woman or the man must fall ineluctably into patterns or must recharge the circuit of reproduction. If there's a risk there's not an inevitable trap: may women be spared the pressure, under the guise of consciousness-raising, of a supplement of interdictions. Either you want a kid or you don't—*that's your business*. Let nobody threaten you; in satisfying your desire, let not the fear of becoming the accomplice to a sociality succeed the old-time fear of being "taken." And man, are you still going to bank on everyone's blindness and passivity, afraid lest the child make a father and, consequently, that in having a kid the woman land herself more than one bad deal by engendering all at once child—mother—father—family? No; it's up to you to break the old circuits. It will be up to man and woman to render obsolete the former relationship and all its consequences, to consider the launching of a brand-new subject, alive, with defamilialization. Let us demater-paternalize rather than deny woman, in an effort to avoid the co-optation of procreation, a thrilling era of the body. Let us defetishize. Let's get away from the dialectic which has it that the only good father is a dead one, or that the child is the death of his parents. The child is the other, but the other without violence, bypassing loss, struggle. We're fed up with the reuniting of bonds forever to be severed, with the litany of castration that's handed down and genealogized. We won't advance backward anymore; we're not going to repress something so simple as the desire for life. Oral drive, anal drive, vocal drive—all these drives are our strengths, and among them is the gestation drive—just like the desire to write: a desire to live self from within, a desire for the swollen belly, for language, for blood. We are not going to refuse, if it should happen to strike our fancy, the unsurpassed pleasures of pregnancy which have actually been always exaggerated or conjured away—or cursed—in the classic texts. For if there's one thing that's been repressed here's just the place to find it: in the taboo of the pregnant woman. This says a lot about the power she seems invested with at the time, because it has always been suspected, that, when pregnant, the woman not only doubles her market value, but—what's more important—takes on intrinsic value as a woman in her own eyes and, undeniably, acquires body and sex.

There are thousands of ways of living one's pregnancy; to have or not to have with that still invisible other a relationship of another intensity. And if you don't have that particular yearning, it doesn't mean that you're in any way lacking. Each body distributes in its own special way, without model or norm, the nonfinite and changing totality of its desires. Decide for yourself on your position in the arena of contradictions, where pleasure and reality embrace. Bring the other to life. Women know how to live detachment; giving birth is neither losing nor increasing. It's adding to life an other. Am I dreaming? Am I mis-recognizing? You, the defenders of "theory," the sacrosanct yes-men of Concept, enthroners of the phallus (but not of the penis):

Once more you'll say that all this smacks of "idealism," or what's worse, you'll sputter that I'm a "mystic."

And what about the libido? Haven't I read the "Signification of the Phallus"? And what about separation, what about that bit of self for which, to be born, you undergo an ablation—an ablation, so they say, to be forever commemorated by your desire?

Besides, isn't it evident that the penis gets around in my texts, that I give it a place and appeal? Of course I do. I want all. I want all of me with all of him. Why should I deprive myself of a part of us? I want all of us. Woman of course has a desire for a "loving desire" and not a jealous one. But not because she is gelded; not because she's deprived and needs to be filled out, like some wounded person who wants to console herself or seek vengeance: I don't want a penis to decorate my body with. But I do desire the other for the other, whole and entire, male or female; because living means wanting everything that is, everything that lives, and wanting it alive. Castration? Let others toy with it. What's a desire originating from a lack? A pretty meager desire.

The woman who still allows herself to be threatened by the big dick, who's still impressed by the commotion of the phallic stance, who still leads a loyal master to the beat of the drum: that's the woman of yesterday. They still exist, easy and numerous victims of the oldest of farces: either they're cast in the original silent version in which, as titanesses lying under the mountains they make with their quivering, they never see erected that theoretic monument to the golden phallus looming, in the old manner, over their bodies. Or, coming today out of their *infans* period and into the second, "enlightened" version of their virtuous debasement, they see themselves suddenly assaulted by the builders of the analytic empire and, as soon as they've begun to formulate the new desire, naked, nameless, so happy at making an appearance, they're taken in their bath by the new old men, and then, whoops! Luring them with flashy signifiers, the demon of interpretation—oblique, decked out in modernity—sells them the same old handcuffs, baubles, and chains. Which castration do you prefer? Whose degrading do you like better, the father's or the mother's? Oh, what pwetty eyes, you pwetty little girl. Here, buy my glasses and you'll see the Truth-Me-Myself tell you everything you should know. Put them on your nose and take a fetishist's look (you are me, the other analyst—that's what I'm telling you) at your body and the body of the other. You see? No? Wait, you'll have everything explained to you, and you'll know at last which sort of neurosis you're related to. Hold still, we're going to do your portrait, so that you can begin looking like it right away.

Yes, the naives to the first and second degree are still legion. If the New Women, arriving now, dare to create outside the theoretical, they're called in by the cops of the signifier, fingerprinted, remonstrated, and brought into the line of order that they are supposed to know; assigned by force of trickery to a precise place in the chain that's always formed for the benefit of a privileged signifier. We are pieced back to the string which leads back, if not to the Name-of-the-Father, then, for a new twist, to the place of the phallic-mother.

Beware, my friend, of the signifier that would take you back to the authority of a signified! Beware of diagnoses that would reduce your generative powers. "Common" nouns are also proper nouns that disparage your singularity by classifying it into species. Break out of the circles; don't remain within the psychoanalytic closure. Take a look around, then cut through!

And if we are legion, it's because the war of liberation has only made as yet a tiny breakthrough. But women are thronging to it. I've seen them, those who will be neither dupe nor domestic, those who will not fear the risk of being a woman; will not fear any risk, any desire, any space still unexplored in themselves, among themselves and others or anywhere else. They do not fetishize, they do not deny, they do not hate. They observe, they approach, they try to see the other woman, the child, the lover—not to strengthen their own narcissism or verify the solidity or weakness of the master, but to make love better, to invent.

Other love.—In the beginning are our differences. The new love dares for the other, wants the other, makes dizzying, precipitous flights between knowledge and invention. The woman arriving over and over again does not stand still; she's everywhere, she exchanges, she is the desire-that-gives. (Not enclosed in the paradox of the gift that takes nor under the illusion of unitary fusion. We're past that.) She comes in, comes-in-between herself me and you, between the other me where one is always infinitely more than one and more than me, without the fear of ever reaching a limit; she thrills in our becoming. And we'll keep on becoming! She cuts through defensive loves, motherages, and devourations: beyond selfish narcissism, in the moving, open, transitional space, she runs her risks. Beyond the struggle-to-the-death that's been removed to the bed, beyond the love-battle that claims to represent exchange, she scorns at an Eros dynamic that would be fed by hatred. Hatred: a heritage, again, a remainder, a duping subservience to the phallus. To love, to watch-think-seek the other in the other, to despecularize, to unhoard. Does this seem difficult? It's not impossible, and this is what nourishes life—a love that has no commerce with the apprehensive desire that provides against the lack and stultifies the strange; a love that rejoices in the exchange that multiplies. Wherever history still unfolds as the history of death, she does not tread. Opposition, hierarchizing exchange, the struggle for mastery which can end only in at least one death (one master—one slave, or two nonmasters ≠ two dead)—all that comes from a period in time governed by phallocentric values. The fact that this period extends into the present doesn't prevent woman from starting the history of life somewhere else. Elsewhere, she gives. She doesn't "know" what she's giving, she doesn't measure it; she gives, though, neither a counterfeit impression nor something she hasn't got. She gives more, with no assurance that she'll get back even some unexpected profit from what she puts out. She gives that there may be life, thought, transformation. This is an "economy" that can no longer be put in economic terms. Wherever she loves, all the old concepts of management are left behind. At the end of a more or less conscious computation, she finds not her sum but her differences. I am for you what you want me to be at the moment you look at me in a way you've never seen me before: at every instant. When I write, it's everything that we don't know we can be that is written out of me, without exclusions, without stipulation, and everything we will be calls us to the unflagging, intoxicating, unappeasable search for love. In one another we will never be lacking.

Nora

Historian, teacher, and editor, Pierre Nora (1931–   ) is a major figure of contemporary intellectual life in France. Working in the prestigious publishing house of Gallimard, he has spurred the publications of historians like Maurice Agulhon, Michel Foucault, and Emmanuel LeRoy-Ladurie. In 1980, he launched a magazine, *Le Débat;* its purpose was to stimulate intellectual debate that could go beyond limits set by Marxist, psychoanalytical, and Deconstructionist dominance of the intellectual scene.

The essay printed below is excerpted from Nora's introduction to the first number of *Le Débat*. It examines, in historical context, the function of intellectuals in modern society, and the changes wrought by contemporary developments.

But Nora's pages have to be read in context, and the context, like that of Wagner's *Götterdammerung,* is the twilight of an idea and of the caste that carried it. The idea was Liberalism, and the caste is that of the intellectuals.

Stimulated by sensibilities new to mankind, the eighteenth century had generated moral arguments that continued to dominate the culture and politics of the nineteenth and twentieth centuries. Liberalism was their major expression, and Liberalism meant freedom, first for me, then for others. It framed its ends in the concept of the nation, ideally the democratic nation, within which men were first declared free and equal, then delivered from the public and private forces that make them less so. Abolishing autocracy opened the way to democracy, allegedly meant to grow ever more democratic. Abolishing privilege was a first step too, to abolishing exploitation: of slaves, of children, of a long list of injured, insulted, and oppressed. My right to freedom demonstrates the equal rights of others. The rights of free white men, who were first in line, came to highlight the rights of other categories: races, classes, species, even women.

When in 1789 Jeremy Bentham published his *Principles of Morals and Legislation*, he argued for animal rights by referring to the rights of slaves, whom the French had just emancipated by appealing to the rights of individual human beings—themselves the reflection of the abstract rights of man:

> The French have already discovered that the blackness of skin is no reason why a human being should be abandoned without redress to the caprice of a tormentor. . . . The day may come when the rest of the animal creation may acquire those rights which never could have been withholden from them by the hand of tyranny. . . . The question is not, Can they *reason*? nor, Can they *talk*? but, Can they *suffer*?

So, after freedom *to* talk and act, freedom *from* adversity, misery, discomfort, vexations, and anguish became a major liberal concern, and the progressive liberation of mankind from suffering was written into the purpose of History.

But all this was argued and pursued with a logic grounded in the belief in a historical process that progressed in time, and Liberalism found its firm base in national community. It could be formulated in coherent terms, based on definable concepts like justice, progress, fatherland; and further based on the reason that allowed us to formulate them and recognized them. Beginning in the late nineteenth century, culminating a century later, such concepts cracked and crumbled under the assault of relativism. So did the self-confidence of those who articulated liberal theology and spread it abroad: the intellectuals, no longer sure either of their terminology or their role. Patriotism, freedom, rationality, once firm and unequivocal, became precarious notions. An age seemed to be ending: that of Liberalism (and its offspring, Marxism), of the nation, of history, and of intellectuals—or at least of the social and cultural functions they had fulfilled. That is the context of Nora's reflections.

About Intellectuals

So there is something like an intellectual power. And I imagine that a magazine that aims at a concourse of intelligences and that places its birth under

---

Source: Pierre Nora, "Que peuvent les intellectuels?" *Le Débat*, 1, March 1980, pp. 3–17. Translated by Eugen Weber; reprinted by permission of Pierre Nora.

the zodiac sign of intellect would not represent an insignificant part of it. But let us take a closer look.

The word "power" belongs to the register of politics and to the vocabulary of the State. What relation can there be between the intellectual act and the exercise of authority? The law, if you ignore it, reminds you of its existence, but no one is obliged to become acquainted with the productions of the mind. The world of books is, by its very nature, the realm of liberty; the world of politics, that of constraints. The universe of power is ruled by scarcity; that of letters, sciences and arts by productivity indefinitely open to desires and to talents. The world of power is governed by a visible institutionalized hierarchy defined by progressions, positions, careers, tables of organization. The world of the mind is constituted by incomparable creations, by reputations that are made and unmade. We cannot compare lectors and electors, an influence to an authority, reception by a public to coercive power, the handling of ideas and words to the manipulation of men and things.

Certainly, there is no shortage of intellectuals ready to place their fame at the service of a political cause or to use their prestige to political ends. The multiplication of the number of students, the favor of the media, may even have created a degree of intellectual stardom that turns certain thinkers into quasi-political personalities. Too bad for the victims of vanity. It is also possible that today, through a complex organization of the market of symbolic goods and in limited circles, intellectuals and politicians share something of the magic of those few who seem to be able to do anything they want. But it is only the confusion of our time or the jealousy of frustration that opens the way from superficial resemblance to natural identification of one power with the other, that dares to speak of *intellectual* power as one element of *power* as such.

It is easy to see how contemporary intellectuals may withdraw into subjectivity and insist that they speak only for themselves. This retreat reflects their disavowal of a cause that is not [or no longer] their own. Ever since modern intellectuals have existed, which really means since the beginnings of representative democracy, political commitment has appeared to them as representing true ambition and ultimate justification. The political disalignment of recent years has withdrawn their political ardor within the sphere of their own peculiar activities, and has increased the care they lavish on its public expression. Those who only yesterday would have placed their talent at the service of the masses, devote their militant capacity to the service of their own glory with an assiduity beyond all praise. Whether it concerns the technique of the coup d'état, the infiltration of the media, flanking or outflanking operations, weary leninists are left aghast and out of breath. The very title of Thinking Masters [or Masters of Thought—*Maîtres Penseurs*] may have officially inaugurated the age of internal politicization of cultural life. After all, one has to have a little fun; and the preceding generation, my own, did not abstain from "seizing power" just because it was busy denouncing every kind of power. And since there is nothing left in political life to sustain agitators, there is every reason why they should express themselves elsewhere. A complete democracy, checked and ruled by the regular play of its institutions (like the United States, for example), excludes in a certain fashion the appearance of those unexpected expressions by which men of talent attract to their benefit first attention, then interest, then desire, then the will to servitude of their fellows. The situation controls you, you never control the situation. In a democratic regime which prohibits the affirmation of raw power, it is normal that genuine politics should take refuge in intellectual life.

The media have served this tendency. It is less easy to discuss books—which one would have to read first—than to interview their authors. By its very principle, the magic of television brings things closer and distances them at the same time. It distorts the causes, and neglects the works for the sake of presences which it prefers. It promotes the producer at the expense of the product. It creates that universe of the elect, of the separated: the precise presence of political personalities, accessible yet inapprehensible. It offers an unequalled sphere of communication to these professionals of communication. And since the elect are few, it replaces discussion between professionals, and the intellectual pluralism of different points of view, by monopolies of monocratic monologs.

The disappearance of a common language would render discussion between professionals awkward in any case. Language was connected with tradition, but tradition has broken. The intellectual alters when the literate world crumbles. There has rarely been a time when there was so little common ground to defend, and so much—everything—to reinvent alone. No more intellectual administrators of tradition. That is finished. No one would dare to bother us unless they had to offer at least a radically fresh start for thought. The civic role of the intellectual, his social function, have been stripped down and revealed. The obliteration of Rome and Athens as models of civilization, the end of the humanities as mistresses of national education, and, most profound, the disappearance of the rhetorical ideal as backbone of French intellectual tradition—this republican and bourgeois matrix that stretched straight from the elementary school teacher to the greatest writer—have completely subverted the original model. Or, rather, there is no more model. Every intellectual tends to be himself alone, his own beginning, his own end. There used to be places of worship, a language and offices of the creed. No university, no chapel, no academy would, today, pretend to such a role.

The shift from literature to comprehension has done the rest. Until Sartre—who played a crucial role in this respect—French intellectual tradition set itself carefully apart from the University. This was different from what happened in many other countries, especially Germany. Today, the University has absorbed everything, even if it is no longer the same university. In this connection, the influence of the "human sciences" [or social "sciences"] which began around 1950 and is now treading water, proved capital. It blurred the clear old frontier that distinguished the specialist from the man of letters, the erudite from the inspired, the researcher from the expert, the professor from the writer. It replaced these distinctions by a frontier, internal to a university that is breaking up, more subtle and less visible to the wider public. The contemporary intellectual flourishes over a university in ruins. The old system established a very clear separation between the intellectual who could talk of everything while knowing nothing, and the scholarly professor, prisoner of a narrow domain. Warranted or not, scientific justification and the equally new prestige of nurturing institutions—labs, seminars, centers and institutes—began to alter decisively the definition of the intellectual. . . . Positive knowledge as the source of legitimacy has radically modified intellectual identity.

The contemporary conjunction of these two poles, university and intelligentsia, has ended a division that illegitimated each a little bit. The prestige of the intellectual undergoes a transformation; reinforced on the personal plane by the sanction of a knowledge that is not him, it is diminished on the individual plane by his folkloric charisma. Social function has become the determining factor. It is the end of the leisure class. The intellectual is no longer an idler, a rentier; he has become a functionary, an expert, an administrative potentate (though free not to use his power), rather than lord, master, or good bourgeois. His legitimacy heretofore came from owing nothing to the State; today it is just the opposite. . . . The institutional legitimation of competence has become an integral part of the definition of the intellectual.

There is no doubt that what the intellectual has gained on one hand he has lost on the other. There may be Master Thinkers. There are no more masters of thought. The intellectual oracle has had his day. No one would think of going to ask Michel Foucault, as they once asked Sartre, whether to join the Foreign Legion or to arrange a girlfriend's abortion. However great the Master's prestige, it is no longer sacerdotal. . . . In the vast transfer from the "literary" to the "scientific," an essential dimension of the intellectuals' magic has disappeared: the ethical function. The human (or social) sciences, psychoanalysis in the lead, but also economics, history and linguistics, have killed duty and introspection, the two pillars of old psychology, on behalf of an allegedly exact science of one's self. The morality of everyday life has ceased to be an intellectual problem.

Politicization, massmediatization, sociabilization, bureaucratization, the condition of the intellectual has certainly changed—changed to the point where we have to ask whether we face a simple degradation of the traditional image, the forfeiture of intellectual hegemony, or whether the recent evolution has not brought to light a tendency present since our beginnings. Perhaps erasing everything that hitherto concealed the reality of intellectuals may permit us today—and only today—to better understand their original nature. Just as the Old Regime was only perceived for what it was at the moment when nobody upheld it any more, it may be only today, for reasons that we have to penetrate, that the intellectual phenomenon appears as a phenomenon, and not a matter of course.

The intellectuals are in a fix—deadlock, dilemma, impasse. The only means for them to escape the discredit in which they have enclosed themselves and us with them (since none of us can pretend to be anything else) may be to try to say who we are and what we are.

Within this modest servant of the intellect a despot dwells. And nowhere has this despot expressed himself more fully than in the French tradition.

Let me explain myself. The democratic state which, of all old Catholic nations, France was the first to experience, expressed itself by a swift and definitive break between spiritual and temporal power. The temporal power of the classic monarch included the spiritual, even if that was delegated. The order of ultimate ends was, once and for all, inscribed in the order of society, the intellectuals (anachronistic though it be to use the term) defined themselves exclusively within the sphere of power, or else outside the world. Better still, there were no intellectuals. The new fact, radically new in the dynamics of modern societies, is that the democratic power, in its very principle, deprived itself of the ability to express what society should be. "Ultimate ends": the political power of democracy does not recognize that kind of language. It is not up to a president of the republic to say what French democracy is, or should be. If he says that sort of thing, it is only in order to open a discussion in which he does not pretend to have the last word. This democracy, in its functioning, expresses the society. It issues from it, it reflects the general balance of forces at a given moment, but it cannot in any way, without denying itself, without foundering into some form of totalitarianism, impose a doctrinal orientation. The only spiritual elaboration permitted to it is the cult of the nation, because the nation was the ideal and limiting form whose contours democracy adopted, and whose possibilities it exhausted. But the nation has, by its nature, left plenty of scope for the establishment of a spiritual power which also appeals to society, and which also connects with the [democratic] mechanism of delegation and representation.

This appeal to society has been made historically and successively in the name of reason, of progress, of science, of liberty, of justice, of the direction of history, and of the interest of the masses. But, contrary to what they pretend, the intellectuals no more stand for what this society thinks of itself than political power represents the general expression of the popular will. That is a role which the Church should, normally, have played. But the religious power was, in France, too imbricated in the old political regime for the abolition of the one not to inform the other. That is not the case in Protestant countries, notably in the United States, where the incorporation of religion in the very principles of democracy has prevented the development of what in France are called intellectuals. The only historical comparison, and it is illuminating, is with nineteenth-century Russia, which is precisely the homeland of the "intelligentsia."

There was thus in France, as in Russia, a possibility for "intellectuals" to occupy the terrain. Yet, just as there is a representative *political* power, there has been, since the eighteenth century, a representative *intellectual* power. The intellectual, like the politician, appeals to the people, but he does it to distinguish himself from the people whilst expressing it. According to the times, and for different reasons, the people is called opinion, readers, colleagues, students, public, all of whom provide instances of consecration. One way or another, the legitimation of the intellectual is always conferred by success. [Sales in particular confer] a legitimacy based on a type of suffrage that one can debate but cannot reject. That's the way it is.

One cannot say it too often: the criteria that classical sociology provides for defining intellectuals in France are an aberration. It is the nature of the discourse that makes the intellectual; it is on immanent and representative criteria that the public perceives the justification of the discourse. It is the others who declare you an intellectual, never yourself. One understands the feverishness of present authors. It is not on posterity that they can rely for endorsements, there is no more more Posterity than there is Tradition. And the only bill one can draw on this absence is the capital of notoriety immediately acquired. Hence the jealousy and jockeying within a narrow milieu; hence the harrowing libidinal investment in the least pagelet published: the permanent Opera. Hence also the consoling fact that everybody can always become the intellectual of someone. The consecration descends upon you without having been sought. Brigitte Bardot may some day be elected to the Collège de France. Simone Signoret is virtually there already. The intellectual is the one in whose discourse the public hears, directly or indirectly, the echo of its ultimate ends. One is intellectual only on the basis of elective criteria.

The key of this representative mechanism is opposition. The intellectual is an opponent by nature even if he is not a political opponent, because he has to extricate his own autonomy from the political sphere. He has to be elsewhere, he has to display a power that is distinct. And those whom we see least, are those who are in the strongest position. The "great intellectual" is not the one most frequently displayed on TV screens or invited to the presidential palace; but the personality one dare not invite, who knows how to keep aloof. Stressing one's difference from power feeds one's own power.

The history of intellectuals does not begin when the philosophers of the Enlightenment begin to think *against* the powers that be. It begins when the effective effacement of divine right institutes in society a two-power regime. Tocqueville has explained this in a famous chapter: the power of intellectuals established itself in the void left by the dominant class. So, the rise of political democracy went hand in hand with the distinction of intellectuals. On the political plane, whether I am for or against, my intellectual power is nil. But I am the other of the political power, the double it cannot do without. If it becomes me, it is Hitler, Stalin, Mao or Khomeini—all, themselves, authors, poets, thinkers. From Voltaire to Sartre, from Marx to Zola, the political enlistment of intellectuals in the democratic battle, did not signify the truth of the intellectual. On the contrary, it helped to conceal the internal problem of intellectual democracy. That is why we had to await the vast and recent perturbation of the intelligentsia's political investment in the left which rendered obvious, urgent and explosive the problem that the very existence of intellectuals raised since the very beginning. The Republic *in* the Letters is the order of the day.

For the true paradox of intellectual life, and one that the French case illustrates in an exemplary manner, is that, in its very principle, it seems to postulate a democracy. Yet democracy is precisely what the verity of the intellectual act, imperialist and solitary, tyrannical and jealous, excludes in fact. Intellectuals tend to evoke the most amiable of images: cultivated, playful, fair-play. Yet there is a profound contradiction between the progressive and moderating role that the enlistment of intellectuals has given them in the past two centuries, and the transcendental carnivorous spirit, which in his profoundest reaches, endows a man with the predatory and anti-natural vocation to think and write. Essentially (that is, in essence), an intellectual does not oppose political power; it is other intellectuals he opposes and, accessorily, his public. A virtual paranoiac lies hidden in the most tranquil of intellectuals, a mixture of the archaic tyrant and the half-crazed Emperor of the late Roman Empire. King Voltaire. Political democracy hems individual ambitions within the limits of its juridical limitations. The intellectual act, on the contrary, knows no limitations. It exists by denying the elementary fact that one thinks in the midst of others. An immense political education campaign has exorcized on a narrow strip of an endangered planet the hallucinations of pure power. But all this time the intellectual tradition has merely exalted in those who profess to write the murderous narcissism of solitary domination. Today, I can only think by preventing others from thinking. I only speak to you to tell you that you will never know. Every intellectual pursues the death of the other; that's how we have been made. . . .

Intellectuals have not accomplished their democratic revolution. There used to be, once, an absolute monarchy and a republic of letters; now, we have a political republic and a despotism of letters. In brief, the progressive democratization of politics, to which intellectuals contributed their share, went with a progressive despotization of the intellectual. Not an extraordinary blockage if you think of it, in a society that recognizes no divine right. Without divine right, where would worldly tyranny exercise itself, if not on the ultimate realms of the spirit? There is a close link between the status of intellectuals and the imaginary realm of absolute power. This is the link that has to be destroyed.

Such an enterprise would make no sense, were we not carried, all of us, intellectuals or not, by a movement of history that is not ourselves. To understand or to plumb this movement, we must return from the psychology of imagination to the effective exercise of what has been, up to the present, this celebrated "intellectual power" in relation to "society." Two things distinguish secular spiritual power from religious power: on one hand the disappearance of a final fixed point, the God of Christian theology; on the other hand the absence of homogeneity within the social body that incarnates the secular spirit. Rules of access to political power used to be simpler, because power itself, in its sacred heart and head, lay beyond profane covetousness. Rules of access to the clergy were simpler too. Social order, monarchic order and divine order marched in lockstep under heavens of similarly immutable intelligibility. The effacement of the divine as keystone of the whole hierarchy tore apart temporal and spiritual, political and intellectual. It also opened an endless inquiry about the nature of this new society, and launched the obsession of its future. Indeed, it constituted, established, this nature as an autosociety where it became possible for men to exercise power. Power had been a simple instrument of upkeep. It became an instrument of transformation. But to what end, and to do what? In a nutshell, the birth of modern historical consciousness overturned our investment in time: a history made to last became a history made to change. Those who were called philosophers in the eighteenth century, doctrinaires in the nineteenth century, intellectuals at the dawn of the twentieth century, were simply the interpreters and guides of this change, the guardians of the sense of history.

Yet, unlike the clergy, intellectuals have had neither rules of access, nor a source of authority that was given once and for all. And even though in every epoch and despite differing opinions they were able to share a common body of ideas—the "unsurpassable horizon" of their time—what was it that could be found in history that could ever guarantee their point of view *about* history? This is the ambiguity that rules over intellectuals and that constitutes their essence. The ambiguity is inherent to what they are, and it prohibits any kind of definition, be it ideological, sociological, or existential. They exist at one and the same time *within* history and *outside* history. Within history because they are its familiar product and even the inventors of the concept; outside history, whose verbal expression they provide without anyone having given them the right to do so. Consubstantial with history and external to it, secreted by historical sensibility and charged with its expression. Perpetual representatives of something other than themselves, and never representing anything other than themselves. Impressed by a sense that makes sense only when they express it. Here lies the essential ambiguity that allows intellectuals, now at a high price and now for free, simultaneously to claim the monopoly of historical truth and escape the sanction of its verification, to claim the privilege of the legislator and the immunities of the law.

The only gangway between the two types of modern power will have been the national formula: synthesis, compromise, reconciliation. The nation looks like a ballet of the spheres: spiritual within the temporal sphere, historical within the geographical, ideological within the fleshly, indefiniteness within delimitation, the universal within the particular, the eternal within the chronological. The nation, mystery of modern times, is the radically original post-ideological formula that only long-established habit prevents us from questioning with the wonder it deserves. It has represented the only ideology that a political democracy could allow itself to create, and also the minimal political framework that would not constrain the continuous operation of power bouncing off society. We think of nation (political fact) and society (intellectual construct) as one. Yet their identity is hardly evident. Alone in history, the nation permits the reconciliation of that continuity which the government of men demands with the ever-renewed discontinuity of social perspectives. A fixed, stable, final harmony, risen from the depths of ages, but also a historical category absolutely undefinable except when it becomes immediately palpable to all in its spiritualized form: *the fatherland*. The nation, sole repository of that familiar miracle: the constitution of a history in history.

The formula has worked marvelously well. It reached its golden age in the great republican synthesis achieved on the eve of the First World War. Its expression was found in the struggle for secular power that proved a powerful factor of national integration, both political and spiritual; and in a powerful educational system infused in every part and at every level by the civic imperative. It also expressed itself in the success, at every political crisis, of liberal forms of government, and in the flaring up of every kind of patriotic myth. And it expressed itself in the powerful ideological charge all political parties carried, as in the profound national assimilation of socialist internationalism of the Jaurès school. Intellectuals were never more divided over the concept of the fatherland than they were in those days, but their relation to politics, their relation to history, were never so dependent on national concepts. You might even say that here is where intellectual and national concepts meet: in February 1898, with the Dreyfus Affair in full cry, in the wake of Zola's *J'Accuse*. That is when, almost simultaneously under the pen of Barrès and of Clemenceau, the word "intellectual," used only as an adjective until that time, enters the public vocabulary. And with it, soon after, the term "avant-garde."

This solemn date marks one central turning point in a chronology (still to be drawn) of cultural crossroads and junctures of historical sensibility among intellectuals. One would have to establish just how and why displacing the center of gravity from "literature" to "science" (vague and undefinable though the expression be), ushered in a new stage that mutates or ends right now, under our gaze. What did these sciences called human (or social) have in common, when compared to a relatively univocal definition of literature in the singular? What bestows on the declarations of those who profess them, economists or sociologists, historians, psychoanalysts, ethnologists or linguists, that ideological aura which their scientific ambitions should have denied them? Are all ethnologists intellectuals, are all historians or linguists intellectuals, simply because of their discipline, when the peculiarity of a discipline is to parcel out knowledge and to raise doubts about those who claim to master its whole? Finally: what relations of reciprocal jointing or exclusion, or of internal dissymetry, exist between these "sciences," between history and the others, or psychoanalysis, each with its hard kernel and its soft frontiers— unless we ought to say the opposite? Vast questions . . . Let us just say, for the moment, that the intellectual pertinence of the "human sciences," their relation to the ultimate ends of history, appears to be related to the abuse of the word "science," and that the more scientific the human sciences look to public opinion, the less so they are. . . .

The only basic certitudes these sciences have contributed to the general public is that men spoke a language different from what they thought, acted for motives they ignored, tended towards results they had not wanted, and ignored the history that they made. Something to make you think, in effect. Something to enslave you to the masters of suspicion. Something to endow quaint subjects as exotic as Bororo myth, as microscopic as the use of the ergative in Caucasian languages, with that thrill of interest that colors the uncertain identity of the present. Yet, in the context that interests us, the internal organization of this anthropology remains to be traced. What, for example, might be the relation of history to History? Or that of biology to History? These are not empty questions, since it is from such relations that the professional of a discipline derives his intellectual authority. It is not indifferent to note that the topic of "intellectual power" (or authority, or control), so urgent and devastating today, with its train of hierarchic and inequalitarian connotations, with its stock of castrating images, with the visions of domination and perversity it carries, owes its efficacy to the symbolic centrality of psychoanalysis in our culture, and specifically of psychoanalysis in the version of [Jacques] Lacan.

Between the eighteenth century and the dawn of what we might call the age of human sciences, various kinds of historical relations to History have differed from each other. Yet, however much they differed, they shared one fundamental aspect: a fixed point of reference. In the uncertainty of its determinism as in the vast realm of its possibilities, the very notion of history offered one enduring, unfailing vision: the perspective of a *future*. Uncertain future, always under debate, but whose distant certainty began to depend on mankind. Control of the future governed both the analysis of the present and the historical investment of the past. No intellectual without an idea of the future, without a secret of the present, without knowledge of the past.

Since the eighteenth century there have been roughly three models that permitted one to think the future: one could imagine—hence expect and favor—the *restoration* of the old state of things. One could imagine *progress*, technical and scientific, moral or political, and set its limits here or there. One could finally imagine *revolution*, in diverse forms, all of which would constitute a point zero or *omega* of History. These three models are dead; and the future, that future which defined the end of history in both senses of the term, died with them. The counterpoint that accompanies the background noise of the human sciences is the historical liquefaction of those traditional benchmarks which, since the French Revolution, guaranteed the destiny of society, dictating in one infallible continuity the judgment of the present, the imagination of the future, and the reconstitution of the past.

History has finally discovered itself, only to deny itself. It had projected its conclusion in the very act of its birth. In the very first of his lessons on *The Philosophy of History*, Hegel announced both the advent of History and the end of universal History. But perspectives of finality are foreign to our day. The future, the thinkable future that had been truly the new idea of revolutionary Europe, lies behind us. It foundered in the calamities of our century, leaving us to face a future without face or name, uncontrollable, undefined.

This is what has abolished the historical figure of the "despotic" intellectual. [This is the] liberating shipwreck which has inaugurated the democratic revolution of spiritual power and summoned intellectuals to a new historical role: *within* history and only within history. Assuming, that is, that we still choose to call them "history" and "intellectual." History, nation, democracy, intellectuals, made up a historical constellation every term of which now drifts to a new redefinition, whose very meaning capsizes in search for a new meaning. Our only task is to live up to what is happening through us. To understand what is happening: we are living the end of historical finality.

A second age of historical consciousness has begun: an age of exploration.

Havel

Liberalism accompanied equality; equality implied equal justice for all. But equal justice meant more than laws and principles equally applied; it called for social justice. And the organic image first of the nation, then of mankind, demanded that all parts of the national (and eventually of the human) body or family share in the common welfare, in the commonwealth. First Socialism, then Communism and Fascism, were to draw the conclusions of this logic. Liberalism had proved too slow and inefficient at solving the problems it articulated and that, to some extent, it caused.

If freedom could not bring freedom, maybe coercion would prove more effective. Where reasoned arguments did not triumph, force should do the trick. Catastrophic violence would succeed where progressive gradualism had failed. First Bolshevism, then Fascism, set out to realize history, to build the future, by forcing men to be free. They claimed to love mankind, but they distrusted men, who had to be harnessed before mankind could be saved. Opium of the befuddled masses, Bolshevik, Fascist, Nazi doctrines offered explanations, compensations, promises, and satisfactions that were more apparent, more accessible, more acceptable, than bewilderingly complicated analyses or plans. Bolshevism, Fascism, and Nazism achieved spectacular success and ended in disaster just as spectacular. The latter two in destructive war, the former in chaos and discredit. As a Polish workman put it during a strike at the Lenin shipyards in Gdansk, in May 1988, "Forty years of socialism, and there's still no toilet paper." Let alone food.

The Czechs had endured the passage of Nazism before they fell to Communism. Vaclav Havel (1936–   ) is one of the country's leading playwrights. Consistently critical of the Communist regime, his plays and his writings banned in his home country, harassed and frequently detained by the police, imprisoned for years for criminal subversion, he stubbornly insisted on such outdated notions as individual experience, responsibility, conscience, the freedom to live and work in his own country and to think as he likes. In 1984, one year after his last release from prison, he explained to the foreign producer of one more play that had been banned at home that his writings focused on

> people's arduous struggle to protect their own identity from impersonal power which seeks to take it away from them; on the strange contradiction between people's actual capacities and the role they are obliged to play by reason of their environment, their destiny and their own work; on how easy it is in theory to know how to live one's life, but how difficult it is to do so in practice; on the tragic incapacity of people to understand each other, even when they wish each other the best; on human loneliness, fear and cowardice, etc., etc.—and finally, of course (and most importantly), on the tragi-comic and absurd dimensions of all these themes.

Also written in 1984, his essay on "Politics and Conscience," much of which is reprinted here, reflects some of the same concerns. Destined for the conferment of an honorary doctorate by the University of Toulouse, Havel was not allowed to attend the ceremony. "Politics and Conscience," like Havel's other writings, circulated at home only in private copies. But it made plain, as does the quotation above, that old-fashioned beliefs, concepts, values, may not be as irrelevant (let alone as dead) as they have been declared. In times of real crisis, intellectual games have to be suspended; serious thought recognizes an identity to be protected. We face moral duties, dilemmas, decisions not as relative and ambiguous inventions but as immediate challenges, and some of us reclaim action not as a product of vacillating consensus but as affirmation of self, personality, and values just as real as the stubborn individual who makes them.

In 1990, Vaclav Havel was elected the first president of a newly free Czechoslovak republic.

Politics and Conscience

I

As a boy, I lived for some time in the country and I clearly remember an experience from those days: I used to walk to school in a nearby village along a cart track through the fields and, on the way, see on the horizon a huge smokestack of some hurriedly built factory, in all likelihood in the service of war. It spewed dense brown smoke and scattered it across the sky. Each time I saw it, I had an intense sense of something profoundly wrong, of humans

---

Source: From *Open Letters* by Vaclav Havel, trans. by Paul Wilson et al. Copyright © 1991 by Vaclav Havel. Reprinted by permission of Alfred A. Knopf Inc.

soiling the heavens. I have no idea whether there was something like a science of ecology in those days; if there was, I certainly knew nothing of it. Still that "soiling the heavens" offended me spontaneously. It seemed to me that, in it, humans are guilty of something, that they destroy something important, arbitrarily disrupting the natural order of things, and that such things cannot go unpunished. To be sure, my revulsion was largely aesthetic; I knew nothing then of the noxious emissions which would one day devastate our forests, exterminate game and endanger the health of people.

If a medieval man were to see something like that suddenly on the horizon—say, while out hunting—he would probably think it the work of the Devil and would fall on his knees and pray that he and his kin be saved.

What is it, actually, that the world of the medieval peasant and that of a small boy have in common? Something substantive, I think. Both the boy and the peasant are far more intensely rooted in what some philosophers call "the natural world," or *Lebenswelt,* than most modern adults. They have not yet grown alienated from the world of their actual personal experience, the world which has its morning and its evening, its *down* (the earth) and its *up* (the heavens), where the sun rises daily in the east, traverses the sky and sets in the west, and where concepts like "at home" and "in foreign parts," good and evil, beauty and ugliness, near and far, duty and work, still mean something living and definite. They are still rooted in a world which knows the dividing line between all that is intimately familiar and appropriately a subject of our concern, and that which lies beyond its horizon, that before which we should bow down humbly because of the mystery about it. Our "I" primordially attests to that world and personally certifies it; that is the world of our lived experience, a world not yet indifferent since we are personally bound to it in our love, hatred, respect, contempt, tradition, in our interests and in that pre-reflective meaning-fulness from which culture is born. That is the realm of our induplicable, inalienable and non-transferable joy and pain, a world in which, through which and for which we are somehow answerable, a world of personal responsibility. In this world, categories like justice, honour, treason, friendship, infidelity, courage or empathy have a wholly tangible content, relating to actual persons and important for actual life. At the basis of this world are values which are simply there, perennially, before we ever speak of them, before we reflect upon them and inquire about them. It owes its internal coherence to something like a "pre-speculative" assumption that the world functions and is generally possible at all only because there is something beyond its horizon, something beyond or above it that might escape our understanding and our grasp but, for just that reason, firmly grounds this world, bestows upon it its order and measure, and is the hidden source of all the rules, customs, commandments, prohibitions and norms that hold within it. The natural world, in virtue of its very being, bears within it the presupposition of the absolute which grounds, delimits, animates and directs it, without which it would be unthinkable, absurd and superfluous, and which we can only quietly respect. Any attempt to spurn it, master it or replace it with something else, appears, within the framework of the natural world, as an expression of *hubris* for which humans must pay a heavy price, as did Don Juan and Faust.

To me, personally, the smokestack soiling the heavens is not just a regrettable lapse of a technology that failed to include "the ecological factor" in its calculation, one which can be easily corrected with the appropriate filter. To me it is more, the symbol of an age which seeks to transcend the boundaries of the natural world and its norms and to make it into a merely private concern, a matter of subjective preference and private feeling, of the illusions, prejudices and whims of a "mere" individual. It is a symbol of an epoch which denies the binding importance of personal experience—including the experience of mystery and of the absolute—and displaces the personally experienced absolute as the measure of the world with a new, man-made absolute, devoid of mystery, free of the "whims" of subjectivity and, as such, impersonal and inhuman. It is the absolute of so-called objectivity: the objective, rational cognition of the scientific model of the world.

Modern science, constructing its universally valid image of the world, thus crashes through the bounds of the natural world which it can understand only as a prison of prejudices from which we must break out into the light of objectively verified truth. The natural world appears to it as no more than an unfortunate left-over from our backward ancestors, a fantasy of their childish immaturity. With that, of course, it abolishes as mere fiction even the innermost foundation of our natural world; it kills God and takes his place on the vacant throne so that henceforth it would be science which would hold the order of being in its hand as its sole legitimate guardian and be the sole legitimate arbiter of all relevant truth. For after all, it is only science that rises above all individual subjective truths and replaces them with a superior, trans-subjective, trans-personal truth which is truly objective and universal.

Modern rationalism and modern science, though the work of man that, as all human works, developed within our natural world, now systematically leave it behind, deny it, degrade and defame it—and, of course, at the same time colonize it. A modern man, whose natural world has been properly conquered by science and technology, objects to the smoke from the smokestack only if the stench penetrates his apartment. In no case, though, does he take offence at it *metaphysically* since he knows that the factory to which the smokestack belongs manufactures things that he needs. As a man of the technological era, he can conceive of a remedy only within the limits of technology—say, a catalytic scrubber fitted to the chimney.

Lest you misunderstand: I am not proposing that humans abolish smokestacks or prohibit science or generally return to the Middle Ages. Besides, it is not by accident that some of the most profound discoveries of modern science render the myth of objectivity surprisingly problematic and, via a remarkable detour, return us to the human subject and his world. I wish no more than to consider, in a most general and admittedly schematic outline, the spiritual framework of modern civilization and the source of its present crisis. And though the primary focus of these reflections will be the political rather than ecological aspect of this crisis, I might, perhaps, clarify my starting point with one more ecological example. For centuries, the basic component of European agriculture had been the family farm. In Czech, the older term for it was *grunt*—which itself is not without its etymological interest. The word, taken from the German *Grund*, actually means ground or foundation and, in Czech, acquired a peculiar semantic colouring. As the colloquial synonym for "foundation," it points out the "groundedness" of the ground, its indubitable, traditional and pre-speculatively given authenticity and veridicality. Certainly, the family farm was a source of endless and intensifying social conflict of all kinds. Still, we cannot deny it one thing: it was rooted in the nature of its place, appropriate, harmonious, personally tested by generations of farmers and certified by the results of their husbandry. It also displayed a kind of optimal mutual proportionality in extent and kind of all that belonged to it; fields, meadows, boundaries, woods, cattle, domestic animals, water, toads and so on. For centuries no farmer made it the topic of a scientific study. Nevertheless, it constituted a generally satisfying economic and ecological system, within which everything was bound together by a thousand threads of mutual and meaningful connection, guaranteeing its stability as well as the stability of the product of the farmer's husbandry. Unlike present-day "agribusiness," the traditional family farm was energetically self-sufficient. Though it was subject to common calamities, it was not guilty of them—unfavourable weather, cattle disease, wars and other catastrophes lay outside the farmer's province.

Certainly, modern agricultural and social science could also improve agriculture in a thousand ways, increasing its productivity, reducing the amount of sheer drudgery, and eliminating the worst social inequities. But this is possible only on the assumption that modernization, too, will be guided by a certain humility and respect for the mysterious order of nature and for the appropriateness which derives from it and which is intrinsic to the natural world of personal experience and responsibility. Modernization must not be simply an arrogant, megalomaniac and brutal invasion by an impersonally objective science, represented by a newly graduated agronomist or a bureaucrat in the service of the "scientific world view."

That is just what happened to our country: our word for it was "collectivization." Like a tornado, it raged through the Czechoslovak countryside thirty years ago, leaving not a stone in place. Among its consequences were, on the one hand, tens of thousands of lives devastated by prison, sacrificed on the altar of a scientific Utopia about brighter tomorrows. On the other hand, the level of social conflict and the amount of drudgery in the countryside did in truth decrease while agricultural productivity rose quantitatively. That, though, is not why I mention it. My reason is something else: thirty years after the tornado swept the traditional family farm off the face of the earth, scientists are amazed to discover what even a semi-literate farmer previously knew—that human beings must pay a heavy price for every attempt to abolish, radically, once for all and without trace, the humbly respected boundary of the natural world, with its tradition of scrupulous personal acknowledgement. They must pay for the attempt to seize nature, to leave not a remnant of it in human hands, to ridicule its mystery; they must pay for the attempt to abolish Gold and to play at being God. The price, in fact, fell due. With hedges ploughed under and woods cut down, wild birds have died out and, with them, a natural, unpaid protector of the crops against harmful insects. Huge unified fields have led to the inevitable annual loss of millions of cubic yards of topsoil that have taken centuries to accumulate; chemical fertilizers and pesticides have catastrophically poisoned all vegetable products, the earth and the waters. Heavy machinery systematically presses down the soil, making it impenetrable to air and thus infertile; cows in gigantic dairy farms suffer neuroses and lose their milk while agriculture siphons off ever more energy from industry—manufacture of machines, artificial fertilizers, rising transportation costs in an age of growing local specialization, and so on. In short, the prognoses are terrifying and no one knows what surprises coming years and decades may bring.

It is paradoxical: people in the age of science and technology live in the conviction that they can improve their lives because they are able to grasp and exploit the complexity of nature and the general laws of its functioning. Yet it is precisely these laws which, in the end, tragically catch up with them and get the better of them. People thought they could explain and conquer nature—yet the outcome is that they destroyed it and disinherited themselves from it. But what are the prospects for man "outside nature"? It is, after all, precisely the sciences that are most recently discovering that the human body is actually only a particularly busy intersection of billions of organic micro-bodies, of their complex mutual contacts and influences, together forming that incredible megaorganism we call the "biosphere" in which our planet is blanketed.

The fault is not one of science as such but of the arrogance of man in the age of science. Man simply is not God, and playing God has cruel consequences. Man has abolished the absolute horizon of his relations, denied his personal "pre-objective" experience of the lived world, while relegating personal conscience and consciousness to the bathroom, as something so private that it is no one's business. Man rejected his responsibility as a "subjective illusion"—and in place of it installed what is now proving to be the most dangerous illusion of all: the fiction of objectivity stripped of all that is concretely human, of a rational understanding of the cosmos, and of an abstract schema of a putative "historical necessity." As the apex of it all, man has constructed a vision of a purely scientifically calculable and technologically achievable "universal welfare," demanding no more than that experimental institutes invent it while industrial and bureaucratic factories turn it into reality. That millions of people will be sacrificed to this illusion in scientifically directed concentration camps is not something that concerns our "modern man" unless by chance he himself lands behind barbed wire and is thrown drastically back upon his natural world. The phenomenon of empathy, after all, belongs with that abolished realm of personal prejudice which had to yield to science, objectivity, historical necessity, technology, system and the *"apparat"*—and those, being impersonal, cannot worry. They are abstract and anonymous, ever utilitarian and thus also ever *a priori* innocent.

And as for the future? Who, personally, would care about it or even personally worry about it when the perspective of eternity is one of the things locked away in the bathroom, if not expelled outright into the realm of fairy tales? If a contemporary scientist thinks at all of what will be in two hundred years, he does so solely as a personally disinterested observer, who, basically, could not care less whether he is doing research on the metabolism of the flea, on the radio signals of pulsars or on the global reserves of natural gas. And a modern politician? He has absolutely no reason to care, especially if it might interfere with his chances in an election, as long as he lives in a country where there are elections. . . .

II

A Czech philosopher, Václav Bělohradský, suggestively unfolded the thought that the rationalistic spirit of modern science, founded on abstract reason and on the presumption of impersonal objectivity, has, beside its father in the natural sciences, Galileo, also a father in politics—Machiavelli, who first formulated, albeit with an undertone of malicious irony, a theory of politics as a rational technology of power. We could say that, for all the complex historical detours, the origin of the modern state and of modern political power may be sought precisely here, that is, once again in a moment when human reason begins to "free" itself from the human being as such, from his personal experience, personal conscience and personal responsibility and so also from that to which, within the framework of the natural world, all responsibility is uniquely related, his absolute horizon. Just as the modern scientists set apart the actual human being as the subject of the lived experience of the world, so, ever more evidently, do both the modern state and modern politics.

To be sure, this process of anonymization and depersonalization of power and its reduction to a mere technology of rule and manipulation, has a thousand masks, variants and expressions. In one case it is covert and inconspicuous, while in another case it is just the contrary, entirely overt; in one case it sneaks up on us along subtle and devious paths, in another case it is brutally direct. Essentially, though, it is the same universal trend. It is the essential trait of all modern civilization, growing directly from its spiritual structure, rooted in it by a thousand tangled tendrils and inseparable even in thought from its technological nature, its mass characteristics and its consumer orientation.

The rulers and leaders were once personalities in their own right, with concrete human faces, still in some sense personally responsible for their deeds, good and ill, whether they had been installed by dynastic tradition, by the will of the people, by a victorious battle or by intrigue. But they have been replaced in modern times by the manager, the bureaucrat, the *apparatchik*—a professional ruler, manipulator and expert in the techniques of management, manipulation and obfuscation, filling a depersonalized intersection of functional relations, a cog in the machinery of state caught up in a predetermined role. This professional ruler is an "innocent" tool of an "innocent" anonymous power, legitimized by science, cybernetics, ideology, law, abstraction and objectivity—that is, by everything except personal responsibility to human beings as persons and neighbours. A modern politician is transparent: behind his judicious mask and affected diction there is not a trace of a human being rooted by his loves, passions, interests, personal opinions, hatred, courage or cruelty in the order of the natural world. All that he, too, locks away in his private bathroom. If we glimpse anything at all behind the mask, it will be only a more or less competent power technician. System, ideology and *apparat* have deprived humans—rulers as well as the ruled—of their conscience, of their common sense and natural speech and thereby, of their actual humanity. States grow ever more machine-like, men are transformed into statistical choruses of voters, producers, consumers, patients, tourists or soldiers. In politics, good and evil, categories of the natural world and therefore obsolete remnants of the past, lose all absolute meaning; the sole method of politics is quantifiable success. Power is *a priori* innocent because it does not grow from a world in which words like guilt and innocence retain their meaning.

This impersonal power has achieved what is its most complete expression so far in the totalitarian systems. As Bělohradský points out, the depersonalization of power and its conquest of human conscience and human speech have been successfully linked to an extra-European tradition of a "cosmological" conception of the empire (identifying the empire, as the sole true centre of the world, with the world as such, and considering the human as its exclusive property). But, as the totalitarian systems clearly illustrate, this does not mean that the modern impersonal power is itself an extra-European affair. The truth is the very opposite: it was precisely Europe, and the European West, that provided and frequently forced on the world all that today has become the basis of such power: natural science, rationalism, scientism, the industrial revolution, and also revolution as such, as a fanatical abstraction, through the displacement of the natural world to the bathroom down to the cult of consumption, the atomic bomb and Marxism. And it is Europe—democratic western Europe—which today stands bewildered in the face of this ambiguous export. The contemporary dilemma, whether to resist this reverse expansionism of its erstwhile export or to yield to it, attests to this. Should rockets, now aimed at Europe thanks to its export of spiritual and technological potential, be countered by similar and better rockets, thereby demonstrating a determination to defend such values as Europe has left, at the cost of entering into an utterly immoral game being forced upon it? Or should Europe retreat, hoping that the responsibility for the fate of the planet demonstrated thereby will infect, by its miraculous power, the rest of the world?

I think that, with respect to the relation of western Europe to the totalitarian systems, no error could be greater than the one looming largest: that of a failure to understand the totalitarian systems for what they ultimately are—a convex mirror of all modern civilization and a harsh, perhaps final call for a global recasting of that civilization's self-understanding. If we ignore that, then it does not make any essential difference which form Europe's efforts will take. It might be the form of taking the totalitarian systems, in the spirit of Europe's own rationalistic tradition, as some locally idiosyncratic attempt at achieving "general welfare," to which only men of ill-will attribute expansionist tendencies. Or, in the spirit of the same rationalistic tradition, though this time in the Machiavellian conception of politics as the technology of power, one might perceive the totalitarian regimes as a purely external threat by expansionist neighbours who can be driven back within acceptable bounds by an appropriate demonstration of power, without having to be considered more deeply. The first alternative is that of the person who reconciles himself to the chimney belching smoke, even though that smoke is ugly and smelly, because in the end it serves a good purpose, the production of commonly needed goods. The second alternative is that of the man who thinks that it is simply a matter of a technological flaw, which can be eliminated by technological means, such as a filter or a scrubber.

The reality, I believe, is unfortunately more serious. The chimney "soiling the heavens" is not just a technologically corrigible flaw of design, or a tax paid for a better consumerist tomorrow, but a symbol of a civilization which has renounced the absolute, which ignores the natural world and disdains its imperatives. So, too, the totalitarian systems warn of something far more serious than Western rationalism is willing to admit. They are, most of all, a convex mirror of the inevitable consequences of rationalism, a grotesquely magnified image of its own deep tendencies, an extremist offshoot of its own development and an ominous product of its own expansion. They are a deeply informative reflection of its own crisis. Those regimes are not merely dangerous neighbours and even less some kind of an avant-garde of world progress. Alas, just the opposite: they are the avant-garde of a global crisis of this civilization, first European, then Euro-American, and ultimately global. They are one of the possible futurological studies of the Western world, not in the sense that one day they will attack and conquer it, but in a far deeper sense—that they illustrate graphically to what the "eschatology of the impersonal," as Bělohradský calls it, can lead.

It is the total rule of a bloated, anonymously bureaucratic power, not yet irresponsible but already operating outside all conscience, a power grounded in an omnipresent ideological fiction which can rationalize anything without ever having to brush against the truth. Power as the omnipresent monopoly of control, repression and fear; power which makes thought, morality and privacy a state monopoly and so dehumanizes them; power which long since has ceased to be the matter of a group of arbitrary rulers but which, rather, occupies and swallows up everyone so that all should become integrated within it, at least through their silence. No one actually possesses such power, since it is the power itself which possesses everyone; it is a monstrosity which is not guided by humans but which, on the contrary, drags all persons along with its "objective" self-momentum—objective in the sense of being cut off from all human standards, including human reason and hence entirely irrational—to a terrifying, unknown future.

Let me repeat: it is a great reminder to contemporary civilization. Perhaps somewhere there may be some generals who think it would be best to dispatch such systems from the face of the earth and then all would be well. But that is no different from an ugly woman trying to get rid of her ugliness by smashing the mirror which reminds her of it. Such a "final solution" is one of the typical dreams of impersonal reason—capable, as the term "final solution" graphically reminds us, of transforming its dreams into reality and thereby reality into a nightmare. It would not only fail to resolve the crisis of the present world but, assuming anyone survived at all, would only aggravate it. By burdening the already heavy account of this civilization with further millions of dead, it would not block its essential trend to totalitarianism but would rather accelerate it. It would be a Pyrrhic victory, because the victors would emerge from a conflict inevitably resembling their defeated opponents far more than anyone today is willing to admit or able to imagine. Just as a minor example: imagine what a huge Gulag Archipelago would have to be built in the West, in the name of country, democracy, progress and war discipline, to contain all who refuse to take part in the effort, whether from naivety, principle, fear or ill-will!

No evil has ever been eliminated by suppressing its symptoms. We need to address the cause itself. . . .

III

. . . Patočka once wrote that a life not willing to sacrifice itself to what makes it meaningful is not worth living. It is just in the world of such lives and of such a "peace"—that is, under the "rule of everydayness"—that wars happen most easily. In such a world, there is no moral barrier against them, no barrier guaranteed by the courage of supreme sacrifice. The door stands wide open for the irrational "securing of our interests." The absence of heroes who know what they are dying for is the first step on the way to the mounds of corpses of those who are slaughtered like cattle. The slogan "better Red than dead" does not irritate me as an expression of surrender to the Soviet Union, but it terrifies me as an expression of the renunciation by Western people of any claim to a meaningful life and of their acceptance of impersonal power as such. For what the slogan really says is that nothing is worth giving one's life for. However, without the horizon of the highest sacrifice, all sacrifice becomes senseless. Then nothing is worth anything. Nothing means anything. The result is a philosophy of sheer negation of our humanity. In the case of Soviet totalitarianism, such a philosophy does no more than offer a little political assistance. With respect to Western totalitarianism, it is what constitutes it, directly and primordially.

In short, I cannot overcome the impression that Western culture is threatened far more by itself than by SS–20 rockets. When a French leftist student told me with a sincere glow in his eyes that the Gulag was a tax paid for the ideals of socialism and that Solzhenitsyn is just a personally embittered man, he cast me into a deep gloom. Is Europe really incapable of learning from its own history? Can't that dear lad ever understand that even the most promising project of "general well-being" convicts itself of inhumanity the moment it demands a single involuntary death—that is, one which is not a conscious sacrifice of a life to its meaning? Is he really incapable of comprehending that until he finds himself incarcerated in some Soviet-style jail near Toulouse? Did the newspeak of our world so penetrate natural human speech that two people can no longer communicate even such a basic experience?

IV

I presume that after all these stringent criticisms, I am expected to tell just what I consider to be a meaningful alternative for Western humanity today in face of the political dilemmas of the contemporary world.

As all I have said suggests, it seems to me that all of us, East and West, face one fundamental task from which all else should follow. That task is one of resisting vigilantly, thoughtfully and attentively, but at the same time with total dedication, at every step and everywhere, the irrational momentum of anonymous, impersonal and inhuman power—the power of ideologies, systems, *apparat*, bureaucracy, artificial languages and political slogans. We must resist their complex and wholly alienating pressure, whether it takes the form of consumption, advertising, repression, technology, or cliché—all of which are the blood brothers of fanaticism and the wellspring of totalitarian thought. We must draw our standards from our natural world, heedless of ridicule, and reaffirm its denied validity. We must honour with the humility of the wise the bounds of that natural world and the mystery which lies beyond them, admitting that there is something in the order of being which evidently exceeds all our competence; relating ever again to the absolute horizon of our existence which, if we but will, we shall constantly rediscover and experience; making values and imperatives into the starting point of all our acts, of all our personally attested, openly contemplated and ideologically uncensored lived experience. We must trust the voice of our conscience more than that of all abstract speculations and not invent other responsibilities than the one to which the voice calls us. We must not be ashamed that we are capable of love, friendship, solidarity, sympathy and tolerance, but just the opposite: we must set these fundamental dimensions of our humanity free from their "private" exile and accept them as the only genuine starting point of meaningful human community. We must be guided by our own reason and serve the truth under all circumstances as our own essential experience.

I know all that sounds very general, very indefinite and very unrealistic, but . . . if I may say so, I know what I am talking about. . . .

. . . A reaffirmed human responsibility is the most natural barrier to all irresponsibility. If, for instance, the spiritual and technological potential of the advanced world is spread truly responsibly, not solely under the pressure of a selfish interest in profits, we can prevent its irresponsible transformation into weapons of destruction. It surely makes much more sense to operate in the sphere of causes than simply to respond to their effects. By then, as a rule, the only possible response is by equally immoral means. To follow that path means to continue spreading the evil of irresponsibility in the world, and so to produce precisely the poison on which totalitarianism feeds.

I favour "anti-political politics," that is, politics not as the technology of power and manipulation, of cybernetic rule over humans or as the art of the useful, but politics as one of the ways of seeking and achieving meaningful lives, of protecting them and serving them. I favour politics as practical morality, as service to the truth, as essentially human and humanly measured care for our fellow humans. It is, I presume, an approach which, in this world, is extremely impractical and difficult to apply in daily life. Still, I know no better alternative. . . .

Afterthought

Still glides the stream and shall forever glide.
The form remains, the function never dies.
While we—the brave, the mighty and the wise—
We men who in our morn of youth defied the elements
Must vanish. Be it so!
Enough that something from our hands have power
To live, and act, and serve the future hour
And that—as toward the silent tomb we go—
Through love, through hope, and faith's unending dower,
We feel that we are greater than we know.

—William Wordsworth